# An Ancient Way of Life

## 4<sup>th</sup> Edition

## Ted M. Preston, Ph.D.
Rio Hondo College

A Local Source Textbook™ Company

# An Ancient Way Of Life

# Preface to the 4ᵗʰ Edition

The fourth edition of this text corrects minor errors from the third. Several chapters have undergone some expansion and revisions, including the addition of Empedocles to the pre-Socratic chapter.

Perhaps the most substantial change to this edition is the inclusion of several non-European philosophical sources. I present this new material with a multipart disclaimer: (1) I'm not an expert on East Asian or Nahua philosophy, nor will I pretend to be. For that reason (and others), my discussion of these philosophers and their ideas will be brief, and will admittedly merely scratch the surface. It should go without saying that the depth of their ideas runs deeper than our treatment, and I encourage interested readers to pursue books (or professors) with a dedicated specialization in those philosophers. (2) I am including these additional sources not only because they are interesting, but to make clear that philosophy was not unique to the ancient Mediterranean region, and that deep thinkers have undoubtedly existed across all the continents at various times. (3) Despite showing similarities between some of these philosophers and ancient Western philosophers, I am not implying that there is any sort of actual intellectual connection between them, that somehow ideas were shared across thousands of miles, or that anyone "stole" ideas from anyone else. It is safe to assume that the similarities, where they exist, are a fascinating coincidence.

These changes are the product of the "living laboratory" provided by my students, for whom I am grateful.

# Acknowledgments

This book, and the motivation behind it, would not have been possible without the inspiration and assistance provided by several people. I would like to thank one of my mentors, Dr. David Glidden, for rescuing me from Nietzsche studies, and introducing me to the formal study of philosophy as a "way of life." I would like to thank my colleague Dr. Adam Wetsman for creating Gnutext and making this book, and others, possible—not to mention his excellent editing skills. I would also like to thank my colleague Professor Scott Dixon for being a kindred spirit and a true Aristotelian friend. Finally, I would like to thank my students, for whom I write. The sparks of interest and understanding in your eyes inspire me to teach and write in ways that will reach you where you are.

# Table of Contents

# Philosophical Timeline (partial)

- <u>Thales</u> of Miletus (c. 624 – 546 BC).
    - Tengh Shih (sixth century BCE)
- <u>Pythagoras</u> of Samos (c. 580 – c. 500 BC).
    - Confucius (traditionally 551–479 BCE)
- <u>Heraclitus</u> of Ephesus (c. 535 – c. 475 BC).
- <u>Parmenides</u> of Elea (c. 515 – 450 BC).
- <u>Zeno of Elea</u> (c. 490 – 430 BC).
- <u>Protagoras</u> of Abdera (c. 481 – 420 BC).
- <u>Socrates</u> of Athens (c. 470 – 399 BC).
    - Mozi (c. 470–c. 390 BCE)
- <u>Leucippus</u> of Miletus (First half of the 5th century BC).
- <u>Thrasymachus</u> of Miletus (c. 459 - c. 400 BC).
- <u>Democritus</u> of Abdera (c. 450 – 370 BC).
- <u>Antisthenes</u> (c. 444 – 365 BC)..
- <u>Plato</u> (c. 427 – 347 BC).
- <u>Diogenes of Sinope</u> (c. 399 – 323 BC).
- <u>Aristotle</u> (c. 384 – 322 BC).

## Hellenistic era philosophers

- Chuang-Tzu (369 - 286 BCE).
- <u>Pyrrho</u> of Elis (c. 360 – 270 BC).
- <u>Epicurus</u> (c. 341 – 270 BC).
- <u>Zeno of Citium</u> (c. 333 – 264 BC).
- <u>Chrysippus</u> of Soli (c. 280 – 207 BC).
- <u>Carneades</u> (c. 214 – 129 BC).

## Roman era philosophers

- <u>Lucretius</u> (c. 99 – 55 BC).
- <u>Cicero</u> (c. 106 BC – 43 BC)
- <u>Seneca the Younger</u> (c. 4 BC – 65 AD).
- <u>Epictetus</u> (c. 55 – 135).
- <u>Marcus Aurelius</u> (121–180).
- <u>Sextus Empiricus</u> (fl. during the 2nd and possibly the 3rd centuries AD).

## And beyond. . .

- Wonhyo (617–686 CE)

# Introduction

Among many, philosophy has a reputation for being "useless," or at least "impractical." Philosophy is an intellectual diversion, at best, and a waste of time, at worst. Philosophers are socially awkward people who crawl up inside their own heads, have deep thoughts, and then crawl back out with nothing to show for it. This perception is (sadly) aided by the way many of my "peers" teach philosophy (let alone "live" it), but, I do not share that perception of philosophy. Indeed, my goal is to demonstrate the practical value of philosophy.

I can't claim that practical approach as my own novel invention. It's a very old idea, actually, and the *original* approach to philosophy as it developed thousands of years ago in ancient Greece and Rome. In this book I will provide a brief and introductory overview of that ancient approach to philosophy as a "way of life," as our philosophical ancestors conceived it, and as it developed from the theoretical inquiries of the pre-Socratic philosophers, through the system building of Plato and Aristotle, and into the therapeutic efforts of the Hellenistic schools. Before any further explanation, I want to provide a taste of some ancient philosophy, in the words of the philosophers themselves.

> *Those who have learned the principles and nothing else are eager to throw them up immediately, just as persons with a weak stomach throw up their food. First digest your principles, and then you will surely not throw them up this way. Otherwise they are mere vomit, foul stuff and unfit to eat. But after you have digested these principles, show us some change in your governing principles that is due to them; as the athletes show their shoulders as the results of their exercising and eating.[1]*

> *A carpenter does not come up to you and say, "listen to me discourse about the art of carpentry," but he makes a contract for a house and builds it...Do the same thing yourself. Eat like a man, drink like a man...get married, have children, take part in civic life, learn how to put up with insults, and tolerate other people.[2]*

> *If philosophical theories seduce you, sit down and go over them again and again in your mind. But never call yourself a philosopher, and never allow yourself to be called a philosopher.[3]*

> *Vain is the word of a philosopher which does not heal any suffering of man. For just as there is no profit in medicine if it does not expel the diseases of the body, so there is no profit in philosophy either, if it does not expel the*

---

[1] Epictetus, *Discourses* III.21.
[2] Ibid.
[3] Ibid., 21,23.

*suffering of the mind.[4]*

*I think there is no one who has rendered worse service to the human race than those who have learned philosophy as a mercenary trade.[5]*

*Philosophy is no trick to catch the public; it is not devised for show. It is a matter, not of words, but of facts. It is not pursued in order that the day may yield some amusement before it is spent, or that our leisure may be relieved of a tedium that irks us. It moulds and constructs the soul; it orders our life, guides our conduct, shows us what we should do and what we should leave undone; it sits at the helm and directs our course as we waver amid uncertainties. Without it, no one can live fearlessly or in peace of mind. Countless things that happen every hour call for advice; and such advice is to be sought in philosophy.[6]*

*Most people imagine that philosophy consists in delivering discourses from the heights of a chair, and in giving classes based on texts. But what these people utterly miss is the uninterrupted philosophy which we see being practiced every day in a way which is perfectly equal to itself. . . . Socrates did not set up a grandstand for his audience and did not sit upon a professorial chair; he had no fixed timetables for talking or walking with his friends. Rather, he did philosophy sometimes by joking with them, and finally by going to prison and drinking poison. He was the first to show that at all times and in every place, in everything that happens to us, daily life gives us the opportunity to do philosophy.[7]*

Notice the unavoidable and obvious theme of practical benefit. This is no aberration. *Ancient philosophy* was done for the sake of becoming wise, and wisdom was desired for its incredibly important role in living an excellent life. Philosophy that did not make you better was not true philosophy. Philosophy that amounted to nothing more than pretty speeches and complicated arguments had missed the point. This theme will get explored in much greater detail in later chapters, but you should keep it in mind as you read the remainder of this book.

## Great Minds Think Alike!

At the time of the Spanish conquest of the valley of Mexico, there were numerous peoples (perhaps most well-known among them were the Aztecs)

---

[4] Epicurus, *Extant Remains, Fragments*, p. 133.
[5] Seneca, *Letters to Lucilius*, 108,36.
[6] Ibid., 16,3
[7] Plutarch, *Whether a Man Should Engage in Politics When He Is Old*, 26, 79.

linked by a common language: Nahuatl. The language is still spoken in various forms by approximately 1.5 million people, most of whom reside in central Mexico. The legacy of this language has made its way into the English language as well with words such as avocado, chocolate, chili, and tomato, among others. In addition to being linked by language, these peoples also inherited many traditions and ideas of the ancient Toltecs.

Spanish missionaries began a project of interviewing Nahua people and recording their accounts of Nahuatl culture, including their cosmology and accounts of "wise men." Presented in the form of songs transmitted by an oral tradition, and recorded as poems, these accounts echo the same sort of cultural development that occurred in the ancient Mediterranean: the transition from mythological and religious explanation to what we would recognize as "philosophical" explanation.[8]

> The Nahuas' first attempts to understand the origin of the universe, its essence, a natural phenomenon took the form of the great body of myths, generally thought to be part of their Toltec heritage. While the majority of the people unquestioningly accepted the myths as valid cosmogonic explanations, the tlamatinime eventually began to analyze the ancient concepts inherent in them, not for the purpose of denying their validity, but in order to delve deeper into the meaning of their symbols. Inevitably, they came upon certain problems in the traditional accounts of the origin, immutability and change, and ultimate fate of the world. In expressing their doubts in formulating their new ideas, however, they continue to use the language of myth.[9]

The exact content and timing of Nahuatl ideas is evasive, as the recorded accounts reflect the understanding of them as it was just prior to the 16th century, and it is unknown to what extent these ideas had changed or been faithfully transmitted in the centuries prior. In addition, little is known of the particular philosophers themselves, since their doctrines were handed down by students who didn't mention names, and the ideas were collectively attributed to whole generations of wise men. In this sense, there are no individuals that might stand out like a "Socrates." For these reasons, no attempt will be made to offer anything resembling a date, or a name, to the particular poems or ideas we will consider, including the following:

---

[8] And we would be prudent to recall that there is nothing resembling a sharp line demarcating "mythological" explanation from "philosophical" explanation in the Mediterranean either. The language used by Heraclitus and Parmenides, for example, sounds downright mystical, as will that of Plotinus centuries later.

[9] Miguel León-Portilla, *Aztec Thought and Culture*. Translated by Jack Emory Davis. University of Oklahoma press, 1990.p.25.).

1.  "The wise man: a light, a torch, a stout torch that does not smoke.
2.  A perforated mirror, a mirror pierced on both sides.
3.  His are the black and red ink, his are the illuminated manuscripts, he studies the illuminated manuscripts.
4.  He himself is writing and wisdom.
5.  He is the path, the true way for others.
6.  He directs people and things; he is a guide in human affairs.
7.  The wise man is careful (like a physician) and preserves tradition.
8.  He is the handed-down wisdom; he teaches it; he follows the path of truth.
9.  Teacher of truth, he never ceases to admonish.
10. He makes wise the countenances of others; to them he gives a face; he leads them to develop it.
11. He opens their ears; he enlightens them.
12. He is the teacher of guides; he shows in their path.
13. One depends upon him.
14. He puts a mirror before others, he makes them prudent, cautious; he causes a face to appear on them.
15. He attends to things; he regulates their path, he arranges and commands.
16. He applies his light to the world.
17. He knows what is above us (and) in the region of the dead.
18. He is a serious man.
19. Everyone is comforted by him, corrected, taught.
20. Thanks to him people humanize their will and receive a strict education.
21. He comforts the heart, he comforts the people, he helps, gives remedies, heals everyone."[10]

Here are just a few observations:

- In line 1, there is a reference to "the wise man." The Nahuatl word here is "tlamatini." In context, this is the equivalent of "philosopher."
- The tlamatini is being overtly compared to a physician, in lines 7 and 21; as someone who has wisdom and (more importantly) uses that wisdom to provide healing. This is a wonderful similarity to the ancient Mediterranean understanding of philosophy as "medicine for the soul."

---

[10] Codice Matritense de la Real Academia, VIII,fol.118, r.- 118,v. trans. by Leon-Portilla 1963.

- In lines 9, 10, 11, 12, and 13 the tlamatini is identified as a teacher and guide, and someone who "never ceases to admonish." There are some clear analogies with Socrates here.
- In line 14 the tlamatini is described as offering a mirror before other people, forcing them to see themselves. I can't help but think of the Socratic injunction to "know thyself" in this context.
- In lines 5, 8, and 9 the tlamatini is credited with knowing and teaching the truth – as distinct from falsehoods. Here we have an analogy with the philosopher as a seeker after truth, as compared to others who either don't know the truth or who do not teach it in any event. Contrast the praises of the tlamatini offered above with the account of the "false wise man" offered in some other verses.

*The false wise man, like an ignorant physician,*
*a man without understanding, claims to*
*know about God.*
*He has his own traditions, and keeps them secretly.*
*He is a boaster, vanity is his.*
*He makes things complicated; he brags and exaggerates.*
*He is a river, a Rocky Hill (a dangerous man).*
*A lover of darkness and corners,*
*a mysterious wizard, a magician, a witch doctor,*
*a public thief, he takes things.*
*A destroyer, a destroyer of faces.*
*He leaves the people astray; and he causes others to lose their faces.*
*He hides things, he makes them difficult.*
*He entangles them with difficulty; he destroys them;*
*he causes the people to perish; he mysteriously puts an*
*and to everything.*[11]

In sharp contrast to the tlamatini, the "amo qualli tlamatini" (not good wise man) is presented in ways analogous to the sophists of the ancient Mediterranean. Plato will famously uses Socrates to critique the sophists as both ignorant and dangerous. Here, the "false wise man" is described as an ignorant physician, as someone who lacks understanding but who claims to possess it. He operates from vanity, and rather than improving the conditions of others, he makes things worse. He is described as someone who makes things complicated, rather than clarifying them, and is someone who leads people astray rather than as a competent guide.

---

[11] Ibid., fol.188,v

This (unfavorable) comparison continues, emphasizing even more the tlamatini as a healer in contrast to the "false physician."

> *The true doctor.*
> *He is a wise man (tlamatini);*
> *he imparts life.*
> *A tried specialist,*
> *he has worked with herbs, stones, trees, and roots.*
> *His remedies have been tested;*
> *he examines, he experiments.*
> *he alleviates sickness.*
> *He massages aches and sets broken bones.*
> *He administers purges and potions;*
> *he bleeds his patients;*
> *he cuts and he sews the wound;*
> *he brings about reactions;*
> *he stanches the bleeding with ashes.*
> *The false physician.*
> *He ridicules and deceives the people;*
> *he brings on indigestion;*
> *he makes illness worse;*
> *his medicines are fatal.*
> *He has dark secrets he will not reveal;*
> *he is a sorcerer and a witch;*
> *he is familiar with the noxious herbs and possesses their seeds,*
> *he practices divination with knotted ropes.*
> *He makes sickness worse;*
> *his herbs and seeds poison and his cures kill."[12]*

In addition to the tlamatini being a true physician, as opposed to a false one, there is even a clearly indicated difference in methodology between the tlamatini and the "false wise man." The tlamatini uses reason, and his conclusions are evidence-based! "His remedies have been tested; he examines, he experiments." In contrast to this, the "false wise man" is called a sorcerer with "dark secrets he will not reveal."

Without making too much of the analogy, in both the ancient Mediterranean as well as these poems exalting the tlamatini, we see in emphasis on the use of reason in defending positions, as opposed to appeals to authority or divine agents.

---

[12] Ibid., p. 26-27.

We will begin our treatment of philosophy with a brief discussion of its birth, and how it changed the way people thought. We will consider several prominent philosophers who came before Socrates, then Socrates himself, and then several more that came after. We will finish this exploration by moving from Greece to Rome, to see how philosophy continued to develop and took an even more obviously practical turn.

# Chapter 1: The Birth of Philosophy

*Comprehension questions you should be able to answer after reading this chapter:*

1. How was "philosophical" explanation different from that of the poets?

2. What does each of the following philosophers identify as the "first principle," the most fundamental "substance" or basis of reality? Thales, Pythagoras, Heraclitus, Parmenides, Democritus.

3. Thales not only claims that water is the most fundamental substance, but offers an argument for his view. How would you summarize his argument?

4. Why did Pythagoras think that math was the basis of reality?

5. What did Heraclitus think about change? About permanence?

6. Why did Parmenides and Zeno think that the senses were unreliable and that change is an illusion?

7. What are the properties of "The One" ("Being") according to Parmenides? How does he try to "prove" them?

8. What is the purpose of Zeno's paradoxes? How are they supposed to work?

9. What are the four "roots" according to Empedocles?

10. Explain Empedocles' "evolutionary" account of the origin of all the different kinds of living creatures.

11. What are atoms, according to Democritus & Leucippus? Explain the relationship between atoms and what we observe in Nature (e.g., "permanence," "change").

It seems reasonable to suppose that for as long as humans have been able to think, some people have had "deep thoughts." It's also presumptuous to think that the first "deep thoughts" arose in the ancient Mediterranean region. However, we do have an historical record for this time and region that does reveal a remarkable shift in the way people understood their world and its operations, and we can call this the birth of "philosophy"—at least in the West.

In Greece, specifically, prior to philosophy, intellectual and moral authority was associated with celebrated poets, such as Homer or Hesiod (for both of whom, the dates of their lives are fuzzy, at best—*very* roughly 750-650 BCE). Poets and poems (e.g., The Odyssey, the Illiad, Achilles, Ulysses, etc.) served a variety of functions far beyond entertainment. They were the communities' source for history, "science," religion, and morality. Poets were no ordinary people. They were inspired by the Muses (goddesses of inspiration) in a fashion akin to divine inspiration. They spoke, therefore, with a special authority. Poets provided models of virtue and vice to be emulated or shunned (e.g., Achilles), and they explained the nature and operations of the world through myths. *These myths tried to explain the unfamiliar by appealing to the familiar.* For example, that strange glowing ball that seems to travel across the sky? A fiery chariot driven each day by the god Apollo. Unexpected events, such as natural disasters or diseases, were the outcome of the gods' fickle and changing tempers.

The problem, though, of appealing to gods and spirits to explain all the operations of nature and events that transpired, is that these explanations didn't seem to really explain all that much. "The gods did it" doesn't really provide much more understanding of an event than the event offered by itself. Moreover, the inconsistency observed in the world, when the only explanation was "the will of the gods," was a source of confusion and frustration. To remedy this, some poets placed even the gods under the power of the "Fates." *The Fates represented an implicit, objective ordering principle, a source of "justice," as it were, to which even the gods were subject.*

Having now taken the fateful cultural step of supposing that there is some "larger" principle than the anthropomorphic, all-too-human gods with which to interpret reality, the task now shifted to figuring out just what that larger underlying and ordering principle *is*.

Many individuals came forward to offer their answers. They include Thales, Anaximander, Pythagoras, Xenophenes, Heraclitus, Parmenides, Empedocles, Zeno, and Democritus, among others. We will focus on only a few of those, and even with those only to a small extent. I focus on only a few, and only in limited fashion, for several reasons. For one, as is the case with most of the pre-Socratic philosophers, what little we know of them comes from literal fragments of their works, or their descriptions by other philosophers (such as Aristotle) or historians (such as Herodotus)—and often these accounts serve to critique the views of these philosophers. One wonders, therefore, whether the summaries of their views are as charitable as they should be. A good friend and colleague of mine once remarked to me that a whole lot of theory is attributed to these people on the basis of very little actual writing! To attempt to say a lot about whom we know so little seems presumptuous.

In addition, most approaches to ancient philosophy in general, and the pre-Socratics in particular, seem to rely on a simple presentation of all of the known thinkers in chronological order. The problem with that approach is that without any basic context or theme, it seems to be an experience in mere trivia. "Thales thought reality was ultimately water, whereas Heraclitus favored fire." This is fine if our goal is to fare well in philosophical trivial pursuit, but that is not my aim with regard to studying philosophy.

Instead, I consider only a handful, in brief, and with an ulterior motive for each. Several philosophers from this time period have been omitted, and even those who are being described are being given scandalously brief treatment. I confess that if you are looking for a book that attempts to delve deeply into the murky waters of pre-Socratic philosophy, this is not that book.

I will begin with Thales, because philosophy is said to have begun with Thales, and I think he deserves the gesture of respect. He also set the tone for philosophy as we recognize it today, and is relevant for that reason. I will then consider Pythagoras, Heraclitus, and Parmenides (along with his sidekick, Zeno) primarily because of the role they play in Plato's thought—someone much more important, in my estimation. I will also give Democritus a brief treatment, primarily because of the influence he had on Epicurus (who will receive much more attention in a later chapter).

## Thales

Thales is generally accepted as the first (known, recognized) philosopher. He lived roughly from 624 BCE to 546 BCE, and made his home in Miletus (on the East coast of present-day Turkey).

Thales flourished in a time of great thinkers across the globe. He was a contemporary of the prophet Jeremiah, the Persian prophet Zoroaster, Gautama Siddhartha (Buddha), and Confucius. He is notable, among other things, for his apparent prediction of a solar eclipse on May 23rd, 585 BCE. What is significant about this prediction is that he did not attribute it to some sort of divine foretelling, but rather saw it as the result of (and indicator of) a consistent, impersonal natural order of things—a "Nature" subject to investigation, generalization, and prediction.

Some of you might be thinking that this sounds more like science, than philosophy. Fair enough. But, keep but mind that "science" did not yet exist in Thales' time, and that the methodology that we regard as science first developed and emerged from within the philosophical community. As another credit to Thales, though, some also credit him with being the first (known, recognized) scientist. Thales, and his peers and "descendants," would conduct their inquiries in a wholly new literary style, as well. Rather than writing in verse, like the poets, they (most of them, at least) wrote in prose—another departure from custom.

What's important about Thales is that he accepts *that reality is something stable and subject to understanding.* Though the world is filled with a multiplicity of various things, he seeks a "unity" behind this multiplicity, some organizing principle that will explain all things and their operations. This most basic metaphysical question of "what is that organizing principle?" inspired a search that still takes place today, whether by philosophers or physicists.

Thales not only posed the question of what is the one, common element that unifies Nature, but offered an answer: *water.*

Yes, water. Since we have no surviving writings from Thales himself, we must take the word of others, such as Aristotle:

*Of the first philosophers, then, most thought the principles (tas archas) which were of the nature of matter (tas en hulês) were the only principles of all things (archas pantôn)....Yet they do not all agree as to the number and the nature of these principles. Thales, the founder of this type of philosophy, says the principle is water (for which reason he declared that the earth rests on water), getting the notion perhaps from seeing that the nutriment of all things is moist, and that heat itself is generated from the moist and kept alive by it (and that from which they come to be is a principle of all things). He got his notion from this fact, and from the fact that the seeds of all things have a moist nature, and that water is the origin of the nature of moist things.*

*Some think that even the ancients who lived long before the present generation, and first framed accounts of the gods, had a similar view of nature; for they made Ocean and Tethys the parents of creation, and described the oath of the gods as being by water, to which they give the name of Styx; for what is oldest is most honorable, and the most honorable thing is that by which one swears. It may perhaps be uncertain whether this opinion about nature is primitive and ancient, but Thales at any rate is said to have declared himself thus about the first cause. Hippo no one would think fit to include among these thinkers, because of the paltriness of his thought.[13]*

Joining Aristotle in affirming that Thales' identified water as the first principle is Hippolytus:

*It is said that Thales of Miletus, one of the seven wise men, was the first to undertake the study of physical philosophy. He said that the archê (principle) and the end of all things is water. All things acquire firmness as this solidifies, and again as it is melted their existence is*

---

[13] Aristotle, *Metaphysics*, 983b -984a

*threatened; to this are due earthquakes and whirlwinds and movements of the stars. And all things are movable and in a fluid state, the character of the compound being determined by the nature of the principle from which it springs.*[14]

*Reality, at its most fundamental level, is water.* Before you so quickly dismiss his answer, though, consider the following (and give the guy a break—he came up with his answer about 2500 years ago!):

- Water is essential for all living things. ("He got his notion from this fact, and from the fact that the seeds of all things have a moist nature, and that water is the origin of the nature of moist things.")

- Things could exist in three different states (known at that time time): solid, liquid, and air/gas. Water (and seemingly only water) could exist in all three. Water can evaporate and become air (steam), or condense from air and become water (rain), or freeze and become solid (ice). ("All things acquire firmness as this solidifies, and again as it is melted their existence is threatened.")

- When water evaporates, it often leaves sediment—giving the impression that earth comes from water. Similarly, if one digs deeply into the earth, one finds water.

- Water seems to be "self-moving" (i.e., it seems to flow all on its own via rain or rivers), and therefore could account for motion and change in the world. ("And all things are movable and in a fluid state.")

It is worth noting that Thales imbues water with properties and a significance that exceeds what most of think of as water, today. Aristotle attributes to Thales the belief that "All things are full of gods" (Aristotle, On the Soul, 405a 19). Hippolytus says something similar of him: "This principle [water] is God, and it has neither beginning nor end" (Refutation of all Heresies, 1). A quotation attributed to Aetius of Antioch further clarifies this view by saying of him the following: "Thales said that the mind in the universe is God, and the all is endowed with soul and is full of spirits; and its divine moving power pervades the elementary water."

The reasoning seems to be something like this: Only souls can cause motion. For any case of motion, there must a soul causing it. The soul responsible for motion is God. Anything eternal is divine. (According to Clement of Alexandria: "For Thales being asked, What is the divinity? said, 'What has neither beginning nor end.'"). Water (as the first principle) is eternal. Therefore water is divine. Therefore, water is the God responsible for motion. Water is the "soul" of all things, present in all things. God is fragmented into the animating souls of all

---

[14] Hippolytus, *Refutation of All Heresies*, 1; Dox. 555.

things. Therefore, all things are "full of gods." This is very special water, indeed!

Today, I suspect it would be difficult to find many who would enthusiastically endorse "water" as the ultimate explanation of everything, but Thales' particular answer is less important than the pattern he established. His theory was *monistic* (i.e., appealed to only one principle), and therefore simple. His theory was *materialist* (i.e., that one substance is physical). His theory was considered interesting and worthy of thought even if it was "purely theoretical" and not obviously of practical benefit. For possibly the first time, an interest in understanding, for understanding's sake, entered into the mental life of the Greeks. What's more, this understanding was rational. *It was supported by reasons, as opposed to an appeal to tradition or authority, and was subject to examination and debate*—as would all philosophical theories to come after him.

That there would be debate should come as no surprise. The poets had simply appealed to the authority of the Muses to support their interpretation of events in terms of the will of the gods. Thales and other philosophers made no such appeal to authority. On what basis, then, could they claim to *know* the "nature" of Nature (what Nature is *really* like)? This not only introduced the field of epistemology, but inspired the reasoned defenses and critiques for which philosophy has become well known.

Thales set the tone and modeled the kind of approach that philosophy still follows to this day. If for no other reason, then, Thales is monumentally important to the history of Western philosophy.

## Pythagoras

As far as allegedly-vegetarian "cult" leaders obsessed with mathematics are concerned, it doesn't get much better than Pythagoras. Pythagoras lived (roughly) from 571-497 BCE. He was born on the island of Samos, near Miletus (Thales' home), but later moved to a Greek colony in Southern Italy. Pythagoras was a historical contemporary of the Buddha, as well as the Old Testament prophets Haggai and Zechariah.

Most of us have encountered him by virtue of his famous Pythagorean Theorem ($a^2 + b^2 = c^2$)—and here, already, we encounter our first challenge. Pythagoras, over time, took on a mythic/mystic status. Actual miracles were attributed to him! So many legends arose concerning Pythagoras that it is uncertain what about his life, or even teachings, is true, attributable to him, or to "pythagoreans." His school had a tendency to attribute all new ideas to him, even years after his death, as a gesture of respect. Even the Pythagorean Theorem itself, bearing his name, might not have been discovered by him. The story according to which he sacrificed 100 oxen at its discovery (if true) could merely have been a testimony to his excitement that the theorem has been discovered, not necessarily that he did so himself. While we have to tread carefully with any of these pre-Socratic figures, we must be especially hesitant with Pythagoras.

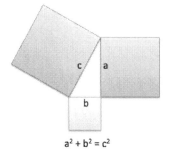

$$a^2 + b^2 = c^2$$

Whereas Thales identified water as the first organizing principle in terms of a substance, Pythagoras sought the nature of "form" itself. His answer focused on mathematics. Once again we must rely on Aristotle:

> *Contemporaneously with these philosophers and before them, the so-called Pythagoreans, who were the first to take up mathematics, not only advanced this study, but also having been brought up in it they thought its principles (archas) were the principles of all things. Since of these principles numbers are by nature the first, and in numbers they seemed to see many resemblances to the things that exist and come into being—more than in fire and earth and water (such and such a modification of numbers being justice, another being soul and reason, another being opportunity— and similarly almost all other things being numerically expressible); since, again, they saw that the modifications and the ratios of the musical scales were expressible in numbers;—since, then, all other things seemed in their whole nature to be modeled on numbers, and numbers seemed to be the first things in the whole of nature, they supposed the elements of numbers to be the elements of all things, and the whole heaven to be a musical scale and a number.*[15]

Pythagoras observed that *reality is mathematical in nature*. It is structured geometrically. Mathematical points can produce lines. Combinations of lines can produce plane figures. Combinations of plane figures produce solid objects (just think of 3D rendering, today). Interestingly, we can think of math without thereby thinking of physical objects. For example, I can complete equations and ponder the properties of mathematical abstractions without explicitly or even implicitly imagining actual physical objects that correspond to those abstractions. I can add 2 and 2 to get 4 without having to think of 2 books and another 2 books making a total of 4 books. We can't, however, seem to think of objects without at least implicitly making use of math (e.g., the geometry that describes the objects' extension). He also noted the mathematical structure of music (e.g., that particular ratios of lengths of string on an instrument produce predictable changes in sound, such as how doubling the length of a string lowers the sound

---

[15] Aristotle, *Metaphysics*, 985b 23-986a 3

by an octave), and inferred something akin to spiritual significance from that by virtue of their hypothesized "harmony of the spheres." This theory claimed that the distances between planets were in proportion to notes in the musical scale. Moreover, he thought that the human body could be in or out of "harmony," and this corresponded to health or sickness. Music (and math) was at the center of existence. Indeed, Pythagoras (or at least, "Pythagoreans") developed a complicated cosmology based on math.

> *Evidently, then, these thinkers also consider that number is the principle both as matter for things and as forming both their modifications and their permanent states, and hold that the elements of number are the even and the odd, and that of these the latter is limited, and the former unlimited; and that the One proceeds from both of these (for it is both even and odd), and number from the One; and that the whole heaven, as has been said, is numbers.[16]*

Mystic and mysterious though it may be, the idea seems to be something like this: there has always existed, as a sort of disordered, passive, prime matter, the principle of the unlimited (the "even"). Co-eternal with the unlimited is the (active) principle of the limited ("odd") which imposes order on the unlimited. "The One" derives from these two opposing principles. For some reason, the even (unlimited) was associated with evil, and the limited (odd) with good. "Evil belongs to the class of the unlimited, as the Pythagoreans conjectured, and good to that of the limited."[17]

Therefore, "the One" is both good and evil, and order is associated with good, and disorder with evil. The limited (odd) is also associated with the "Monad" (not to be confused with the One!), and the unlimited with the "Dyad." According to Aetius of Antioch, "Pythagoras held that one of the first principles, the Monad, is God and the good, which is the origin of the One, and is itself intelligence; but the undefined Dyad is a deity and the evil, surrounding which is the mass of matter." Also, from Diogenes Laertius:

> *The principle of all things is the Monad or unit; arising from this Monad, the undefined Dyad or two serves as material substratum to the Monad, which is cause; from the Monad and undefined Dyad spring numbers; from numbers point; from points, lines; from line plane figures; from plane figures, solid figures; from solid figures, sensible bodies, the elements which are four, fire, water, earth and air; these elements interchange and turn into one another completely, and combine to create a universe animate, intelligent, spherical.[18]*

Beyond his inspiration for math majors, I find him most interesting for the

---

[16] Aristotle, *Metaphysics*, 986a 15-21
[17] Aristotle, *Nicomachean Ethics*,1106b29.
[18] Diogenes Laertius, *Lives of Eminent Philosophers*, VIII. 25

influence he had on Plato. We will consider Plato in a later chapter, but for now it's worth pointing out some of Pythagoras' ideas that will be encountered once again when we turn our attention to Plato:

- Pythagoras was a dualist, and conceived of the body as a "prison" for the soul.

- He believed the soul was immortal, and was reincarnated.

According to Xenophanes' account: "And now I will turn to another tale and point the way.... Once they say that he (Pythagoras) was passing by when a dog was being beaten and spoke this word: "Stop! Don't beat it! For it is the soul of a friend that I recognized when I heard its voice."

- *He conceived of "salvation" in terms of philosophical enlightenment.* Indeed, some claim that he was the first to refer to himself as a "philosopher"—a "lover of wisdom." This is terribly important, as the vision of philosophy as a means of living a better life might have started with Pythagoras.

- He developed a vision of an ideal society.

- He regarded women as equal to men.

- He thought property should be held in common.

- He proposed a rigid class system.

When you study Plato, and specifically when you read the Republic, think of these ideas and note how they reappear in Plato's own work.

## Heraclitus

If being an influence on Plato is enough to get Pythagoras mentioned, it will be enough for Heraclitus as well—though Plato was certainly not the only philosopher (ancient or otherwise) to be influenced by him. When we turn our attention to Plato, consider how Plato tries to address the issue of "change," and then remember Heraclitus.

Heraclitus lived in Ephesis (North of Miletus) from (roughly) 540-480 BCE. In sharp contrast to Thales' water, *Heraclitus proposes fire as the first principle,* the *"Logos."* "This world did none of gods or men make, but it always was and is and shall be: an ever living fire, kindling in measures and going out in measures (Fragment 30)."

According to Simplicius, "Heraclitus ... made fire the *archê*, and out of fire they produce existing things by thickening and thinning, and resolve them into fire again, on the assumption that fire is the one, underlying *physis*."[19] And, from Diogenes Laertius: "Fire is the element; all things are an exchange for fire and come into being by rarefaction and condensation."[20]

---

[19] Simplicius, *On Aristotle's Physics*, 23.23
[20] Diogenes Laertius, *Lives of Eminent Philosophers*, 9. 8

The notion (if taken literally) seems to be that fire, when compressed, turned into "denser" elements—but these then (eventually) revert back to fire. "All things are an equal exchange for fire and fire for all things, as goods are for gold and gold for goods (Fragment 90)."

One of the primary questions for pre-Socratic philosophers (and many who came after them) was how to understand "change." What is the nature of change, how is it possible? This would occupy philosophers for centuries. Fire, probably best understood symbolically, represented change and strife for Heraclitus. All Things Are in Flux. As Plato characterizes the view of Cratylus, a disciple of Heraclitus: "All things flow and nothing stands."[21]  Elsewhere in Plato we have another, similar metaphor: "All things move like flowing streams."[22] Heraclitus apparently thought that there is *only* change. *Permanence is an illusion.*

> *Moreover, the view is actually held by some [i.e. Heraclitus] that not merely some things but all things in the world are in motion and always in motion, though we cannot apprehend the fact by sense perception.*[23]

He famously said that "we step and do not step into the same rivers, we are and are not." More colloquially, one cannot step into the same river twice. At first glance, a river seems stable and permanent, but closer inspection reveals that it is in flux. A simple explanation for this is that the river is constantly changing, so it's no longer the same river the second time you step. Additionally, one could argue that you have changed as well, so that you are no longer the same "you" who is doing the stepping.

The flux/change Heraclitus speaks of is also associated with strife—though he rejects any negative connotation for strife. "It is necessary to know that war is common and right, is strife and that all things happen by strife and necessity (Fragment 80)." Opposition and strife are only apparent, but not "real." All things are regulated by the Logos ("Fire"), and are of Logos. "Unity" emerges from apparent tension, just as there is an implicit unity underlying the apparent tension, as the following fragments attest.

> *The hot substance and the cold form what we might call a hot-cold continuum, a single entity (Fragment 126).*

> *Night and day, which Hesiod had made parent and child, are, and must always have been, essentially connected and interdependent (Fragment 57).*

---

21 Plato, *Cratylus*, 401d
22 Plato, *Theaetetus*, 161d.
23 Aristotle, *Physics*, 253b 9

*Out of all things there comes a unity, and out of a unity all things (Fragment 10).*
*They do not apprehend how being at variance it agrees with itself: there is a palintonos (counter-stretched) harmony, as in the bow and the lyre.*[24]

This last fragment offers a metaphor for the unity that comes from tension: the bow could not exist, as a bow, if not for the tension between the wood and the bowstring. Change, strife, "opposing" forces "pushing" and "pulling" on each other –that is what is "real," the truth hidden to our senses, masked by the illusion of permanency. Given his emphasis on change, perhaps we can see why he chose fire as his "first principle." Fire is constantly changing, after all. He also had a cyclical vision of the universe and its history, believing that endless cycles of fiery destruction and rebirth occur. This model was incorporated into later Stoic thought, and had a profound influence on Nietzsche (i.e., his doctrine of the eternal recurrence).

## Parmenides and Zeno

Although the year of his birth is uncertain, Parmenides is thought to have lived in Elea (Southern Italy) from (roughly) 515-450 BCE. He was a younger contemporary of Heraclitus, and an older contemporary of Socrates. He allegedly came to Athens with his student, Zeno, and spoke with a young Socrates—though the meeting is dubious. Instead, the apocryphal meeting is likely a gesture of respect from Plato—especially considering that Parmenides "instructs" Socrates in the dialogue, and Socrates speaks of him in complimentary fashion. "Parmenides seems to me to be, in Homer's words, 'one to be venerated' and also 'awful'. For I met him when I was very young and he was very old, and he appeared to me to possess an absolutely noble depth of mind."[25]

Parmenides composed a poem called "On Nature," of which only 160 (of perhaps 3,000) lines have survived.[26] The poem distinguishes the "Way of Truth" from the "Way of Seeming" ("Way of Opinion"). The writing style exhibited in the poem is abstract, and quasi-religious.

Abstract, or not, Parmenides was a metaphysician who would be profoundly influential to many philosophers who followed. *Parmenides claimed that the first principle is "The One," or "Being." This Being is uncreated, unchangeable and imperishable, one and indivisible, motionless, and also a finite body.* Note how several of the properties he ascribes to Being are those that later theologians will ascribe to God (e.g., uncreated, imperishable), or that will be incorporated by

---

[24] Hippolytus, *Refutations of all Heresies*, 9. 9.

[25] Plato, *Parmenides*, 184e

[26] If these numbers are accurate, it underscores my point about interpreting these philosophers on the basis of scant textual evidence. Our understanding of Parmenides' view is (in terms of primary text) is based on 5% of the original work!

later philosophers (e.g., Aristotle's notion of the unmoved Mover).[27]

Parmenides central, seismic revelation is that "it is." Or, perhaps more helpfully: "What is, is." Aristotle will eventually enshrine this insight as the law of identity (A is A). The rest of Parmenides' ideas all derive from this single, basic insight. What is, is—and this means that it can't be what it is not, or fail to be what it is. What is cannot be other than what it is.

What "is not" (i.e., "nothing") does not exist—it is not any-*thing* that either is or could be. Nothing is not even something that we can conceive, since, if we can conceive it, it is *something* that we conceive! In short, Being is, and Nothing cannot exist.

It is on this basis that Parmenides, in direct opposition to Heraclitus, ultimately rejects change. "Undiscerning crowds, in whose eyes it is, and is not, the same and not the same, all things travel in opposite directions." Our senses tell us that things come into existence, and then go out of existence (i.e., that something "is" *and* "is not"). Change requires that something go from what it is, to what it is not. What is (Being), though, simply *is*.

> It is [i.e. what is], is uncreated and indestructible; for it is complete, immovable, and without end. Nor was it ever, nor will it be; for now it is, all at once, a continuous one. For what kind of origin for it will you look for? In what way and from what source could it have drawn its increase? I shall not let you say nor think that it came from what is not; for it can neither be thought nor uttered that anything is not. And, if it came from nothing, what need could have made it arise later rather than sooner? Therefore must it either be altogether or be not at all. Nor will the force of truth suffer anything to arise besides itself from that which is not. Wherefore, Justice does not loose her fetters and let anything come into being or pass away, but holds it fast. Our judgment thereon depends on this: "Is it or is it not?" Surely it is adjudged, as it must be, that we are to set aside the one way as unthinkable and nameless (for it is no true way), and that the other path is real and true. How, then, can what is be going to be in the future? Or how could it come into being? If it came into being, it is not; nor is it if it is going to be in the future. Thus is becoming extinguished and passing away not to be heard of.

As Aristotle describes it: "First, if it comes into being from something, then it does not come into being at all, since it already exists; second, if it comes into being from nothing, then it cannot come into being, since something cannot come from nothing."[28]

Another reason Parmenides thought something can't come from nothing is that there would be no explanation as to the timing of something coming into

---

[27] The 20th century philosopher, Martin Heidegger, wrote a book on Parmenides. He was clearly influenced by him, including, presumably and unfortunately, with respect to obscure writing style. . . .

[28] Aristotle, *Physics*, 187a 34.

existence. "And, if it came from nothing, what need could have made it arise later rather than sooner?"

Being, therefore is eternal. It is uncreated, never coming into existence (for it would have to have come from Nothing, which is impossible). Nor can it go out of existence, for it would become nothing—which is not any "thing" that can be. "Thus is becoming extinguished and passing away not to be heard of."

Not only change, but time (if understood in terms of change), is an illusion. "Nor was it ever, nor will it be; for now it is, all at once, a continuous one." Since being can't come into Being, or cease to be, but just "is," Being "is" all at once, entirely, wholly, with neither parts nor change, neither growth nor decay. "Therefore must it either be altogether or be not at all." Since "not at all" is no option, Being must be "altogether." "If it came into being, it is not; nor is it if it is going to be in the future." Being is thought to be "complete, immovable." "Wherefore, Justice does not loose her fetters and let anything come into being or pass away, but holds it fast."

In addition, Being has no parts, but is indivisible. "Nor is it divisible, since it is all alike, and there is no more of it in one place than in another, to hinder it from holding together, nor less of it, but everything is full of what is. Wherefore it is wholly continuous; for what is, is in contact with what is." Since Being is all that is, there is no-thing that could separate Being from itself.

Parmenides describes the "completeness" of Being as analogous to a sphere: "Since, then, it has a furthest limit, it is complete on every side, like the mass of a rounded sphere, equally poised from the center in every direction; for it cannot be greater or smaller in one place than in another. For there is no nothing that could keep it from reaching out equally, nor can anything that is be more here and less there than what is, since it is all inviolable. For the point from which it is equal in every direction tends equally to the limits."

We don't have to take him literally—though it is possible that he really did conceive of Being as a finite (actual) sphere. A non-literal option would be to think of the sphere as a symbol of the fact that Being "cannot be greater or smaller in one place rather than another." Spheres are equal and identical in every direction (from the center—until the circumference of the sphere is reached).

Because Being is unchanging, Parmenides takes the opposite view of Heraclitus: *reality is permanent and unchanging, change is the illusion*. Obviously, this flies in the face of our direct observation of change, so we have here an early example of reason being privileged over experience and sense testimony. If reason tells us that reality is unchanging, and our senses tell us change occurs, then so much the worse for our senses!

Another famous philosopher, Zeno (490-430 BCE), was a follower and capable defender of Parmenides. *Zeno's infamous paradoxes were meant to demonstrate the unreliability of the senses, and that change is an illusion*. To demonstrate the unreliability of the senses, he offers us the "millet seed" paradox. Actually, Aristotle offers us an account of the millet seed paradox in his own work (*Physics*) that we can hope is a fair rendering:

Zeno: Tell me Protagoras, does a single millet seed make a noise as it falls, or does 1/10,000 of a millet?

Protagoras: No.

Zeno: Does a bushel of millet seed make a noise as it falls, or not?

Protagoras: Yes, a bushel makes a noise.

Zeno: But isn't there a ratio (logos) between a bushel of millet seed, and one seed, and 1/10,000 of a seed?

Protagoras: Yes, there is.

Zeno: So won't there be the same ratio of sounds between them, for the sounds are in proportion to what makes the sound? And if this is so, if the bushel of millet seed makes a noise so will a single seed and 1/10,000 of a seed.

The moral of this story is that "reason" tells us that the single seed makes a sound. Our ears tell us otherwise. Therefore, the senses are unreliable. To illustrate the illusion of change, he offers us the "foot race" paradox—also recounted by Aristotle:

*Second is the one called 'Achilles': this is that the slowest runner never will be overtaken by the fastest; for it is necessary for the one chasing to come first to where the one fleeing started from, so that it is necessary for the slower runner always to be ahead some (Physics. 6.9.239ᵇ14–18).*

By way of explanation (and analogy), suppose that the Roadrunner is going to race Wile E. Coyote (I certainly hope you readers get the Warner Brothers cartoon reference). The Roadrunner is going to be a good sport, however, and gives the Coyote a head start. According to the paradox, even though the Roadrunner is faster, he will never overtake the Coyote. Why?

At the start of the race (time $t_1$), the Coyote (C) is in the lead over the Roadrunner (R).

In the next moment of the race (time $t_2$), both R and C have advanced. R has reached C's starting point, but C has moved forward as well, and is now slightly less ahead of R.

R          C

In the next moment of the race (time $t_3$), the same sort of advancement occurs again.

R          C

This process continues, with the distance between them getting ever smaller—but never reducing to nothing. There will always be some tiny distance the Roadrunner has to cross before he can reach the Coyote, and will therefore never overtake him. Of course, in a different paradox, Zeno establishes that no one (neither Roadrunner nor Coyote, using our examples) can ever complete the race anyway, so it's all a moot point as far as racing is concerned.

And yet, our senses clearly indicate that races can be completed and that runners can pass each other, that change is possible. Reason tells us otherwise, by virtue of these paradoxes. Therefore, the senses are unreliable and change is an illusion of those unreliable senses.

The significance of both Parmenides and Zeno is that they were, perhaps, the first to being attention to the philosophical significance of words and concepts (e.g., "being," "is"). They also zealously pursued logical conclusions, even at the expense of common sense. Finally, their blatantly counter-intuitive conclusions inspired rigorous counter-examples from those seeking to refute them. In essence, everyone else had to rise to the challenge presented by their arguments—a tactic (and benefit) produced by the Skeptics later on. In fact, the distinction between appearance and reality as detailed by Parmenides and Zeno is what makes Skepticism possible.

## Empedocles

Empedocles (492 – 432 BCE) was a Sicilian philosopher known for two (partially) surviving poems: "On Nature," and "Purifications." Although these poems exist only as fragments, we actually have more fragments from Empedocles than from any other pre-Socratic philosopher.

His significance is unquestionable, being mentioned by both Plato and Aristotle. His status, it seems, went far beyond recognition as a philosopher. Indeed, he had a fantastic (and very much questionable) reputation for someone who ended plagues, revived the dead, and magically diverted the course of the stream. He also proclaimed himself to be an immortal God! Despite that title, he died – though his death was itself a source of mystery, with some sources saying he died by drowning, others by hanging, others by virtue of a broken leg (presumably by infection), and still another by having thrown himself into a volcano. Apocryphal stories notwithstanding, his legacy endures.

Perhaps his most recognizable contribution to the Western philosophical tradition is by virtue of being the first to propose that everything is ultimately composed of four basic "roots:" earth, air, fire, and water.[29] These are the four basic, indestructible "elements" from which all things are composed. Each compound, he thought, has a "theoretically" specifiable ratio of roots. For example, he claimed that bone was composed of four parts fire, two parts of earth, and two parts water. Flesh and blood on the other hand are composed of equal parts fire, air, and water.

## Great Minds Think Alike!

A significant aspect of Nahua cosmology is their account of change. In an amazing coincidence, these agents of change are the four elements: earth, air/wind, fire, and water – the very same "roots" proposed by Empedocles in the ancient Mediterranean.

> closely related to the theory of cyclical development is the concept of the four elements symbolized in the Historia de los Mexicanos by the four sons of Ometéotl. By an amazing parallelism, these elements – earth, wind, fire and water – are the same for hypothesized as the roots (ritsomata) of all things by the Greek philosopher Empedocles and transmitted to Western thought through Aristotle. Eduard Seler said of the relationship between the cosmic periods in the four elements: "these four distinct prehistoric or pre-'s cosmic ages of the Mexicans, each one oriented toward a different direction of the heavens, are astonishingly related to the four elements, water, earth, wind, and fire, known to classical antiquity in which even now constitute the way that the civilized peoples of East Asia look upon nature.[30]

In addition to these four roots, he proposed two fundamental forces: love (*philia*) and strife (*neikos*). Love is an attractive force, and forms compounds by mixing roots together. Strife, in contrast, is a repulsive force which separates compounds into their constituent roots. He deduced that these are equal forces, since otherwise the cosmos would be either a single mixture (if love dominates) or entirely separated into the four roots (if strife dominates).

---

[29] The first, that is, at least according to Aristotle: *Metaphysics* A4 985a31-33
[30] Quoted in in Leon-Portilla, Miguel (1963). *Aztec Thought and Culture.* Translated by Jack Emory Davis. University of Oklahoma Press, Norman. p.46.

astronomy, and who foretold the eclipses and motions of the sun, as Eudemus relates in his history of the discoveries made in astronomy; on which account Xenophanes and Herodotus praise him greatly; and Heraclitus and Democritus confirm this statement.

III.   Some again (one of whom is Choerilus the poet) say that he was the first person who affirmed that the souls of men were immortal; and he was the first person, too, who discovered the path of the sun from one end of the ecliptic to the other; and who, as one account tells us, defined the magnitude of the sun as being seven hundred and twenty times as great as that of the moon. He was also the first person who called the last day of the month the thirtieth. And likewise the first to converse about natural philosophy, as some say. But Aristotle and Hippias say that he attributed souls also to lifeless things, forming his conjecture from the nature of the magnet, and of amber. And Pamphila relates that he, having learnt geometry from the Egyptians, was the first person to describe a right-angled triangle in a circle, and that he sacrificed an ox in honour of his discovery. But others, among whom is Apollodorus the calculator, say that it was Pythagoras who made this discovery. It was Thales also who carried to their greatest point of advancement the discoveries which Callimachus in his iambics says were first made by Euphorbus the Phrygian, such as those of the scalene angle, and of the triangle, and of other things which relate to investigations about lines. He seems also to have been a man of the greatest wisdom in political matters. For when Croesus sent to the Milesians to invite them to an alliance, he prevented them from agreeing to it, which step of his, as Cyrus got the victory, proved the salvation of the city. But Clytus relates, as Heraclides assures us, that he was attached to a solitary and recluse life.

IV.   Some assert that he was married, and that he had a son named Cybisthus; others, on the contrary, say that he never had a wife, but that he adopted the son of his sister; and that once being asked why he did not himself become a father, he answered, that it was because he was fond of children. They say, too, that when his mother exhorted him to marry, he said, "No, by Jove, it is not yet time." And afterwards, when he was past his youth, and she was again pressing him earnestly, he said, "It is no longer time."

V.   Hieronymus, of Rhodes, also tells us, in the second book of his Miscellaneous Memoranda, that when he was desirous to show that it was easy to get rich, he, foreseeing that there would be a great crop of olives, took some large plantations of olive trees, and so made a great deal of money.

VI.   He asserted water to be the principle of all things, and that the world had life, and was full of daemons: they say, too, that he was the original definer of the seasons of the year, and that it was he who divided the year into three hundred and sixty-five days. And he never had any teacher except during the time that he went to Egypt, and associated with the priests. Hieronymus also says that he measured the Pyramids: watching their shadow, and calculating when they were of the same size as that was. He lived with Thrasybulus the tyrant of Miletus, as we are informed by Minyas.

VII.   Now it is known to every one what happened with respect to the tripod that was found by the fishermen and sent to the wise men by the people of the Milesians, For they say that some Ionian youths bought a cast of their nets from some Milesian fishermen. And when the tripod was drawn up in the net there was a dispute about it; until the Milesians sent to Delphi: and the God gave them the following answer:

You ask about the tripod, to whom you shall present it;
'Tis for the wisest, I reply, that fortune surely meant it.

Accordingly they gave it to Thales, and he gave it to someone, who again handed it over to another, till it came to Solon. But he said that it was the God himself who was the first in wisdom; and so he sent it to Delphi. But Callimachus gives a different account of this in his Iambic taking the tradition which he mentions from Leander the Milesian; for he says that a certain Arcadian of the name of Bathycles, when dying, left a goblet behind him with an injunction that it should be given to the first of the wise men. And it was given to Thales, and went the whole circle till it came back to Thales, on which he sent it to Apollo Didymaeus, adding (according to Callimachus,) the following distich:

Thales, who's twice received me as a prize,
Gives me to him who rules the race of Neleus.
And the prose inscription runs thus:

Thales the son of Examyas, a Milesian, offers this to Apollo Didymaeus, having twice received it from the Greeks as the reward for virtue.

And the name of the son of Bathycles who carved the goblet about from one to the other, was Thyrion, as Eleusis tells us in his History of Achilles. And Alexander the Myndian agrees with him in the ninth book of his Traditions. But Eudoxus of Cnidos, and Euanthes of Miletus, say that one of the friends of Croesus received from the king a golden goblet, for the purpose of giving it to the wisest of the Greeks; and that he gave it to Thales, and that it came round to Chilon, and that he inquired of the God at Delphi who was wiser than himself; and that the God replied, Myson, whom we shall mention hereafter. (He is the man whom Eudoxus places among the seven wise men instead of Cleobulus ; but Plato inserts his name instead of Periander.) The God accordingly made this reply concerning him:

I say that Myson the Aetoean sage,
The citizen of Chen, is wiser far
In his deep mind than you.
The person who went to the temple to ask the question was Anacharsis ; but

again Daimachus the Platonic philosopher, and Clearchus, state that the goblet was sent by Croesus to Pittacus, and so was carried round to the different men. But Andron, in his book called The Tripod, says that the Argives offered the tripod as a prize for excellence to the wisest of the Greeks; and that Aristodemus, a Spartan, was judged to deserve it, but that he yielded the palm to Chilon; and Alcaeus mentions Aristodemus in these lines:

And so they say Aristodemus once
Uttered a truthful speech in noble Sparta:
'Tis money makes the man; and he who's none,
Is counted neither good nor honourable.

But some say that a vessel fully loaded was sent by Periander to Thrasybulus the tyrant of the Milesians; and that as the ship was wrecked in the sea, near the island of Cos, this tripod was afterwards found by some fishermen. Phanodicus says that it was found in the sea near Athens, and so brought into the city; and then, after an assembly had been held to decide on the disposal, it was sent to Bias—and the reason why we will mention in our account of Bias. Others say that this goblet had been made by Vulcan and presented by the Gods to Pelops, on his marriage; and that subsequently it came into the possession of Menelaus, and was taken away by Paris when he carried off Helen, and was thrown into the sea near Cos by her, as she said that it would become a cause of battle. And after some time, some of the citizens of Lebedos having bought a net, this tripod was brought up in it; and as they quarrelled with the fishermen about it, they went to Cos; and not being able to get the matter settled there, they laid it before the Milesians, as Miletus was their metropolis; and they sent ambassadors, who were treated with neglect, on which account they made war on the Coans; and after each side had met with many revolutions of fortune, an oracle directed that the tripod should be given to the wisest; and then both parties agreed that it belonged to Thales: and he, after it had gone the circuit of all the wise men, presented it to the Didymaean Apollo. Now, the assignation of the oracle was given to the Coans in the following words:

The war between the brave Ionian race
And the proud Meropes will never cease,
Till the rich golden tripod which the God,
Its maker, cast beneath the briny waves,
Is from your city sent, and justly given
To that wise being who knows all present things,
And all that's past, and all that is to come.

And the reply given to the Milesians was
You ask about the tripod
and so on, as I have related it before. And now we have said enough on this subject.

But Hermippus, in his Lives, refers to Thales what has been by some people reported of Socrates; for he recites that he used to say that he thanked fortune for three things: first of all, that he had been born a man and not a beast; secondly, that he was a man and not a woman; and thirdly, that he was a Greek and not a barbarian.

VIII.  It is said that once he was led out of his house by an old woman for the purpose of observing the stars, and he fell into a ditch and bewailed himself, on which the old woman said to him—"Do you, O Thales, who cannot see what is under your feet, think that you shall understand what is in heaven?" Timon also knew that he was an astronomer, and in his Silli he praises him, saying:

Like Thales, wisest of the seven sages,
That great astronomer.

And Lobon, of Argos, says, that which was written by him extends to about two hundred verses; and that the following inscription is engraved upon his statue:

Miletus, fairest of Ionian cities,
Gave birth to Thales, great astronomer,
Wisest of mortals in all kinds of knowledge.

IX.  And these are quoted as some of his lines :
It is not many words that real wisdom proves;
Breathe rather one wise thought,
Select one worthy object,
So shall you best the endless prate of silly men reprove.—

And the following are quoted as sayings of his: "God is the most ancient of all things, for he had no birth: the world is the most beautiful of things, for it is the work of God: place is the greatest of things, for it contains all things: intellect is the swiftest of things, for it runs through everything: necessity is the strongest of things, for it rules everything: time is the wisest of things, for it finds out everything."

He said also that there was no difference between life and death. "Why, then," said some one to him, "do not you die?" "Because," said he, "it does make no difference." A man asked him which was made first, night or day, and he replied "Night was made first by one day." Another man asked him whether a man who did wrong, could escape the notice of the Gods. "No, not even if he thinks wrong," said he. An adulterer inquired of him whether he should swear that he had not committed adultery. "Perjury," said he, "is no worse than adultery." When he was asked what was very difficult, he said, "To know one's self." And what was easy, "To advise another." What was most pleasant? "To be successful." To the question, "What is the divinity?" he replied "That which has neither beginning nor end." When asked what hard thing he had seen, he said, "An old man a tyrant."

When the question was put to him how a man might most easily endure misfortune, he said, "If he saw his enemies more unfortunate still." When asked how men might live most virtuously and most justly, he said, "If we never do ourselves what we blame in others." To the question, "Who was happy?" he made answer. "He who is healthy in his body, easy in his circumstances, and well-instructed as to his mind." He said that men ought to remember those friends who were absent as well as those who were present, and not to care about adorning their faces, but to be beautified by their studies. "Do not," said he, "get rich by evil actions, and let not any one ever be able to reproach you with speaking against those who partake of your friendship. All the assistance that you give to your parents, the same you have a right to expect from your children." He said that the reason of the Nile overflowing, was, that its streams were beaten back by the Etesian winds blowing in a contrary direction.

X.  Apollodorus, in his Chronicles, says, that Thales was born in the first year of the thirty-fifth Olympiad; and he died at the age of seventy-eight years, or according to the statement of Sosicrates, at the age of ninety; for he died in the fifty-eighth Olympiad, having lived in the time of Croesus, to whom he promised that he would enable him to pass the Halys without a bridge, by turning the course of the river.

XI.   There have also been other men of the name of Thales, as Demetrius of Magnesia says, in his Treatise on People and Things of the Same Name; of whom five are particularly mentioned, an orator of Calatia of a very affected style of eloquence; a painter of Sicyon, a great man; the third was one who lived in very ancient times, in the age of Homer and Hesiod and Lycurgus ; the fourth is a man who is mentioned by Duris in his work On Painting; the fifth is a more modern person, of no great reputation, who is mentioned by Dionysius in his Criticisms.

XII.   But this wise Thales died while present as a spectator at a gymnastic contest, being worn out with heat and thirst and weakness, for he was very old, and the following inscription was placed on his tomb:

You see this tomb is small—but recollect,
The fame of Thales reaches to the skies.

I have also myself composed this epigram on him in the first book of my epigrams or poems in various metres:

O mighty sun our wisest Thales sat
    Spectator of the games, when you did seize upon him;
But you were right to take him near yourself,
    Now that his aged sight could scarcely reach to heaven.

XIII.   The apophthegm, "know yourself," is his; though Antisthenes in his Successions, says that it belongs to Phemonoe, but that Chilon appropriated it as his own.

XIV.   Now concerning the seven, (for it is well here to speak of them all together,) the following traditions are handed down. Damon the Cyrenaean, who wrote about the philosophers, reproaches them all, but most especially the seven. And Anaximenes says, that they all applied themselves to poetry. But Dicaearchus says, that they were neither wise men nor philosophers, but merely shrewd men, who had studied legislation. And Archetimus, the Syracusian, wrote an account of their having a meeting at the palace of Cypselus, at which he says that he himself was present. Ephorus says that they all except Thales met at the court of Croesus. And some say that they also met at the Pandionium,(1) and at Corinth, and at Delphi. There is a good deal of disagreement between different writers with respect to their apophthegms, as the same one is attributed by them to various authors. For instance there is the epigram:

Chilon, the Spartan sage, this sentence said:
Seek no excess—all timely things are good

There is also a difference of opinion with respect to their number. Leander inserts in the number instead of Cleobulus and Myson, Leophantus Gorsias, a native of either Lebedos or Ephesus; and Epimenides, the Cretan; Plato, in his Protagoras, reckons Myson among them instead of Periander. And Ephorus mentions Anacharsis in the place of Myson; some also add Pythagoras to the number. Dicaearchus speaks of four, as universally agreed upon, Thales, Bias, Pittacus, and Solon; and then enumerates six more, of whom we are to select three, namely, Aristodemus, Pamphilus, Chilon the Lacedaemonian, Cleobulus, Anacharsis, and Periander. Some add Acusilaus of Argos, the son of Cabas, or Scabras. But Hermippus, in his Treatise on the Wise Men says that there were altogether seventeen, out of whom different authors selected different individuals to make up the seven. These seventeen were Solon, Thales, Pittacus, Bias, Chilon, Myson, Cleobulus, Periander, Anacharsis, Acusilaus, Epimenides, Leophantus, Pherecydes, Aristodemus, Pythagoras, Lasus the son of Charmantides, or Sisymbrinus, or as Aristoxenus calls him the son of Chabrinus, a citizen of Hermione, and Anaxagoras. But Hippobotus in his Description of the Philosophers enumerates among them Orpheus, Linus, Solon, Periander, Anacharsis, Cleobulus, Myson, Thales, Bias, Pittacus, Epicharmus, and Pythagoras.

XV.   The following letters are preserved as having been written by Thales:

THALES TO PHERECYDES.
I hear that you are disposed, as no other Ionian has been, to discourse to the Greeks about divine things, and perhaps it will be wiser of you to reserve for your own friends what you write rather than to entrust it to any chance people, without any advantage. If therefore it is agreeable to you, I should be glad to become a pupil of yours as to the matters about which you write; and if you invite

me I will come to you to Syros; for Solon the Athenian and I must be out of our senses if we sailed to Crete to investigate the history of that country, and to Egypt for the purpose of conferring with the priests and astronomers who are to be found there, and yet are unwilling to make a voyage to you; for Solon will come too, if you will give him leave, for as you are fond of your present habitation you are not likely to come to Ionia, nor are you desirous of seeing strangers; but you rather, as I hope, devote yourself wholly to the occupation of writing. We, on the other hand, who write nothing, travel over all Greece and Asia

THALES TO SOLON.

XVI.  If you should leave Athens it appears to me that you would find a home at Miletus among the colonists of Athens more suitably than anywhere else, for here there are no annoyances of any kind. And if you are indignant because we Milesians are governed by a tyrant, (for you yourself hate all despotic rulers), still at all events you will find it pleasant to live with us for your companions. Bias has also written to invite you to Priene, and if you prefer taking up your abode in the city of the Prieneans, then we ourselves will come thither and settle near you.

## LIFE OF PYTHAGORAS

I. SINCE we have now gone through the Ionian philosophy, which was derived from Thales, and the lives of the several illustrious men who were the chief ornaments of that school; we will now proceed to treat of the Italian School, which was founded by Pythagoras, the son of Mnesarchus, a seal engraver, as he is recorded to have been by Hermippus; a native of Samos, or as Aristoxenus asserts, a Tyrrhenian, and a native of one of the islands which the Athenians occupied after they had driven out the Tyrrhenians. But some authors say that he was the son of Marmacus, the son of Hippasus, the son of Euthyphron, the son of Cleonymus, who was an exile from Phlias; and that Marmacus settled in Samos, and that from this circumstance Pythagoras was called a Samian. After that he migrated to Lesbos, having come to Pherecydes with letters of recommendation from Zoilus, his uncle. And having made three silver goblets, he carried them to Egypt as a present for each of the three priests. He had brothers, the eldest of whom was named Eunomus, the middle one Tyrrhenus, and a slave named Zamolxis, to whom the Getae sacrifice, believing him to be the same as Saturn, according to the account of Herodotus (Herod. iv. 93.).

II. He was a pupil, as I have already mentioned, of Pherecydes, the Syrian; and after his death he came to Samos, and became a pupil of Hermodamas, the descendant of Creophylus, who was by this time an old man.

III. And as he was a young man, and devoted to learning, he quitted his country, and got initiated into all the Grecian and barbarian sacred mysteries. Accordingly, he went to Egypt, on which occasion Polycrates gave him a letter of introduction to Amasis; and he learnt the Egyptian language, as Antipho tells us, in his treatise on those men who have been conspicuous for virtue, and he associated with the Chaldaeans and with the Magi.

Afterwards he went to Crete, and in company with Epimenides, he descended into the Idaean cave, (and in Egypt too, he entered into the holiest parts of their temples,) and learned all the most secret mysteries that relate to their Gods. Then he returned back again to Samos, and finding his country reduced under the absolute dominion of Polycrates, he set sail, and fled to Crotona in Italy. And there, having given laws to the Italians, he gained a very high reputation, together with his scholars, who were about three hundred in number, and governed the republic in a most excellent manner; so that the constitution was very nearly an aristocracy.

V. Heraclides Ponticus says, that he was accustomed to speak of himself in this manner; that he had formerly been Aethalides, and had been accounted the son of Mercury; and that Mercury had desired him to select any gift he pleased except immortality. And that he accordingly had requested that whether living or dead, he might preserve the memory of what had happened to him. While, therefore, he was alive, he recollected everything; and when he was dead, he retained the same memory. And at a subsequent period he passed into Euphorbus, and was wounded by Menelaus. And while he was Euphorbus, he used to say that he had formerly been Aethalides; and that he had received as a gift from Mercury the perpetual transmigration of his soul, so that it was constantly transmigrating and passing into whatever plants or animals it pleased; and he had also received the gift of knowing and recollecting all that his soul had suffered in hell, and what sufferings too are endured by the rest of the souls.

But after Euphorbus died, he said that his soul had passed into Hermotimus; and when he wished to convince people of this, he went into the territory of the Branchidae, and going into the temple of Apollo, he showed his shield which Menelaus had dedicated there as an offering. For he said that he, when he sailed from Troy, had offered up his shield which was already getting worn out, to Apollo, and that nothing remained but the ivory face which was on it. And when Hermotimus died, then he said that he had become Pyrrhus, a fisherman of Delos; and that he still recollected everything, how he had been formerly Aethalides, then Euphorbus, then Hermotimus, and then Pyrrhus. And when Pyrrhus died, he became Pythagoras, and still recollected all the circumstances that I have been mentioning.

V. Now, some people say that Pythagoras did not leave behind him a single book; but they talk foolishly; for Heraclitus, the natural philosopher, speaks plainly enough of him, saying, "Pythagoras, the Son of Mnesarchus, was the most learned of all men in history; and having selected from these writings, he thus formed his own wisdom and extensive learning, and mischievous art." And he speaks thus, because Pythagoras, in the beginning of his treatise on Natural Philosophy, writes in the following manner: "By the air which I breathe, and by the water which I drink, I will not endure to be blamed on account of this discourse."

And there are three volumes extant written by Pythagoras. One on Education; one on Politics; and one on Natural Philosophy. But the treatise which is now extant under the name of Pythagoras is the work of Lysis, of Tarentum, a philosopher of the Pythagorean School, who fled to Thebes, and became the master of Epaminondas. And Heraclides, the son of Sarapion, in his Abridgment of Sotion, says that he wrote a poem in epic verse on the Universe; and besides that a sacred poem, which begins thus:

Dear youths, I warn you cherish peace divine,
And in your hearts lay deep these words of mine.

A third about the Soul; a fourth on Piety; a fifth entitled Helothales, which was the name of the father of Epicharmus, of Cos; a sixth called Crotona, and other poems too. But the mystic discourse which is extant under his name, they say is really the work of Hippasus, having been composed with a view to bring Pythagoras into disrepute. There were also many other books composed by Aston, of Crotona, and attributed to Pythagoras.

Aristoxenus asserts that Pythagoras derived the greater part of his ethical doctrines from Themistoclea, the priestess at Delphi. And Ion, of Chios, in his Victories, says that he wrote some poems and attributed them to Orpheus. They also say that the poem called the Scopeadae is by him, which begins thus:

Behave not shamelessly to any one.
VI. And Sosicrates, in his Successions, relates that he, having being asked by Leon, the tyrant of the Phliasians, who he was, replied, "A philosopher." And adds, that he used to compare life to a festival. "And as some people came to a festival to contend for the prizes, and others for the purposes of traffic, and the best as spectators; so also in life, the men of slavish dispositions," said he, "are born hunters after glory and covetousness, but philosophers are seekers after truth." And thus he spoke on this subject. But in the three treatises above mentioned, the following principles are laid down by Pythagoras generally.

He forbids men to pray for anything in particular for themselves, because they do not know what is good for them. He calls drunkenness an expression identical with ruin, and rejects all superfluity, saying, "That no one ought to exceed the proper quantity of meat and drink." And on the subject of venereal pleasures, he speaks thus: "One ought to sacrifice to Venus in the winter, not in the summer; and in autumn and spring in a lesser degree. But the practice is pernicious at every season, and is never good for the health." And once, when he was asked when a man might indulge in the pleasures of love, he replied, "Whenever you wish to be weaker than yourself."

VII. And he divides the life of man thus. A boy for twenty years ; a young man (neaniskos) for twenty years; a middle-aged man (neanias) for twenty years; an old man for twenty years. And these different ages correspond proportionably to the seasons: boyhood answers to spring; youth to summer; middle age to autumn; and old age to winter. And he uses neaniskos here as equivalent to meirakion and neanias as equivalent to anêr.

VIII. He was the first person, as Timaeus says, who asserted that the property of friends is common, and that friendship is equality. And his disciples used to put all their possessions together into one store, and use them in common; and for five years they kept silence, doing nothing but listen to discourses, and never once seeing Pythagoras, until they were approved; after that time they were admitted into his house, and allowed to see him. They also abstained from the use of cypress coffins, because the sceptre of Jupiter was made of that wood, as Hermippus tells us in the second book of his account of Pythagoras.

IX. He is said to have been a man of the most dignified appearance, and his disciples adopted an opinion respecting him, that he was Apollo who had come from the Hyperboreans; and it is said, that once when he was stripped naked, he was seen to have a golden thigh. And there were many people who affirmed, that when he was crossing the river Nessus it addressed him by his name.

X. Timaeus, in the tenth book of his Histories, tells us, that he used to say that women who were married to men had the names of the Gods, being successively called virgins, then nymphs, and subsequently mothers.

XI. It was Pythagoras also who carried geometry to perfection, after Moeris had first found out the principles of the elements of that science, as Aristiclides tells us in the second book of his History of Alexander; and the part of the science to which Pythagoras applied himself above all others was arithmetic. He also discovered the numerical relation of sounds on a single string: he also studied medicine. And Apollodorus, the logician, records of him, that he sacrified a hecatomb, when he had discovered that the square of the hypothenuse of a right-angled triangle is equal to the squares of the sides containing the right angle. And there is an epigram which is couched in the following terms:

When the great Samian sage his noble problem found,
A hundred oxen dyed with their life-blood the ground.

XII. He is also said to have been the first man who trained athletes on meat; and Eurymenes was the first man, according to the statement of Favorinus, in the third book of his commentaries, who ever did submit to this diet, as before that time men used to train themselves on dry figs and moist cheese, and wheaten bread; as the same Favorinus infor s us in the eighth book of his Universal History. But some authors state that a trainer of the name of Pythagoras certainly did train his athletes on this system, but that it was not our philosopher; for that he even forbade men to kill animals at all, much less would have allowed his disciples to eat then, as having a right to live in common with mankind. And this was his pretext; but in reality, he prohibited the eating of animals, because he wished to train and accustom men to simplicity of life, so that all their food should be easily procurable, as it would be, if they ate only such things as required no fire to dress them, and if they drank plain water; for from this diet they would derive health of body and acuteness of intellect.

The only altar at which he worshipped was that of Apollo the Father, at Delos, which is at the back of the altar of Ceratinus, because wheat, and barley, and cheese-cakes are the only offerings laid upon it, being not dressed by fire; and no victim is ever slain there as Aristotle tells us in his Constitution of the Delians. They say, too, that he was the first person who asserted that the soul went a necessary circle, being changed about and confined at different times in different bodies.

XIII. He was also the first person who introduced measures and weights among the Greeks; as Aristoxenus the musician informs us.

XIV. Parmenides, too, assures us, that he was the first person who asserted the identity of Hesperus and Lucifer.

XV. And he was so greatly admired, that they used to say that his friends looked on all his sayings as the oracles of God. And he himself says in his writings, that he had come among men after having spent two hundred and seven years in the shades below. Therefore the Lucanians and the Peucetians, and the Messapians, and the Romans, flocked around him, coming with eagerness to hear his discourses; but until the time of Philolaus, there were no doctrines of Pythagoras ever divulged; and he was the first person who published the three celebrated books which Plato wrote to have purchased for him for a hundred minae. Nor were the number of his scholars who used to come to him by night fewer than six hundred. And if any of them had ever been permitted to see him, they wrote of it to their friends, as if they had gained some great advantage.

The people of Metapontum used to call his house the temple of Ceres; and the street leading to it they called the street of the Muses, as we are told by Favorinus in his Universal History.

And the rest of the Pythagoreans used to say, according to the account given by Aristoxenus, in the tenth book of his Laws on Education, that his precepts ought not to be divulged to all the world; and Xenophilus, the Pythagorean, when he was asked what was the best way for a man to educate his son, said, "That he must first of all take care that he was born in a city which enjoyed good laws."

Pythagoras, too, formed many excellent men in Italy, by his precepts, and among them Zaleucus, and Charondas, the lawgivers.

XVI. For he was very eminent for his power of attracting friendships; and among other things, if ever he heard that any one had any community of symbols with him, he at once made him a companion and a friend.

XVII. Now, what he called his symbols were such as these. "Do not stir the fire with a sword." "Do not sit down on a bushel." "Do not devour your heart." "Do not aid men in discarding a burden, but in increasing one." "Always have your bed packed up." "Do not bear the image of a God on a ring." "Efface the traces of a pot in the ashes." "Do not wipe a seat with a lamp." "Do not make water in the sunshine." "Do not walk in the main street." "Do not offer your right hand lightly." "Do not cherish swallows under your roof." "Do not cherish birds with crooked talons." "Do not defile; and do not stand upon the parings of your nails or the cuttings of your hair." "Avoid a sharp sword." "When you are travelling abroad, look not back at your own borders." Now the precept not to stir fire with a sword meant, not to provoke the anger or swelling pride of powerful men; not to violate the beam of the balance meant, not to transgress fairness and justice; not to sit on a bushel is to have an equal care for the present and for the future, for by the bushel is meant one's daily food. By not devouring one's heart, he intended to show that we ought not to waste away our souls with grief and sorrow. In the precept that a man when travelling abroad should not turn his eyes back, he recommended those who were departing from life not to be desirous to live, and not to be too much attracted by the pleasures here on earth. And the other symbols may be explained in a similar manner, that we may not be too prolix here.

XVIII. And above all things, he used to prohibit the eating of the erythinus, and the melanurus; and also, he enjoined his disciples to abstain from the hearts of animals, and from beans. And Aristotle informs us, that he sometimes used also to add to these prohibitions paunches and mullet. And some authors assert that he himself used to be contented with honey and honeycomb, and bread, and that he never drank wine in the day time. And his desert was usually vegetables, either boiled or raw; and he very rarely ate fish. His dress was white, very clean, and his bed-clothes were also white, and woollen, for linen had not yet been introduced into that country. He was never known to have eaten too much, or to have drunk too much, or to indulge in the pleasures of love. He abstained wholly from laughter, and from all such indulgences as jests and idle stories. And when he was angry, he never chastised any one, whether slave or freeman. He used to call admonishing, feeding storks.

He used to practise divination, as far as auguries and auspices go, but not by means of burnt offerings, except only the burning of frankincense. And all the sacrifices which he offered consisted of inanimate things. But some, however, assert that he did sacrifice animals, limiting himself to cocks, and sucking kids, which are called apalioi, but that he very rarely offered lambs. Aristoxenus, however, affirms that he permitted the eating of all other animals, and only abstained from oxen used in agriculture, and from rams.

XIX. The same author tells us, as I have already mentioned, that he received his doctrines from Themistoclea, at Delphi. And Hieronymus says, that when he descended to the shades below, he saw the soul of Hesiod bound to a brazen pillar, and gnashing its teeth; and that of Homer suspended from a tree, and snakes around it, as a punishment for the things that they had said of the Gods. And that those people also were punished who refrained from commerce with their wives; and that on account of this he was greatly honoured by the people of Crotona.

But Aristippus, of Cyrene, in his Account of Natural Philosophers, says that Pythagoras derived his name from the fact of his speaking (agoreuein) truth no less than the God at Delphi (tou pythiou).

It is said that he used to admonish his disciples to repeat these lines to themselves whenever they returned home to their houses:

In what have I transgress'd? What have I done?
What that I should have done have I omitted?

And that he used to forbid them to offer victims to the Gods, ordering them to worship only at those altars which were unstained with blood. He forbade them also to swear by the Gods; saying, "That every man ought so to exercise himself, as to be worthy of belief without an oath." He also taught men that it behoved them to honour their elders, thinking that which was precedent in point of time more honourable; just as in the world, the rising of the sun was more so than the setting; in life, the beginning more so than the end; and in animals, production more so than destruction.

Another of his rules was that men should honour the Gods above the daemones, heroes above men; and of all men parents were entitled to the highest degree of reverence. Another, that people should associate with one another in such a way as not to make their friends enemies, but to render their enemies friends. Another was that they should think nothing exclusively their own. Another was to assist the law, and to make war upon lawlessness. Not to destroy or injure a cultivated tree, nor any animal either which does not injure men. That modesty and decorum consisted in never yielding to laughter, and yet not looking stern. He taught that men should avoid too much flesh, that they should in travelling let rest and exertion alternate; that they should exercise memory; that they should never say or do anything in anger; that they should not pay respect to every kind of divination; that they should use songs set to the lyre; and by hymns to the Gods and to eminent men, display a reasonable gratitude to them.

He also forbade his disciples to eat beans, because, as they were flatulent, they greatly partook of animal properties [he also said that men kept their stomachs in better order by avoiding them]; and that such abstinence made the visions which appear in one's sleep gentle and free from agitation. Alexander also says, in his Successions of Philosophers, that he found the following dogmas also set down in the Commentaries of Pythagoras:

That the monad was the beginning of everything. From the monad proceeds an indefinite duad, which is subordinate to the monad as to its cause. That from the monad and the indefinite duad proceed numbers. And from numbers signs. And from these last, lines of which plane figures consist. And from plane figures are derived solid bodies. And from solid bodies sensible bodies, of which last there are four elements; fire, water, earth, and air. And that the world, which is endued with life, and intellect, and which is of a spherical figure, having the earth, which is also spherical, and inhabited all over in its centre, results from a combination of these elements, and derives its motion from them; and also that there are antipodes, and that what is below, as respects us, is above in respect of them.

He also taught that light and darkness, and cold and heat, and dryness and moisture, were equally divided in the world; and that, while heat was predominant it was summer; while cold had the mastery it was winter; when dryness prevailed it was spring; and when moisture preponderated, winter. And while all these qualities were on a level, then was the loveliest season of the year; of which the flourishing spring was the wholesome period, and the season of autumn the most pernicious one. Of the day, he said that the flourishing period was the morning, and the fading one the evening; on which account that also was the least healthy time.

Another of his theories was, that the air around the earth was immoveable, and pregnant with disease; and that everything in it was mortal; but that the upper air was in perpetual motion, and pure and salubrious; and that everything in that was immortal, and on that account divine. And that the sun, and the moon, and the stars, were all Gods; for in them the warm principle predominates which is the cause of life. And that the moon derives its light from the sun. And that there is a relationship between men and the Gods, because men partake of the divine principle; on which account also, God exercises his providence for our advantage. Also, that fate is the cause of the arrangement of the world both generally and particularly. Moreover, that a ray from the sun penetrated both the cold aether and the dense aether; and they call the air (aêr) the cold aether (psychron aithera), and the sea and moisture they call the dense aether (pachun aethera). And this ray descends into the depths, and in this way vivifies everything. And everything which partakes of the principle of heat lives, on which account also plants are animated beings; but that all living things have not necessarily souls. And that the soul is a something torn off from the aether, both warm and cold, from its partaking of the cold aether. And that the soul is something different from life. Also, that it is immortal, because that from which it has been detached is immortal.

Also, that animals are born from one another by seeds, and that it is impossible for there to be any spontaneous production by the earth. And that seed is a drop from the brain which contains in itself a warm vapour; and that when this is applied to the womb, it transmits virtue, and moisture, and blood from the brain, from which flesh, and sinews, and bones, and hair, and the whole body are produced. And from the vapour is produced the soul, and also sensation. And that the infant first becomes a solid body at the end of forty days; but, according to the principles of harmony, it is not perfect till seven, or perhaps nine, or at most ten months, and then it is brought forth. And that it contains in itself all the principles of life, which are all connected together, and by their union and combination form a harmonious whole, each of them, developing itself at the appointed time.

The senses in general, and especially the sight, are a vapour of excessive warmth, and on this account a man is said to see through air, and through water. For the hot principle is opposed by the cold one; since, if the vapour in the eyes were cold, it would have the same temperature as the air, and so would be dissipated. As it is, in some passages he calls the eyes the gates of the sun. And he speaks in a similar manner of hearing, and of the other senses.

He also says that the soul of man is divided into three parts; into intuition (nous), and reason (phren) and mind (thymos), and that the first and last divisions are found also in other animals, but that the middle one, reason, is only found in man. And that the chief abode of the soul is in those parts of the body which are between the heart and the brain. And that that portion of it which is in the heart is the mind (thymos); but that deliberation (nous), and reason (phren), reside in the brain:

Moreover, that the senses are drops from them; and that the reasoning sense is immortal, but the others are mortal. And that the soul is nourished by the blood; and that reasons are the winds of the soul. That it is invisible, and so are its reasons, since the aether itself is invisible. That the links of the soul are the veins, and the arteries and the nerves. But that when it is vigorous, and is by itself in a quiescent state, then its links are words and actions. That when it is cast forth upon the earth it wanders about, resembling the body. Moreover, that Mercury is the steward of the souls, and that on this account he has the name of Conductor, and Commercial, and Infernal, since it is he who conducts the souls from their bodies, and from earth, and sea; and that he conducts the pure souls to the highest region, and that he does not allow the impure ones to approach them, nor to come near one another; but commits them to be bound in indissoluble fetters by the Furies. The Pythagoreans also assert, that the whole air is full of souls, and that these are those which are accounted daemones, and heroes. Also, that it is by them that dreams are sent among men, and also the tokens of disease and health; these last too, being sent not only to men, but to sheep also and other cattle. Also, that it is they who are concerned with purifications, and expiations, and all kinds of divination, and oracular predictions, and things of that kind.

They also say, that the most important privilege in man is the being able to persuade his soul to either good or bad. And that men are happy when they have a good soul; yet, that they are never quiet, and that they never retain the same mind long. Also, that an oath is justice; and that on that account, Jupiter is called Jupiter of Oaths (Orkios). Also, that virtue is harmony, and health, and universal good, and God; on which account everything owes its existence and consistency to harmony. Also, that friendship is a harmonious equality.

Again, they teach that one ought not to pay equal honours to Gods and to heroes; but that one ought to honour the Gods at all times, extolling them with praises, clothed in white garments, and keeping one's body chaste; but that one ought not to pay such honour to the heroes till after midday. Also, that a state of purity is brought about by purifications, and washings, and sprinklings, and by a man's purifying himself from all funerals, or concubinage, or pollution of every kind, and by abstaining from all flesh that has either been killed or died of itself, and from mullets, and from melanuri, and from eggs, and from such animals as lay eggs, and from beans, and from other things which are prohibited by those who have the charge of the mysteries in the temples.

And Aristotle says, in his treatise on Beans, that Pythagoras enjoined his disciples to abstain from beans, either because they resemble some part of the human body, or because they are like the gates of hell (for they are the only plants without parts); or because they dry up other plants, or because they are representatives of universal nature, or because they are used in elections in oligarchical governments. He also forbade his disciples to pick up what fell from the table, for the sake of accustoming them not to eat immoderately, or else because such things belong to the dead.

But Aristophanes says, that what falls belongs to the heroes; saying, in his Heroes:

Never taste the things which fall
From the table on the floor.

He also forbade his disciples to eat white poultry, because a cock of that colour was sacred to Month, and was also a suppliant. He was also accounted a good animal; and he was sacred to the God Month, for he indicates the time.

The Pythagoreans were also forbidden to eat of all fish that were sacred; on the ground that the same animals ought not to be served up before both Gods and men just as the same things do not belong to freemen and to slaves. Now, white is an indication of a good nature, and black of a bad one. Another of the precepts of Pythagoras was, that men ought not to break bread; because in ancient times friends used to assemble around one loaf, as they even now do among the barbarians. Nor would he allow men to divide bread which unites them. Some think that he laid down this rule in reference to the judgment which takes place in hell; some because this practice engenders timidity in war. According to others, what is alluded to is the Union, which presides over the government of the universe.

Another of his doctrines was, that of all solid figures the sphere was the most beautiful; and of all plane figures, the circle. That old age and all diminution were similar, and also increase and youth were identical. That health was the permanence of form, and disease the destruction of it. Of salt his opinion was, that it ought to be set before people as a reminder of justice; for salt preserves everything which it touches, and it is composed of the purest particles of water and sea.

These are the doctrines which Alexander asserts that he discovered in the Pythagorean treatises; and Aristotle gives a similar account of them.

XX. Timon, in his Silli, has not left unnoticed the dignified appearance of Pythagoras, when he attacks him on other points. And his words are these:

Pythagoras, who often teaches
Precepts of magic, and with speeches
Of long high-sounding diction draws,
From gaping crowds, a vain applause.

And respecting his having been different people at different times, Xenophanes adds his evidence in an elegiac poem which commences thus:

Now I will on another subject touch,
And lead the way.
And the passage in which he mentions Pythagoras is as follows ;

They say that once as passing by he saw
A dog severely beaten, he did pity him,
And spoke as follows to the man who beat him:
"Stop now, and beat him not; since in his body,
Abides the soul of a dear friend of mine,
Whose voice I recognized as he was crying."
These are the words of Xenophanes.

Cratinus also ridiculed him in his Pythagorean Woman; but in his Tarentines, he speaks thus:

They are accustomed, if by chance they see
A private individual abroad,
To try what powers of argument he has,
How he can speak and reason: and they bother him
With strange antitheses and forced conclusions,
Errors, comparisons, and magnitudes,

Till they have filled and quite perplex'd his mind.
And Innesimachus says in his Alcmaeon:

As we do sacrifice to the Phoebus whom
Pythagoras worships, never eating aught
Which has the breath of life.
Austophon says in his Pythagorean:

A. He said that when he did descend below
Among the shades in Hell, he there beheld
All men who e'er had died; and there he saw,
That the Pythagoreans differ'd much
From all the rest; for that with them alone
Did Pluto deign to eat, much honouring
Their pious habits.
B. He's a civil God,
If he likes eating with such dirty fellows.
And again, in the same play he says:

They eat
Nothing but herbs and vegetables, and drink
Pure water only. But their lice are such,
Their cloaks so dirty, and their unwash'd scent
So rank, that no one of our younger men
Will for a moment bear them.

XXI. Pythagoras died in this manner. When he was sitting with some of his
companions in Milo's house, some one of those whom he did not think worthy of
admission into it, was excited by envy to set fire to it. But some say that the people
of Crotona themselves did this, being afraid lest he might aspire to the tyranny.
And that Pythagoras was caught as he was trying to escape; and coming to a place
full of beans, he stopped there, saying that it was better to be caught than to
trample on the beans, and better to be slain than to speak; and so he was
murdered by those who were pursuing him. And in this way, also, most of his
companions were slain; being in number about forty; but that a very few did
escape, among whom were Archippus, of Tarentum, and Lysis, whom I have
mentioned before.

But Dicaearchus relates that Pythagoras died afterwards, having escaped as
far as the temple of the Muses, at Metapontum, and that he died there of
starvation, having abstained from food for forty days. And Heraclides says, in his
abridgment of the life of Satyrus, that after he had buried Pherecydes in Delos, he
returned to Italy, and finding there a superb banquet prepared at the house of
Milo, of Cortona, he left Crotona, and went to Metapontum, and there put an end
to his life by starvation, not wishing to live any longer. But Hermippus says, that
when there was war between the people of Agrigentum and the Syracusans,

Pythagoras went out with his usual companions, and took the part of the Agrigentines; and as they were put to flight, he ran all round a field of beans, instead of crossing it, and so was slain by the Syracusans; and that the rest, being about five-and-thirty in number, were burnt at Tarentum, when they were trying to excite a sedition in the state against the principal magistrates.

Hermippus also relates another story about Pythagoras. For he says that when he was in Italy, he made a subterraneous apartment, and charged his mother to write an account of everything that took place, marking the time of each on a tablet, and then to send them down to him, until he came up again; and that his mother did so; and that Pythagoras came up again after a certain time, lean, and reduced to a skeleton; and that he came into the public assembly, and said that he had arrived from the shades below, and then he recited to them all that had happened during his absence. And they, being charmed by what he told them, wept and lamented, and believed that Pythagoras was a divine being; so that they even entrusted their wives to him, as likely to learn some good from him; and that they too were called Pythagoreans. And this is the story of Hermippus.

XXII. And Pythagoras had a wife, whose name was Theano; the daughter of Brontinus, of Crotona. But some say that she was the wife of Brontinus, and only a pupil of Pythagoras. And he had a daughter named Damo, as Lysis mentions in his letter to Hipparchus; where he speaks thus of Pythagoras: "And many say that you philosophize in public, as Pythagoras also used to do; who, when he had entrusted his Commentaries to Damo, his daughter, charged her to divulge them to no person out of the house. And she, though she might have sold his discourses for much money, would not abandon them, for she thought poverty and obedience to her father's injunctions more valuable than gold; and that too, though she was a woman."

He had also a son, named Telauges, who was the successor of his father in his school, and who, according to some authors, was the teacher of Empedocles. At least Hippobotus relates that Empedocles said

"Telauges, noble youth, whom in due time,
Theano bore to wise Pythagoras."

But there is no book extant, which is the work of Telauges, though there are some extant, which are attributed to his mother Theano. And they tell a story of her, that once, when she was asked how long a woman ought to be absent from her husband to be pure, she said, the moment she leaves her own husband, she is pure; but she is never pure at all, after she leaves any one else. And she recommended a woman, who was going to her husband, to put off her modesty with her clothes, and when she left him, to resume it again with her clothes; and when she was asked, "What clothes?" she said, "Those which cause you to be called a woman."

XXIII. Now Pythagoras, as Heraclides, the son of Sarapian, relates, died when he was eighty years of age; according to his own account of his age, but according to the common account, he was more than ninety. And we have written a sportive epigram on him, which is couched in the following terms:

You're not the only man who has abstained
From living food, for so likewise have we;
And who, I'd like to know did ever taste
Food while alive, most sage Pythagoras?
When meat is boil'd, or roasted well and salted,
I don't think it can well be called living.
Which, therefore, without scruple then we eat it,
And call it no more living flesh, but meat.
And another, which runs thus:

Pythagoras was so wise a man, that he
Never eat meat himself, and called it sin.
And yet he gave good joints of beef to others.
So that I marvel at his principles;
Who others wronged, by teaching them to do
What he believed unholy for himself.
And another, as follows:

Should you Phythagoras' doctrine wish to know,
Look on the centre of Euphorbus' shield.
For he asserts there lived a man of old,
And when he had no longer an existence,
He still could say that he had been alive,
Or else he would not still be living now.
And this one too:

Alas! alas! why did Pythagoras hold
Beans in such wondrous honour? Why, besides,
Did he thus die among his choice companions?
There was a field of beans; and so the sage,
Died in the common road of Agrigentum,
Rather than trample down his favourite beans.

XXIV. And he flourished about the sixtieth Olympiad and his system lasted for nine or ten generations. And the last of the Pythagoreans, whom Aristoxenus knew, were Xenophilus, the Chalcidean, from Thrace; and Phanton, the Phliasian, and Echurates, and Diodes, and Polymnestus, who were also Phliasians, and they were disciples of Philolaus and Eurytus, of Tarentum.

XXV. And there were four men of the name of Pythagoras, about the same time, at no great distance from one another. One was a native of Crotona, a man who attained tyrannical power; the second was a Phliasian, a trainer of wrestlers, as some say; the third was a native of Zacynthus; the fourth was this our philosopher, to whom they say the mysteries of philosophy belong, in whose time that proverbial phrase, "Ipse dixit," was introduced into ordinary life. Some also affirm, that there was another man of the name of Pythagoras, a statuary of Rhodes; who is believed to have been the first discoverer of rhythm and proportion; and another was a Samian statuary; and another an orator, of no reputation; and another was a physician, who wrote a treatise on Squills; and also some essays on Homer; and another was a man, who wrote a history of the affairs of the Dorians, as we are told by Dionysius.

But Eratosthenes says, as Favorinus quotes him, in the eighth book of his Universal History, that this philosopher, of whom we are speaking, was the first man who ever practised boxing in a scientific manner, in the forty-eighth Olympiad, having his hair long, and being clothed in a purple robe; and that he was rejected from the competition among boys, and being ridiculed for his application, he immediately entered among the men, and came off victorious. And this statement is confirmed among other things, by the epigram which Theaetetus composed:

Stranger, if e'er you knew Pythagoras,
Pythagoras, the man with flowing hair,
The celebrated boxer, erst of Samos;
I am Pythagoras. And if you ask
A citizen of Elis of my deeds,
You'll surely think he is relating fables.

Favorinus says, that he employed definitions, on account of the mathematical subjects to which he applied himself. And that Socrates and those who were his pupils, did so still more; and that they were subsequently followed in this by Aristotle and the Stoics.

He too, was the first person, who ever gave the name of kosmos to the universe, and the first who called the earth round; though Theophrastus attributes this to Parmenides, and Zeno to Hesiod. They say too, that Cylon used to be a constant adversary of his, as Antidicus was of Socrates. And this epigram also used to be repeated, concerning Pythagoras the athlete:

Pythagoras of Samos, son of Crates,
Came while a child to the Olympic games,
Eager to battle for the prize in boxing.

XXVI. There is a letter of this philosopher extant, which is couched in the following terms:-

## PYTHAGORAS TO ANAXIMENES.

"You too, my most excellent friend, if you were not superior to Pythagoras, in birth and reputation, would have migrated from Miletus and gone elsewhere. But now the reputation of your father keeps you back, which perhaps would have restrained me too, if I had been like Anaximenes. But if you, who are the most eminent man, abandon the cities, all their ornaments will be taken from them; and the Median power will be more dangerous to them. Nor is it always seasonable to be studying astronomy, but it is more honourable to exhibit a regard for one's country. And I myself am not always occupied about speculations of my own fancy, but I am busied also with the wars which the Italians are waging against one another."

But since we have now finished our account of Pythagoras, we must also speak of the most eminent of the Pythagoreans. After whom, we must mention those who are spoken of more promiscuously in connection with no particular school; and then we will connect the whole series of philosophers worth speaking of, till we arrive at Epicurus, as we have already promised.

Now Jelanges and Theano we have mentioned; and we must now speak of Empedocles, in the first place, for, according to some accounts, he was a pupil of Pythagoras.

## LIFE OF HERACLITUS

I. HERACLITUS was the son of Blyson, or, as some say, of Heraceon, and a citizen of Ephesus. He flourished about the sixty-ninth olympiad.

II. He was above all men of a lofty and arrogant spirit, as is plain from his writings, in which he says, "Abundant learning does not form the mind; for if it did, it would have instructed Hesiod, and Pythagoras, and likewise Xenophanes, and Hecataeus. For the only piece of real wisdom is to know that idea, which by itself will govern everything on every occasion. He used to say, too, that Homer deserved to be expelled from the games and beaten, and Archilochus likewise. He used also to say, "It is more necessary to extinguish insolence, than to put out a fire." Another of his sayings was, "The people ought to fight for the law, as for their city." He also attacks the Ephesians for having banished his companion Hermodorus, when he says, "The Ephesians deserve to have all their youth put to death, and all those who are younger still banished from their city, inasmuch as they have banished Hermodorus, the best man among them, saying, "Let no one of us be pre-eminently good; and if there be any such person, let him go to another city and another people."

And when he was requested to make laws for them, he refused, because the city was already immersed in a thoroughly bad constitution. And having retired to the temple of Diana with his children he began to play at dice; and when all the Ephesians flocked round him, he said, "You wretches, what are you wondering at? is it not better to do this, than to meddle with public affairs in your company?"

III. And at last becoming a complete misanthrope, he used to live, spending his time in walking about the mountains; feeding on grasses and plants, and in consequence of these habits, he was attacked by the dropsy, and so then he returned to the city, and asked the physicians, in a riddle, whether they were able to produce a drought after wet weather. And as they did not understand him, he shut himself up in a stable for oxen, and covered himself with cow-dung, hoping to cause the wet to evaporate from him, by the warmth that this produced. And as he did himself no go good in this way, he died, having lived seventy years; and we have written an epigram upon him which runs thus:

I've often wondered much at Heraclitus,
That he should chose to live so miserably,
And die by such a miserable fate.
For fell disease did master all his body,
With water quenching all the light of his eyes,
And bringing darkness o'er his mind and body.

But Hermippus states, that what he asked the physicians was this, whether any one could draw off the water by depressing his intestines? and when they answered that they could not, he placed himself in the sun, and ordered his servants to plaster him over with cow-dung; and being stretched out in that way, on the second day he died, and was buried in the market-place. But Neanthes, of Cyzicus says, that as he could not tear off the cow-dung, he remained there, and on account of the alteration in his appearance, he was not discovered, and so was devoured by the dogs.

IV. And he was a wonderful person, from his boyhood, since, while he was young, he used to say that he knew nothing but when he had grown up, he then used to affirm that he knew everything. And he was no one's pupil, but he used to say, that he himself had investigated every thing, and had learned everything of himself. But Sotion relates, that some people affirmed that he had been a pupil of Xenophanes. And that Ariston, stated in his account of Heraclitus, that he was cured of the dropsy, and died of some other disease. And Hippobotus gives the same account.

V. There is a book of his extant, which is about nature generally, and it is divided into three discourses; one on the Universe; one on Politics; and one on Theology. And he deposited this book in the temple of Diana, as some authors report, having written it intentionally in an obscure style, in order that only those who were able men might comprehend it, and that it might not be exposed to ridicule at the hands of the common people. Timon attacks this man also, saying:

Among them came that cuckoo Heraclitus
The enigmatical obscure reviler
Of all the common people.

Theophrastus asserts, that it was out of melancholy that be left some of his works half finished, and wrote several, in completely different styles; and Antisthenes, in his Successions, adduces as a proof of his lofty spirit, the fact, that he yielded to his brother the title and privileges of royalty.1

And his book had so high a reputation, that a sect arose in consequence of it, who were called after his own name, Heracliteans.

VI. The following may be set down in a general manner as his main principles: that everything is created from fire, and is dissolved into fire; that everything happens according to destiny, and that all existing things are harmonized, and made to agree together by opposite tendencies; and that all things are full of souls and daemones. He also discussed all the passions which exist in the world, and used also to contend that the sun was of that precise magnitude of which he appears to be. One of his sayings too was, that no one, by whatever road he might travel, could ever possibly find out the boundaries of the soul, so deeply hidden are the principles which regulate it. He used also to call opinion the sacred disease; and to say that eye-sight was often deceived. Sometimes, in his writings, he expresses himself with great brilliancy and clearness; so that even the most stupid man may easily understand him, and receive an elevation of soul from him. And his conciseness, and the dignity of his style, are incomparable.

In particulars, his doctrines are of this kind. That fire is an element, and that it is by the changes of fire that all things exist; being engendered sometimes by rarity, sometimes by density. But he explains nothing clearly. He also says, that everything is produced by contrariety, and that everything flows on like a river; that the universe is finite, and that there is one world, and that that is produced from fire, and that the whole world is in its turn again consumed by fire at certain periods, and that all this happens according to fate. That of the contraries, that which leads to production is called war and contest, and that which leads to the conflagration is called harmony and peace; that change is the road leading upward, and the road leading downward; and that the whole world exists according to it.

For that fire, when densified becomes liquid, and becoming concrete, becomes also water; again, that the water when concrete is turned to earth, and that this is the road down; again, that the earth itself becomes fused, from which water is produced, and from that everything else is produced; and then he refers almost everything to the evaporation which takes place from the sea; and this is the road which leads upwards. Also, that there are evaporations, both from earth and sea, some of which are bright and clear, and some are dark; and that the fire is increased by the dark ones, and the moisture by the others. But what the space which surrounds us is, he does not explain. He states, however, that there are vessels in it, turned with their hollow part towards us; in which all the bright evaporations are collected, and form flames, which are the stars; and that the brightest of these flames, and the hottest, is the light of the sun ; for that all the other stars are farther off from the earth; and that on this account, they give less light and warmth; and that the moon is nearer the earth, but does not move through a pure space; the sun, on the other hand, is situated in a transparent space, and one free from all admixture, preserving a well proportioned distance from us, on which account it gives us more light and more heat. And that the sun and moon are eclipsed, when the before-mentioned vessels are turned upwards. And that the different phases of the moon take place every month, as its vessel keeps gradually turning round. Moreover, that day and night, and months and years, and rains and winds, and things of that kind, all exist according to, and are caused by, the different evaporations.

For that the bright evaporation catching fire in the circle of the sun causes day, and the predominance of the opposite one causes night; and again, from the bright one the heat is increased so as to produce summer, and from the dark one the cold gains strength and produces winter; and he also explains the causes of the other phenomena in a corresponding manner.

But with respect to the earth, he does not explain at all of what character it is, nor does he do so in the case of the vessels; and these were his main doctrines.

VII. Now, what his opinion about Socrates was, and what expressions he used when he met with a treatise of his which Euripides brought him, according to the story told by Ariston, we have detailed in our account of Socrates. Seleucus, the grammarian, however, says that a man of the name of Croton, in his Diver, relates that it was a person of the name of Crates who first brought this book into Greece; and that he said that he wanted some Delian diver who would not be drowned in it. And the book is described under several titles; some calling it the Muses, some a treatise on Nature; but Diodotus calls it--

A well compacted helm to lead a man
Straight through the path of life.

Some call it a science of morals, the arrangement of the changes2 of unity and of everything.

VIII. They say that when he was asked why he preserved Silence, he said, "That you may talk."

IX. Darius was very desirous to enjoy his conversation; and wrote thus to him:--

### KING DARIUS, THE SON OF HYSTASPES, ADDRESSES HERACLITUS OF EPHESUS, THE WISE MAN, GREETING HIM.

"You have written a book on Natural Philosophy, difficult to understand and difficult to explain. Accordingly, if in some parts it is explained literally, it seems to disclose a very important theory concerning the universal world, and all that is contained in it, as they are placed in a state of most divine motion. But commonly, the mind is kept in suspense, so that those who have studied your work the most, are not able precisely to disentangle the exact meaning of your expressions. Therefore, king Darius, the son of Hystaspes wishes to enjoy the benefit of hearing you discourse, and of receiving some Grecian instruction. Come, therefore, quickly to my sight, and to my royal palace; for the Greeks in general, do not accord to wise men the distinction which they deserve, and disregard the admirable expositions delivered by them, which are, however, worthy of being seriously listened to and studied; but with me you shall have every kind of distinction and honour, and you shall enjoy every day honourable and worthy conversation, and your pupils' life shall become virtuous, in accordance with your precepts."

### HERACLITUS, OF EPHESUS, TO KING DARIUS, THE SON OF HYSTASPES, GREETING.

"All the men that exist in the world, are far removed from truth and just dealings; but they are full of evil foolishness, which leads them to insatiable covetousness and vain-glorious ambition. I, however, forgetting all their worthlessness, and shunning satiety, and who wish to avoid all envy on the part of my countrymen, and all appearance of arrogance, will never come to Persia, since I am quite contented with a little, and live as best suits my own inclination."

X. This was the way in which the man behaved even to the king. And Demetrius, in his treatise on People of the same Name, says that he also despised the Athenians among whom he had a very high reputation. And that though he was himself despised by the Ephesians, he nevertheless preferred his own home. Demetrius Phaleruus also mentions him in his Defence of Socrates.

XI. There were many people who undertook to interpret his book. For Antisthenes and Heraclides, Ponticus, and Cleanthes, and Sphaerus the Stoic; and besides them Pausanias, who was surnamed Heraclitistes, and Nicomedes, and Dionysius, all did so. And of the grammarians, Diodotus undertook the same task; and he says that the subject of the book is not natural philosophy, but politics; and that all that is said in it about natural philosophy, is only by way of illustration. And Hieronymus tells us, that a man of the name of Scythenus, an iambic poet, attempted to render the book into verse.

XII. There are many epigrams extant which were written upon him, and this is one of them:

I who lie here am Heraclitus, spare me
Ye rude unlettered men: 'Twas not for you
That I did labour, but for wiser people.
One man may be to me a countless host,
And an unnumbered multitude be no one;
And this I still say in the shades below.
And there is another expressed thus:

Be not too hasty, skimming o'er the book
Of Heraclitus; 'tis a difficult road,
For mist is there, and darkness hard to pierce.
But if you have a guide who knows his system,
Then everything is clearer than the sun.

XIII. There were five people of the name of Heraclitus. The first was this philosopher of ours. The second a lyric poet, who wrote a panegyrical hymn on the Twelve Gods. The third was an Elegiac poet, of Halicarnassus; on whom Callimachus wrote the following epigram:

I heard, O Heraclitus, of your death,
And the news filled my eyes with mournful tears,
When I remembered all the happy hours
When we with talk beguiled the setting sun.
You now are dust; but still the honeyed voice
Of your sweet converse doth and will survive;
Nor can fell death, which all things else destroys,
Lay upon that his ruthless conquering grasp.

The fourth was a Lesbian, who wrote a history of Macedonia. The fifth was a man who blended jest with earnest; and who, having been a harp-player, abandoned that profession for a serio-comic style of writing.

## LIFE OF PARMENIDES

I. PARMENIDES, the son of Pyres, and a citizen of Elea, was a pupil of Xenophanes. And Theophrastus, in his Abridgment, says that he was also a pupil of Anaximander. However, though he was a pupil of Xenophanes he was not afterwards a follower of his; but he attached himself to Aminias, and Diochartes the Pythagorean, as Sotion relates, which last was a poor but honourable and virtuous man. And he it was whose follower he became, and after he was dead he erected a shrine, or hêrôon, in his honour. And so Parmenides, who was of a noble family and possessed of considerable wealth, was induced, not by Xenophanes but by Aminias, to embrace the tranquil life of a philosopher.

II. He was the first person who asserted that the earth was of a spherical form; and that it was situated in the centre of the universe. He also taught that there were two elements, fire and earth; and that one of them occupies the place of the maker, the other that of the matter. He also used to teach that man was originally made out of clay; and that they were composed of two parts, the hot and the cold; of which, in fact, everything consists. Another of his doctrines was, that the mind and the soul were the same thing, as we are informed by Theophrastus, in his Natural Philosophy, when he enumerates the theories of nearly all the different philosophers.

He also used to say that philosophy was of a twofold character; one kind resting on certain truth, the other on opinion. On which account he says some where:

> And 'twill be needful for you well to know,
> The fearless heart of all-convincing truth:
> Also the opinions, though less sure, of men,
> Which rest upon no certain evidence.

III. Parmenides too philosophizes in his poems; as Hesiod and Xenophanes, and Empedocles used to. And he used to say that argument was the test of truth; and that the sensations were not trustworthy witnesses. Accordingly, he says:

> Let not the common usages of men
> Persuade your better taught experience,
> To trust to men's unsafe deceitful sight,
> Or treacherous ears, or random speaking tongue:
> Reason alone will prove the truth of facts.
> On which account Timon says of him:
>
> The vigorous mind of wise Parmenides,
> Who classes all the errors of the thoughts
> Under vain phantasies.

Plato inscribed one of his dialogues with his name--Parmenides or an essay on Ideas. He flourished about the sixty-ninth Olympiad. He appears to have been the first person who discovered that Hesperus and Lucifer were the same star, as Favorinus records, in the fifth book of his Commentaries. Some, however, attribute this discovery to Pythagoras. And Callimachus asserts that the poem in which this doctrine is promulgated is not his work.

IV. He is said also to have given laws to his fellow-citizens, as Speusippus records, in his account of the Philosophers. He was also the first employer of the question called the Achilles, as Favorinus assures us in his Universal History.

V. There was also another Parmenides, an orator, who wrote a treatise on the art of Oratory.

## LIFE OF ZENO, THE ELEATIC

I. ZENO was a native of Elea. Apollodorus, in his Chronicles, says that he was by nature the son of Teleutagoras, but by adoption the son of Parmenides.

II. Timon speaks thus of him and Melissus:--

Great is the strength, invincible the might
Of Zeno, skilled to argue on both sides
Of any question, th' universal critic;
And of Melissus too. They rose superior
To prejudice in general; only yielding
To very few.

And Zeno had been a pupil of Parmenides, and had been on other accounts greatly attached to him.

III. He was a tall man, as Plato tells us in his Parmenides, and the same writer, in his Phaedrus, calls him also the Eleatic Palamedes.

IV. Aristotle, in his Sophist, says that he was the inventor of dialectics, as Empedocles was of rhetoric. And he was a man of the greatest nobleness of spirit, both in philosophy and in politics. There are also many books extant, which are attributed to him, full of great learning and wisdom.

V. He, wishing to put an end to the power of Nearches, the tyrant (some, however, call the tyrant Diomedon), was arrested, as we are informed by Heraclides, in his abridgment of Satyrus. And when he was examined, as to his accomplices, and as to the arms which he was taking to Lipara, he named all the friends of the tyrant as his accomplices, wishing to make him feel himself alone. And then, after he had mentioned some names, he said that he wished to whisper something privately to the tyrant; and when he came near him he bit him, and would not leave his hold till he was stabbed. And the same thing happened to Aristogiton, the tyrant slayer. But Demetrius, in his treatise on People of the same Name, says that it was his nose that he bit off.

Moreover, Antisthenes, in his Successions, says that after he had given him information against his friends, he was asked by the tyrant if there was any one else. And he replied, "Yes, you, the destruction of the city." And that he also said to the bystanders, "I marvel at your cowardice, if you submit to be slaves to the tyrant out of fear of such pains as I am now enduring." And at last he bit off his tongue and spit it at him; and the citizens immediately rushed forward, and slew the tyrant with stones. And this is the account that is given by almost every one.

But Hermippus says, that he was put into a mortar, and pounded to death.

And we ourselves have written the following epigram on him:

> Your noble wish, O Zeno, was to slay
> A cruel tyrant, freeing Elea
> From the harsh bonds of shameful slavery,
> But you were disappointed; for the tyrant
> Pounded you in a mortar. I say wrong,
> He only crushed your body, and not you.

VI. And Zeno was an excellent man in other respects: and he was also a despiser of great men in an equal degree with Heraclitus; for he, too, preferred the town which was formerly called Hyele, and afterwards Elea, being a colony of the Phocaeans, and his own native place, a poor city possessed of no other importance than the knowledge of how to raise virtuous citizens, to the pride of the Athenians; so that he did not often visit them, but spent his life at home.

VII. He, too, was the first man who asked the question called Achilles,1 though Favorinus attributes its first use to Parmenides, and several others.

VIII. His chief doctrines were, that there were several worlds, and that there was no vacuum; that the nature of all things consisted of hot and cold, and dry and moist, these elements interchanging their substances with one another; that man was made out of the earth, and that his soul was a mixture of the before-named elements in such a way that no one of them predominated.

IX. They say that when he was reproached, he was indignant; and that when some one blamed him, he replied, "If when I am reproached, I am not angered, then I shall not be pleased when I am praised."

X. We have already said in our account of the Cittiaean, that there were eight Zenos; but this one flourished about the seventy-ninth Olympiad.

## LIFE OF DEMOCRITUS

I. DEMOCRITUS was the son of Hegesistratus, but as some say, of Athenocrites, and, according to other accounts, of Damasippus. He was a native of Abdera, or, as it is stated by some authors, a citizen of Miletus.

II. He was a pupil of some of the Magi and Chaldaeans, whom Xerxes had left with his father as teachers, when he had been hospitably received by him, as Herodotus informs us;1 and from these men he, while still a boy, learned the principles of astronomy and theology. Afterwards, his father entrusted him to Leucippus, and to Anaxagoras, as some authors assert, who was forty years older than he. And Favorinus, in his Universal History, says that Democritus said of Anaxagoras, that his opinions about the sun and moon were not his own, but were old theories, and that he had stolen them. And that he used also to pull to pieces his assertions about the composition of the world, and about mind, as he was hostile to him, because he had declined to admit him as a pupil. How then can he have been a pupil of his, as some assert? And Demetrius in his treatise on People of the same Name, and Antisthenes in his Successions, both affirm that he travelled to Egypt to see the priests there, and to learn mathematics of them; and that he proceeded further to the Chaldeans, and penetrated into Persia, and went as far as the Persian Gulf. Some also say that he made acquaintance with the Gymnosophists in India, and that he went to Aethiopia.

III. He was one of three brothers who divided their patrimony among them; and the most common story is, that he took the smaller portion, as it was in money, because he required money for the purpose of travelling; though his brothers suspected him of entertaining some treacherous design. And Demetrius says, that his share amounted to more than a hundred talents, and that he spent the whole of it.

IV. He also says, that he was so industrious a man, that he cut off for himself a small portion of the garden which surrounded his house, in which there was a small cottage, and shut himself up in it. And on one occasion, when his father brought him an ox to sacrifice, and fastened it there, he for a long tim did not discover it, until his father having roused him, on the pretext of the sacrifice, told him what he had done with the ox.

V. He further asserts, that it is well known that he went to Athens, and as he despised glory, he did not desire to be known; and that he became acquainted with Socrates, without Socrates knowing who he was. "For I came," says he, "to Athens, and no one knew me." "If," says Thrasylus, "the Rivals is really the work of Plato, then Democritus must be the anonymous interlocutor, who is introduced in that dialogue, besides Aenopides and Anaxagoras, the one I mean who, in the conversation with Socrates, is arguing about philosophy, and whom the philosopher tells, that a philosopher resembles a conqueror in the Pentathlum." And he was veritably a master of five branches of philosophy. For he was thoroughly acquainted with physics, and ethics, and mathematics and the whole encyclic system, and indeed be was thoroughly experienced and skilful in every kind of art. He it was who was the author of the saying, "Speech is the shadow of action." But Demetrius Phalereus, in his Defence of Socrates, affirms that he never came to Athens at all. And that is a still stranger circumstance than any, if he despised so important a city, not wishing to derive glory from the place in which he was, but preferring rather himself to invest the place with glory.

VI. And it is evident from his writings, what sort of man he was. "He seems," says Thrasylus, "to have been also an admirer of the Pythagoreans." And he mentions Pythagoras himself, speaking of him with admiration, in the treatise which is inscribed with his name. And he appears to have derived all his doctrines from him to such a degree, that one would have thought that he had been his pupil, if the difference of time did not prevent it. At all events, Glaucus, of Rhegium, who was a contemporary of his, affirms that he was pupil of some of the Pythagorean school.

And Apollodorus, of Cyzicus, says that he was intimate with Philolaus; "He used to practise himself," says Antisthenes, "in testing perceptions in various manners; sometimes retiring into solitary places, and spending his time even among tombs."

VII. And he further adds, that when he returned from his travels, he lived in a most humble manner; like a man who had spent all his property, and that on account of his poverty, he was supported by his brother Damasus. But when he had foretold some future event, which happened as he had predicted, and had in consequence become famous, he was for all the rest of his life thought worthy of almost divine honours by the generality of people. And as there was a law, that a man who had squandered the whole of his patrimony, should not be allowed funeral rites in his country, Antisthenes says, that he, being aware of this law, and not wishing to be exposed to the calumnies of those who envied him, and would be glad to accuse him, recited to the people his work called the Great World, which is far superior to all his other writings, and that as a reward for it he was presented with five hundred talents; and not only that, but he also had some brazen statues erected in his honour. And when he died, he was buried at the public expense; after having attained the age of more than a hundred years. But Demetrius says, that it was his relations who read the Great World, and that they were presented with a hundred talents only; and Hippobotus coincides in this statement.

VIII. And Aristoxenus, in his Historic Commentaries, says that Plato wished to burn all the writings of Democritus that he was able to collect; but that Amyclas and Cleinias, the Pythagoreans, prevented him, as it would do no good; for that copies of his books were already in many hands. And it is plain that that was the case; for Plato, who mentions nearly all the ancient philosophers, nowhere speaks of Democritus; not even in those passages where he has occasion to contradict his theories, evidently, because he said that if he did, he would be showing his disagreement with the best of all philosophers; a man whom even Timon praises in the following terms:

Like that Democritus, wisest of men,
Sage ruler of his speech; profound converser,
Whose works I love to read among the first.

IX. But he was, according to the statement made by himself in the Little World, a youth when Anaxagoras was an old man, being forty years younger than he was. And he says, that he composed the Little World seven hundred and thirty years after the capture of Troy. And he must have been born, according to the account given by Apollodorus in his Chronicles, in the eightieth Olympiad; but, as

Thrasylus says, in his work entitled the Events, which took place before the reading of the books of Democritus, in the third year of the seventy-seventh olympiad, being, as it is there stated, one year older than Socrates. He must therefore have been a contemporary of Archelaus, the pupil of Anaxagoras, and of Aenopides, for he makes mention of this latter. He also speaks of the theories of Parmenides and Zeno, on the subject of the One, as they were the men of the highest reputation in histories, and he also speaks of Protagoras of Abdera, who confessedly lived at the same time as Socrates.

X. Athenodorus tells us, in the eighth book of his Conversations, that once, when Hippocrates came to see him, he ordered some milk to be brought; and that, when he saw the milk, he said that it was the milk of a black goat, with her first kid; on which Hippocrates marvelled at his accurate knowledge. Also, as a young girl came with Hippocrates, on the first day, he saluted her thus, "Good morning, my maid; but on the next day, "Good morning, woman;" for, indeed, she had ceased to be a maid during the night.

XI. And Hermippus relates, that Democritus died in the following manner: he was exceedingly old, and appeared at the point of death; and his sister was lamenting that he would die during the festival of the Thesmophoria,2 and so prevent her from discharging her duties to the Goddess; and so he bade her be of good cheer, and desired her to bring him hot loaves every day. And, by applying these to his nostrils, he kept himself alive even over the festival. But when the days of the festival were passed (and it lasted three days), then he expired, without any pain, as Hipparchus assures us, having lived a hundred and nine years. And we have written an epigram upon him in our collection of poems in every metre, which runs thus:

What man was e'er so wise, who ever did
So great a deed as this Democritus?
Who kept off death, though present for three days,
And entertained him with hot steam of bread.
Such was the life of this man.

XII. Now his principal doctrines were these. That atoms and the vacuum were the beginning of the universe; and that everything else existed only in opinion. That the worlds were infinite, created, and perishable. But that nothing was created out of nothing, and that nothing was destroyed so as to become nothing. That the atoms were infinite both in magnitude and number, and were borne about through the universe in endless revolutions. And that thus they produced all the combinations that exist; fire, water, air, and earth; for that all these things are only combinations of certain atoms; which combinations are incapable of being affected by external circumstances, and are unchangeable by reason of their solidity. Also, that the sun and the moon are formed by such revolutions and round bodies; and in like manner the soul is produced; and that the soul and the mind are identical; that we see by the falling of visions across our sight; and that everything that happens, happens of necessity. Motion, being the cause of the production of everything, which he calls necessity. The chief good he asserts to be cheerfulness; which, however, he does not consider the same as pleasure; as some people, who have misunderstood him, have fancied that he meant; but he understands by cheerfulness, a condition according to which the soul lives calmly and steadily, being disturbed by no fear, or superstition, or other passion. He calls this state euthymia, and euestô, and several other names. Everything which is made he looks upon as depending for its existence on opinion; but atoms and the vacuum he believes exist by nature. These were his principal opinions.

XIII. Of his books, Thrasylus has given a regular catalogue, in the same way that he has arranged the works of Plato, dividing them into four classes.

Now these are his ethical works. The Pythagoras; a treatise on the Disposition of the Wise Man; an essay on those in the Shades Below; the Tritogeneia (this is so called because from Minerva three things are derived which hold together all human affairs); a treatise on Manly Courage or Valour: the Horn of Amalthea; an essay on Cheerfulness; a volume of Ethical Commentaries. A treatise entitled, For Cheerfulness, (euestô) is not found.

These are his writings on natural philosophy. The Great World (which Theophrastus asserts to be the work of Leucippus); the Little World; the Cosmography; a treatise on the Planets; the first book on Nature; two books on the Nature of Man, or on Flesh; an essay on the Mind; one on the Senses (some people join these two together in one volume, which they entitle, on the Soul); a treatise on Juices; one on Colours; one on the Different Figures; one on the Changes of Figures; the Cratynteria (that is to say, an essay, approving of what has been said in preceding ones); a treatise on Phaenomenon, or on Providence; three books on Pestilences, or Pestilential Evils; a book of Difficulties. These are his books on natural philosophy.

His miscellaneous works are these. Heavenly Causes; Aërial Causes; Causes affecting Plane Surfaces; Causes referring to Fire, and to what is in Fire; Causes affecting Voices; Causes affecting Seeds, and Plants, and Fruits; three books of Causes affecting Animals; Miscellaneous Causes; a treatise on the Magnet. These are his miscellaneous works.

His mathematical writings are the following. A treatise on the Difference of Opinion, or on the Contact of the Circle and the Sphere; one on Geometry; one on Numbers; one on Incommensurable Lines, and Solids, in two books; a volume called Explanations; the Great Year, or the Astronomical Calendar; a discussion on the Clepsydra; the Map of the Heavens; Geography; Polography; Artmography, or a discussion on Rays of Light. These are his mathematical works.

His works on music are the following. A treatise on Rhythm and Harmony; one on Poetry; one on the beauty of Epic Poems; one on Euphonious and

Discordant Letters; one on Homer, or on Propriety of Diction3 and Dialects; one on Song, one on Words; the Onomasticon. These are his musical works.

The following are his works on art. Prognostics; a treatise on the Way of Living, called also Diaetetics, or the Opinions of a Physician; Causes relating to Unfavourable and Favourable Opportunities; a treatise on Agriculture, called also the Georgic; one on Painting; Tactics, and Fighting in heavy Armour. These are his works on such subjects.

Some authors also give a list of some separate treatises which they collect from his Commentaries. A treatise on the Sacred Letters seen at Babylon; another on the Sacred Letters seen at Meroe; the Voyage round the Ocean; a treatise on History; a Chaldaic Discourse; a Phrygian Discourse; a treatise on Fever; an essay on those who are attacked with Cough after illness; the Principles of Laws; Things made by Hand, or Problems.

As to the other books which some writers ascribed to him, some are merely extracts from his other writings, and some are confessedly the work of others. And this is a sufficient account of his writings.

XIV. There were six people of the name of Democritus. The first was this man of whom we are speaking; the second was a musician of Chios, who lived about the same time; the third was a sculptor who is mentioned by Antigonus; the fourth is a man who wrote a treatise on the Temple at Ephesus, and on the city of Samothrace; the fifth was an epigrammatic poet, of great perspicuity and elegance; the sixth was a citizen of Pergamus, who wrote a treatise on Oratory.

## LIFE OF EMPEDOCLES

LI. Empedocles was, according to Hippobotus, the son of Meton and grandson of Empedocles, and was a native of Agrigentum. This is confirmed by Timaeus in the fifteenth book of his Histories, and he adds that Empedocles, the poet's grandfather, had been a man of distinction. Hermippus also agrees with Timaeus. So, too, Heraclides, in his treatise On Diseases, says that he was of an illustrious family, his grandfather having kept racehorses. Eratosthenes also in his Olympic Victories records, on the authority of Aristotle, that the father of Meton was a victor in the 71st Olympiad.

LII. The grammarian Apollodorus in his Chronology tells us that

He was the son of Meton, and Glaucus says he went to Thurii, just then founded.

Then farther on he adds:

Those who relate that, being exiled from his home, he went to Syracuse and fought in their ranks against the Athenians seem, in my judgement at least, to be completely mistaken. For by that time either he was no longer living or in extreme old age, which is inconsistent with the story.

For Aristotle and Heraclides both affirm that he died at the age of sixty. The victor with the riding horse in the 71st Olympiad was

This man's namesake and grandfather,

so that Apollodorus in one and the same passage indicates the date as well as the fact.

LIII. But Satyrus in his Lives states that Empedocles was the son of Exaenetus and himself left a son named Exaenetus, and that in the same Olympiad Empedocles himself was victorious in the horse-race and his son in wrestling, or, as Heraclides in his Epitome has it, in the foot-race. I found in the Memorabilia of Favorinus a statement that Empedocles feasted the sacred envoys on a sacrificial ox made of honey and barley-meal, and that he had a brother named Callicratides. Telauges, the son of Pythagoras, in his letter to Philolaus calls Empedocles the son of Archinomus.

LIV. That he belonged to Agrigentum in Sicily he himself testifies at the beginning of his Purifications:

My friends, who dwell in the great city sloping down to yellow Acragas, hard by the citadel.

So much for his family.

Timaeus in the ninth book of his Histories says he was a pupil of Pythagoras, adding that, having been convicted at that time of stealing his discourses, he was, like Plato, excluded from taking part in the discussions of the school; and further, that Empedocles himself mentions Pythagoras in the lines:

And there lived among them a man of superhuman knowledge, who verily possessed the greatest wealth of wisdom.

Others say that it is to Parmenides that he is here referring.

LV. Neanthes states that down to the time of Philolaus and Empedocles all Pythagoreans were admitted to the discussions. But when Empedocles himself made them public property by his poem, they made a law that they should not be imparted to any poet. He says the same thing also happened to Plato, for he too was excommunicated. But which of the Pythagoreans it was who had Empedocles for a pupil he did not say. For the epistle commonly attributed to Telauges and the statement that Empedocles was the pupil of both Hippasus and Brontinus he held to be unworthy of credence.

Theophrastus affirms that he was an admirer of Parmenides and imitated him in his verses, for Parmenides too had published his treatise On Nature in verse.

LVI. But Hermippus's account is that he was an admirer not so much of Parmenides as of Xenophanes, with whom in fact he lived and whose writing of poetry he imitated, and that his meeting with the Pythagoreans was subsequent. Alcidamas tells us in his treatise on Physics that Zeno and Empedocles were pupils of Parmenides about the same time, that afterwards they left him, and that, while Zeno framed his own system, Empedocles became the pupil of Anaxagoras and Pythagoras, emulating the latter in dignity of life and bearing, and the former in his physical investigations.

LVII. Aristotle in his Sophist calls Empedocles the inventor of rhetoric as Zeno of dialectic. In his treatise On Poets he says that Empedocles was of Homer's school and powerful in diction, being great in metaphors and in the use of all other poetical devices. He also says that he wrote other poems, in particular the invasion of Xerxes and a hymn to Apollo, which a sister of his (or, according to Hieronymus, his daughter) afterwards burnt. The hymn she destroyed unintentionally, but the poem on the Persian war deliberately, because it was unfinished.

LVIII. And in general terms he says he wrote both tragedies and political discourses. But Heraclides, the son of Sarapion, attributes the tragedies to a different author. Hieronymus declares that he had come across forty-three of these plays, while Neanthes tells us that Empedocles wrote these tragedies in his youth, and that he, Neanthes, was acquainted with seven of them.

Satyrus in his Lives says that he was also a physician and an excellent orator: at all events Gorgias of Leontini, a man pre-eminent in oratory and the author of a treatise on the art, had been his pupil. Of Gorgias Apollodorus says in his Chronology that he lived to be one hundred and nine.

LIX. Satyrus quotes this same Gorgias as saying that he himself was present when Empedocles performed magical feats. Nay more: he contends that Empedocles in his poems lays claim to this power and to much besides when he says:

And thou shalt learn all the drugs that are a defence to ward off ills and old age, since for thee alone shall I accomplish all this. Thou shalt arrest the violence of the unwearied winds that arise and sweep the earth, laying waste the cornfields with their blasts; and again, if thou so will, thou shalt call back winds in requital. Thou shalt make after the dark rain a seasonable drought for men, and again after the summer drought thou shalt cause tree-nourishing streams to pour from the sky. Thou shalt bring back from Hades a dead man's strength.

LX. Timaeus also in the eighteenth book of his Histories remarks that Empedocles has been admired on many grounds. For instance, when the etesian winds once began to blow violently and to damage the crops, he ordered asses to be flayed and bags to be made of their skin. These he stretched out here and there on the hills and headlands to catch the wind and, because this checked the wind, he was called the "wind-stayer." Heraclides in his book On Diseases says that he furnished Pausanias with the facts about the woman in a trance. This Pausanias, according to Aristippus and Satyrus, was his bosom-friend, to whom he dedicated his poem On Nature thus:

LXI.

Give ear, Pausanias, thou son of Anchitus the wise!

Moreover he wrote an epigram upon him:

The physician Pausanias, rightly so named, son of Anchitus, descendant of Asclepius, was born and bred at Gela. Many a wight pining in fell torments did he bring back from Persephone's inmost shrine.

At all events Heraclides testifies that the case of the woman in a trance was such that for thirty days he kept her body without pulsation though she never breathed; and for that reason Heraclides called him not merely a physician but a diviner as well, deriving the titles from the following lines also:

LXII. My friends, who dwell in the great city sloping down to yellow Acragas, hard by the citadel, busied with goodly works, all hail! I go about among you an immortal god, no more a mortal, so honoured of all, as is meet, crowned with fillets and flowery garlands. Straightway as soon as I enter with these, men and women, into flourishing towns, I am reverenced and tens of thousands follow, to learn where is the path which leads to welfare, some desirous of oracles, others suffering from all kinds of diseases, desiring to hear a message of healing.

LXIII. Timaeus explains that he called Agrigentum great, inasmuch as it had 800,000 inhabitants. Hence Empedocles, he continues, speaking of their luxury, said, "The Agrigentines live delicately as if tomorrow they would die, but they build their houses well as if they thought they would live for ever."

It is said that Cleomenes the rhapsode recited this very poem, the Purifications, at Olympia: so Favorinus in his Memorabilia. Aristotle too declares him to have been a champion of freedom and averse to rule of every kind, seeing that, as Xanthus relates in his account of him, he declined the kingship when it was offered to him, obviously because he preferred a frugal life.

LXIV. With this Timaeus agrees, at the same time giving the reason why Empedocles favoured democracy, namely, that, having been invited to dine with one of the magistrates, when the dinner had gone on some time and no wine was put on the table, though the other guests kept quiet, he, becoming indignant, ordered wine to be brought. Then the host confessed that he was waiting for the servant of the senate to appear. When he came he was made master of the revels, clearly by the arrangement of the host, whose design of making himself tyrant was but thinly veiled, for he ordered the guests either to drink wine or have it poured over their heads. For the time being Empedocles was reduced to silence; the next day he impeached both of them, the host and the master of the revels, and secured their condemnation and execution. This, then, was the beginning of his political career.

LXV. Again, when Acron the physician asked the council for a site on which to build a monument to his father, who had been eminent among physicians, Empedocles came forward and forbade it in a speech where he enlarged upon equality and in particular put the following question: "But what inscription shall we put upon it? Shall it be this?

Acron the eminent physician of Agrigentum, son of Acros, is buried beneath the steep eminence of his most eminent native city?"

Others give as the second line:

Is laid in an exalted tomb on a most exalted peak. Some attribute this couplet to Simonides.

LXVI. Subsequently Empedocles broke up the assembly of the Thousand three years after it had been set up, which proves not only that he was wealthy but that he favoured the popular cause. At all events Timaeus in his eleventh and twelfth books (for he mentions him more than once) states that he seems to have held opposite views when in public life and when writing poetry. In some passages one may see that he is boastful and selfish. At any rate these are his words:

All hail! I go about among you an immortal god, no more a mortal, etc.

At the time when he visited Olympia he demanded an excessive deference, so that never was anyone so talked about in gatherings of friends as Empedocles.

LXVII. Subsequently, however, when Agrigentum came to regret him, the descendants of his personal enemies opposed his return home; and this was why he went to Peloponnesus, where he died. Nor did Timon let even him alone, but fastens upon him in these words:

Empedocles, too, mouthing tawdry verses; to all that had independent force, he gave a separate existence; and the principles he chose need others to explain them.

As to his death different accounts are given.

Thus Heraclides, after telling the story of the woman in a trance, how that Empedocles became famous because he had sent away the dead woman alive, goes on to say that he was offering a sacrifice close to the field of Peisianax. Some of his friends had been invited to the sacrifice, including Pausanias.

LXVIII. Then, after the feast, the remainder of the company dispersed and retired to rest, some under the trees in the adjoining field, others wherever they chose, while Empedocles himself remained on the spot where he had reclined at table. At daybreak all got up, and he was the only one missing. A search was made, and they questioned the servants, who said they did not know where he was. Thereupon someone said that in the middle of the night he heard an exceedingly loud voice calling Empedocles. Then he got up and beheld a light in the heavens and a glitter of lamps, but nothing else. His hearers were amazed at what had occurred, and Pausanias came down and sent people to search for him. But later he bade them take no further trouble, for things beyond expectation had happened to him, and it was their duty to sacrifice to him since he was now a god.

LXIX. Hermippus tells us that Empedocles cured Panthea, a woman of Agrigentum, who had been given up by the physicians, and this was why he was offering sacrifice, and that those invited were about eighty in number. Hippobotus, again, asserts that, when he got up, he set out on his way to Etna; then, when he had reached it, he plunged into the fiery craters and disappeared, his intention being to confirm the report that he had become a god. Afterwards the truth was known, because one of his slippers was thrown up in the flames; it had been his custom to wear slippers of bronze. To this story Pausanias is made (by Heraclides) to take exception.

LXX. Diodorus of Ephesus, when writing of Anaximander, declares that Empedocles emulated him, displaying theatrical arrogance and wearing stately robes. We are told that the people of Selinus suffered from pestilence owing to the noisome smells from the river hard by, so that the citizens themselves perished and their women died in childbirth, that Empedocles conceived the plan of bringing two neighbouring rivers to the place at his own expense, and that by this admixture he sweetened the waters. When in this way the pestilence had been stayed and the Selinuntines were feasting on the river bank, Empedocles appeared; and the company rose up and worshipped and prayed to him as to a god. It was then to confirm this belief of theirs that he leapt into the fire.

LXXI. These stories are contradicted by Timaeus, who expressly says that he left Sicily for Peloponnesus and never returned at all; and this is the reason Timaeus gives for the fact that the manner of his death is unknown. He replies to Heraclides, whom he mentions by name, in his fourteenth book. Pisianax, he says, was a citizen of Syracuse and possessed no land at Agrigentum. Further, if such a story had been in circulation, Pausanias would have set up a monument to his friend, as to a god, in the form of a statue or shrine, for he was a wealthy man. "How came he," adds Timaeus, "to leap into the craters, which he had never once mentioned though they were not far off ? He must then have died in Peloponnesus.

LXII. It is not at all surprising that his tomb is not found; the same is true of many other men." After urging some such arguments Timaeus goes on to say, "But Heraclides is everywhere just such a collector of absurdities, telling us, for instance, that a man dropped down to earth from the moon."

Hippobotus assures us that formerly there was in Agrigentum a statue of Empedocles with his head covered, and afterwards another with the head uncovered in front of the Senate House at Rome, which plainly the Romans had removed to that site. For portrait-statues with inscriptions are extant even now. Neanthes of Cyzicus, who tells about the Pythagoreans, relates that, after the death of Meton, the germs of a tyranny began to show themselves, that then it was Empedocles who persuaded the Agrigentines to put an end to their factions and cultivate equality in politics.

LXIII. Moreover, from his abundant means he bestowed dowries upon many of the maidens of the city who had no dowry. No doubt it was the same means that enabled him to don a purple robe and over it a golden girdle, as Favorinus relates in his Memorabilia, and again slippers of bronze and a Delphic laurel-wreath. He had thick hair, and a train of boy attendants. He himself was always grave, and kept this gravity of demeanour unshaken. In such sort would he appear in public; when the citizens met him, they recognized in this demeanour the stamp, as it were, of royalty. But afterwards, as he was going in a carriage to Messene to attend some festival, he fell and broke his thigh; this brought an illness which caused his death at the age of seventy-seven. Moreover, his tomb is in Megara.

LXIV. As to his age, Aristotle's account is different, for he makes him to have been sixty when he died; while others make him one hundred and nine. He flourished in the 84th Olympiad.Demetrius of Troezen in his pamphlet Against the Sophists said of him, adapting the words of Homer:

He tied a noose that hung aloft from a tall cornel-tree and thrust his neck into it, and his soul went down to Hades.

In the short letter of Telauges which was mentioned above it is stated that by reason of his age he slipped into the sea and was drowned. Thus and thus much of his death.

There is an epigram of my own on him in my Pammetros in a satirical vein, as follows:

LXXV. Thou, Empedocles, didst cleanse thy body with nimble flame, fire didst thou drink from everlasting bowls. I will not say that of thine own will thou didst hurl thyself into the stream of Etna; thou didst fall in against thy will when thou wouldst fain not have been found out.

And another:

Verily there is a tale about the death of Empedocles, how that once he fell from a carriage and broke his right thigh. But if he leapt into the bowls of fire and so took a draught of life, how was it that his tomb was shown still in Megara ?

LXVI. His doctrines were as follows, that there are four elements, fire, water, earth and air, besides friendship by which these are united, and strife by which they are separated. These are his words:

Shining Zeus and life-bringing Hera, Aidoneus and Nestis, who lets flow from her tears the source of mortal life,

where by Zeus he means fire, by Hera earth, by Aidoneus air, and by Nestis water.

"And their continuous change," he says, "never ceases," as if this ordering of things were eternal. At all events he goes on:

At one time all things uniting in one through Love, at another each carried in a different direction through the hatred born of strife.

LXVII. The sun he calls a vast collection of fire and larger than the moon; the moon, he says, is of the shape of a quoit, and the heaven itself crystalline. The soul, again, assumes all the various forms of animals and plants. At any rate he says:

Before now I was born a boy and a maid, a bush and a bird, and a dumb fish leaping out of the sea.

His poems On Nature and Purifications run to 5000 lines, his Discourse on Medicine to 600. Of the tragedies we have spoken above.

# Chapter 2: Socrates and the Sophists

> *Comprehension questions you should be able to answer after reading this chapter:*
>
> 1. Who were the Sophists, and what were the cultural conditions that made them possible?
>
> 2. What did Protagoras mean when he said that "man is the measure of all things?"
>
> 3. Why is it difficult to know what Socrates' actually believed?
>
> 4. What are the features of the "Socratic method?"
>
> 5. Why was Socrates' death inspirational to so many?

If we accept the narrative from the previous section, ancient Greek intellectual culture had become focused on unraveling the truth about the cosmos, identifying the "logos' that gave rational structure and order to the universe—and then the Sophists came along....

From a socio-historical perspective, we might consider several possible contributors to the rise of sophistry. Ancient Greece had grown more cosmopolitan, and came into ever greater contact with other cultures and traditions. The rise of democracy meant an increased number of voices that not only were heard, but that asserted an equal claim to be heard. Even among the philosophers there was a dizzying diversity of opinions.

"Reality is water."

"No, it's fire."

"Actually, it's 'apeiron.'"

"What the heck is 'apeiron?' Never mind. Regardless, permanence is an illusion."

"On the contrary, it is change that is the illusion."

To make things more maddening, these contradictory positions were being presented via rigorous argumentation. An interesting and compelling case could be made for each. In sum, the ancient Greek world found itself flooded with, and grappling with, pluralism: a diversity of different ideas and values. Given such a cultural and intellectual backdrop, perhaps it should come as no surprise that some thinkers gave up on the search for The Truth.

The Sophists, to use an uncomfortable analogy, were what we might expect if a typical university philosophy professor today mated with an equally typical lawyer. We can imagine the offspring to be a very intelligent person, capable of arguing any and every side of a debate, and focused primarily on "victory" as opposed to truth. Such were the Sophists. Among the most famous of them were

Protagoras, Gorgias, and Thrasymachus. If you read much Plato, you'll encounter these names as characters in his dialogues. Indeed, both Protagoras and Gorgias have entire dialogues named after them. Of course, these Sophists always appeared as the antagonists, doing (ill-fated) intellectual battle with the hero, Socrates....

What Sophists had in common with modern day philosophy professors is that they taught in exchange for money. What they had in common with (stereotypical) modern day lawyers is that they were (generally) willing to take any side in a debate, or court case, if the price was right.

In their defense, *most Sophists were either skeptics or epistemic relativists.* That is, they either believed that "the truth" was unknowable, or else that truth is a matter of perspective. In either case, there is no (knowable) "right" answer to our deep questions, nor any (knowable) "right" outcome to a lawsuit. If "Truth" could not be the arbiter of such things, then we must default to persuasiveness instead. Rhetoric might be more important than reason, if there is no "Truth" to be discovered. Victory, not accuracy, is the only outcome to be pursued and obtained.

Why come to such (possibly depressing) conclusions? Remember the foundation already laid by the pre-Socratics: the distinction between appearance and reality emphasized by those such as Heraclitus, Parmenides, and Zeno make skepticism not only possible, but compelling. If we have no clear access to "reality," and must operate solely by "appearances," and if the world appears differently on the basis of who is making the perception, then perhaps the sensible approach to take is that "truth" is simply a matter of perception.

One notable Sophist, Protagoras (490 - 420 BCE) is credited with the claim that "man is the measure of all things." By this, he meant that *perception is relative to the individual doing the perceiving*, and therefore any contact with reality is unique to that individual. Since perception is our only contact with the world, "reality" is relative to the individual who perceives it. Values are also relative. There is no Nature (*physis*), objective and independent of human traditions, perceptions, and decisions, out there for us to discover. Instead, such things are a matter of convention (*nomos*) or custom. Morality is subjective, but there is a pragmatic value to adhering to shared social conventions for the sake of peace and order.

## Great Minds Think Alike!

The sophists were the notorious "rivals" to Socrates. They were hardly unique in their outlook, however. Roughly a century before Protagoras (i.e. in the sixth century BCE), the Chinese sophist Teng Shih lived and wrote in the province of Cheng.

Although his moral subjectivism invites comparison with Protagoras, his alleged methods also invite comparison to the ancient Skeptics. According to a historical record known as The Lu-Sze-Chun-Chiu, "he could argue a right to be wrong, and wrong to be right. With him right and wrong had no fixed standard and 'yea' and 'nay' changed every day. What he wished to win was always one; and whom he desired to punish was always punished."

The Sophists were important to philosophy—and just not as Socrates' sparring partners in many of Plato's dialogues. The Sophists raised important questions in epistemology, ethics, and politics—divisions of philosophy that had been generally overshadowed by metaphysics. They encouraged the study of logic, rhetoric, and grammar, and helped to clear out naïve traditions and dogmatic assumptions. It is in such a climate that we encounter their primary antagonist: Socrates.

## Socrates

Socrates (470 - 399 BCE), pictured here, is the iconic "philosopher" in the West, but he was also a man. He was a husband and father of three children. He was an itinerant teacher who seemed to rely on the support of his wealthier friends, as he charged nothing to those he "instructed." He served in the military, and his courage in war was recognized. He never wrote anything himself. All we think we know about him comes from the writing of others, most notably Plato, but also Aristophanes and Xenophon. Finally, he was put on trial for atheism and corrupting the youth of Athens. After being convicted and sentenced to death, he drank hemlock and died.

Socrates presents an interpretation problem. As already mentioned, he didn't write philosophical texts or dialogues himself. He is lampooned in Aristophanes' *Clouds*, and presented as a serious philosopher by both Xenophon and Plato. Our greatest source for all things Socrates is his student Plato, but Plato was roughly 45 years younger than Socrates, and was only 25 when Socrates was tried and executed. Plato was only a young child when most of the events and conversations reported in his dialogues could have actually taken place. It's unlikely that a five year old Plato was not only present for all these conversations, but memorized them precisely that he might write them down some decades later. We have, then, *"the problem of Socrates:" what did Socrates himself really believe and teach and say*? How much of Plato's "Socrates" is actually Socrates, and not just Plato wearing a "Socrates" mask? We can't know for sure. What we can know, however, is that Socrates (whatever he said!) was a hugely influential and revered figure for ancient philosophers, as all the philosophical schools to come after him (except for Epicureanism) either traced themselves back to Socrates himself, or at least claimed that Socrates was an embodiment of their ideals.

Socrates is most well-known for the *"Socratic method."* Socrates, himself (according to legend), claimed to know nothing (and from this it is easy to see the lineage the Skeptics traced back to him), and also claimed to be seeking knowledge from those with whom he spoke. Socrates starts from the position of (alleged) ignorance, all due to a fateful prophecy he received:

> *You must have known Chaerephon; he was early a friend of mine, and also a friend of yours, for he shared in the recent exile of the people, and returned with you. Well, Chaerephon, as you know, was very impetuous in all his doings, and he went to Delphi and boldly asked the oracle to tell him whether -- as I was saying, I must beg you not to interrupt -- he asked the oracle to tell him whether anyone was wiser than I was, and the Pythian prophetess answered, that there was no man wiser. Chaerephon is dead himself; but his brother, who is in court, will confirm the truth of what I am saying.*

> *Why do I mention this? Because I am going to explain to you why I have such an evil name. When I heard the answer, I said to myself, What can the god mean? and what is the interpretation of his riddle? for I know that I have no wisdom, small or great. What then can he mean when he says that I am the wisest of men? And yet he is a god, and cannot lie; that would be against his nature. After long consideration, I thought of a method of trying the question. I reflected that if I could only find a man wiser than myself, then I might go to the god with a refutation in my hand. I should say to him, 'Here is a man who is wiser than I am; but you said that I was the wisest.' Accordingly I went to one who had the reputation of wisdom, and observed him -- his name I need not mention; he was a politician whom I selected for examination -- and the result was as follows: When I began to talk with him, I could not help thinking that he was not really wise, although he was thought wise by many, and still wiser by himself; and thereupon I tried to explain to him that he thought himself wise, but was not really wise; and the consequence was that he hated me, and his enmity was shared by several who were present and heard me. So I left him, saying to myself, as I went away: Well, although I do not suppose that either of us knows anything really beautiful and good, I am better off than he is, -- for he knows nothing, and thinks that he knows; I neither know nor think that I know. In this latter particular, then, I seem to have slightly the advantage of him.[38]*

Being proclaimed the wisest of all, Socrates sought a counter-example—someone who would prove wiser than he. So, he spoke with all sorts of prominent people, people who claimed to be wise, in an effort to confirm their wisdom. The result was always the same: by virtue of his interrogation, they were revealed to be lacking in wisdom after all. His method was notorious:

---

[38] Plato, *Apology.*

1. Ask a question concerning an important issue (all while claiming not to have an answer himself)
2. Attack whatever answers (often definitions) are provided by identifying logical flaws (e.g., circularity, definition by example, etc.).
3. Employ a *reductio ad absurdum* argument to reveal further flaws, and/or use counter-examples to the same effect.
4. Thereby cause his sparring partner to cede defeat.

Consider the following example from the *Apology*:

*But still I should like to know, Meletus, in what I am affirmed to corrupt the young. I suppose you mean, as I infer from your indictment, that I teach them not to acknowledge the gods which the state acknowledges, but some other new divinities or spiritual agencies in their stead. These are the lessons by which I corrupt the youth, as you say.*

*Yes, that I say emphatically.*

*Then, by the gods, Meletus, of whom we are speaking, tell me and the court, in somewhat plainer terms, what you mean! for I do not as yet understand whether you affirm that I teach other men to acknowledge some gods, and therefore that I do believe in gods, and am not an entire atheist -- this you do not lay to my charge, -- but only you say that they are not the same gods which the city recognizes -- the charge is that they are different gods. Or, do you mean that I am an atheist simply, and a teacher of atheism?*

*I mean the latter -- that you are a complete atheist.*

*What an extraordinary statement! Why do you think so, Meletus? Do you mean that I do not believe in the godhead of the sun or moon, like other men?*

*I assure you, judges, that he does not: for he says that the sun is stone, and the moon earth.*

*Friend Meletus, you think that you are accusing Anaxagoras: and you have but a bad opinion of the judges, if you fancy them illiterate to such a degree as not to know that these doctrines are found in the books of Anaxagoras the Clazomenian, which are full of them. And so, forsooth, the youth are said to be taught them by Socrates, when there are not unfrequently exhibitions of them at the theatre (Probably in allusion to Aristophanes who caricatured, and to Euripides who borrowed the notions of Anaxagoras, as well as to other dramatic poets.) (price of admission one drachma at the most); and they might pay their money, and laugh at Socrates if he pretends to father these extraordinary views. And so, Meletus, you really think that I do not believe in any god?*

*I swear by Zeus that you believe absolutely in none at all.*

*Nobody will believe you, Meletus, and I am pretty sure that you do not believe yourself. I cannot help thinking, men of Athens, that Meletus is reckless and impudent, and that he has written this indictment in a spirit of mere wantonness and youthful bravado. Has he not compounded a riddle, thinking to try me? He said to himself: -- I shall see whether the wise Socrates will discover my facetious contradiction, or whether I shall be able to deceive him and the rest of them. For he certainly does appear to me to contradict himself in the indictment as much as if he said that Socrates is guilty of not believing in the gods, and yet of believing in them -- but this is not like a person who is in earnest.*

*I should like you, O men of Athens, to join me in examining what I conceive to be his inconsistency; and do you, Meletus, answer. And I must remind the audience of my request that they would not make a disturbance if I speak in my accustomed manner:*

*Did ever man, Meletus, believe in the existence of human things, and not of human beings?...I wish, men of Athens, that he would answer, and not be always trying to get up an interruption. Did ever any man believe in horsemanship, and not in horses? or in flute-playing, and not in flute-players? No, my friend; I will answer to you and to the court, as you refuse to answer for yourself. There is no man who ever did. But now please to answer the next question: Can a man believe in spiritual and divine agencies, and not in spirits or demigods?*

*He cannot.*

*How lucky I am to have extracted that answer, by the assistance of the court! But then you swear in the indictment that I teach and believe in divine or spiritual agencies (new or old, no matter for that); at any rate, I believe in spiritual agencies, -- so you say and swear in the affidavit; and yet if I believe in divine beings, how can I help believing in spirits or demigods; -- must I not? To be sure I must; and therefore I may assume that your silence gives consent. Now what are spirits or demigods? Are they not either gods or the sons of gods?*

*Certainly they are.*

*But this is what I call the facetious riddle invented by you: the demigods or spirits are gods, and you say first that I do not believe in gods, and then again that I do believe in gods; that is, if I believe in demigods. For if the demigods are the illegitimate sons of gods, whether by the nymphs or by any other mothers, of whom they are said to be the sons -- what human being will ever believe that there are no gods if they are the sons of gods?*

*You might as well affirm the existence of mules, and deny that of horses and asses. Such nonsense, Meletus, could only have been intended by you to make trial of me. You have put this into the indictment because you had nothing real of which to accuse me. But no one who has a particle of understanding will ever be convinced by you that the same men can believe in divine and superhuman things, and yet not believe that there are gods and demigods and heroes.*

At this point, Meletus already looks ridiculous, given that he has been reduced to the absurd position that although Socrates believes in no gods at all, he nevertheless believes in the offspring of gods! This process will continue until it becomes obvious to any impartial observer that Socrates is not guilty of the charges brought against him—not that it helped him in that case.

There are various ways to interpret his argumentative approach, with the least charitable being that Socrates was some sort of bully who preferred clever arguments over fists. If Plato's account of Socrates (especially in the *Apology*) is remotely accurate, Socrates saw himself to be on a divine mission.

*And so I go about the world, obedient to the god, and search and make enquiry into the wisdom of any one, whether citizen or stranger, who appears to be wise; and if he is not wise, then in vindication of the oracle I show him that he is not wise; and my occupation quite absorbs me, and I have no time to give either to any public matter of interest or to any concern of my own, but I am in utter poverty by reason of my devotion to the god.*

He also saw himself in service to Athens, and believed that his confrontations and interrogations were efforts to improve the very souls of those with whom he spoke.

*Men of Athens, I honour and love you; but I shall obey God rather than you, and while I have life and strength I shall never cease from the practice and teaching of philosophy, exhorting any one whom I meet and saying to him after my manner: You, my friend, -- a citizen of the great and mighty and wise city of Athens, -- are you not ashamed of heaping up the greatest amount of money and honour and reputation, and caring so little about wisdom and truth and the greatest improvement of the soul, which you never regard or heed at all? And if the person with whom I am arguing, says: Yes, but I do care; then I do not leave him or let him go at once; but I proceed to interrogate and examine and cross-examine him, and if I think that he has no virtue in him, but only says that he has, I reproach him with undervaluing the greater, and overvaluing the less. And I shall repeat the same words to every one whom I meet, young and old, citizen and alien, but especially to the citizens, inasmuch as they are my brethren. For know that this is the command of God; and I believe that no greater good has ever happened in the state than my service to the God. For I do nothing but go about persuading you all, old and young alike, not to take thought for your persons or your properties, but first and chiefly to care about the greatest improvement of the soul. I tell you that virtue is not given by money, but that from virtue comes money and every other good of man, public as well as private.*

Although it is impossible to know, with certainty, what Socrates himself affirmed (not only because of the difficulty of sorting him out from Plato, but also because he claimed to know nothing himself!), we can infer (via Plato) *that he seems to have believed that knowledge is innately within us, and is remembered rather than discovered*, as is evident in his conversation with Meno (found in the dialogue of that same name).

*Soc: ...So with virtue now. I don't know what it is. You may have known before you came into contact with me, but now you look as if you don't. Nevertheless I am ready to carry out, together with you, a joint investigation and inquiry into what it is.*

*Meno: But how will you look for something when you don't in the least know what it is? How on earth are you going to set up something you don't know as the object of your search? To put it another way, even if you come right up against it, how will you know that what you have found is the thing you didn't know?*

*Soc: I know what you mean. Do you realize that what you are bringing up is the trick argument that a man cannot try to discover either what he knows or what he does not know? He would not seek what he knows, for since he knows it there is no need of the inquiry, nor what he does not know, for in that case he does not even know what he is to look for.*

*Meno: Well, do you think it a good argument?*

*Soc: No.*

*Meno: Can you explain how it fails?*

*Soc: I can. I have heard from men and women who understand the truths of religion....Pindar speaks of it too, and many another of the poets who are divinely inspired. What they say is this--see whether you think they are speaking the truth. They say that the soul of man is immortal. At one time it comes to an end--that which is called death--and at another is born again, but is never finally exterminated....Thus the soul, since it is immortal and has been born many times, and has seen all things both here and in the other world, has learned everything that is. So we need not be surprised if it can recall the knowledge of virtue or anything else which, as we see, it once possessed. All nature is akin, and the soul has learned everything, so that when a man has recalled a single piece of knowledge--learned it, in ordinary language--there is no reason why he should not find out all the rest, if he keeps a stout heart and does not grow weary of the search, for seeking and learning are in fact nothing but recollection.[39]*

This view of knowledge as recollection of things already known explains why rather than telling people things, he would question them so that they could recall the truth of matters themselves. Because people already *know* the truth, including moral truths (but have just forgotten), *he believed that vice was always due to error.* No one chooses to do evil willingly, just as no one would willingly choose sickness over health. Instead, people do bad things because they just don't know ("remember") any better. If evil-doers could be properly educated, they would change their ways. Presumably, this interpretation would have applied to the jurors who convicted him of atheism and corrupting the youth—they simply didn't understand what they were doing.

It seems suitable, in an obvious sort of way, to end our brief treatment of Socrates with his death. Despite his superior arguments, Socrates was convicted on the charges brought against him. When given an opportunity to propose his own punishment, he first suggested that his "punishment" be free public meals for the rest of his life! At the urging of Plato and others present, he then suggested a modest fine. He refused to cower and plead for mercy, confident in his own righteousness. When the sentence of death was pronounced, he did not cower then either. Instead, he offered an argument for why death is not a bad thing.

*Let us reflect in another way, and we shall see that there is great reason to hope that death is a good; for one of two things -- either death is a state of nothingness and utter unconsciousness, or, as men say, there is a change and migration of the soul from this world to another. Now if you suppose that there is no consciousness, but a sleep like the sleep of him who is undisturbed even by dreams, death will be an unspeakable gain. For if a person were to select the night in which his sleep was undisturbed even by dreams, and were to compare with this the other days and nights of his life, and then were to tell us how many days and nights he had passed in the course of his life better and more pleasantly than this one, I think that any man, I will not say a private man, but even the great king will not find many such days or nights, when compared with the others. Now if death be of such a nature, I say that to die is gain; for eternity is then only a single night. But if death is the journey to another place, and there, as men say, all the dead abide, what good, O my friends and judges, can be greater than this? If indeed when the pilgrim arrives in the world below, he is delivered from the professors of justice in this world, and finds the true judges who are said to give judgment there, . . . Above all, I shall then be able to continue my search into true and false knowledge; as in this world, so also in the next; and I shall find out who is wise, and who pretends to be wise,*

---

[39] Plato, *Meno* 80c-81e.

*and is not. What would not a man give, O judges, to be able to examine the leader of the great Trojan expedition; or Odysseus or Sisyphus, or numberless others, men and women too! What infinite delight would there be in conversing with them and asking them questions! In another world they do not put a man to death for asking questions: assuredly not. For besides being happier than we are, they will be immortal, if what is said is true.*

Perhaps more important and impressive than his words, were his deeds. In another dialogue written by Plato (*Crito*), one of Socrates' friends visits him in prison prior to his execution with plans for his escape. Rather than seizing the opportunity to save his own life, Socrates seizes one last opportunity to offer moral instruction. *He demonstrates that it is not life that is to be valued, but a good and just life.* Socrates imagines himself being interrogated by the laws of Athens themselves should he escape.

*Consider, Socrates, if this is true, that in your present attempt you are going to do us wrong. For, after having brought you into the world, and nurtured and educated you, and given you and every other citizen a share in every good that we had to give, we further proclaim and give the right to every Athenian, that if he does not like us when he has come of age and has seen the ways of the city, and made our acquaintance, he may go where he pleases and take his goods with him; and none of us laws will forbid him or interfere with him. Any of you who does not like us and the city, and who wants to go to a colony or to any other city, may go where he likes, and take his goods with him. But he who has experience of the manner in which we order justice and administer the State, and still remains, has entered into an implied contract that he will do as we command him. And he who disobeys us is, as we maintain, thrice wrong: first, because in disobeying us he is disobeying his parents; secondly, because we are the authors of his education; thirdly, because he has made an agreement with us that he will duly obey our commands; and he neither obeys them nor convinces us that our commands are wrong; and we do not rudely impose them, but give him the alternative of obeying or convincing us; that is what we offer and he does neither. These are the sort of accusations to which, as we were saying, you, Socrates, will be exposed if you accomplish your intentions; you, above all other Athenians." Suppose I ask, why is this? they will justly retort upon me that I above all other men have acknowledged the agreement. "There is clear proof," they will say, "Socrates, that we and the city were not displeasing to you. Of all Athenians you have been the most constant resident in the city, which, as you never leave, you may be supposed to love. For you never went out of the city either to see the games, except once when you went to the Isthmus, or to any other place unless when you were on military service; nor did you travel as other men do. Nor had you any curiosity to know other States or their laws: your affections did not go beyond us and our State; we were your especial favorites, and you acquiesced in our government of you; and this is the State in which you begat your children, which is a proof of your satisfaction. Moreover, you might, if you had liked, have fixed the penalty at banishment in the course of the trial-the State which refuses to let you go now would have let you go then. But you pretended that you preferred death to exile, and that you were not grieved at death. And now you have forgotten these fine sentiments, and pay no respect to us, the laws, of whom you are the destroyer; and are doing what only a miserable slave would do, running away and turning your back upon the compacts and agreements which you made as a citizen. And first of all answer this very question: Are we right in saying that you agreed to be governed according to us in deed, and not in word only? Is that true or not?*[40]

If Socrates were to escape from his sentence, he would not only violate the laws of his city-State, he would reveal himself to be a fraud. He had long claimed that death was not a bad thing, and that *nothing in life or death could truly harm a virtuous person*. If he were to flee death, his actions would contradict his words. Deeds, not mere words.

In his death, Socrates' philosophy and status as a philosopher is arguably most evident. It is one thing to be clever and gifted in speech. The Sophists could all be described so. A true philosopher, on the other hand, *lives* his (or her) philosophy. Or, in Socrates' case, dies for it.

Pythagoras *might* have been the first to seek "salvation" in philosophy, but Socrates was the first to provide a living (and dying) testimony to how philosophy can transform one's life. Small wonder that nearly every philosophical school to come would point to him as either founder or inspiration. He exerted obvious influence on his most famous pupil, Plato (and Plato's most famous pupil: Aristotle). When Arcesilaus converted Plato's Academy to Skepticism, they stressed Socrates' own denial of wisdom and his ceaseless questioning. One of Socrates' associates, Antisthenes, contributed to the Cynic school, which emphasized Socrates' simple lifestyle and insistence that virtue is sufficient for happiness. The Cynics then transmitted Socrates to the Stoics, who emphasized Socrates' claim that virtue is the only true good, as well as his call for a life lived in accordance with reason. Socrates, whether via his words or his example, transcended the death imposed upon him to become the icon of the Western philosopher.

---

[40] Plato, *Crito.*

*Plato (424 BCE – 328 BCE) is a very well-known ancient Greek philosopher and student of the possibly more well-known Socrates. Because Socrates wrote nothing himself, most of what we think we know about Socrates comes from the writings of others, most notably Plato. Socrates appears as the main character in numerous Platonic dialogues, including the Apology. Not to be confused with apologizing, the "Apology" comes from the Greek word ἀπολογία ("apologia") meaning to give a "reasoned defense." Here, Socrates is giving a "reasoned defense" of his teachings and activities. Although ultimately condemned by the laws and jurors of Athens, he remains steadfast in his devotion to his "higher" calling.*

# Plato's *Apology*

### [*The Dialogues of Plato*]

How you, O Athenians, have been affected by my accusers, I cannot tell; but I know that they almost made me forget who I was -- so persuasively did they speak; and yet they have hardly uttered a word of truth. But of the many falsehoods told by them, there was one which quite amazed me; -- I mean when they said that you should be upon your guard and not allow yourselves to be deceived by the force of my eloquence. To say this, when they were certain to be detected as soon as I opened my lips and proved myself to be anything but a great speaker, did indeed appear to me most shameless -- unless by the force of eloquence they mean the force of truth; for is such is their meaning, I admit that I am eloquent. But in how different a way from theirs! Well, as I was saying, they have scarcely spoken the truth at all; but from me you shall hear the whole truth: not, however, delivered after their manner in a set oration duly ornamented with words and phrases. No, by heaven! but I shall use the words and arguments which occur to me at the moment; for I am confident in the justice of my cause (Or, I am certain that I am right in taking this course.): at my time of life I ought not to be appearing before you, O men of Athens, in the character of a juvenile orator -- let no one expect it of me. And I must beg of you to grant me a favour: -- If I defend myself in my accustomed manner, and you hear me using the words which I have been in the habit of using in the agora, at the tables of the money-changers, or anywhere else, I would ask you not to be surprised, and not to interrupt me on this account. For I am more than seventy years of age, and appearing now for the first time in a court of law, I am quite a stranger to the language of the place; and therefore I would have you regard me as if I were really a stranger, whom you would excuse if he spoke in his native tongue, and after the fashion of his country: -- Am I making an unfair request of you? Never mind the manner, which may or may not be good; but think only of the truth of my words, and give heed to that: let the speaker speak truly and the judge decide justly.

And first, I have to reply to the older charges and to my first accusers, and then I will go on to the later ones. For of old I have had many accusers, who have accused me falsely to you during many years; and I am more afraid of them than of Anytus and his associates, who are dangerous, too, in their own way. But far more dangerous are the others, who began when you were children, and took possession of your minds with their falsehoods, telling of one Socrates, a wise man, who speculated about the heaven above, and searched into the earth beneath, and made the worse appear the better cause. The disseminators of this tale are the accusers whom I dread; for their hearers are apt to fancy that such enquirers do not believe in the existence of the gods. And they are many, and their charges against me are of ancient date, and they were made by them in the days when you were more impressible than you are now -- in childhood, or it may have been in youth -- and the cause when heard went by default, for there was none to answer. And hardest of all, I do not know and cannot tell the names of my accusers; unless in the chance case of a Comic poet. All who from envy and malice have persuaded you -- some of them having first convinced themselves -- all this class of men are most difficult to deal with; for I cannot have them up here, and cross-examine them, and therefore I must simply fight with shadows in my own defence, and argue when there is no one who answers. I will ask you then to assume with me, as I was saying, that my opponents are of two kinds; one recent, the other ancient: and I hope that you will see the propriety of my answering the latter first, for these accusations you heard long before the others, and much oftener.

Well, then, I must make my defence, and endeavour to clear away in a short time, a slander which has lasted a long time. May I succeed, if to succeed be for my good and yours, or likely to avail me in my cause! The task is not an easy one; I quite understand the nature of it. And so leaving the event with God, in obedience to the law I will now make my defence.

I will begin at the beginning, and ask what is the accusation which has given rise to the slander of me, and in fact has encouraged Meletus to proof this charge against me. Well, what do the slanderers say? They shall be my prosecutors, and I will sum up their words in an affidavit: 'Socrates is an evil-doer, and a curious person, who searches into things under the earth and in heaven, and he makes the worse appear the better cause; and he teaches the aforesaid doctrines to others.' Such is the nature of the accusation: it is just what you have yourselves seen in the comedy of Aristophanes (Aristoph., Clouds.), who has introduced a man whom he calls Socrates, going about and saying that he walks in air, and talking a deal of nonsense concerning matters of which I do not pretend to know either much or little -- not that I mean to speak disparagingly of any one who is a student of natural philosophy. I should be very sorry if Meletus could bring so grave a charge against me. But the simple truth is, O Athenians, that I have nothing to do with physical speculations. Very many of those here present are witnesses to the truth of this, and to them I appeal. Speak then, you who have heard me, and tell your neighbours whether any of you have ever known me hold forth in few words or in many upon such matters...You hear their answer. And from what they say of this part of the charge you will be able to judge of the truth of the rest.

As little foundation is there for the report that I am a teacher, and take money; this accusation has no more truth in it than the other. Although, if a man were really able to instruct mankind, to receive money for giving instruction would, in my opinion, be an honour to him. There is Gorgias of Leontium, and Prodicus of Ceos, and Hippias of Elis, who go the round of the cities, and are able to persuade the young men to leave their own citizens by whom they might be taught for nothing, and come to them whom they not only pay, but are thankful if they may be allowed to pay them. There is at this time a Parian philosopher residing in Athens, of whom I have heard; and I came to hear of him in this way: -- I came across a man who has spent a world of money on the Sophists, Callias, the son of Hipponicus, and knowing that he had sons, I asked him: 'Callias,' I said, 'if your two sons were foals or calves, there would be no difficulty in finding some one to put over them; we should hire a trainer of horses, or a farmer probably, who would improve and perfect them in their own proper virtue and excellence; but as they are human beings, whom are you thinking of placing over them? Is there any one who understands human and political virtue? You must have thought about the matter, for you have sons; is there any one?' 'There is,' he said. 'Who is he?' said I; 'and of what country? and what does he charge?' 'Evenus the Parian,' he replied; 'he is the man, and his charge is five minae.' Happy is Evenus, I said to myself, if he really has this wisdom, and teaches at such a moderate charge. Had I the same, I should have been very proud and conceited; but the truth is that I have no knowledge of the kind.

I dare say, Athenians, that some one among you will reply, 'Yes, Socrates, but what is the origin of these accusations which are brought against you; there must have been something strange which you have been doing? All these rumours and this talk about you would never have arisen if you had been like other men: tell us, then, what is the cause of them, for we should be sorry to judge hastily of you.' Now I regard this as a fair challenge, and I will endeavour to explain to you the reason why I am called wise and have such an evil fame. Please to attend then. And although some of you may think that I am joking, I declare that I will tell you the entire truth. Men of Athens, this reputation of mine has come of a certain sort of wisdom which I possess. If you ask me what kind of wisdom, I reply, wisdom such as may perhaps be attained by man, for to that extent I am inclined to believe that I am wise; whereas the persons of whom I was speaking have a superhuman wisdom which I may fail to describe, because I have it not myself; and he who says that I have, speaks falsely, and is taking away my character. And here, O men of Athens, I must beg you not to interrupt me, even if I seem to say something extravagant. For the word which I will speak is not mine. I will refer you to a witness who is worthy of credit; that witness shall be the God of Delphi -- he will tell you about my wisdom, if I have any, and of what sort it is. You must have known Chaerephon; he was early a friend of mine, and also a friend of yours, for he shared in the recent exile of the people, and returned with you. Well, Chaerephon, as you know, was very impetuous in all his doings, and he went to Delphi and boldly asked the oracle to tell him whether -- as I was saying, I must beg you not to interrupt -- he asked the oracle to tell him whether anyone was wiser than I was, and the Pythian prophetess answered, that there was no man wiser. Chaerephon is dead himself; but his brother, who is in court, will confirm the truth of what I am saying.

Why do I mention this? Because I am going to explain to you why I have such an evil name. When I heard the answer, I said to myself, What can the god mean? and what is the interpretation of his riddle? for I know that I have no wisdom, small or great. What then can he mean when he says that I am the wisest of men? And yet he is a god, and cannot lie; that would be against his nature. After long consideration, I thought of a method of trying the question. I reflected that if I could only find a man wiser than myself, then I might go to the god with a refutation in my hand. I should say to him, 'Here is a man who is wiser than I am; but you said that I was the wisest.' Accordingly I went to one who had the reputation of wisdom, and observed him -- his name I need not mention; he was a politician whom I selected for examination -- and the result was as follows: When I began to talk with him, I could not help thinking that he was not really wise, although he was thought wise by many, and still wiser by himself; and thereupon I tried to explain to him that he thought himself wise, but was not really wise; and the consequence was that he hated me, and his enmity was shared by several who were present and heard me. So I left him, saying to myself, as I went away: Well, although I do not suppose that either of us knows anything really beautiful and good, I am better off than he is, -- for he knows nothing, and thinks that he knows; I neither know nor think that I know. In this latter particular, then, I seem to have slightly the advantage of him. Then I went to another who had still higher pretensions to wisdom, and my conclusion was exactly the same. Whereupon I made another enemy of him, and of many others besides him.

Then I went to one man after another, being not unconscious of the enmity which I provoked, and I lamented and feared this: but necessity was laid upon me, -- the word of God, I thought, ought to be considered first. And I said to myself, Go I must to all who appear to know, and find out the meaning of the oracle. And I swear to you, Athenians, by the dog I swear! -- for I must tell you the truth -- the result of my mission was just this: I found that the men most in repute were all but the most foolish; and that others less esteemed were really wiser and better. I will tell you the tale of my wanderings and of the 'Herculean' labours, as I may call them, which I endured only to find at last the oracle irrefutable. After the politicians, I went to the poets; tragic, dithyrambic, and all sorts. And there, I said to myself, you will be instantly detected; now you will find out that you are more ignorant than they are. Accordingly, I took them some of the most elaborate passages in their own writings, and asked what was the meaning of them -- thinking that they would teach me something. Will you believe me? I am almost ashamed to confess the truth, but I must say that there is hardly a person present who would not have talked better about their poetry than they did themselves. Then I knew that not by wisdom do poets write poetry, but by a sort of genius and inspiration; they are like diviners or soothsayers who also say many fine things, but do not understand the meaning of them. The poets appeared to me to be much in the same case; and I further observed that upon the strength of their poetry they believed themselves to be the wisest of men in other things in which they were not wise. So I departed, conceiving myself to be superior to them for the same reason that I was superior to the politicians.

At last I went to the artisans. I was conscious that I knew nothing at all, as I may say, and I was sure that they knew many fine things; and here I was not mistaken, for they did know many things of which I was ignorant, and in this they certainly were wiser than I was. But I observed that even the good artisans fell into the same error as the poets; -- because they were good workmen they thought that they also knew all sorts of high matters, and this defect in them overshadowed their wisdom; and therefore I asked myself on behalf of the oracle, whether I would like to be as I was, neither having their knowledge nor their ignorance, or like them in both; and I made answer to myself and to the oracle that I was better off as I was.

This inquisition has led to my having many enemies of the worst and most dangerous kind, and has given occasion also to many calumnies. And I am called wise, for my hearers always imagine that I myself possess the wisdom which I find wanting in others: but the truth is, O men of Athens, that God only is wise; and by his answer he intends to show that the wisdom of men is worth little or nothing; he is not speaking of Socrates, he is only using my name by way of illustration, as if he said, He, O men, is the wisest, who, like Socrates, knows that his wisdom is in truth worth nothing. And so I go about the world, obedient to the god, and search and make enquiry into the wisdom of any one, whether citizen or stranger, who appears to be wise; and if he is not wise, then in vindication of the oracle I show him that he is not wise; and my occupation quite absorbs me, and I have no time to give either to any public matter of interest or to any concern of my own, but I am in utter poverty by reason of my devotion to the god.

There is another thing: -- young men of the richer classes, who have not much to do, come about me of their own accord; they like to hear the pretenders examined, and they often imitate me, and proceed to examine others; there are plenty of persons, as they quickly discover, who think that they know something, but really know little or nothing; and then those who are examined by them instead of being angry with themselves are angry with me: This confounded Socrates, they say; this villainous misleader of youth! -- and then if somebody asks them, Why, what evil does he practise or teach? they do not know, and cannot tell; but in order that they may not appear to be at a loss, they repeat the ready-made charges which are used against all philosophers about teaching things up in the clouds and under the earth, and having no gods, and making the worse appear the better cause; for they do not like to confess that their pretence of knowledge has been detected -- which is the truth; and as they are numerous and ambitious and energetic, and are drawn up in battle array and have persuasive tongues, they have filled your ears with their loud and inveterate calumnies. And this is the reason why my three accusers, Meletus and Anytus and Lycon, have set upon me; Meletus, who has a quarrel with me on behalf of the poets; Anytus, on behalf of the craftsmen and politicians; Lycon, on behalf of the rhetoricians: and as I said at the beginning, I cannot expect to get rid of such a mass of calumny all in a moment. And this, O men of Athens, is the truth and the whole truth; I have concealed nothing, I have dissembled nothing. And yet, I know that my plainness of speech makes them hate me, and what is their hatred but a proof that I am speaking the truth? -- Hence has arisen the prejudice against me;

and this is the reason of it, as you will find out either in this or in any future enquiry.

I have said enough in my defence against the first class of my accusers; I turn to the second class. They are headed by Meletus, that good man and true lover of his country, as he calls himself. Against these, too, I must try to make a defence: -- Let their affidavit be read: it contains something of this kind: It says that Socrates is a doer of evil, who corrupts the youth; and who does not believe in the gods of the state, but has other new divinities of his own. Such is the charge; and now let us examine the particular counts. He says that I am a doer of evil, and corrupt the youth; but I say, O men of Athens, that Meletus is a doer of evil, in that he pretends to be in earnest when he is only in jest, and is so eager to bring men to trial from a pretended zeal and interest about matters in which he really never had the smallest interest. And the truth of this I will endeavour to prove to you.

Come hither, Meletus, and let me ask a question of you. You think a great deal about the improvement of youth?

Yes, I do.

Tell the judges, then, who is their improver; for you must know, as you have taken the pains to discover their corrupter, and are citing and accusing me before them. Speak, then, and tell the judges who their improver is. -- Observe, Meletus, that you are silent, and have nothing to say. But is not this rather disgraceful, and a very considerable proof of what I was saying, that you have no interest in the matter? Speak up, friend, and tell us who their improver is.

The laws.

But that, my good sir, is not my meaning. I want to know who the person is, who, in the first place, knows the laws.

The judges, Socrates, who are present in court.

What, do you mean to say, Meletus, that they are able to instruct and improve youth?

Certainly they are.

What, all of them, or some only and not others?

All of them.

By the goddess Here, that is good news! There are plenty of improvers, then. And what do you say of the audience, -- do they improve them?

Yes, they do.

And the senators?

Yes, the senators improve them.

But perhaps the members of the assembly corrupt them? -- or do they too improve them?

They improve them.

Then every Athenian improves and elevates them; all with the exception of myself; and I alone am their corrupter? Is that what you affirm?

That is what I stoutly affirm.

I am very unfortunate if you are right. But suppose I ask you a question: How about horses? Does one man do them harm and all the world good? Is not the exact opposite the truth? One man is able to do them good, or at least not many; -- the trainer of horses, that is to say, does them good, and others who have to do with them rather injure them? Is not that true, Meletus, of horses, or of any other animals? Most assuredly it is; whether you and Anytus say yes or no. Happy indeed would be the condition of youth if they had one corrupter only, and all the rest of the world were their improvers. But you, Meletus, have sufficiently shown that you never had a thought about the young: your carelessness is seen in your not caring about the very things which you bring against me.

And now, Meletus, I will ask you another question -- by Zeus I will: Which is better, to live among bad citizens, or among good ones? Answer, friend, I say; the question is one which may be easily answered. Do not the good do their neighbours good, and the bad do them evil?

Certainly.

And is there anyone who would rather be injured than benefited by those who live with him? Answer, my good friend, the law requires you to answer -- does any one like to be injured?

Certainly not.

And when you accuse me of corrupting and deteriorating the youth, do you allege that I corrupt them intentionally or unintentionally?

Intentionally, I say.

But you have just admitted that the good do their neighbours good, and the evil do them evil. Now, is that a truth which your superior wisdom has recognized thus early in life, and am I, at my age, in such darkness and ignorance as not to know that if a man with whom I have to live is corrupted by me, I am very likely to be harmed by him; and yet I corrupt him, and intentionally, too -- so you say, although neither I nor any other human being is ever likely to be convinced by you. But either I do not corrupt them, or I corrupt them unintentionally; and on either view of the case you lie. If my offence is unintentional, the law has no cognizance of unintentional offences: you ought to have taken me privately, and warned and admonished me; for if I had been better advised, I should have left off doing what I only did unintentionally -- no doubt I should; but you would have nothing to say to me and refused to teach me. And now you bring me up in this court, which is a place not of instruction, but of punishment.

It will be very clear to you, Athenians, as I was saying, that Meletus has no care at all, great or small, about the matter. But still I should like to know, Meletus, in what I am affirmed to corrupt the young. I suppose you mean, as I infer from your indictment, that I teach them not to acknowledge the gods which the state acknowledges, but some other new divinities or spiritual agencies in their stead. These are the lessons by which I corrupt the youth, as you say.

Yes, that I say emphatically.

Then, by the gods, Meletus, of whom we are speaking, tell me and the court, in somewhat plainer terms, what you mean! for I do not as yet understand whether you affirm that I teach other men to acknowledge some gods, and therefore that I do believe in gods, and am not an entire atheist -- this you do not lay to my charge, -- but only you say that they are not the same gods which the city recognizes -- the charge is that they are different gods. Or, do you mean that I am an atheist simply, and a teacher of atheism?

I mean the latter -- that you are a complete atheist.

What an extraordinary statement! Why do you think so, Meletus? Do you mean that I do not believe in the godhead of the sun or moon, like other men?

I assure you, judges, that he does not: for he says that the sun is stone, and the moon earth.

Friend Meletus, you think that you are accusing Anaxagoras: and you have but a bad opinion of the judges, if you fancy them illiterate to such a degree as not to know that these doctrines are found in the books of Anaxagoras the Clazomenian, which are full of them. And so, forsooth, the youth are said to be taught them by Socrates, when there are not unfrequently exhibitions of them at the theatre (Probably in allusion to Aristophanes who caricatured, and to Euripides who borrowed the notions of Anaxagoras, as well as to other dramatic poets.) (price of admission one drachma at the most); and they might pay their money, and laugh at Socrates if he pretends to father these extraordinary views. And so, Meletus, you really think that I do not believe in any god?

I swear by Zeus that you believe absolutely in none at all.

Nobody will believe you, Meletus, and I am pretty sure that you do not believe yourself. I cannot help thinking, men of Athens, that Meletus is reckless and impudent, and that he has written this indictment in a spirit of mere wantonness and youthful bravado. Has he not compounded a riddle, thinking to try me? He said to himself: -- I shall see whether the wise Socrates will discover my facetious contradiction, or whether I shall be able to deceive him and the rest of them. For he certainly does appear to me to contradict himself in the indictment as much as if he said that Socrates is guilty of not believing in the gods, and yet of believing in them -- but this is not like a person who is in earnest.

I should like you, O men of Athens, to join me in examining what I conceive to be his inconsistency; and do you, Meletus, answer. And I must remind the audience of my request that they would not make a disturbance if I speak in my accustomed manner:

Did ever man, Meletus, believe in the existence of human things, and not of human beings?...I wish, men of Athens, that he would answer, and not be always trying to get up an interruption. Did ever any man believe in horsemanship, and not in horses? or in flute-playing, and not in flute- players? No, my friend; I will answer to you and to the court, as you refuse to answer for yourself. There is no man who ever did. But now please to answer the next question: Can a man believe in spiritual and divine agencies, and not in spirits or demigods?

He cannot.

How lucky I am to have extracted that answer, by the assistance of the court! But then you swear in the indictment that I teach and believe in divine or spiritual agencies (new or old, no matter for that); at any rate, I believe in spiritual agencies, -- so you say and swear in the affidavit; and yet if I believe in divine beings, how can I help believing in spirits or demigods; -- must I not? To be sure I must; and therefore I may assume that your silence gives consent. Now what are spirits or demigods? Are they not either gods or the sons of gods?

Certainly they are.

But this is what I call the facetious riddle invented by you: the demigods or spirits are gods, and you say first that I do not believe in gods, and then again that

I do believe in gods; that is, if I believe in demigods. For if the demigods are the illegitimate sons of gods, whether by the nymphs or by any other mothers, of whom they are said to be the sons -- what human being will ever believe that there are no gods if they are the sons of gods? You might as well affirm the existence of mules, and deny that of horses and asses. Such nonsense, Meletus, could only have been intended by you to make trial of me. You have put this into the indictment because you had nothing real of which to accuse me. But no one who has a particle of understanding will ever be convinced by you that the same men can believe in divine and superhuman things, and yet not believe that there are gods and demigods and heroes.

I have said enough in answer to the charge of Meletus: any elaborate defence is unnecessary, but I know only too well how many are the enmities which I have incurred, and this is what will be my destruction if I am destroyed; -- not Meletus, nor yet Anytus, but the envy and detraction of the world, which has been the death of many good men, and will probably be the death of many more; there is no danger of my being the last of them.

Some one will say: And are you not ashamed, Socrates, of a course of life which is likely to bring you to an untimely end? To him I may fairly answer: There you are mistaken: a man who is good for anything ought not to calculate the chance of living or dying; he ought only to consider whether in doing anything he is doing right or wrong -- acting the part of a good man or of a bad. Whereas, upon your view, the heroes who fell at Troy were not good for much, and the son of Thetis above all, who altogether despised danger in comparison with disgrace; and when he was so eager to slay Hector, his goddess mother said to him, that if he avenged his companion Patroclus, and slew Hector, he would die himself -- 'Fate,' she said, in these or the like words, 'waits for you next after Hector;' he, receiving this warning, utterly despised danger and death, and instead of fearing them, feared rather to live in dishonour, and not to avenge his friend. 'Let me die forthwith,' he replies, 'and be avenged of my enemy, rather than abide here by the beaked ships, a laughing-stock and a burden of the earth.' Had Achilles any thought of death and danger? For wherever a man's place is, whether the place which he has chosen or that in which he has been placed by a commander, there he ought to remain in the hour of danger; he should not think of death or of anything but of disgrace. And this, O men of Athens, is a true saying.

Strange, indeed, would be my conduct, O men of Athens, if I who, when I was ordered by the generals whom you chose to command me at Potidaea and Amphipolis and Delium, remained where they placed me, like any other man, facing death -- if now, when, as I conceive and imagine, God orders me to fulfil the philosopher's mission of searching into myself and other men, I were to desert my post through fear of death, or any other fear; that would indeed be strange, and I might justly be arraigned in court for denying the existence of the gods, if I disobeyed the oracle because I was afraid of death, fancying that I was wise when I was not wise. For the fear of death is indeed the pretence of wisdom, and not real wisdom, being a pretence of knowing the unknown; and no one knows whether death, which men in their fear apprehend to be the greatest evil, may not be the greatest good. Is not this ignorance of a disgraceful sort, the ignorance which is the conceit that a man knows what he does not know? And in this respect only I believe myself to differ from men in general, and may perhaps claim to be wiser than they are: -- that whereas I know but little of the world below, I do not suppose that I know: but I do know that injustice and disobedience to a better, whether God or man, is evil and dishonourable, and I will never fear or avoid a possible good rather than a certain evil. And therefore if you let me go now, and are not convinced by Anytus, who said that since I had been prosecuted I must be put to death; (or if not that I ought never to have been prosecuted at all); and that if I escape now, your sons will all be utterly ruined by listening to my words -- if you say to me, Socrates, this time we will not mind Anytus, and you shall be let off, but upon one condition, that you are not to enquire and speculate in this way any more, and that if you are caught doing so again you shall die; -- if this was the condition on which you let me go, I should reply: Men of Athens, I honour and love you; but I shall obey God rather than you, and while I have life and strength I shall never cease from the practice and teaching of philosophy, exhorting any one whom I meet and saying to him after my manner: You, my friend, -- a citizen of the great and mighty and wise city of Athens, -- are you not ashamed of heaping up the greatest amount of money and honour and reputation, and caring so little about wisdom and truth and the greatest improvement of the soul, which you never regard or heed at all? And if the person with whom I am arguing, says: Yes, but I do care; then I do not leave him or let him go at once; but I proceed to interrogate and examine and cross-examine him, and if I think that he has no virtue in him, but only says that he has, I reproach him with undervaluing the greater, and overvaluing the less. And I shall repeat the same words to every one whom I meet, young and old, citizen and alien, but especially to the citizens, inasmuch as they are my brethren. For know that this is the command of God; and I believe that no greater good has ever happened in the state than my service to the God. For I do nothing but go about persuading you all, old and young alike, not to take thought for your persons or your properties, but first and chiefly to care about the greatest improvement of the soul. I tell you that virtue is not given by money, but that from virtue comes money and every other good of man, public as well as private. This is my teaching, and if this is the doctrine which corrupts the youth, I am a mischievous person. But if any one says that this is not my teaching, he is speaking an untruth. Wherefore, O men of Athens, I say to you, do as Anytus bids or not as Anytus bids, and either acquit me or not; but whichever you do, understand that I shall never alter my ways, not even if I have to die many times.

Men of Athens, do not interrupt, but hear me; there was an understanding between us that you should hear me to the end: I have something more to say, at which you may be inclined to cry out; but I believe that to hear me will be good for you, and therefore I beg that you will not cry out. I would have you know, that if you kill such an one as I am, you will injure yourselves more than you will injure me. Nothing will injure me, not Meletus nor yet Anytus -- they cannot, for a bad man is not permitted to injure a better than himself. I do not deny that Anytus may, perhaps, kill him, or drive him into exile, or deprive him of civil rights; and he may imagine, and others may imagine, that he is inflicting a great injury upon him: but there I do not agree. For the evil of doing as he is doing -- the evil of unjustly taking away the life of another -- is greater far.

And now, Athenians, I am not going to argue for my own sake, as you may think, but for yours, that you may not sin against the God by condemning me, who am his gift to you. For if you kill me you will not easily find a successor to me, who, if I may use such a ludicrous figure of speech, am a sort of gadfly, given to the state by God; and the state is a great and noble steed who is tardy in his motions owing to his very size, and requires to be stirred into life. I am that gadfly which God has attached to the state, and all day long and in all places am always fastening upon you, arousing and persuading and reproaching you. You will not easily find another like me, and therefore I would advise you to spare me. I dare say that you may feel out of temper (like a person who is suddenly awakened from sleep), and you think that you might easily strike me dead as Anytus advises, and then you would sleep on for the remainder of your lives, unless God in his care of you sent you another gadfly. When I say that I am given to you by God, the proof of my mission is this: -- if I had been like other men, I should not have neglected all my own concerns or patiently seen the neglect of them during all these years, and have been doing yours, coming to you individually like a father or elder brother, exhorting you to regard virtue; such conduct, I say, would be unlike human nature. If I had gained anything, or if my exhortations had been paid, there would have been some sense in my doing so; but now, as you will perceive, not even the impudence of my accusers dares to say that I have ever exacted or sought pay of any one; of that they have no witness. And I have a sufficient witness to the truth of what I say -- my poverty.

Some one may wonder why I go about in private giving advice and busying myself with the concerns of others, but do not venture to come forward in public and advise the state. I will tell you why. You have heard me speak at sundry times and in divers places of an oracle or sign which comes to me, and is the divinity which Meletus ridicules in the indictment. This sign, which is a kind of voice, first began to come to me when I was a child; it always forbids but never commands me to do anything which I am going to do. This is what deters me from being a politician. And rightly, as I think. For I am certain, O men of Athens, that if I had engaged in politics, I should have perished long ago, and done no good either to you or to myself. And do not be offended at my telling you the truth: for the truth is, that no man who goes to war with you or any other multitude, honestly striving against the many lawless and unrighteous deeds which are done in a state, will save his life; he who will fight for the right, if he would live even for a brief space, must have a private station and not a public one.

I can give you convincing evidence of what I say, not words only, but what you value far more--actions. Let me relate to you a passage of my own life which will prove to you that I should never have yielded to injustice from any fear of death, and that 'as I should have refused to yield' I must have died at once. I will tell you a tale of the courts, not very interesting perhaps, but nevertheless true. The only office of state which I ever held, O men of Athens, was that of senator: the tribe Antiochis, which is my tribe, had the presidency at the trial of the generals who had not taken up the bodies of the slain after the battle of

Arginusae; and you proposed to try them in a body, contrary to law, as you all thought afterwards; but at the time I was the only one of the Prytanes who was opposed to the illegality, and I gave my vote against you; and when the orators threatened to impeach and arrest me, and you called and shouted, I made up my mind that I would run the risk, having law and justice with me, rather than take part in your injustice because I feared imprisonment and death. This happened in the days of the democracy. But when the oligarchy of the Thirty was in power, they sent for me and four others into the rotunda, and bade us bring Leon the Salaminian from Salamis, as they wanted to put him to death. This was a specimen of the sort of commands which they were always giving with the view of implicating as many as possible in their crimes; and then I showed, not in word only but in deed, that, if I may be allowed to use such an expression, I cared not a straw for death, and that my great and only care was lest I should do an unrighteous or unholy thing. For the strong arm of that oppressive power did not frighten me into doing wrong; and when we came out of the rotunda the other four went to Salamis and fetched Leon, but I went quietly home. For which I might have lost my life, had not the power of the Thirty shortly afterwards come to an end. And many will witness to my words.

Now do you really imagine that I could have survived all these years, if I had led a public life, supposing that like a good man I had always maintained the right and had made justice, as I ought, the first thing? No indeed, men of Athens, neither I nor any other man. But I have been always the same in all my actions, public as well as private, and never have I yielded any base compliance to those who are slanderously termed my disciples, or to any other. Not that I have any regular disciples. But if any one likes to come and hear me while I am pursuing my mission, whether he be young or old, he is not excluded. Nor do I converse only with those who pay; but any one, whether he be rich or poor, may ask and answer me and listen to my words; and whether he turns out to be a bad man or a good one, neither result can be justly imputed to me; for I never taught or professed to teach him anything. And if any one says that he has ever learned or heard anything from me in private which all the world has not heard, let me tell you that he is lying.

But I shall be asked, Why do people delight in continually conversing with you? I have told you already, Athenians, the whole truth about this matter: they like to hear the cross-examination of the pretenders to wisdom; there is amusement in it. Now this duty of cross-examining other men has been imposed upon me by God; and has been signified to me by oracles, visions, and in every way in which the will of divine power was ever intimated to any one. This is true, O Athenians, or, if not true, would be soon refuted. If I am or have been corrupting the youth, those of them who are now grown up and have become sensible that I gave them bad advice in the days of their youth should come forward as accusers, and take their revenge; or if they do not like to come themselves, some of their relatives, fathers, brothers, or other kinsmen, should say what evil their families have suffered at my hands. Now is their time. Many of them I see in the court. There is Crito, who is of the same age and of the same deme with myself, and there is Critobulus his son, whom I also see. Then again there is Lysanias of Sphettus,

who is the father of Aeschines -- he is present; and also there is Antiphon of
Cephisus, who is the father of Epigenes; and there are the brothers of several who
have associated with me. There is Nicostratus the son of Theosdotides, and the
brother of Theodotus (now Theodotus himself is dead, and therefore he, at any
rate, will not seek to stop him); and there is Paralus the son of Demodocus, who
had a brother Theages; and Adeimantus the son of Ariston, whose brother Plato
is present; and Aeantodorus, who is the brother of Apollodorus, whom I also see.
I might mention a great many others, some of whom Meletus should have
produced as witnesses in the course of his speech; and let him still produce them,
if he has forgotten -- I will make way for him. And let him say, if he has any
testimony of the sort which he can produce. Nay, Athenians, the very opposite is
the truth. For all these are ready to witness on behalf of the corrupter, of the
injurer of their kindred, as Meletus and Anytus call me; not the corrupted youth
only -- there might have been a motive for that -- but their uncorrupted elder
relatives. Why should they too support me with their testimony? Why, indeed,
except for the sake of truth and justice, and because they know that I am speaking
the truth, and that Meletus is a liar.

Well, Athenians, this and the like of this is all the defence which I have to
offer. Yet a word more. Perhaps there may be some one who is offended at me,
when he calls to mind how he himself on a similar, or even a less serious occasion,
prayed and entreated the judges with many tears, and how he produced his
children in court, which was a moving spectacle, together with a host of relations
and friends; whereas I, who am probably in danger of my life, will do none of
these things. The contrast may occur to his mind, and he may be set against me,
and vote in anger because he is displeased at me on this account. Now if there be
such a person among you, -- mind, I do not say that there is, -- to him I may fairly
reply: My friend, I am a man, and like other men, a creature of flesh and blood,
and not 'of wood or stone,' as Homer says; and I have a family, yes, and sons, O
Athenians, three in number, one almost a man, and two others who are still
young; and yet I will not bring any of them hither in order to petition you for an
acquittal. And why not? Not from any self-assertion or want of respect for you.
Whether I am or am not afraid of death is another question, of which I will not
now speak. But, having regard to public opinion, I feel that such conduct would
be discreditable to myself, and to you, and to the whole state. One who has
reached my years, and who has a name for wisdom, ought not to demean himself.
Whether this opinion of me be deserved or not, at any rate the world has decided
that Socrates is in some way superior to other men. And if those among you who
are said to be superior in wisdom and courage, and any other virtue, demean
themselves in this way, how shameful is their conduct! I have seen men of
reputation, when they have been condemned, behaving in the strangest manner:
they seemed to fancy that they were going to suffer something dreadful if they
died, and that they could be immortal if you only allowed them to live; and I think
that such are a dishonour to the state, and that any stranger coming in would have
said of them that the most eminent men of Athens, to whom the Athenians
themselves give honour and command, are no better than women. And I say that
these things ought not to be done by those of us who have a reputation; and if

they are done, you ought not to permit them; you ought rather to show that you are far more disposed to condemn the man who gets up a doleful scene and makes the city ridiculous, than him who holds his peace.

But, setting aside the question of public opinion, there seems to be something wrong in asking a favour of a judge, and thus procuring an acquittal, instead of informing and convincing him. For his duty is, not to make a present of justice, but to give judgment; and he has sworn that he will judge according to the laws, and not according to his own good pleasure; and we ought not to encourage you, nor should you allow yourselves to be encouraged, in this habit of perjury -- there can be no piety in that. Do not then require me to do what I consider dishonourable and impious and wrong, especially now, when I am being tried for impiety on the indictment of Meletus. For if, O men of Athens, by force of persuasion and entreaty I could overpower your oaths, then I should be teaching you to believe that there are no gods, and in defending should simply convict myself of the charge of not believing in them. But that is not so -- far otherwise. For I do believe that there are gods, and in a sense higher than that in which any of my accusers believe in them. And to you and to God I commit my cause, to be determined by you as is best for you and me.

...

There are many reasons why I am not grieved, O men of Athens, at the vote of condemnation. I expected it, and am only surprised that the votes are so nearly equal; for I had thought that the majority against me would have been far larger; but now, had thirty votes gone over to the other side, I should have been acquitted. And I may say, I think, that I have escaped Meletus. I may say more; for without the assistance of Anytus and Lycon, any one may see that he would not have had a fifth part of the votes, as the law requires, in which case he would have incurred a fine of a thousand drachmae.

And so he proposes death as the penalty. And what shall I propose on my part, O men of Athens? Clearly that which is my due. And what is my due? What return shall be made to the man who has never had the wit to be idle during his whole life; but has been careless of what the many care for -- wealth, and family interests, and military offices, and speaking in the assembly, and magistracies, and plots, and parties. Reflecting that I was really too honest a man to be a politician and live, I did not go where I could do no good to you or to myself; but where I could do the greatest good privately to every one of you, thither I went, and sought to persuade every man among you that he must look to himself, and seek virtue and wisdom before he looks to his private interests, and look to the state before he looks to the interests of the state; and that this should be the order which he observes in all his actions. What shall be done to such an one? Doubtless some good thing, O men of Athens, if he has his reward; and the good should be of a kind suitable to him. What would be a reward suitable to a poor man who is your benefactor, and who desires leisure that he may instruct you? There can be no reward so fitting as maintenance in the Prytaneum, O men of Athens, a reward which he deserves far more than the citizen who has won the prize at Olympia in the horse or chariot race, whether the chariots were drawn by two horses or by many. For I am in want, and he has enough; and he only gives you the appearance of happiness, and I give you the reality. And if I am to estimate the penalty fairly, I should say that maintenance in the Prytaneum is the just return.

Perhaps you think that I am braving you in what I am saying now, as in what I said before about the tears and prayers. But this is not so. I speak rather because I am convinced that I never intentionally wronged any one, although I cannot convince you -- the time has been too short; if there were a law at Athens, as there is in other cities, that a capital cause should not be decided in one day, then I believe that I should have convinced you. But I cannot in a moment refute great slanders; and, as I am convinced that I never wronged another, I will assuredly not wrong myself. I will not say of myself that I deserve any evil, or propose any penalty. Why should I? because I am afraid of the penalty of death which Meletus proposes? When I do not know whether death is a good or an evil, why should I propose a penalty which would certainly be an evil? Shall I say imprisonment? And why should I live in prison, and be the slave of the magistrates of the year -- of the Eleven? Or shall the penalty be a fine, and imprisonment until the fine is paid? There is the same objection. I should have to lie in prison, for money I have none, and cannot pay. And if I say exile (and this may possibly be the penalty which you will affix), I must indeed be blinded by the love of life, if I am so irrational as to expect that when you, who are my own citizens, cannot endure my discourses and words, and have found them so grievous and odious that you will have no more of them, others are likely to endure me. No indeed, men of Athens, that is not very likely. And what a life should I lead, at my age, wandering from city to city, ever changing my place of exile, and always being driven out! For I am quite sure that wherever I go, there, as here, the young men will flock to me; and if I drive them away, their elders will drive me out at their request; and if I let them come, their fathers and friends will drive me out for their sakes.

Some one will say: Yes, Socrates, but cannot you hold your tongue, and then you may go into a foreign city, and no one will interfere with you? Now I have great difficulty in making you understand my answer to this. For if I tell you that to do as you say would be a disobedience to the God, and therefore that I cannot hold my tongue, you will not believe that I am serious; and if I say again that daily to discourse about virtue, and of those other things about which you hear me examining myself and others, is the greatest good of man, and that the unexamined life is not worth living, you are still less likely to believe me. Yet I say what is true, although a thing of which it is hard for me to persuade you. Also, I have never been accustomed to think that I deserve to suffer any harm. Had I money I might have estimated the offence at what I was able to pay, and not have been much the worse. But I have none, and therefore I must ask you to proportion the fine to my means. Well, perhaps I could afford a mina, and therefore I propose that penalty: Plato, Crito, Critobulus, and Apollodorus, my friends here, bid me say thirty minae, and they will be the sureties. Let thirty minae be the penalty; for which sum they will be ample security to you.

...

Not much time will be gained, O Athenians, in return for the evil name which you will get from the detractors of the city, who will say that you killed Socrates, a wise man; for they will call me wise, even although I am not wise, when they want to reproach you. If you had waited a little while, your desire would have been fulfilled in the course of nature.For I am far advanced in years, as you may perceive, and not far from death. I am speaking now not to all of you, but only to those who have condemned me to death. And I have another thing to say to them: you think that I was convicted because I had no words of the sort which would have procured my acquittal -- I mean, if I had thought fit to leave nothing undone or unsaid. Not so; the deficiency which led to my conviction was not of words -- certainly not. But I had not the boldness or impudence or inclination to address you as you would have liked me to do, weeping and wailing and lamenting, and saying and doing many things which you have been accustomed to hear from others, and which, as I maintain, are unworthy of me. I thought at the time that I ought not to do anything common or mean when in danger: nor do I now repent of the style of my defence; I would rather die having spoken after my manner, than speak in your manner and live. For neither in war nor yet at law ought I or any man to use every way of escaping death. Often in battle there can be no doubt that if a man will throw away his arms, and fall on his knees before his pursuers, he may escape death; and in other dangers there are other ways of escaping death, if a man is willing to say and do anything. The difficulty, my friends, is not to avoid death, but to avoid unrighteousness; for that runs faster than death. I am old and move slowly, and the slower runner has overtaken me, and my accusers are keen and quick, and the faster runner, who is unrighteousness, has overtaken them. And now I depart hence condemned by you to suffer the penalty of death, -- they too go their ways condemned by the truth to suffer the penalty of villainy and wrong; and I must abide by my award -- let them abide by theirs. I suppose that these things may be regarded as fated, -- and I think that they are well.

And now, O men who have condemned me, I would fain prophesy to you; for I am about to die, and in the hour of death men are gifted with prophetic power. And I prophesy to you who are my murderers, that immediately after my departure punishment far heavier than you have inflicted on me will surely await you. Me you have killed because you wanted to escape the accuser, and not to give an account of your lives. But that will not be as you suppose: far otherwise. For I say that there will be more accusers of you than there are now; accusers whom hitherto I have restrained: and as they are younger they will be more inconsiderate with you, and you will be more offended at them. If you think that by killing men you can prevent some one from censuring your evil lives, you are mistaken; that is not a way of escape which is either possible or honourable; the easiest and the noblest way is not to be disabling others, but to be improving yourselves. This is the prophecy which I utter before my departure to the judges who have condemned me.

Friends, who would have acquitted me, I would like also to talk with you about the thing which has come to pass, while the magistrates are busy, and before I go to the place at which I must die. Stay then a little, for we may as well talk with one another while there is time. You are my friends, and I should like to show you the meaning of this event which has happened to me. O my judges -- for you I may truly call judges -- I should like to tell you of a wonderful circumstance. Hitherto the divine faculty of which the internal oracle is the source has constantly been in the habit of opposing me even about trifles, if I was going to make a slip or error in any matter; and now as you see there has come upon me that which may be thought, and is generally believed to be, the last and worst evil. But the oracle made no sign of opposition, either when I was leaving my house in the morning, or when I was on my way to the court, or while I was speaking, at anything which I was going to say; and yet I have often been stopped in the middle of a speech, but now in nothing I either said or did touching the matter in hand has the oracle opposed me. What do I take to be the explanation of this silence? I will tell you. It is an intimation that what has happened to me is a good, and that those of us who think that death is an evil are in error. For the customary sign would surely have opposed me had I been going to evil and not to good.

Let us reflect in another way, and we shall see that there is great reason to hope that death is a good; for one of two things -- either death is a state of nothingness and utter unconsciousness, or, as men say, there is a change and migration of the soul from this world to another. Now if you suppose that there is no consciousness, but a sleep like the sleep of him who is undisturbed even by dreams, death will be an unspeakable gain. For if a person were to select the night in which his sleep was undisturbed even by dreams, and were to compare with this the other days and nights of his life, and then were to tell us how many days and nights he had passed in the course of his life better and more pleasantly than this one, I think that any man, I will not say a private man, but even the great king will not find many such days or nights, when compared with the others. Now if death be of such a nature, I say that to die is gain; for eternity is then only a single night. But if death is the journey to another place, and there, as men say, all the dead abide, what good, O my friends and judges, can be greater than this? If indeed when the pilgrim arrives in the world below, he is delivered from the professors of justice in this world, and finds the true judges who are said to give judgment there, Minos and Rhadamanthus and Aeacus and Triptolemus, and other sons of God who were righteous in their own life, that pilgrimage will be worth making. What would not a man give if he might converse with Orpheus and Musaeus and Hesiod and Homer? Nay, if this be true, let me die again and again. I myself, too, shall have a wonderful interest in there meeting and conversing with Palamedes, and Ajax the son of Telamon, and any other ancient hero who has suffered death through an unjust judgment; and there will be no small pleasure, as I think, in comparing my own sufferings with theirs. Above all, I shall then be able to continue my search into true and false knowledge; as in this world, so also in the next; and I shall find out who is wise, and who pretends to be wise, and is not. What would not a man give, O judges, to be able to examine the leader of the great Trojan expedition; or Odysseus or Sisyphus, or numberless others, men and women too! What infinite delight would there be in conversing with them and asking them questions! In another world they do not put a man to death for asking questions: assuredly not. For besides being happier than we are, they will be immortal, if what is said is true.

Wherefore, O judges, be of good cheer about death, and know of a certainty, that no evil can happen to a good man, either in life or after death. He and his are not neglected by the gods; nor has my own approaching end happened by mere chance. But I see clearly that the time had arrived when it was better for me to die and be released from trouble; wherefore the oracle gave no sign. For which reason, also, I am not angry with my condemners, or with my accusers; they have done me no harm, although they did not mean to do me any good; and for this I may gently blame them.

Still I have a favour to ask of them. When my sons are grown up, I would ask you, O my friends, to punish them; and I would have you trouble them, as I have troubled you, if they seem to care about riches, or anything, more than about virtue; or if they pretend to be something when they are really nothing, -- then reprove them, as I have reproved you, for not caring about that for which they ought to care, and thinking that they are something when they are really nothing. And if you do this, both I and my sons will have received justice at your hands.

The hour of departure has arrived, and we go our ways -- I to die, and you to live. Which is better God only knows.

# Chapter 3: Plato

---

*Comprehension questions you should be able to answer after reading this chapter:*

1. Why did Thrasymachus believe that justice is "the will of the stronger," and how does Socrates refute this position?

2. What did Glaucon think justice is, and how does the Myth of Gyges' Ring reinforce his point?

3. What is the point of Socrates' extended political analogy in the *Republic*?

4. What is the "principle of specialization", and why is it important?

5. What are the three classes in the *Republic*? What are the three parts of the soul? What do they have to do with each other?

6. What is the "noble lie," and what is its purpose?

7. Why does Plato (as Socrates) think epistemic relativism is false?

8. What are the "Forms," and what is their relationship to particular objects?

9. What is the point of the "allegory of the cave?"

10. Why is it that only philosophers have "knowledge?"

11. What is "justice" in the *Republic*? What is "justice" in the soul?

12. What are some of the differences between the city-state proposed in the *Republic* and that proposed in the *Laws*?

---

We already discussed Plato a little bit in the previous chapter in the context of his friend and mentor, Socrates. Now we turn to Plato himself, where he will continue the tradition of Socrates in seeking the Truth with regard to goodness, justice, etc.

Plato is undeniably a giant in the history of Western philosophy. Perhaps humorously, "Plato" was actually his nickname, meaning "broad-shouldered"—so it seems his physical stature rivaled his intellectual stature. He lived from 428-348 BCE and was the son of a wealthy, aristocratic family. He initially studied philosophy under a Heraclitean philosopher, but at around the age of twenty began to study with Socrates. After Socrates' execution, he traveled and became influenced by Pythagorean philosophy in what is now Italy. He was summoned by Dionysius the Elder ("the

tyrant of Syracuse") to promote philosophy at his court, but his efforts were not well-received, and he returned to Athens. He started his own school on a site sacred to the hero Academus, thus explaining how his school became known as the "Academy." It's worth pointing out that our contemporary use of "academy" as synonymous with a place of learning traces back to Plato's own school. This Academy is generally regarded as the first "university" in the Western world.

Plato was a prolific philosopher and writer, and we are fortunate that so many of his works survived the passage and trials of time. He was a systematic and comprehensive philosopher, writing on virtually every topic of the time. Indeed, one well-known approach to teaching introduction to philosophy courses is to teach just the *Republic*, with the idea being that it contains everything a new philosopher needs to experience. Alfred North Whitehead went so far as to say that "the safest general characterization of the European philosophical tradition is that it consists of a series of footnotes to Plato." High praise, indeed.

Known mostly for his dialogues, his work can be divided into three periods: early, middle, and late. The "early" dialogues (where there is the most confidence that Socrates is being presented authentically) include: *Apology, Crito, Euthyphro, Laches, Charmides, Ion, Hippias Minor, Lysis, Euthydemus, Protagoras*, and *Gorgias*. The middle dialogues (for which Socrates' authentic representation is less certain) include: *Meno, Hippias Major, Cratylus, Phaedo, Symposium*, and the *Republic*. The later dialogues (in which most believe Plato has found his own voice, and uses Socrates more as a mouthpiece, if at all) include: *Parmenides, Phaedrus, Theatetus, Sophist, Statesman, Timaeus, Philebus*, and the *Laws*.

No book of this kind should even pretend to offer a thorough and systemic presentation of Plato's thought, and I have no such pretensions. Instead, in what follows, I will offer a brief overview of some of Plato's central ideas, primarily as presented in the *Republic*, with a clear emphasis on his account of justice, and those other ideas that are important with regard to understanding his account of justice. It must be noted that his views changed over time, and were not always presented in the same way. His prescriptions for government and rulership, for example, change somewhat from the *Republic* to the *Laws*. In the *Republic*, enlightened Philosopher Kings rule with the aim of promoting harmony and preventing strife and factionalism (*Republic* 462a-b), but in the *Laws* this function is assumed by good and just laws instead (*Laws* 715c-d)—though the central focus of preventing "disharmony" is the same in both cases. Keeping in mind such adjustments to his thoughts, the *Republic* offers a fine introduction to Plato's system, as well as to philosophy in general. It even makes for an enjoyable read!

## The Republic[41]

The very first line of the Republic inspires controversy for those paying

---

[41] Quotations from the *Republic* that follow are from a public domain translation. I use that translation in this book so as to keep the cost of this book low. I have not, however, included the full text of that version in this book as a primary source reading, unlike several other texts. In my own classes, I will sometimes

attention.

> *I went down yesterday to the Piraeus with Glaucon the son of Ariston, that*
> *I might offer up my prayers to the goddess (Bendis, the Thracian Artemis.);*
> *and also because I wanted to see in what manner they would celebrate the*
> *festival, which was a new thing. (327a[42])*

The opening scene of the Republic has Socrates returning from a celebration in honor of Athens' recognition of a new god: Bendis. Why is this controversial? If you recall the *Apology*, one of the charges leveled against Socrates involved the introduction of "new gods" as one of the means by which he corrupted the youth of Athens.

> *I suppose you mean, as I infer from your indictment, that I teach them not*
> *to acknowledge the gods which the state acknowledges, but some other*
> *new divinities or spiritual agencies in their stead. These are the lessons by*
> *which I corrupt the youth, as you say.*

Granted, Socrates later twists his accuser into mental pretzels by getting him to claim that Socrates both believes in new gods and demigods, in addition to being a complete atheist, but the ironic point remains for those interested in seeing it: Socrates was brought up on charges for (among other things) "introducing new gods," and the very first line of the *Republic* shows a formal, official celebration of a new god in Athens! Clearly introducing new gods is only a serious offense when it's (allegedly) done by Socrates!

The *Republic* is filled with gems like this, if only one reads slowly and

---

instead require my students to purchase a hard copy of the *Republic*. The reason why is simple: the free public domain version doesn't use the "Stephanus" pagination that I explain in the next footnote. When I quote from it, I am forced to cross-reference it with another translation in order to provide that pagination. It would be far too much work to do so for the entire text, and the Stephanus pagination is useful enough that I judge it to be worth the $10 (roughly) for the hardcopy. For those who would like the free version anyway, it may be found at the following URL: http://www.gutenberg.org/files/1497/1497-h/1497-h.htm

[42] A note on pagination: this reference is an instance of what is known as "Stephanus pagination." The *Republic* is an ancient text that was been translated numerous times and edited into countless editions. Page numbers will vary, of course, based on things like paper and font size, as well as the inclusion of notes or explanatory essays. To make sure that everyone reading Plato will be able to find the correct reference, regardless of which translation or edition one has, scholars make use of the "Stephanus pagination" found in the margins in nearly every edition of any of Plato's works. In this way, we can all make sure we're referring to the same sections, no matter which version of the *Republic* we have. It's a wonderfully convenient convention that I will use throughout this book.

carefully. I will not focus on many more of them, and will instead emphasize the general arguments, but I encourage you to allow yourself to enjoy the *Republic* as you might enjoy a good meal. Savor each bite rather than finishing it as quickly as possible (let alone skipping the meal altogether).

One final bit of irony: although the theme of the *Apology*[43] is clearly to vindicate Socrates and reveal that the charges brought against him were unjustifiable, the *Republic* actually reveals that Socrates does, in fact, introduce "new gods" to Athens. Though he is vindicated by virtue of his devotion to "The Good," this understanding of goodness and morality is, in a fact, a sharp and radical departure from the vision of the local gods revered in Athens at the time. While not an atheist, Socrates vision of "God" as presented in the *Republic* certainly is "new."

Socrates is returning from this celebration with Glaucon (Plato's half-brother) when he is spotted by Polemarchus, the son of Cephalus. Polemarchus sends his slave to detain Socrates, and then insists that Socrates and Glaucon join him at his house where numerous others await. There is something a bit disturbing about the encounter, as Polemarchus (playfully?) seems to be forcing Socrates to join him.

> *Polemarchus said to me: I perceive, Socrates, that you and your companion are already on your way to the city.*

> *You are not far wrong, I said.*

> *But do you see, he rejoined, how many we are?*

> *Of course.*

> *And are you stronger than all these? for if not, you will have to remain where you are. (327a)*

In perhaps another reference to the *Apology*, Socrates suggests that he might persuade them to let him (and Glaucon) go, but Polemarchus retorts that they will refuse to listen to him, and therefore be incapable of persuasion—much like the jurors were not persuaded by Socrates defense of himself at his trial.

Whether playful or serious, Socrates goes with them and finds himself brought into their lengthy and lofty discussions of the nature of justice. Before Socrates takes center stage and offers his massive account of justice, several others give it a try. They are Cephalus, Polemarchus, Thrasymachus, Glaucon, and Adeimantus.[44] We will consider each in turn.

---

[43] Don't be confused by the word. "Apology" in this sense doesn't to apologize for something, but rather is derived from the Greek word *apologia*, which means a reasoned defense.

[44] Adeimantus was also one of Plato's brothers.

## Cephalus

Plato is clever in how he introduces justice as a topic of conversation. It might well have seemed forced if he had Socrates walk into the home and then immediately be asked by some other toga-wearing gentleman, "what is justice?" Instead, Cephalus, who is an elderly man, chides Socrates for not visiting more often, and claims that his "declining interest in physical pleasures is exactly matched by increasing desire for and enjoyment of conversation."

Socrates is polite and respectful of his elder, so he asks how he is doing and what he thinks of old age. Cephalus points out that many of his fellow senior citizens, when they get together, just complain about their families and grumble about being old, but he, himself, finds old age to be no burden—so long as one is disciplined and good-tempered (and it doesn't hurt, either, if one is rich, as he was).

Socrates seizes on this mention of wealth, and asks Cephalus what he thinks the greatest benefit of that wealth is to him. Cephalus answers by first pointing out that as one grows older, thoughts of death and what might await beyond death come more frequently, and with greater anxiety. He quotes Pindar as saying, in effect, that knowledge that one has been morally good is a comfort in old age. In this context, the benefit of his wealth has been that he can be more confident that he will not leave life with unpaid debts, including various sacrificial offerings to the gods.[45]

In what might well be an uncharitable maneuver, Socrates takes this to be a definition of goodness (justice[46]) itself: discharging one's debts and obligations. In the same breath, Socrates criticizes this definition in his usual style: by providing a counter-example. Suppose one had borrowed a weapon from a friend, and that friend then went insane and came asking for his weapon. Surely it would not be good (just) to pay him back what he is owed, in that case.

Cephalus, who had never sought an argument about justice in the first place, hasn't acquired any new interest in the face of Socrates' refutation. He immediately excuses himself to go attend yet another religious ceremony (to discharge another debt?), and leaves his son, Polemarchus, to deal with Socrates.

---

[45] The readers of the *Republic*, when it was written, would have been aware of what actually happened to Cephalus and his family, and it is likely that Plato relies on this. After Athens was conquered, Cephalus' family fortune was lost, and his son, Polemarchus, was executed. Plato's first readers would have known, in their own time, that what Cephalus seemed to think most important were all contingent, fleeting, and easily lost.

[46] Although "good" and "just" often have distinct meanings today, in the context of the *Republic* they mean essentially the same thing. For the remainder of this chapter, please understand the word justice also means moral goodness, and vice versa.

## Polemarchus

Taking over for his father (who never sought the debate in the first place), Polemarchus defends a variation of his father's claim by appealing to the poet, Simonides, to whom he attributes the following interpretation of justice: "friends owe friends good deeds, not bad ones (332a)." This is later clarified to mean that we should do good for friends, and bad for enemies. More generally, give to each their due.

Socrates' immediately begins his usual strategy of developing a counter-example (334c-e).

*And so, you and Homer and Simonides are agreed that justice is an art of theft; to be practised however 'for the good of friends and for the harm of enemies,'—that was what you were saying?*

*No, certainly not that, though I do not now know what I did say; but I still stand by the latter words.*

*Well, there is another question: By friends and enemies do we mean those who are so really, or only in seeming?*

*Surely, he said, a man may be expected to love those whom he thinks good, and to hate those whom he thinks evil.*

*Yes, but do not persons often err about good and evil: many who are not good seem to be so, and conversely?*

*That is true.*

*Then to them the good will be enemies and the evil will be their friends?*

*True.*

*And in that case they will be right in doing good to the evil and evil to the good?*

*Clearly.*

*But the good are just and would not do an injustice?*

*True.*

*Then according to your argument it is just to injure those who do no wrong?*

*Nay, Socrates; the doctrine is immoral.*

*Then I suppose that we ought to do good to the just and harm to the unjust?*

*I like that better.*

But see the consequence:—Many a man who is ignorant of human nature has friends who are bad friends, and in that case he ought to do harm to them; and he has good enemies whom he ought to benefit; but, if so, we shall be saying the very opposite of that which we affirmed to be the meaning of Simonides.

Socrates' criticism of this particular interpretation of justice is probably less important than the assumption and strategy that now appears for the first time in the *Republic*, but upon which he will rely throughout the remainder of the work: *justice is an "art" with a single focus, analogous to other arts.* Justice, therefore, is like cooking, or carpentry, or medicine, in that it has a focus and persons are evaluated in terms of their skill in this art by virtue of how well they achieve its end. Someone who produces bad-tasting food is not a good cook, and someone who can cure no disease is a poor doctor.

The context in which this analogy arises is that Polemarchus seeks to revise his definition in response to Socrates' counter-example. Justice, now, requires that one do good to those who are truly friends, and harm those who are truly enemies. Socrates' continues his assault (335b-e):

*When horses are injured, are they improved or deteriorated?*

*The latter.*

*Deteriorated, that is to say, in the good qualities of horses, not of dogs?*

*Yes, of horses.*

*And dogs are deteriorated in the good qualities of dogs, and not of horses?*

*Of course.*

*And will not men who are injured be deteriorated in that which is the proper virtue of man?*

*Certainly.*

*And that human virtue is justice?*

*To be sure.*

*Then men who are injured are of necessity made unjust?*

*That is the result.*

*But can the musician by his art make men unmusical?*

*Certainly not.*

*Or the horseman by his art make them bad horsemen?*

*Impossible.*

*And can the just by justice make men unjust, or speaking generally, can the good by virtue make them bad?*

*Assuredly not.*

*Any more than heat can produce cold?*

*It cannot.*

*Or drought moisture?*

*Clearly not.*

*Nor can the good harm any one?*

*Impossible.*

*And the just is the good?*

*Certainly.*

*Then to injure a friend or any one else is not the act of a just man, but of the opposite, who is the unjust?*

*I think that what you say is quite true, Socrates.*

*Then if a man says that justice consists in the repayment of debts, and that good is the debt which a just man owes to his friends, and evil the debt which he owes to his enemies,—to say this is not wise; for it is not true, if, as has been clearly shown, the injuring of another can be in no case just.*

At this point, Socrates has done two very important things: he has declared (or at least assumed that) justice is a skill, and he has claimed that it is never just or right to harm another. A just person is one who improves others, who helps others. Justice, like medicine, is for the sake of the patient. At this point in the conversation, the most notorious (and famous) of Socrates' sparring partners in the *Republic* bursts into the conversation.

## Thrasymachus

*Several times in the course of the discussion Thrasymachus had made an attempt to get the argument into his own hands, and had been put down by the rest of the company, who wanted to hear the end. But when Polemarchus and I had done speaking and there was a pause, he could no longer hold his peace; and, gathering himself up, he came at us like a wild beast, seeking to devour us. We were quite panic-stricken at the sight of him (336b).*

Socrates claims to be terrified as Thrasymachus (a well-known sophist) berates him for doing that for which Socrates was most well-known: asking questions and refuting everyone else's answers without ever offering up any of his own. Despite this (accurate) observation, within just a few paragraphs Thrasymachus is already offering his own view of justice for Socrates to critique anyway, and Socrates remains in his usual role of asking questions and refuting answers.

Perhaps to remind us all that Thrasymachus was a Sophist, Plato has him demand some sort of payment for the instruction he is about to offer, and Glaucon offers to compensate him, along with others, given that Socrates is perpetually poor. Thrasymachus relents and offers his infamous claim that "morality is nothing other than the advantage of the other party (338c)." He then, literally, asks why they have not applauded him.

*According to Thrasymachus, justice (morality) is nothing other than the will of the stronger.* Might makes right. "Justice" is simply a pretty label that we attach to the preferences and values of the ruling party (whether individual, as in a king or dictator, or group, as in an oligarchy or democracy). Whoever is in charge, wherever they might be, promote their own interests and call that "justice." When someone else takes over, they do the same thing.

In response, to Thrasymachus' position, Socrates begins his predictable line of attack. He first gets Thrasymachus to acknowledge that those in power sometimes make mistakes about what is to their advantage, and that subjects are to obey those laws anyway—and that it is right for them to do so. Accordingly, even though "justice" is defined as the advantage of the stronger, it is nevertheless "just" to do things which are actually to their disadvantage.

Socrates continues by once again making reference to justice as a skill and begins with analogy. Medicine considers the welfare of the body, not the welfare of medicine. In other words, a doctor, when she is practicing medicine, is not aimed at wealth or prestige, but at healing the sick. Also, medicine is for the advantage of the "weaker" party. It serves the patient (the one who is sick), not the doctor (the one who is well).

By analogy, *Socrates claims, rulers, when they practice the craft of ruling, consider not their own welfare, but that of their subjects.* Justice, then, is not concerned with the advantage of the stronger (i.e., the ruler), but, if anyone at all, of the weaker (i.e., the ruled).

Thrasymachus immediately offers an analogy of his own: shepherds are indeed concerned with their welfare of their flock, but only so that they can sell or eat them later! Thrasymachus then does something unusual: he seems to shift his usage of "moral" and "immoral." Though he has defined morality (justice) as the advantage of the stronger party, he now begins to claim that "immorality" is beneficial—and by "immorality" it is clear that he means specific things like theft, fraud, deceit, etc. The corrupt politician who embezzles and takes bribes is benefitted, while the honest politician loses out on those benefits. He claims that everyone recognizes that immorality is advantageous, but we publicly denounce it out of fear of being the victim of it.

Socrates proceeds to attack both points. First, with regard to the shepherd analogy, Socrates claims that different skills are at work. Medical doctors, for example, are concerned with the success of their practice. However, a *different* skill is employed when the doctor is considering and working on the financial success of her practice. When she is doing *medicine*, her craft focuses on healing the body. Similarly, the shepherd, when acting as a shepherd, is focused on the well-being of the flock. When the shepherd turns his attention to making a profit, a different skill is employed. Socrates suggests that something like "money-making" is this overarching (different) skill that conjoins with every other craft. Carpentry concerns working with wood, but to be a financially successful carpenter requires the skill of "money-making." When working with the wood, though, the skill is carpentry, not money-making. Rulers, *qua* rulers, are not working to their own benefit. When they do, they are exercising a different skill.

> Then now, Thrasymachus, there is no longer any doubt that neither arts nor governments provide for their own interests; but, as we were before saying, they rule and provide for the interests of their subjects who are the weaker and not the stronger—to their good they attend and not to the good of the superior. And this is the reason, my dear Thrasymachus, why, as I was just now saying, no one is willing to govern; because no one likes to take in hand the reformation of evils which are not his concern without remuneration. For, in the execution of his work, and in giving his orders to another, the true artist does not regard his own interest, but always that of his subjects; and therefore in order that rulers may be willing to rule, they must be paid in one of three modes of payment, money, or honour, or a penalty for refusing. (346e-347a)

Moving to Thraymachus' second point, that immorality is more beneficial to the individual than morality, Socrates once again resorts to analogy. After all, if something is like something else in one respect, it might be like it in another as well. He considers a band of pirates or thieves, and gets Thrasymachus to acknowledge that if the members were to wrong one another, they would be less successful as a group "because immorality makes for mutual conflict, hatred, and antagonism, while moral behavior makes for concord and friendship (351d)." Analogously, *when immorality arises in a single individual, it will generate internal division*, conflict, and discord. In addition to generating internal hostility, immorality will generate hostility between the immoral person and moral persons. If we acknowledge that the gods are moral, then this would mean conflict with the gods as well.

> *And we have admitted that justice is the excellence of the soul, and injustice the defect of the soul?*
>
> *That has been admitted.*
>
> *Then the just soul and the just man will live well, and the unjust man will live ill?*
>
> *That is what your argument proves.*
>
> *And he who lives well is blessed and happy, and he who lives ill the reverse of happy?*
>
> *Certainly.*
>
> *Then the just is happy, and the unjust miserable?*
>
> *So be it.*
>
> *But happiness and not misery is profitable.*
>
> *Of course.*
>
> *Then, my blessed Thrasymachus, injustice can never be more profitable than justice.*

At this point, it would seem that Socrates has refuted Thrasymachus' position and has demonstrated that injustice is not more profitable than justice, and that true rulership looks not to the advantage of the ruler, but of the ruled (the "weaker party"). Moreover, Socrates has reiterated his notion of justice (goodness, morality) as a skill, and has introduced his notion of virtue as a healthy, integrated soul. Both of these ideas will continue to be prominent throughout the rest of the *Republic*.

## Glaucon & Adeimantus

Thrasymachus, despite his fearsome entrance into the conversation, now wants only to done with it. In fact, he tries several times to get up and leave, only to be prevented by others. It might seem that Socrates is victorious, but some disagree. Socrates, for one, acknowledges that, thus far, he hasn't actually learned what justice *is*—only what it is *not*. Others, such as Glaucon (Plato's half-brother), believe that Thrasymachus gave up the fight too quickly.

> *Thrasymachus seems to me, like a snake, to have been charmed by your voice sooner than he ought to have been; but to my mind the nature of justice and injustice have not yet been made clear. Setting aside their rewards and results, I want to know what they are in themselves, and how they inwardly work in the soul. If you, please, then, I will revive the argument of Thrasymachus. And first I will speak of the nature and origin of justice according to the common view of them. Secondly, I will show that all men who practise justice do so against their will, of necessity, but not as a good. And thirdly, I will argue that there is reason in this view, for the life of the unjust is after all better far than the life of the just—if what they say is true, Socrates, since I myself am not of their opinion. But still I acknowledge that I am perplexed when I hear the voices of Thrasymachus and myriads of others dinning in my ears; and, on the other hand, I have never yet heard the superiority of justice to injustice maintained by any one in a satisfactory way. I want to hear justice praised in respect of itself; then I shall be satisfied, and you are the person from whom I think that I am most likely to hear this; and therefore I will praise the unjust life to the utmost of my power, and my manner of speaking will indicate the manner in which I desire to hear you too praising justice and censuring injustice. (358b-c)*

Glaucon appears to be in the awkward position of believing that a view of justice similar to Thrasymachus' might well be true, but hopes that it is not. So, he proposes to revive (a variation of) Thrasymachus' view in hopes that Socrates will demonstrate, once and for all, that justice is something more noble.

*Glaucon distinguishes three different ways in which something can be perceived as good. Some things are good for their own sake, and not for their consequences* (e.g., simple pleasures). *Other things are good both for their own sake as well as for their consequences* (e.g., health). *Finally, some things are good only for their consequences* (e.g., a polio vaccine). Glaucon wonders into which of these categories should justice be placed?

His own proposal is that it falls into the third: justice is good only for its consequences. His brother Adeimantus will second this and claim that justice is valuable only for its external rewards, and what would be best is to have the *reputation* of being just, while actually being unjust. In such a case, one would reap the award of being unjust, while also reaping the rewards of being seen as just.

To support this notion of justice, *Glaucon offers a very early (as in, Ancient) presentation of the "**social contract**" theory in political philosophy, while presupposing what appears to be the "psychological egoist" interpretation of human nature.*

> *They say that to do injustice is, by nature, good; to suffer injustice, evil; but that the evil is greater than the good. And so when men have both done and*

*suffered injustice and have had experience of both, not being able to avoid the one and obtain the other, they think that they had better agree among themselves to have neither; hence there arise laws and mutual covenants; and that which is ordained by law is termed by them lawful and just. This they affirm to be the origin and nature of justice;—it is a mean or compromise, between the best of all, which is to do injustice and not be punished, and the worst of all, which is to suffer injustice without the power of retaliation; and justice, being at a middle point between the two, is tolerated not as a good, but as the lesser evil, and honoured by reason of the inability of men to do injustice. For no man who is worthy to be called a man would ever submit to such an agreement if he were able to resist; he would be mad if he did. Such is the received account, Socrates, of the nature and origin of justice. (358e-359b)*

In other words, we "play nicely" with each other because it's necessary; it's in our own best interest to do so. Although we would all like to have sufficient power to do whatever we want, whenever we want, without anyone having the power to stop us, that just isn't possible. In addition, we fear being the victim of just that sort of powerful person, of being unable to protect ourselves and retaliate against those who would try to take advantage of us. As a compromise, we settle at a mid-point between these two extremes by means of a series of promises. I won't kill you, so long as you don't kill me. I won't take your stuff so long as you don't take mine. We enact, in effect, a "social contract" for the sake of safety, stability, and security—and we honor the contract not because we want to, but because we have to, because we lack the power to defy it.

To reinforce his argument, Glaucon appeals to the Myth of Gyges' ring, and invites us to consider the thought experiment that follows.

*Now that those who practise justice do so involuntarily and because they have not the power to be unjust will best appear if we imagine something of this kind: having given both to the just and the unjust power to do what they will, let us watch and see whither desire will lead them; then we shall discover in the very act the just and unjust man to be proceeding along the same road, following their interest, which all natures deem to be their good, and are only diverted into the path of justice by the force of law. The liberty which we are supposing may be most completely given to them in the form of such a power as is said to have been possessed by Gyges, the ancestor of Croesus the Lydian. According to the tradition, Gyges was a shepherd in the service of the king of Lydia; there was a great storm, and an earthquake made an opening in the earth at the place where he was feeding his flock. Amazed at the sight, he descended into the opening, where, among other marvels, he beheld a hollow brazen horse, having doors, at which he stooping and looking in saw a dead body of stature, as appeared to him, more than human, and having nothing on but a gold ring; this he took from the finger of the dead and reascended. Now the shepherds met together, according to custom, that they might send their monthly report about the flocks to the king; into their assembly he came having the ring on his finger, and as he was sitting among them he chanced to turn the collet of the ring inside his hand, when instantly he became invisible to the rest of the company and they began to speak of him as if he were no longer present. He was astonished at this, and again touching the ring he turned the collet outwards and reappeared; he made several trials of the ring, and always with the same result—when he turned the collet inwards he became invisible, when outwards he reappeared. Whereupon he contrived to be chosen one of the messengers who were sent to the court; whereas soon as he arrived he seduced the queen, and with her help conspired against the king and slew him, and took the kingdom. Suppose now that there were two such magic rings, and the just put on one of them and the unjust the other; no man can be imagined to be of such an iron nature that he would stand fast in justice. No man would keep his hands off what was not his own when he could safely take what he liked out of the market, or go into houses and lie with any one at his pleasure, or kill or release from prison whom he would, and in all respects be like a God among men. Then the actions of the just would be as the actions of the unjust; they would both come at last to the same point. And this we may truly affirm to be a great proof that a man is just, not willingly or because he thinks that justice is any good to him individually, but of necessity, for wherever any one thinks that he can safely be unjust, there he is unjust. For all men believe in their hearts that injustice is far more profitable to the individual than justice, and he who argues as I have been supposing, will say that they are right. If you could imagine any one obtaining this power of becoming invisible, and never doing any wrong or touching what was another's, he would be thought by the lookers-on to be a most wretched idiot, although they would praise him to one another's faces, and keep up appearances with one another from a fear that they too might suffer injustice. Enough of this. (359d-360d)*

Before we come to any harsh judgments against Gyges, remember that Glaucon recommends a thought experiment. Imagine there are two such magic rings, each of which renders the wearer invisible. These days, we might need to get a little more sophisticated. Perhaps you suppose that even invisible persons might still leave behind fingerprints, or hair samples, or other means by which a clever forensic investigator could identify a perpetrator. They're magic rings. We can make them do whatever we want! Suppose the rings render the wearer invisible, magically cloaks any heat signatures, erases fingerprints, eliminates DNA evidence, etc. Now, give one of the two rings to someone whom you regard as tremendously virtuous and just. Give the other to someone quite the opposite: a vicious and unjust jerk. What, do you suppose, each would do with the ring? Glaucon believes that both the "just" and the "unjust" would come "at last to the same point." That is, they would each, eventually, do the same thing: whatever it is that each wanted. To make matters more interesting, give yourself one of the rings.

The outcome of Glaucon's thought experiment provides a particular insight into human nature. If it is true that any one of us would ultimately and inevitably abuse the power of Gyges' ring, then the reason why most of us usually obey the rules and "play nice" with one another is fear. Although we would like to be able to do whatever we want, to whomever we want, whenever we want, we recognize that just isn't possible. None of us is Superman. However powerful a given individual might be, she isn't bulletproof (to put it bluntly). No matter how wealthy, how powerful, how well-connected, each one of us is all-too-human, and all-too-vulnerable. Realizing that, and wishing to minimize the risk we face from others, we make mutual promises to "play nice." I won't rob you so long as you don't rob me. I won't kill you, so long as you don't kill me. We surrender some of our own power, and our own freedom, when we make those promises, but in exchange for that we gain security. We behave ourselves because it is in our self-interest to do so. If it were no longer necessary, no longer in our self-interest (e.g., if we had Gyges' ring), we would no longer be inclined to "play nice." All of this is meant to demonstrate that justice is valued not for its own sake, but because of the beneficial consequences it generates. In the context of the "nature" v. "convention" debate, Glaucon seems to be arguing in favor of convention as regards justice: laws exist merely as a necessary compromise due to our inability to fulfill our true heart's desires.[47]

The final challenge thrown at Socrates' feet will produce the answer that occupies the rest of the *Republic*.

> *And therefore, I say, not only prove to us that justice is better than injustice, but show what they either of them do to the possessor of them, which makes the one to be a good and the other an evil, whether seen or unseen by gods and men. (367e)*

## Socrates

Thus far, I have presented the first two books of the *Republic* in considerable detail. That strategy is about to change. Most of the rest of the *Republic* is the development of an extended analogy between the soul and the State for the purpose of identifying and understanding justice. Rather than proceed through this argument book by book (let alone line by line), I am going to present the analogy itself, in as clear a fashion as I can manage. This will involve skipping over large chunks of the *Republic*, and addressing some ideas out of order. I believe, though, that the end result will be a clearer and more precise presentation of the key material.

I have already mentioned an extended analogy. Socrates claims that the analogy will assist in understanding the nature of justice.

---

[47] This possibly pessimistic (or possibly accurate) interpretation of human nature as that of desire-satisfying individuals who can only be entrusted to live cooperatively if provided the threat of punishment and the force of law will find voice in such later political philosophers as Hobbes and Machiavelli.

*Glaucon and the rest entreated me by all means not to let the question drop, but to proceed in the investigation. They wanted to arrive at the truth, first, about the nature of justice and injustice, and secondly, about their relative advantages. I told them, what I really thought, that the enquiry would be of a serious nature, and would require very good eyes. Seeing then, I said, that we are no great wits, I think that we had better adopt a method which I may illustrate thus; suppose that a short-sighted person had been asked by some one to read small letters from a distance; and it occurred to some one else that they might be found in another place which was larger and in which the letters were larger—if they were the same and he could read the larger letters first, and then proceed to the lesser—this would have been thought a rare piece of good fortune.*

*Very true, said Adeimantus; but how does the illustration apply to our enquiry?*

*I will tell you, I replied; justice, which is the subject of our enquiry, is, as you know, sometimes spoken of as the virtue of an individual, and sometimes as the virtue of a State.*

*True, he replied.*

*And is not a State larger than an individual?*

*It is.*

*Then in the larger the quantity of justice is likely to be larger and more easily discernible. I propose therefore that we enquire into the nature of justice and injustice, first as they appear in the State, and secondly in the individual, proceeding from the greater to the lesser and comparing them.* (368d-369a)

*Socrates proposes to spend a significant amount of time and energy developing a vision of an ideal State on the assumption that there is a meaningful analogy between the State and the individual.* If true, then what we learn about justice in the case of this ideal State can be applied to our understanding of justice for the individual soul.

Before delving into the analogy itself, I want to say a few things about how to interpret what Socrates is doing. Some interpreters of the *Republic* take the political philosophy very seriously, believe that Plato (via Socrates) is presenting a serious attempt at State-building, and then (usually) critique that vision as either hopelessly utopian, or fascist. Other interpreters claim that no serious political philosophy is intended, and that all of the discussion of the State, its policies and structures and so on, is solely for the sake of the analogy. Therefore, we are not to take seriously anything Socrates says about politics except in regards to how it motivates the analogy with the individual soul. Within the

*Republic* itself, Plato has Socrates acknowledge the ideal/utopian nature of the project.

> *you mean the city whose establishment we have described, the city whose home is in the ideal; for I think that it can be found nowhere on earth." "Well," said I, "perhaps there is a pattern of it laid up in heaven for him who wishes to contemplate it and so beholding to constitute himself its citizen. But it makes no difference whether it exists now or ever will come into being ... (592a-b).*

The ideal Republic is found nowhere on Earth, and might never exist, for that matter—but there might, nevertheless, be an ideal "form" of government, against which all actual governments may be evaluated. In that sense, some actual statecraft might be intended.

My own view as to how seriously we are to take the political philosophy in the *Republic* is unsettled, but that unsettled-ness mirrors, in my opinion, the condition of the debate. My own opinion is that it's clear that he intends the analogy (he says so, explicitly!), so we must interpret most of the *Republic* with that analogy in mind. However, in some places he goes into political detail that would be unnecessary if his *sole* purpose was to develop an analogy. So, my own sense is that the primary purpose of this lengthy section of the *Republic* is (ultimately) to understand justice in the soul, but that there might well be some sincere effort at political philosophy as well. Having built it up so much by now, let's finally get into the analogy itself.

After describing how a community might develop with regard to its needs and division of labor, *Socrates ultimately divides his ideal community into three classes:*

1. Guardians
2. Auxiliaries
3. Producers

The Guardians are the ruling class, drawn from the Auxiliaries by virtue of having demonstrated the proper traits. Auxiliaries are warriors, in effect both military and police in one. The Producers are everyone else. It's easy to think of Producers as only "blue collar," working class types such as factory workers, farmers, etc. However, lawyers and bankers are also "Producers" in this framework. Basically, anyone who isn't an Auxiliary or Guardian is a Producer, by default.

## The Principle of Specialization (POS)

These divisions are not arbitrary, nor is the selection process by which one is placed into his or her class. Selection is driven by what we might call the "principle of specialization." This principle plays a very important (and persistent) role in Socrates' argument. The first indicator of this principle in the text is found at 370b-c:

> *...we are not all alike; there are diversities of natures among us which are adapted to different occupations.... And if so, we must infer that all things are produced more plentifully and easily and of a better quality when one man does one thing which is natural to him and does it at the right time, and leaves other things. (370b-c)*

*Different people are best-suited for different roles in society.* Some people are "natural" leaders. Others lack leadership ability, but are courageous and strong and would excel at military work. Still others lack either, but are skilled at some trade or craft. For the good of the community, individuals should do that for which they are best suited. If someone who is not suitable for leadership aspires to, and acquires, a leadership position anyway, the community suffers. The community suffers if cowards become soldiers. Natural leaders "waste" their talents when they become doctors instead. On the assumption that the good of the whole (the community) is more important than the good of the individual, individuals should be put to use in the way that best serves their community.

Remember, though, that the basic point of all this political talk is to develop an analogy by which to understand the individual soul. *Socrates claims that the soul is likewise divisible into three parts that just so happen to correspond to the three divisions in society.*[48] These three parts of the soul are as follows:

1. Reason
2. Spirit (or passion)
3. Appetite (or desire)

This tripartite understanding of the soul is employed not only in the *Republic*, but in another of Plato's works as well: *Phaedrus*. There, he employs a different analogy. The soul is like a chariot with two horses and one charioteer. One of the horses represents the appetitive/desirous part of the soul, and is the source of our instinctive desires. The other horse represents the spirited part of the soul, and is the source of our motivation and desire for personal glory. The charioteer represents the rational part of the soul, and the source of understanding and wisdom, and our desire for one's overall good.

In case it wasn't obvious, the Guardians in the community correspond to Reason in the soul. The Auxiliaries correspond to the spirited/passionate part of the soul. The Producers correspond to the appetitive/desirous part of the soul.

1. Guardians      Reason
2. Auxiliaries    Spirit/Passion
3. Producers      Appetite/desire

---

[48] An argument for this tripartite model of the soul may be found on 439c-441b, for those who are interested.

Despite the fact that the point of the society-building exercise is supposed to be to develop an analogy with the soul, Socrates proceeds to develop this ideal society in exhausting detail—which makes it difficult to dismiss his efforts as being aimed *solely* at developing the analogy.

## Life in the *Republic*

His ideal society, to the extent that we take it seriously, might seem shockingly totalitarian to our delicate, democratic sensibilities. Although the Producers are largely free to live as they please (subject to their basic class restrictions, of course), the lives of the Auxiliaries and Guardians are thoroughly regulated. I will offer a brief description in what follows, and you should assume that these policies apply to both the Guardians and Auxiliaries unless I specifically indicate otherwise.

They will live "spartan" lives. In Plato's own time, this expression had a more poignant meaning, of course, as Sparta had recently warred with, and defeated, Athens. However, the contemporary usage of the term is accurate. They will have no private possessions, nor private homes (416a-417b, 462c). They will live together, in barracks, and all of their possessions will be provided to them by the State. These possessions will be the basic necessities of life and of their profession. For example, Auxiliaries will be supplied armor and weapons in addition to basic daily needs. These items technically belong to the State, and have merely been "checked out" for use, in much the same way that a soldier in the U.S. military doesn't own "his" firearm. The purpose of limiting their personal possessions is to prevent them from being motivated by greed. After all, in real life leaders have a tendency to use their power to promote themselves, to acquire personal wealth and connections—and warriors might allow their personal ambition to inspire them to seize leadership (and the wealth and power it offers) by means of a military coup. If these two classes have been raised without personal possessions, they will (presumably) lack those temptations.

> Then now let us consider what will be their way of life, if they are to realize our idea of them. In the first place, none of them should have any property of his own beyond what is absolutely necessary; neither should they have a private house or store closed against any one who has a mind to enter; their provisions should be only such as are required by trained warriors, who are men of temperance and courage; they should agree to receive from the citizens a fixed rate of pay, enough to meet the expenses of the year and no more; and they will go to mess and live together like soldiers in a camp. Gold and silver we will tell them that they have from God; the diviner metal is within them, and they have therefore no need of the dross which is current among men, and ought not to pollute the divine by any such earthly admixture; for that commoner metal has been the source of many unholy deeds, but their own is undefiled. And they alone of all the citizens may not touch or handle silver or gold, or be under the same roof with them, or wear them, or drink from them. And this will be their

*salvation, and they will be the saviours of the State. But should they ever acquire homes or lands or moneys of their own, they will become housekeepers and husbandmen instead of guardians, enemies and tyrants instead of allies of the other citizens; hating and being hated, plotting and being plotted against, they will pass their whole life in much greater terror of internal than of external enemies, and the hour of ruin, both to themselves and to the rest of the State, will be at hand. (416e)*

Just as they will have no private possessions, nor will they have private relationships. By virtue of what can only be described as a eugenics program, they will have non-exclusive "marriages" selected by Guardians on the basis of what will produce the best offspring. These pairings will not be permanent or exclusive, so as to prevent jealousies and possessiveness from developing. This line of reasoning extends to the offspring of those pairings as well. Those children will be raised in common, with no knowledge of the identity of their biological parents (nor will those parents know which child is their own—so as to prevent thoughts of "their own" from arising at all)(457d). Perhaps disturbingly, this system aimed at what is best for the community will also weed out some children as unfit. "Inferior" offspring will not be "brought up." They will be "hidden away in some secret and secluded spot." This includes not only offspring resulting from unsuitable pairings, but also children with disabilities resulting from proper pairings (459e, 460c). To be clear, what we're talking about is killing "unfit" babies—though the actual process probably would have been more passive, merely leaving them out to die of exposure. All this would be done secretly, of course, to avoid disturbing the populace.

Oddly enough, the rulers (Guardians) and warriors (Auxiliaries) of this "ideal" State seem to have the least freedom and least luxuries of anyone in their community. Plato/Socrates was aware of this:

*Here Adeimantus interposed a question: How would you answer, Socrates, said he, if a person were to say that you are making these people miserable, and that they are the cause of their own unhappiness; the city in fact belongs to them, but they are none the better for it; whereas other men acquire lands, and build large and handsome houses, and have everything handsome about them, offering sacrifices to the gods on their own account, and practising hospitality; moreover, as you were saying just now, they have gold and silver, and all that is usual among the favourites of fortune; but our poor citizens are no better than mercenaries who are quartered in the city and are always mounting guard?*

*Yes, I said; and you may add that they are only fed, and not paid in addition to their food, like other men; and therefore they cannot, if they would, take a journey of pleasure; they have no money to spend on a mistress or any other luxurious fancy, which, as the world goes, is thought to be happiness; and many other accusations of the same nature might be added....*

*If we proceed along the old path, my belief, I said, is that we shall find the answer. And our answer will be that, even as they are, our guardians may very likely be the happiest of men; but that our aim in founding the State was not the disproportionate happiness of any one class, but the greatest happiness of the whole;... (419a-420c)*

I assume that the typical reader of this text is an American, or at least living in the United States of America. We are accustomed to a cultural norm of individualism, according to which we tend to focus on the individual, first and foremost, and then consider the needs of the broader community as something "extra," something to be promoted so long as it's not overly much at the expense of the individual. This would have been an utterly alien concept to the Greeks of Plato's time. There was much more emphasis on the group, whether it be the larger community (city state) or family. Given our own contemporary sensibilities, this claim that the aim of this ideal State is the happiness of the whole, not of any one class or individual, and that it's acceptable to impose burdens on some for the sake of the many, might sound disturbingly totalitarian—and the Guardians and Auxiliaries are subject to even more controls than these.

For example, their lives will be subject to vigorous training with regard to physical exercise, music, culture, and philosophy. The very best persons will excel in all of these, and these persons are naturally suited to be Guardians (412a-b). Training will aim at avoiding extremes. Exclusive focus on physical exercise produces brutality (411c-e), while exclusive focus on cultural studies produces "shamefully soft" characters (410d).

Training will be coeducational. The *Republic* is surprisingly "progressive" with regard to gender equality.

*Let us further suppose the birth and education of our women to be subject to similar or nearly similar regulations; then we shall see whether the result accords with our design.*

*What do you mean?*

*What I mean may be put into the form of a question, I said: Are dogs divided into hes and shes, or do they both share equally in hunting and in keeping watch and in the other duties of dogs? or do we entrust to the males the entire and exclusive care of the flocks, while we leave the females at home, under the idea that the bearing and suckling their puppies is labour enough for them?*

*No, he said, they share alike; the only difference between them is that the males are stronger and the females weaker.*

*But can you use different animals for the same purpose, unless they are bred and fed in the same way?*

*You cannot.*

*Then, if women are to have the same duties as men, they must have the same nurture and education?*

*Yes....*

*Then let us put a speech into the mouths of our opponents. They will say: 'Socrates and Glaucon, no adversary need convict you, for you yourselves, at the first foundation of the State, admitted the principle that everybody was to do the one work suited to his own nature.' And certainly, if I am not mistaken, such an admission was made by us. 'And do not the natures of men and women differ very much indeed?' And we shall reply: Of course they do. Then we shall be asked, 'Whether the tasks assigned to men and to women should not be different, and such as are agreeable to their different natures?' Certainly they should. 'But if so, have you not fallen into a serious inconsistency in saying that men and women, whose natures are so entirely different, ought to perform the same actions?'—What defence will you make for us, my good Sir, against any one who offers these objections?...*

*And if, I said, the male and female sex appear to differ in their fitness for any art or pursuit, we should say that such pursuit or art ought to be assigned to one or the other of them; but if the difference consists only in women bearing and men begetting children, this does not amount to a proof that a woman differs from a man in respect of the sort of education she should receive; and we shall therefore continue to maintain that our guardians and their wives ought to have the same pursuits....*

*And if so, my friend, I said, there is no special faculty of administration in a state which a woman has because she is a woman, or which a man has by virtue of his sex, but the gifts of nature are alike diffused in both; all the pursuits of men are the pursuits of women also, but in all of them a woman is inferior to a man. (451d-455e)*

Because what is relevant to the class divisions (and therefore to the training and education received by each class) are the traits suitable to each class, and because reproductive organs are relevant only to the task of conceiving and bearing children, there should be no difference, on the basis of sex or gender alone, with regard to class or training. Instead, we should recognize that some females are suitable for being Guardians, and some are not, in just the same way that some men are and some are not.

Although Plato's Socrates might seem quite the progressive or feminist in this sense, he's quite the "totalitarian" in others. For example, Socrates argues that young people are impressionable, and that it's important to control the messages they hear. If you suspect he's talking about censorship, you are correct.

*You know also that the beginning is the most important part of any work, especially in the case of a young and tender thing; for that is the time at which the character is being formed and the desired impression is more readily taken.*

*Quite true.*

*And shall we just carelessly allow children to hear any casual tales which may be devised by casual persons, and to receive into their minds ideas for the most part the very opposite of those which we should wish them to have when they are grown up?*

*We cannot.*

*Then the first thing will be to establish a censorship of the writers of fiction, and let the censors receive any tale of fiction which is good, and reject the bad; and we will desire mothers and nurses to tell their children the authorised ones only. (377b-c)*

In one of the lengthier tangents of the *Republic*, Socrates offers a sustained critique of the poets (a primary rival to philosophers with regard to moral influence). The poets, including legends such as Hesiod and Homer, were, in effect, professional liars—and their lies produce harmful effects in the populace. For example, the poets tell stories of the gods, such as Zeus, engaging in all kinds of scandalous and immoral behavior. What a terrible example this offers to young people!

*First of all, I said, there was that greatest of all lies in high places, which the poet told about Uranus, and which was a bad lie too,—I mean what Hesiod says that Uranus did, and how Cronus retaliated on him. The doings of Cronus, and the sufferings which in turn his son inflicted upon him, even if they were true, ought certainly not to be lightly told to young and thoughtless persons; if possible, they had better be buried in silence.... Yes, Adeimantus, they are stories not to be repeated in our State; the young man should not be told that in committing the worst of crimes he is far from doing anything outrageous; and that even if he chastises his father when he does wrong, in whatever manner, he will only be following the example of the first and greatest among the gods. (378a-b)*

Even should the story be true, some truths are better left not communicated—especially to the young who are so easily influenced. We must admit that this view is not so outrageous or ancient. After all, many people today are concerned about the effect that violent video games or violent (or sexually explicit) lyrics in music has on children. Is it so outlandish to suspect that if a young person continuously listens to music that glorifies the "gangster" lifestyle that he or she might be influenced to emulate it?

Of course, if young people are so impressionable, they are bound to be "impressed" by *something*. This is why the ideal State in the *Republic* doesn't merely ban certain stories, but will actively promote others. Such stories should inspire courage and remove fear of death (386b), remove the "horror of Hades" (387d), remove embarrassing stories of eminent men (387d, 389a, 389e), encourage discipline (390d), and discourage mercenary or greedy natures (390e). In addition, in order to promote a deep sense of community, Plato has Socrates offer the "*noble lie.*"

A lie? But hasn't Socrates criticized the poets for lying? Yes, but the State is a special case.

> *Then if any one at all is to have the privilege of lying, the rulers of the State should be the persons; and they, in their dealings either with enemies or with their own citizens, may be allowed to lie for the public good (389c).*

What sort of lie does Socrates have in mind? One that will attempt (at least over time) to erase personal ambitions and replace them with a sense of solidarity and common purpose, and one which will reinforce the rigid class structure of the Republic.

> *How then may we devise one of those needful falsehoods of which we lately spoke—just one royal lie which may deceive the rulers, if that be possible, and at any rate the rest of the city?...*
>
> *Speak, he said, and fear not.*
>
> *Well then, I will speak, although I really know not how to look you in the face, or in what words to utter the audacious fiction, which I propose to communicate gradually, first to the rulers, then to the soldiers, and lastly to the people. They are to be told that their youth was a dream, and the education and training which they received from us, an appearance only; in reality during all that time they were being formed and fed in the womb of the earth, where they themselves and their arms and appurtenances were manufactured; when they were completed, the earth, their mother, sent them up; and so, their country being their mother and also their nurse, they are bound to advise for her good, and to defend her against attacks, and her citizens they are to regard as children of the earth and their own brothers.*
>
> *You had good reason, he said, to be ashamed of the lie which you were going to tell.*
>
> *True, I replied, but there is more coming; I have only told you half. Citizens, we shall say to them in our tale, you are brothers, yet God has framed you differently. Some of you have the power of command, and in the composition of these he has mingled gold, wherefore also they have the*

*greatest honour; others he has made of silver, to be auxiliaries; others again who are to be husbandmen and craftsmen he has composed of brass and iron; and the species will generally be preserved in the children. But as all are of the same original stock, a golden parent will sometimes have a silver son, or a silver parent a golden son. And God proclaims as a first principle to the rulers, and above all else, that there is nothing which they should so anxiously guard, or of which they are to be such good guardians, as of the purity of the race. They should observe what elements mingle in their offspring; for if the son of a golden or silver parent has an admixture of brass and iron, then nature orders a transposition of ranks, and the eye of the ruler must not be pitiful towards the child because he has to descend in the scale and become a husbandman or artisan, just as there may be sons of artisans who having an admixture of gold or silver in them are raised to honour, and become guardians or auxiliaries. For an oracle says that when a man of brass or iron guards the State, it will be destroyed. Such is the tale; is there any possibility of making our citizens believe in it?*

*Not in the present generation, he replied; there is no way of accomplishing this; but their sons may be made to believe in the tale, and their sons' sons, and posterity after them.*

*I see the difficulty, I replied; yet the fostering of such a belief will make them care more for the city and for one another. (414c-415d)*

While Socrates acknowledges the practical difficulty of getting the present generation to accept such a fantastic story, later generations will simply grow up hearing it as the true origin of their community—and all of this serves the greater good of their community.

Remember: a key principle motivating this entire discussion is the "principle of specialization," according to which persons are best-suited for certain roles in the community, and the community is best served by people knowing and fulfilling their respective roles. This theme is reinforced continuously in the *Republic* (370a-c, 374a, 375a, 406c, 421c, 423d, 433a).

If the goal is to produce the ideal State, and to organize it for the good of the community, then it's obvious that the issue of who should run this State will be very important. Perhaps not surprisingly, Socrates claims that only philosophers are qualified for this task.

*Unless communities have philosophers as kings, or the people who are currently called kings and rulers practice philosophy with enough integrity, . . . there can be no end to political troubles. (473d)*

What is so special about philosophers that would make them suitable Guardians? *Socrates claims that only philosophers have knowledge, while everyone else makes do with mere belief.* Moreover, he argues that only philosophers will be capable of being virtuous and expert rulers. First, he claims that philosophers love every kind of learning (474c-475c), and that no one else does (475c-480a). Then, he claims that the love of *every* kind of learning produces knowledge of ethical matters, and therefore virtue (485a-486e). Therefore, the love of every kind of learning makes one a virtuous and expert ruler. Accordingly, one is a virtuous and expert ruler if and only if one is a philosopher.

Among their many other excellent qualities, philosophers have a passion for wisdom. This reduces other passions (485d-e), and produces courage (486b) and temperance (485e). Still, Socrates has to admit that this is not the common view of philosophers. Indeed, they are often scorned and rejected by the public.[49]

> For any one of us might say, that although in words he is not able to meet you at each step of the argument, he sees as a fact that the votaries of philosophy, when they carry on the study, not only in youth as a part of education, but as the pursuit of their maturer years, most of them become strange monsters, not to say utter rogues, and that those who may be considered the best of them are made useless to the world by the very study which you extol. (487c-d)

In other words, philosophers have the reputation of being weird and useless—or worse! In defense of philosophers, Socrates argues by way of analogy.

> I perceive, I said, that you are vastly amused at having plunged me into such a hopeless discussion; but now hear the parable, and then you will be still more amused at the meagreness of my imagination: for the manner in which the best men are treated in their own States is so grievous that no single thing on earth is comparable to it; and therefore, if I am to plead their cause, I must have recourse to fiction, and put together a figure made up of many things, like the fabulous unions of goats and stags which are found in pictures. Imagine then a fleet or a ship in which there is a captain who is taller and stronger than any of the crew, but he is a little deaf and has a similar infirmity in sight, and his knowledge of navigation is not much better. The sailors are quarrelling with one another about the steering—every one is of opinion that he has a right to steer, though he has never learned the art of navigation and cannot tell who taught him or when he learned, and will further assert that it cannot be taught, and they are ready to cut in pieces any one who says the contrary. They throng about the captain, begging and praying him to commit the helm to them; and if at any time they do not prevail, but others are preferred to them, they kill the others or throw them overboard, and having first chained up the noble captain's senses with drink or some narcotic drug, they mutiny and take possession of the ship and make free with the stores; thus, eating and drinking, they proceed on their voyage in such manner as might be expected of them. Him who is their partisan and cleverly aids them in their

---

[49] It's hard not to think of Socrates' own trial and execution at this point.

*plot for getting the ship out of the captain's hands into their own whether by force or persuasion, they compliment with the name of sailor, pilot, able seaman, and abuse the other sort of man, whom they call a good-for-nothing; but that the true pilot must pay attention to the year and seasons and sky and stars and winds, and whatever else belongs to his art, if he intends to be really qualified for the command of a ship, and that he must and will be the steerer, whether other people like or not—the possibility of this union of authority with the steerer's art has never seriously entered into their thoughts or been made part of their calling. Now in vessels which are in a state of mutiny and by sailors who are mutineers, how will the true pilot be regarded? Will he not be called by them a prater, a star-gazer, a good-for-nothing?*

*Of course, said Adeimantus.*

*Then you will hardly need, I said, to hear the interpretation of the figure, which describes the true philosopher in his relation to the State; for you understand already. (488a-489b)*

In a corrupt community, amidst corrupt and blinded people, a truly wise person who be perceived as and treated as a fool. At this point, one might think Socrates is merely engaging in some special pleading, or even some sort of *ad hominem* attack. Philosophers are poorly regarded because everyone else is a fool? To shore up his position, Socrates needs to demonstrate that philosophers, as philosophers, really are people who have knowledge, and that not everyone is equally qualified with regard to knowledge, or rulership.

Among other things, this is going to require a rejection of epistemic relativism. If "all truth is relative," as many of the Sophists claimed, then it would appear to be the case that no one person is any more qualified with regard to knowledge than is anyone else. All perspectives are equal. Socrates dismisses this view, however, as absurd on its surface. In another Platonic dialogue (*Theaetetus*), Socrates considers the relativism of the Sophist, Protagoras.

*Protagoras, for his part, admitting as he does that everybody's opinion is true, must acknowledge the truth of his opponent's belief about his own belief, where they think he is wrong. . . . That is to say, he would acknowledge his own belief to be false, if he admits that the belief of those who think him wrong is true. (171a-b)*

*There is something seemingly self-refuting, or internally inconsistent, with epistemic relativism. Since all opinions are equally true, it is simultaneously and equally true that epistemic relativism is, itself, both true and false.* Beyond this conceptual puzzle, Socrates points out that we do not, in fact, regard all opinions as equally true. If you are not a medical doctor and you think you are healthy, but a medical doctor tells you that you have cancer, do you really regard your respective opinions as equally true? Don't we recognize legitimate expertise in a great many areas of inquiry? If our subject is Plato's philosophy, do we really believe that each person's position is equally true regarding that philosophical system? The opinions of the physicist who has specialized in string theory and the opinion of the philosopher who has specialized in Plato are equally true with regard to Plato? I think a tiger looks friendly, but a trained animal handler warns me that the tiger is about to rip my face off. Equally true opinions? Presumably not. If we acknowledge that different people have different degrees of expertise with regard to different skills, then it would stand to reason that not all people are equally equipped to rule a community (i.e., be a Guardian), and that not all people are even equally equipped to discuss and identify knowledge itself. If "philosophers" are those best equipped to perceive the Truth of things, then it is they who should lead rather than some popularly elected politician. *Truth* is not up to a majority vote!

This relativism is even more egregious when the issue at stake is morality itself. Socrates seizes the opportunity to take another shot at his Sophist rivals.

> *Why, that all those mercenary individuals, whom the many call Sophists and whom they deem to be their adversaries, do, in fact, teach nothing but the opinion of the many, that is to say, the opinions of their assemblies; and this is their wisdom. I might compare them to a man who should study the tempers and desires of a mighty strong beast who is fed by him—he would learn how to approach and handle him, also at what times and from what causes he is dangerous or the reverse, and what is the meaning of his several cries, and by what sounds, when another utters them, he is soothed or infuriated; and you may suppose further, that when, by continually attending upon him, he has become perfect in all this, he calls his knowledge wisdom, and makes of it a system or art, which he proceeds to teach, although he has no real notion of what he means by the principles or passions of which he is speaking, but calls this honourable and that dishonourable, or good or evil, or just or unjust, all in accordance with the tastes and tempers of the great brute. Good he pronounces to be that in which the beast delights and evil to be that which he dislikes; and he can give no other account of them except that the just and noble are the necessary, having never himself seen, and having no power of explaining to others the nature of either, or the difference between them, which is immense. (493a-c)*

These intellectual mercenaries know nothing of good or evil, justice or injustice. Instead, they merely observe what actually happens in the world, what people like and dislike, and proclaim those things to be good or bad, just or unjust. They perceive cultural and individual differences in practices and values, and conclude something like moral subjectivism or cultural relativism. Socrates, however, disagrees with the strategy of identifying what is just or unjust with the events of this constantly changing world—and this is a problem not merely with respect to moral knowledge.

One of the problems with recognizing "The Truth" (aside from lack of training and qualification) is that the world we experience is constantly in flux, and insufficiently stable so as to provide for knowledge. Plato, ultimately, rejects sense experience as a means of knowledge, because the senses show us only the world of change, and our perceptions are relative to the perceiver. For example, consider hot coffee. Whether or not it is hot depends not only on when the measurement is taken, but also on who is making the determination. My former father-in-law would literally heat his coffee in the microwave until it boiled. Only then did he consider it sufficiently hot. I, on the other hand, consider that to be an example of coffee that is scalding, rather than "hot." Which one of us is right, and when would we have been right?

It might sound like we're backsliding into epistemic relativism again, or into skepticism. Plato does not intend that outcome, though. Knowledge, he claims, is objective, universal, unchanging, grounded in Reason, and is ultimately unavailable to the senses. *Knowledge will not pertain to the particular, constantly changing "things" we experience in the world of the senses, but instead to unchanging universal concepts that inform our understanding of particular things in the first place.* What we are now delving into is Plato's theory of the Forms.

## The Forms

We encounter all kinds of circles in daily life. There is a mirror on my desk that I'm looking at right now. It's in the shape of a circle. The lid of my coffee cup is a circle. Doughnuts are circles, as are tires, as are wedding rings. What each one of these particular objects has in common (among other things) is that they are circular. We have a concept, an ideal, of a circle, and because each of these objects matches up (to an extent) with that concept, we recognize them as circular. None of those objects is itself a perfect circle, but each one approximates a circle—or else we never would have described it as circular.

This notion is clear from Socrates basic line of inquiry in most of the dialogues. He always seems to seek the "universal" behind the "particular." Consider, for example, his famous investigation of piety in *Euthyphro*.

*And what is piety, and what is impiety?*

*Piety is doing as I am doing; that is to say, prosecuting any one who is guilty of murder, sacrilege, or of any similar crime-whether he be your father or mother, or whoever he may be-that makes no difference; and not to prosecute them is impiety....*

*I dare say; and you shall tell me them at some other time when I have leisure. But just at present I would rather hear from you a more precise answer, which you have not as yet given, my friend, to the question, What is "piety"? When asked, you only replied, Doing as you do, charging your father with murder.*

*And what I said was true, Socrates.*

*No doubt, Euthyphro; but you would admit that there are many other pious acts?*

*There are.*

*Remember that I did not ask you to give me two or three examples of piety, but to explain the general idea which makes all pious things to be pious. Do you not recollect that there was one idea which made the impious impious, and the pious pious?*

*I remember.*

*Tell me what is the nature of this idea, and then I shall have a standard to which I may look, and by which I may measure actions, whether yours or those of any one else, and then I shall be able to say that such and such an action is pious, such another impious.*[50]

Socrates is assuming that there is some property of "piety" that manifests in any number of acts. It is not identical to any particular of those acts, but those acts simply are "pious" to the extent that they exemplify that quality of piety. An individual act may be pious, or impious depending on circumstances. I might be pious one moment, but impious the next. Piety itself, however, is unchanging.

*Plato suggests that our concepts*, not only of piety or circles, but of all sorts of other things: human, chair, Christmas tree, greeting card, television set, onion ring, etc., *are "universals" that are exemplified (to varying degrees) by particular things* (e.g., actual onion rings, or chairs). He refers to these ideals, these concepts, as "Forms."

According to this theory, there is a Form of a chair. This is what allows us to recognize objects as chairs. Particular objects are related to their Forms in a variety of ways. Particular things (e.g., the chair I am sitting on at this moment) resemble the Form of a chair (otherwise I'd call it something else!). In a very abstract sort of way Plato claims that Forms cause particulars in the sort of way that a statue causes its shadow. Particulars "participate" in their Forms to varying degrees, and this is the means by which we evaluate them. For example, at dog shows various particular dogs are judged by how well they exemplify their breed. Those that "participate" very well in their breed would be regarded as excellent examples of that breed, whereas a "mutt" wouldn't "participate" well at all. Finally, Forms are what make particulars

---

[50] Plato, *Euthyphro.*

intelligible to us at all. In that Forms are concepts, they are make thought and speech possible. Try to describe an object (e.g., a chair, a doughnut, a human being, etc.) without appealing to concepts. What could you possibly say? The thing I am sitting on is a chair. Oops. I'm not allowed to say chair. OK, it's a piece of furniture. Oops. I can't appeal to "furniture." It's underneath me. Oops. "Underneath" is a concept too. It's supportive. Oops. Gray. Oops. Etc.

At this point, we could simply understand Forms as concepts, and not have anything too controversial on our hands—but Plato does not avoid controversy. Plato doesn't merely claim that the Forms are concepts, in the sense of universal ideas; he argues that they exist, independently of our thoughts, in another realm of existence distinct from the physical world. The physical world is the one we encounter by sense experience. It is constantly changing, and doesn't permit knowledge to be acquired. This is where Plato honors Heraclitus (remember him?). The intelligible world, on the other hand, is non-physical, eternal, unchanging, and intelligible to Reason. This is where Plato honors Parmenides (remember him?). Parmenides and Heraclitus represented two opposite camps, one of which claiming that everything is in flux and the other claiming that there is no change at all. Plato thinks they were both on to something, but also both incorrect. Heraclitus was right about the physical world of sense experience. Parmenides was right about the mental world of the Forms. The correct view is the one that combines both into a single vision of a dualistic reality.

## Great Minds Think Alike?

Mozi flourished in the fifth century BCE, roughly around the same time as Socrates. He and his followers are credited, even more so than Confucius, with initiating philosophical argumentation and debate in China. They developed an explicit consequentialist ethical theory, as well as theories of language and knowledge.

A central task of Mohism was to establish objective standards for judgment, especially moral judgment. The standard to which they would ultimately appeal was the "benefit" (li) of "all under heaven." Here we can clearly see a consequentialist approach very similar to utilitarianism.

*The task of the benevolent is surely to diligently seek to promote the benefit of the world and eliminate harm to the world and to take this as a model (fa) throughout the world. Does it benefit people? Then do it. Does it not benefit people? Then stop.[51]*

To justify this standard, they appealed to the will/intention of "Heaven" (Tian). On the assumption that Heaven is the wisest judge, the judgments of Heaven will provide a reliable criterion for moral judgments.

---

[51] Mozi, Book 32, "Condemning Music."

A central goal for the Mohists was moral and political order – something they believed would benefit "everyone under heaven." This order is achieved by establishing our objective moral standards which will promote unity and agreement (and eliminate confusion and conflict). The Confucian standard which represented the primary rival at the time, was li (ritual) established by the traditional culture. The Mohists acknowledgeD the existence of multiple perspectives with respect to cultural values, at roughly the same time Herodotus was doing the same in Greece, to demonstrate the ineffectiveness of this appeal to ritual.

*This is what's called deeming their habits convenient and their customs righteous. In the past, east of Yue there was the country of Gai Shu. When their eldest son was born, they chopped them up and ate him, calling this "advantageous to the younger brothers." When their grandfather died, they carried off their grandmother and abandoned her, saying, "one cannot live with the wife of a ghost." These practices superiors took as government policy and subordinates took us custom, performing them without ceasing and maintain them without choosing something else. Yet how could these really be the Way of benevolence and righteousness?![52]*

In other words, the mere fact that a community has been practicing a ritual/custom should not be taken to mean that that practice is correct. Instead, the Mohists will seek objective standards that transcend individual cultures and rituals, in the form of what they call "*fa*" (models, or standards).

*Those in the world who perform task cannot do without models (fa) and standards. There is no one who can accomplish their task without models and standards. Even officers serving as generals or ministers, they all have models; even the hundred artist inns performing the tasks, they to all have models. The hundred artisans make squares with a set square, circles for the compass, straight lines with a string, vertical lines with the plumb line, and flat services with the level. Whether skilled artisans or unskilled artisans, all take these five is models. The Skilled are able to conform to them. The unskilled, though unable to conform to them, by following them in performing their tasks still surpass what they can do by themselves. Thus the hundred artisans in performing their tasks all have models to measure by. Now for the greatest to order the world in those the next level down to order great states without models to measure by, this is to be less discriminating than the hundred artisans.[53]*

---

[52] Ibid., Book 25, "Moderation in Burial."
[53] Ibid., Book 4, "Models and Standards."

Clearly, Fa represent objective standards. Much as a straight line is determined to be straight by appealing to a ruler, and a surface flat by appealing to a level, judgments can be determined to be correct by appealing to the appropriate models/standards. What will provide these models/standards? The best, wisest, and most reliable source possible: Heaven (Tian-- thought to be a quasi-personal god).

> *That being so, then what is acceptable to take is a model for order? So I say, nothing is like modeling on Heaven. Heaven's conduct is broad and partial; its favors are rich and incur no debt; its brightness endures without fading. So the sage-kings modeled themselves on it.*[54]

Fa represent a fascinating philosophical concept, as they provide both practical guidelines as well as criteria for both judgment and action. They provide not only guidance to behavior, but also the very standard of correctness by which to measure both our actions and our judgments.

"Fa" is very wide ranging in meaning, including basically *any* criterion or paradigm that helps us to make correct judgments. This includes not just the standard of Heaven, but the (correct) examples of political rulers, parents, tools (such as a ruler), analogies, etc.

With respect to moral decision-making, the function of these models/standards is fairly clear. With respect to providing criteria for judgment in general, however, the concept is a bit more complex. The Mohists appeared to have understood judgment (of all kinds) as a process of distinguishing relevantly similar kinds of things from dissimilar things, reliably distinguishing "this" (shi) from "not"(fei).

> *Thus our Master Mozi's having Heaven's intent, to give an analogy, is no different from the wheelwright's having a compass or the carpenter's having a set square. Now the wheelwright grasps his compass and uses it to measure the round not round in the world, saying, "what conforms to my compass, call it "round," what doesn't conform to my compass, call it "not round.""" Hence round and not round can both be known. What is the reason for this? It's that the fa for "round" is clear.*[55]

The Mohists understand knowledge as the ability to reliably make these sorts of proper distinctions. Not quite a "correspondence theory," instead they offer what is known today as a "reliabilist" account of knowledge.[56] With

---

[54] Ibid.

[55] Ibid., Book 27, "Heaven's Intent."

[56] As a contemporary example, Robert Nozick (1981) proposed what he called a

respect to justifying one's judgments, this also is understood in terms of fa – specifically the ability to cite a suitable fa when making a distinction/judgment.

Because of their emphasis on the actual (reliable) ability to make distinctions, the Mohist theory of knowledge is practical, more so than theoretical or representational. To know something is not a matter of having some sort of concept in one's mind that corresponds to reality, but is rather a stable disposition to correctly distinguish certain kinds of things from other things.

*Our Master Mozi said, "Now the blind say, 'What's bright is white, and what's dark is black.' Even the clear-sighted have no grounds for changing this. But collect white and black things together and make the blind select from among them, and they cannot know. So as to my saying the blind don't know white and black, it's not by their naming, it's by their selecting.*[57]

This is an interesting example. From a certain (correspondence) perspective, a blind person's claim that what is dark is black "corresponds to reality," and is therefore a true statement that might technically count as knowledge. However, a genuinely blind person, despite correctly understanding the concepts/meanings of dark and black, cannot reliably distinguish things that are dark from things that are not, and things that are black, from things that are not. Therefore, they don't actually *know* that what is dark is black.

Note how different this is from Plato's "semantic" approach to knowledge. Again and again throughout various dialogues, we see Socrates interrogating people to see if they have a correct and consistent definition of a key concept. "Knowing" a concept amounted to perceiving its "essence" (Form) and being able to articulate that essence.

In contrast to this, the Mohists don't ask for definitions, descriptions, or the essence of the term in question. They focused on the ability to reliably distinguish a thing from something that is not that thing. This can be facilitated by finding appropriate models and then teaching everyone to apply them.

It's plausible that someone could correctly distinguish in this sort of way, without "understanding" in the way we might normally think of that word. Children, for example, can correctly recognize straight lines with the help of the ruler, without being able to articulate just what a "straight" line is.

---

"tracking" theory. In addition to truth and belief, Nozick's conditions for knowledge were: (1) if P were not true then S would not believe that P, and (2) if P were true, S would believe that P.

[57] Mozi, Book 47, "Valuing Duty."

Similarly, someone might be able to correctly and reliably distinguish righteousness (yi) from unrighteousness without any sort of sophisticated understanding of "righteousness" itself – so long as they have been provided an effective standard (fa).

It's important to recognize the work that "reliable" does here. A lucky guess will not count for the Mohists any more than it would count for someone subscribing to Plato's definition of knowledge as "justified true belief."[58]

> *Now suppose there is a person here, who, seeing a little black, says "Black," but seeing much black, says "White." Then surely we'd take this person to not know the distinction between white and black. Tasting a little of something bitter, he says "Bitter," but tasting much of something bitter, he says, "Sweet." Then surely we'd take this person to not know the distinction between sweet and bitter.59*

The error being exhibited in this example is understood not as a lack of correspondence between the person's belief and reality, but rather as a lack of skill. Someone who successfully bakes one cake out of 100 would not be regarded as a skilled baker, and someone who only rarely, in practice, makes correct distinctions (such as between things that are bitter and things that are sweet) should not be regarded as someone who "knows" bitterness and sweetness.

Mohists offer three fa by which "the distinctions between "this" and "not" and benefit and harm... Can be clearly known."60 Statements must have a:

1.   root: historical precedent provided by moral exemplars who reliably distinguished in the past.
2.   source: empirical basis capable of being checked against what people can see and hear.
3.   use: demonstration of benefit (li).[61]

This appeal to and use of fa extends to the Mohists' understanding of logic as well. Their model of reasoning involves citing one or more fa by which to distinguish "this" from "not" (including moral judgments that would conclude that something is righteous (yi) or not righteous), then indicating how a particular example either does or does not conform to the fa, and then finally

---

[58]Technically, "true belief with an account."

[59] Mozi, Book 17, "Condemning Aggression."

[60] Ibid., Book 35, "Condemning Fatalism."

[61] Arguably, the third fa holds priority, given the Mohists' multiple appeal to benefit throughout their writings, and the fact that they do not endorse any sort of unthinking appeal to authority.

concluding that the example therefore is either "this" or "not."

If we compare this to the standard form of a syllogism in ancient Greece, with a major premise, minor premise, and a conclusion, then the citing of a fa would correspond to the major premise, the application of the example to the fa would be the minor premise, and the conclusion be the distinguishing of the example as either "this" or "not."

What does any of this have to do with philosophers, and their being the only people who have knowledge? We're getting there! Consider yet another of Plato's allegories—perhaps his most famous: the *allegory of the cave*. It is worth quoting at length.

> *And now, I said, let me show in a figure how far our nature is enlightened or unenlightened:—Behold! human beings living in a underground den, which has a mouth open towards the light and reaching all along the den; here they have been from their childhood, and have their legs and necks chained so that they cannot move, and can only see before them, being prevented by the chains from turning round their heads. Above and behind them a fire is blazing at a distance, and between the fire and the prisoners there is a raised way; and you will see, if you look, a low wall built along the way, like the screen which marionette players have in front of them, over which they show the puppets.*

> *I see.*

> *And do you see, I said, men passing along the wall carrying all sorts of vessels, and statues and figures of animals made of wood and stone and various materials, which appear over the wall? Some of them are talking, others silent.*

> *You have shown me a strange image, and they are strange prisoners.*

> *Like ourselves, I replied; and they see only their own shadows, or the shadows of one another, which the fire throws on the opposite wall of the cave?*

> *True, he said; how could they see anything but the shadows if they were never allowed to move their heads?*

> *And of the objects which are being carried in like manner they would only see the shadows?*

> *Yes, he said.*

*And if they were able to converse with one another, would they not suppose that they were naming what was actually before them?*

*Very true.*

*And suppose further that the prison had an echo which came from the other side, would they not be sure to fancy when one of the passers-by spoke that the voice which they heard came from the passing shadow?*

*No question, he replied.*

*To them, I said, the truth would be literally nothing but the shadows of the images.*

*That is certain.*

*And now look again, and see what will naturally follow if the prisoners are released and disabused of their error. At first, when any of them is liberated and compelled suddenly to stand up and turn his neck round and walk and look towards the light, he will suffer sharp pains; the glare will distress him, and he will be unable to see the realities of which in his former state he had seen the shadows; and then conceive some one saying to him, that what he saw before was an illusion, but that now, when he is approaching nearer to being and his eye is turned towards more real existence, he has a clearer vision,—what will be his reply? And you may further imagine that his instructor is pointing to the objects as they pass and requiring him to name them,—will he not be perplexed? Will he not fancy that the shadows which he formerly saw are truer than the objects which are now shown to him?*

*Far truer.*

*And if he is compelled to look straight at the light, will he not have a pain in his eyes which will make him turn away to take refuge in the objects of vision which he can see, and which he will conceive to be in reality clearer than the things which are now being shown to him?*

*True, he said.*

*And suppose once more, that he is reluctantly dragged up a steep and rugged ascent, and held fast until he is forced into the presence of the sun himself, is he not likely to be pained and irritated? When he approaches the light his eyes will be dazzled, and he will not be able to see anything at all of what are now called realities.*

*Not all in a moment, he said.*

*He will require to grow accustomed to the sight of the upper world. And first he will see the shadows best, next the reflections of men and other objects in the water, and then the objects themselves; then he will gaze upon the light of the moon and the stars and the spangled heaven; and he will see the sky and the stars by night better than the sun or the light of the sun by day?*

*Certainly.*

*Last of all he will be able to see the sun, and not mere reflections of him in the water, but he will see him in his own proper place, and not in another; and he will contemplate him as he is.*

*Certainly.*

*He will then proceed to argue that this is he who gives the season and the years, and is the guardian of all that is in the visible world, and in a certain way the cause of all things which he and his fellows have been accustomed to behold?*

*Clearly, he said, he would first see the sun and then reason about him. And when he remembered his old habitation, and the wisdom of the den and his fellow-prisoners, do you not suppose that he would felicitate himself on the change, and pity them?*

*Certainly, he would.*

*And if they were in the habit of conferring honours among themselves on those who were quickest to observe the passing shadows and to remark which of them went before, and which followed after, and which were together; and who were therefore best able to draw conclusions as to the future, do you think that he would care for such honours and glories, or envy the possessors of them? Would he not say with Homer,*

*'Better to be the poor servant of a poor master,'*

*and to endure anything, rather than think as they do and live after their manner?*

*Yes, he said, I think that he would rather suffer anything than entertain these false notions and live in this miserable manner.*

*Imagine once more, I said, such an one coming suddenly out of the sun to be replaced in his old situation; would he not be certain to have his eyes full of darkness?*

*To be sure, he said.*

*And if there were a contest, and he had to compete in measuring the shadows with the prisoners who had never moved out of the den, while his sight was still weak, and before his eyes had become steady (and the time which would be needed to acquire this new habit of sight might be very considerable), would he not be ridiculous? Men would say of him that up he went and down he came without his eyes; and that it was better not even to think of ascending; and if any one tried to loose another and lead him up to the light, let them only catch the offender, and they would put him to death. (514a-517a)*

It is impossible not to recall the trial and death of Socrates yet again. This allegory attempts to depict the plight of humanity. The vast majority of us are the prisoners in the cave. What we think is knowledge is just the shadowy reflections of copies of real things, symbolic of the mere opinions taught to us by those in positions of power and influence. The objects from which the shadows are cast are themselves still only copies of the real objects as they exist outside the cave. The shadows we see, then, are just copies of copies, at least two steps removed from truth. Those who parade these objects and cast the shadows before us are symbolic of illegitimate rulers. The philosopher is the prisoner who manages to break free, who ascends from the cave to behold things are they really are (i.e., who perceives the "Forms," and, who thereby alone has knowledge). Finally, the sun which illuminates those objects is the Form of the Good itself (to be discussed later). Not surprisingly, if the philosopher returns to the cave to explain things to the rest of the prisoners, he's going to sound "crazy," and will be persecuted— just as Socrates was. Also notice that the philosopher doesn't bring light to the cave, but tries to bring prisoners upward into the light.

Compelling as this allegory might be, we still don't have an explanation (beyond metaphor) as to why the philosopher really does have knowledge while the rest of us have mere opinion. This brings us back to the Forms. *Only the Forms provide knowledge.* Particulars are those imperfect, temporary, changing copies of the Forms that we experience in the sensory world. In the allegory of the cave, particulars are represented by the shadows cast on the walls. The Forms are represented by the original, "real" objects found on the surface. Only the philosopher gets past the shadows to the real thing, only the philosopher gets a glimpse of the forms (by means of Reason, not sight, of course). Therefore, only the philosopher can acquire knowledge.

Another way to represent this is by means of his *"Divided Line"* (also worth quoting at length).

*You have to imagine, then, that there are two ruling powers, and that one of them is set over the intellectual world, the other over the visible. I do not say heaven, lest you should fancy that I am playing upon the name ('ourhanoz, orhatoz'). May I suppose that you have this distinction of the visible and intelligible fixed in your mind?*

*I have.*

*Now take a line which has been cut into two unequal parts, and divide each of them again in the same proportion, and suppose the two main divisions to answer, one to the visible and the other to the intelligible, and then compare the subdivisions in respect of their clearness and want of clearness, and you will find that the first section in the sphere of the visible consists of images. And by images I mean, in the first place, shadows, and in the second place, reflections in water and in solid, smooth and polished bodies and the like: Do you understand?*

*Yes, I understand.*

*Imagine, now, the other section, of which this is only the resemblance, to include the animals which we see, and everything that grows or is made. Very good.*

*Would you not admit that both the sections of this division have different degrees of truth, and that the copy is to the original as the sphere of opinion is to the sphere of knowledge?*

*Most undoubtedly.*

*Next proceed to consider the manner in which the sphere of the intellectual is to be divided.*

*In what manner?*

*Thus:—There are two subdivisions, in the lower of which the soul uses the figures given by the former division as images; the enquiry can only be hypothetical, and instead of going upwards to a principle descends to the other end; in the higher of the two, the soul passes out of hypotheses, and goes up to a principle which is above hypotheses, making no use of images as in the former case, but proceeding only in and through the ideas themselves.*

*I do not quite understand your meaning, he said.*

*Then I will try again; you will understand me better when I have made some preliminary remarks. You are aware that students of geometry, arithmetic, and the kindred sciences assume the odd and the even and the figures and three kinds of angles and the like in their several branches of science; these are their hypotheses, which they and every body are supposed to know, and therefore they do not deign to give any account of them either to themselves or others; but they begin with them, and go on until they arrive at last, and in a consistent manner, at their conclusion?*

*Yes, he said, I know.*

*And do you not know also that although they make use of the visible forms and reason about them, they are thinking not of these, but of the ideals which they resemble; not of the figures which they draw, but of the absolute square and the absolute diameter, and so on—the forms which they draw or make, and which have shadows and reflections in water of their own, are converted by them into images, but they are really seeking to behold the things themselves, which can only be seen with the eye of the mind?*

*That is true.*

*And of this kind I spoke as the intelligible, although in the search after it the soul is compelled to use hypotheses; not ascending to a first principle, because she is unable to rise above the region of hypothesis, but employing the objects of which the shadows below are resemblances in their turn as images, they having in relation to the shadows and reflections of them a greater distinctness, and therefore a higher value. (509d-511a)*

### The Divided Line

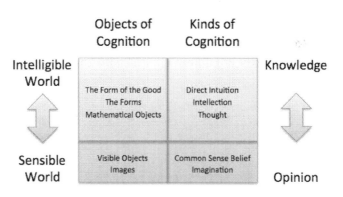

On the left side of the line, we are dealing with metaphysics, the nature of reality. The "higher" up one goes, the more "real" something is. On the right side of the line, we are dealing with epistemology. The higher up one goes, the closer one is to knowledge. The upper portion of the figure represents the intelligible world (the world of the Forms), while the lower portion represents the physical world (the world of the senses). Starting with the metaphysical side, at the very bottom we have mere images. These would include shadows, reflections, dreams, mirages, etc. They have some "reality," but are faint copies of other, more real, things. Above images, but still part of the physical world, we have all visible things—the objects we encounter by means of our senses. A statue is "more real" than its shadow, in this sense.

As we continue to ascend, we go beyond the physical world and enter the world of ideas, the Forms. We encounter mathematical objects, which are not physical, but are "real," and that provide the structure and reality to their physical counterparts. Above mathematical objects are the Forms themselves, our concepts of all the things we encounter in the physical world. *At the very peak of reality is the Form of the Good itself, that which gives reality and understanding to everything "beneath" it.*

On the right side of the line, we are dealing with epistemology, the nature of belief and knowledge. At the very bottom we have imagining, conjecture, and general ignorance. Above mere conjecture we have common sense beliefs, beliefs for which we are confident and that must even be true. As we continue to ascend we go beyond the world of the senses and enter the intelligible realm. We encounter abstract reasoning, and then finally reach direct intuition (pure "perception") of the Forms. Knowledge.

The ascent up the divided line mirrors the ascent out of the cave. In each case, the "higher" one goes, the more "real" are the things one encounters, and the closer one gets to knowledge. The philosopher is the one who has managed to climb out of the cave, who has moved beyond mere appearances and "common sense" and glimpsed the Forms, including the Form of the Good itself.

The Form of the Good is, well, a bit weird. The Form of the Good is represented by the Sun (507c-509b). The Sun is what the philosopher sees when he has emerged from the cave. It illuminates all the other objects (Forms), and is "higher" than them. Just what the Form of the Good *is* though is probably not altogether clear. Using our everyday sense of "good" in a moral context, it might be confused with other forms, such as justice, or piety, or generosity. But, if all such traits have their own Forms, what is left over for the Form of the Good itself?

A Form is the universal that gives unity to particulars. "Piety," for example, is the property which all pious acts or persons share in. The Form of piety is the absolute best with regards to piousness, because it is the yardstick against which all pious acts are measured, and that which gives meaning to piety in the first place. Procedurally, we observe many things that we call pious, and then we identify their common feature in order to intuit the Form of piety itself. With regard to the Forms, we observe many things (Form of piety, Form of circularity, etc.) that we call Forms. They appear to have something in common—namely, their "Form-ness." *The Form of the Good is, for lack of a better expression, the Form of Form-ness itself.* But, because Forms are the "best" of whatever they represent, the Form of Form-ness is the property of being best—the Form of "The Good."

This is, admittedly, an unusual use of the term "good." Later thinkers, such as Plotinus, would make the Form of the Good into a divine principle, and Christian theologians (such as St. Augustine) would claim that what Plato calls the Form of the Good is actually God. Plato himself, though, had no such anthropomorphic vision in mind. The Form of the Good is not a person, but an abstract entity—the Form of Form-ness (best-ness, Good-ness) itself.

Those who "see" the Form of the Good are those who have attained the highest level of philosophical abstraction. If it's impressive to ascend from the "shadows" or mere imaginings and opinion to knowledge of things are they really are (Forms), how much more impressive to have ascended higher still (the highest, in fact), to understand the Form that informs all the other Forms? Philosophers have glimpsed the "highest" degrees of both reality and knowledge, at this point—but it's no wonder that when they return to the cave to tell the rest of the prisoners about it, they're regarded as crazy. . . .

"Craziness" aside, imagine that the Republic (or a close approximation) to it, could be founded. Plato imagines and explains how such a State could decline through various inferior forms of government, and in so doing possibly provides clues as to how to prevent such a decline.

The ideal Republic is a sort of aristocratic meritocracy in which an elite, superior, wise, and virtuous few rule for the sake of the common good, and maintain social harmony. To continue with the state-individual analogy, a corresponding individual is one who is ruled by reason, and whose inner life is harmonious and well-regulated, much as the life of the Republic is disciplined and well-regulated, with each class following the principle of specialization.

Should the principle of specialization not be followed, however, there will be widespread societal ramifications.

| Society | Mental Trait | Reason for Decline |
|---|---|---|
| Aristocratic Meritocracy | "regal," reason, moral, harmonious | Conflict, envy, loss of PS (547b-548b) |
| Timocracy | "timarchic," competitive, passionate | Greed, wealth (550d-551b) |
| Oligarchy/ Plutocracy | "oligarchic," thrifty, ascetic | Corruption, envious revolution (555c-557a) |
| Democracy | "democratic," ruled by unnecessary desires | Corrupt "champion of the people" (565d-567d) |
| Dictatorship | "dictatorial," frenzied, maniacal | |

As stated, the ideal Republic is an aristocratic meritocracy in which people are sorted into their proper class by adhering to the principle of specialization, and harmony is maintained so long as each class performs its proper function. Should the POS be abandoned, or be insufficiently enforced, the Republic will degenerate into a lower form of State.

How does this happen? Any meritocracy has the innate tendency to cease to be a meritocracy within a single generation.

Imagine a utopia in which only the very best, most-suitable and talented people become leaders in politics and business. The very best and brightest among us become wealthy and powerful as a result, and, arguably, they deserve it. And then they have children. . . .

The children of these wealthy, powerful, best and brightest, will start out life with an undeniable advantage over their peers. There is no guarantee, however, that those qualities that made their parents the "best and brightest," will be inherited by those children. For example, the hotel magnate Conrad Hilton (1887–1979) was arguably a skilled and hard-working businessman. His children and their descendants (literally) inherited the wealth and influence he acquired by virtue of his skills and character. His great grand-daughter is Paris Hilton, known more for her scandals and her "famous-for-being-famous" antics than much else—and his great grand-son (Conrad Hughes Hilton—named after him, no less!) was arrested by the FBI for disrupting a British Airways flight in 2014. He (allegedly) threatened flight attendants, saying "I could get you all fired in five minutes. I know your boss. My father will pay this out, he has done it before. Dad paid $300,000 last time."[62] He also vowed to "own anyone on this flight" and referred to the passengers as "peasants."

The point of this is not to disparage any particular person or family, but merely to point out there is no magical guarantee that "greatness" is automatically transmitted to one's descendants. In order to maintain a genuine meritocracy, there must a constant sorting, filtering, and redistributing to make sure that only the "best" remain at the "top," and that each person performs the task to which they are best-suited—no matter who their mother or father happened to be.

This is precisely what is *supposed* to happen in the *Republic*, of course. But, the human beings living within and (in some cases) ruling the Republic are human beings, after all. It might be overly tempting to a Guardian to make sure his or her own child be raised up a Guardian as well, even if that child properly should be placed in the Producer class. It's possible that some Producers or Auxiliaries might covet the power that Guardians wield, and maneuver to somehow change their station—or perhaps facilitate their children doing so. Perhaps either Guardians or Auxiliaries will come to covet the greater wealth (and personal possessions!) allowed to the Producers, and will desire to have a nice (private) home, and the ability to throw parties too.

For any of these reasons the POS might cease to be followed, and some of the *wrong* people start ruling the society. Because they aren't *properly* Guardians, they are motivated not solely (or even primarily) by the public good, but are motivated instead by wealth or power, they begin to change the laws and policies of the Republic—by allowing Guardians to acquire wealth and property, for example. This new kind of society rewards ambition and "spiritedness," and it is those previously sorted into the Auxiliary class who come to power. The result is no longer an aristocratic meritocracy, but a "timocracy."

A timocracy (of which Sparta was an example) is a government ruled by the warrior class, and, not surprisingly, emphasizing "warrior" traits. He supposes that Auxiliaries (now rulers) will look down on Producers, and mistrust Guardians. They will also desire to accumulate wealth to accompany their power. While they might have courage in abundance, these new rulers lack wisdom and moderation. Because of the pleasure derived from accumulating and spending wealth, money comes to be valued more than virtue, and laws and customs are

---

[62]http://www.latimes.com/local/lanow/la-me-ln-paris-hilton-conrad-hilton-charged-20150203-story.html

changed once again to favor the accumulation of wealth—but specifically in ways that favor their own class, and that restrict political power to the wealthy only. When this happens, the timocracy degenerates into an oligarchy.

An oligarchy (or plutocracy) is the rule of a wealthy elite. A report released in 2014 by researchers from Princeton and Northwestern Universities concluded that, on the basis of objective measures, the United States is not actually a democracy, but an oligarchy. "The central point that emerges from our research is that economic elites and organised groups representing business interests have substantial independent impacts on US government policy, while mass-based interest groups and average citizens have little or no independent influence."[63] Laws and policies do not generally reflect the will of the "people" so much as the will of wealthy corporate interests and other influential groups. "When a majority of citizens disagrees with economic elites and/or with organized interests, they generally lose. Moreover, because of the strong status quo bias built into the US political system, even when fairly large majorities of Americans favour policy change, they generally do not get it."

Setting aside the proper classification of the United States, Plato's critique of oligarchies, in general, is consistent with his emphasis on the POS, in general. When the poor are excluded from rulership, regardless of merit, people who should rule, don't. When the rich are empowered to rule, regardless of merit, people who shouldn't rule, do.

As of 2012, the median net worth for lawmakers in the U.S. House and Senate was just over $1 million.[64] Incoming Congressional "freshmen" had a net worth that was exactly $1 million *more* than the average American household.[65] While it is possible that wealth and fitness for rulership correlate, this is by no means an obvious truth—and a system that reserves rulership exclusively for the wealthy makes precisely that controversial assumption.

Plato predicts that the increasing gap between the wealthy and the rest of the society will produce class divisions and tension. As of 2012, conflict between the rich and the poor surpassed conflict on the basis of race or immigration status as being the greatest source of tension in American society.[66] The poor, Plato predicts, increasingly desperate and resentful, will develop a revolutionary spirit that will threaten the internal stability of the society. Should a revolution actually occur, and the poor overthrow the rich (probably seizing and dividing their property, as was the case in the French Revolution and numerous Communist revolutions), a "democracy" is established."

In Plato's ranking, democracy is the second-worst form of government,

---

[63]http://journals.cambridge.org/download.php?file=%2FPPS%2FPPS12_03%2FS1537592714001595a.pdf&code=a7337ff4942bb8b23f42f347c677729f
[64]http://www.nytimes.com/2014/01/10/us/politics/more-than-half-the-members-of-congress-are-millionaires-analysis-finds.html?_r=0
[65]http://www.usnews.com/news/articles/2013/01/18/the-five-poorest-us-senators
[66] http://www.nytimes.com/2012/01/12/us/more-conflict-seen-between-rich-and-poor-survey-finds.html

second only to a dictatorship. "What could be so bad about democracy?" you might wonder.

Plato has several "problems" with democracy. For one, democracy seems to presuppose that we are all equally suited to govern, and this flies in the face of the basic idea behind the principle of specialization. According to the POS, we are *not* all equally suited to do *anything*. Just as some people are better suited for combat, and others better suited for trades, so too are some of us better suited to rule. If rulership is a skill like another, it is just plain false that we are all qualified to participate in rulership. Given the incredibly high stakes of rulership (i.e., the very well-being of the community itself!), Plato would think it both misguided and dangerous to set aside the POS.

In addition, it's important to note that Plato's usage of "democracy" might be different from your own. He is not referring to some sort of idealistic system in which each person freely and equally participates in political decision-making in the mutual pursuit of life, liberty, and happiness (though he would have reservations about that, as well, given his emphasis on the POS). Instead, the "democracy" to which Plato refers is more like anarchic mob rule. Plato thought that democracy led to the pursuit of excessive freedom, and this ultimately resulted in anarchy.

"Freedom" is the supreme value in this system, but this freedom is unchecked by virtue or even laws. People wantonly pursue their own desires and self-interests. When we are all "equal" (i.e., where each is thought to have both an equal right and an equal capacity to rule), the result is that we pursue power and personal benefit, rather than the public good. In other words, democracy lends itself to corruption. The resulting lack of discipline causes society to descend deeper and deeper into chaos, until a powerful individual seizes power in the name of order and security. A dictatorship is born.

The lowest form of government, a dictatorship is the tyrannical rule of a single individual who originally claimed power in the name of the "people," but quickly rules for his own benefit instead.

History has provided us real-world candidates for each of the government types Plato proposes. The primary difference between them lies in who is ruling, and for whom (and for what) they are ruling. This method of classification will be revived by Plato's most famous student, Aristotle, in a later chapter. For Plato, however, the Republic represents not only the ideal society, but the ideal type of person—the only types, in each case, where justice is fully actualized.

## Justice

Much more detail is possible with regard to the account of the ideal State (and various supporting ideas) in the *Republic*, but for our purposes the current detail is sufficient, and we shall finally begin to connect this attempt at political philosophy to the basic analogy with the human soul which is supposed to have inspired all this State-building in the first place.

*But in reality justice was such as we were describing, being concerned however, not with the outward man, but with the inward, which is the true self and concernment of man: for the just man does not permit the several elements within him to interfere with one another, or any of them to do the work of others,—he sets in order his own inner life, and is his own master and his own law, and at peace with himself; and when he has bound together the three principles within him, which may be compared to the higher, lower, and middle notes of the scale, and the intermediate intervals—when he has bound all these together, and is no longer many, but has become one entirely temperate and perfectly adjusted nature, then he proceeds to act, if he has to act, whether in a matter of property, or in the treatment of the body, or in some affair of politics or private business; always thinking and calling that which preserves and co-operates with this harmonious condition, just and good action, and the knowledge which presides over it, wisdom, and that which at any time impairs this condition, he will call unjust action, and the opinion which presides over it ignorance.*

*You have said the exact truth, Socrates.*

*Very good; and if we were to affirm that we had discovered the just man and the just State, and the nature of justice in each of them, we should not be telling a falsehood?*

*Most certainly not.*

*May we say so, then?*

*Let us say so.*

*And now, I said, injustice has to be considered.*

*Clearly.*

*Must not injustice be a strife which arises among the three principles—a meddlesomeness, and interference, and rising up of a part of the soul against the whole, an assertion of unlawful authority, which is made by a rebellious subject against a true prince, of whom he is the natural vassal,— what is all this confusion and delusion but injustice, and intemperance and cowardice and ignorance, and every form of vice? (443d-444b)*

Remember that, in the community, there are three classes and people are assigned to the class for which they are properly suited. For the good of the community, Producers should not perform the tasks of Guardians, nor vice versa. *A "just" State is one in which each class is successfully fulfilling its proper function.* Socrates is advancing a view of justice, then, that translates to something like "internal harmony." An unjust State, by contrast, is one that lacks such harmonious integration. Justice (internal harmony) is a virtue in the State because the proper arrangement of its parts makes its citizens good (to the extent such is possible).

We can say the same of the individual soul. *A just soul is one whose parts are in harmony.* Each class has a role to fulfill, just as each part of the soul has a role to fulfill. Each class has a virtue that corresponds to its own proper functioning, just as each part of the soul has its own virtue. Justice, for both the community and the individual, is when each part is virtuous and fulfilling its proper function.

| Virtue | Part of the Soul | Manifestation in the Community |
|--------|------------------|-------------------------------|
| Wisdom | Reason | Thoughtful/resourceful care by the Guardians (428d) |
| Courage | Spirit/Passion | Lawful bravery of the Auxiliaries (429d) |
| Temperance | Appetite/Desire | Obedience of the Producers (431a-c) |
| Justice | Proper harmony | Following the principle of specialization among three parts |

Justice in the individual soul is understood as internal harmony. This organization makes a person good because it emphasizes and exercises reason (paradigmatically, when contemplating the Forms). When reason rules the soul, based on its knowledge of the Forms—particularly the Form of the Good—the individual's life is arranged so as to promote reason and the Good. When we understand justice (morality) as "harmony," in this sense, one of the most basic and important questions of ethics has an answer. The question is "why be moral?" The answer is as obvious as is the answer to the question "why be healthy?"

*Still our old question of the comparative advantage of justice and injustice has not been answered: Which is the more profitable, to be just and act justly and practise virtue, whether seen or unseen of gods and men, or to be unjust and act unjustly, if only unpunished and unreformed?*

*In my judgment, Socrates, the question has now become ridiculous. We know that, when the bodily constitution is gone, life is no longer endurable, though pampered with all kinds of meats and drinks, and having all wealth and all power; and shall we be told that when the very essence of the vital principle is undermined and corrupted, life is still worth having to a man, if only he be allowed to do whatever he likes with the single exception that he is not to acquire justice and virtue, or to escape from injustice and vice; assuming them both to be such as we have described (445a-b)?*

Justice is a sort of health for the soul. Injustice is a sort of sickness. When we act rightly, we nurture the rational part of our soul (589b). When we act immorally, we feed the appetitive part of the soul, which Socrates likens to a many-headed monster (589a). In the State, the role of education and law is to provide external constraints on the "monster," if necessary (590d-591b).

That a healthy soul is preferable to an unhealthy one should be as apparent as a healthy body being preferable to an unhealthy body. The practical value of philosophy is evident: philosophy is the means by which we "ascend" out of the "cave," acquire knowledge, and achieve harmony in our soul. The challenge that Glaucon (and Adeimantus) had set before Socrates was to demonstrate not only the nature of justice, but also why justice is to be preferred for its own sake, and over injustice. This is Socrates' answer to that challenge, as presented by Plato.

## The Laws

The entirety of this chapter, thus far, has focused on the account of justice and vision of political philosophy that Plato articulates in the *Republic*. As mentioned at the beginning of the chapter, however, the *Republic* was not Plato's only contribution to political philosophy, nor was it his last. Indeed, the *Laws* was written later, and was considered unfinished at the time of Plato's death.

We will not consider the *Laws* in detail or at length. Instead, we will consider a very brief overview of some basic ideas, focusing primarily on how the *Laws* relates to the *Republic*.

Although there remains some scholarly debate, the generally predominant view amongst Plato scholars is that while the *Republic* is a statement of the ideally best State, the *Laws* is a more practical concession to what is best among what is actually feasible. The radical assumptions and demands made by the *Republic* were recognized as possibly unrealistic even within the text of the *Republic* itself. As an example, in the *Republic*, the Guardians and Auxiliaries have no personal property, nor do they even have their own spouses or children.

> *That State and polity come first, and those laws are best, where there is observed as carefully as possible throughout the whole State the old saying that "friends have all things really in common." As to this condition,—whether it anywhere exists now, or ever will exist,—in which there is community of wives, children, and all chattels, and all that is called "private" is everywhere and by every means rooted out of our life, and so far as possible it is contrived that even things naturally "private" have become in a way "communized"...*[67]

This describes what is actually promoted in the *Republic*, suggesting that the model in the *Republic* is the "best." Within the *Laws*, though, second and even third best options are offered, and the details of the city-state as regards private property aligns with the "second best" option. This lends itself to the very reasonable interpretation that the city-state sketched out in the *Laws* is presented as a more modest (though still idealistic!), and therefore more realistic, alternative.[68]

---

[67] *Laws*, Book 5, 739b-c.

[68] Another interpretation of the "second-best" label attached to the *Laws* is that, in the *Republic*, there are no codified laws, per se. Instead, philosopher kings (Guardians) rule by enlightened fiat. In the *Laws*, however, the "eternal" laws of the "Forms" come down to Earth, and are recorded as legislation to be followed. The only "philosophy" that takes place occurs in the public "preludes" meant as

As was the case with the *Republic*, the *Laws* is written as a dialogue—although Socrates no longer appears as the protagonist but has been replaced by the "Athenian Stranger" (thought to represent Plato himself). The other two participants are Kleinias (from Crete) and Megillus (from Sparta). Kleinias is to found a new colony, and the conversation between the three concerns how best to structure the government and laws of this new city-state.

The central goal of the *Republic* was internal harmony (achieved via the Principle of Specialization), and a similar unity of purpose is desired and pursued in the *Laws*. "That is to say, we should state that he enacted laws with an eye not to some one fraction, and that the most paltry, of goodness, but to goodness as a whole"[69]

Although the city-state will be brand-new, there is no pretense that the citizens can be convinced of a "noble lie" (as was proposed in the *Republic*). No invented mythology will offer reason for their union and camaraderie, and it is presumed that they will arrive at their new city-state with both memories and material possessions intact.

The land of this new city-state will be divided into 5,040 equal plots, and given (permanently) to each colonist and his heirs. The owners will not be permitted to either sell off all (or any portion) of their land, nor acquire any additional land. In this way, some measure of equality will be maintained, and massive differences in wealth will be prevented since no family will be allowed to accumulate more land, and none can be without their family plot. Indeed, there is a strict cap on accumulated wealth in that no citizen will be allowed to acquire any more than four times the natural wealth of his land. Any wealth generated beyond that will be placed into a common fund. Although, technically, this plot is allotted to the family in question, it is officially still the common-property of the city-state itself, and all members will be expected to contribute from their land to the common good (and will be supported by their community, as needed).

The ostensive point of this strict regulation of wealth and property is to prevent class divisions, envy, and conflict. This is not to say that there will be difference amongst persons, nor any classes within the city-state, however. There will be four classes of citizens, based on their wealth. The first class has wealth worth between 3 and 4 times the value of their plot of land. The second class has wealth worth between 2 and 3 times the value of their plot. The third class has wealth worth between 1 and 2 times the value of their plot—with the lowest class having wealth equal to their plot. There is general equality between men and women (as was the case in the *Republic*), and marriages are to be arranged in the interest of the common good (rather than personal preference—also like the *Republic*).

In addition to the 5,040 families/citizens, there will be many resident-foreigners allowed to live and work within the city-state. They will not be allowed to own land, nor participate in politics, but will instead work in trade and other

---

arguments in favor of the laws. This demotion of philosophizing to a supporting role for laws is "second-best," according to some scholars, such as Ernest Baker.
[69] *Laws*, Book 1, 630e.

money-making endeavors. A large population of slaves (considered property, not citizens) will do most of the physical/menial labor, allowing the citizens to have as much leisure time as possible, that they might attend to the important affairs of the city-state, and participate in political activities.

A notable difference between the *Laws* and the *Republic* is the greater role allowed to (and greater demands placed upon) each citizen. Recall that in the *Republic*, only the Guardian class had only political decision-making power (or responsibility). Everyone else was either a soldier (Auxiliary), or Producer. As of the *Laws*, however, each citizen (theoretically) has the right and responsibility to participate in the political process, to some degree. The result is that rather than a "meritocratic aristocracy" advocated in the *Republic*, we have a mix of aristocracy and democracy. The political structure of the fledgling city-state will include the following:

- The General Assembly: consisting of all citizens who are serving (or who have served) in the military. They elect most of the city's officers and magistrates, as well as judging public offenses and giving rewards of merit.
- The Guardians of the Laws: an elite group of 37 citizens who must be at least fifty years old when elected, and serve from the time of their election until the age of seventy. These Guardians supervise magistrates, exercise control over citizens in the form of fines for those who spend excessively, and by overseeing foreign travel requests. They exercise judicial authority over "difficult" or especially important trials. Finally, and perhaps most importantly, they are tasked with revising and supplementing the initial founding laws, as needed.
- The Council: 360 citizens, composed of 90 citizens elected from each of the four social classes to serve one-year terms. They are responsible for supervising elections, calling and dissolving the Assembly, and receiving foreign ambassadors.
- Miscellaneous selected Officials: Generals, Judges, Priests, and Regulators who fulfill various other functions.
- The Nocturnal Council: perhaps ominous-sounding, the "Nocturnal Council" (so-called because they will meet in the hour before dawn) is a group of the ten oldest Guardians, their selected "interns" (who must be at least 30 years or older), and a handful of especially distinguished/decorated citizens, and is responsible for making sure that the city-state and its laws consistently aims at virtue.[70]

---

[70] The precise role and scope of power of this Nocturnal Council is subject to debate, ranging from interpretations according to which they are the true wielders of power, serving the same role as the Philosopher Kings in the Republic, to a more modest interpretation according to which they are merely wise and respected advisors.

The "Athenian" (i.e., Plato) claims that virtue (i.e., courage, moderation, wisdom, and justice) ought to be the goal of the lawgivers. Indeed, "every legislator who is worth his salt will most assuredly legislate always with a single eye to the highest goodness and to that alone"[71] Laws are only *true* laws when they have the *eudaimonia* (flourishing) of their citizens as their goal.[72] Quite *consistent* with the *Republic* is the notion, presented in the *Laws*, that there is an ideal against which the actual may be evaluated. "Ideally," the best ruler a city-state could have is a god. In actuality, it's unlikely that Apollo or Zeus will personally rule this newly founded city-state, but, fortunately, Reason is presented as the immortal/godly element within us all. Therefore, a city-state ruled by Reason is the next best thing to being ruled by a god. Laws consistent with Reason, then, are the only laws worthy of being called laws. There is no mistaking this: Reason provides the *physis* (nature) against which laws will be judged. In the nature v. convention debate, Plato once again comes down firmly on the side of nature.

## Conclusion

It is difficult to overstate Plato's significance in the history of Western philosophy. In a very real sense he "did it all," and, in a meaningful sense, much of philosophy since Plato has been a reaction to what he produced whether as elaboration or rejection and criticism. Plato's dualistic understanding of reality ("physical" v. "spiritual," "body v. "soul") as well as his clear hierarchy ("spiritual" over "physical," "soul" over "body") exerted profound influence on Christian thought once St. Augustine had "Christianized" Plato. His thorough treatment of epistemology, his quest for enlightenment depicted throughout his dialogues, and his discussion of the individual v. the collective, among others, have continued to be characteristic of philosophy ever since.

Plato's political philosophy is based off a premise that factionalism and division are the greatest dangers to the city-state—more dangerous even than war and foreign threats. He argued that genuine social harmony and political stability can't be achieved by one class or faction subduing others and "winning" for the sake of their own cause, but instead that lasting peace is better achieved through genuine cooperation and friendship of all factions within the city-state.[73] To promote internal harmony, he offers enlightened rule by philosopher kings in the *Republic*, but as of the *Laws* he tries to achieve that same harmony by turning to a more traditional polity, consisting of a mixed constitution including elements of oligarchy, aristocracy, and democracy. This sort of mixed polity is precisely what will be advocated by Plato's student, Aristotle, as we will see in our next chapter.

---

[71] *Laws*, Book 1, 630c.

[72] Ibid., 631b.

[73] See, for example, *Republic* 462a-b and *Laws* 628a-b. This concern with internal stability will be a recurring theme over the next couple millennia.

# Chapter 4: Aristotle

*Comprehension questions you should be able to answer after reading this chapter:*

1. What are Aristotle's four kinds of "cause," and what is an example for each?

2. What does each of the following mean? *Telos, areté, eudaimonia.*

3. How does one become virtuous, according to Aristotle (be sure to include a discussion of the Golden Mean)?

4. What is "*phronesis*," and what is its relationship to the Golden Mean?

5. What does it mean to say that the *Politics* is part of the same project as the *Nicomachean Ethics*?

6. What is a "*polis*," and how is it different from a mere "State"?

7. What does Aristotle mean when he says humans are "naturally" political?

8. Why would the United States (arguably) not be considered a *polis*?

9. How do the four kinds of "causes" apply to the *polis*?

10. Explain Aristotle's defense of "natural slavery."

11. In what ways do both oligarchies and democracies have mistaken understandings of the proper *telos* of the *polis*?

12. What is a polity/mixed-constitution, and how is it a "second-best" constitution?

13. Explain Aristotle's favoring of the middle-class, in a polity.

If all philosophy is a "footnote to Plato," something equally clever should be coined for his most celebrated student, Aristotle. Aristotle was so revered as a philosopher that St. Thomas Aquinas referred to him simply as "The Philosopher" within his own works. Indeed, Aquinas' efforts at "Christianizing" Aristotle revolutionized Christian theology and brought about a renaissance of interest in Aristotle.

Aristotle lived from 384 BCE to 323 BCE. At around the age of 18, he began studying under Plato. He studied and taught at Plato's Academy until the time of Plato's death, when curriculum disagreements between Aristotle and Plato's successor to head the Academy (Plato's own nephew, Speussipus) inspired Aristotle to split from the Academy. There might also have been a bit of resentment involved, as Aristotle had been a strong candidate for the position as well. Aristotle took on the job of tutor to no less a youth than Alexander the Great. He eventually opened his own school (the *Lyceum*) and his followers became known as "Peripatetics," due to their habit of walking the gardens (*peripatoi* = covered walk) while having their deep philosophical conversations.

Aristotle favored an empirical approach to knowledge (in contrast to his mentor, Plato). That is, the source of knowledge will be data collected from sense experience. Correctly interpreted, this will provide theoretical as well as scientific knowledge. As an example of his dedication to this method, he spent several years studying marine organisms, in effect inventing what we now know as the discipline of marine biology. He was confident that from observations of particular things, we could gain insight into universal concepts. For example, to gain insight into politics, in general, he studied the particular constitutions of 158 existing states. As another example, we will learn about morality, in general, by studying actual people and how they behave. Moreover, his ethical system will be about people and for people as they (and we) actually live.

It is no coincidence that I mention ethics and political philosophy at the same time, with regard to Aristotle: he saw them as parts of the same exploration of moral theory. Indeed, the content of the *Politics* was seen, by Aristotle, as a continuation of the *Nicomachean Ethics*. For that reason, we will spend what might seem like a surprising amount of time (for a book on political philosophy) building the ethical foundations offered in the *Nicomachean Ethics*, before moving on to "official" political theory. This is not merely for the sake of trivia, but is necessary in order to properly understand the stance Aristotle takes with regards to political institutions.

Aristotle did not limit himself to ethics, politics, and marine biology. If it existed as a subject of inquiry, he pursued it. A "renaissance man" a millennia and a half before the Renaissance, Aristotle studied and wrote about physics, "metaphysics," poetry, theater, and music, logic and rhetoric and linguistics, politics and government, ethics, biology, and zoology. His collected works are numerous and varied, and include many subjects not typically associated (today) with philosophy. His writing about what we now call metaphysics is called *metaphysics*. I suspect you can infer the significance of that. He works in "natural philosophy" include *Physics, Meteorology, On the Heavens*, and *On Generation and Corruption*. Writings on animals include *History of Animals, Parts of Animals, Movement of Animals, Progression of Animals*, and *Generation of Animals*. His many works on humans include *De Anima, Sense and Sensibilia, On Memory, On Sleep, On Dreams, On Divination in Sleep, On Length and Shortness of Life, On Youth, Old Age, and Death, On Respiration*, and *On Breath*. In aesthetics he offers us *Rhetoric* and *Poetics*. Concerning ethics and politics we have *Nicomachean Ethics, Eudemian Ethics*, and *The Politics*. Finally, dealing with what we now call logic: *Categories, On Interpretation, Prior Analytics, Posterior Analytics, Topics*, and *Sophistical Refutations*.

Other achievements of Aristotle, dealing more perhaps with language than "logic," include his recognition that "is" has many uses in language. Notice the word "is" as it appears in each of the ten questions below. Now notice the very different sorts of answers one would give, depending on the use of the word "is." These correspond to different modes of thought and language—but not just that: they also correspond to different modes of being. Aristotle is engaged with not only philosophy of logic, but also ontology, not just the linguistic classification of predicate terms, but listing the ways in which things can exist.

| Question | Typical Answer | Category |
|---|---|---|
| 1. What is X? | human, dog, baseball | Substance (being) |
| 2. How large is X? | 5'6" tall, 30' long | Quantity (amount) |
| 3. What is X like? | Wise, round | Quality (what kind) |
| 4. How is X related? | Greater, half | Relation (relation to) |
| 5. Where is X? | At work, at home | Place |
| 6. When does (did) X exist? | Today, last year | Time |
| 7. What position is X in? | Sitting, prone | Position |
| 8. What condition is X in? | Clothed, blossoming | State (having) |
| 9. What is X doing? | Writing, running | Action (doing) |
| 10. How is X acted upon? | Being interrupted, being fed | Passivity (being affected) |

The "problem of change" was a persistent and important philosophical problem for ancient philosophers. How do we account for change? Is change an illusion? Is permanence an illusion? Parmenides, for example, argued against change because change would require a transition from that which "is not" to that which "is." But, Aristotle thought Parmenides' view of change was too simple. There are two kinds of change to consider: one in which P becomes Q, and one in which Q comes to be from P.

In the first case (P becomes Q), we have an alteration in a substance—for example, I (the author) become muscular. In the second case, we have something coming into being—for example, a baby being born. In neither case, does "being" come from "not-being," does that which "is" come from that which "is not"—at least not in any ontologically significant sense. In both cases, something (a substance) has persisted. In the event of my becoming muscular, a substance (my body) has been altered in terms of quality: non-muscular to muscular. In the event of a baby being born, two substances (a sperm and an egg) have been altered in such a way that they are now (becoming) a baby. At no point was "nothing" producing "something." In both cases, potential was being actualized. I was always potentially muscular. The change is simply the actualization of that potential. A sperm and egg are (typically) potentially "babies." At conception, the actualization of that potential begins. Parmenides seems to be restricting "is" to just one usage: the existence or non-existing of a substance—but there are many other ways in which a thing "is" (i.e., those nine other categories!). A change in quality (e.g., non-muscular to muscular) is a change *of* a substance, not the miraculous appearance (from nothing) of a wholly new one.

A related and important of Aristotle's philosophy is his understanding of "substance" and "essence." Each physical thing (each "substance") can be understood in terms of two aspects: form, and matter.

*The "form" of a substance is its essence, that which makes it what it is, and not something else.* Each substance must be understood in terms of its essence. We understand tables in terms of their "tableness," dogs in terms of their "dogness," and people in terms of their "humanness." A dog's essence is what makes it a dog rather than a cat. Alter a thing's essence, and it is no longer that same thing, but something else.

*The "matter" of a substance is the material of which it is composed, and that which distinguishes one particular thing from another* (even if they share the same essence). For example, two different cats are both understood in terms of their "catness" (essence), but what makes them two different cats is they don't share the same matter. Putting the metaphysical vocabulary aside, this is a pretty simple idea. *Form and matter are each indispensable aspects of any and every thing. You can't separate them.* There is no such thing (for Aristotle) as a form without matter (some sort of disembodied, abstract essence), nor is there any such thing as formless matter.

This is where Aristotle rejects Plato's theory of the Forms. Plato treated Forms as independently existing abstract objects occupying some other purely mental realm. Aristotle, in contrast, believed that a form cannot exist apart from the matter for which it provides structure and meaning. The "forms" (generally understood as an "essence," by Aristotle) exist in real things. Our minds are capable of sufficient abstraction that we can identify the "essence" of a thing and recognize it as that which all particulars of the same kind have in common. This is just a fancy way of saying that we can identify an abstract concept of "chair," distinct from any particular chair—but which all chairs exhibit to some degree— without needing to imagine that there is some additional mental thing (the Form of the Chair) that exists "out there" in some purely mental realm. "Chairness" exists only in actual chairs, but we can think of "chairness" as a concept, in the abstract.

We can further understand matter in terms of potentiality and actuality (as mentioned earlier). Potentiality is associated with matter, while actuality is associated with form. To understand change and process (for Aristotle) is to understand movement from potentiality, to actuality. For example, an acorn is potentially an oak tree. It becomes an oak tree when its potential is actualized. How does something move from potentiality to actuality? Through causation.

Aristotle provides us with *four* different notions of "cause."

## Causation

1. Material cause
2. Efficient cause
3. Formal cause
4. Final cause

*A thing's Material cause is its matter*, the raw materials of which it is made. Using the example of a statue, its Material cause is marble (or whatever kind of stone the sculptor used). *An Efficient cause is a thing's origin*—the process responsible for it being what it is. In the case of the statue, its Efficient cause is the sculptor and her tools. *The Formal cause is a thing's essence,* the governing idea giving it its structure and form. For the statue, its Formal cause is the vision of the completed sculpture entertained by the sculptor. Finally, we have the Final cause. *The Final cause is the end or purpose ("telos") that the thing is to fulfill.* With the statue, perhaps its Final cause is to depict the likeness of Aristotle. For our purposes, focus on that idea of a Final cause.

When we combine Aristotle's notion of a final cause, and his notion of essence/form, we get his teleology: the goal-oriented structure of the universe.

## *Telos*

*The essence of each kind of substance includes its "inner drive" to develop in a certain kind of way, to actualize its potential.* For example, part of the essence of an acorn is its *telos* (Final cause)—namely, to become an oak tree. All things have a "*telos*" relating to their essence. The *telos* of an acorn is to become an oak tree, the *telos* of a knife is to cut. Human beings also have an essence, and a potential to actualize.

To understand the essence of humans, and our *telos*, we have to understand Aristotle's different categories of soul (I know, we're diverting into quite a lot of ancient philosophy, but trust me—his ethics will make much more sense thanks to these details). Don't think that Aristotle is getting religious when he discusses souls. As a biologist, his understanding of "souls" was naturalistic. A soul was not some sort of spirit that flies away when the body dies and goes to heaven. Instead, for living things, the soul just was the "essence" (form) of that kind of living thing. Because there is no such thing as form apart from matter, clearly, Aristotle's notion of the soul is not anything that could somehow survive the death of the body. That would literally make no sense to him.

*There are three basic kinds of souls: vegetative, animal, and rational.* Vegetative souls (sometimes called nutritive souls) are the essences of different kinds of plants. Vegetative souls make possible growth and nourishment. Anything capable of growth, therefore, can be understood in terms of a vegetative soul. Some living things are capable of more than growth, though. Animals, unlike plants, are also capable of perception, motion, and expression. An animal soul, then, is the kind of essence that makes such things possible. Animals, therefore, are to be understood in terms of both animal and vegetative souls, whereas plants are understood only in terms of vegetative souls. Finally, some living things (e.g., humans) are capable of more than growth, motion, perception, and expression. We are also capable of thinking, judging, belief-formation—in short, Reason. Rational souls make this possible. Humans, then, (exclusively, according to Aristotle) have aspects of all three types.

Since a thing's potential is determined by its essence, and a thing's *telos* is determined by its potential, our own *telos* (our Final cause) is likewise determined by our essence, by the kind of thing that we are. Since that which makes humans distinctly human, and different from every other living thing, is our capacity for Reason, it should come as no surprise that Reason will play a significant role in our *telos*. Once again, the practical benefit of philosophy is clear: philosophical contemplation is not only the means by which we can understand our *telos*, but, as the highest use of Reason, is the clearest expression of a fully actualized human being.

In addition to each thing having a *telos* (an end, a purpose), *each thing has an "excellence" (in Greek, "areté")* that serves that *telos*. Just like the *telos*, a thing's *areté* is likewise based on its essence, and is that by which we evaluate the quality of the thing with regard to its *telos*. That sounds complicated, but it's really fairly simple. A knife's *telos* is to cut. Its *areté* will be that which makes it excellent with regard to cutting. "Sharpness" seems like a pretty good candidate for its *areté*! The *telos* of an eyeball is to see. An eyeball's *areté*, then, will be that which makes it excellent with regard to seeing. An ophthalmologist could surely discuss this better than I, but I would assume that the overall shape of the eye, the transparency of its lens (e.g., not having any cataracts), and other such things would constitute the *areté* of an eyeball. The example that will matter to us, of course, is that of a human being. What is our *telos*? What is our *areté*?

## *Eudaimonia*

Aristotle, like many ancient philosophers, believed that the ultimate "end" in life, life's ultimate goal and purpose, was *"eudaimonia."* This is sometimes translated as happiness, but that's misleading. To render it "happiness" suggests that *eudaimonia* is a feeling, or, worse yet, that's it's just a fancy Greek word for pleasure. Not so. *Eudaimonia is better translated as "flourishing."* It refers to an overall quality of one's life. Thus, one is not *"eudaimon"* on Monday, but not so much on Tuesday. It is one's whole life that is either *"eudaimon,"* or not.

There are several ways to try to capture the meaning of a life that is *"eudaimon."* Some of them have become cliché's, but they'll suffice. Realizing your potential. Being fully alive. Thriving. Being all you can be. Exemplifying what it is to be human.

Why is *eudaimonia* our *telos*? Because all other "ends" have only instrumental value. That is, we pursue them for the sake of something else. Success, for its own sake? Wealth, for its own sake? A good reputation, for its own sake? Education, for its own sake? All these things are valuable, to be sure, and certainly worthy of attainment, but for each of them there is an implicit "because." Wealth is desirable because it enables one to live comfortably, and to pursue the things important to her. Education is valuable because it better allows us to understand ourselves, and the world. But what about *eudaimonia*? This rich notion of "happiness" involving one's entire being, culminating in a truly excellent life? Because? Just because, it seems. *Aristotle thought that eudaimonia was intrinsically valuable, pursued for its own sake—the ultimate "end" to which all other worthy ends point.*

Assuming Aristotle is right about that, what it means for a human to flourish will be defined by a human's essence. Reason is uniquely human, so our flourishing must involve Reason, a life in which our behavior and our character is determined and governed by Reason rather than our appetites. For Aristotle, this is what it means to be virtuous.

## Virtue

Virtue will be the most important ingredient in a life that is *eudaimon*. Without it, *eudaimonia* will be impossible. With it, *eudaimonia* is not guaranteed, but virtue is the most reliable means to a life that is *eudaimon*. Note that even virtue does not guarantee *eudaimonia*. Aristotle recognized that other factors, admittedly often beyond our control, influence our ability to flourish as well. For Aristotle, these other factors included political stability, wealth, beauty, reputation, having a good family, having good friends, etc. For many of us, some of the elements of this list seem unfair, or even outrageous. Wealth? Why not? Being wealthy certainly doesn't guarantee an excellent character (in fact, it can be an obstacle to it), but being desperately poor probably doesn't help either! Health? Sick people can certainly have excellent character, and illness can often be a means to developing courage, patience, and other virtues. However, a life wracked with pain and suffering can hardly be called an excellent life. Beauty? Let's face it: attractive people have an easier time in life. That might be unfair, but it seems to be true. If you are considered attractive, you reap numerous benefits that others do not. Studies indicate that those perceived as being attractive have an easier time getting jobs (and better jobs), are promoted more often, receive better treatment from the police and the legal system, have more choices in romantic partners, and are even perceived as being more intelligent and morally better! All Aristotle is recognizing here is that the recipe for an excellent life includes several ingredients. Virtue is the most important, by far—but it's not the only ingredient.

Given that the most important ingredient is also the one over which we have the most control, it makes sense for us to focus on having a good character. Those with good character possess the virtues among their character traits. *Virtues are simply dispositions (habits) to behave in certain ways*. The virtues are positive dispositions, such as honesty, respectfulness, generosity, courage, etc. There are also negative dispositions (vices) such as disloyalty, cowardice, greediness, etc. Generally speaking, we want to display the virtues, and not the vices.

Aristotle had a particular understanding of the virtues. First, he thought there were two kinds: intellectual, and moral.

*Intellectual virtues are based on excellence in reasoning, and can be taught.* Prudence is an example of an intellectual virtue. *The moral virtues, on the other hand, can't be taught (not directly, at least), but must be lived and practiced in order for one to acquire them.* You could read a very well-written book on courage, for example, without it making you one bit more courageous. The way we acquire those sorts of virtues is by practicing them. We become courageous by putting ourselves in fearsome situations, and then overcoming that fear. We become honest by telling the truth. Aristotle says, "It is right, then, to say that by doing what is just a man becomes just, and temperate by doing what is temperate, while without doing thus he has no chance of ever becoming good. But most men, instead of doing thus, fly to theories, and fancy that they are philosophizing and that this will make them good, like a sick man who listens attentively to what the doctor says and then disobeys all his orders. This sort of philosophizing will no more produce a healthy habit of mind than this sort of treatment will produce a healthy habit of body."[74]

When I lie, I am training myself to be a liar. When I steal, I am training myself to be a thief. When I act without compassion, I am training myself to be cold and cruel. If those are all traits I would like to avoid, I had better practice their opposites! Practice, then, is essential in acquiring the virtues—and they are not our virtues until they become habitual. To say that it is habitual means that in order to qualify as generous, for example, you have to be generous most of the time. Being generous one time in your life doesn't earn you the right to be labeled generous!

Habit covers one half of Aristotle's particular understanding of virtue. The other half refers to the "mean." For Aristotle, a virtue is a character trait that hits the "mean" and is manifested in habitual action, or what he called "habituation."

This doctrine of the "mean" is often referred to as *"the Golden Mean." According to this doctrine, we should choose the "mean" over the extremes of excess and deficit.* The extremes of excess and deficiency occur when we're ruled by desires/emotions and not reason. This reminds us of the central role of reason in human excellence. Virtue serves to correct these disorders by helping us to resist our impulses and desires that interfere with us living the good life. For example, the virtue of courage corrects for inappropriate fear. The virtue of temperance corrects our impulses to overindulge or to seek immediate and harmful pleasures. The mean shows us a rational course of action by choosing between the two competing desire extremes (e.g., fear and wrath), letting neither desire have complete control.

## Great Minds Think Alike!

Confucius (551 – 479 BCE) is arguably the most famous of East Asian philosophers. His influence on Chinese culture and thought has spanned millennia, and is arguably without peer.

Confucius personally experienced poverty in his youth, along with other hardships and political abuse. As a young man he accepted an administrative position in local government which allowed him to observe the in adequacy of the government of his time. This inspired him to recognize the need for social reform, and the development of a humanistic philosophy.

His philosophical system is decidedly humanist, looking to humans as the ultimate source of values rather than nature (by means of some sort of "naturalism"), or spirits or gods (by means of some sort of

---

[74] *Nicomachean Ethics*, 1105b4-5.

"supernaturalism"). His approach calls us to look to the best of human practices and traditions to find proper principles of what is good and how to flourish.

One of his principles should sound familiar, as it is a doctrine of the "Golden Mean." "To go beyond is as wrong as to fall short."[75] Similar to Aristotle, though developed roughly two centuries *before* Aristotle's, this doctrine of the Golden Mean focuses on living a life of balance and moderation, avoiding extremes of excess and deficiency. Doing so produces inner harmony, and by virtue of this inner harmony we are able to live in harmony with others.

That virtue is seen as a "mean" is interesting, and unusual. Most people see virtue as the opposite of a vice. Aristotle sees virtue as the mean between two vices, one of excess, and one of deficiency. The following is a list of virtues entertained by Aristotle. Note that the virtue is depicted as a mean between two vices.

| Issue | Vice (Deficiency) | Virtue (Mean) | Vice (Excess) |
|---|---|---|---|
| Fear | Cowardice | Courage | Foolhardiness |
| Pleasure/Pain | Inhibition | Temperance | Overindulgence |
| Spending | Miserliness | Liberality | Extravagance |
| Spending (major) | Shabbiness | Magnificence | Vulgarity |
| Ambition | Lack of ambition | Proper ambition | Over-Ambition |
| Self-esteem | Meekness | Magnanimity | Vanity |
| Anger | Timidity | Righteous indignation | Hot-temperedness |
| Conversation | Boorishness | Wittiness | Buffoonery |
| Social Conduct | Crankiness | Friendliness | Obsequiousness |

Notice, for example, that courage is not the opposite of cowardice, but rather the mean between cowardice (excessive fear) and foolhardiness (bravado). Being temperate doesn't mean that you never indulge any desires, but enjoy sensual delights appropriately (at the right times, and in the right amounts).

The mean is the "perfect" thing for a particular person to do in a specific situation. Note the relativity of this. Courage is different for different people. Someone with agoraphobia shows courage simply by stepping outside. A very sociable person, on the other hand, must take a very different sort of risk in order to display courage. What might count as a generous donation from you or me is probably quite different from what would qualify as a generous donation from

---

[75] Confucius, *Analects*, XI, 15, 3.

Bill Gates.

A morally admirable person is one who has learned (over time, and with experience) what it means to be virtuous, and how to apply that understanding in ever-changing circumstances, reliably finding "just the right way" to behave, so much so that it is habitual, a reliable feature of her very character. Her reason commands her passions and appetites, and she avoids extreme emotional responses in either direction, hitting the "mean" instead. It tends to be the "extremes" in life that get us into trouble. As a result, she is not led off her path or distracted from her pursuit of the good life. With the addition of some favorable circumstances, her life could be *eudaimon*.

Although the Golden Mean sounds mathematical, it falls short of providing us a formula, or even any concrete list of "thou shalt nots." In fairness to Aristotle, he thought ethics could not be understood in that way. Ethics is not like math. If any analogy is to be made, the ancients (including Aristotle) preferred the analogy to medicine. Indeed, philosophy was often referred to as "medicine for the soul."

There is a science to medicine, to be sure, but a good doctor isn't one who has memorized all the I.C.D. codes, nor is the good psychiatrist the one who has memorized the DSM-IVTR. What makes medicine so interesting (and challenging) is those darn patients! Each one is subtly different, though their symptoms might be quite similar. Excellent doctors are the ones that can synthesize their theoretical understanding with the practical information and context before them. Martha Nussbaum, a contemporary philosopher and expert on Aristotle put it this way: "Excellent ethical choice cannot be captured completely in general rules because-like medicine-it is a matter of fitting one's choice to the complex requirements of a concrete situation, taking all of its contextual features into account."

Wisdom (understood as "practical wisdom," *phronesis*) was regarded by Aristotle as the "master" virtue. Without it, none of the other virtues enjoy guidance, and we won't know how to implement them. For example, the "Golden Mean" is the virtuous avoidance of two extremes (vices). Too much "courage" becomes recklessness, and too little becomes cowardice. How much is enough, though? We need *phronesis* to discern the answer to that question.

Similarly, virtues often come into conflict with each other. Kindness is a virtue, but so is honesty. Imagine you have a friend who is going out for the evening, and she asks you how she looks. You think her outfit is unflattering. The honest answer might not be kind, but the kind answer might not be honest. Which virtue should prevail, in such a situation of conflict? Once again, *phronesis* is needed to resolve that dilemma—and no simple, formulaic answer is possible. To know the right thing to do will require that you know your friend very well. Is she very sensitive? Will an honest answer crush her self-esteem? Will it ruin the friendship? Will she be grateful for the honest feedback? Also, you would need to know the situation. How important are her plans? Is it just an average night out, with nothing at stake? Is she on a first date? Is she interviewing for a job? Does she have other options? If you tell her the outfit is unflattering, is there anything else she could wear instead, that would be appropriate and more flattering? An understanding of all these things (and probably more) is needed, in order to discern the right course of action, for that person, in that situation. Someone who can reliably discern that right thing to do, is wise.

Returning to the example of courage, Aristotle can urge us to be courageous, but that's going to sound pretty hollow until we have a context in which to understand courage. What it means to be courageous will vary from one person to the next, from one circumstance to the next—and that's why we can't get specific "rules" from virtue approaches, like "always rush into battle." Sometimes it might be courageous to rush into battle, but other times that will be stupidity. Towards the end of the 2003 film, The Last Samurai, all of the samurai from the last holdout clan resisting "reform" enter battle knowing it will be their last, knowing they will die. This might well be courage, as they are overcoming fear of death for the sake of their principles. However, after much success in the battle, they end their fight with a cavalry charge into a line of Gatling guns. They are cut down with only one character (the main one) managing to survive. It's questionable whether that final charge was "courageous," as a case could certainly be made that it was more foolhardy. After all, courage doesn't require one to abandon sound tactics. Was their charge courageous, or reckless? No obvious and indisputable answer is available, as virtue is a subtle thing.

This is not to say that Aristotle (and virtue ethicists, in general) provides no moral guidance. For Aristotle, guidance was everywhere. Look around Athens and take note of those who are esteemed, and those who are held in disgrace. There are already people deemed virtuous. Be like those people. Robert Solomon (a contemporary American philosopher) thinks the alleged threat of virtue vagueness is overstated.

> When we discuss the virtues in general, they can become vague and we can begin to think that almost anything can be a virtue somewhere, under some conditions, but when we look at particular communities and their practices, this vagueness is dispelled and the virtues emerge with remarkable clarity and strictness.

We all have moral role-models in our lives, whether they are friends, family members, teachers or priests or mentors, historical figures, or even fictional characters. Each one of us is capable of thinking of a person (perhaps several) of whom we would say, "that person is an excellent human being. I wish I were more like him (or her)." Even the "What Would Jesus Do" (WWJD) movement expresses this theme. By modeling our behavior on those who have already achieved a level of personal excellence, we can practice and pursue that excellence ourselves. This is not unlike a golfer trying to model her swing after Tiger Wood's, or a pianist studying the technique of Little Richard. Perhaps looking for "human virtues" is to overreach, but to seek after what it means to be an admirable person within your own community is not so difficult.

Speaking of community, it would be a mistake to think that Aristotle's understanding of ethics is somehow focused exclusively on the self in isolation. Aristotle was especially and overtly sensitive to the demands of community.

> *The complete good is thought to be self-sufficient. Now by self-sufficient we do not mean that which is sufficient for a man all by himself, for one who lives a solitary life, but also for parents, children, wife, and in general for friends and fellow citizens, since, a human being by nature is a political animal.*[76]

Aristotle even ties the flourishing of the individual to the flourishing of his greater society. As such, one cannot be happy unless a similar happiness is realized in the greater society. Since our *eudaimonia* is affected by life circumstances (e.g., health, political stability, wealth, etc.), a "bad" society will interfere with personal flourishing. One can be virtuous in spite of bad circumstances, but one would be impaired in the practice of one's virtue.

Still others argue that, far from being in conflict with community, the pursuit of private perfection is necessary for an excellent community. Stanley Cavell (another contemporary philosopher) argues (at least with respect to democratic societies) that our democratic institutions and principles will only be as strong and just as are the individuals who run, apply, and criticize them. Perfectionism is needed to create the sort of character needed for a healthy democracy. Second, relying solely upon institutional principles of justice inspires complacency in the face of the many sorts of injustices and brutality we witness that are not excluded by institutional principles of justice alone. "The perfectionist will never be satisfied with himself and the system as long as any injustice or misery exists. Reproaching himself and the system for not doing better, he will constantly struggle to better himself and others. Democracy, if it is to realize the best justice possible, needs this vigilance and supererogation."[77]

The virtue approach encourages individual greatness—but not solely for our own sake, as if there is some forced choice between self and society. Instead, this approach recognizes that we are social creatures, and must understand ourselves as part of a community. Our flourishing is tied to others. Excellent individuals make for excellent communities, and excellent communities facilitate excellent individuals.

## Politics

Having shifted to discussion about the relationship between the individual and the community, it is finally time to officially turn our attention to Aristotle's *Politics*. As mentioned briefly at the beginning of this chapter, the *Politics* was

---

[76] Aristotle, *Nicomachean Ethics*, 1097b6.

[77] Richard Shusterman, summarizing Stanley Cavell, in *Practicing Philosophy: Pragmatism and the Philosophical Life*, Routledge, 1996, p.100.

intended as a continuation of the same project begun in the *Nicomachean Ethics*.

Recall that the theme of the *Nicomachean Ethics* discussed above was *eudaimonia*, and how best to achieve and live that sort of life. Because we are, by our very nature, social animals, according to Aristotle, this flourishing can't be achieved in isolation, but can only take place within a community. His agenda in the *Politics*, then, is to determine what kind of political community will best serve that end. Indeed, this is foreshadowed in the *Nicomachean Ethics* when, in the last ("practical application") chapters of the work, Aristotle focuses not on individuals' opportunities for moral self-improvement, but on opportunities for legislators to craft institutions and laws that will promote virtue.

Already, we have a significant contrast between Aristotle's understanding of politics and that assumed by most "modern" political philosophers (i.e., from roughly the Renaissance until today).

One of the most central questions for modern political philosophers is "what justifies the State?" This assumes that the State is something artificial, constructed by persons for some purpose, and that the purpose must outweigh the "inconvenience" of submitting to the authority of that State and its laws.

For Aristotle, though, politics is not (ideally) about control or power, but involves free and equal citizens "ruling and being ruled in turn." Indeed, the use of force by one party to exert control over another within the same community was, for Aristotle, a sign that the State was failing. Tyranny, though a form of government, is not "politics" in Aristotle's usage. The State is not a "contract" for the sake of security (personal or property), but a self-sufficient community of persons with a shared set of core values. When citizens resort to force to pursue their vision of the good life, it is obvious that there is no longer a *collective* vision of the good life in operation.

For Aristotle, (like many ancient political theorists), the paradigm isn't one of obligation and justification, but one of flourishing—and which type of government (and laws) best promote that flourishing. The legislator's task is to frame a society that will make the good life possible for its citizens. Indeed, Aristotle claims that a State comes into being for the sake of life (i.e., survival), but it exists with the aim/goal (*telos*) of a *good* life (*Politics*, 1252b).

Recall from much earlier this chapter we understood a thing's *telos* as its aim, goal, or purpose. This is one kind of cause/explanation described by Aristotle: the Final Cause. We can fruitfully apply his four kinds of cause/explanation to the *polis*, as well.

The Material Cause of the *polis* is the individual citizens and the natural resources of the community. The Formal Cause is the constitution of the *polis*, understood not merely as a written document, but as the organizing principle of the community, analogous to the soul's relationship to the body (as understood by Aristotle). The Efficient Cause of the State is the ruler himself, including, possibly, the very founder of the constitution of that *polis* (revealing that legislation is conceived as a craft, analogous to sculpting). Lastly, as already mentioned, the Final Cause of the *polis* is the promotion/cultivation of virtue in its citizens.

Once our basic physical (survival) needs are met, the *polis* exists for the sake of acquiring virtue and living an excellent life. Because we are rational animals, the exercise of reason is necessary for a complete (good) life. This includes rational deliberation about goodness and justice, among other things. But, we need a community in order to discuss and deliberate over such things.

Aristotle claims that we are "naturally" political, social, and rational animals. Clearly, he is making claims about human nature—but it is important to distinguish Aristotle's understanding of this from what other philosophers might intend by it.

Other philosophers, such as Hobbes and Machiavelli, will start with a particular understanding of human nature (e.g., that we are "naturally" egoistic), and then develop their visions of the State and of laws to account for this. Aristotle's claims about human nature, however, refer back to our previous discussion of potentiality and our *telos*. To say that we are "naturally" political and rational is to claim that it is part of our *telos* to develop our reasoning faculty and to participate in a political community. We are *potentially* rational and political in that sense, but of course there is no guarantee that we will fulfill our *telos*! Indeed, an important function of the *polis* is to help us to do exactly that.

Recall that virtue was thought necessary for flourishing, but note that many of the particular virtues require interaction with others. An excellent life will be one in which one has an opportunity to exhibit (and does, in fact, exhibit) various virtues such as justice, generosity, etc. How can anyone be generous without others with whom to be generous? How can each be given their due ("justice") in a society consisting of just one person? From Aristotle's perspective, we not only naturally desire the (good) company of others, such as friends, but we *need* the company of others, within a community, just to live a complete and virtuous life.

In fairness, the "need" Aristotle had in mind is much more specific than merely living in community with others. Not just any sort of community will suffice. Specifically, we need to live in a "*polis.*" A *polis*, technically, just means something like a "city-state," or "political community," but in practice Aristotle intends "*polis*" to refer to a political community that aims at the virtue and flourishing of its citizens, and this will require the community to have certain features.

Aristotle envisions not just a loose confederation of people cooperating for the sake of mutual self-interest. Friendship is the "glue" that will bind the *polis* together as a community. In a political context, friendship is harmonious agreement amongst citizens concerning their shared values and how best to govern for the sake of those values. A "friendship" based on mere (perceived) usefulness or necessity is too vulnerable to slipping into conflict and factionalism. Genuine friendship between citizens is so important that Aristotle thinks legislators should actively cultivate it by means of laws and activities, in an effort to transform potentially competing individuals into a moral *community*.

Since the good life is a life of moral and intellectual virtue, an individual must be free and autonomous so as to direct his or her life by practical reason (*phronēsis*; wisdom). However, the best exercise of practical reason (according to Aristotle) is the application of wisdom to the common good within a community: "to deliberate well about what is good and advantageous for oneself, not in particular areas such as what promotes health or strength, but with a view to living well overall."[78]

In other words, active political participation is part of an excellent life. This should not be confused with mere "voting." Obviously, someone who is banned from any political participation at all, such as subjects of a dictator or monarch, is being deprived an important aspect of an excellent life, but it's also not enough just to vote for a candidate who will then represent your interests (or not!) from then on. A representative democracy like the United States is not a "*polis*" (using Aristotle's understanding) for a variety of reasons.

In the first place, considering just Presidential elections, the voter turnout among eligible voters was only 51.8% in 2012. The Midterm election of 2014 saw a participation rate of 33.24%.[79] Participation in State and Local elections is notoriously worse. Although (most) American citizens *may* vote, only a slim majority of us bother to, in the best of circumstances.

Even when we do vote, there is no guarantee that we do so on the basis of "deliberation." How many voters truly understand the "issues" when they vote, and can offer a reasoned defense for their vote? How many simply vote for their party's candidate, come what may? How many of those candidates have even offered clear, reasoned presentations of their views in the first place?

Even when we do vote, and even when we do have good reasons to support our vote, given a representative system such as that of the United States, we are merely electing someone to do the deliberation *on our behalf*! Under the most ideal interpretation, our elected officials will reason carefully, deliberate, and then make political decisions—but in that case only they are exercising their practical reason in the way Aristotle prescribes. The rest of us do not.

The United States is not a *polis* because of its size and plurality of values, as well. The assumption for Aristotle (and many other Ancient political theorists too) was that the city-state they envisioned would be quite small by our standards—one in which the citizens (generally) know one another, and in which all can be recruited for a town meeting by a single herald. All the citizens could gather together in one location and be addressed by speakers for the sake of political decision-making. Whether deliberating on laws, or issuing judgments in trials, the premise is that the citizens are all familiar with the details of the issues or case, and even know the history and character of the persons in question— something that is difficult in large communities. "Both in order to give decisions in matters of disputed rights, and to distribute the offices of government according to the merit of candidates, the citizens of a state must know one another's characters."[80]

Perhaps a close analogy to this is "Small Town America," where we can envision a local city council meeting in which all the citizens of that town gather to speak their minds on some local city ordinance, where voters all know the candidates for local office, or in which a local criminal trial includes jurors who

---

[78] *Nicomachean Ethics*, 1140a25-28.

[79] http://www.idea.int/vt/countryview.cfm?CountryCode=US

[80] Aristotle, *Politics*, 1326a-b.

all know the defendant and witnesses. Such is certainly not the case when we climb to State or National politics! Electing representatives seems to lack the sort of direct participation Aristotle has in mind, but perhaps this can be supplemented by participating in campaigns, in activity on behalf of political parties (e.g., "phone banking"), by participating in and contributing to "interest groups," by focusing on local elections and political processes, etc.

Aside from participation issues, a key feature of the *polis* is a common set of values that guides the political vision of the community, and given the plurality of worldviews and value systems found in the United States (and other large, cosmopolitan States), it is far from obvious that we are all guided by the same vision. "[A] city is excellent, at any rate, by its citizens' - those sharing in the regime - being excellent; and in our case all the citizens share in the regime."[81] That is, a *polis* is a "partnership" amongst persons with similar values, who get together to reflect upon those values, and deliberate upon which policies will best promote them.

Once again, we can imagine a hypothetical town in "Small Town America," where, for better, or for worse, "everyone" shares in common some basic, core values. The community is presumably homogenous with respect to religion and culture (generally conceived), and even if they disagree as to how best implement their values, the values themselves are a "given." Also once again, that certainly ceases to be the case once we start to think of larger political communities such as the State of California—let alone the Nation, as a whole.

Perhaps interestingly, those who advocate for "State's rights" or "local control" with regard to politics are drawing upon an Aristotelian legacy, whether they realize it or not. Those who claim that local officials and citizens are better equipped to make political decisions for their own citizens (as opposed to "Big Government" bureaucrats in Washington, for example), and those who argue that local communities (at least individual States) should be allowed to express their own values in their own (local) laws, even when those laws and values might be different in other States, are making claims consistent with Aristotle's vision the *polis*. An easy application of this would be those who advocate that "social issues," such as same-sex marriage, abortion, the legal status of marijuana, physician-assisted suicide, or even racial segregation, should be left to each State to decide for itself, based on their own values.[82] Should residents find those laws objectionable, they are free to move to another State that is more to their own liking. . . .

In the spirit of fairness, an appeal to "State's rights" is not merely (or always) some sort of political "dog whistle" to reference racism, segregation,

---

[81] Ibid., 1332a34.

[82] Infamous desegregation opponent Governor George Wallace of Alabama is known for having declared "Segregation now! Segregation tomorrow! Segregation forever!" in a 1963 address, but later remarked that he should have said, "States' rights now! States' rights tomorrow! States' rights forever!" (Carter, Dan T. *From George Wallace to Newt Gingrich: Race in the Conservative Counterrevolution*, 1963-1994. p. 1.)

discrimination against gays, etc.—and this is so not merely because the appeal can refer to "liberal" issues such as marijuana legalization as well. More charitably, an appeal to State's rights can be an appeal to the idea that political communities *should* be communities with shared values, and a one-size-fits-all, top-down approach might ignore that. Perhaps some communities, like Portland, Oregon, are ones in which mandatory recycling, extensive accommodations to bicycle riders, and legalized marijuana cultivation "works,"[83] but perhaps those same values (and the laws that promote or protect them) don't fit in Dallas, Texas?

If you think that the political community should be guided by shared values, and that the laws should promote those values, then it's clear that there must be agreement on what those values are—and this is probably implausible given larger communities where a variety of values is likely to be found.

There is no pretense of value-neutrality with regard to the government and laws of the *polis*. The function of the *polis* is moral perfection. It must, necessarily, aim at moral education. Laws are intended to shape character, and good legislators will enact laws that aim to make citizens virtuous by habituating them to good acts.

For better or for worse, the United States is a pluralistic society with a variety of competing visions of the good life. It would be difficult to pinpoint a singular "common good" towards which we all aim, and for the sake of which we all partner. The preceding analysis of the U.S. society is not meant as a criticism, but rather as an argument that the vision of the *polis* espoused by Aristotle is something different than what we experience in the United States—and in some cases, as we will soon see, that is probably a good thing!

As we have seen, political communities can fail to qualify as a *polis* for a variety of reasons, including size, lack of shared values, and inadequate levels of political participation. There is another way in which a community fails to qualify as a *polis*, though. Not every political organization serves to fulfill our *telos*. Aristotle distinguishes several different kinds of State based on who rules, and for what purpose.

| State | Who rules? | For what purpose? |
|---|---|---|
| Tyranny | one person | self-interest |
| Kingship | one person | collective interest |
| Oligarchy | a wealthy minority | self-interest |
| Aristocracy | a virtuous minority | collective interest |
| Populist democracy | many (usually poor) | self-interest |
| Polity | many | collective interest |

Aristotle recognizes that all six of those types of State exist (with numerous variations), but believes that only some of them are legitimate, with the rest being

---

[83] Please note that these are intentionally non-controversial examples. Clearly, the stakes are much higher when the difference in community standards isn't concerning recycling, but about which human beings have basic rights!

deviant or corrupted versions of "proper" government types. All of the "good" constitutions (i.e., kingship, aristocracy, and polity) exhibit justice (in some sense) and promote friendship (harmony) because of their emphasis on the common good.

When one person rules for the common good, that is kingship or monarchy. When the one person rules in his own interests, however, we have a tyranny. When a minority of the population rule for the common good, and when that minority rules because of their virtue and merit, we have an aristocracy; but, when the minority rules for their own interests, and they rule because of their wealth rather than their virtue or merit, we have an oligarchy. Finally, when the "many" rule for the sake of the common good, we have a polity—the system that Aristotle seems to be advocating (despite the fact that a majority of the population, being slaves and resident aliens, don't seem to count towards this "many!"). But, when the "many" is a mere majority ruling for their own good (e.g., the poor ruling for the sake of the poor), we have a (populist) democracy instead.

To contemporary (American) ears, the claim that "democracy" is a degenerative form of government might sound shocking. Isn't democracy the "best" form of government, the hope of the free world? Why would Aristotle have a problem with democracy?

In some respects, Aristotle's concerns about democracy echo those of his teacher, Plato. Plato condemned democracy because, among other things, it is a system that fails to recognize that rulership is a skill that requires expertise, like any other—and democracy falsely claims that all persons are equally qualified to exercise that skill.

For Aristotle (and Plato), the State exists to promote and cultivate virtue in its citizens. Laws are to mold and shape us into being better people, according to the standards of our shared community values. Such laws are necessary since most citizens are not already "virtuous" by means of their own efforts.

Most of us think of happiness in terms of desire-satisfaction, and seek a life of pleasure. In Plato's *Republic*, Plato has Socrates make the potentially surprising claim that neither the "sophists," nor any individual citizen, can "corrupt" the youth and turn them away from civic virtue.[84] This power lies in the hands of the

---

[84] The irony here is tangible. Recall that Socrates was executed for, among other things, "corrupting the youth"—a power that Plato denies Socrates (or anyone) could have. "Or are you too one of the multitude who believe that there are young men who are corrupted by the sophists, and that there are sophists in private life who corrupt to any extent worth mentioning, and that it is not rather the very men who talk in this strain who are the chief sophists and educate most effectively and mould to their own heart's desire young and old, men and women?' 'When?' said he. 'Why, when,' I said, 'the multitude are seated together in assemblies or in court-rooms or theaters or camps or any other public gathering of a crowd, and with loud uproar censure some of the things that are said and done and approve others, both in excess, with full-throated clamor and clapping of hands, and thereto the rocks and the region round about re-echoing redouble the din of the censure and the praise (*Republic* 492a-c).'"

"multitude," instead. Both Plato and Aristotle seem to think that the mass of public opinion is too powerful for any individual to subvert—which means that public moral values have to be steered and firmly established from the start, by means of good (enlightened) legislation and educational programs.

Since most of us aren't professional philosophers who have already discerned the good life, we need to be steered by laws and the threat of punishment to make good choices. Of course, those who *make* these laws will need to be virtuous, in order to make sure that the laws are correctly formed and implemented. This means that legislators must be virtuous, well-educated, and wise. Not everyone is going to be equally virtuous, well-educated, and wise! Therefore, not everyone is well-suited to be legislators.

A problem with both oligarchy and democracy is that they have a mistaken vision of the proper *telos* of the *polis*, which in turns results in a mistaken application of distributive justice. The State should distribute "awards" in proportion to the contribution one makes to the State, and we evaluate contributions by appealing to the *telos* of the State: cultivating virtue. Oligarchs mistakenly view the purpose of the State as maximizing wealth.[85] However, someone who donates the most amount of money to public accounts does not deserve the greatest "award" (or political influence) because "revenue" is not the *telos* of the State.

Where democracy errs is in thinking that the *telos* of *the polis* is to promote and maximize liberty and equality, and therefore that all persons should have equal status and privileges—but this is just as misguided, in its own way, as was the vision promoted by the oligarchs.

Where a democracy gets it "wrong" is in taking one measure in which people are equal (i.e., all citizens are equally free), and using it as the basis for another equal distribution: political decision-making. But, just because people are equal in one respect doesn't entail that they should be equal in another, nor does being "superior" in one respect (e.g., wealth) entail that one is superior in others (e.g., virtue).

Worse, when "freedom" is taken as the relevant measure and qualification for political decision-making, freedom becomes the *telos*, the "end" towards which political decisions are oriented. Freedom then, according to Aristotle's vision, becomes interpreted as the absence of control, the freedom to do whatever one desires—but this is the abandonment of moral discipline, and amounts to anarchy.[86] If everyone pursues their own vision of "the good," and is left to their own devices to do so, the *polis* has literally ceased to exist.

Instead, the greatest awards should go to those who most contribute to virtue—and it is for this reason that Aristotle is sympathetic to the idea of an

---

[85] Think of how the current Republican political party exalts "job creators" and, at times, literally describe the wealthiest as the "best" of us.

[86] For the sake of historical accuracy, neither contemporary democracy, nor even the democracies of Aristotle's own history, amounted to "anarchy." The liberty to pursue one's own values, while indeed anathema to a *polis*, will become quite desirable centuries later with the birth of classical liberalism.

enlightened aristocracy (*aristoi*—literally, "best persons") ruling the *polis*. For a genuine, *polis*, however, Aristotle claims that "it is clear that the best constitution is that organization by which everyone, whoever he is, would do the best things and live a blessed life."[87] In order for a person to cultivate virtue and exercise practical reason so as to live that blessed life, they must have the leisure time and resources necessary to develop those traits—and here we start to run into some potentially uncomfortable "tensions" in his *polis*.

Citizenship in the *polis*, for Aristotle, will be confined to males of "leisure" who are capable of rationally deliberating on the proper "end" (*telos*) of life. In order to have the leisure time necessary to develop virtue and to deliberate about and participate in political affairs, one can't really have a "normal job." Perhaps not coincidentally, Aristotle is advocating the lifestyle of his own aristocratic social class—a life of "gentlemanly leisure" that affords people like Aristotle the opportunity to study philosophy under teachers like Plato, because household slaves tend to the mundane needs of his estate!

The preceding statement was not merely an exaggeration meant to provoke you. Aristotle is serious about that aspect of the *polis*. In the previous chapter, we saw how Plato recommended in the *Laws* a small city state in which slaves and resident-aliens did all the physical labor and attended to most of the economic activities of the community so that the elite, leisured class of citizens could cultivate their virtue and participate governing. Aristotle makes a similar proposal: all necessary economic functions will be completed by slaves and resident aliens (both being non-citizens, of course) so that citizens (specifically, *males*) have sufficient leisure time to participate in the pursuit of their common good.[88]

As it turns out, the *polis* is only "that organization by which everyone, whoever he is, would do the best things and live a blessed life" if, by "everyone" we understand only a tiny, privileged minority of the total population. These aristocrats are at liberty to be virtuous and "live a blessed life" because the majority are not.

Perhaps ironically, Aristotle criticizes Plato for doing essentially the same thing. "He makes one body of persons the permanent rulers of his state [thus rejecting the principle of 'ruling and being ruled in turn']. This is a system which must breed discontent and dissension . . . ."[89] This criticism applies both the Guardians in the *Republic* as well as the leisured citizens (buttressed by their slaves and resident alien workers) in the *Laws*—but why wouldn't this apply equally to Aristotle's own *polis* for the very same reasons?

## Slavery

Having discussed slavery, without commentary thus far, in the context of both Plato's *Laws* and now Aristotle's *Politics*, it is time to offer a brief account

---

[87] Aristotle, *Politics*, 1324a23-25.
[88] Ibid., 1329a24-26.
[89] Ibid.,1264b25.

(and critique) of Aristotle's defense of slavery. With very little effort, I think it can easily be shown to be incoherent, and is revealed to be an unfortunate, all-too-human "blind spot" to which even brilliant philosophers such as Aristotle are subject.

Aristotle described slaves as "animate property (1253b2)." He holds that there are "natural slaves," and he contrasts this with those who become slaves by convention (law). It is always the "natural slave" that he has in mind when defending slavery. A "natural slave" is described as follows (1254a6):

1. "anybody who by his nature is not his own man, but another's"
2. "anybody who, being a man, is an article of property"

This is embarrassingly circular, of course, if offered as an argument for what makes someone a natural slave. A natural slave is someone who is another man's property? There is nothing yet "natural" about this, since anyone could be captured and placed into a condition of slavery, thereby making a person a "natural slave," by these standards! This is not what Aristotle meant, and in his defense he recognizes the need to establish whether any such persons as natural slaves even exist.

As it turns out, Aristotle claims that makes a human a natural slave is that he (or she) "is entirely without the faculty of deliberation (1260a7)."[90] For such humans, "the condition of slavery is both beneficial and just (1255a)." Apparently, a natural slave is some sort of mentally defective human who is "*entirely without*" the ability to deliberate. There are, of course, some people who, as a result of serious developmental delays or mental disorders, are arguably incapable of deliberating on their own behalf. In the vast majority of cases, such persons are in the care of others, wards of the State, supervised in board-and-care facilities, etc. The problem, of course, is that such persons constitute a tiny fraction of the adult population of the adult community, whereas the slave population Aristotle has in mind is larger than the free citizens! Moreover, such "natural slaves," even if they were numerous, would clearly be incapable of performing all the labor (both skilled and unskilled) needed to maintain the community and homes within the *polis*—due to the very cognitive deficiencies that make them "natural slaves" in the first place!

Lamentably, his rationalization of slavery on the basis of the existence of "natural slaves" found new traction nearly two thousand years later in the context of the American slavery.

*There is one strong argument in favor of negro slavery over all other*

---

[90] He also claims that women have a form of deliberative faculty which is "inconclusive"—a claim that supports, of course, his claim that males are the natural rulers of females, and that females are generally incapable of the feats of reason that males can perform—a claim that contemporary Aristotle expert and philosopher Martha Nussbaum capably refutes by both *her* standing in the philosophical community as well as the profundity of *her* many books.

*slavery: that he, being unfitted for the mechanic arts, for trade, and all skillful pursuits, leaves those pursuits to be carried on by the whites; and does not bring all industry into disrepute, as in Greece and Rome, where the slaves were not only the artists and mechanics, but also the merchants.*

*Whilst, as a general and abstract question, negro slavery has no other claims over other forms of slavery, except that from inferiority, or rather peculiarity, of race, almost all negroes require masters, whilst only the children, the women, the very weak, poor, and ignorant, &c., among the whites, need some protective and governing relation of this kind. . . .* [91]

Modern (utilitarian) philosopher, John Stuart Mill, acknowledges this unfortunate philosophical "kinship."

*There was a time when the division of mankind into two classes, a small one of masters and a numerous one of slaves, appeared, even to the most cultivated minds, to be a natural, and the only natural, condition of the human race. No less an intellect, and one which contributed no less to the progress of human thought, than Aristotle, held this opinion without doubt or misgiving. . . . But why need I go back to Aristotle? Did not the slaveowners of the Southern United States maintain the same doctrine, with all the fanaticism with which men cling to the theories that justify their passions and legitimate their personal interests? Did they not call heaven and earth to witness that the dominion of the white man over the black is natural, that the black race is by nature incapable of freedom, and marked out for slavery? some even going so far as to say that the freedom of manual labourers is an unnatural order of things anywhere.* [92]

Aristotle's defense of slavery is, to be blunt, indefensible. It is an unfortunate (and unmistakable) conceit of his classism and ethnocentrism that he could rationalize the subjugation of a multitude of people who clearly don't satisfy even his own definition of a "natural slave," for the sake of the "good life" for the elite ruling minority.

While it might be tempting to simply forgive Aristotle's "blind spot" with regard to slavery, and try to work with his political vision without the slaves, this is more easily said than done. After all, for a community to properly be a *polis*, the citizens must collectively participate in politics for the common good, and individually cultivate their own virtue. If we eliminate the slave working class, and consider everyone a citizen and a participant in the pursuit of the good life, who is performing all the "day jobs" needed to keep the society operating? Perhaps some sort of system of shared labor could be implemented, so that everyone has a "day job" but also enough leisure time to develop their virtue and

---

[91] George Fitzhugh, *Cannibals All! Or, Slaves Without Masters*: Electronic Edition (1806 -1881), p.297.

[92] John Stuart Mill, *The Subjugation of Women* (1869), paragraph 1.9.

participate in politics in an informed way. This is certainly possible, but would presumably require a pretty intrusive and ambitious system of work requirements and redistribution of wealth in order to facilitate every citizen having a chance to meaningfully participate in the life of the *polis*. This is not an objection, mind you—but merely a recognition of an issue of distributive justice that would need to be addressed in order to have a *polis* without slavery (or its equivalent).

In fairness, one could argue that a critique (and the inevitable demise) of Aristotle's breathtakingly elitist vision of citizenship is contained within his own text. He does hold up aristocracy as an ideal, in which case comes the probably offensive package of "natural slaves," and a majority of residents (e.g., women, slaves, resident aliens, and artisans), who have no participation in governing, and for whom, therefore, the fulfillment of their own potential (as rational, political animals) is denied. But, he also admits that "ruling and being ruled in turn" is as essential feature of a good constitution—and this, of course, is an alternative to aristocracy. At times, he holds up the *telos* of the *polis* to be only the attainment of virtue (favoring aristocracy), but at other times he holds up a more "complex" *telos* that includes not only virtue, but also wealth and equality—and this will favor a so-called "mixed constitution" (even if it is "second best").

The mixed constitution is so-called because it is a mix of aristocratic, oligarchic, and democratic themes. It is born from a recognition of seemingly inevitable factionalism and class division in any actual State. Ideally, no such divisions would exist, but, in the "real world," they inevitably arise. The task, then, is to forge a State that can manage those factions and remain just and stable. Essential to the success and stability of a mixed constitution is the existence of a large middle class.

## The Middle Class

Presumably less offensive than the adaptation of Aristotle in the defense of American slavery is the adaptation of his appreciation of the middle class. In the United States, both major political parties angle to present themselves as the true supporters of the middle class, and both tend to emphasize the value and importance of the middle class in terms of the American economy and society, overall.[93] Today's Democrats and Republicans are hardly the first to voice appreciation of the middle class, however. Aristotle's discussion of the middle-class is worth quoting at length:

> *In all states therefore there exist three divisions of the state, the very rich, the very poor, and thirdly those who are between the two. Since then it is admitted that what is moderate or in the middle is best, it is manifest that*

---

[93] The American middle class shrank from 61% to 51% from 1971 to 2011—though it remains the (slim) majority.
http://money.cnn.com/2012/08/22/news/economy/middle-class-pew/index.html?iid=EL

*the middle amount of all of the good things of fortune is the best amount to possess. For this degree of wealth is the readiest to obey reason, whereas for a person who is exceedingly beautiful or strong or nobly born or rich, or the opposite—exceedingly poor or weak or of very mean station, it is difficult to follow the bidding of reason; for the former turn more to insolence and grand wickedness, and the latter overmuch to malice and petty wickedness, and the motive of all wrongdoing is either insolence or malice. And moreover the middle class are the least inclined to shun office and to covet office, and both these tendencies are injurious to states. And in addition to these points, those who have an excess of fortune's goods, strength, wealth, friends and the like, are not willing to be governed and do not know how to be and they have acquired this quality even in their boyhood from their homelife, which was so luxurious that they have not got used to submitting to authority even in school, while those who are excessively in need of these things are too humble. Hence the latter class do not know how to govern but know how to submit to government of a servile kind, while the former class do not know how to submit to any government, and only know how to govern in the manner of a master. The result is a state consisting of slaves and masters, not of free men, and of one class envious and another contemptuous of their fellows. This condition of affairs is very far removed from friendliness, and from political partnership—for friendliness is an element of partnership, since men are not willing to be partners with their enemies even on a journey. But surely the ideal of the state is to consist as much as possible of persons that are equal and alike, and this similarity is most found in the middle classes; therefore the middle-class state will necessarily be best constituted in respect of those elements of which we say that the state is by nature composed. And also this class of citizens have the greatest security in the states; for they do not themselves covet other men's goods as do the poor, nor do the other classes covet their substance as the poor covet that of the rich; and because they are neither plotted against nor plotting they live free from danger. Because of this it was a good prayer of Phocylides— "In many things the middle have the best; Be mine a middle station.*

*It is clear therefore also that the political community administered by the middle class is the best, and that it is possible for those states to be well governed that are of the kind in which the middle class is numerous, and preferably stronger than both the other two classes, or at all events than one of them, for by throwing in its weight it sways the balance and prevents the opposite extremes from coming into existence. Hence it is the greatest good fortune if the men that have political power possess a moderate and sufficient substance, since where some own a very great deal of property and others none there comes about either an extreme democracy or an unmixed oligarchy, or a tyranny may result from both of the two extremes, for tyranny springs from both democracy and oligarchy of the most unbridled kind, but much less often from the middle forms of constitution and those near to them. The cause of this we will speak of later in our treatment of political revolutions. That the middle form of constitution is the best is evident; for it alone is free from faction, since where the middle class is numerous, factions and party divisions among the citizens are least likely to occur. And the great states are more free from faction for the same reason, because the middle class is numerous, whereas in the small states it is easy to divide the whole people into two parties leaving nothing in between, and also almost everybody is needy or wealthy. Also democracies are more secure and more long-lived than oligarchies owing to the citizens of the middle class (for they are more numerous and have a larger share of the honors in democracies than in oligarchies, since when the poor are in a majority without the middle class, adversity sets in and they are soon ruined.*[94]

A summary of the merits of the middle class, as described by Aristotle, is as follows:

- They are most ready to listen to reason
- They suffer least from ambition and envy
- They are more obedient
- They are (relatively) equal peers
- They enjoy greater security/stability
- They neither plot nor are plotted against

While the middle-class might lack some of the "aristocratic" virtues like "magnificence,"[95] they are capable of justice and other virtues, and, by preventing extreme factionalism between the rich and poor, present a stabilizing influence for their society. Indeed, we find an echo of the Golden Mean in Aristotle's appreciation of the middle class. If the very rich is one extreme, and the very poor is the other, then the middle class will be the mean between those two extremes. Communities are well-served when they "hit the mean." The middle class will be able to act as the mediator between the rich and the poor. In contrast, when the middle class is small and politically weak, economic inequalities will tend to grow more severe, and the community is likely to slide into corrupt rule either by oligarchs or by the "mob."

Even with a mixed-constitution/polity, Aristotle still advocates the cultivation of shared values. Although allowing political contributions from all social classes might mean that it not exclusively the virtuous aristocrats who make political decisions, this promotion of greater equality could result in greater

---

[94] *Politics*, 1295b4-15.

[95] This is just to say that it takes a lot of disposable income to be "magnificent" with your resources. Someone like Bill Gates can fund global philanthropic organizations, but a typical high school teacher, while capable of generosity (relative to her own resources), could never do anything so "grand."

friendship and harmony across the classes, and maybe even the overall promotion of virtue after all.

## Conclusion

Aristotle's impact on philosophy, like that of his teacher, Plato, is hard to overstate. A systematic and empirically-minded thinker, Aristotle's prominence would be rivaled only by Plato for centuries after his death. His domination of physics would not end until Galileo supplanted him some two *thousand* years later. His contributions to logic, epistemology, metaphysics, and ethics provide a model for enquiry, and fodder for critique and commentary, to this day. His understanding of causation informs contemporary cosmological arguments for God's existence (for example), and his emphasis on virtue has borne fruit in the currently flourishing field of virtue ethics. Logic students still learn "Aristotle's laws" and construct "squares of opposition."

In the field of Politics, Aristotle has been a source of inspiration for literally thousands of years. Today, he is the philosophical inspiration for contemporary conservative philosophers like Leo Strauss (and his neo-conservative heirs) as well as (classically) liberal philosophers such as Martha Nussbaum. His emphasis on a community of shared values, and the government as having a role in actively promoting certain values over others finds him at odds with contemporary libertarianism.

During the Medieval period, St. Thomas Aquinas leaned heavily on Aristotle in the formulation of his own system, including his political theory. Aquinas was provided with a Latin translation of the *Politics*. He arguably fused the insights of that work with those of St. Augustine's *City of God* into what remains the core substance of Catholic political theory to this day!

Just as Plato was Socrates' student, Aristotle (384 BCE – 322 BCE) was Plato's student. Aristotle is also tremendously important in the history of Western philosophy, and is often understood as a practical, empirical contrast to his idealist teacher. Aristotle seemed to study and be an expert on virtually everything, ranging from physics to poetry, to marine biology, to logic, and to ethics (to name just a few). Aristotle's thought shaped much of medieval philosophy and was so respected that Aquinas refers to him simply as "the philosopher." In the first excerpt from his Nicomachean Ethics, Aristotle argues that happiness (eudaimonia) is the ultimate aim of all our actions. Given that we are rational and social animals, this fulfillment of our "end" (telos) will require a life of reason and relationships. Virtue (arete) is the most important ingredient in living an excellent life (i.e,. one that achieves eudaimonia). Intellectual virtues might be taught, but moral virtues must be practiced and trained. One means of training is to pursue the "golden mean" in our actions. In the second set of excerpts from the Politics (in the provided text, the title is translated as "A Treatise on Government"), we have samples of Aristotle criticizing Plato's versions of the ideal state, Aristotle's discussion of the major types of constitutions and their features, his controversial treatment of slavery, and his own vision for the best (achievable) political community.

# *The Nichomachean Ethics* of Aristotle

### [Translation by F.H. Peters, M.A. 5th edition; London: Kegan Paul, Trench, Truebner & Co., 1893]

BOOK I.
THE END.
1.
In all he does man seeks same good as end or means.

Every art and every kind of inquiry, and likewise every act and purpose, seems to aim at some good: and so it has been well said that the good is that at which everything aims.

But a difference is observable among these aims or ends. What is aimed at is sometimes the exercise of a faculty, sometimes a certain result beyond that exercise. And where there is an end beyond the act, there the result is better than the exercise of the faculty.

Now since there are many kinds of actions and many arts and sciences, it follows that there are many ends also; *e.g.* health is the end of medicine, ships of shipbuilding, victory of the art of war, and wealth of economy.

But when several of these are subordinated to some one art or science,—as the making of bridles and other trappings to the art of horsemanship, and this in turn, along with all else that the soldier does, to the art of war, and so on,—then the end of the master-art is always more desired than the ends of the subordinate arts, since these are pursued for its sake. And this is equally true whether the end in view be the mere exercise of a faculty or something beyond that, as in the above instances.

2.

THE end is THE good; our subject is this and its science Politics.

If then in what we do there be some end which we wish for on its own account, choosing all the others as means to this, but not every end without exception as a means to something else (for so we should go on *ad infinitum,* and desire would be left void and objectless),—this evidently will be the good or the best of all things. And surely from a practical point of view it much concerns us to know this good; for then, like archers shooting at a definite mark, we shall be more likely to attain what we want.

If this be so, we must try to indicate roughly what it is, and first of all to which of the arts or sciences it belongs.

It would seem to belong to the supreme art or science, that one which most of all deserves the name of master-art or master-science.

Now Politics seems to answer to this description. For it prescribes which of the sciences a state needs, and which each man shall study, and up to what point; and to it we see subordinated even the highest arts, such as economy, rhetoric, and the art of war.

Since then it makes use of the other practical sciences, and since it further ordains what men are to do and from what to refrain, its end must include the ends of the others, and must be the proper good of man.

For though this good is the same for the individual and the state, yet the good of the state seems a grander and more perfect thing both to attain and to secure; and glad as one would be to do this service for a single individual, to do it for a people and for a number of states is nobler and more divine.

This then is the aim of the present inquiry, which is a sort of political inquiry.

3.

Exactness not permitted by subject nor to be expected by student, who needs experience and training.

We must be content if we can attain to so much precision in our statement as the subject before us admits of; for the same degree of accuracy is no more to be expected in all kinds of reasoning than in all kinds of handicraft.

Now the things that are noble and just (with which Politics deals) are so various and so uncertain, that some think these are merely conventional and not natural distinctions.

There is a similar uncertainty also about what is good, because good things often do people harm: men have before now been ruined by wealth, and have lost their lives through courage.

Our subject, then, and our data being of this nature, we must be content if we can indicate the truth roughly and in outline, and if, in dealing with matters that are not amenable to immutable laws, and reasoning from premises that are but probable, we can arrive at probable conclusions.

The reader, on his part, should take each of my statements in the same spirit; for it is the mark of an educated man to require, in each kind of inquiry, just so much exactness as the subject admits of: it is equally absurd to accept probable reasoning from a mathematician, and to demand scientific proof from an orator.

But each man can form a judgment about what he knows, and is called "a good judge" of that—of any special matter when he has received a special education therein, "a good judge" (without any qualifying epithet) when he has received a universal education. And hence a young man is not qualified to be a student of Politics; for he lacks experience of the affairs of life, which form the data and the subject-matter of Politics.

Further, since he is apt to be swayed by his feelings, he will derive no benefit from a study whose aim is not speculative but practical.

But in this respect young in character counts the same as young in years; for the young man's disqualification is not a matter of time, but is due to the fact that feeling rules his life and directs all his desires. Men of this character turn the knowledge they get to no account in practice, as we see with those we call incontinent; but those who direct their desires and actions by reason will gain much profit from the knowledge of these matters.

So much then by way of preface as to the student, and the spirit in which he must accept what we say, and the object which we propose to ourselves.

4.

Men agree that the good is happiness, but differ as to what this is.

4. Since—to resume—all knowledge and all purpose aims at some good, what is this which we say is the aim of Politics; or, in other words, what is the highest of all realizable goods?

As to its name, I suppose nearly all men are agreed; for the masses and the men of culture alike declare that it is happiness, and hold that to "live well" or to "do well" is the same as to be "happy."

But they differ as to what this happiness is, and the masses do not give the same account of it as the philosophers.

The former take it to be something palpable and plain, as pleasure or wealth or fame; one man holds it to be this, and another that, and often the same man is of different minds at different times,—after sickness it is health, and in poverty it is wealth; while when they are impressed with the consciousness of their ignorance, they admire most those who say grand things that are above their comprehension.

Some philosophers, on the other hand, have thought that, beside these several good things, there is an "absolute" good which is the cause of their goodness.

As it would hardly be worth while to review all the opinions that have been held, we will confine ourselves to those which are most popular, or which seem to have some foundation in reason.

We must reason from facts accepted without question by the man of trained character.

But we must not omit to notice the distinction that is drawn between the method of proceeding from your starting-points or principles, and the method of working up to them. Plato used with fitness to raise this question, and to ask whether the right way is from or to your starting-points, as in the race-course you may run from the judges to the boundary, or *vice versâ.*

Well, we must start from what is known.

But "what is known" may mean two things: "what is known to us," which is one thing, or "what is known" simply, which is another.

I think it is safe to say that *we* must start from what is known to *us*.

And on this account nothing but a good moral training can qualify a man to study what is noble and just—in a word, to study questions of Politics. For the undemonstrated fact is here the starting-point, and if this undemonstrated fact be sufficiently evident to a man, he will not require a "reason why." Now the man who has had a good moral training either has already arrived at starting-points or principles of action, or will easily accept them when pointed out. But he who neither has them nor will accept them may hear what Hesiod says —

"The best is he who of himself doth know;
Good too is he who listens to the wise;
But he who neither knows himself nor heeds
The words of others, is a useless man."

5.

The good cannot be pleasure, nor honour, nor virtue.

Let us now take up the discussion at the point from which we digressed.

It seems that men not unreasonably take their notions of the good or happiness from the lives actually led, and that the masses who are the least refined suppose it to be pleasure, which is the reason why they aim at nothing higher than the life of enjoyment.

For the most conspicuous kinds of life are three: this life of enjoyment, the life of the statesman, and, thirdly, the contemplative life.

The mass of men show themselves utterly slavish in their preference for the life of brute beasts, but their views receive consideration because many of those in high places have the tastes of Sardanapalus.

Men of refinement with a practical turn prefer honour; for I suppose we may say that honour is the aim of the statesman's life.

But this seems too superficial to be the good we are seeking: for it appears to depend upon those who give rather than upon those who receive it; while we have a presentiment that the good is something that is peculiarly a man's own and can scarce be taken away from him.

Moreover, these men seem to pursue honour in order that they may be assured of their own excellence,—at least, they wish to be honoured by men of sense, and by those who know them, and on the ground of their virtue or excellence. It is plain, then, that in their view, at any rate, virtue or excellence is better than honour; and perhaps we should take this to be the end of the statesman's life, rather than honour.

But virtue or excellence also appears too incomplete to be what we want; for it seems that a man might have virtue and yet be asleep or be inactive all his life, and, moreover, might meet with the greatest disasters and misfortunes; and no one would maintain that such a man is happy, except for argument's sake. But we will not dwell on these matters now, for they are sufficiently discussed in the popular treatises.

The third kind of life is the life of contemplation: we will treat of it further on.

As for the money-making life, it is something quite contrary to nature; and wealth evidently is not the good of which we are in search, for it is merely useful as a means to something else. So we might rather take pleasure and virtue or excellence to be ends than wealth; for they are chosen on their own account. But it seems that not even they are the end, though much breath has been wasted in attempts to show that they are.

6.

Various arguments to show against the Platonists that there cannot be one universal good.

Dismissing these views, then, we have now to consider the "universal good," and to state the difficulties which it presents; though such an inquiry is not a pleasant task in view of our friendship for the authors of the doctrine of ideas. But we venture to think that this is the right course, and that in the interests of truth we ought to sacrifice even what is nearest to us, especially as we call ourselves philosophers. Both are dear to us, but it is a sacred duty to give the preference to truth.

In the first place, the authors of this theory themselves did not assert a common idea in the case of things of which one is prior to the other; and for this reason they did not hold one common idea of numbers. Now the predicate good is applied to substances and also to qualities and relations. But that which has independent existence, what we call "substance," is logically prior to that which is relative; for the latter is an offshoot as it were, or [in logical language] an accident of a thing or substance. So [by their own showing] there cannot be one common idea of these goods.

Secondly, the term good is used in as many different ways as the term "is" or "being:" we apply the term to substances or independent existences, as God, reason; to qualities, as the virtues; to quantity, as the moderate or due amount; to relatives, as the useful; to time, as opportunity; to place, as habitation, and so on. It is evident, therefore, that the word good cannot stand for one and the same notion in all these various applications; for if it did, the term could not be applied in all the categories, but in one only.

Thirdly, if the notion were one, since there is but one science of all the things that come under one idea, there would be but one science of all goods; but as it is, there are many sciences even of the goods that come under one category; as, for instance, the science which deals with opportunity in war is strategy, but in disease is medicine; and the science of the due amount in the matter of food is medicine, but in the matter of exercise is the science of gymnastic.

Fourthly, one might ask what they mean by the "absolute:" in "absolute man" and "man" the word "man" has one and the same sense; for in respect of manhood there will be no difference between them; and if so, neither will there be any difference in respect of goodness between "absolute good" and "good."

Fifthly, they do not make the good any more good by making it eternal; a white thing that lasts a long while is no whiter than what lasts but a day.

There seems to be more plausibility in the doctrine of the Pythagoreans, who [in their table of opposites] place the one on the same side with the good things [instead of reducing all goods to unity]; and even Speusippus seems to follow them in this.

However, these points may be reserved for another occasion; but objection may be taken to what I have said on the ground that the Platonists do not speak in this way of all goods indiscriminately, but hold that those that are pursued and welcomed on their own account are called good by reference to one common form or type, while those things that tend to produce or preserve these goods, or to prevent their opposites, are called good only as means to these, and in a different sense.

It is evident that there will thus be two classes of goods: one good in themselves, the other good as means to the former. Let us separate then from the things that are merely useful those that are good in themselves, and inquire if they are called good by reference to one common idea or type.

Now what kind of things would one call "good in themselves"?

Surely those things that we pursue even apart from their consequences, such as wisdom and sight and certain pleasures and certain honours; for although we sometimes pursue these things as means, no one could refuse to rank them among the things that are good in themselves.

If these be excluded, nothing is good in itself except the idea; and then the type or form will be meaningless.

If however, these are ranked among the things that are good in themselves, then it must be shown that the goodness of all of them can be defined in the same terms, as white has the same meaning when applied to snow and to white lead.

But, in fact, we have to give a separate and different account of the goodness of honour and wisdom and pleasure.

Good, then, is not a term that is applied to all these things alike in the same sense or with reference to one common idea or form.

But how then do these things come to be called good? for they do not appear to have received the same name by chance merely. Perhaps it is because they all proceed from one source, or all conduce to one end; or perhaps it is rather in virtue of some analogy, just as we call the reason the eye of the soul because it bears the same relation to the soul that the eye does to the body, and so on.

But we may dismiss these questions at present; for to discuss them in detail belongs more properly to another branch of philosophy.

Even if there were, it would not help us here.

And for the same reason we may dismiss the further consideration of the idea; for even granting that this term good, which is applied to all these different things, has one and the same meaning throughout, or that there is an absolute good apart from these particulars, it is evident that this good will not be anything that man can realize or attain: but it is a good of this kind that we are now seeking.

It might, perhaps, be thought that it would nevertheless be well to make ourselves acquainted with this universal good, with a view to the goods that are attainable and realizable. With this for a pattern, it may be said, we shall more readily discern our own good, and discerning achieve it.

There certainly is some plausibility in this argument, but it seems to be at variance with the existing sciences; for though they are all aiming at some good and striving to make up their deficiencies, they neglect to inquire about this universal good. And yet it is scarce likely that the professors of the several arts and sciences should not know, nor even look for, what would help them so much.

And indeed I am at a loss to know how the weaver or the carpenter would be furthered in his art by a knowledge of this absolute good, or how a man would be rendered more able to heal the sick or to command an army by contemplation of the pure form or idea. For it seems to me that the physician does not even seek for health in this abstract way, but seeks for the health of man, or rather of some particular man, for it is individuals that he has to heal.

7.

The good is the final end, and happiness is this.

Leaving these matters, then, let us return once more to the question, what this good can be of which we are in search.

It seems to be different in different kinds of action and in different arts,—one thing in medicine and another in war, and so on. What then is the good in each of these cases? Surely that for the sake of which all else is done. And that in medicine is health, in war is victory, in building is a house,—a different thing in each different case, but always, in whatever we do and in whatever we choose, the end. For it is always for the sake of the end that all else is done.

If then there be one end of all that man does, this end will be the realizable good,—or these ends, if there be more than one.

By this generalization our argument is brought to the same point as before. This point we must try to explain more clearly.

We see that there are many ends. But some of these are chosen only as means, as wealth, flutes, and the whole class of instruments. And so it is plain that not all ends are final.

But the best of all things must, we conceive, be something final.

If then there be only one final end, this will be what we are seeking,—or if there be more than one, then the most final of them.

Now that which is pursued as an end in itself is more final than that which is pursued as means to something else, and that which is never chosen as means than that which is chosen both as an end in itself and as means, and that is strictly final which is always chosen as an end in itself and never as means.

Happiness seems more than anything else to answer to this description: for we always choose it for itself, and never for the sake of something else; while honour and pleasure and reason, and all virtue or excellence, we choose partly indeed for themselves (for, apart from any result, we should choose each of them), but partly also for the sake of happiness, supposing that they will help to make us happy. But no one chooses happiness for the sake of these things, or as a means to anything else at all.

We seem to be led to the same conclusion when we start from the notion of self-sufficiency.

The final good is thought to be self-sufficing [or all-sufficing]. In applying this term we do not regard a man as an individual leading a solitary life, but we also take account of parents, children, wife, and, in short, friends and fellow-citizens generally, since man is naturally a social being. Some limit must indeed be set to this; for if you go on to parents and descendants and friends of friends, you will never come to a stop. But this we will consider further on: for the present we will take self-sufficing to mean what by itself makes life desirable and in want of nothing. And happiness is believed to answer to this description.

And further, happiness is believed to be the most desirable thing in the world, and that not merely as one among other good things: if it were merely one among other good things [so that other things could be added to it], it is plain that the addition of the least of other goods must make it more desirable; for the addition becomes a surplus of good, and of two goods the greater is always more desirable.

Thus it seems that happiness is something final and self-sufficing, and is the end of all that man does.

To find it we ask, What is man's function?

But perhaps the reader thinks that though no one will dispute the statement that happiness is the best thing in the world, yet a still more precise definition of it is needed.

This will best be gained, I think, by asking, What is the function of man? For as the goodness and the excellence of a piper or a sculptor, or the practiser of any art, and generally of those who have any function or business to do, lies in that function, so man's good would seem to lie in his function, if he has one.

But can we suppose that, while a carpenter and a cobbler has a function and a business of his own, man has no business and no function assigned him by nature? Nay, surely as his several members, eye and hand and foot, plainly have each his own function, so we must suppose that man also has some function over and above all these.

What then is it?

Life evidently he has in common even with the plants, but we want that which is peculiar to him. We must exclude, therefore, the life of mere nutrition and growth.

Next to this comes the life of sense; but this too he plainly shares with horses and cattle and all kinds of animals.

There remains then the life whereby he acts—the life of his rational nature, with its two sides or divisions, one rational as obeying reason, the other rational as having and exercising reason.

But as this expression is ambiguous, we must be understood to mean thereby the life that consists in the exercise of the faculties; for this seems to be more properly entitled to the name.

The function of man, then, is exercise of his vital faculties [or soul] on one side in obedience to reason, and on the other side with reason.

But what is called the function of a man of any profession and the function of a man who is good in that profession are generically the same, *e.g.* of a harper and of a good harper; and this holds in all cases without exception, only that in the case of the latter his superior excellence at his work is added; for we say a harper's function is to harp, and a good harper's to harp well.

(Man's function then being, as we say, a kind of life—that is to say, exercise of his faculties and action of various kinds with reason—the good man's function is to do this well and beautifully [or nobly]. But the function of anything is done well when it is done in accordance with the proper excellence of that thing.)

Resulting definition of happiness.

If this be so the result is that the good of man is exercise of his faculties in accordance with excellence or virtue, or, if there be more than one, in accordance with the best and most complete virtue.

But there must also be a full term of years for this exercise; for one swallow or one fine day does not make a spring, nor does one day or any small space of time make a blessed or happy man.

This, then, may be taken as a rough outline of the good; for this, I think, is the proper method,—first to sketch the outline, and then to fill in the details. But it would seem that, the outline once fairly drawn, any one can carry on the work and fit in the several items which time reveals to us or helps us to find. And this indeed is the way in which the arts and sciences have grown; for it requires no extraordinary genius to fill up the gaps.

We must bear in mind, however, what was said above, and not demand the same degree of accuracy in all branches of study, but in each case so much as the subject-matter admits of and as is proper to that kind of inquiry. The carpenter and the geometer both look for the right angle, but in different ways: the former only wants such an approximation to it as his work requires, but the latter wants to know what constitutes a right angle, or what is its special quality; his aim is to find out the truth. And so in other cases we must follow the same course, lest we spend more time on what is immaterial than on the real business in hand.

Nor must we in all cases alike demand the reason why; sometimes it is enough if the undemonstrated fact be fairly pointed out, as in the case of the starting-points or principles of a science. Undemonstrated facts always form the first step or starting-point of a science; and these starting-points or principles are arrived at some in one way, some in another—some by induction, others by perception, others again by some kind of training. But in each case we must try to apprehend them in the proper way, and do our best to define them clearly; for they have great influence upon the subsequent course of an inquiry. A good start is more than half the race, I think, and our starting-point or principle, once found, clears up a number of our difficulties.

8.

This view harmonizes various current views.

We must not be satisfied, then, with examining this starting-point or principle of ours as a conclusion from our data, but must also view it in its relation to current opinions on the subject; for all experience harmonizes with a true principle, but a false one is soon found to be incompatible with the facts.

Now, good things have been divided into three classes, external goods on the one hand, and on the other goods of the soul and goods of the body; and the goods of the soul are commonly said to be goods in the fullest sense, and more good than any other.

But "actions and exercises of the vital faculties or soul" may be said to be "of the soul." So our account is confirmed by this opinion, which is both of long standing and approved by all who busy themselves with philosophy.

But, indeed, we secure the support of this opinion by the mere statement that certain actions and exercises are the end; for this implies that it is to be ranked among the goods of the soul, and not among external goods.

Our account, again, is in harmony with the common saying that the happy man lives well and does well; for we may say that happiness, according to us, is a living well and doing well.

And, indeed, all the characteristics that men expect to find in happiness seem to belong to happiness as we define it.

Some hold it to be virtue or excellence, some prudence, others a kind of wisdom; others, again, hold it to be all or some of these, with the addition of pleasure, either as an ingredient or as a necessary accompaniment; and some even include external prosperity in their account of it.

Now, some of these views have the support of many voices and of old authority; others have few voices, but those of weight; but it is probable that neither the one side nor the other is entirely wrong, but that in some one point at least, if not in most, they are both right.

First, then, the view that happiness is excellence or a kind of excellence harmonizes with our account; for "exercise of faculties in accordance with excellence" belongs to excellence.

But I think we may say that it makes no small difference whether the good be conceived as the mere possession of something, or as its use—as a mere habit or trained faculty, or as the exercise of that faculty. For the habit or faculty may be present, and yet issue in no good result, as when a man is asleep, or in any other way hindered from his function; but with its exercise this is not possible, for it must show itself in acts and in good acts. And as at the Olympic games it is not the fairest and strongest who receive the crown, but those who contend (for among these are the victors), so in life, too, the winners are those who not only have all the excellences, but manifest these in deed.

And, further, the life of these men is in itself pleasant. For pleasure is an affection of the soul, and each man takes pleasure in that which he is said to love,—he who loves horses in horses, he who loves sight-seeing in sight-seeing, and in the same way he who loves justice in acts of justice, and generally the lover of excellence or virtue in virtuous acts or the manifestation of excellence.

And while with most men there is a perpetual conflict between the several things in which they find pleasure, since these are not naturally pleasant, those who love what is noble take pleasure in that which is naturally pleasant. For the manifestations of excellence are naturally pleasant, so that they are both pleasant to them and pleasant in themselves.

Their life, then, does not need pleasure to be added to it as an appendage, but contains pleasure in itself.

Indeed, in addition to what we have said, a man is not good at all unless he takes pleasure in noble deeds. No one would call a man just who did not take pleasure in doing justice, nor generous who took no pleasure in acts of generosity, and so on.

If this be so, the manifestations of excellence will be pleasant in themselves. But they are also both good and noble, and that in the highest degree—at least, if the good man's judgment about them is right, for this is his judgment.

Happiness, then, is at once the best and noblest and pleasantest thing in the world, and these are not separated, as the Delian inscription would have them to

be:—
- "What is most just is noblest, health is best,
- Pleasantest is to get your heart's desire."

For all these characteristics are united in the best exercises of our faculties; and these, or some one of them that is better than all the others, we identify with happiness.

But nevertheless happiness plainly requires external goods too, as we said; for it is impossible, or at least not easy, to act nobly without some furniture of fortune. There are many things that can only be done through instruments, so to speak, such as friends and wealth and political influence: and there are some things whose absence takes the bloom off our happiness, as good birth, the blessing of children, personal beauty; for a man is not very likely to be happy if he is very ugly in person, or of low birth, or alone in the world, or childless, and perhaps still less if he has worthless children or friends, or has lost good ones that he had.

As we said, then, happiness seems to stand in need of this kind of prosperity; and so some identify it with good fortune, just as others identify it with excellence.

9.

It happiness acquired, or the gift of Gods or of chance?

This has led people to ask whether happiness is attained by learning, or the formation of habits, or any other kind of training, or comes by some divine dispensation or even by chance.

Well, if the Gods do give gifts to men, happiness is likely to be among the number, more likely, indeed, than anything else, in proportion as it is better than all other human things.

This belongs more properly to another branch of inquiry; but we may say that even if it is not heavensent, but comes as a consequence of virtue or some kind of learning or training, still it seems to be one of the most divine things in the world; for the prize and aim of virtue would appear to be better than anything else and something divine and blessed.

Again, if it is thus acquired it will be widely accessible; for it will then be in the power of all except those who have lost the capacity for excellence to acquire it by study and diligence.

And if it be better that men should attain happiness in this way rather than by chance, it is reasonable to suppose that it is so, since in the sphere of nature all things are arranged in the best possible way, and likewise in the sphere of art, and of each mode of causation, and most of all in the sphere of the noblest mode of causation. And indeed it would be too absurd to leave what is noblest and fairest to the dispensation of chance.

But our definition itself clears up the difficulty;* for happiness was defined as a certain kind of exercise of the vital faculties in accordance with excellence or virtue. And of the remaining goods [other than happiness itself], some must be present as necessary conditions, while others are aids and useful instruments to happiness. And this agrees with what we said at starting. We then laid down that the end of the art political is the best of all ends; but the chief business of that art is to make the citizens of a certain character—that is, good and apt to do what is noble. It is not without reason, then, that we do not call an ox, or a horse, or any brute happy; for none of them is able to share in this kind of activity.

For the same reason also a child is not happy; he is as yet, because of his age, unable to do such things. If we ever call a child happy, it is because we hope he will do them. For, as we said, happiness requires not only perfect excellence or virtue, but also a full term of years for its exercise. For our circumstances are liable to many changes and to all sorts of chances, and it is possible that he who is now most prosperous will in his old age meet with great disasters, as is told of Priam in the tales of Troy; and a man who is thus used by fortune and comes to a miserable end cannot be called happy.

10.

Can no man be called happy during life?

Are we, then, to call no man happy as long as he lives, but to wait for the end, as Solon said?

And, supposing we have to allow this, do we mean that he actually is happy after he is dead? Surely that is absurd, especially for us who say that happiness is a kind of activity or life.

But if we do not call the dead man happy, and if Solon meant not this, but that only then could we safely apply the term to a man, as being now beyond the reach of evil and calamity, then here too we find some ground for objection. For it is thought that both good and evil may in some sort befall a dead man (just as they may befall a living man, although he is unconscious of them), *e.g.* honours rendered to him, or the reverse of these, and again the prosperity or the misfortune of his children and all his descendants.

But this, too, has its difficulties; for after a man has lived happily to a good old age, and ended as he lived, it is possible that many changes may befall him in the persons of his descendants, and that some of them may turn out good and meet with the good fortune they deserve, and others the reverse. It is evident too that the degree in which the descendants are related to their ancestors may vary to any extent. And it would be a strange thing if the dead man were to change with these changes and become happy and miserable by turns. But it would also be strange to suppose that the dead are not affected at all, even for a limited time, by the fortunes of their posterity.

But let us return to our former question; for its solution will, perhaps, clear up this other difficulty.

The saying of Solon may mean that we ought to look for the end and then call a man happy, not because he now is, but because he once was happy.

But surely it is strange that when he is happy we should refuse to say what is true of him, because we do not like to apply the term to living men in view of the changes to which they are liable, and because we hold happiness to be something that endures and is little liable to change, while the fortunes of one and the same man often undergo many revolutions: for, it is argued, it is plain that, if we follow the changes of fortune, we shall call the same man happy and miserable many times over, making the happy man "a sort of chameleon and one who rests on no sound foundation."

We reply that it cannot be right thus to follow fortune. For it is not in this that our weal or woe lies; but, as we said, though good fortune is needed to complete man's life, yet it is the excellent employment of his powers that constitutes his happiness, as the reverse of this constitutes his misery.

But the discussion of this difficulty leads to a further confirmation of our account. For nothing human is so constant as the excellent exercise of our faculties. The sciences themselves seem to be less abiding. And the highest of these exercises are the most abiding, because the happy are occupied with them most of all and most continuously (for this seems to be the reason why we do not forget how to do them).

The happy man, then, as we define him, will have this required property of permanence, and all through life will preserve his character; for he will be occupied continually, or with the least possible interruption, in excellent deeds and excellent speculations; and, whatever his fortune be, he will take it in the noblest fashion, and bear himself always and in all things suitably, since he is truly good and "foursquare without a flaw."

But the dispensations of fortune are many, some great, some small. The small ones, whether good or evil, plainly are of no weight in the scale; but the great ones, when numerous, will make life happier if they be good; for they help to give a grace to life themselves, and their use is noble and good; but, if they be evil, will enfeeble and spoil happiness; for they bring pain, and often impede the exercise of our faculties.

But nevertheless true worth shines out even here, in the calm endurance of many great misfortunes, not through insensibility, but through nobility and greatness of soul. And if it is what a man does that determines the character of his life, as we said, then no happy man will become miserable; for he will never do what is hateful and base. For we hold that the man who is truly good and wise will bear with dignity whatever fortune sends, and will always make the best of his circumstances, as a good general will turn the forces at his command to the best account, and a good shoemaker will make the best shoe that can be made out of a given piece of leather, and so on with all other crafts.

If this be so, the happy man will never become miserable, though he will not be truly happy if he meets with the fate of Priam.

But yet he is not unstable and lightly changed: he will not be moved from his happiness easily, nor by any ordinary misfortunes, but only by many heavy ones; and after such, he will not recover his happiness again in a short time, but if at all, only in a considerable period, which has a certain completeness, and in which he attains to great and noble things.

We shall meet all objections, then, if we say that a happy man is "one who exercises his faculties in accordance with perfect excellence, being duly furnished with external goods, not for any chance time, but for a full term of years:" to which perhaps we should add, "and who shall continue to live so, and shall die as he lived," since the future is veiled to us, but happiness we take to be the end and in all ways perfectly final or complete.

If this be so, we may say that those living men are blessed or perfectly happy who both have and shall continue to have these characteristics, but happy as men only.

11.

Cannot the fortunes of survivors affect the dead?

Passing now from this question to that of the fortunes of descendants and of friends generally, the doctrine that they do not affect the departed at all seems too cold and too much opposed to popular opinion. But as the things that happen to them are many and differ in all sorts of ways, and some come home to them more and some less, so that to discuss them all separately would be a long, indeed an endless task, it will perhaps be enough to speak of them in general terms and in outline merely.

Now, as of the misfortunes that happen to a man's self, some have a certain weight and influence on his life, while others are of less moment, so is it also with what happens to any of his friends. And, again, it always makes much more difference whether those who are affected by an occurrence are alive or dead than it does whether a terrible crime in a tragedy be enacted on the stage or merely supposed to have already taken place. We must therefore take these differences into account, and still more, perhaps, the fact that it is a doubtful question whether the dead are at all accessible to good and ill. For it appears that even if anything that happens, whether good or evil, does come home to them, yet it is something unsubstantial and slight to them if not in itself; or if not that, yet at any rate its influence is not of that magnitude or nature that it can make happy those who are not, or take away their happiness from those that are.

It seems then—to conclude—that the prosperity, and likewise the adversity, of friends does affect the dead, but not in such a way or to such an extent as to make the happy unhappy, or to do anything of the kind.

12.

Happiness as absolute end is above praise.

These points being settled, we may now inquire whether happiness is to be ranked among the goods that we praise, or rather among those that we revere; for it is plainly not a mere potentiality, but an actual good.

What we praise seems always to be praised as being of a certain quality and having a certain relation to something. For instance, we praise the just and the courageous man, and generally the good man, and excellence or virtue, because of what they do or produce; and we praise also the strong or the swiftfooted man, and so on, because he has a certain gift or faculty in relation to some good and admirable thing.

This is evident if we consider the praises bestowed on the Gods. The Gods are thereby made ridiculous by being made relative to man; and this happens because, as we said, a thing can only be praised in relation to something else.

If, then, praise be proper to such things as we mentioned, it is evident that to the best things is due, not praise, but something greater and better, as our usage shows; for the Gods we call blessed and happy, and "blessed" is the term we apply to the most godlike men.

And so with good things: no one praises happiness as he praises justice, but calls it blessed, as something better and more divine.

On these grounds Eudoxus is thought to have based a strong argument for the claims of pleasure to the first prize: for he maintained that the fact that it is not praised, though it is a good thing, shows that it is higher than the goods we praise, as God and the good are higher; for these are the standards by reference to which we judge all other things,—giving praise to excellence or virtue, since it makes us apt to do what is noble, and passing encomiums on the results of virtue, whether these be bodily or psychical.

But to refine on these points belongs more properly to those who have made a study of the subject of encomiums; for us it is plain from what has been said that happiness is one of the goods which we revere and count as final.

And this further seems to follow from the fact that it is a starting-point or principle: for everything we do is always done for its sake; but the principle and cause of all good we hold to be something divine and worthy of reverence.

13.

Division of the faculties and resulting division of the virtues.

Since happiness is an exercise of the vital faculties in accordance with perfect virtue or excellence, we will now inquire about virtue or excellence; for this will probably help us in our inquiry about happiness.

And indeed the true statesman seems to be especially concerned with virtue, for he wishes to make the citizens good and obedient to the laws. Of this we have an example in the Cretan and the Lacedæmonian lawgivers, and any others who have resembled them. But if the inquiry belongs to Politics or the science of the state, it is plain that it will be in accordance with our original purpose to pursue it.

The virtue or excellence that we are to consider is, of course, the excellence of man; for it is the good of man and the happiness of man that we started to seek. And by the excellence of man I mean excellence not of body, but of soul; for happiness we take to be an activity of the soul.

If this be so, then it is evident that the statesman must have some knowledge of the soul, just as the man who is to heal the eye or the whole body must have some knowledge of them, and that the more in proportion as the science of the state is higher and better than medicine. But all educated physicians take much pains to know about the body.

As statesmen [or students of Politics], then, we must inquire into the nature of the soul, but in so doing we must keep our special purpose in view and go only so far as that requires; for to go into minuter detail would be too laborious for the present undertaking.

Now, there are certain doctrines about the soul which are stated elsewhere with sufficient precision, and these we will adopt.

Two parts of the soul are distinguished, an irrational and a rational part.

Whether these are separated as are the parts of the body or any divisible thing, or whether they are only distinguishable in thought but in fact inseparable, like concave and convex in the circumference of a circle, makes no difference for our present purpose.

Of the irrational part, again, one division seems to be common to all things that live, and to be possessed by plants—I mean that which causes nutrition and growth; for we must assume that all things that take nourishment have a faculty of this kind, even when they are embryos, and have the same faculty when they are full grown; at least, this is more reasonable than to suppose that they then have a different one.

The excellence of this faculty, then, is plainly one that man shares with other beings, and not specifically human.

And this is confirmed by the fact that in sleep this part of the soul, or this faculty, is thought to be most active, while the good and the bad man are undistinguishable when they are asleep (whence the saying that for half their lives there is no difference between the happy and the miserable; which indeed is what we should expect; for sleep is the cessation of the soul from those functions in respect of which it is called good or bad), except that they are to some slight extent roused by what goes on in their bodies, with the result that the dreams of the good man are better than those of ordinary people.

However, we need not pursue this further, and may dismiss the nutritive principle, since it has no place in the excellence of man.

But there seems to be another vital principle that is irrational, and yet in some way partakes of reason. In the case of the continent and of the incontinent man alike we praise the reason or the rational part, for it exhorts them rightly and urges them to do what is best; but there is plainly present in them another principle besides the rational one, which fights and struggles against the reason. For just as a paralyzed limb, when you will to move it to the right, moves on the contrary to the left, so is it with the soul; the incontinent man's impulses run counter to his reason. Only whereas we see the refractory member in the case of the body, we do not see it in the case of the soul. But we must nevertheless, I think, hold that in the soul too there is something beside the reason, which opposes and runs counter to it (though in what sense it is distinct from the reason does not matter here).

It seems, however, to partake of reason also, as we said: at least, in the continent man it submits to the reason; while in the temperate and courageous man we may say it is still more obedient; for in him it is altogether in harmony with the reason.

The irrational part, then, it appears, is twofold. There is the vegetative faculty, which has no share of reason; and the faculty of appetite or of desire in general, which in a manner partakes of reason or is rational as listening to reason and submitting to its sway,—rational in the sense in which we speak of rational obedience to father or friends, not in the sense in which we speak of rational apprehension of mathematical truths. But all advice and all rebuke and exhortation testify that the irrational part is in some way amenable to reason.

If then we like to say that this part, too, has a share of reason, the rational part also will have two divisions: one rational in the strict sense as possessing reason in itself, the other rational as listening to reason as a man listens to his father.

Now, on this division of the faculties is based the division of excellence; for we speak of intellectual excellences and of moral excellences; wisdom and understanding and prudence we call intellectual, liberality and temperance we call moral virtues or excellences. When we are speaking of a man's moral character we do not say that he is wise or intelligent, but that he is gentle or temperate. But we praise the wise man, too, for his habit of mind or trained faculty; and a habit or trained faculty that is praiseworthy is what we call an excellence or virtue.

BOOK II.
MORAL VIRTUE.
1.
Moral virtue is acquired by the repetition of the corresponding acts.

Excellence, then, being of these two kinds, intellectual and moral intellectual excellence owes its birth and growth mainly to instruction, and so requires time and experience, while moral excellence is the result of habit or custom (ἔθος), and has accordingly in our language received a name formed by a slight change from ἔθος.

From this it is plain that none of the moral excellences or virtues is implanted in us by nature; for that which is by nature cannot be altered by training. For instance, a stone naturally tends to fall downwards, and you could not train it to rise upwards, though you tried to do so by throwing it up ten thousand times, nor could you train fire to move downwards, nor accustom anything which naturally behaves in one way to behave in any other way.

The virtues, then, come neither by nature nor against nature, but nature gives the capacity for acquiring them, and this is developed by training.

Again, where we do things by nature we get the power first, and put this power forth in act afterwards: as we plainly see in the case of the senses; for it is not by constantly seeing and hearing that we acquire those faculties, but, on the contrary, we had the power first and then used it, instead of acquiring the power by the use. But the virtues we acquire by doing the acts, as is the case with the arts too. We learn an art by doing that which we wish to do when we have learned it; we become builders by building, and harpers by harping. And so by doing just acts we become just, and by doing acts of temperance and courage we become temperate and courageous.

This is attested, too, by what occurs in states; for the legislators make their citizens good by training; *i.e.* this is the wish of all legislators, and those who do not succeed in this miss their aim, and it is this that distinguishes a good from a bad constitution.

Again, both the moral virtues and the corresponding vices result from and are formed by the same acts; and this is the case with the arts also. It is by harping that good harpers and bad harpers alike are produced: and so with builders and the rest; by building well they will become good builders, and bad builders by building badly. Indeed, if it were not so, they would not want anybody to teach them, but would all be born either good or bad at their trades. And it is just the same with the virtues also. It is by our conduct in our intercourse with other men that we become just or unjust, and by acting in circumstances of danger, and training ourselves to feel fear or confidence, that we become courageous or cowardly. So, too, with our animal appetites and the passion of anger; for by behaving in this way or in that on the occasions with which these passions are concerned, some become temperate and gentle, and others profligate and ill-tempered. In a word, acts of any kind produce habits or characters of the same kind.

Hence we ought to make sure that our acts be of a certain kind; for the resulting character varies as they vary. It makes no small difference, therefore, whether a man be trained from his youth up in this way or in that, but a great difference, or rather all the difference.

2.

These acts must be such as reason prescribes; they can't be defined exactly, but must be neither too much nor too little.

But our present inquiry has not, like the rest, a merely speculative aim; we are not inquiring merely in order to know what excellence or virtue is, but in order to become good; for otherwise it would profit us nothing. We must ask therefore about these acts, and see of what kind they are to be; for, as we said, it is they that determine our habits or character.

First of all, then, that they must be in accordance with right reason is a common characteristic of them, which we shall here take for granted, reserving for future discussion* the question what this right reason is, and how it is related to the other excellences.

But let it be understood, before we go on, that all reasoning on matters of practice must be in outline merely, and not scientifically exact: for, as we said at starting, the kind of reasoning to be demanded varies with the subject in hand; and in practical matters and questions of expediency there are no invariable laws, any more than in questions of health.

And if our general conclusions are thus inexact, still more inexact is all reasoning about particular cases; for these fall under no system of scientifically established rules or traditional maxims, but the agent must always consider for himself what the special occasion requires, just as in medicine or navigation.

But though this is the case we must try to render what help we can.

First of all, then, we must observe that, in matters of this sort, to fall short and to exceed are alike fatal. This is plain (to illustrate what we cannot see by what we can see) in the case of strength and health. Too much and too little exercise alike destroy strength, and to take too much meat and drink, or to take too little, is equally ruinous to health, but the fitting amount produces and increases and preserves them. Just so, then, is it with temperance also, and courage, and the other virtues. The man who shuns and fears everything and never makes a stand, becomes a coward; while the man who fears nothing at all, but will face anything, becomes foolhardy. So, too, the man who takes his fill of any kind of pleasure, and abstains from none, is a profligate, but the man who shuns all (like him whom we call a "boor") is devoid of sensibility. Thus temperance and courage are destroyed both by excess and defect, but preserved by moderation.

But habits or types of character are not only produced and preserved and destroyed by the same occasions and the same means, but they will also manifest themselves in the same circumstances. This is the case with palpable things like strength. Strength is produced by taking plenty of nourishment and doing plenty of hard work, and the strong man, in turn, has the greatest capacity for these. And the case is the same with the virtues: by abstaining from pleasure we become temperate, and when we have become temperate we are best able to abstain. And so with courage: by habituating ourselves to despise danger, and to face it, we become courageous; and when we have become courageous, we are best able to face danger.

3.

Virtue is in various ways concerned with pleasure and pain.

The pleasure or pain that accompanies the acts must be taken as a test of the formed habit or character.

He who abstains from the pleasures of the body and rejoices in the abstinence is temperate, while he who is vexed at having to abstain is profligate; and again, he who faces danger with pleasure, or, at any rate, without pain, is courageous, but he to whom this is painful is a coward.

For moral virtue or excellence is closely concerned with pleasure and pain. It is pleasure that moves us to do what is base, and pain that moves us to refrain from what is noble. And therefore, as Plato says, man needs to be so trained from his youth up as to find pleasure and pain in the right objects. This is what sound education means.

Another reason why virtue has to do with pleasure and pain, is that it has to do with actions and passions or affections; but every affection and every act is accompanied by pleasure or pain.

The fact is further attested by the employment of pleasure and pain in correction; they have a kind of curative property, and a cure is effected by administering the opposite of the disease.

Again, as we said before, every type of character [or habit or formed faculty] is essentially relative to, and concerned with, those things that form it for good or for ill; but it is through pleasure and pain that bad characters are formed—that is to say, through pursuing and avoiding the wrong pleasures and pains, or pursuing and avoiding them at the wrong time, or in the wrong manner, or in any other of the various ways of going wrong that may be distinguished.

And hence some people go so far as to define the virtues as a kind of impassive or neutral state of mind. But they err in stating this absolutely, instead of qualifying it by the addition of the right and wrong manner, time, etc.

We may lay down, therefore, that this kind of excellence [*i.e.* moral excellence] makes us do what is best in matters of pleasure and pain, while vice or badness has the contrary effect. But the following considerations will throw additional light on the point.

There are three kinds of things that move us to choose, and three that move us to avoid them: on the one hand, the beautiful or noble, the advantageous, the pleasant; on the other hand, the ugly or base, the hurtful, the painful. Now, the good man is apt to go right, and the bad man to go wrong, about them all, but especially about pleasure: for pleasure is not only common to man with animals, but also accompanies all pursuit or choice; since the noble, and the advantageous also, are pleasant in idea.

Again, the feeling of pleasure has been fostered in us all from our infancy by our training, and has thus become so engrained in our life that it can scarce be washed out. And, indeed, we all more or less make pleasure our test in judging of actions. For this reason too, then, our whole inquiry must be concerned with these matters; since to be pleased and pained in the right or the wrong way has great influence on our actions.

Again, to fight with pleasure is harder than to fight with wrath (which Heraclitus says is hard), and virtue, like art, is always more concerned with what is harder; for the harder the task the better is success. For this reason also, then, both [moral] virtue or excellence and the science of the state must always be concerned with pleasures and pains; for he that behaves rightly with regard to them will be good, and he that behaves badly will be bad.

We will take it as established, then, that [moral] excellence or virtue has to do with pleasures and pains; and that the acts which produce it develop it, and also, when differently done, destroy it; and that it manifests itself in the same acts which produced it.

4.

The conditions of virtuous action as distinct from artistic production.

But here we may be asked what we mean by saying that men can become just and temperate only by doing what is just and temperate: surely, it may be said, if their acts are just and temperate, they themselves are already just and temperate, as they are grammarians and musicians if they do what is grammatical and musical.

We may answer, I think, firstly, that this is not quite the case even with the arts. A man may do something grammatical [or write something correctly] by chance, or at the prompting of another person: he will not be grammatical till he not only does something grammatical, but also does it grammatically [or like a grammatical person], *i.e.* in virtue of his own knowledge of grammar.

But, secondly, the virtues are not in this point analogous to the arts. The products of art have their excellence in themselves, and so it is enough if when produced they are of a certain quality; but in the case of the virtues, a man is not said to act justly or temperately [or like a just or temperate man] if what he does merely be of a certain sort—he must also be in a certain state of mind when he does it; *i.e.*, first of all, he must know what he is doing; secondly, he must choose it, and choose it for itself; and, thirdly, his act must be the expression of a formed and stable character. Now, of these conditions, only one, the knowledge, is necessary for the possession of any art; but for the possession of the virtues knowledge is of little or no avail, while the other conditions that result from repeatedly doing what is just and temperate are not a little important, but all-important.

The thing that is done, therefore, is called just or temperate when it is such as the just or temperate man would do; but the man who does it is not just or temperate, unless he also does it in the spirit of the just or the temperate man.

It is right, then, to say that by doing what is just a man becomes just, and temperate by doing what is temperate, while without doing thus he has no chance of ever becoming good.

But most men, instead of doing thus, fly to theories, and fancy that they are philosophizing and that this will make them good, like a sick man who listens attentively to what the doctor says and then disobeys all his orders. This sort of philosophizing will no more produce a healthy habit of mind than this sort of treatment will produce a healthy habit of body.

5.

Virtue not an emotion, nor a faculty, but a trained faculty or habit.

We have next to inquire what excellence or virtue is.

A quality of the soul is either (1) a passion or emotion, or (2) a power or faculty, or (3) a habit or trained faculty; and so virtue must be one of these three. By (1) a passion or emotion we mean appetite, anger, fear, confidence, envy, joy, love, hate, longing, emulation, pity, or generally that which is accompanied by pleasure or pain; (2) a power or faculty is that in respect of which we are said to be capable of being affected in any of these ways, as, for instance, that in respect of which we are able to be angered or pained or to pity; and (3) a habit or trained faculty is that in respect of which we are well or ill regulated or disposed in the matter of our affections; as, for instance, in the matter of being angered, we are ill regulated if we are too violent or too slack, but if we are moderate in our anger we are well regulated. And so with the rest.

Now, the virtues are not emotions, nor are the vices—(1) because we are not called good or bad in respect of our emotions, but are called so in respect of our virtues or vices; (2) because we are neither praised nor blamed in respect of our emotions (a man is not praised for being afraid or angry, nor blamed for being angry simply, but for being angry in a particular way), but we are praised or blamed in respect of our virtues or vices; (3) because we may be angered or frightened without deliberate choice, but the virtues are a kind of deliberate choice, or at least are impossible without it; and (4) because in respect of our emotions we are said to be moved, but in respect of our virtues and vices we are not said to be moved, but to be regulated or disposed in this way or in that.

For these same reasons also they are not powers or faculties; for we are not called either good or bad for being merely capable of emotion, nor are we either praised or blamed for this. And further, while nature gives us our powers or faculties, she does not make us either good or bad. (This point, however, we have already treated.)

If, then, the virtues be neither emotions nor faculties, it only remains for them to be habits or trained faculties.

6.

viz., the habit of choosing the mean.

We have thus found the genus to which virtue belongs; but we want to know, not only that it is a trained faculty, but also what species of trained faculty it is.

We may safely assert that the virtue or excellence of a thing causes that thing both to be itself in good condition and to perform its function well. The excellence of the eye, for instance, makes both the eye and its work good; for it is by the excellence of the eye that we see well. So the proper excellence of the horse makes a horse what he should be, and makes him good at running, and carrying his rider, and standing a charge.

If, then, this holds good in all cases, the proper excellence or virtue of man will be the habit or trained faculty that makes a man good and makes him perform his function well.

How this is to be done we have already said, but we may exhibit the same conclusion in another way, by inquiring what the nature of this virtue is.

Now, if we have any quantity, whether continuous or discrete,* it is possible to take either a larger [or too large], or a smaller [or too small], or an equal [or fair] amount, and that either absolutely or relatively to our own needs.

By an equal or fair amount I understand a mean amount, or one that lies between excess and deficiency.

By the absolute mean, or mean relatively to the thing itself, I understand that which is equidistant from both extremes, and this is one and the same for all.

By the mean relatively to us I understand that which is neither too much nor too little for us; and this is not one and the same for all.

For instance, if ten be larger [or too large] and two be smaller [or too small], if we take six we take the mean relatively to the thing itself [or the arithmetical mean]; for it exceeds one extreme by the same amount by which it is exceeded by the other extreme: and this is the mean in arithmetical proportion.

But the mean relatively to us cannot be found in this way. If ten pounds of food is too much for a given man to eat, and two pounds too little, it does not follow that the trainer will order him six pounds: for that also may perhaps be too much for the man in question, or too little; too little for Milo, too much for the beginner. The same holds true in running and wrestling.

And so we may say generally that a master in any art avoids what is too much and what is too little, and seeks for the mean and chooses it—not the absolute but the relative mean.

If, then, every art or science perfects its work in this way, looking to the mean and bringing its work up to this standard (so that people are wont to say of a good work that nothing could be taken from it or added to it, implying that excellence is destroyed by excess or deficiency, but secured by observing the mean; and good artists, as we say, do in fact keep their eyes fixed on this in all that they do), and if virtue, like nature, is more exact and better than any art, it follows that virtue also must aim at the mean—virtue of course meaning moral virtue or excellence; for it has to do with passions and actions, and it is these that admit of excess and deficiency and the mean. For instance, it is possible to feel fear, confidence, desire, anger, pity, and generally to be affected pleasantly and painfully, either too much or too little, in either case wrongly; but to be thus affected at the right times, and on the right occasions, and towards the right persons, and with the right object, and in the right fashion, is the mean course and the best course, and these are characteristics of virtue. And in the same way our outward acts also admit of excess and deficiency, and the mean or due amount.

Virtue, then, has to deal with feelings or passions and with outward acts, in which excess is wrong and deficiency also is blamed, but the mean amount is praised and is right—both of which are characteristics of virtue.

Virtue, then, is a kind of moderation (μεσότης τις), inasmuch as it aims at the mean or moderate amount (τὸ μέσον).

Again, there are many ways of going wrong (for evil is infinite in nature, to use a Pythagorean figure, while good is finite), but only one way of going right; so that the one is easy and the other hard—easy to miss the mark and hard to hit. On this account also, then, excess and deficiency are characteristic of vice, hitting the mean is characteristic of virtue:

"Goodness is simple, ill takes any shape."

Virtue, then, is a habit or trained faculty of choice, the characteristic of which lies in moderation or observance of the mean relatively to the persons concerned, as determined by reason, *i.e.* by the reason by which the prudent man would determine it. And it is a moderation, firstly, inasmuch as it comes in the middle or mean between two vices, one on the side of excess, the other on the side of defect; and, secondly, inasmuch as, while these vices fall short of or exceed the due measure in feeling and in action, it finds and chooses the mean, middling, or moderate amount.

Regarded in its essence, therefore, or according to the definition of its nature, virtue is a moderation or middle state, but viewed in its relation to what is best and right it is the extreme of perfection.

But it is not all actions nor all passions that admit of moderation; there are some whose very names imply badness, as malevolence, shamelessness, envy, and, among acts, adultery, theft, murder. These and all other like things are blamed as being bad in themselves, and not merely in their excess or deficiency. It is impossible therefore to go right in them; they are always wrong: rightness and wrongness in such things (*e.g.* in adultery) does not depend upon whether it is the right person and occasion and manner, but the mere doing of any one of them is wrong.

It would be equally absurd to look for moderation or excess or deficiency in unjust cowardly or profligate conduct; for then there would be moderation in excess or deficiency, and excess in excess, and deficiency in deficiency.

The fact is that just as there can be no excess or deficiency in temperance or courage because the mean or moderate amount is, in a sense, an extreme, so in these kinds of conduct also there can be no moderation or excess or deficiency, but the acts are wrong however they be done. For, to put it generally, there cannot be moderation in excess or deficiency, nor excess or deficiency in moderation.

7.

This must be applied to the several virtues.

But it is not enough to make these general statements [about virtue and vice]: we must go on and apply them to particulars [*i.e.* to the several virtues and vices]. For in reasoning about matters of conduct general statements are too vague, and do not convey so much truth as particular propositions. It is with particulars that conduct is concerned: our statements, therefore, when applied to these particulars, should be found to hold good.

These particulars then [*i.e.* the several virtues and vices and the several acts and affections with which they deal], we will take from the following table.

Moderation in the feelings of fear and confidence is courage: of those that exceed, he that exceeds in fearlessness has no name (as often happens), but he that exceeds in confidence is foolhardy, while he that exceeds in fear, but is deficient in confidence, is cowardly.

Moderation in respect of certain pleasures and also (though to a less extent) certain pains is temperance, while excess is profligacy. But defectiveness in the matter of these pleasures is hardly ever found, and so this sort of people also have as yet received no name: let us put them down as "void of sensibility."

In the matter of giving and taking money, moderation is liberality, excess and deficiency are prodigality and illiberality. But both vices exceed and fall short in giving and taking in contrary ways: the prodigal exceeds in spending, but falls short in taking; while the illiberal man exceeds in taking, but falls short in spending. (For the present we are but giving an outline or summary, and aim at nothing more; we shall afterwards treat these points in greater detail.)

But, besides these, there are other dispositions in the matter of money: there is a moderation which is called magnificence (for the magnificent is not the same as the liberal man: the former deals with large sums, the latter with small), and an excess which is called bad taste or vulgarity, and a deficiency which is called meanness; and these vices differ from those which are opposed to liberality: how they differ will be explained later.

With respect to honour and disgrace, there is a moderation which is high-mindedness, an excess which may be called vanity, and a deficiency which is little-mindedness.

But just as we said that liberality is related to magnificence, differing only in that it deals with small sums, so here there is a virtue related to high-mindedness, and differing only in that it is concerned with small instead of great honours. A man may have a due desire for honour, and also more or less than a due desire: he that carries this desire to excess is called ambitious, he that has not enough of it is called unambitious, but he that has the due amount has no name. There are also no abstract names for the characters, except "ambition," corresponding to ambitious. And on this account those who occupy the extremes lay claim to the middle place. And in common parlance, too, the moderate man is sometimes called ambitious and sometimes unambitious, and sometimes the ambitious man is praised and sometimes the unambitious. Why this is we will explain afterwards; for the present we will follow out our plan and enumerate the other types of character.

In the matter of anger also we find excess and deficiency and moderation. The characters themselves hardly have recognized names, but as the moderate man is here called gentle, we will call his character gentleness; of those who go into extremes, we may take the term wrathful for him who exceeds, with wrathfulness for the vice, and wrathless for him who is deficient, with wrathlessness for his character.

Besides these, there are three kinds of moderation, bearing some resemblance to one another, and yet different. They all have to do with intercourse in speech and action, but they differ in that one has to do with the truthfulness of this intercourse, while the other two have to do with its pleasantness—one of the two with pleasantness in matters of amusement, the other with pleasantness in all the relations of life. We must therefore speak of these qualities also in order that we may the more plainly see how, in all cases, moderation is praiseworthy, while the extreme courses are neither right nor praiseworthy, but blamable.

In these cases also names are for the most part wanting, but we must try, here as elsewhere, to coin names ourselves, in order to make our argument clear and easy to follow.

In the matter of truth, then, let us call him who observes the mean a true [or truthful] person, and observance of the mean truth [or truthfulness]: pretence, when it exaggerates, may be called boasting, and the person a boaster; when it understates, let the names be irony and ironical.

With regard to pleasantness in amusement, he who observes the mean may be called witty, and his character wittiness; excess may be called buffoonery, and the man a buffoon; while boorish may stand for the person who is deficient, and boorishness for his character.

With regard to pleasantness in the other affairs of life, he who makes himself properly pleasant may be called friendly, and his moderation friendliness; he that exceeds may be called obsequious if he have no ulterior motive, but a flatterer if he has an eye to his own advantage; he that is deficient in this respect, and always makes himself disagreeable, may be called a quarrelsome or peevish fellow.

Moreover, in mere emotions and in our conduct with regard to them, there are ways of observing the mean; for instance, shame (αἰδώς), is not a virtue, but yet the modest (αἰδήμων) man is praised. For in these matters also we speak of this man as observing the mean, of that man as going beyond it (as the shame-faced man whom the least thing makes shy), while he who is deficient in the feeling, or lacks it altogether, is called shameless; but the term modest (αἰδήμων) is applied to him who observes the mean.

Righteous indignation, again, hits the mean between envy and malevolence. These have to do with feelings of pleasure and pain at what happens to our neighbours. A man is called righteously indignant when he feels pain at the sight of undeserved prosperity, but your envious man goes beyond him and is pained by the sight of any one in prosperity, while the malevolent man is so far from being pained that he actually exults in the misfortunes of his neighbours.

But we shall have another opportunity of discussing these matters.

As for justice, the term is used in more senses than one; we will, therefore, after disposing of the above questions, distinguish these various senses, and show how each of these kinds of justice is a kind of moderation.

And then we will treat of the intellectual virtues in the same way.

8.

The two vicious extremes are opposed to one another and to the intermediate virtue.

There are, as we said, three classes of disposition, viz. two kinds of vice, one marked by excess, the other by deficiency, and one kind of virtue, the observance of the mean. Now, each is in a way opposed to each, for the extreme dispositions are opposed both to the mean or moderate disposition and to one another, while the moderate disposition is opposed to both the extremes. Just as a quantity which is equal to a given quantity is also greater when compared with a less, and less when compared with a greater quantity, so the mean or moderate dispositions exceed as compared with the defective dispositions, and fall short as compared with the excessive dispositions, both in feeling and in action; *e.g.* the courageous man seems foolhardy as compared with the coward, and cowardly as compared with the foolhardy; and similarly the temperate man appears profligate in comparison with the insensible, and insensible in comparison with the profligate man; and the liberal man appears prodigal by the side of the illiberal man, and illiberal by the side of the prodigal man.

And so the extreme characters try to displace the mean or moderate character, and each represents him as falling into the opposite extreme, the coward calling the courageous man foolhardy, the foolhardy calling him coward, and so on in other cases.

But while the mean and the extremes are thus opposed to one another, the extremes are strictly contrary to each other rather than to the mean; for they are further removed from one another than from the mean, as that which is greater than a given magnitude is further from that which is less, and that which is less is further from that which is greater, than either the greater or the less is from that which is equal to the given magnitude.

Sometimes, again, an extreme, when compared with the mean, has a sort of resemblance to it, as foolhardiness to courage, or prodigality to liberality; but there is the greatest possible dissimilarity between the extremes.

Again, "things that are as far as possible removed from each other" is the accepted definition of contraries, so that the further things are removed from each other the more contrary they are.

In comparison with the mean, however, it is sometimes the deficiency that is the more opposed, and sometimes the excess; *e.g.* foolhardiness, which is excess, is not so much opposed to courage as cowardice, which is deficiency; but insensibility, which is lack of feeling, is not so much opposed to temperance as profligacy, which is excess.

The reasons for this are two. One is the reason derived from the nature of the matter itself: since one extreme is, in fact, nearer and more similar to the mean, we naturally do not oppose it to the mean so strongly as the other; *e.g.* as foolhardiness seems more similar to courage and nearer to it, and cowardice more dissimilar, we speak of cowardice as the opposite rather than the other: for that which is further removed from the mean seems to be more opposed to it.

This, then, is one reason, derived from the nature of the thing itself. Another reason lies in ourselves: and it is this—those things to which we happen to be more prone by nature appear to be more opposed to the mean: *e.g.* our natural inclination is rather towards indulgence in pleasure, and so we more easily fall into profligate than into regular habits: those courses, then, in which we are more apt to run to great lengths are spoken of as more opposed to the mean; and thus profligacy, which is an excess, is more opposed to temperance than the deficiency is.

9.

The mean hard to hit, and is a matter of perception, not of reasoning.

We have sufficiently explained, then, that moral virtue is moderation or observance of the mean, and in what sense, viz. (1) as holding a middle position between two vices, one on the side of excess, and the other on the side of deficiency, and (2) as aiming at the mean or moderate amount both in feeling and in action.

And on this account it is a hard thing to be good; for finding the middle or the mean in each case is a hard thing, just as finding the middle or centre of a circle is a thing that is not within the power of everybody, but only of him who has the requisite knowledge.

Thus any one can be angry—that is quite easy; any one can give money away or spend it: but to do these things to the right person, to the right extent, at the right time, with the right object, and in the right manner, is not what everybody can do, and is by no means easy; and that is the reason why right doing is rare and praiseworthy and noble.

He that aims at the mean, then, should first of all strive to avoid that extreme which is more opposed to it, as Calypso* bids Ulysses—

"Clear of these smoking breakers keep thy ship."

For of the extremes one is more dangerous, the other less. Since then it is hard to hit the mean precisely, we must "row when we cannot sail," as the proverb has it, and choose the least of two evils; and that will be best effected in the way we have described.

And secondly we must consider, each for himself, what we are most prone to—for different natures are inclined to different things—which we may learn by the pleasure or pain we feel. And then we must bend ourselves in the opposite direction; for by keeping well away from error we shall fall into the middle course, as we straighten a bent stick by bending it the other way.

But in all cases we must be especially on our guard against pleasant things, and against pleasure; for we can scarce judge her impartially. And so, in our behaviour towards her, we should imitate the behaviour of the old counsellors towards Helen, and in all cases repeat their saying: if we dismiss her we shall be less likely to go wrong.

This then, in outline, is the course by which we shall best be able to hit the mean.

But it is a hard task, we must admit, especially in a particular case. It is not easy to determine, for instance, how and with whom one ought to be angry, and upon what grounds, and for how long; for public opinion sometimes praises those who fall short, and calls them gentle, and sometimes applies the term manly to those who show a harsh temper.

In fact, a slight error, whether on the side of excess or deficiency, is not blamed, but only a considerable error; for then there can be no mistake. But it is hardly possible to determine by reasoning how far or to what extent a man must err in order to incur blame; and indeed matters that fall within the scope of perception never can be so determined. Such matters lie within the region of particulars, and can only be determined by perception.

So much then is plain, that the middle character is in all cases to be praised, but that we ought to incline sometimes towards excess, sometimes towards deficiency; for in this way we shall most easily hit the mean and attain to right doing....

# *A Treatise on Government*[96]
# Aristotle

**[Translated From The Greek Of Aristotle By William Ellis, A.M. London &.Toronto Published By J M Dent & Sons Ltd. &.In New York By E. P. Dutton &. Co. First Issue Of This Edition 1912 Reprinted 1919, 1923, 1928]**

## BOOK I
## CHAPTER I

As we see that every city is a society, and every society Ed. is established for some good purpose; for an apparent [Bekker 1252a] good is the spring of all human actions; it is evident that this is the principle upon which they are every one founded, and this is more especially true of that which has for its object the best possible, and is itself the most excellent, and comprehends all the rest. Now this is called a city, and the society thereof a political society; for those who think that the principles of a political, a regal, a family, and a herile government are the same are mistaken, while they suppose that each of these differ in the numbers to whom their power extends, but not in their constitution: so that with them a herile government is one composed of a very few, a domestic of more, a civil and a regal of still more, as if there was no difference between a large family and a small city, or that a regal government and a political one are the same, only that in the one a single person is continually at the head of public affairs; in the other, that each member of the state has in his turn a share in the government, and is at one time a magistrate, at another a private person, according to the rules of political science. But now this is not true, as will be evident to any one who will consider this question in the most approved method. As, in an inquiry into every other subject, it is necessary to separate the different parts of which it is compounded, till we arrive at their first elements, which are the most minute parts thereof; so by the same proceeding we shall acquire a knowledge of the primary parts of a city and see wherein they differ from each other, and whether the rules of art will give us any assistance in examining into each of these things which are mentioned.

## CHAPTER II

Now if in this particular science any one would attend to its original seeds, and their first shoot, he would then as in others have the subject perfectly before him; and perceive, in the first place, that it is requisite that those should be joined together whose species cannot exist without each other, as the male and the female, for the business of propagation; and this not through choice, but by that natural impulse which acts both upon plants and animals also, for the purpose of their leaving behind them others like themselves. It is also from natural causes that some beings command and others obey, that each may obtain their mutual

[96]http://www.gutenberg.org/ebooks/6762

safety; for a being who is endowed with a mind capable of reflection and forethought is by nature the superior and governor, whereas he whose excellence is merely corporeal is formed to be a slave; whence it follows that the different state of master [1252b] and slave is equally advantageous to both. But there is a natural difference between a female and a slave: for nature is not like the artists who make the Delphic swords for the use of the poor, but for every particular purpose she has her separate instruments, and thus her ends are most complete, for whatsoever is employed on one subject only, brings that one to much greater perfection than when employed on many; and yet among the barbarians, a female and a slave are upon a level in the community, the reason for which is, that amongst them there are none qualified by nature to govern, therefore their society can be nothing but between slaves of different sexes. For which reason the poets say, it is proper for the Greeks to govern the barbarians, as if a barbarian and a slave were by nature one. Now of these two societies the domestic is the first, and Hesiod is right when he says, "First a house, then a wife, then an ox for the plough," for the poor man has always an ox before a household slave. That society then which nature has established for daily support is the domestic, and those who compose it are called by Charondas *homosipuoi*, and by Epimenides the Cretan *homokapnoi*; but the society of many families, which was first instituted for their lasting, mutual advantage, is called a village, and a village is most naturally composed of the descendants of one family, whom some persons call homogalaktes, the children and the children's children thereof: for which reason cities were originally governed by kings, as the barbarian states now are, which are composed of those who had before submitted to kingly government; for every family is governed by the elder, as are the branches thereof, on account of their relationship thereunto, which is what Homer says, "Each one ruled his wife and child;" and in this scattered manner they formerly lived. And the opinion which universally prevails, that the gods themselves are subject to kingly government, arises from hence, that all men formerly were, and many are so now; and as they imagined themselves to be made in the likeness of the gods, so they supposed their manner of life must needs be the same. And when many villages so entirely join themselves together as in every respect to form but one society, that society is a city, and contains in itself, if I may so speak, the end and perfection of government: first founded that we might live, but continued that we may live happily. For which reason every city must be allowed to be the work of nature, if we admit that the original society between male and female is; for to this as their end all subordinate societies tend, and the end of everything is the nature of it. For what every being is in its most perfect state, that certainly is the nature of that being, whether it be a man, a horse, or a house: besides, whatsoever produces the final cause and the end which we [1253a] desire, must be best; but a government complete in itself is that final cause and what is best. Hence it is evident that a city is a natural production, and that man is naturally a political animal, and that whosoever is naturally and not accidentally unfit for society, must be either inferior or superior to man: thus the man in Homer, who is reviled for being "without society, without law, without family." Such a one must naturally be of a quarrelsome disposition, and as solitary as the birds. The gift of speech also evidently proves that man is a more social animal than the bees, or any of the herding cattle: for nature, as we say, does nothing in vain, and man is the only animal who enjoys it. Voice indeed, as being the token of pleasure and pain, is imparted to others also, and thus much their nature is capable of, to perceive pleasure and pain, and to impart these sensations to others; but it is by speech that we are enabled to express what is useful for us, and what is hurtful, and of course what is just and what is unjust: for in this particular man differs from other animals, that he alone has a perception of good and evil, of just and unjust, and it is a participation of these common sentiments which forms a family and a city. Besides, the notion of a city naturally precedes that of a family or an individual, for the whole must necessarily be prior to the parts, for if you take away the whole man, you cannot say a foot or a hand remains, unless by equivocation, as supposing a hand of stone to be made, but that would only be a dead one; but everything is understood to be this or that by its energic qualities and powers, so that when these no longer remain, neither can that be said to be the same, but something of the same name. That a city then precedes an individual is plain, for if an individual is not in himself sufficient to compose a perfect government, he is to a city as other parts are to a whole; but he that is incapable of society, or so complete in himself as not to want it, makes no part of a city, as a beast or a god. There is then in all persons a natural impetus to associate with each other in this manner, and he who first founded civil society was the cause of the greatest good; for as by the completion of it man is the most excellent of all living beings, so without law and justice he would be the worst of all, for nothing is so difficult to subdue as injustice in arms: but these arms man is born with, namely, prudence and valour, which he may apply to the most opposite purposes, for he who abuses them will be the most wicked, the most cruel, the most lustful, and most gluttonous being imaginable; for justice is a political virtue, by the rules of it the state is regulated, and these rules are the criterion of what is right.

## CHAPTER III

SINCE it is now evident of what parts a city is composed, it will be necessary to treat first of family government, for every city is made up of families, and every family [1253b] has again its separate parts of which it is composed. When a family is complete, it consists of freemen and slaves; but as in every subject we should begin with examining into the smallest parts of which it consists, and as the first and smallest parts of a family are the master and slave, the husband and wife, the father and child, let us first inquire into these three, what each of them may be, and what they ought to be; that is to say, the herile, the nuptial, and the paternal. Let these then be considered as the three distinct parts of a family: some think that the providing what is necessary for the family is something different from the government of it, others that this is the greatest part of it; it shall be considered separately; but we will first speak of a master and a slave, that we may both understand the nature of those things which are absolutely necessary, and also try if we can learn anything better on this subject than what is already known. Some persons have thought that the power of the master over his slave originates from his superior knowledge, and that this knowledge is the same in the master, the magistrate, and the king, as we have already said; but others think that herile government is contrary to nature, and that it is the law which makes one man a slave and another free, but that in nature there is no difference; for which reason that power cannot be founded in justice, but in force.

**CHAPTER IV**

Since then a subsistence is necessary in every family, the means of procuring it certainly makes up part of the management of a family, for without necessaries it is impossible to live, and to live well. As in all arts which are brought to perfection it is necessary that they should have their proper instruments if they would complete their works, so is it in the art of managing a family: now of instruments some of them are alive, others inanimate; thus with respect to the pilot of the ship, the tiller is without life, the sailor is alive; for a servant is as an instrument in many arts. Thus property is as an instrument to living; an estate is a multitude of instruments; so a slave is an animated instrument, but every one that can minister of himself is more valuable than any other instrument; for if every instrument, at command, or from a preconception of its master's will, could accomplish its work (as the story goes of the statues of Daedalus; or what the poet tells us of the tripods of Vulcan, "that they moved of their own accord into the assembly of the gods "), the shuttle would then weave, and the lyre play of itself; nor would the architect want servants, or the [1254a] master slaves. Now what are generally called instruments are the efficients of something else, but possessions are what we simply use: thus with a shuttle we make something else for our use; but we only use a coat, or a bed: since then making and using differ from each other in species, and they both require their instruments, it is necessary that these should be different from each other. Now life is itself what we use, and not what we employ as the efficient of something else; for which reason the services of a slave are for use. A possession may be considered in the same nature as a part of anything; now a part is not only a part of something, but also is nothing else; so is a possession; therefore a master is only the master of the slave, but no part of him; but the slave is not only the slave of the master, but nothing else but that. This fully explains what is the nature of a slave, and what are his capacities; for that being who by nature is nothing of himself, but totally another's, and is a man, is a slave by nature; and that man who is the property of another, is his mere chattel, though he continues a man; but a chattel is an instrument for use, separate from the body.

**CHAPTER V**

But whether any person is such by nature, and whether it is advantageous and just for any one to be a slave or no, or whether all slavery is contrary to nature, shall be considered hereafter; not that it is difficult to determine it upon general principles, or to understand it from matters of fact; for that some should govern, and others be governed, is not only necessary but useful, and from the hour of their birth some are marked out for those purposes, and others for the other, and there are many species of both sorts. And the better those are who are governed the better also is the government, as for instance of man, rather than the brute creation: for the more excellent the materials are with which the work is finished, the more excellent certainly is the work; and wherever there is a governor and a governed, there certainly is some work produced; for whatsoever is composed of many parts, which jointly become one, whether conjunct or separate, evidently show the marks of governing and governed; and this is true of every living thing in all nature; nay, even in some things which partake not of life, as in music; but this probably would be a disquisition too foreign to our present purpose. Every living thing in the first place is composed of soul and body, of these the one is by nature the governor, the other the governed; now if we would know what is natural, we ought to search for it in those subjects in which nature appears most perfect, and not in those which are corrupted; we should therefore examine into a man who is most perfectly formed both in soul and body, in whom this is evident, for in the depraved and vicious the body seems [1254b] to rule rather than the soul, on account of their being corrupt and contrary to nature. We may then, as we affirm, perceive in an animal the first principles of herile and political government; for the soul governs the body as the master governs his slave; the mind governs the appetite with a political or a kingly power, which shows that it is both natural and advantageous that the body should be governed by the soul, and the pathetic part by the mind, and that part which is possessed of reason; but to have no ruling power, or an improper one, is hurtful to all; and this holds true not only of man, but of other animals also, for tame animals are naturally better than wild ones, and it is advantageous that both should be under subjection to man; for this is productive of their common safety: so is it naturally with the male and the female; the one is superior, the other inferior; the one governs, the other is governed; and the same rule must necessarily hold good with respect to all mankind. Those men therefore who are as much inferior to others as the body is to the soul, are to be thus disposed of, as the proper use of them is their bodies, in which their excellence consists; and if what I have said be true, they are slaves by nature, and it is advantageous to them to be always under government. He then is by nature formed a slave who is qualified to become the chattel of another person, and on that account is so, and who has just reason enough to know that there is such a faculty, without being indued with the use of it; for other animals have no perception of reason, but are entirely guided by appetite, and indeed they vary very little in their use from each other; for the advantage which we receive, both from slaves and tame animals, arises from their bodily strength administering to our necessities; for it is the intention of nature to make the bodies of slaves and freemen different from each other, that the one should be robust for their necessary purposes, the others erect, useless indeed for what slaves are employed in, but fit for civil life, which is divided into the duties of war and peace; though these rules do not always take place, for slaves have sometimes the bodies of freemen, sometimes the souls; if then it is evident that if some bodies are as much more excellent than others as the statues of the gods excel the human form, every one will allow that the inferior ought to be slaves to the superior; and if this is true with respect to the body, it is still juster to determine in the same manner, when we consider the soul; though it is not so easy to perceive the beauty of [1255a] the soul as it is of the body. Since then some men are slaves by nature, and others are freemen, it is clear that where slavery is advantageous to any one, then it is just to make him a slave.

## CHAPTER VI
But it is not difficult to perceive that those who maintain the contrary opinion have some reason on their side; for a man may become a slave two different ways; for he may be so by law also, and this law is a certain compact, by which whatsoever is taken in battle is adjudged to be the property of the conquerors: but many persons who are conversant in law call in question this pretended right, and say that it would be hard that a man should be compelled by violence to be the slave and subject of another who had the power to compel him, and was his superior in strength; and upon this subject, even of those who are wise, some think one way and some another; but the cause of this doubt and variety of opinions arises from hence, that great abilities, when accompanied with proper means, are generally able to succeed by force: for victory is always owing to a superiority in some advantageous circumstances; so that it seems that force never prevails but in consequence of great abilities. But still the dispute concerning the justice of it remains; for some persons think, that justice consists in benevolence, others think it just that the powerful should govern: in the midst of these contrary opinions, there are no reasons sufficient to convince us, that the right of being master and governor ought not to be placed with those who have the greatest abilities. Some persons, entirely resting upon the right which the law gives (for that which is legal is in some respects just), insist upon it that slavery occasioned by war is just, not that they say it is wholly so, for it may happen that the principle upon which the wars were commenced is unjust; moreover no one will say that a man who is unworthily in slavery is therefore a slave; for if so, men of the noblest families might happen to be slaves, and the descendants of slaves, if they should chance to be taken prisoners in war and sold: to avoid this difficulty they say that such persons should not be called slaves, but barbarians only should; but when they say this, they do nothing more than inquire who is a slave by nature, which was what we at first said; for we must acknowledge that there are some persons who, wherever they are, must necessarily be slaves, but others in no situation; thus also it is with those of noble descent: it is not only in their own country that they are Esteemed as such, but everywhere, but the barbarians are respected on this account at home only; as if nobility and freedom were of two sorts, the one universal, the other not so. Thus says the Helen of Theodectes:
"Who dares reproach me with the name of slave? When from the  immortal gods, on either side, I draw my lineage."
Those who express sentiments like these, shew only that they distinguish the slave and the freeman, the noble and the ignoble from each other by their virtues and their [1255b] vices; for they think it reasonable, that as a man begets a man, and a beast a beast, so from a good man, a good man should be descended; and this is what nature desires to do, but frequently cannot accomplish it. It is evident then that this doubt has some reason in it, and that these persons are not slaves,

and those freemen, by the appointment of nature; and also that in some instances it is sufficiently clear, that it is advantageous to both parties for this man to be a slave, and that to be a master, and that it is right and just, that some should be governed, and others govern, in the manner that nature intended; of which sort of government is that which a master exercises over a slave. But to govern ill is disadvantageous to both; for the same thing is useful to the part and to the whole, to the body and to the soul; but the slave is as it were a part of the master, as if he were an animated part of his body, though separate. For which reason a mutual utility and friendship may subsist between the master and the slave, I mean when they are placed by nature in that relation to each other, for the contrary takes place amongst those who are reduced to slavery by the law, or by conquest.

...

## CHAPTER XII

There are then three parts of domestic government, the masters, of which we have already treated, the fathers, and the husbands; now the government of the wife and children should both be that of free persons, but not the [1259b] same; for the wife should be treated as a citizen of a free state, the children should be under kingly power; for the male is by nature superior to the female, except when something happens contrary to the usual course of nature, as is the elder and perfect to the younger and imperfect. Now in the generality of free states, the governors and the governed alternately change place; for an equality without any preference is what nature chooses; however, when one governs and another is governed, she endeavours that there should be a distinction between them in forms, expressions, and honours; according to what Amasis said of his laver. This then should be the established rule between the man and the woman. The government of children should be kingly; for the power of the father over the child is founded in affection and seniority, which is a species of kingly government; for which reason Homer very properly calls Jupiter "the father of gods and men," who was king of both these; for nature requires that a king should be of the same species with those whom he governs, though superior in some particulars, as is the case between the elder and the younger, the father and the son.

## CHAPTER XIII

It is evident then that in the due government of a family, greater attention should be paid to the several members of it and their virtues than to the possessions or riches of it; and greater to the freemen than the slaves: but here some one may doubt whether there is any other virtue in a slave than his organic services, and of higher estimation than these, as temperance, fortitude, justice, and such-like habits, or whether they possess only bodily qualities: each side of the question has its difficulties; for if they possess these virtues, wherein do they differ from freemen? and that they do not, since they are men, and partakers of reason, is absurd. Nearly the same inquiry may be made concerning a woman and a child, whether these also have their proper virtues; whether a woman ought to be temperate, brave, and just, and whether a child is temperate or no; and indeed this inquiry ought to be general, whether the virtues of those who, by nature, either govern or are governed, are the same or different; for if it is necessary that both of them should partake of the fair and good, why is it also necessary that, without exception, the one should govern, the other always be governed? for this cannot arise from their possessing these qualities in different degrees; for to govern, and to be governed, are things different in species, but more or less are not. And yet it is wonderful that one party ought to have them, and the other not; for if he who is to govern should not be temperate and just, how can he govern well? or if he is to be governed, how can he be governed well? for he who is intemperate [1260a] and a coward will never do what he ought: it is evident then that both parties ought to be virtuous; but there is a difference between them, as there is between those who by nature command and who by nature obey, and this originates in the soul; for in this nature has planted the governing and submitting principle, the virtues of which we say are different, as are those of a rational and an irrational being. It is plain then that the same principle may be extended farther, and that there are in nature a variety of things which govern and are governed; for a freeman is governed in a different manner from a slave, a male from a female, and a man from a child: and all these have parts of mind within them, but in a different manner. Thus a slave can have no power of determination, a woman but a weak one, a child an imperfect one. Thus also must it necessarily be with respect to moral virtues; all must be supposed to possess them, but not in the same manner, but as is best suited to every one's employment; on which account he who is to govern ought to be perfect in moral virtue, for his business is entirely that of an architect, and reason is the architect; while others want only that portion of it which may be sufficient for their station; from whence it is evident, that although moral virtue is common to all those we have spoken of, yet the temperance of a man and a woman are not the same, nor their courage, nor their justice, though Socrates thought otherwise; for the courage of the man consists in commanding, the woman's in obeying; and the same is true in other particulars: and this will be evident to those who will examine different virtues separately; for those who use general terms deceive themselves when they say, that virtue consists in a good disposition of mind, or doing what is right, or something of this sort. They do much better who enumerate the different virtues as Georgias did, than those who thus define them; and as Sophocles speaks of a woman, we think of all persons, that their 'virtues should be applicable to their characters, for says he,

"Silence is a woman's ornament,"

but it is not a man's; and as a child is incomplete, it is evident that his virtue is not to be referred to himself in his present situation, but to that in which he will be complete, and his preceptor. In like manner the virtue of a slave is to be referred to his master; for we laid it down as a maxim, that the use of a slave was to employ him in what you wanted; so that it is clear enough that few virtues are wanted in his station, only that he may not neglect his work through idleness or fear: some person may question if what I have said is true, whether virtue is not necessary for artificers in their calling, for they often through idleness neglect their work, but the difference between them is very great; for a slave is connected with you for life, but the artificer not so nearly: as near therefore as the artificer approaches to the situation of a slave, just so much ought he to have of the virtues of one; for a mean artificer is to a certain point a slave; but then a slave is one of those things which are by nature what they are, but this is not true [1260b] of a shoemaker, or any other artist. It is evident then that a slave ought to be trained to those virtues which are proper for his situation by his master; and not by him who has the power of a master, to teach him any particular art. Those therefore are in the wrong who would deprive slaves of reason, and say that they have only to follow their orders; for slaves want more instruction than children, and thus we determine this matter. It is necessary, I am sensible, for every one who treats upon government, to enter particularly into the relations of husband and wife, and of parent and child, and to show what are the virtues of each and their respective connections with each other; what is right and what is wrong; and how the one ought to be followed, and the other avoided. Since then every family is part of a city, and each of those individuals is part of a family, and the virtue of the parts ought to correspond to the virtue of the whole; it is necessary, that both the wives and children of the community should be instructed correspondent to the nature thereof, if it is of consequence to the virtue of the state, that the wives and children therein should be virtuous, and of consequence it certainly is, for the wives are one half of the free persons; and of the children the succeeding citizens are to be formed. As then we have determined these points, we will leave the rest to be spoken to in another place, as if the subject was now finished; and beginning again anew, first consider the sentiments of those who have treated of the most perfect forms of government.

## BOOK II
## CHAPTER I

Since then we propose to inquire what civil society is of all others best for those who have it in their power to live entirely as they wish, it is necessary to examine into the polity of those states which are allowed to be well governed; and if there should be any others which some persons have described, and which appear properly regulated, to note what is right and useful in them; and when we point out wherein they have failed, let not this be imputed to an affectation of wisdom, for it is because there are great defects in all those which are already established, that I have been induced to undertake this work. We will begin with that part of the subject which naturally presents itself first to our consideration. The members of every state must of necessity have all things in common, or some things common, and not others, or nothing at all common. To have nothing in common is evidently impossible, for society itself is one species of [1261a] community; and the first thing necessary thereunto is a common place of habitation, namely the city, which must be one, and this every citizen must have a share in. But in a government which is to be well founded, will it be best to admit of a community in everything which is capable thereof, or only in some particulars, but in others not? for it is possible that the citizens may have their wives, and children, and goods in common, as in Plato's Commonwealth; for in that Socrates affirms that all these particulars ought to be so. Which then shall we prefer? the custom which is already established, or the laws which are proposed in that treatise?

## CHAPTER II

Now as a community of wives is attended with many other difficulties, so neither does the cause for which he would frame his government in this manner seem agreeable to reason, nor is it capable of producing that end which he has proposed, and for which he says it ought to take place; nor has he given any particular directions for putting it in practice. Now I also am willing to agree with Socrates in the principle which he proceeds upon, and admit that the city ought to be one as much as possible; and yet it is evident that if it is contracted too much, it will be no longer a city, for that necessarily supposes a multitude; so that if we proceed in this manner, we shall reduce a city to a family, and a family to a single person: for we admit that a family is one in a greater degree than a city, and a single person than a family; so that if this end could be obtained, it should never be put in practice, as it would annihilate the city; for a city does not only consist of a large number of inhabitants, but there must also be different sorts; for were they all alike, there could be no city; for a confederacy and a city are two different things; for a confederacy is valuable from its numbers, although all those who compose it are men of the same calling; for this is entered into for the sake of mutual defence, as we add an additional weight to make the scale go down. The same distinction prevails between a city and a nation when the people are not collected into separate villages, but live as the Arcadians. Now those things in which a city should be one are of different sorts, and in preserving an alternate reciprocation of power between these, the safety thereof consists (as I have already mentioned in my treatise on Morals), for amongst freemen and equals this is absolutely necessary; for all cannot govern at the same time, but either by the year, or according to some other regulation or time, by which means every one in his turn will be in office; as if the shoemakers and carpenters should exchange occupations, and not always be employed in the same calling. But as it is evidently better, that these should continue to exercise their respective trades; so also in civil society, where it is possible, it would be better that the government should continue in the same hands; but where it [1261b] is not (as nature has made all men equal, and therefore it is just, be the administration good or bad, that all should partake of it), there it is best to observe a rotation, and let those who are their equals by turns submit to those who are at that time magistrates, as they will, in their turns, alternately be governors and governed, as if they were different men: by the same method different persons will execute different offices. From hence it is evident, that a city cannot be one in the manner that some persons propose; and that what has been said to be the greatest good which it could enjoy, is absolutely its destruction, which cannot be: for the good of anything is that which preserves it. For another reason also it is clear, that it is not for the best to endeavour to make a city too much one, because a family is more sufficient in itself than a single person, a city than a family; and indeed Plato supposes that a city owes its existence to that sufficiency in themselves which the members of it enjoy. If then this sufficiency is so desirable, the less the city is one the better.

## CHAPTER III

But admitting that it is most advantageous for a city to be one as much as possible, it does not seem to follow that this will take place by permitting all at once to say this is mine, and this is not mine (though this is what Socrates regards as a proof that a city is entirely one), for the word All is used in two senses; if it means each individual, what Socrates proposes will nearly take place; for each person will say, this is his own son, and his own wife, and his own property, and of everything else that may happen to belong to him, that it is his own. But those who have their wives and children in common will not say so, but all will say so, though not as individuals; therefore, to use the word all is evidently a fallacious mode of speech; for this word is sometimes used distributively, and sometimes collectively, on account of its double meaning, and is the cause of inconclusive syllogisms in reasoning. Therefore for all persons to say the same thing was their own, using the word all in its distributive sense, would be well, but is impossible: in its collective sense it would by no means contribute to the concord of the state. Besides, there would be another inconvenience attending this proposal, for what is common to many is taken least care of; for all men regard more what is their own than what others share with them in, to which they pay less attention than is incumbent on every one: let me add also, that every one is more negligent of what another is to see to, as well as himself, than of his own private business; as in a family one is often worse served by many servants than by a few. Let each citizen then in the state have a thousand children, but let none of them be considered as the children of that individual, but let the relation of father and child be common to them all, and they will all be neglected. Besides, in consequence of this, [1262a] whenever any citizen behaved well or ill, every person, be the number what it would, might say, this is my son, or this man's or that; and in this manner would they speak, and thus would they doubt of the whole thousand, or of whatever number the city consisted; and it would be uncertain to whom each child belonged, and when it was born, who was to take care of it: and which do you think is better, for every one to say this is mine, while they may apply it equally to two thousand or ten thousand; or as we say, this is mine in our present forms of government, where one man calls another his son, another calls that same person his brother, another nephew, or some other relation, either by blood or marriage, and first extends his care to him and his, while another regards him as one of the same parish and the same tribe; and it is better for any one to be a nephew in his private capacity than a son after that manner. Besides, it will be impossible to prevent some persons from suspecting that they are brothers and sisters, fathers and mothers to each other; for, from the mutual likeness there is between the sire and the offspring, they will necessarily conclude in what relation they stand to each other, which circumstance, we are informed by those writers who describe different parts of the world, does sometimes happen; for in Upper Africa there are wives in common who yet deliver their children to their respective fathers, being guided by their likeness to them. There are also some mares and cows which naturally bring forth their young so like the male, that we can easily distinguish by which of them they were impregnated: such was the mare called Just, in Pharsalia.

## CHAPTER IV
Besides, those who contrive this plan of community cannot easily avoid the following evils; namely, blows, murders involuntary or voluntary, quarrels, and reproaches, all which it would be impious indeed to be guilty of towards our fathers and mothers, or those who are nearly related to us; though not to those who are not connected to us by any tie of affinity: and certainly these mischiefs must necessarily happen oftener amongst those who do not know how they are connected to each other than those who do; and when they do happen, if it is among the first of these, they admit of a legal expiation, but amongst the latter that cannot be done. It is also absurd for those who promote a community of children to forbid those who love each other from indulging themselves in the last excesses of that passion, while they do not restrain them from the passion itself, or those intercourses which are of all things most improper, between a Father and a son, a brother and a brother, and indeed the thing itself is most absurd. It is also ridiculous to prevent this intercourse between the nearest relations, for no other reason than the violence of the pleasure, while they think that the relation of father and daughter, the brother and sister, is of no consequence at all. It seems also more advantageous for the state, that the husbandmen should have their wives and children in common than the military, for there will be less affection [1262b] among them in that case than when otherwise; for such persons ought to be under subjection, that they may obey the laws, and not seek after innovations. Upon the whole, the consequences of such a law as this would be directly contrary to those things which good laws ought to establish, and which Socrates endeavoured to establish by his regulations concerning women and children: for we think that friendship is the greatest good which can happen to any city, as nothing so much prevents seditions: and amity in a city is what Socrates commends above all things, which appears to be, as indeed he says, the effect of friendship; as we learn from Aristophanes in the Erotics, who says, that those who love one another from the excess of that passion, desire to breathe the same soul, and from being two to be blended into one: from whence it would necessarily follow, that both or one of them must be destroyed. But now in a city which admits of this community, the tie of friendship must, from that very cause, be extremely weak, when no father can say, this is my son; or son, this is my father; for as a very little of what is sweet, being mixed with a great deal of water is imperceptible after the mixture, so must all family connections, and the names they go by, be necessarily disregarded in such a community, it being then by no means necessary that the father should have any regard for him he called a son, or the brothers for those they call brothers. There are two things which principally inspire mankind with care and love of their offspring, knowing it is their own, and what ought to be the object of their affection, neither of which can take place in this sort of community. As for exchanging the children of the artificers and husbandmen with those of the military, and theirs reciprocally with these, it will occasion great confusion in

whatever manner it shall be done; for of necessity, those who carry the children must know from whom they took and to whom they gave them; and by this means those evils which I have already mentioned will necessarily be the more likely to happen, as blows, incestuous love, murders, and the like; for those who are given from their own parents to other citizens, the military, for instance, will not call them brothers, sons, fathers, or mothers. The same thing would happen to those of the military who were placed among the other citizens; so that by this means every one would be in fear how to act in consequence of consanguinity. And thus let us determine concerning a community of wives and children.

## CHAPTER V

We proceed next to consider in what manner property should be regulated in a state which is formed after the most perfect mode of government, whether it should be common or not; for this may be considered as a separate question from what had been determined concerning [1263a] wives and children; I mean, whether it is better that these should be held separate, as they now everywhere are, or that not only possessions but also the usufruct of them should be in common; or that the soil should have a particular owner, but that the produce should be brought together and used as one common stock, as some nations at present do; or on the contrary, should the soil be common, and should it also be cultivated in common, while the produce is divided amongst the individuals for their particular use, which is said to be practised by some barbarians; or shall both the soil and the fruit be common? When the business of the husbandman devolves not on the citizen, the matter is much easier settled; but when those labour together who have a common right of possession, this may occasion several difficulties; for there may not be an equal proportion between their labour and what they consume; and those who labour hard and have but a small proportion of the produce, will certainly complain of those who take a large share of it and do but little for that. Upon the whole, as a community between man and man so entire as to include everything possible, and thus to have all things that man can possess in common, is very difficult, so is it particularly so with respect to property; and this is evident from that community which takes place between those who go out to settle a colony; for they frequently have disputes with each other upon the most common occasions, and come to blows upon trifles: we find, too, that we oftenest correct those slaves who are generally employed in the common offices of the family: a community of property then has these and other inconveniences attending it.

But the manner of life which is now established, more particularly when embellished with good morals and a system of equal laws, is far superior to it, for it will have the advantage of both; by both I mean properties being common, and divided also; for in some respects it ought to be in a manner common, but upon the whole private: for every man's attention being employed on his own particular concerns, will prevent mutual complaints against each other; nay, by this means industry will be increased, as each person will labour to improve his own private property; and it will then be, that from a principle of virtue they will mutually perform good offices to each other, according to the proverb, "All things are common amongst friends;" and in some cities there are traces of this custom to be seen, so that it is not impracticable, and particularly in those which are best governed; some things are by this means in a manner common, and others might be so; for there, every person enjoying his own private property, some things he assists his friend with, others are considered as in common; as in Lacedaemon, where they use each other's slaves, as if they were, so to speak, their own, as they do their horses and dogs, or even any provision they may want in a journey.

It is evident then that it is best to have property private, but to make the use of it common; but how the citizens are to be brought to it is the particular [1263b] business of the legislator. And also with respect to pleasure, it is unspeakable how advantageous it is, that a man should think he has something which he may call his own; for it is by no means to no purpose, that each person should have an affection for himself, for that is natural, and yet to be a self-lover is justly censured; for we mean by that, not one that simply loves himself, but one that loves himself more than he ought; in like manner we blame a money-lover, and yet both money and self is what all men love. Besides, it is very pleasing to us to oblige and assist our friends and companions, as well as those whom we are connected with by the rights of hospitality; and this cannot be done without the establishment of private property, which cannot take place with those who make a city too much one; besides, they prevent every opportunity of exercising two principal virtues, modesty and liberality. Modesty with respect to the female sex, for this virtue requires you to abstain from her who is another's; liberality, which depends upon private property, for without that no one can appear liberal, or do any generous action; for liberality consists in imparting to others what is our own.

This system of polity does indeed recommend itself by its good appearance and specious pretences to humanity; and when first proposed to any one, must give him great pleasure, as he will conclude it to be a wonderful bond of friendship, connecting all to all; particularly when any one censures the evils which are now to be found in society, as arising from properties not being common, I mean the disputes which happen between man and man, upon their different contracts with each other; those judgments which are passed in court in consequence of fraud, and perjury, and flattering the rich, none of which arise from properties being private, but from the vices of mankind. Besides, those who live in one general community, and have all things in common, oftener dispute with each other than those who have their property separate; from the very small number indeed of those who have their property in common, compared with those where it is appropriated, the instances of their quarrels are but few. It is also but right to mention, not only the inconveniences they are preserved from who live in a communion of goods, but also the advantages they are deprived of; for when the whole comes to be considered, this manner of life will be found impracticable.

We must suppose, then, that Socrates's mistake arose from the principle he set out with being false; we admit, indeed, that both a family and a city ought to be one in some particulars, but not entirely; for there is a point beyond which if a city proceeds in reducing itself to one, it will be no longer a city.

There is also another point at which it will still continue to be a city, but it will approach so near to not being one, that it will be worse than none; as if any one should reduce the voices of those who sing in concert to one, or a verse to a foot. But the people ought to be made one, and a community, as I have already said, by education; as property at Lacedaemon, and their public tables at Crete, were made common by their legislators. But yet, whosoever shall introduce any education, and think thereby to make his city excellent and respectable, will be absurd, while he expects to form it by such regulations, and not by manners, philosophy, and laws. And whoever [1264a] would establish a government upon a community of goods, ought to know that he should consult the experience of many years, which would plainly enough inform him whether such a scheme is useful; for almost all things have already been found out, but some have been neglected, and others which have been known have not been put in practice. But this would be most evident, if any one could see such a government really established: for it would be impossible to frame such a city without dividing and separating it into its distinct parts, as public tables, wards, and tribes; so that here the laws will do nothing more than forbid the military to engage in agriculture, which is what the Lacedaemonians are at present endeavouring to do.

Nor has Socrates told us (nor is it easy to say) what plan of government should be pursued with respect to the individuals in the state where there is a community of goods established; for though the majority of his citizens will in general consist of a multitude of persons of different occupations, of those he has determined nothing; whether the property of the husbandman ought to be in common, or whether each person should have his share to himself; and also, whether their wives and children ought to be in common: for if all things are to be alike common to all, where will be the difference between them and the military, or what would they get by submitting to their government? and upon what principles would they do it, unless they should establish the wise practice of the Cretans? for they, allowing everything else to their slaves, forbid them only gymnastic exercises and the use of arms. And if they are not, but these should be in the same situation with respect to their property which they are in other cities, what sort of a community will there be? in one city there must of necessity be two, and those contrary to each other; for he makes the military the guardians of the state, and the husbandman, artisans, and others, citizens; and all those quarrels, accusations, and things of the like sort, which he says are the bane of other cities, will be found in his also: notwithstanding Socrates says they will not want many laws in consequence of their education, but such only as may be necessary for regulating the streets, the markets, and the like, while at the same time it is the education of the military only that he has taken any care of. Besides, he makes the husbandmen masters of property upon paying a tribute; but this would be likely to make them far more troublesome and high-spirited than the Helots, the Penestise, or the slaves which others employ; nor has he ever determined whether it is necessary to give any attention to them in these particulars, nor thought of what is connected therewith, their polity, their education, their laws; besides, it is of no little consequence, nor is it easy to determine, how these should be framed so as to preserve the community of the military.

Besides, if he makes the wives common, while the property [1264b] continues separate, who shall manage the domestic concerns with the same care which the man bestows upon his fields? nor will the inconvenience be remedied by making property as well as wives common; and it is absurd to draw a comparison from the brute creation, and say, that the same principle should regulate the connection of a man and a woman which regulates theirs amongst whom there is no family association.

It is also very hazardous to settle the magistracy as Socrates has done; for he would have persons of the same rank always in office, which becomes the cause of sedition even amongst those who are of no account, but more particularly amongst those who are of a courageous and warlike disposition; it is indeed evidently necessary that he should frame his community in this manner; for that golden particle which God has mixed up in the soul of man flies not from one to the other, but always continues with the same; for he says, that some of our species have gold, and others silver, blended in their composition from the moment of their birth: but those who are to be husbandmen and artists, brass and iron; besides, though he deprives the military of happiness, he says, that the legislator ought to make all the citizens happy; but it is impossible that the whole city can be happy, without all, or the greater, or some part of it be happy. For happiness is not like that numerical equality which arises from certain numbers when added together, although neither of them may separately contain it; for happiness cannot be thus added together, but must exist in every individual, as some properties belong to every integral; and if the military are not happy, who else are so? for the artisans are not, nor the multitude of those who are employed in inferior offices. The state which Socrates has described has all these defects, and others which are not of less consequence.

## CHAPTER VI

It is also nearly the same in the treatise upon Laws which was writ afterwards, for which reason it will be proper in this place to consider briefly what he has there said upon government, for Socrates has thoroughly settled but very few parts of it; as for instance, in what manner the community of wives and children ought to be regulated, how property should be established, and government conducted.

Now he divides the inhabitants into two parts, husbandmen and soldiers, and from these he select a third part who are to be senators and govern the city; but he has not said whether or no the husbandman and artificer shall have any or what share in the government, or whether they shall have arms, and join with the others in war, or not. He thinks also that the women ought to go to war, and have the same education as the soldiers; as to other particulars, he has filled his treatise with matter foreign to the purpose; and with respect to education, he has only said what that of the guards ought to be.

[1265a] As to his book of Laws, laws are the principal thing which that contains, for he has there said but little concerning government; and this government, which he was so desirous of framing in such a manner as to impart

to its members a more entire community of goods than is to be found in other cities, he almost brings round again to be the same as that other government which he had first proposed; for except the community of wives and goods, he has framed both his governments alike, for the education of the citizens is to be the same in both; they are in both to live without any servile employ, and their common tables are to be the same, excepting that in that he says the women should have common tables, and that there should be a thousand men-at-arms, in this, that there should be five thousand.

All the discourses of Socrates are masterly, noble, new, and inquisitive; but that they are all true it may probably be too much to say. For now with respect to the number just spoken of, it must be acknowledged that he would want the country of Babylonia for them, or some one like it, of an immeasurable extent, to support five thousand idle persons, besides a much greater number of women and servants. Every one, it is true, may frame an hypothesis as he pleases, but yet it ought to be possible. It has been said, that a legislator should have two things in view when he frames his laws, the country and the people. He will also do well, if he has some regard to the neighbouring states, if he intends that his community should maintain any political intercourse with them, for it is not only necessary that they should understand that practice of war which is adapted to their own country, but to others also; for admitting that any one chooses not this life either in public or private, yet there is not the less occasion for their being formidable to their enemies, not only when they invade their country, but also when they retire out of it.

It may also be considered whether the quantity of each person's property may not be settled in a different manner from what he has done it in, by making it more determinate; for he says, that every one ought to have enough whereon to live moderately, as if any one had said to live well, which is the most comprehensive expression. Besides, a man may live moderately and miserably at the same time; he had therefore better have proposed, that they should live both moderately and liberally; for unless these two conspire, luxury will come in on the one hand, or wretchedness on the other, since these two modes of living are the only ones applicable to the employment of our substance; for we cannot say with respect to a man's fortune, that he is mild or courageous, but we may say that he is prudent and liberal, which are the only qualities connected therewith.

It is also absurd to render property equal, and not to provide for the increasing number of the citizens; but to leave that circumstance uncertain, as if it would regulate itself according to the number of women who [1265b] should happen to be childless, let that be what it would because this seems to take place in other cities; but the case would not be the same in such a state which he proposes and those which now actually unite; for in these no one actually wants, as the property is divided amongst the whole community, be their numbers what they will; but as it could not then be divided, the supernumeraries, whether they were many or few, would have nothing at all. But it is more necessary than even to regulate property, to take care that the increase of the people should not exceed a certain number; and in determining that, to take into consideration those children who will die, and also those women who will be barren; and to neglect this, as is done in several cities, is to bring certain poverty on the citizens; and poverty is the cause of sedition and evil. Now Phidon the Corinthian, one of the oldest legislators, thought the families and the number of the citizens should continue the same; although it should happen that all should have allotments at the first, disproportionate to their numbers.

In Plato's Laws it is however different; we shall mention hereafter what we think would be best in these particulars. He has also neglected in that treatise to point out how the governors are to be distinguished from the governed; for he says, that as of one sort of wool the warp ought to be made, and of another the woof, so ought some to govern, and others to be governed. But since he admits, that all their property may be increased fivefold, why should he not allow the same increase to the country? he ought also to consider whether his allotment of the houses will be useful to the community, for he appoints two houses to each person, separate from each other; but it is inconvenient for a person to inhabit two houses. Now he is desirous to have his whole plan of government neither a democracy nor an oligarchy, but something between both, which he calls a polity, for it is to be composed of men-at-arms. If Plato intended to frame a state in which more than in any other everything should be common, he has certainly given it a right name; but if he intended it to be the next in perfection to that which he had already framed, it is not so; for perhaps some persons will give the preference to the Lacedaemonian form of government, or some other which may more completely have attained to the aristocratic form.

Some persons say, that the most perfect government should be composed of all others blended together, for which reason they commend that of Lacedaemon; for they say, that this is composed of an oligarchy, a monarchy, and a democracy, their kings representing the monarchical part, the senate the oligarchical; and, that in the ephori may be found the democratical, as these are taken from the people. But some say, that in the ephori is absolute power, and that it is their common meal and daily course of life, in which the democratical form is represented. It is also said in this treatise of [1266a] Laws, that the best form of government must, be one composed of a democracy and a tyranny; though such a mixture no one else would ever allow to be any government at all, or if it is, the worst possible; those propose what is much better who blend many governments together; for the most perfect is that which is formed of many parts. But now in this government of Plato's there are no traces of a monarchy, only of an oligarchy and democracy; though he seems to choose that it should rather incline to an oligarchy, as is evident from the appointment of the magistrates; for to choose them by lot is common to both; but that a man of fortune must necessarily be a member of the assembly, or to elect the magistrates, or take part in the management of public affairs, while others are passed over, makes the state incline to an oligarchy; as does the endeavouring that the greater part of the rich may be in office, and that the rank of their appointments may correspond with their fortunes.

The same principle prevails also in the choice of their senate; the manner of electing which is favourable also to an oligarchy; for all are obliged to vote for those who are senators of the first class, afterwards they vote for the same number out of the second, and then out of the third; but this compulsion to vote at the election of senators does not extend to the third and fourth classes and the first and second class only are obliged to vote for the fourth. By this means he says he shall necessarily have an equal number of each rank, but he is mistaken—for the majority will always consist of those of the first rank, and the most considerable people; and for this reason, that many of the commonalty not being obliged to it, will not attend the elections. From hence it is evident, that such a state will not consist of a democracy and a monarchy, and this will be further proved by what we shall say when we come particularly to consider this form of government.

There will also great danger arise from the manner of electing the senate, when those who are elected themselves are afterwards to elect others; for by this means, if a certain number choose to combine together, though not very considerable, the election will always fall according to their pleasure. Such are the things which Plato proposes concerning government in his book of Laws.

...

## BOOK III
## CHAPTER I

Every one who inquires into the nature of government, and what are its different forms, should make this almost his first question, What is a city? For upon this there is a dispute: for some persons say the city did this or that, while others say, not the city, but the oligarchy, or the tyranny. We see that the city is the only object which both the politician and legislator have in view in all they do: but government is a certain ordering of those who inhabit a city. As a city is a collective body, and, like other wholes, composed of many parts, it is evident our first inquiry must be, what a citizen is: for a city is a certain number of citizens. So that we must consider whom we ought to call citizen, and who is one; for this is often doubtful: for every one will not allow that this character is applicable to the same person; for that man who would be a citizen in a republic would very often not be one in an oligarchy. We do not include in this inquiry many of those who acquire this appellation out of the ordinary way, as honorary persons, for instance, but those only who have a natural right to it.

Now it is not residence which constitutes a man a citizen; for in this sojourners and slaves are upon an equality with him; nor will it be sufficient for this purpose, that you have the privilege of the laws, and may plead or be impleaded, for this all those of different nations, between whom there is a mutual agreement for that purpose, are allowed; although it very often happens, that sojourners have not a perfect right therein without the protection of a patron, to whom they are obliged to apply, which shows that their share in the community is incomplete. In like manner, with respect to boys who are not yet enrolled, or old men who are past war, we admit that they are in some respects citizens, but not completely so, but with some exceptions, for these are not yet arrived to years of maturity, and those are past service; nor is there any difference between them. But what we mean is sufficiently intelligible and clear, we want a complete citizen, one in whom there is no deficiency to be corrected to make him so. As to those who are banished, or infamous, there may be the same objections made and the same answer given. There is nothing that more characterises a complete citizen than having a share in the judicial and executive part of the government.

With respect to offices, some are fixed to a particular time, so that no person is, on any account, permitted to fill them twice; or else not till some certain period has intervened; others are not fixed, as a juryman's, and a member of the general assembly: but probably some one may say these are not offices, nor have the citizens in these capacities any share in the government; though surely it is ridiculous to say that those who have the principal power in the state bear no office in it. But this objection is of no weight, for it is only a dispute about words; as there is no general term which can be applied both to the office of a juryman and a member of the assembly. For the sake of distinction, suppose we call it an indeterminate office: but I lay it down as a maxim, that those are citizens who could exercise it. Such then is the description of a citizen who comes nearest to what all those who are called citizens are. Every one also should know, that of the component parts of those things which differ from each other in species, after the first or second remove, those which follow have either nothing at all or very little common to each.

Now we see that governments differ from each other in their form, and that some of them are defective, others [1275b] as excellent as possible: for it is evident, that those which have many deficiencies and degeneracies in them must be far inferior to those which are without such faults. What I mean by degeneracies will be hereafter explained. Hence it is clear that the office of a citizen must differ as governments do from each other: for which reason he who is called a citizen has, in a democracy, every privilege which that station supposes. In other forms of government he may enjoy them; but not necessarily: for in some states the people have no power; nor have they any general assembly, but a few select men.

The trial also of different causes is allotted to different persons; as at Lacedaemon all disputes concerning contracts are brought before some of the ephori: the senate are the judges in cases of murder, and so on; some being to be heard by one magistrate, others by another: and thus at Carthage certain magistrates determine all causes. But our former description of a citizen will admit of correction; for in some governments the office of a juryman and a member of the general assembly is not an indeterminate one; but there are particular persons appointed for these purposes, some or all of the citizens being appointed jurymen or members of the general assembly, and this either for all causes and all public business whatsoever, or else for some particular one: and this may be sufficient to show what a citizen is; for he who has a right to a share in the judicial and executive part of government in any city, him we call a citizen of that place; and a city, in one word, is a collective body of such persons sufficient in themselves to all the purposes of life.

## CHAPTER II

In common use they define a citizen to be one who is sprung from citizens on both sides, not on the father's or the mother's only. Others carry the matter still further, and inquire how many of his ancestors have been citizens, as his grandfather, great-grandfather, etc., but some persons have questioned how the first of the family could prove themselves citizens, according to this popular and careless definition. Gorgias of Leontium, partly entertaining the same doubt, and partly in jest, says, that as a mortar is made by a mortar-maker, so a citizen is made by a citizen-maker, and a Larisssean by a Larisssean-maker. This is indeed a very simple account of the matter; for if citizens are so, according to this definition, it will be impossible to apply it to the first founders or first inhabitants of states, who cannot possibly claim in right either of their father or mother. It is probably a matter of still more difficulty to determine their rights as citizens who are admitted to their freedom after any revolution in the state. As, for instance, at Athens, after the expulsion of the tyrants, when Clisthenes enrolled many foreigners and city-slaves amongst the tribes; and the doubt with respect to them was, not whether they were citizens or no, but whether they were legally so or not. Though indeed some persons may have this further [1276a] doubt, whether a citizen can be a citizen when he is illegally made; as if an illegal citizen, and one who is no citizen at all, were in the same predicament: but since we see some persons govern unjustly, whom yet we admit to govern, though not justly, and the definition of a citizen is one who exercises certain offices, for such a one we have defined a citizen to be, it is evident, that a citizen illegally created yet continues to be a citizen, but whether justly or unjustly so belongs to the former inquiry.

## CHAPTER III

It has also been doubted what was and what was not the act of the city; as, for instance, when a democracy arises out of an aristocracy or a tyranny; for some persons then refuse to fulfil their contracts; as if the right to receive the money was in the tyrant and not in the state, and many other things of the same nature; as if any covenant was founded for violence and not for the common good. So in like manner, if anything is done by those who have the management of public affairs where a democracy is established, their actions are to be considered as the actions of the state, as well as in the oligarchy or tyranny.

And here it seems very proper to consider this question, When shall we say that a city is the same, and when shall we say that it is different?

It is but a superficial mode of examining into this question to begin with the place and the people; for it may happen that these may be divided from that, or that some one of them may live in one place, and some in another (but this question may be regarded as no very knotty one; for, as a city may acquire that appellation on many accounts, it may be solved many ways); and in like manner, when men inhabit one common place, when shall we say that they inhabit the same city, or that the city is the same? for it does not depend upon the walls; for I can suppose Peloponnesus itself surrounded with a wall, as Babylon was, and every other place, which rather encircles many nations than one city, and that they say was taken three days when some of the inhabitants knew nothing of it: but we shall find a proper time to determine this question; for the extent of a city, how large it should be, and whether it should consist of more than one people, these are particulars that the politician should by no means be unacquainted with. This, too, is a matter of inquiry, whether we shall say that a city is the same while it is inhabited by the same race of men, though some of them are perpetually dying, others coming into the world, as we say that a river or a fountain is the same, though the waters are continually changing; or when a revolution takes place shall we [1276b] say the men are the same, but the city is different: for if a city is a community, it is a community of citizens; but if the mode of government should alter, and become of another sort, it would seem a necessary consequence that the city is not the same; as we regard the tragic chorus as different from the comic, though it may probably consist of the same performers: thus every other community or composition is said to be different if the species of composition is different; as in music the same hands produce different harmony, as the Doric and Phrygian. If this is true, it is evident, that when we speak of a city as being the same we refer to the government there established; and this, whether it is called by the same name or any other, or inhabited by the same men or different. But whether or no it is right to dissolve the community when the constitution is altered is another question.

**CHAPTER IV**
What has been said, it follows that we should consider whether the same virtues which constitute a good man make a valuable citizen, or different; and if a particular inquiry is necessary for this matter we must first give a general description of the virtues of a good citizen; for as a sailor is one of those who make up a community, so is a citizen, although the province of one sailor may be different from another's (for one is a rower, another a steersman, a third a boatswain, and so on, each having their several appointments), it is evident that the most accurate description of any one good sailor must refer to his peculiar abilities, yet there are some things in which the same description may be applied to the whole crew, as the safety of the ship is the common business of all of them, for this is the general centre of all their cares: so also with respect to citizens, although they may in a few particulars be very different, yet there is one care common to them all, the safety of the community, for the community of the citizens composes the state; for which reason the virtue of a citizen has necessarily a reference to the state. But if there are different sorts of governments, it is evident that those actions which constitute the virtue of an excellent citizen in one community will not constitute it in another; wherefore the virtue of such a one cannot be perfect: but we say, a man is good when his virtues are perfect; from whence it follows, that an excellent citizen does not possess that virtue which constitutes a good man. Those who are any ways doubtful concerning this question may be convinced of the truth of it by examining into the best formed states: for, if it is impossible that a city should consist entirely of excellent citizens (while it is necessary that every one should do well in his calling, in which consists his excellence, as it is impossible that all the citizens should have the same [1277a] qualifications) it is impossible that the virtue of a citizen and a good man should be the same; for all should possess the virtue of an excellent citizen: for from hence necessarily arise the perfection of the city: but that every one should possess the virtue of a good man is impossible

without all the citizens in a well-regulated state were necessarily virtuous. Besides, as a city is composed of dissimilar parts, as an animal is of life and body; the soul of reason and appetite; a family of a man and his wife—property of a master and a slave; in the same manner, as a city is composed of all these and many other very different parts, it necessarily follows that the virtue of all the citizens cannot be the same; as the business of him who leads the band is different from the other dancers. From all which proofs it is evident that the virtues of a citizen cannot be one and the same. But do we never find those virtues united which constitute a good man and excellent citizen? for we say, such a one is an excellent magistrate and a prudent and good man; but prudence is a necessary qualification for all those who engage in public affairs. Nay, some persons affirm that the education of those who are intended to command should, from the beginning, be different from other citizens, as the children of kings are generally instructed in riding and warlike exercises; and thus Euripides says:

"... No showy arts Be mine, but teach me what the state requires."

As if those who are to rule were to have an education peculiar to themselves. But if we allow, that the virtues of a good man and a good magistrate may be the same, and a citizen is one who obeys the magistrate, it follows that the virtue of the one cannot in general be the same as the virtue of the other, although it may be true of some particular citizen; for the virtue of the magistrate must be different from the virtue of the citizen. For which reason Jason declared that was he deprived of his kingdom he should pine away with regret, as not knowing how to live a private man. But it is a great recommendation to know how to command as well as to obey; and to do both these things well is the virtue of an accomplished citizen. If then the virtue of a good man consists only in being able to command, but the virtue of a good citizen renders him equally fit for the one as well as the other, the commendation of both of them is not the same. It appears, then, that both he who commands and he who obeys should each of them learn their separate business: but that the citizen should be master of and take part in both these, as any one may easily perceive; in a family government there is no occasion for the master to know how to perform the necessary offices, but rather to enjoy the labour of others; for to do the other is a servile part. I mean by the other, the common family business of the slave.

There are many sorts of slaves; for their employments are various: of these the handicraftsmen are one, who, as their name imports, get their living by the labour of their hands, and amongst these all mechanics are included; [1277b] for which reasons such workmen, in some states, were not formerly admitted into any share in the government; till at length democracies were established: it is not therefore proper for any man of honour, or any citizen, or any one who engages in public affairs, to learn these servile employments without they have occasion for them for their own use; for without this was observed the distinction between a master and a slave would be lost. But there is a government of another sort, in which men govern those who are their equals in rank, and freemen, which we call a political government, in which men learn to command by first submitting to obey, as a good general of horse, or a commander-in-chief, must acquire a knowledge of their duty by having been long under the command of another, and the like in every appointment in the army: for well is it said, no one knows how to command who has not himself been under command of another. The virtues of those are indeed different, but a good citizen must necessarily be endowed with them; he ought also to know in what manner freemen ought to govern, as well as be governed: and this, too, is the duty of a good man. And if the temperance and justice of him who commands is different from his who, though a freeman, is under command, it is evident that the virtues of a good citizen cannot be the same as justice, for instance but must be of a different species in these two different situations, as the temperance and courage of a man and a woman are different from each other; for a man would appear a coward who had only that courage which would be graceful in a woman, and a woman would be thought a talker who should take as large a part in the conversation as would become a man of consequence.

The domestic employments of each of them are also different; it is the man's business to acquire subsistence, the woman's to take care of it. But direction and knowledge of public affairs is a virtue peculiar to those who govern, while all others seem to be equally requisite for both parties; but with this the governed have no concern, it is theirs to entertain just notions: they indeed are like flute-makers, while those who govern are the musicians who play on them. And thus much to show whether the virtue of a good man and an excellent citizen is the same, or if it is different, and also how far it is the same, and how far different.

## CHAPTER V

But with respect to citizens there is a doubt remaining, whether those only are truly so who are allowed to share in the government, or whether the mechanics also are to be considered as such? for if those who are not permitted to rule are to be reckoned among them, it is impossible that the virtue of all the citizens should be the same, for these also are citizens; and if none of them are admitted to be citizens, where shall they be ranked? for they are neither [1278a] sojourners nor foreigners? or shall we say that there will no inconvenience arise from their not being citizens, as they are neither slaves nor freedmen: for this is certainly true, that all those are not citizens who are necessary to the existence of a city, as boys are not citizens in the same manner that men are, for those are perfectly so, the others under some conditions; for they are citizens, though imperfect ones: for in former times among some people the mechanics were either slaves or foreigners, for which reason many of them are so now: and indeed the best regulated states will not permit a mechanic to be a citizen; but if it be allowed them, we cannot then attribute the virtue we have described to every citizen or freeman, but to those only who are disengaged from servile offices. Now those who are employed by one person in them are slaves; those who do them for money are mechanics and hired servants: hence it is evident on the least reflection what is their situation, for what I have said is fully explained by appearances. Since the number of communities is very great, it follows necessarily that there will be many different sorts of citizens, particularly of those who are governed by others, so that in one state it may be necessary to admit mechanics and hired servants to be citizens, but in others it may be impossible;

as particularly in an aristocracy, where honours are bestowed on virtue and dignity: for it is impossible for one who lives the life of a mechanic or hired servant to acquire the practice of virtue. In an oligarchy also hired servants are not admitted to be citizens; because there a man's right to bear any office is regulated by his fortune; but mechanics are, for many citizens are very rich.

There was a law at Thebes that no one could have a share in the government till he had been ten years out of trade. In many states the law invites strangers to accept the freedom of the city; and in some democracies the son of a free-woman is himself free. The same is also observed in many others with respect to natural children; but it is through want of citizens regularly born that they admit such: for these laws are always made in consequence of a scarcity of inhabitants; so, as their numbers increase, they first deprive the children of a male or female slave of this privilege, next the child of a free-woman, and last of all they will admit none but those whose fathers and mothers were both free.

That there are many sorts of citizens, and that he may be said to be as completely who shares the honours of the state, is evident from what has been already said. Thus Achilles, in Homer, complains of Agamemnon's treating him like an unhonoured stranger; for a stranger or sojourner is one who does not partake of the honours of the state: and whenever the right to the freedom of the city is kept obscure, it is for the sake of the inhabitants. [1278b] From what has been said it is plain whether the virtue of a good man and an excellent citizen is the same or different: and we find that in some states it is the same, in others not; and also that this is not true of each citizen, but of those only who take the lead, or are capable of taking the lead, in public affairs, either alone or in conjunction with others.

## CHAPTER VI

Having established these points, we proceed next to consider whether one form of government only should be established, or more than one; and if more, how many, and of what sort, and what are the differences between them. The form of government is the ordering and regulating of the city, and all the offices in it, particularly those wherein the supreme power is lodged; and this power is always possessed by the administration; but the administration itself is that particular form of government which is established in any state: thus in a democracy the supreme power is lodged in the whole people; on the contrary, in an oligarchy it is in the hands of a few. We say then, that the form of government in these states is different, and we shall find the same thing hold good in others. Let us first determine for whose sake a city is established; and point out the different species of rule which man may submit to in social life.

I have already mentioned in my treatise on the management of a family, and the power of the master, that man is an animal naturally formed for society, and that therefore, when he does not want any foreign assistance, he will of his own accord desire to live with others; not but that mutual advantage induces them to it, as far as it enables each person to live more agreeably; and this is indeed the great object not only to all in general, but also to each individual: but it is not merely matter of choice, but they join in society also, even that they may be able to live, which probably is not without some share of merit, and they also support civil society, even for the sake of preserving life, without they are grievously overwhelmed with the miseries of it: for it is very evident that men will endure many calamities for the sake of living, as being something naturally sweet and desirable. It is easy to point out the different modes of government, and we have already settled them in our exoteric discourses. The power of the master, though by nature equally serviceable, both to the master and to the slave, yet nevertheless has for its object the benefit of the master, while the benefit of the slave arises accidentally; for if the slave is destroyed, the power of the master is at an end: but the authority which a man has over his wife, and children, and his family, which we call domestic government, is either for the benefit of those who are under subjection, or else for the common benefit of the whole: but its particular object is the benefit of the governed, as we see in other arts; in physic, for instance, and the gymnastic exercises, wherein, if any benefit [1279a] arise to the master, it is accidental; for nothing forbids the master of the exercises from sometimes being himself one of those who exercises, as the steersman is always one of the sailors; but both the master of the exercises and the steersman consider the good of those who are under their government. Whatever good may happen to the steersman when he is a sailor, or to the master of the exercises when he himself makes one at the games, is not intentional, or the object of their power; thus in all political governments which are established to preserve and defend the equality of the citizens it is held right to rule by turns. Formerly, as was natural, every one expected that each of his fellow-citizens should in his turn serve the public, and thus administer to his private good, as he himself when in office had done for others; but now every one is desirous of being continually in power, that he may enjoy the advantage which he makes of public business and being in office; as if places were a never-failing remedy for every complaint, and were on that account so eagerly sought after.

It is evident, then, that all those governments which have a common good in view are rightly established and strictly just, but those who have in view only the good of the rulers are all founded on wrong principles, and are widely different from what a government ought to be, for they are tyranny over slaves, whereas a city is a community of freemen.

## CHAPTER VII

Having established these particulars, we come to consider next the different number of governments which there are, and what they are; and first, what are their excellencies: for when we have determined this, their defects will be evident enough.

It is evident that every form of government or administration, for the words are of the same import, must contain a supreme power over the whole state, and this supreme power must necessarily be in the hands of one person, or a few, or many; and when either of these apply their power for the common good, such states are well governed; but when the interest of the one, the few, or the many who enjoy this power is alone consulted, then ill; for you must either affirm that those who make up the community are not citizens, or else let these share in the advantages of government. We usually call a state which is governed by one person for the common good, a kingdom; one that is governed by more than one, but by a few only, an aristocracy; either because the government is in the hands of the most worthy citizens, or because it is the best form for the city and its inhabitants. When the citizens at large govern for the public good, it is called a state; which is also a common name for all other governments, and these distinctions are consonant to reason; for it will not be difficult to find one person, or a very few, of very distinguished abilities, but almost impossible to meet with the majority [1279b] of a people eminent for every virtue; but if there is one common to a whole nation it is valour; for this is created and supported by numbers: for which reason in such a state the profession of arms will always have the greatest share in the government.

Now the corruptions attending each of these governments are these; a kingdom may degenerate into a tyranny, an aristocracy into an oligarchy, and a state into a democracy. Now a tyranny is a monarchy where the good of one man only is the object of government, an oligarchy considers only the rich, and a democracy only the poor; but neither of them have a common good in view.

## CHAPTER VIII

It will be necessary to enlarge a little more upon the nature of each of these states, which is not without some difficulty, for he who would enter into a philosophical inquiry into the principles of them, and not content himself with a superficial view of their outward conduct, must pass over and omit nothing, but explain the true spirit of each of them. A tyranny then is, as has been said, a monarchy, where one person has an absolute and despotic power over the whole community and every member therein: an oligarchy, where the supreme power of the state is lodged with the rich: a democracy, on the contrary, is where those have it who are worth little or nothing. But the first difficulty that arises from the distinctions which we have laid down is this, should it happen that the majority of the inhabitants who possess the power of the state (for this is a democracy) should be rich, the question is, how does this agree with what we have said? The same difficulty occurs, should it ever happen that the poor compose a smaller part of the people than the rich, but from their superior abilities acquire the supreme power; for this is what they call an oligarchy; it should seem then that our definition of the different states was not correct: nay, moreover, could any one suppose that the majority of the people were poor, and the minority rich, and then describe the state in this manner, that an oligarchy was a government in which the rich, being few in number, possessed the supreme power, and that a democracy was a state in which the poor, being many in number, possessed it, still there will be another difficulty; for what name shall we give to those states we have been describing? I mean, that in which the greater number are rich, and that in which the lesser number are poor (where each of these possess the supreme power), if there are no other states than those we have described. It seems therefore evident to reason, that whether the supreme power is vested in the hands of many or few may be a matter of accident; but that it is clear enough, that when it is in the hands of the few, it will be a government of the rich; when in the hands of the many, it will be a government of the poor; since in all countries there are many poor and few rich: it is not therefore the cause that has been already assigned (namely, the number of people in power) that makes the difference between the two governments; but an oligarchy and democracy differ in this from each other, in the poverty of those who govern in the one, and the riches 1280a of those who govern in the other; for when the government is in the hands of the rich, be they few or be they more, it is an oligarchy; when it is in the hands of the poor, it is a democracy: but, as we have already said, the one will be always few, the other numerous, but both will enjoy liberty; and from the claims of wealth and liberty will arise continual disputes with each other for the lead in public affairs.

**CHAPTER IX**
Let us first determine what are the proper limits of an oligarchy and a democracy, and what is just in each of these states; for all men have some natural inclination to justice; but they proceed therein only to a certain degree; nor can they universally point out what is absolutely just; as, for instance, what is equal appears just, and is so; but not to all; only among those who are equals: and what is unequal appears just, and is so; but not to all, only amongst those who are unequals; which circumstance some people neglect, and therefore judge ill; the reason for which is, they judge for themselves, and every one almost is the worst judge in his own cause. Since then justice has reference to persons, the same distinctions must be made with respect to persons which are made with respect to things, in the manner that I have already described in my Ethics.

As to the equality of the things, these they agree in; but their dispute is concerning the equality of the persons, and chiefly for the reason above assigned; because they judge ill in their own cause; and also because each party thinks, that if they admit what is right in some particulars, they have done justice on the whole: thus, for instance, if some persons are unequal in riches, they suppose them unequal in the whole; or, on the contrary, if they are equal in liberty, they suppose them equal in the whole: but what is absolutely just they omit; for if civil society was founded for the sake of preserving and increasing property, every one's right in the city would be equal to his fortune; and then the reasoning of those who insist upon an oligarchy would be valid; for it would not be right that he who contributed one mina should have an equal share in the hundred along with him who brought in all the rest, either of the original money or what was afterwards acquired.

Nor was civil society founded merely to preserve the lives of its members; but that they might live well: for otherwise a state might be composed of slaves, or the animal creation: but this is not so; for these have no share in the happiness of it; nor do they live after their own choice; nor is it an alliance mutually to defend each other from injuries, or for a commercial intercourse: for then the Tyrrhenians and Carthaginians, and all other nations between whom treaties of commerce subsist, would be citizens of one city; for they have articles to regulate their exports and imports, and engagements for mutual protection, and alliances for mutual defence; but [1280b] yet they have not all the same magistrates established among them, but they are different among the different people; nor does the one take any care, that the morals of the other should be as they ought, or that none of those who have entered into the common agreements should be unjust, or in any degree vicious, only that they do not injure any member of the confederacy. But whosoever endeavours to establish wholesome laws in a state, attends to the virtues and the vices of each individual who composes it; from whence it is evident, that the first care of him who would found a city, truly deserving that name, and not nominally so, must be to have his citizens virtuous; for otherwise it is merely an alliance for self-defence; differing from those of the same cast which are made between different people only in place: for law is an agreement and a pledge, as the sophist Lycophron says, between the citizens of their intending to do justice to each other, though not sufficient to make all the citizens just and good: and that this is faact is evident, for could any one bring different places together, as, for instance, enclose Megara and Corinth in a wall, yet they would not be one city, not even if the inhabitants intermarried with each other, though this inter-community contributes much to make a place one city. Besides, could we suppose a set of people to live separate from each other, but within such a distance as would admit of an intercourse, and that there were laws subsisting between each party, to prevent their injuring one another in their mutual dealings, supposing one a carpenter, another a husbandman, shoemaker, and the like, and that their numbers were ten thousand, still all that they would have together in common would be a tariff for trade, or an alliance for mutual defence, but not the same city. And why? not because their mutual intercourse is not near enough, for even if persons so situated should come to one place, and every one should live in his own house as in his native city, and there should be alliances subsisting between each party to mutually assist and prevent any injury being done to the other, still they would not be admitted to be a city by those who think correctly, if they preserved the same customs when they were together as when they were separate.

It is evident, then, that a city is not a community of place; nor established for the sake of mutual safety or traffic with each other; but that these things are the necessary consequences of a city, although they may all exist where there is no city: but a city is a society of people joining together with their families and their children to live agreeably for the sake of having their lives as happy and as independent as possible: and for this purpose it is necessary that they should live in one place and intermarry with each other: hence in all cities there are family-meetings, clubs, sacrifices, and public entertainments to promote friendship; for a love of sociability is friendship itself; so that the end then for which a city is established is, that the inhabitants of it may live happy, and these things are conducive to that end: for it is a community of families and villages for the sake of a perfect independent life; that is, as we have already said, for the sake of living well and happily. It is not therefore founded for the purpose of men's merely [1281a] living together, but for their living as men ought; for which reason those who contribute most to this end deserve to have greater power in the city than those who are their equals in family and freedom, but their inferiors in civil virtue, or those who excel them in wealth but are below them in worth. It is evident from what has been said, that in all disputes upon government each party says something that is just.

## CHAPTER X

It may also be a doubt where the supreme power ought to be lodged. Shall it be with the majority, or the wealthy, with a number of proper persons, or one better than the rest, or with a tyrant? But whichever of these we prefer some difficulty will arise. For what? shall the poor have it because they are the majority? they may then divide among themselves, what belongs to the rich: nor is this unjust; because truly it has been so judged by the supreme power. But what avails it to point out what is the height of injustice if this is not? Again, if the many seize into their own hands everything which belongs to the few, it is evident that the city will be at an end. But virtue will never destroy what is virtuous; nor can what is right be the ruin of the state: therefore such a law can never be right, nor can the acts of a tyrant ever be wrong, for of necessity they must all be just; for he, from his unlimited power, compels every one to obey his command, as the multitude oppress the rich. Is it right then that the rich, the few, should have the supreme power? and what if they be guilty of the same rapine and plunder the possessions of the majority, that will be as right as the other: but that all things of this sort are wrong and unjust is evident. Well then, these of the better sort shall have it: but must not then all the other citizens live unhonoured, without sharing the offices of the city; for the offices of a city are its honours, and if one set of men are always in power, it is evident that the rest must be without honour. Well then, let it be with one person of all others the fittest for it: but by this means the power will be still more contracted, and a greater number than before continue unhonoured. But some one may say, that it is wrong to let man have the supreme power and not the law, as his soul is subject to so many passions. But if this law appoints an aristocracy, or a democracy, how will it help us in our present doubts? for those things will happen which we have already mentioned.

## CHAPTER XI

Other particulars we will consider separately; but it seems proper to prove, that the supreme power ought to be lodged with the many, rather than with those of the better sort, who are few; and also to explain what doubts (and probably just ones) may arise: now, though not one individual of the many may himself be fit for the supreme power, yet when these many are joined together, it does not follow but they may be better qualified for it than those; and this not separately, but as a collective body; as the public suppers exceed those which are given at one person's private expense: for, as they are many, each person brings in his share of virtue and wisdom; and thus, coming together, they are like one man made up of a multitude, with many feet, many hands, and many intelligences: thus is it with respect to the manners and understandings of the multitude taken together; for which reason the public are the best judges of music and poetry; for some understand one part, some another, and all collectively the whole; and in this particular men of consequence differ from each of the many; as they say those who are beautiful do from those who are not so, and as fine pictures excel any natural objects, by collecting the several beautiful parts which were dispersed among different originals into one, although the separate parts, as the eye or any other, might be handsomer than in the picture.

But if this distinction is to be made between every people and every general assembly, and some few men of consequence, it may be doubtful whether it is true; nay, it is clear enough that, with respect to a few, it is not; since the same conclusion might be applied even to brutes: and indeed wherein do some men differ from brutes? Not but that nothing prevents what I have said being true of the people in some states. The doubt then which we have lately proposed, with all its consequences, may be settled in this manner; it is necessary that the freemen who compose the bulk of the people should have absolute power in some things; but as they are neither men of property, nor act uniformly upon principles of virtue, it is not safe to trust them with the first offices in the state, both on account of their iniquity and their ignorance; from the one of which they will do what is wrong, from the other they will mistake: and yet it is dangerous to allow them no power or share in the government; for when there are many poor people who are incapable of acquiring the honours of their country, the state must necessarily have many enemies in it; let them then be permitted to vote in the public assemblies and to determine causes; for which reason Socrates, and some other legislators, gave them the power of electing the officers of the state, and also of inquiring into their conduct when they came out of office, and only prevented their being magistrates by themselves; for the multitude when they are collected together have all of them sufficient understanding for these purposes, and, mixing among those of higher rank, are serviceable to the city, as some things, which alone are improper for food, when mixed with others make the whole more wholesome than a few of them would be.

But there is a difficulty attending this form of government, for it seems, that the person who himself was capable of curing any one who was then sick, must be the best judge whom to employ as a physician; but such a one must be himself a physician; and the same holds true in every other practice and art: and as a physician ought [1282a] to give an account of his practice to a physician, so ought it to be in other arts: those whose business is physic may be divided into three sorts, the first of these is he who makes up the medicines; the second prescribes, and is to the other as the architect is to the mason; the third is he who understands the science, but never practises it: now these three distinctions may be found in those who understand all other arts; nor have we less opinion of their judgment who are only instructed in the principles of the art than of those who practise it: and with respect to elections the same method of proceeding seems right; for to elect a proper person in any science is the business of those who are skilful therein; as in geometry, of geometricians; in steering, of steersmen: but if some individuals should know something of particular arts and works, they do not know more than the professors of them: so that even upon this principle neither the election of magistrates, nor the censure of their conduct, should be entrusted to the many.

But probably all that has been here said may not be right; for, to resume the argument I lately used, if the people are not very brutal indeed, although we allow that each individual knows less of these affairs than those who have given particular attention to them, yet when they come together they will know them better, or at least not worse; besides, in some particular arts it is not the workman only who is the best judge; namely, in those the works of which are understood by those who do not profess them: thus he who builds a house is not the only judge of it, for the master of the family who inhabits it is a better; thus also a steersman is a better judge of a tiller than he who made it; and he who gives an entertainment than the cook. What has been said seems a sufficient solution of this difficulty; but there is another that follows: for it seems absurd that the power of the state should be lodged with those who are but of indifferent morals, instead of those who are of excellent characters. Now the power of election and censure are of the utmost consequence, and this, as has been said, in some states they entrust to the people; for the general assembly is the supreme court of all, and they have a voice in this, and deliberate in all public affairs, and try all causes, without any objection to the meanness of their circumstances, and at any age: but their treasurers, generals, and other great officers of state are taken from men of great fortune and worth. This difficulty also may be solved upon the same principle; and here too they may be right, for the power is not in the man who is member of the assembly, or council, but the assembly itself, and the council, and the people, of which each individual of the whole community are the parts, I mean as senator, adviser, or judge; for which reason it is very right, that the many should have the greatest powers in their own hands; for the people, the council, and the judges are composed of them, and the property of all these collectively is more than the property of any person or a few who fill the great offices of the state: and thus I determine these points.

The first question that we stated shows plainly, that the supreme power should be lodged in laws duly made and that the magistrate or magistrates, either one or more, should be authorised to determine those cases which the laws cannot particularly speak to, as it is impossible for them, in general language, to explain themselves upon everything that may arise: but what these laws are which are established upon the best foundations has not been yet explained, but still remains a matter of some question: but the laws of every state will necessarily be like every state, either trifling or excellent, just or unjust; for it is evident, that the laws must be framed correspondent to the constitution of the government; and, if so, it is plain, that a well-formed government will have good laws, a bad one, bad ones.

## CHAPTER XII

Since in every art and science the end aimed at is always good, so particularly in this, which is the most excellent of all, the founding of civil society, the good wherein aimed at is justice; for it is this which is for the benefit of all. Now, it is the common opinion, that justice is a certain equality; and in this point all the philosophers are agreed when they treat of morals: for they say what is just, and to whom; and that equals ought to receive equal: but we should know how we are to determine what things are equal and what unequal; and in this there is some difficulty, which calls for the philosophy of the politician. Some persons will probably say, that the employments of the state ought to be given according to every particular excellence of each citizen, if there is no other difference between them and the rest of the community, but they are in every respect else alike: for justice attributes different things to persons differing from each other in their character, according to their respective merits. But if this is admitted to be true, complexion, or height, or any such advantage will be a claim for a greater share of the public rights. But that this is evidently absurd is clear from other arts and sciences; for with respect to musicians who play on the flute together, the best flute is not given to him who is of the best family, for he will play never the better for that, but the best instrument ought to be given to him who is the best artist.

If what is now said does not make this clear, we will explain it still further: if there should be any one, a very excellent player on the flute, but very deficient in family and beauty, though each of them are more valuable endowments than a skill in music, and excel this art in a higher degree than that player excels others, yet the best flutes ought to be given to him; for the superiority [1283a] in beauty and fortune should have a reference to the business in hand; but these have none. Moreover, according to this reasoning, every possible excellence might come in comparison with every other; for if bodily strength might dispute the point with riches or liberty, even any bodily strength might do it; so that if one person excelled in size more than another did in virtue, and his size was to qualify him to take place of the other's virtue, everything must then admit of a comparison with each other; for if such a size is greater than virtue by so much, it is evident another must be equal to it: but, since this is impossible, it is plain that it would be contrary to common sense to dispute a right to any office in the state from every superiority whatsoever: for if one person is slow and the other swift, neither is the one better qualified nor the other worse on that account, though in the gymnastic races a difference in these particulars would gain the prize; but a pretension to the offices of the state should be founded on a superiority in those qualifications which are useful to it: for which reason those of family, independency, and fortune, with great propriety, contend with each other for them; for these are the fit persons to fill them: for a city can no more consist of all poor men than it can of all slaves But if such persons are requisite, it is evident that those also who are just and valiant are equally so; for without justice and valour no state can be supported, the former being necessary for its existence, the latter for its happiness.

## CHAPTER XIII

It seems, then, requisite for the establishment of a state, that all, or at least many of these particulars should be well canvassed and inquired into; and that virtue and education may most justly claim the right of being considered as the necessary means of making the citizens happy, as we have already said. As those who are equal in one particular are not therefore equal in all, and those who are unequal in one particular are not therefore unequal in all, it follows that all those governments which are established upon a principle which supposes they are, are erroneous.

We have already said, that all the members of the community will dispute with each other for the offices of the state; and in some particulars justly, but not so in general; the rich, for instance, because they have the greatest landed property, and the ultimate right to the soil is vested in the community; and also because their fidelity is in general most to be depended on. The freemen and men of family will dispute the point with each other, as nearly on an equality; for these latter have a right to a higher regard as citizens than obscure persons, for honourable descent is everywhere of great esteem: nor is it an improper conclusion, that the descendants of men of worth will be men of worth themselves; for noble birth is the fountain of virtue to men of family: for the same reason also we justly say, that virtue has a right to put in her pretensions. Justice, for instance, is a virtue, and so necessary to society, that all others must yield her the precedence.

Let us now see what the many have to urge on their side against the few; and they may say, that if, when collectively taken, they are compared with them, they are stronger, richer, and better than they are. But should it ever happen that all these should inhabit the [1283b] same city, I mean the good, the rich, the noble, as well as the many, such as usually make up the community, I ask, will there then be any reason to dispute concerning who shall govern, or will there not? for in every community which we have mentioned there is no dispute where the supreme power should be placed; for as these differ from each other, so do those in whom that is placed; for in one state the rich enjoy it, in others the meritorious, and thus each according to their separate manners. Let us however consider what is to be done when all these happen at the same time to inhabit the same city. If the virtuous should be very few in number, how then shall we act? shall we prefer the virtuous on account of their abilities, if they are capable of governing the city? or should they be so many as almost entirely to compose the state?

There is also a doubt concerning the pretensions of all those who claim the honours of government: for those who found them either on fortune or family have nothing which they can justly say in their defence; since it is evident upon their principle, that if any one person can be found richer than all the rest, the right of governing all these will be justly vested in this one person. In the same manner, one man who is of the best family will claim it from those who dispute the point upon family merit: and probably in an aristocracy the same dispute might arise on the score of virtue, if there is one man better than all the other men of worth who are in the same community; it seems just, by the same reasoning, that he should enjoy the supreme power. And upon this principle also, while the many suppose they ought to have the supreme command, as being more powerful than the few, if one or more than one, though a small number should be found stronger than themselves, these ought rather to have it than they.

All these things seem to make it plain, that none of these principles are justly founded on which these persons would establish their right to the supreme power; and that all men whatsoever ought to obey them: for with respect to those who claim it as due to their virtue or their fortune, they might have justly some objection to make; for nothing hinders but that it may sometimes happen, that the many may be better or richer than the few, not as individuals, but in their collective capacity.

As to the doubt which some persons have proposed and objected, we may answer it in this manner; it is this, whether a legislator, who would establish the most perfect system of laws, should calculate them for the use of the better part of the citizens, or the many, in the circumstances we have already mentioned? The rectitude of anything consists in its equality; that therefore which is equally right will be advantageous to the whole state, and to every member of it in common.

Now, in general, a citizen is one who both shares in the government and also in his turn submits to be governed; [1284a] their condition, it is true, is different in different states: the best is that in which a man is enabled to choose and to persevere in a course of virtue during his whole life, both in his public and private state. But should there be one person, or a very few, eminent for an uncommon degree of virtue, though not enough to make up a civil state, so that the virtue of the many, or their political abilities, should be too inferior to come in comparison with theirs, if more than one; or if but one, with his only; such are not to be considered as part of the city; for it would be doing them injustice to rate them on a level with those who are so far their inferiors in virtue and political abilities, that they appear to them like a god amongst men. From whence it is evident, that a system of laws must be calculated for those who are equal to each other in nature and power. Such men, therefore, are not the object of law; for they are themselves a law: and it would be ridiculous in any one to endeavour to include them in the penalties of a law: for probably they might say what Antisthenes tells us the lions did to the hares when they demanded to be admitted to an equal share with them in the government. And it is on this account that democratic states have established the ostracism; for an equality seems the principal object of their government. For which reason they compel all those who are very eminent for their power, their fortune, their friendships, or any other cause which may give them too great weight in the government, to submit to the ostracism, and leave the city for a stated time; as the fabulous histories relate the Argonauts served Hercules, for they refused to take him with them in the ship Argo on account of his superior valour. For which reason those who hate a tyranny and find fault with the advice which Periander gave to Thrasybulus, must not think there was nothing to be said in its defence; for the story goes, that Periander said nothing to the messenger in answer to the business he was consulted about, but striking off those ears of corn which were higher than the rest, reduced the whole crop to a level; so that the messenger, without knowing the cause of what was done, related the fact to Thrasybulus, who understood by it that he must take off all the principal men in the city. Nor is this serviceable to tyrants only; nor is it tyrants only who do it; for the same thing is practised both in oligarchies and democracies: for the ostracism has in a manner nearly the same power, by restraining and banishing those who are too great; and what is done in one city is done also by those who have the supreme power in separate states; as the Athenians with respect to the Samians, the Chians, and the Lesbians; for when they suddenly acquired the superiority over all Greece, they brought the other states into subjection, contrary to the treaties which subsisted between them. The King of Persia also very often reduces the Medes and Babylonians when they assume upon their former power: [1284b] and this is a principle which all governments whatsoever keep in their eye; even those which are best administered, as well as those which are not, do it; these for the sake of private utility, the others for the public good.

The same thing is to be perceived in the other arts and sciences; for a painter would not represent an animal with a foot disproportionally large, though he had drawn it remarkably beautiful; nor would the shipwright make the prow or any other part of the vessel larger than it ought to be; nor will the master of the band permit any who sings louder and better than the rest to sing in concert with them. There is therefore no reason that a monarch should not act in agreement with free states, to support his own power, if they do the same thing for the benefit of their respective communities; upon which account when there is any acknowledged difference in the power of the citizens, the reason upon which the ostracism is founded will be politically just; but it is better for the legislator so to establish his state at the beginning as not to want this remedy: but if in course of time such an inconvenience should arise, to endeavour to amend it by some such correction. Not that this was the use it was put to: for many did not regard the benefit of their respective communities, but made the ostracism a weapon in the hand of sedition.

It is evident, then, that in corrupt governments it is partly just and useful to the individual, though probably it is as clear that it is not entirely just: for in a well-governed state there may be great doubts about the use of it, not on account of the pre-eminence which one may have in strength, riches, or connection: but when the pre-eminence is virtue, what then is to be done? for it seems not right to turn out and banish such a one; neither does it seem right to govern him, for that would be like desiring to share the power with Jupiter and to govern him: nothing then remains but what indeed seems natural, and that is for all persons quietly to submit to the government of those who are thus eminently virtuous, and let them be perpetually kings in the separate states.

...

## CHAPTER XV

...

Now the first thing which presents itself to our consideration is this, whether it is best to be governed by a good man, or by good laws? Those who prefer a kingly government think that laws can only speak a general language, but cannot adapt themselves to particular circumstances; for which reason it is absurd in any science to follow written rule; and even in Egypt the physician was allowed to alter the mode of cure which the law prescribed to him, after the fourth day; but if he did it sooner it was at his own peril: from whence it is evident, on the very same account, that a government of written laws is not the best; and yet general reasoning is necessary to all those who are to govern, and it will be much more perfect in those who are entirely free from passions than in those to whom they are natural. But now this is a quality which laws possess; while the other is natural to the human soul. But some one will say in answer to this, that man will be a better judge of particulars. It will be necessary, then, for a king to be a lawgiver, and that his laws should be published, but that those should have no authority which are absurd, as those which are not, should. But whether is it better for the community that those things which cannot possibly come under the cognisance of the law either at all or properly should be under the government of every worthy citizen, as the present method is, when the public community, in their general assemblies, act as judges and counsellors, where all their determinations are upon particular cases, for one individual, be he who he will, will be found, upon comparison, inferior to a whole people taken collectively: but this is what a city is, as a public entertainment is better than one man's portion: for this reason the multitude judge of many things better than any one single person. They are also less liable to corruption from their numbers, as water is from its quantity: besides, the judgment of an individual must necessarily be perverted if he is overcome by anger or any other passion; but it would be hard indeed if the whole community should be misled by anger. Moreover, let the people be free, and they will do nothing but in conformity to the law, except only in those cases which the law cannot speak to. But though what I am going to propose may not easily be met with, yet if the majority of the state should happen to be good men, should they prefer one uncorrupt governor or many equally good, is it not evident that they should choose the many? But there may be divisions among [1286b] these which cannot happen when there is but one. In answer to this it may be replied that all their souls will be as much animated with virtue as this one man's.

If then a government of many, and all of them good men, compose an aristocracy, and the government of one a kingly power, it is evident that the people should rather choose the first than the last; and this whether the state is powerful or not, if many such persons so alike can be met with: and for this reason probable it was, that the first governments were generally monarchies; because it was difficult to find a number of persons eminently virtuous, more particularly as the world was then divided into small communities; besides, kings were appointed in return for the benefits they had conferred on mankind; but such actions are peculiar to good men: but when many persons equal in virtue appeared at the time, they brooked not a superiority, but sought after an equality and established a free state; but after this, when they degenerated, they made a property of the public; which probably gave rise to oligarchies; for they made wealth meritorious, and the honours of government were reserved for the rich: and these afterwards turned to tyrannies and these in their turn gave rise to democracies; for the power of the tyrants continually decreasing, on account of their rapacious avarice, the people grew powerful enough to frame and establish democracies: and as cities after that happened to increase, probably it was not easy for them to be under any other government than a democracy. But if any person prefers a kingly government in a state, what is to be done with the king's children? Is the family also to reign? But should they have such children as some persons usually have, it will be very detrimental. It may be said, that then the king who has it in his power will never permit such children to succeed to his kingdom. But it is not easy to trust to that; for it is very hard and requires greater virtue than is to be met with in human nature. There is also a doubt concerning the power with which a king should be entrusted: whether he should be allowed force sufficient to compel those who do not choose to be obedient to the laws, and how he is to support his government? for if he is to govern according to law and do nothing of his own will which is contrary thereunto, at the same time it will be necessary to protect that power with which he guards the law, This matter however may not be very difficult to determine; for he ought to have a proper power, and such a one is that which will be sufficient to make the king superior to any one person or even a large part of the community, but inferior to the whole, as the ancients always appointed guards for that person whom they created aesumnetes or tyrant; and some one advised the Syracusians, when Dionysius asked for guards, to allow him such.

## CHAPTER XVI

[1287a] We will next consider the absolute monarch that we have just mentioned, who does everything according to his own will: for a king governing under the direction of laws which he is obliged to follow does not of himself create any particular species of government, as we have already said: for in every state whatsoever, either aristocracy or democracy, it is easy to appoint a general for life; and there are many who entrust the administration of affairs to one person only; such is the government at Dyrrachium, and nearly the same at Opus. As for an absolute monarchy as it is called, that is to say, when the whole state is wholly subject to the will of one person, namely the king, it seems to many that it is unnatural that one man should have the entire rule over his fellow-citizens when the state consists of equals: for nature requires that the same right and the same rank should necessarily take place amongst all those who are equal by nature: for as it would be hurtful to the body for those who are of different constitutions to observe the same regimen, either of diet or clothing, so is it with respect to the honours of the state as hurtful, that those who are equal in merit should be unequal in rank; for which reason it is as much a man's duty to submit to command as to assume it, and this also by rotation; for this is law, for order is law; and it is more proper that law should govern than any one of the citizens: upon the same principle, if it is advantageous to place the supreme power in some particular persons, they should be appointed to be only guardians, and the servants of the laws, for the supreme power must be placed somewhere; but they say, that it is unjust that where all are equal one person should continually enjoy it. But it seems unlikely that man should be able to adjust that which the law cannot determine; it may be replied, that the law having laid down the best rules possible, leaves the adjustment and application of particulars to the discretion of the magistrate; besides, it allows anything to be altered which experience proves may be better established. Moreover, he who would place the supreme power in mind, would place it in God and the laws; but he who entrusts man with it, gives it to a wild beast, for such his appetites sometimes make him; for passion influences those who are in power, even the very best of men: for which reason law is reason without desire.

The instance taken from the arts seems fallacious: wherein it is said to be wrong for a sick person to apply for a remedy to books, but that it would be far more eligible to employ those who are skilful in physic; for these do nothing contrary to reason from motives of friendship but earn their money by curing the sick, whereas those who have the management of public affairs do many things through hatred or favour. And, as a proof of what we have advanced, it may be observed, that whenever a sick person suspects that his physician has been persuaded by his enemies to be guilty of any foul practice to him in his profession, he then rather chooses to apply to books for his cure: and not only this [1287b] but even physicians themselves when they are ill call in other physicians: and those who teach others the gymnastic exercises, exercise with those of the same profession, as being incapable from self-partiality to form a proper judgment of what concerns themselves. From whence it is evident, that those who seek for what is just, seek for a mean; now law is a mean. Moreover; the moral law is far superior and conversant with far superior objects than the written law; for the supreme magistrate is safer to be trusted to than the one, though he is inferior to the other. But as it is impossible that one person should have an eye to everything himself, it will be necessary that the supreme magistrate should employ several subordinate ones under him; why then should not this be done at first, instead of appointing one person in this manner? Besides, if, according to what has been already said, the man of worth is on that account fit to govern, two men of worth are certainly better than one: as, for instance, in Homer, "Let two together go:" and also Agamemnon's wish; "Were ten such faithful counsel mine!" Not but that there are even now some particular magistrates invested with supreme power to decide, as judges, those things which the law cannot, as being one of those cases which comes not properly under its jurisdiction; for of those which can there is no doubt: since then laws comprehend some things, but not all, it is necessary to enquire and consider which of the two is preferable, that the best man or the best law should govern; for to reduce every subject which can come under the deliberation of man into a law is impossible.

No one then denies, that it is necessary that there should be some person to decide those cases which cannot come under the cognisance of a written law: but we say, that it is better to have many than one; for though every one who decides according to the principles of the law decides justly; yet surely it seems absurd to suppose, that one person can see better with two eyes, and hear better with two ears, or do better with two hands and two feet, than many can do with many: for we see that absolute monarchs now furnish themselves with many eyes and ears and hands and feet; for they entrust those who are friends to them and their government with part of their power; for if they are not friends to the monarch, they will not do what he chooses; but if they are friends to him, they are friends also to his government: but a friend is an equal and like his friend: if then he thinks that such should govern, he thinks that his equal also should govern. These are nearly the objections which are usually made to a kingly power.

...

## CHAPTER XVIII

Since then we have said that there are three sorts of regular governments, and of these the best must necessarily be that which is administered by the best men (and this must be that which happens to have one man, or one family, or a number of persons excelling all the rest in virtue, who are able to govern and be governed in such a manner as will make life most agreeable, and we have already shown that the virtue of a good man and of a citizen in the most perfect government will be the same), it is evident, that in the same manner, and for those very qualities which would procure a man the character of good, any one would say, that the government of a state was a well-established aristocracy or kingdom; so that it will be found to be education and [1288b] morals that are almost the whole which go to make a good man, and the same qualities will make a good citizen or good king.

These particulars being treated of, we will now proceed to consider what sort of government is best, how it naturally arises, and how it is established; for it is necessary to make a proper inquiry concerning this.

## BOOK IV
## CHAPTER I

In every art and science which is not conversant in parts but in some one genus in which it is complete, it is the business of that art alone to determine what is fitted to its particular genus; as what particular exercise is fitted to a certain particular body, and suits it best: for that body which is formed by nature the most perfect and superior to others necessarily requires the best exercise-and also of what one kind that must be which will suit the generality; and this is the business of the gymnastic arts: and although any one should not desire to acquire an exact knowledge and skill in these exercises, yet it is not, on that account, the less necessary that he who professes to be a master and instruct the youth in them should be perfect therein: and we see that this is what equally befalls the healing, shipbuilding, cloth-making, and indeed all other arts; so that it evidently belongs to the same art to find out what kind of government is best, and would of all others be most correspondent to our wish, while it received no molestation from without: and what particular species of it is adapted to particular persons; for there are many who probably are incapable of enjoying the best form: so that the legislator, and he who is truly a politician, ought to be acquainted not only with that which is most perfect imaginable, but also that which is the best suited to any given circumstances. There is, moreover, a third sort, an imaginary one, and he ought, if such a one should be presented to his consideration, to be able to discern what sort of one it would be at the beginning; and, when once established, what would be the proper means to preserve it a long time. I mean, for instance, if a state should happen not to have the best form of government, or be deficient in what was necessary, or not receive every advantage possible, but something less. And, besides all this, it is necessary to know what sort of government is best fitting for all cities: for most of those writers who have treated this subject, however speciously they may handle other parts of it, have failed in describing the practical parts: for it is not enough to be able to perceive what is best without it is what can be put in practice. It should also be simple, and easy for all to attain to. But some seek only the most subtile forms of government. Others again, choosing [1289a] rather to treat of what is common, censure those under which they live, and extol the excellence of a particular state, as the Lacedaemonian, or some other: but every legislator ought to establish such a form of government as from the present state and disposition of the people who are to receive it they will most readily submit to and persuade the community to partake of: for it is not a business of less trouble to correct the mistakes of an established government than to form a new one; as it is as difficult to recover what we have forgot as to learn anything afresh. He, therefore, who aspires to the character of a legislator, ought, besides all we have already said, to be able to correct the mistakes of a government already established, as we have before mentioned. But this is impossible to be done by him who does not know how many different forms of government there are: some persons think that there is only one species both of democracy and oligarchy; but this is not true: so that every one should be acquainted with the difference of these governments, how great they are, and whence they arise; and should have equal knowledge to perceive what laws are best, and what are most suitable to each particular government: for all laws are, and ought to be, framed agreeable to the state that is to be governed by them, and not the state to the laws: for government is a certain ordering in a state which particularly respects the magistrates in what manner they shall be regulated, and where the supreme power shall be placed; and what shall be the final object which each community shall have in view; but the laws are something different from what regulates and expresses the form of the constitution-it is their office to direct the conduct of the magistrate in the execution of his office and the punishment of offenders. From whence it is evident, that the founders of laws should attend both to the number and the different sorts of government; for it is impossible that the same laws should be calculated for all sorts of oligarchies and all sorts of democracies, for of both these governments there are many species, not one only.

## CHAPTER II

Since, then, according to our first method in treating of the different forms of government, we have divided those which are regular into three sorts, the kingly, the aristocratical, the free states, and shown the three excesses which these are liable to: the kingly, of becoming tyrannical; the aristocratical, oligarchical; and the free state, democratical: and as we have already treated of the aristocratical and kingly; for to enter into an inquiry what sort of government is best is the same thing as to treat of these two expressly; for each of them desires to be established upon the principles of virtue: and as, moreover, we have already determined wherein a kingly power and an aristocracy differ from each other, and when a state may be said to be governed by a king, it now remains that we examine into a free state, and also these other governments, an oligarchy, a democracy, and a [1289b] tyranny; and it is evident of these three excesses which must be the worst of all, and which next to it; for, of course, the excesses of the best and most holy must be the worst; for it must necessarily happen either that the name of king only will remain, or else that the king will assume more power than belongs to him, from whence tyranny will arise, the worst excess imaginable, a government the most contrary possible to a free state. The excess next hurtful is an oligarchy; for an aristocracy differs much from this sort of government: that which is least so is a democracy. This subject has been already treated of by one of those writers who have gone before me, though his sentiments are not the same as mine: for he thought, that of all excellent constitutions, as a good oligarchy or the like, a democracy was the worst, but of all bad ones, the best.

Now I affirm, that all these states have, without exception, fallen into excess; and also that he should not have said that one oligarchy was better than another, but that it was not quite so bad. But this question we shall not enter into at present. We shall first inquire how many different sorts of free states there are; since there are many species of democracies and oligarchies; and which of them is the most comprehensive, and most desirable after the best form of government; or if there is any other like an aristocracy, well established; and also which of these is best adapted to most cities, and which of them is preferable for particular persons: for, probably, some may suit better with an oligarchy than a democracy, and others better with a democracy than an oligarchy; and afterwards in what manner any one ought to proceed who desires to establish either of these states, I mean every species of democracy, and also of oligarchy. And to conclude, when we shall have briefly gone through everything that is necessary, we will endeavour to point out the sources of corruption, and stability, in government, as well those which are common to all as those which are peculiar to each state, and from what causes they chiefly arise.

...

## CHAPTER VIII

It now remains for us to treat of that government which is particularly called a free state, and also of a tyranny; and the reason for my choosing to place that free state here is, because this, as well as those aristocracies already mentioned, although they do not seem excesses, yet, to speak true, they have all departed from what a perfect government is. Nay, they are deviations both of them equally from other forms, as I said at the beginning. It is proper to mention a tyranny the last of all governments, for it is of all others the least like one: but as my intention is to treat of all governments in general, for this reason that also, as I have said, will be taken into consideration in its proper place.

I shall now inquire into a free state and show what it is; and we shall the better understand its positive nature as we have already described an oligarchy and a democracy; for a free state is indeed nothing more than a mixture of them, and it has been usual to call those which incline most to a democracy, a free state; those which incline most to an oligarchy, an aristocracy, because those who are rich are generally men of family and education; besides, they enjoy those things which others are often guilty of crimes to procure: for which reason they are regarded as men of worth and honour and note.

Since, then, it is the genius of an aristocracy to allot the larger part of the government to the best citizens, they therefore say, that an oligarchy is chiefly composed of those men who are worthy and honourable: now it [1294a] seems impossible that where the government is in the hands of the good, there the laws should not be good, but bad; or, on the contrary, that where the government is in the hands of the bad, there the laws should be good; nor is a government well constituted because the laws are, without at the same time care is taken that they are observed; for to enforce obedience to the laws which it makes is one proof of a good constitution in the state-another is, to have laws well calculated for those who are to abide by them; for if they are improper they must be obeyed: and this may be done two ways, either by their being the best relative to the particular state, or the best absolutely. An aristocracy seems most likely to confer the honours of the state on the virtuous; for virtue is the object of an aristocracy, riches of an oligarchy, and liberty of a democracy; for what is approved of by the majority will prevail in all or in each of these three different states; and that which seems good to most of those who compose the community will prevail: for what is called a state prevails in many communities, which aim at a mixture of rich and poor, riches and liberty: as for the rich, they are usually supposed to take the place of the worthy and honourable. As there are three things which claim an equal rank in the state, freedom, riches, and virtue (for as for the fourth, rank, it is an attendant on two of the others, for virtue and riches are the origin of family), it is evident, that the conjuncture of the rich and the poor make up a free state; but that all three tend to an aristocracy more than any other, except that which is truly so, which holds the first rank.

We have already seen that there are governments different from a monarchy, a democracy, and an oligarchy; and what they are, and wherein they differ from each other; and also aristocracies and states properly so called, which are derived from them; and it is evident that these are not much unlike each other.

...

## CHAPTER XI

We proceed now to inquire what form of government and what manner of life is best for communities in general, not adapting it to that superior virtue which is above the reach of the vulgar, or that education which every advantage of nature and fortune only can furnish, nor to those imaginary plans which may be formed at pleasure; but to that mode of life which the greater part of mankind can attain to, and that government which most cities may establish: for as to those aristocracies which we have now mentioned, they are either too perfect for a state to support, or one so nearly alike to that state we now going to inquire into, that we shall treat of them both as one.

The opinions which we form upon these subjects must depend upon one common principle: for if what I have said in my treatise on Morals is true, a happy life must arise from an uninterrupted course of virtue; and if virtue consists in a certain medium, the middle life must certainly be the happiest; which medium is attainable [1295b] by every one. The boundaries of virtue and vice in the state must also necessarily be the same as in a private person; for the form of government is the life of the city. In every city the people are divided into three sorts; the very rich, the very poor, and those who are between them. If this is universally admitted, that the mean is best, it is evident that even in point of fortune mediocrity is to be preferred; for that state is most submissive to reason; for those who are very handsome, or very strong, or very noble, or very rich; or, on the contrary; those who are very poor, or very weak, or very mean, with difficulty obey it; for the one are capricious and greatly flagitious, the other rascally and mean, the crimes of each arising from their different excesses: nor will they go through the different offices of the state; which is detrimental to it: besides, those who excel in strength, in riches, or friends, or the like, neither know how nor are willing to submit to command: and this begins at home when they are boys; for there they are brought up too delicately to be accustomed to obey their preceptors: as for the very poor, their general and excessive want of what the rich enjoy reduces them to a state too mean: so that the one know not how to command, but to be commanded as slaves, the others know not how to submit to any command, nor to command themselves but with despotic power.

A city composed of such men must therefore consist of slaves and masters, not freemen; where one party must hate, and the other despise, where there could be no possibility of friendship or political community: for community supposes affection; for we do not even on the road associate with our enemies. It is also the genius of a city to be composed as much as possible of equals; which will be most so when the inhabitants are in the middle state: from whence it follows, that that city must be best framed which is composed of those whom we say are naturally its proper members. It is men of this station also who will be best assured of safety and protection; for they will neither covet what belongs to others, as the poor do; nor will others covet what is theirs, as the poor do what belongs to the rich; and thus, without plotting against any one, or having any one plot against them, they will live free from danger: for which reason Phocylides wisely wishes for the middle state, as being most productive of happiness. It is plain, then, that the most perfect political community must be amongst those who are in the middle rank, and those states are best instituted wherein these are a larger and more respectable part, if possible, than both the other; or, if that cannot be, at least than either of them separate; so that being thrown into the balance it may prevent either scale from preponderating.

It is therefore the greatest happiness which the citizens can enjoy to possess a moderate and convenient fortune; for when some possess too much, and others nothing at [1296a] all, the government must either be in the hands of the meanest rabble or else a pure oligarchy; or, from the excesses of both, a tyranny; for this arises from a headstrong democracy or an oligarchy, but very seldom when the members of the community are nearly on an equality with each other. We will assign a reason for this when we come to treat of the alterations which different states are likely to undergo. The middle state is therefore best, as being least liable to those seditions and insurrections which disturb the community; and for the same reason extensive governments are least liable to these inconveniences; for there those in a middle state are very numerous, whereas in small ones it is easy to pass to the two extremes, so as hardly to have any in a medium remaining, but the one half rich, the other poor: and from the same principle it is that democracies are more firmly established and of longer continuance than oligarchies; but even in those when there is a want of a proper number of men of middling fortune, the poor extend their power too far, abuses arise, and the government is soon at an end.

We ought to consider as a proof of what I now advance, that the best lawgivers themselves were those in the middle rank of life, amongst whom was Solon, as is evident from his poems, and Lycurgus, for he was not a king, and Charondas, and indeed most others. What has been said will show us why of so many free states some have changed to democracies, others to oligarchies: for whenever the number of those in the middle state has been too small, those who were the more numerous, whether the rich or the poor, always overpowered them and assumed to themselves the administration of public affairs; from hence arose either a democracy or an oligarchy. Moreover, when in consequence of their disputes and quarrels with each other, either the rich get the better of the poor, or the poor of the rich, neither of them will establish a free state; but, as the record of their victory, one which inclines to their own principles, and form either a democracy or an oligarchy.

Those who made conquests in Greece, having all of them an eye to the respective forms of government in their own cities, established either democracies or oligarchies, not considering what was serviceable to the state, but what was similar to their own; for which reason a government has never been established where the supreme power has been placed amongst those of the middling rank, or very seldom; and, amongst a few, one man only of those who have yet been conquerors has been persuaded to give the preference to this order of [1296b] men: it is indeed an established custom with the inhabitants of most cities not to desire an equality, but either to aspire to govern, or when they are conquered, to submit.

Thus we have shown what the best state is, and why. It will not be difficult to perceive of the many states which there are, for we have seen that there are various forms both of democracies and oligarchies, to which we should give the first place, to which the second, and in the same manner the next also; and to observe what are the particular excellences and defects of each, after we have first described the best possible; for that must be the best which is nearest to this, that worst which is most distant from the medium, without any one has a particular plan of his own which he judges by. I mean by this, that it may happen, that although one form of government may be better than another, yet there is no reason to prevent another from being preferable thereunto in particular circumstances and for particular purposes.

## CHAPTER XII

After what has been said, it follows that we should now show what particular form of government is most suitable for particular persons; first laying this down as a general maxim, that that party which desires to support the actual administration of the state ought always to be superior to that which would alter it. Every city is made up of quality and quantity: by quality I mean liberty, riches, education, and family, and by quantity its relative populousness: now it may happen that quality may exist in one of those parts of which the city is composed, and quantity in another; thus the number of the ignoble may be greater than the number of those of family, the number of the poor than that of the rich; but not so that the quantity of the one shall overbalance the quality of the other; those must be properly adjusted to each other; for where the number of the poor exceeds the proportion we have mentioned, there a democracy will rise up, and if the husbandry should have more power than others, it will be a democracy of husbandmen; and the democracy will be a particular species according to that class of men which may happen to be most numerous: thus, should these be the husbandmen, it will be of these, and the best; if of mechanics and those who hire themselves out, the worst possible: in the same manner it may be of any other set between these two. But when the rich and the noble prevail more by their quality than they are deficient in quantity, there an oligarchy ensues; and this oligarchy may be of different species, according to the nature of the prevailing party. Every legislator in framing his constitution ought to have a particular regard to those in the middle rank of life; and if he intends an oligarchy, these should be the object of his laws; if a democracy, to these they should be entrusted; and whenever their number exceeds that of the two others, or at least one of them, they give [1297a] stability to the constitution; for there is no fear that the rich and the poor should agree to conspire together against them, for neither of these will choose to serve the other. If any one would choose to fix the administration on the widest basis, he will find none preferable to this; for to rule by turns is what the rich and the poor will not submit to, on account of their hatred to each other. It is, moreover, allowed that an arbitrator is the most proper person for both parties to trust to; now this arbitrator is the middle rank.

Those who would establish aristocratical governments are mistaken not only in giving too much power to the rich, but also in deceiving the common people; for at last, instead of an imaginary good, they must feel a real evil, for the encroachments of the rich are more destructive to the state than those of the poor.

...

# BOOK V
## CHAPTER I
We have now gone through those particulars we proposed to speak of; it remains that we next consider from what causes and how alterations in government arise, and of what nature they are, and to what the destruction of each state is owing; and also to what form any form of polity is most likely to shift into, and what are the means to be used for the general preservation of governments, as well as what are applicable to any particular state; and also of the remedies which are to be applied either to all in general, or to any one considered separately, when they are in a state of corruption: and here we ought first to lay down this principle, that there are many governments, all of which approve of what is just and what is analogically equal; and yet have failed from attaining thereunto, as we have already mentioned; thus democracies have arisen from supposing that those who are equal in one thing are so in every other circumstance; as, because they are equal in liberty, they are equal in everything else; and oligarchies, from supposing that those who are unequal in one thing are unequal in all; that when men are so in point of fortune, that inequality extends to everything else. Hence it follows, that those who in some respects are equal

with others think it right to endeavour to partake of an equality with them in everything; and those who are superior to others endeavour to get still more; and it is this more which is the inequality: thus most states, though they have some notion of what is just, yet are almost totally wrong; and, upon this account, when either party has not that share in the administration which answers to his expectations, he becomes seditious: but those who of all others have the greatest right to be so are the last that are; namely, those who excel in virtue; for they alone can be called generally superior. There are, too, some persons of distinguished families who, because they are so, disdain to be on an equality with others, for those esteem themselves noble who boast of their ancestors' merit and fortune: these, to speak truth, are the origin and fountain from whence seditions arise. The alterations which men may propose to make in governments are two; for either they may change the state already established into some other, as when they propose to erect an oligarchy where there is a democracy; or a democracy, or free state, where there is an oligarchy, or an aristocracy from these, or those from that; or else, when they have no objection to the established government, which they like very well, but choose to have the sole management in it themselves; either in the hands of a few or one only. They will also raise commotions concerning the degree in which they would have the established power; as if, for instance, the government is an oligarchy, to have it more purely so, and in the same manner if it is a democracy, or else to have it less so; and, in like manner, whatever may be the nature of the government, either to extend or contract its powers; or else to make some alterations in some parts of it; as to establish or abolish a particular magistracy, as some persons say Lysander endeavoured to abolish the kingly power in Sparta; and Pausanias that of the ephori. Thus in Epidamnus there was an alteration in one part of the constitution, for instead of the philarchi they established a senate. It is also necessary for all the magistrates at Athens; to attend in the court of the Helisea when any new magistrate is created: the power of the archon also in that state partakes of the nature of an oligarchy: inequality is always the occasion of sedition, but not when those who are unequal are treated in a different manner correspondent to that inequality. Thus kingly power is unequal when exercised over equals. Upon the whole, those who aim after an equality are the cause of seditions. Equality is twofold, either in number or value. Equality in number is when two things contain the same parts or the same quantity; equality in value is by proportion as two exceeds one, and three two by the same number-thus by proportion four exceeds two, and two one in the same degree, for two is the same part of four that one is of two; that is to say, half. Now, all agree in what is absolutely and simply just; but, as we have already said they dispute concerning proportionate value; for some persons, if they are equal in one respect, think themselves equal in all; others, if they are superior in one thing, think they may claim the superiority in all; from whence chiefly arise two sorts of governments, a democracy and an oligarchy; for nobility and virtue are to be found only [1302a] amongst a few; the contrary amongst the many; there being in no place a hundred of the first to be met with, but enough of the last everywhere. But to establish a government entirely upon either of these equalities is wrong, and this the example of those so established makes evident, for none of them have been stable; and for this reason, that it is impossible that whatever is wrong at the first and in its principles should not at last meet with a bad end: for which reason in some things an equality of numbers ought to take place, in others an equality in value. However, a democracy is safer and less liable to sedition than an oligarchy; for in this latter it may arise from two causes, for either the few in power may conspire against each other or against the people; but in a democracy only one; namely, against the few who aim at exclusive power; but there is no instance worth speaking of, of a sedition of the people against themselves. Moreover, a government composed of men of moderate fortunes comes much nearer to a democracy than an oligarchy, and is the safest of all such states.

## CHAPTER II

Since we are inquiring into the causes of seditions and revolutions in governments, we must begin entirely with the first principles from whence they arise. Now these, so to speak, are nearly three in number; which we must first distinguish in general from each other, and endeavour to show in what situation people are who begin a sedition; and for what causes; and thirdly, what are the beginnings of political troubles and mutual quarrels with each other. Now that cause which of all others most universally inclines men to desire to bring about a change in government is that which I have already mentioned; for those who aim at equality will be ever ready for sedition, if they see those whom they esteem their equals possess more than they do, as well as those also who are not content with equality but aim at superiority, if they think that while they deserve more than, they have only equal with, or less than, their inferiors. Now, what they aim at may be either just or unjust; just, when those who are inferior are seditious, that they may be equal; unjust, when those who are equal are so, that they may be superior. These, then, are the situations in which men will be seditious: the causes for which they will be so are profit and honour; and their contrary: for, to avoid dishonour or loss of fortune by mulcts, either on their own account or their friends, they will raise a commotion in the state. The original causes which dispose men to the things which I have mentioned are, taken in one manner, seven in number, in another they are more; two of which are the same with those that have been already mentioned: but influencing in a different manner; for profit and honour sharpen men against each other; not to get the possession of them for themselves (which was what I just now supposed), but when they see others, some justly, others [1302b] unjustly, engrossing them. The other causes are haughtiness, fear, eminence, contempt, disproportionate increase in some part of the state. There are also other things which in a different manner will occasion revolutions in governments; as election intrigues, neglect, want of numbers, a too great dissimilarity of circumstances.

...

## CHAPTER VIII

We are now to consider upon what the preservation of governments in general and of each state in particular depends; and, in the first place, it is evident that if we are right in the causes we have assigned for their destruction, we know also the means of their preservation; for things contrary produce contraries: but destruction and preservation are contrary to each other. In well-tempered governments it requires as much care as anything whatsoever, that nothing be done contrary to law: and this ought chiefly to be attended to in matters of small consequence; for an illegality that approaches insensibly, approaches secretly, as in a family small expenses continually repeated consume a man's income; for the understanding is deceived thereby, as by this false argument; if every part is little, then the whole is little: now, this in one sense is true, in another is false, for the whole and all the parts together are large, though made up of small parts. The first therefore of anything is what the state ought to guard against. In the next place, no credit ought to be given to those who endeavour to deceive the people with false pretences; for they will be [1308a] confuted by facts. The different ways in which they will attempt to do this have been already mentioned. You may often perceive both aristocracies and oligarchies continuing firm, not from the stability of their forms of government, but from the wise conduct of the magistrates, both towards those who have a part in the management of public affairs, and those also who have not: towards those who have not, by never injuring them; and also introducing those who are of most consequence amongst them into office; nor disgracing those who are desirous of honour; or encroaching on the property of individuals; towards those who have, by behaving to each other upon an equality; for that equality which the favourers of a democracy desire to have established in the state is not only just, but convenient also, amongst those who are of the same rank: for which reason, if the administration is in the hands of many, those rules which are established in democracies will be very useful; as to let no one continue in office longer than six months: that all those who are of the same rank may have their turn; for between these there is a sort of democracy: for which reason demagogues are most likely to arise up amongst them, as we have already mentioned: besides, by this means both aristocracies and democracies will be the less liable to be corrupted into dynasties, because it will not be so easy for those who are magistrates for a little to do as much mischief as they could in a long time: for it is from hence that tyrannies arise in democracies and oligarchies; for either those who are most powerful in each state establish a tyranny, as the demagogues in the one, the dynasties in the other, or the chief magistrates who have been long in power. Governments are sometimes preserved not only by having the means of their corruption at a great distance, but also by its being very near them; for those who are alarmed at some impending evil keep a stricter hand over the state; for which reason it is necessary for those who have the guardianship of the constitution to be able to awaken the fears of the people, that they may preserve it, and not like a night-guard to be remiss in protecting the state, but to make the distant danger appear at hand. Great care ought also to be used to endeavour to restrain the quarrels and disputes of the nobles by laws, as well as to prevent those who are not already engaged in them from taking a part therein; for to perceive an evil at its very first approach is not the lot of every one, but of the politician. To prevent any alteration taking place in an oligarchy or free state on account of the census, if that happens to continue the same while the quantity of money is increased, it will be useful to take a general account of the whole amount of it in former times, to compare it with the present, and to do this every year in those cities where the census is yearly, [1308b] in larger communities once in three or five years; and if the whole should be found much larger or much less than it was at the time when the census was first established in the state, let there be a law either to extend or contract it, doing both these according to its increase or decrease; if it increases making the census larger, if it decreases smaller: and if this latter is not done in oligarchies and free states, you will have a dynasty arise in the one, an oligarchy in the other: if the former is not, free states will be changed into democracies, and oligarchies into free states or democracies. It is a general maxim in democracies, oligarchies, monarchies, and indeed in all governments, not to let any one acquire a rank far superior to the rest of the community, but rather to endeavour to confer moderate honours for a continuance than great ones for a short time; for these latter spoil men, for it is not every one who can bear prosperity: but if this rule is not observed, let not those honours which were conferred all at once be all at once taken away, but rather by degrees. But, above all things, let this regulation be made by the law, that no one shall have too much power, either by means of his fortune or friends; but if he has, for his excess therein, let it be contrived that he shall quit the country. Now, as many persons promote innovations, that they may enjoy their own particular manner of living, there ought to be a particular officer to inspect the manners of every one, and see that these are not contrary to the genius of the state in which he lives, whether it may be an oligarchy, a democracy, or any other form of government; and, for the same reason, those should be guarded against who are most prosperous in the city: the means of doing which is by appointing those who are otherwise to the business and the offices of the state. I mean, to oppose men of account to the common people, the poor to the rich, and to blend both these into one body, and to increase the numbers of those who are in the middle rank; and this will prevent those seditions which arise from an inequality of condition. But above all, in every state it is necessary, both by the laws and every other method possible, to prevent those who are employed by the public from being venal, and this particularly in an oligarchy; for then the people will not be so much displeased from seeing themselves excluded from a share in the government (nay, they will rather be glad to have leisure to attend their private affairs) as at suspecting that the officers of the state steal the public money, then indeed they are afflicted with double concern, both because they are deprived of the honours of the state, and pillaged by those who enjoy them. There is one method of blending together a democracy and an aristocracy, [1309a] if office brought no profit; by which means both the rich and the poor will enjoy what they desire; for to admit all to a share in the government is democratical; that the rich should be in office is aristocratical. This must be done by letting no public employment whatsoever be attended with any emolument; for the poor will not desire to be in office when they can get nothing by it, but had rather attend to their own affairs: but the rich will choose it, as they want nothing of the community. Thus the poor will increase their fortunes by being wholly employed in their own concerns; and the principal part of the people will not be governed by the lower sort. To prevent the exchequer from being defrauded, let all public money be delivered out openly in the face of the whole city, and let copies of the accounts be deposited in the different wards tribes, and divisions. But, as the magistrates are to execute their offices without any advantages, the law ought to provide proper honours for those who execute them well. In democracies also it is necessary that the rich should be protected, by not permitting their lands to be divided, nor even the produce of them, which in some states is done unperceivably. It would be also better if the people would prevent them when they offer to exhibit a number of unnecessary and yet expensive public entertainments of plays, music, processions, and the like. In an oligarchy it is necessary to take great care of the poor, and allot them public employments which are gainful; and, if any of the rich insult them, to let their punishment be severer than if they insulted one of their own rank; and to let estates pass by affinity, and not gift: nor to permit any person to have more than one; for by this means property will be more equally divided, and the greater part of the poor get into better circumstances. It is also serviceable in a democracy and an oligarchy to allot those who take no part in public affairs an equality or a preference in other things; the rich in a democracy, to the poor in an oligarchy: but still all the principal offices in the state to be filled only by those who are best qualified to discharge them.

**CHAPTER IX**

There are three qualifications necessary for those who fill the first departments in government; first of all, an affection for the established constitution; second place, abilities every way completely equal to the business of their office; in the third, virtue and justice correspondent to the nature of that particular state they are placed in; for if justice is not the same in all states, it is evident that there must be different species thereof. There may be some doubt, when all these qualifications do not in the same persons, in what manner the choice shall be made; as for instance, suppose that one person is an accomplished general, but a bad man and no friend to the [1309b] constitution; another is just and a friend to it, which shall one prefer? we should then consider of two qualities, which of them the generality possess in a greater degree, which in a less; for which reason in the choice of a general we should regard his courage more than his virtue as the more uncommon quality; as there are fewer capable of conducting an army than there are good men: but, to protect the state or manage the finances, the contrary rule should be followed; for these require greater virtue than the generality are possessed of, but only that knowledge which is common to all. It may be asked, if a man has abilities equal to his appointment in the state, and is affectionate to the constitution, what occasion is there for being virtuous, since these two things alone are sufficient to enable him to be useful to the public? it is, because those who possess those qualities are often deficient in prudence; for, as they often neglect their own affairs, though they know them and love themselves, so nothing will prevent their serving the public in the same manner. In short, whatsoever the laws contain which we allow to be useful to the state contributes to its preservation: but its first and principal support is (as has been often insisted upon) to have the number of those who desire to preserve it greater than those who wish to destroy it. Above all things that ought not to be forgotten which many governments now corrupted neglect; namely, to preserve a mean. For many things seemingly favourable to a democracy destroy a democracy, and many things seemingly favourable to an oligarchy destroy an oligarchy. Those who think this the only virtue extend it to excess, not considering that as a nose which varies a little from perfect straightness, either towards a hook nose or a flat one, may yet be beautiful and agreeable to look at; but if this particularity is extended beyond measure, first of all the properties of the part is lost, but at last it can hardly be admitted to be a nose at all, on account of the excess of the rise or sinking: thus it is with other parts of the human body; so also the same thing is true with respect to states; for both an oligarchy and a democracy may something vary from their most perfect form and yet be well constituted; but if any one endeavours to extend either of them too far, at first he will make the government the worse for it, but at last there will be no government at all remaining. The lawgiver and the politician therefore should know well what preserves and what destroys a democracy or an oligarchy, for neither the one nor the other can possibly continue without rich and poor: but that whenever an entire equality of circumstances [1310a] prevails, the state must necessarily become of another form; so that those who destroy these laws, which authorise an inequality in property, destroy the government. It is also an error in democracies for the demagogues to endeavour to make the common people superior to the laws; and thus by setting them at variance with the rich, dividing one city into two; whereas they ought rather to speak in favour of the rich. In oligarchies, on the contrary, it is wrong to support those who are in administration against the people. The oaths also which they take in an oligarchy ought to be contrary to what they now are; for, at present, in some places they swear, "I will be adverse to the common people, and contrive all I can against them;" whereas they ought rather to suppose and pretend the contrary; expressing in their oaths, that they will not injure the people. But of all things which I have mentioned, that which contributes most to preserve the state is, what is now most despised, to educate your children for the state; for the most useful laws, and most approved by every statesman, will be of no service if the citizens are not accustomed to and brought up in the principles of the constitution; of a democracy, if that is by law established; of an oligarchy, if that is; for if there are bad morals in one man, there are in the city. But to educate a child fit for the state, it must not be done in the manner which would please either those who have the power in an oligarchy or those who desire a democracy, but so as they may be able to conduct either of these forms of governments. But now the children of the magistrates in an oligarchy are brought up too delicately, and the children of the poor hardy with exercise and labour; so that they are both desirous of and able to promote innovations. In democracies of the purest form they pursue a method which is contrary to their welfare; the reason of which is, that they define liberty wrong: now, there are two things which seem to be the objects of a democracy, that the people in general should possess the supreme power, and all enjoy freedom; for that which is just seems to be equal, and what the people think equal, that is a law: now, their freedom and equality consists in every one's doing what they please: that is in such a democracy every one may live as he likes; "as his inclination guides," in the words of Euripides: but this is wrong, for no one ought to think it slavery to live in subjection to government, but protection. Thus I have mentioned the causes of corruption in different states, and the means of their preservation.

...

## BOOK VII
## CHAPTER I

He who proposes to make that inquiry which is necessary concerning what government is best, ought first to determine what manner of living is most eligible; for while this remains uncertain it will also be equally uncertain what government is best: for, provided no unexpected accidents interfere, it is highly probable, that those who enjoy the best government will live the most happily according to their circumstances; he ought, therefore, first to know what manner of life is most desirable for all; and afterwards whether this life is the same to the man and the citizen, or different. As I imagine that I have already sufficiently shown what sort of life is best in my popular discourses on that subject, I think I may very properly repeat the same here; as most certainly no one ever called in question the propriety of one of the divisions; namely, that as what is good, relative to man, may be divided into three sorts, what is external, what appertains to the body, and what to the soul, it is evident that all these must conspire to make a man happy: for no one would say that a man was happy who had no fortitude, no temperance, no justice, no prudence; but was afraid of the flies that flew round him: nor would abstain from the meanest theft if he was either hungry or dry, or would murder his dearest friend for a farthing; and also was in every particular as wanting in his understanding as an infant or an idiot. These truths are so evident that all must agree to them; though some may dispute about the quantity and the degree: for they may think, that a very little virtue is sufficient for happiness; but for riches, property, power, honour, and all such things, they endeavour to increase them without bounds: but to such we reply, that it is easy to prove from what experience teaches us in these cases, that these external goods produce not virtue, but virtue them. As to a happy life, whether it is to be found in pleasure or virtue or both, certain it is, that those whose morals are most pure, and whose understandings are best cultivated, will enjoy more of it, although their fortune is but moderate than those do who own an exuberance of wealth, are deficient in those; and this utility any one who reflects may easily convince himself of; for whatsoever is external has its boundary, as a machine, and whatsoever is useful in its excess is either necessarily hurtful, or at best useless to the possessor; but every good quality of the soul the higher it is in degree, so much the more useful it is, if it is permitted on this subject to use the word useful as well as noble. It is also very evident, that the accidents of each subject take place of each other, as the subjects themselves, of which we allow they are accidents, differ from each other in value; so that if the soul is more noble than any outward possession, as the body, both in itself and with respect to us, it must be admitted of course that the best accidents of each must follow the same analogy. Besides, it is for the sake of the soul that these things are desirable; and it is on this account that wise men should desire them, not the soul for them. Let us therefore be well assured, that every one enjoys as much happiness as he possesses virtue and wisdom, and acts according to their dictates; since for this we have the example of GOD Himself, *who is completely happy, not from any external good, but in Himself, and because such is His nature. For good fortune is something different from happiness, as every good which depends not on the mind is owing to chance or fortune; but it is not from fortune that any one is wise and just: hence it follows, that that city is happiest which is the best and acts best: for no one can do well who acts not well; nor can the deeds either of man or city be praiseworthy without virtue and wisdom; for whatsoever is just, or wise, or prudent in a man, the same things are just, wise, and prudent in a city.*

Thus much by way of introduction; for I could not but just touch upon this subject, though I could not go through a complete investigation of it, as it properly belongs to another question: let us at present suppose so much, that a man's happiest life, both as an individual and as a citizen, is a life of virtue, accompanied with those enjoyments which virtue usually procures. If [1324a] there are any who are not convinced by what I have said, their doubts shall be answered hereafter, at present we shall proceed according to our intended method.

## CHAPTER II

It now remains for us to say whether the happiness of any individual man and the city is the same or different: but this also is evident; for whosoever supposes that riches will make a person happy, must place the happiness of the city in riches if it possesses them; those who prefer a life which enjoys a tyrannic power over others will also think, that the city which has many others under its command is most happy: thus also if any one approves a man for his virtue, he will think the most worthy city the happiest: but here there are two particulars which require consideration, one of which is, whether it is the most eligible life to be a member of the community and enjoy the rights of a citizen, or whether to live as a stranger, without interfering in public affairs; and also what form of government is to be preferred, and what disposition of the state is best; whether the whole community should be eligible to a share in the administration, or only the greater part, and some only: as this, therefore, is a subject of political examination and speculation, and not what concerns the individual, and the first of these is what we are at present engaged in, the one of these I am not obliged to speak to, the other is the proper business of my present design. It is evident that government must be the best which is so established, that every one therein may have it in his power to act virtuously and live happily: but some, who admit that a life of virtue is most eligible, still doubt which is preferable a public life of active virtue, or one entirely disengaged from what is without and spent in contemplation; which some say is the only one worthy of a philosopher; and one of these two different modes of life both now and formerly seem to have been chosen by all those who were the most virtuous men; I mean the public or philosophic. And yet it is of no little consequence on which side the truth lies; for a man of sense must naturally incline to the better choice; both as an individual and a citizen. Some think that a tyrannic government over those near us is the greatest injustice; but that a political one is not unjust: but that still is a restraint on the pleasures and tranquillity of life. Others hold the quite contrary opinion, and think that a public and active life is the only life for man: for that private persons have no opportunity of practising any one virtue, more than they have who are engaged in public life the management of the [1324b] state. These are their sentiments; others say, that a tyrannical and despotical mode of government is the only happy one; for even amongst some free states the object of their laws seems to be to tyrannise over their neighbours: so that the generality of political institutions, wheresoever dispersed, if they have any one common object in view, have all of them this, to conquer and govern. It is evident, both from the laws of the Lacedaemonians and Cretans, as well as by the manner in which they educated their children, that all which they had in view was to make them soldiers: besides, among all nations, those who have power enough and reduce others to servitude are honoured on that account; as were the Scythians, Persians, Thracians, and Gauls: with some there are laws to heighten the virtue of courage; thus they tell us that at Carthage they allowed every person to wear as many rings for distinction as he had served campaigns. There was also a law in Macedonia, that a man who had not himself killed an enemy should be obliged to wear a halter; among the Scythians, at a festival, none were permitted to drink out of the cup was carried about who had not done the same thing. Among the Iberians, a warlike nation, they fixed as many columns upon a man's tomb as he had slain enemies: and among different nations different things of this sort prevail, some of them established by law, others by custom. Probably it may seem too absurd to those who are willing to take this subject into their consideration to inquire whether it is the business of a legislator to be able to point out by what means a state may govern and tyrannise over its neighbours, whether they will, or will not: for how can that belong either to the politician or legislator which is unlawful? for that cannot be lawful which is done not only justly, but unjustly also: for a conquest may be unjustly made. But we see nothing of this in the arts: for it is the business neither of the physician nor the pilot to use either persuasion or force, the one to his patients, the other to his passengers: and yet many seem to think a despotic government is a political one, and what they would not allow to be just or proper, if exercised over themselves, they will not blush to exercise over others; for they endeavour to be wisely governed themselves, but think it of no consequence whether others are so or not: but a despotic power is absurd, except only where nature has framed the one party for dominion, the other for subordination; and therefore no one ought to assume it over all in general, but those only which are the proper objects thereof: thus no one should hunt men either for food or sacrifice, but what is fit for those purposes, and these are wild animals which are eatable.

Now a city which is well governed might be very [1325a] happy in itself while it enjoyed a good system of laws, although it should happen to be so situated as to have no connection with any other state, though its constitution should not be framed for war or conquest; for it would then have no occasion for these. It is evident therefore that the business of war is to be considered as commendable, not as a final end, but as the means of procuring it. It is the duty of a good legislator to examine carefully into his state; and the nature of the people, and how they may partake of every intercourse, of a good life, and of the happiness which results from it: and in this respect some laws and customs differ from others. It is also the duty of a legislator, if he has any neighbouring states to consider in what manner he shall oppose each of them, or what good offices he shall show them. But what should be the final end of the best governments will be considered hereafter.

## CHAPTER III

We will now speak to those who, while they agree that a life of virtue is most eligible, yet differ in the use of it addressing ourselves to both these parties; for there are some who disapprove of all political governments, and think that the life of one who is really free is different from the life of a citizen, and of all others most eligible: others again think that the citizen is the best; and that it is impossible for him who does nothing to be well employed; but that virtuous activity and happiness are the same thing. Now both parties in some particulars say what is right, in others what is wrong, thus, that the life of a freeman is better than the life of a slave is true, for a slave, as a slave, is employed in nothing honourable; for the common servile employments which he is commanded to perform have nothing virtuous in them; but, on the other hand, it is not true that a submission to all sorts of governments is slavery; for the government of freemen differs not more from the government of slaves than slavery and freedom differ from each other in their nature; and how they do has been already mentioned. To prefer doing of nothing to virtuous activity is also wrong, for happiness consists in action, and many noble ends are produced by the actions of the just and wise. From what we have already determined on this subject, some one probably may think, that supreme power is of all things best, as that will enable a man to command very many useful services from others; so that he who can obtain this ought not to give it up to another, but rather to seize it: and, for this purpose, the father should have no attention or regard for the son, or the son for the father, or friend for friend; for what is best is most eligible: but to be a member of the community and be in felicity is best. What these persons advance might probably be true, if the supreme good was certainly theirs who plunder and use violence to others: but it is [1325b] most unlikely that it should be so; for it is a mere supposition: for it does not follow that their actions are honourable who thus assume the supreme power over others, without they were by nature as superior to them as a man to a woman, a father to a child, a master to a slave: so that he who so far forsakes the paths of virtue can never return back from whence he departed from them: for amongst equals whatever is fair and just ought to be reciprocal; for this is equal and right; but that equals should not partake of what is equal, or like to like, is contrary to nature: but whatever is contrary to nature is not right; therefore, if there is any one superior to the rest of the community in virtue and abilities for active life, him it is proper to follow, him it is right to obey, but the one alone will not do, but must be joined to the other also: and, if we are right in what we have now said, it follows that happiness consists in virtuous activity, and that both with respect to the community as well as the individual an active life is the happiest: not that an active life must necessarily refer to other persons, as some think, or that those studies alone are practical which are pursued to teach others what to do; for those are much more so whose final object is in themselves, and to improve the judgment and understanding of the man; for virtuous activity has an end, therefore is something practical; nay, those who contrive the plan which others follow are more particularly said to act, and are superior to the workmen who execute their designs. But it is not necessary that states which choose to have no intercourse with others should remain inactive; for the several members thereof may have mutual intercourse with each other; for there are many opportunities for this among the different citizens; the same thing is true of every individual: for, was it otherwise, neither could the Deity nor the universe be perfect; to neither of whom can anything external separately exist. Hence it is evident that that very same life which is happy for each individual is happy also for the state and every member of it.

...

**CHAPTER XIII**

We will now show of what numbers and of what sort of people a government ought to consist, that the state may be happy and well administered. As there are two particulars on which the excellence and perfection of everything depend, one of these is, that the object and end proposed should be proper; the other, that the means to accomplish it should be adapted to that purpose; for it may happen that these may either agree or disagree with each other; for the end we propose may be good, but in taking the means to obtain it we may err; at other times we may have the right and proper means in our power, but the end may be bad, and sometimes we may mistake in both; as in the art of medicine the physician does not sometimes know in what situation the body ought to be, to be healthy; nor what to do to procure the end he aims at. In every art and science, therefore, we should be master of this knowledge, namely, the proper end, and the means to obtain it. Now it is evident that all persons are desirous to live well and be happy; but that some have the means thereof in their own power, others not; and this either through nature [1332a] or fortune; for many ingredients are necessary to a happy life; but fewer to those who are of a good than to those who are of a bad disposition. There are others who continually have the means of happiness in their own power, but do not rightly apply them. Since we propose to inquire what government is best, namely, that by which a state may be best administered, and that state is best administered where the people are the happiest, it is evident that happiness is a thing we should not be unacquainted with. Now, I have already said in my treatise on Morals (if I may here make any use of what I have there shown), that happiness consists in the energy and perfect practice of virtue; and this not relatively, but simply; I mean by relatively, what is necessary in some certain circumstances; by simply, what is good and fair in itself: of the first sort are just punishments, and restraints in a just cause; for they arise from virtue and are necessary, and on that account are virtuous; though it is more desirable that neither any state nor any individual should stand in need of them; but those actions which are intended either to procure honour or wealth are simply good; the others eligible only to remove an evil; these, on the contrary, are the foundation and means of relative good. A worthy man indeed will bear poverty, disease, and other unfortunate accidents with a noble mind; but happiness consists in the contrary to these (now we have already determined in our treatise on Morals, that he is a man of worth who considers what is good because it is virtuous as what is simply good; it is evident, therefore, that all the actions of such a one must be worthy and simply good): this has led some persons to conclude, that the cause of happiness was external goods; which would be as if any one should suppose that the playing well upon the lyre was owing to the instrument, and not to the art. It necessarily follows from what has been said, that some things should be ready at hand and others procured by the legislator; for which reason in founding a city we earnestly wish that there may be plenty of those things which are supposed to be under the dominion of fortune (for some things we admit her to be mistress over); but for a state to be worthy and great is not only the work of fortune but of knowledge and judgment also. But for a state to be worthy it is necessary that those citizens which are in the administration should be worthy also; but as in our city every citizen is to be so, we must consider how this may be accomplished; for if this is what every one could be, and not some individuals only, it would be more desirable; for then it would follow, that what might be done by one might be done by all. Men are worthy and good three ways; by nature, by custom, by reason. In the first place, a man ought to be born a man, and not any other animal; that is to say, he ought to have both a body and soul; but it avails not to be only born [1332b] with some things, for custom makes great alterations; for there are some things in nature capable of alteration either way which are fixed by custom, either for the better or the worse. Now, other animals live chiefly a life of nature; and in very few things according to custom; but man lives according to reason also, which he alone is endowed with; wherefore he ought to make all these accord with each other; for if men followed reason, and were persuaded that it was best to obey her, they would act in many respects contrary to nature and custom. What men ought naturally to be, to make good members of a community, I have already determined; the rest of this discourse therefore shall be upon education; for some things are acquired by habit, others by hearing them.

## CHAPTER XIV

As every political community consists of those who govern and of those who are governed, let us consider whether during the continuance of their lives they ought to be the same persons or different; for it is evident that the mode of education should be adapted to this distinction. Now, if one man differed from another as much, as we believe, the gods and heroes differ from men: in the first place, being far their superiors in body; and, secondly, in the soul: so that the superiority of the governors over the governed might be evident beyond a doubt, it is certain that it would be better for the one always to govern, the other always to be governed: but, as this is not easy to obtain, and kings are not so superior to those they govern as Scylax informs us they are in India, it is evident that for many reasons it is necessary that all in their turns should both govern and be governed: for it is just that those who are equal should have everything alike; and it is difficult for a state to continue which is founded in injustice; for all those in the country who are desirous of innovation will apply themselves to those who are under the government of the rest, and such will be their numbers in the state, that it will be impossible for the magistrates to get the better of them. But that the governors ought to excel the governed is beyond a doubt; the legislator therefore ought to consider how this shall be, and how it may be contrived that all shall have their equal share in the administration. Now, with respect to this it will be first said, that nature herself has directed us in our choice, laying down the selfsame thing when she has made some young, others old: the first of whom it becomes to obey, the latter to command; for no one when he is young is offended at his being under government, or thinks himself too good for it; more especially when he considers that he himself shall receive the same honours which he pays when he shall arrive at a proper age. In some respects it must be acknowledged that the governors and the governed are the same, in others they are different; it is therefore necessary that their education should be in [1333a] some respect the same, in others different: as they say, that he will be a good governor who has first learnt to obey. Now of governments, as we have already said, some are instituted for the sake of him who commands; others for him who obeys: of the first sort is that of the master over the servant; of the latter, that of freemen over each other. Now some things which are commanded differ from others; not in the business, but in the end proposed thereby: for which reason many works, even of a servile nature, are not disgraceful for young freemen to perform; for many things which are ordered to be done are not honourable or dishonourable so much in their own nature as in the end which is proposed, and the reason for which they are undertaken. Since then we have determined, that the virtue of a good citizen and good governor is the same as of a good man; and that every one before he commands should have first obeyed, it is the business of the legislator to consider how his citizens may be good men, what education is necessary to that purpose, and what is the final object of a good life. The soul of man may be divided into two parts; that which has reason in itself, and that which hath not, but is capable of obeying its dictates: and according to the virtues of these two parts a man is said to be good: but of those virtues which are the ends, it will not be difficult for those to determine who adopt the division I have already given; for the inferior is always for the sake of the superior; and this is equally evident both in the works of art as well as in those of nature; but that is superior which has reason. Reason itself also is divided into two parts, in the manner we usually divide it; the theoretic and the practical; which division therefore seems necessary for this part also: the same analogy holds good with respect to actions; of which those which are of a superior nature ought always to be chosen by those who have it in their power; for that is always most eligible to every one which will procure the best ends. Now life is divided into labour and rest, war and peace; and of what we do the objects are partly necessary and useful, partly noble: and we should give the same preference to these that we do to the different parts of the soul and its actions, as war to procure peace; labour, rest; and the useful, the noble. The politician, therefore, who composes a body of laws ought to extend his views to everything; the different parts of the soul and their actions; more particularly to those things which are of a superior nature and ends; and, in the same manner, to the lives of men and their different actions.

They ought to be fitted both for labour and war, but rather [1333b] for rest and peace; and also to do what is necessary and useful, but rather what is fair and noble. It is to those objects that the education of the children ought to tend, and of all the youths who want instruction. All the Grecian states which now seem best governed, and the legislators who founded those states, appear not to have framed their polity with a view to the best end, or to every virtue, in their laws and education; but eagerly to have attended to what is useful and productive of gain: and nearly of the same opinion with these are some persons who have written lately, who, by praising the Lacedaemonian state, show they approve of the intention of the legislator in making war and victory the end of his government. But how contrary to reason this is, is easily proved by argument, and has already been proved by facts (but as the generality of men desire to have an extensive command, that they may have everything desirable in the greater abundance; so Thibron and others who have written on that state seem to approve of their legislator for having procured them an extensive command by continually enuring them to all sorts of dangers and hardships): for it is evident, since the Lacedemonians have now no hope that the supreme power will be in their own hand, that neither are they happy nor was their legislator wise. This also is ridiculous, that while they preserved an obedience to their laws, and no one opposed their being governed by them, they lost the means of being honourable: but these people understand not rightly what sort of government it is which ought to reflect honour on the legislator; for a government of freemen is nobler than despotic power, and more consonant to virtue. Moreover, neither should a city be thought happy, nor should a legislator be commended, because he has so trained the people as to conquer their neighbours; for in this there is a great inconvenience: since it is evident that upon this principle every citizen who can will endeavour to procure the supreme power in his own city; which crime the Lacedaemonians accuse Pausanias of, though he enjoyed such great honours.

Such reasoning and such laws are neither political, useful nor true: but a legislator ought to instil those laws on the minds of men which are most useful for them, both in their public and private capacities. The rendering a people fit for war, that they may enslave their inferiors ought not to be the care of the legislator; but that they may not themselves be reduced to slavery by others. In [1334a] the next place, he should take care that the object of his government is the safety of those who are under it, and not a despotism over all: in the third place, that those only are slaves who are fit to be only so. Reason indeed concurs with experience in showing that all the attention which the legislator pays to the business of war, and all other rules which he lays down, should have for their object rest and peace; since most of those states (which we usually see) are preserved by war; but, after they have acquired a supreme power over those around them, are ruined; for during peace, like a sword, they lose their brightness: the fault of which lies in the legislator, who never taught them how to be at rest.

## CHAPTER XV

As there is one end common to a man both as an individual and a citizen, it is evident that a good man and a good citizen must have the same object in view; it is evident that all the virtues which lead to rest are necessary; for, as we have often said, the end of war is peace, of labour, rest; but those virtues whose object is rest, and those also whose object is labour, are necessary for a liberal life and rest; for we want a supply of many necessary things that we may be at rest. A city therefore ought to be temperate, brave, and patient; for, according to the proverb, "Rest is not for slaves;" but those who cannot bravely face danger are the slaves of those who attack them. Bravery, therefore, and patience are necessary for labour, philosophy for rest, and temperance and justice in both; but these chiefly in time of peace and rest; for war obliges men to be just and temperate; but the enjoyment of pleasure, with the rest of peace, is more apt to produce insolence; those indeed who are easy in their circumstances, and enjoy everything that can make them happy, have great occasion for the virtues of temperance and justice. Thus if there are, as the poets tell us, any inhabitants in the happy isles, to these a higher degree of philosophy, temperance, and justice will be necessary, as they live at their ease in the full plenty of every sensual pleasure. It is evident, therefore, that these virtues are necessary in every state that would be happy or worthy; for he who is worthless can never enjoy real good, much less is he qualified to be at rest; but can appear good only by labour and being at war, but in peace and at rest the meanest of creatures. For which reason virtue should not be cultivated as the Lacedaemonians did; for they did not differ from others in their opinion concerning the supreme good, but in [1334b] imagining this good was to be procured by a particular virtue; but since there are greater goods than those of war, it is evident that the enjoyment of those which are valuable in themselves should be desired, rather than those virtues which are useful in war; but how and by what means this is to be acquired is now to be considered. We have already assigned three causes on which it will depend; nature, custom, and reason, arid shown what sort of men nature must produce for this purpose; it remains then that we determine which we shall first begin by in education, reason or custom, for these ought always to preserve the most entire harmony with each other; for it may happen that reason may err from the end proposed, and be corrected by custom. In the first place, it is evident that in this as in other things, its beginning or production arises from some principle, and its end also arises from another principle, which is itself an end. Now, with us, reason and intelligence are the end of nature; our production, therefore, and our manners ought to be accommodated to both these. In the next place, as the soul and the body are two distinct things, so also we see that the soul is divided into two parts, the reasoning and not-reasoning, with their habits which are two in number, one belonging to each, namely appetite and intelligence; and as the body is in production before the soul, so is the not-reasoning part of the soul before the reasoning; and this is evident; for anger, will and desire are to be seen in children nearly as soon as they are born; but reason and intelligence spring up as they grow to maturity. The body, therefore, necessarily demands our care before the soul; next the appetites for the sake of the mind; the body for the sake of the soul.

# Chapter 5: Skepticism

---

*Comprehension questions you should be able to answer after reading this chapter:*

1. What does each of the following mean: *aporia, epoché, ataraxia*?

2. Explain each of the following skeptic modes:

   a) The argument from differences in animals

   b) The argument from the difference between men

   c) The argument from the differences in the senses

   d) The argument based on circumstances

   e) The argument based on positions, distances, and places

   f) The argument based on unwarranted assumption and infinite regress

3. How are the skeptic modes used to "set things in opposition," and how does this produce *aporia*?

4. What is the connection between suspending judgment, and achieving tranquility?

5. What does it mean to "live by appearances?"

6. Did the Skeptics *know* that skepticism was a means to achieve tranquility? Why, or why now?

---

According to legend, Socrates claimed to know "nothing." Some philosophers took that ball and really ran with it! Skepticism was a philosophical school that taught that knowledge was impossible—or, at least that's how it appeared to them, at that moment.

Ancient Skepticism can be divided into two core periods: Academic and Pyrrhonian Skepticism. Academic Skepticism refers to the period (273 BCE through the 1st century BCE) in which Plato's Academy turned "Skeptic." Pyrrhonian Skepticism is named after Pyrrho, and flourished from (roughly) the 1st century BCE through the 3rd century CE.

Arcesilaus (316 – 241 BCE, roughly) was responsible for the Skeptical turn at the Academy during his tenure as its leader. Although he did not refer to himself as a "skeptic" (this vocabulary was added later), his emphasis on Socrates as a critical examiner, questioner, and tester of knowledge claims is certainly consistent with Skeptic themes. Another Academic Skeptic, Carneades (214 – 129 BCE) exemplified what became known as the skeptic method of putting things "in opposition" when he visited Rome around 156 BCE While there, he argued for justice one day, and against justice the very next day. His point was not to somehow reject "justice," but rather to demonstrate that all those who argue for and about justice (including philosophical giants such as Plato himself) don't actually have successful arguments in its defense, or even a clear and accurate concept of what it is.

It is not until Pyrrho (and Pyrrhonian Skepticism), however, that Skepticism develops as a "way of life," analogous to (and in competition with) other such ways of life as Epicureanism and Stoicism. Academic Skepticism was, well, "academic." Arguably, it was scholarly for the sake of scholarship. With Pyrrho, though, skepticism becomes a means to achieve tranquility.

Pyrrho lived (very roughly) from 365-275 BCE, and the accounts of his life (whether embellished or accurate) portray him as a sage, the very portrait of tranquility, undisturbed by emotions, events, and appearances. Some anecdotes take this to the absurd, claiming that his friends had to pull him from the path of an approaching wagon—so "undisturbed" was he. Given his actual philosophy, however, this story seems likely to be a mythologized exaggeration. After all (as we will learn), Pyrrho advocated that we live by appearances, and, given the appearance of an approaching wagon and that it appears preferable to not be run over by a wagon, Pyrrho would have acted accordingly—and gotten the hell out of the way!

Of final mention, we have Sextus Empiricus (160 – 210 CE—roughly). Although of possible interest in his own right, our appreciation of Sextus is due to one of his works: *Outlines of Pyrrhonism*—the only general description of Pyrrhonian skepticism to have survived. Our focus will be the Pyrrhonian variety of Skepticism (as opposed to Academic Skepticism), as detailed by Sextus Empiricus. Any further reference to Skepticism should be assumed to refer to the Pyrrhonian variety, unless otherwise noted.

As might already be evident, Skepticism is a school of thought with a very old and distinguished pedigree. It is also often misunderstood. Today, many people, when they think of a "skeptic," think of a simple nay-sayer—someone who will disagree with whatever she hears just to be difficult. Or, perhaps one thinks of a conspiracy theorist—one, for example, who is "skeptical" that the government wasn't somehow involved in the 9-11 terrorist attacks.

In fact, true Skeptics (in the Ancient sense of the word) will be largely indistinguishable from non-skeptics, except by virtue of some of their phrasings and vocabulary.

Skepticism is a frustratingly difficult system to describe in that it doesn't claim to be a "system" at all. It was not a system of beliefs, nor of doctrines, to be accepted or rejected. Instead, *Skepticism is presented as a way of life that is supposed to lead its practitioners through a state of being "at a loss" (aporia), to a suspension of judgment (epoché), to a state of tranquility (ataraxia).* This way of life involves developing an ability to deploy opposing evidence and arguments, both for and against any claim that went "beyond appearances" (i.e., beyond what was immediately evident), so as to suspend judgment on such issues. This, it was thought, was a cure for the "disease" of dogmatism.

*The Skeptic process*, summarized and simplified, is as follows (for any claim):

1.   "Set things in opposition."
2.   Become "at a loss" (*aporia*) as to the truth of the claim.
3.   Suspend judgment as to the claim (*epoché*), but live by appearances.
4.   Achieve tranquility (*ataraxia*).

At the heart of skepticism, then, is the belief (based on how things appear to the skeptic) that it is never possible to be certain of anything. Even that belief is not thought to be certain—it just appears to be the case. If we can never be certain of anything, a skeptic will think that we can never claim to "know" anything, since we will always lack sufficient justification to go from belief to knowledge.

This is Skepticism, in a nut shell, but several questions arise: why should anyone be skeptical in this way? And, what's the point? What does any of this have to do with "tranquility?"

We'll begin at the beginning. Once we understood how things may be "set in opposition," we will understand why the Skeptics believed knowledge was impossible and why suspension of judgment resulted. Having understood this, perhaps we'll see the connection to tranquility.

So, why would anyone be skeptical in this way? The reasons are better than you might initially suspect.

## Setting things in opposition

*When confronted with a claim (on any subject whatsoever), the Skeptic would be trained to set that claim in opposition.* This process involves any number of skeptical arguments based on a variety of "modes" developed by Skeptics over the centuries. There are several sets of these modes, and two such sets are presented below.

1.   The argument from differences in animals
2.   The argument from the difference between men
3.   The argument from the differences in the senses
4.   The argument based on circumstances
5.   The argument based on positions, distances, and places
6.   The argument based on admixtures
7.   The argument based on the quantities and compoundings of external objects
8.   The argument from relativity
9.   The argument from frequency or rarity of occurrence
10.  The argument from disciplines, customs, laws, myths, and dogmatic notions

The usual tradition amongst the older sceptics is that the "modes" by which "suspension" is supposed to be brought about are ten in number; and they also give them the synonymous names of "arguments" and "positions." They are these: the first, based on the variety in animals; the second, on the differences in human beings; the third, on the different structures of the organs of sense; the fourth, on the circumstantial conditions; the fifth, on positions and intervals and locations; the sixth, on intermixtures; the seventh, on the quantities and formations of the underlying objects; the eighth, on the fact of relativity; the ninth, on the frequency or rarity of occurrence; the tenth, on the disciplines and customs and laws, the legendary beliefs and the dogmatic convictions.[97]

1.  The mode based on disagreement
2.  The mode which produces to infinity
3.  The mode based on relativity
4.  The mode from assumption
5.  The mode from argument in a circle

The mode based upon regress ad infinitum is that whereby we assert that the thing adduced as a proof of the matter proposed needs a further proof, and this again another, and so on ad infinitum, so that the consequence is suspension, as we possess no starting-point for our argument. The mode based upon relativity, as we have already said, is that whereby the object has such or such an appearance in relation to the subject judging and to the concomitant precepts, but as to its real nature we suspend judgement. We have the mode based on hypothesis when the dogmatists, being forced to recede ad infinitum, take as their starting-point something which they do not establish by argument but claim to assume as granted simply and without demonstration. The mode of circular reasoning is the form used when the proof itself which ought to establish the matter of inquiry requires confirmation derived from that matter; in this case, being unable to assume either in order to establish the other, we suspend judgment about both.

The first 10 modes concern "appearances," whereas the second set of 5 concern argument or proof, more generally. Sextus describes all of the above, but to develop all 15 is much more ambitious than is necessary for our purposes. Instead, we will consider just the first 5 modes from the first set, and an even smaller sample from the second.

## 1. The argument from differences in animals

*The first argument (or trope), as we said, is that which shows that the same impressions are not produced by the same objects owing to the differences in animals. ... the differences found in the most important parts of the body, and especially in those of which the natural function is judging and perceiving, are capable of producing a vast deal of divergence in the sense impressions. Thus, sufferers from jaundice declare that objects which seem to us white are yellow, while those whose eyes are bloodshot call them blood-red. Since, then, some animals also have eyes which are yellow, others bloodshot, others albino, others of other colours, they probably, I*

---

[97] Sextus Empiricus, *Outlines of Pyrrhonism*. Book 1.14, 36-38. All future quotations in this chapter are from this same source, unless otherwise indicated.

*suppose, have different perceptions of colour. Moreover, if we bend down over a book after having gazed long and fixedly at the sun, the letters seem to us to be golden in colour and circling round. . . . Again, when we press the eyeball at one side, the forms, figures, and sizes of the objects appear oblong and narrow. So it is probable that all animals which have the pupil of the eye slanting and elongated—such as goats, cats, and similar animals—have impressions of the objects which are different and unlike the notions formed of them by the animals which have round pupils. Mirrors, too, owing to differences in their construction, represent the external objects at one time as very small—as when the mirror is concave—at another time as elongated and narrow—as when the mirror is convex. Some mirrors, too, show the head of the figure reflected at the bottom and the feet at the top. Since, then, some organs of sight actually protrude beyond the face owing to their convexity, while others are quite concave, and others again lie in a level plane—on this account also it is probable that their impressions differ, and that the same objects, as seen by dogs, fishes, lions, men and locusts, are neither equal in size nor similar in shape, but vary according to the image of each object created by the particular sight that receives the impression. . . .*[98]

This mode is perhaps the most obvious and easiest to describe. It is based on the different means of perception employed by different species of animals. Although Sextus offers an unusual argument concerning the (apparent) origin of various species, the most important (and obvious) comes when he calls attention to the common-sense observation that different animals have differently structured sense organs. He observes the differences in pupil size and shape, but our own understanding of biology and zoology dwarfs that available in Sextus' time. We are much more aware of the significant anatomical differences with regard to eyes, ears, nostrils, taste receptors, etc., across various species.

Look at the image of the flower below. What color is it? (Or, if your book is in black and white, what color would you expect a dandelion to be?)

---

[98] Ibid., 40-49.

Yellow, right? Notice the bee on the flower? Because insects, like bees, access a different portion of the spectrum of energy (the UV portion), the flower is more likely to appear "white", with a purple/red patch right in the center. From our perspective, flowers that are a single color actually often light up like a "bulls-eye" to insects.[99] Now ask yourself this question: "What does the flower really look like?" Is it yellow? Or is it white with a red center? Is the bee wrong? Or are you? How can you both be right? As Sextus expresses it:

> But if the same things appear different owing to the variety in animals, we shall indeed be able to state our own impressions of the real object, but as to its essential nature we shall suspend judgment. For we cannot ourselves judge between our own impressions and those of the other animals since we ourselves are involved in the dispute and are, therefore, rather in need of a judge than competent to pass judgment ourselves....[100]

The general point, of course, it that it appears that there is no such thing as a "pure," unmediated perception. Instead, all our perceptions are necessarily (inevitably, unavoidably) *mediated* by our sense organs. To put it bluntly, you can't see without using your eyeballs! Those eyeballs are not "neutral," but instead filter our perceptions based (among other things) on the kind of lens (both literal and figurative) that they are. All our perceptions are filtered by virtue of whatever lenses we happen to be using. It stands to reason, then, that if you change the lens, you change the perception. Different species have different lenses. Indeed, some species have "lenses" that we don't possess at all, such as echolocation. A case can be made that the flower is yellow (based on the kind of lens I'm using), but a case could also be made that it's not yellow (based on the perception resulting from a bee's lens).

The claim that the flower is yellow has been "set in opposition." Having argued both that the flower is, and is not, yellow, I am now "at a loss" (*aporia*) as to the truth of that claim. In other words, I'm not certain. It *appears* yellow, to me, at this moment—but I don't *know* that it's yellow. This causes me to suspend judgment (*epoché*) with regard to that claim, and simply go by appearances. In other words, I will describe the flower as yellow, since that's how it appears to me, but I will suspend judgment as to whether it *really* is yellow. Feeling "tranquil" yet? If not, don't worry. We'll explore the connection to tranquility a bit later. For now, though, let's take a quick tour through four more of those modes. The basic process remains the same. Only the particular argument will

---

[99] Go to http://www.ukchameleons.co.uk/assets/images/tarax_UV.jpg to find an ultraviolet image of a similar flower.
[100] Sextus, Ibid., 59-60.

differ.

## 2.   The argument from the difference between men

*... The second mode is, as we said, that based on the differences in men. For even if we grant for the sake of argument that men are more worthy of credence than irrational animals, we shall find that even our own differences of themselves lead to suspense [of judgement]. For man, you know, is said to be compounded of two things, soul and body, and in both these we differ one from another.*

*Thus, as regards the body, we differ in our figures and "idiosyncrasies," or constitutional peculiarities. The body of an Indian differs in shape from that of a Scythian; and it is said that what causes the variation is a difference in the predominant humours. Owing to this difference in the predominant humours, the sense impressions also come to differ, as we indicated in our first argument. So too, in respect of choice and avoidance of external objects, men exhibit great differences. . . .*

*Seeing, then, that men vary so much in body—to content ourselves with but a few instances of the many collected by the dogmatists—men probably also differ from one another in respect of the soul itself; for the body is a kind of expression of the soul, as in fact is proved by the science of physiognomy. But the greatest proof of the vast and endless differences in men's intelligence is the discrepancy in the statements of the dogmatists concerning the right objects of choice and avoidance, as well as other things. . . .*

*Seeing, then, that choice and avoidance depend on pleasure and displeasure, while pleasure and displeasure depend on sensation and sense impression, whenever some men choose the very things which are avoided by others, it is logical for us to conclude that they are also differently affected by the same things, since otherwise they would all alike have chosen or avoided the same things. But if the same objects affect men differently owing to the differences in the men, then, on this ground also, we shall reasonably be led to suspension of judgement. . . .[101]*

The second mode is similar to the first. Just as we recognize the differences between different species of animals, so too do we recognize the differences between members of the same species—in this case, humans.

There are a variety of ways to understand these differences, all of which lend themselves to the Skeptics point. There are physiological differences, of course, with some being more obvious than others. Sextus notes that "the body of an Indian differs in shape from that of a Scythian." Now, we needn't embrace his

---

[101] Ibid., 79-88.

racial essentialism in order to grasp the point and translate it into more modern vocabulary: there are genetic variations, however slight, across persons. There are differences in sensitivities and training as well. Although the difference between my sense of smell and yours is unlikely to be so striking as the difference between mine and my cat's, there might nevertheless be a difference worth noting. Master Sommeliers are famous for their ability to detect and articulate subtle differences in the taste and smell of wine that most of us mere mortals are unable to perceive. Whether this is the result of differences in physiology, training (or mere bravado) is an interesting question, but the differences do appear to exist.

These differences do not appear to be limited to claims about sense perceptions. Sextus claims that "the greatest proof of the vast and endless differences in men's intelligence is the discrepancy in the statements of the dogmatists concerning the right objects of choice and avoidance, as well as other things." In other words, our "perceptions" of the good life, of what is good and bad, right and wrong, seems to vary, sometimes greatly, sometimes slightly, from one person to the next—and we can find sensible, intelligent people articulating each of these positions. There are smart, sensible people articulating conservative political views, and others articulating liberal views. There are intelligent atheists, and intelligent theists. In the Skeptics own time, Epicureans and Stoics "battled" over their respective visions of *eudaimonia*—with the Skeptics targeting both.

Given these different perceptions, sensory and otherwise, what are we to conclude? Because they can all be "set in opposition," we are "at a loss" as to what is *really* true in regards to these things. So, we "suspend judgment" and live by appearances.

### 3. The argument from the differences in the senses

*That the senses differ from one another is obvious. Thus, to the eye paintings seem to have recesses and projections, but not so to the touch. Honey, too, seems to some, pleasant to the tongue but unpleasant to the eyes—so that it is impossible to say whether it is absolutely pleasant or unpleasant. The same is true of sweet oil, for it pleases the sense of smell but displeases the taste. So too with spurge: since it pains the eyes but causes no pain to any other part of the body, we cannot say whether, in its real nature, it is absolutely painful or painless to bodies. Rainwater, too, is beneficial to the eyes but roughens the windpipe and the lungs—as also does olive oil, though it mollifies the epidermis. The crampfish, also, when applied to the extremities produces cramp, but it can be applied to the rest of the body without hurt. Consequently we are unable to say what is the real nature of each of these things, although it is possible to say what each thing at the moment appears to be. . . .[102]*

---

[102] Ibid., 92-93.

The third mode is a bit silly, on the surface, but quite powerful as soon as we delve to just a little bit of depth. First, the silly. Sextus points out, for example, that "honey is pleasant to the tongue but unpleasant to the eyes—so that it is impossible to say whether it is absolutely pleasant or unpleasant." At first glance, we might think that he is suggesting that although honey tastes good, it doesn't have a pleasant appearance. In context with the rest of that section of the text, though, he seems to be saying something a bit more blunt: if you pour honey on your tongue it's pleasant, but if you pour honey on your eye it's not. This is both true and amusing. With just a small bit of effort, though, we can see that Sextus is making an observation that is much more compelling.

We've already acknowledged that different species employ different "lenses" in the first mode, and that members of the same species employ different lenses as well (in the second mode). This third mode points out that even the same organism employs different lenses. Forget about honey. Instead, look at any flat, solid surface in your environment right now. Do it. Seriously. It can be anything both flat and solid. The surface of a book, or a desk, or table, or counter. Your eyes are telling you it's flat and solid. What do your fingers tell you? If you glide your fingertips across the surface, does it feel exactly as your eyes told you it would? Or, does it have a texture, a tactile impression that your eyes didn't convey? If so, your eyes told you one thing, but your sense of touch another. Which of those two conveyed the truth? Let's make it worse.

Consider flower petals. They typically look pretty smooth, right? What would they feel like? Perhaps still pretty smooth, but maybe a little "velvety?" If we were to magnify the surface of the flower say 1,500 times, one would find that it looks "hilly". The point of this example, and this mode, is the same as the previous two modes: we can "set in opposition" claims about the flower petal based on which sense organ we're using, and whether or not one of those organs (the eye) is looking with the help of an electron microscope. This causes us to be "at a loss" as to the truth of those claims. Therefore, we "suspend judgment" and go by appearances.

### 4. The argument based on circumstances

*In order that we may finally reach suspension by basing our argument on each sense singly, or even by disregarding the senses, we further adopt the fourth mode of suspension. This is the mode based, as we say, on the "circumstances," meaning by "circumstances" conditions or dispositions. And this mode, we say, deals with states that are natural or unnatural, with waking or sleeping, with conditions due to age, motion or rest, hatred or love, emptiness or fulness, drunkenness or soberness, predispositions, confidence or fear, grief or joy. Thus, according as the mental state is natural or unnatural, objects produce dissimilar impressions, as when men in a frenzy or in a state of ecstasy believe they hear demons' voices, while we do not. Similarly they often say that they perceive an odour of storax or frankincense, or some such scent, and many other things, though we fail to perceive them....*[103]

This fourth mode deals with the various conditions and dispositions we might find ourselves subject to and that affect our "lenses." Sextus gives us a brief list of the sorts of conditions he has in mind: waking, sleeping, age, motion, rest, hatred, love, emptiness, fullness, drunkenness, soberness, confidence, fear, grief, joy.

Some of these are probably obvious, and many became part of the long history of skeptical techniques employed for centuries (including, much later, by Descartes). First, consider waking versus sleeping.

Ask yourself this very simple question: have you ever had a dream that was so vivid that, at the time, you didn't know it was a dream and thought it was real? Almost everyone can answer "yes" to that question. Some dreams are so realistic that they produce actual physical effects in us, such as sweating, racing pulse, etc. The power of this observation lies in the realization that, while we are having one of those vivid dreams, we don't know that it's a dream. At the same time, most of

us are confident that what happens in dreams isn't real. For example, it would be hard to find someone who, upon having a dream in which she committed a crime, would feel obligated to go turn herself in to the police. It was "just a dream," after all. If, during those dreams, you don't know that you're dreaming, how do you know you're not dreaming right now? Perhaps you're having a wonderful, amazing dream in which you're reading a philosophy text? Perhaps I'm having a dream in which I'm writing one?

Stepping away from sensory perceptions, consider the effect of age. Isn't it the case that most of us "see" things differently, as we age? Our beliefs and values change, even if subtly, over time—not to mention the impact that something more

blunt such as senility or cataracts could have on our perceptions and beliefs. Or, consider "hate" and "love." It's a cliché, but very often someone whom you love can do no wrong "in your eyes." Emotions provide lenses through which we perceive people and events as well. If I like someone very much, I'm disposed to view that person favorably, and to overlook his or her faults. If, on the other hand, I dislike someone, I'm disposed to view his or her actions more critically, and am much more likely to "see" his or her faults—maybe even faults that aren't (arguably) there, or that have at least been magnified.

Consider the obvious effect of intoxication on beliefs and perceptions. Whether we are talking about mere drunkenness, or powerful hallucinogens, it is obvious that various chemicals can cause us to see, believe, and feel things differently than if we were sober.

Sextus even alludes to mental illness. "Thus, according as the mental state is natural or unnatural, objects produce dissimilar impressions, as when men in a

---

[103] Ibid., 100-101.

frenzy or state of ecstasy believe they hear demons' voices, while we do not."[104]

I used to work as a counselor at a locked-placement psychiatric hospital. The residents there were all seriously mentally ill adults. Nearly all suffered from delusions. I use the word "suffer" intentionally. There is nothing amusing about delusions. They produce great suffering and tragedy in the lives of those who have them. Why? Because profoundly mentally ill people usually don't recognize that their delusions are delusions. They believe they are real, or represent a real image of the world. So, the one poor man who constantly believed that snakes were crawling out of the floor reacted accordingly: with fear. The man who believed he was not a patient, but an employee of the hospital, would become understandably upset when he was not allowed to go home at the end of the day. Those suffering from paranoid delusions, who believed that various forces were conspiring against them, were constantly anxious and fearful of their (imagined) powerful enemies. What made the situation so especially tragic is that the man who believed he was an employee, and not a patient, believed so (seemingly) with just as much confidence as I had in my belief that he was a patient.

The application is simple, if not disturbing: how do you know you're not mentally ill right now, and that all sorts of things that you are believe aren't, in fact, delusions? Perhaps your whole life is one grand delusion, and you're actually restrained and living in a psychiatric hospital right now? If that were the case, and your present perception of reality were delusional, you wouldn't be aware of that fact, after all....

Again, both the process and outcome are the same: because of the mode based on circumstances, we can set in opposition any number of claims. This causes us to be at a loss as to the truth, and therefore suspend judgment and live by appearances.

### 5.   The argument based on positions, distances, and places

*The fifth argument (or trope) is that based on positions, distances, and locations. For owing to each of these, the same objects appear different. For example, the same porch, when viewed from one of its corners, appears curtailed; but viewed from the middle, symmetrical on all sides. And the same ship seems at a distance to be small and stationary; but from close at hand, large and in motion. And the same tower from a distance appears round; but from a near point, quadrangular.*

*These effects are due to distances; among effects due to locations are the following. The light of a lamp appears dim in the sun but bright in the dark; and the same oar, bent when in the water but straight when out of the water; and the egg, soft when inside the fowl but hard when in the air; ...*

*Effects due to positions are such as these: the same painting, when laid flat appears smooth; but when inclined forward at a certain angle, it seems to*

---

[104] Ibid.

*have recesses and prominences. The necks of doves, also, appear different in hue according to the differences in the angle of inclination.*

*Since, then, all apparent objects are viewed in a certain place, and from a certain distance, or in a certain position, and each of these conditions produces a great divergency in the sense impressions, as we mentioned above, we shall be compelled by this mode also to end up in suspension of judgement. For in fact, anyone who purposes to give the preference to any of these impressions will be attempting the impossible. For if he shall deliver his judgement simply and without proof, he will be discredited. And should he, on the other hand, desire to adduce proof, he will confute himself if he says that the proof is false; while if he asserts that the proof is true, he will be asked for a proof of its truth, and again for a proof of this latter proof, since it also must be true, and so on ad infinitum. But to produce proofs to infinity is impossible, so that neither by the use of proofs will he be able to prefer one sense impression to another. If, then, one cannot hope to pass judgement on the aforementioned impressions either with or without proof, the conclusion we are driven to is suspension. For while we can, no doubt, state the nature which each object appears to possess as viewed in a certain position or at a certain distance or in a certain place, what its real nature is we are, for the foregoing reasons, unable to declare. . . .*[105]

Finally from this set, we have the mode based on positions, distances, and places. Again appealing to sensory perceptions, Sextus provides numerous examples of how appearances are subject to the contingencies of our vantage point. Objects appear to be different shapes when viewed up close as opposed to far away, or even from different angles at the same distance. A ship, when far away, appears to be small and stationary, but when much closer appears both larger as well as in motion. A light appears to be dim when viewed in the day but bright when seen at night. An oar appears straight when suspended in the air but bent when seen in the water.

In sum, our senses tell us any number of seemingly contradictory things about what is (allegedly) the same object. It is both large and small, at rest and in motion, dim and bright, etc. Because we can set our claims in opposition, we are at a loss as to the truth and we are caused to suspend judgment and live by.

## Great Minds Think Alike!

The ancient Skeptics argued that knowledge was impossible to attain, and they offered several arguments in support of that conclusion. At roughly the same time (369 - 286 BCE), the philosopher Chuang-Tzu developed a

---

[105] Ibid., 118-123.

philosophy similar to Lao Tzu's Taoism, but with a distinct "skeptical" element.

According to Chuang-Tzu, to become "one with Tao" requires one to adopt the "unlimited" point of view, and abandon the limited point of view.

The limited point of view is the one that does not recognize the Tao, but focuses on distinctions. To argue for the unlimited point of view, he tries to demonstrate the flaws of our ordinary (limited) point of view. He does so in ways unmistakably analogous to both subjectivists such as Protagoras, and skeptics such as Pyrrho.

With respect to values, he acknowledges that judgments about values are subjective and therefore relative. The nature and quality of a thing will vary depending upon one's point of view, but the Tao recognizes no distinctions – all differences are identified as one.

*A road becomes so when people walk on it, and things become so-and-so [to people] because people call them so-and-so. However they become so? They have become so because people say they are so. How have they become not so? They have become not so because [people] say they are not so.*[106]

As an example, he cites that followers of Confucius are confident that our moral sense is capable of providing true knowledge of what is right and wrong. However, this perception is arguably no less relative than any other. He presents a dialogue between a character named Gaptooth who is thought to represent the Confucian point of view, and a character named Wang Ni who is thought to represent his own point of view.

Gaptooth put a question to Wang Ni.
G: 'Would you like to know something of which all things agreed 'That's it?''
W: 'How would I know that?'
G: 'Would you know what you did not know?'
W: 'how would I know that?'
G: 'then does no thing know anything?'
W: 'how would I know that? However, let me try to say it –'how do I know that what I call knowing is not ignorance? How do I know that what I call ignorance is not knowing?'... In my judgment the principles of goodwill and duty, the paths of 'That's it, that's not,' are inextricably confused; how could I know how to discriminate between them?'[107]

---

[106] Wing-tsit Chan, *A Sourcebook in Chinese Philosophy*, Princeton University Press, 1969. p. 184.

[107] John M. Koller and Patricia Koller, *A Sourcebook in Asian Philosophy*,

Much as the ancient Greek skeptics acknowledged of their own philosophy, Chuang Tzu applies the point of the above dialogue even to his own point of view: it, too, is a matter of perspective that cannot be known/proven.

He offers another, similar, argument based on differences in perspectives. It is obvious that things appear differently to different people in different respects and at different times. It is also obvious that if someone had different senses or different experiences that person would perceive things differently. The same thing appears differently based upon the perceiver. Which is the correct appearance? This is precisely the question that ancient Skeptics posed in the ancient Mediterranean at roughly the same time! Chuang Tzu famously illustrates this question of perspectives with his story of the dream of the butterfly.

> Last night Chuang Chou [Chuang Tzu] dreamed he was a butterfly, spirits soaring he was a butterfly (is it that in showing what he was he suited his own fancy?), and did not know about Chou. When all of a sudden he awoke, he was Chou with all his wits about him. He does not know whether he is Chou who dreams he is a butterfly or a butterfly who dreams he is Chou.[108]

Ultimately, we can never really *know* what a thing is, in itself, but we can only know things from the perspective from which we view it. Only by assuming a "perspective-beyond-perspectives" could we know the true nature of the thing. The ordinary point of view does not allow this, and the "unlimited" point of view is recommended instead.

Finally, ancient Greek skeptics believed that there is something therapeutic about suspending judgment. It appears that Chuang Tzu saw a similar value in his own skepticism.

> We say this is right or wrong, and is so or is not so. If the right is really right, and the fact that it is different from the wrong leaves no room for argument. Forget the passage of time (life-and-death) and forget the distinction of right and wrong. Relax in the realm of the infinite and thus abide in the realm of the infinite.[109]

We have considered only five modes from the first list of ten. I will now combine several modes from that second list of five to give us one more

---

Macmillan, 1991. p. 458.

[108] Ibid., p. 460.

[109] Chan, p. 184.

(combined) "mode."

## 1. The argument based on Unwarranted Assumption and Infinite Regress

*"They [skeptics] hand down also two other modes leading to suspension of judgement. Since every object of apprehension seems to be apprehended either through itself or through another object, by showing that nothing is apprehended either through itself or through another thing, they introduce doubt, as they suppose, about everything. That nothing is apprehended through itself is plain, they say, from the controversy which exists amongst the physicists regarding, I imagine, all things, both sensibles and intelligibles; which controversy admits of no settlement because we can neither employ a sensible nor an intelligible criterion, since every criterion we may adopt is controverted and therefore discredited.*

*And the reason why they do not allow that anything is apprehended through something else is this: If that through which an object is apprehended must always itself be apprehended through some other thing, one is involved in a process of circular reasoning or in regress ad infinitum. And if, on the other hand, one should choose to assume that the thing through which another object is apprehended is itself apprehended through itself, this is refuted by the fact that, for the reasons already stated, nothing is apprehended through itself. But as to how what conflicts with itself can possibly be apprehended either through itself or through some other thing we remain in doubt, so long as the criterion of truth or of apprehension is not apparent, and signs, even apart from demonstration, are rejected."[110]*

First, let's consider the formal argument, somewhat "translated" into more contemporary philosophical language, and then we'll dissect it, piece by piece as needed:

1.  If a belief is justified, then it is either a basic justified belief or an inferentially justified belief.
2.  There are no basic justified beliefs.
    Therefore,
3.  If a belief is justified, then it is justified in virtue of belonging to an inferential chain.
4.  All inferential chains are such that either (a) they contain an infinite number of beliefs; (b) they contain circles; or (c) they contain beliefs that are not justified.
5.  No belief is justified in virtue of belonging to an infinite inferential chain.

---

[110] Sextus, 1.16, 178-179.

6. No belief is justified in virtue of belonging to a circular inferential chain.
7. No belief is justified in virtue of belonging to an inferential chain that contains unjustified beliefs.
   Therefore,
8. There are no justified beliefs.

Let's start at the beginning. The first premise claims that in order for a belief to be justified, it is either justified by itself, or by means of other justified beliefs. In the second premise, the skeptics reject the possibility that a belief could be justified just by itself, referring to this as the "mode based on hypothesis, when the dogmatists . . . take as their starting-point something which they do not establish by argument but claim to assume as granted simply and without demonstration."[111] The alleged problem with this is that such a belief has not been justified, but merely asserted—and is therefore without sufficient justification. Therefore, in order for a belief to be justified, it has to be by virtue of an inferential chain of other (justified) beliefs, as stated in the third premise.

In the fourth premise, the skeptics lay out the possibilities: all inferential chains either go on "forever," or involve circular reasoning, or contain ultimately unjustified beliefs. They then proceed to dismiss each of those three options.

In the fifth premise, they reject the legitimacy of an infinite chain. "The mode based upon regress ad infinitum is that whereby we assert that the thing adduced as a proof of the matter proposed needs a further proof, and this again another, and so on ad infinitum, so that the consequence is suspension, as we possess no starting-point for our argument."[112] In other words, if the chain of inference is infinite, it has no "foundation" or "anchor" and is ultimately left unjustified.

The sixth premise rejects inferential chains that involve "circles" as well. "The mode of circular reasoning is the form used when the proof itself which ought to establish the matter of inquiry requires confirmation derived from that matter; in this case, being unable to assume either in order to establish the other, we suspend judgment about both."[113] If you try to justify one belief by means of another belief, and then you justify that second belief by means of the first, you're just "going in a circle," and nothing has been justified.

In the seventh premise, they reject chains that involve unjustified beliefs for the same reason as already mentioned above: an unjustified belief is literally without justification, and can't be (properly) used to justify other beliefs by means of inference.

Therefore, according to this argument, no beliefs are justified, and knowledge appears to be impossible to acquire.

As one final effort, let us consider one last argument that doesn't appear on either list. You will likely love this, or hate it; admire the Skeptics for their cleverness, or curse them for their trickery.

Suppose that a "dogmatist" somehow manages to refute the use of any and

---

[111] Ibid., 1.15, 168.
[112] Ibid., 166.
[113] Ibid., 169.

all of the other skeptical modes and claims that she knows something that cannot be "set in opposition," despite the Skeptic's best efforts. Does the Skeptic have anything left to say? Yes. The Skeptic has what amounts to a secret weapon, a special "last resort" argument. The Skeptic may appeal to a hitherto unknown, but existing, counter-argument.

> *Whenever someone propounds to us an argument which we are not able to refute, we say to him: "Just as before the birth of the founder of the school to which you belong, the argument of the school, which is sound, was not yet apparent, but was nonetheless really there in nature, so likewise it is also possible that the argument opposing the one you are propounding now is really there in nature, but that it is not yet apparent to us, so that we should not yet assent to what now seems to be a strong argument".*[114]

> *since no one is able to visit all humans and determine what pleases the majority, given that it is possible that among some nations of which we have no knowledge the things that are rare among us are usual for the majority, whereas the things which happen to most of us are there rare – as for instance, that most people when bitten by venomous spiders do not suffer whereas some rarely suffer.*[115]

> *even if, with regard to some cases, we cannot immediately state an anomaly, it must be said that it is possible that in some nations unknown to us there is disagreement also about them. Hence, just as, if we had not known, for example, about the Egyptians' custom of marrying their sisters, we would have wrongly affirmed that it is agreed by all that people must not marry their sisters, so likewise, with regard to those things in which no anomalies manifest themselves to us, it is not apposite to affirm that there is no disagreement about them, given that it is possible, as I said, that among some of the nations unknown to us there is disagreement about them..*[116]

> *we declare that it is possible for someone else to be born who is more intelligent than the man whom we say is more intelligent than those of the past and the present. Hence, just as we are required to believe the one who, because of his intelligence, is now said to be wiser than those of the present and the past, so too it is necessary to believe the one who is more intelligent than him that will exist after him. And when that one is born, it is necessary to expect in turn that someone else more intelligent than him will be born, and someone else more intelligent than him, and so on ad infinitum. And it is non-evident whether they will agree with one another or will disagree in what they say. This is why, even if someone is acknowledged to be more*

---

[114] Ibid., 1.13, 34.
[115] Book 1.14, 89.
[116] Book 3.24 ,233.

*intelligent than those of the past and the present, given that we cannot say affirmatively that no one will be more sagacious than him (for that is non-evident), it will always be necessary to wait for the judgment of the one who will later be more intelligent than him and never assent to the one who is presently superior.*[117]

What *is* this counter-argument? I don't know. It's an unknown argument, after all. Imagine the following conversation between Descartes (arguably the most famous refuter of Skepticism) and a very clever Skeptic:

*Descartes: "Skepticism has been defeated. There is one claim that I know, with certainty, at least whenever I utter it or reflect upon it. I am certain that I exist whenever I am thinking. This is indubitable."*

*Skeptic: "You claim to be certain of this because the claim that you exist whenever you are thinking cannot be set in opposition?"*

*Descartes: "Indeed."*

*Skeptic: "Is it even possible, though, that there exists a counter-argument to your claim of which I am presently unaware and that exceeds my skill, as a Skeptic? Is it even possible that, someday, a Skeptic more wise than me will come along who will discover a way, presently unknown to both of us, to set even your claim of your own existence in opposition?"*[118]

At this point, a potentially interesting debate between those who favor Descartes and those who favor the Skeptics might break out. The Skeptic, at least, will claim that it is, of course, at least *possible* that such an argument exists, even if presently unknown. How could we rule it out, categorically? If so, then even very "self-evident" claims such as one's own existence while thinking are not so "evident" after all?

All of our discussion thus far has focused on the process of setting things in opposition—the first stage of the Skeptic process. The second stage, being at a loss (*aporia*) is implied by the first, and has been discussed, at least briefly and tangentially above. It will require far less space and effort.

## Being "at a loss"

*Being "at a loss" is simply the effect of setting claims in opposition by means of the various skeptic modes.* These modes cause us to lose our confidence that any

---

[117] Book 2.5, 40.

[118] For added fun, we can imagine Descartes replying that maybe someone smarter than him, someday, will come up with another argument that can defeat the Skeptics again—but then this just makes the Skeptic's point: we can't be certain of *anything*—not even Skepticism!

particular claim can be known to be true, that any particular "lens" is the "true" lens with which to view and interpret reality.

One thing that is important to note is that *aporia* is not "doubt" in the sense that we often use that term today. Very often, when we say that we "doubt" something what we're really saying is that we deny its truth.

"I'll be there by 5 PM."
"I doubt it."

In that usage, "doubt" means that I think it is false that you will arrive by 5 PM. But, the Skeptics do not mean "doubt" in this way. They are not proclaiming various statements to be false. They are acknowledging that they do not *know* if the claim is true *or* false. Indeed, Pyrrhonian Skeptics wouldn't even go so far as to presume that they even understand the claim, nor any of the particular concepts it invokes. If someone asserts that "the honey is sweet," the Skeptic won't merely be at a loss because she isn't certain whether it really is sweet— she's not even certain if she properly understands "sweetness" and "honey."

*Aporia* is perhaps not best understood as doubt, given all the connotations "doubt" possesses, but rather understand *aporia* as being perplexed, confused, "stymied," stumped, stuck, etc. What follows from this (or, so it appears to the Skeptics) is that one is caused to suspend judgment.

## Suspending Judgment

*As a result of being "at a loss,' the Skeptic is led to "suspend judgment"(epoché)* as to the truth or falsity of the claim. Simply put, she's just not sure, so she's not going to commit herself either way.

On the surface, this might appear to be an absurd, impractical, and maybe even impossible approach to life. After all, what would it mean to not commit yourself either way to the claim that you need to eat to survive? Certain things (such as whether or not one needs to eat) seem like a forced choice. If you refuse to commit to either eating or not eating, you have, by default, committed yourself to not eating. Fortunately, the Skeptics were not as shallow or clumsy as that.

Although we are to suspend judgment as to the ultimate truth or falsity of claims, we are to live by appearances, in the absence of certainty. So, while a Skeptic would not assent to the claim that she needs to eat to survive (just as she would not assent to the claim that she does not need to eat to survive), what she would acknowledge is that it appears (to her, at that moment) that she needs to eat to survive. That's good enough. She'll eat. She's not making any presumptuous statements concerning reality as it really is (and, specifically, as it pertains to human nutritional requirements). All she's claiming is that it appears (to her, at that time) that she needs to eat. Similarly, a Skeptic would suspend judgment as to the sweetness of honey, but he would be just fine with admitting that the honey appears to taste sweet (to him, at that moment). Is honey really sweet? He doesn't know—but it appears to taste sweet to him, at that moment, so he'll just live accordingly. If it appears to him that he desires something sweet, honey would seem to be a decent candidate to satisfy that desire.

Interestingly, if one were to observe a Skeptic's daily life and compare it to that of a non-Skeptic, you would be hard-pressed to discover any obvious, practical differences. The Skeptic will use her senses and reason to live (generally) as everyone else does. Because she's in no position to critique them, the Skeptic will conform to the customs, laws, and institutions of her community. After all, she would be "at a loss" as to whether any other way of life would be preferable. She will follow her natural tendencies and dispositions. In other words, she will eat when hungry, and sleep when tired. In terms of daily life, there is unlikely to be any difference (behaviorally) between her and others. What would be the behavioral difference, for example, between "knowing" the flower is yellow and living by the appearance it is yellow? The only likely observable difference would be one of description: "The flower is yellow" v. "it appears to me, now, that the flower is yellow."

Anyone concerned that the Skeptic will be some sort of behaviorally paralyzed eccentric can rest easy. But, if there's no significant outward difference between the Skeptic and the non-Skeptic, what's the point of being a Skeptic? Benson Mates (a prominent scholar on Pyrrhonian Skepticism) describes it in the following way:

> So the Pyrrhonist's message, insofar as he has one, is something like this: 'At ease! The notion that in order to live well you have to have beliefs about a supposed reality that transcends all appearances is just a mistake. Go by the appearances; put aside your worries about whether they correspond to that so-called 'external world,' which the philosophers never manage to describe in a consistent or fully intelligible way; suspend judgment about all such matters and you will reach the equanimity that we all desire.[119]

## Tranquility

Equanimity? How so? What does suspension of judgment have to do with anything of the kind? Skeptics claimed that it appeared that "tranquilty" (*ataraxia*), in the sense of "peace of mind," or "unperturbedness," resulted from suspending judgment. *When the Skeptic surrendered to appearances, and gave up the pursuit of certainty, tranquility followed.* Since it appears, to the Skeptic, that tranquility is a good thing, then Skepticism appears to be a useful means to achieve that (apparently) desirable end.

We must be clear and fair to the Skeptics. They did not claim (that it appeared to them, at the time) that their method could somehow remove all pain and emotional turmoil from one's life. Injury, disease, starvation, assault, and their like afflict Skeptic and non-Skeptic alike. As Sextus admits:

> We do not suppose, of course, that the Skeptic is wholly untroubled, but we do say that he is troubled only by things unavoidable. For we agree that

---

[119] Benson Mates, *The Skeptic Way*, Oxford University Press, 1996, p.v-vi.

*sometimes he is cold and thirsty and has various feelings like those.*[120]

The difference, according to Skepticism, is that the Skeptic appears to be positioned to lessen the pain that is unavoidable, and eliminate certain pains that are (it would appear) avoidable.

Of those types of suffering which are unavoidable, suspending judgment can make the suffering less than it otherwise might be. For example, to be hungry is to suffer in the literal sense of the actual pain of hunger. Skepticism can't help with that. Non-Skeptics, though, in addition to being physically hungry, might compound their suffering by adding judgments such as "it's terrible to be hungry," or, "it's unjust for me and others to be hungry when others have so much more." Because the Skeptic won't commit to such claims, she is at least spared the additional mental suffering that such commitments might produce.

What of those pains that are entirely avoidable? Those would be the pains that result solely from the frustration and disappointment resulting from our inability to discover (irrefutably) the Truth about the world and how it works, as well what is morally good and bad.

> *All unhappiness comes about because of some perturbation. But in human beings every perturbation is due either to intense pursuit of certain things or to intense avoidance of certain things. All people intensely pursue what they believe to be good and avoid what they assume to be bad. Thus, all unhappiness arises from pursuing good things on the assumption that they are bad. Since, then, the Dogmatist feels sure that this thing is good by nature and that thing is bad by nature, he will always be pursuing the one and avoiding the other, and being perturbed because of this, he will never be happy.*[121]

In a rare editorial moment, I want to take some time to critique Skepticism—or at least put it in some tighter context. Pyrrhonian Skepticism is presented as a way of life, and as a means to better one's condition by virtue of achieving tranquility. Thus, Skepticism presents itself as not merely an academic exercise but as a way to improve your life—or, at least that's how it appears to them at the moment. With any such way of life, the proof is in the pudding. In other words, it should matter whether the system (which doesn't claim to be a system) actually works.

Skepticism is alleged to be helpful with two different kinds of suffering: those that are unavoidable and those that are avoidable. First, let's consider the unavoidable pains.

Let's recall that Skeptics, while suspending judgment, do live by appearances. Ultimately, will there be a tangible difference between the "dogmatists" who claim that they're hungry and that it's bad to be hungry, and the Skeptics who would merely admit that it *appears* that they are hungry and it *appears* to be bad

---

[120] Sextus, 1.12, 29-30.
[121] Sextus, *Against the Mathematicians*, 11.112-113.

to be hungry? After all, the Skeptic has admitted that, outwardly, the life of the Skeptic and the life of the non-Skeptic will be very hard to distinguish. If I'm treading water in the ocean, being threatened by sharks, with no discernible hope of rescue, it's not immediately obvious that my soul will be less "perturbed" if, rather than claiming to *know* I'm in a bad spot, I instead merely acknowledge that it just *appears* that I'm about to be eaten by sharks. Isn't the appearance bad enough?

What of the other type of suffering? The avoidable kind. The suffering that results from not being able to discover certain and irrefutable knowledge about the universe, its operations, and its values. Benson Mates sums up the concern nicely:

> *I have known a few—very few—philosophers to whom the problem of 'our knowledge of the external world' was seriously upsetting; such individuals might indeed find relief in the kind of reflections that constitute the Pyrrhonist point of view. And I can imagine someone being so caught up in certain moral questions of the day—such as whether abortion or suicide under such and such conditions is a bad thing—that he or she would find comfort in suspending judgment, with the thought that the arguments on both sides seem more or less evenly balanced and that the issues seem never to have been satisfactorily defined. But as to the common man, on such questions as whether it is really the case that the honey is sweet or that the wine is sour, it is hard to see why he would be particularly upset by the conflicting evidence, or, if he were, how Pyrrhonism could offer any more help than, perhaps, the advice to stop worrying about that and be content with the appearances.*[122]

I wonder (and this is the editorial part) if Skepticism presents itself as an apparent solution to a problem from which few, if any, actually suffer?

Whatever problems Skepticism might (or might not) have, its impact on Western philosophy is undeniable. In its own time, Skepticism challenged basic epistemological assumptions and gave focus to key epistemological issues (e.g., truth, justification, knowledge, etc.) that haunt philosophers to this day. The Skeptics were ruthless and relentless sparring partners for the other philosophical schools of their time, especially the Stoics. The continued assault on their doctrines by the Skeptics forced these other schools (especially the Stoics) to rigorously develop and defend their systems, thereby adding both strength and depth. Epictetus—a rather prominent Stoic—acknowledges the value of a good sparring partner.

> *What advantage does a wrestler gain from him with whom he exercises himself before the combat? The greatest. And just in the same manner I exercise myself with this man. He exercises me in patience, in gentleness, in meekness. I am to suppose, then, that I gain an advantage from him who*

---

[122] Mates, 63.

*exercises my neck, and puts my back and shoulders in order; so that the trainer may well bid me grapple him, with both hands, and the heavier he is the better for me; and yet it is no advantage to me when I am exercised in gentleness of temper! This is not to know how to gain an advantage from men.*[123]

Finally, the Skeptic's arguments (e.g., their "modes") inspired later generations of Skeptics, and sort-of Skeptics (such as Descartes). Indeed, many of their "modes" found new life during the Renaissance. And, the basic distinction between appearance and reality so thoroughly developed by the Skeptics was profoundly influential on a variety of later philosophical movements such as perspectivism, positivism, and post-modernism—or, at least that's how it appears to me, now.

---

[123] Epictetus, *Discourses*, Book III.xx.9-12.

# Interlude: A Way of Life

*Comprehension questions you should be able to answer after reading this chapter:*

1. Why is it unlikely that merely listening to a philosophy lecture would be sufficient to make it a "way of life?

2. What are "spiritual exercises" (*askesis*), and what is their purpose?

3. What does each of the following mean?

   a. *Areté*
   b. *Askesis*
   c. *Bios*
   d. *Ergon*
   e. *Eudaimonia*
   f. *Logos*
   g. *Philosophia*
   h. *Telos*
   i. *Technē*

Since at least Pythagoras (571 – 495 BCE), there has been something "self-serving" about philosophy—just in the sense that doing philosophy was good for the philosopher. Wisdom was valued not just for the sake of knowing all kinds of cool things, but because it was believed that it contributed to, and was, indeed, necessary for, happiness. Pythagoras sought "salvation" in philosophy.

Socrates (470/469 – 399 BCE) used philosophy to cure ignorance and correct vice, and

Plato (428/427 or 424/423 – 348/347 BCE) conceived of philosophy as the means by which we escape from the fluctuating world of appearance, purify our soul, and acquire true knowledge in contemplation of the Forms.

Aristotle (384 – 322 BCE) regarded philosophical contemplation as the peak of human activity and fulfillment. The practical value of philosophy was clear, but, up to this point, philosophy was often regarded as an exercise in abstraction and theorizing.

While all philosophers used arguments to establish their points, the Skeptics, such as Pyrrho (365 - 275 BCE), began to use philosophical arguments as a therapeutic technique. Their opposing arguments (for and against) a particular claim enabled them to suspend judgment, and achieve tranquility. These arguments could be honed, practiced, and put to use in systematic ways in daily life.

*Most people imagine that philosophy consists in delivering discourses from the heights of a chair, and in giving classes based on texts. But what these people utterly miss is the uninterrupted philosophy which we see being*

*practiced every day in a way which is perfectly equal to itself.... Socrates did not set up a grandstand for his audience and did not sit upon a professorial chair; he had no fixed timetables for talking or walking with his friends. Rather, he did philosophy sometimes by joking with them, and finally by going to prison and drinking poison. He was the first to show that at all times and in every place, in everything that happens to us, daily life gives us the opportunity to do philosophy.*[124]

Rather than thinking of "doing philosophy" in terms of standing in front of people and lecturing from a book (in other words, what *I* do for a living!), Plutarch reminds us that Socrates did neither. He had no fixed schedule, no classroom, and no textbook. He talked with friends and strangers alike, and (arguably) his finest demonstration of philosophy was how he died. Daily life provides occasion for philosophy, and everything we do is an opportunity to practice it. This is undoubtedly in sharp contrast to a vision of philosophy consisting of reading books and arguing about their contents! Instead, philosophy was seen as a practical pursuit, capable of providing practical benefit.

*Vain is the word of a philosopher which does not heal any suffering of man. For just as there is no profit in medicine if it does not expel the diseases of the body, so there is no profit in philosophy either, if it does not expel the suffering of the mind.*[125]

Here, Epicurus is employing the (common, at that time) medical analogy for philosophy. We all recognize that there are diseases and injuries of the body, and a skill and understanding pertaining to those injuries and diseases: medicine. Similarly, there are "diseases and injuries" of the "soul," and a skill and understanding relevant to those ailments: philosophy. Just as we think medicine has failed to do its job if our symptoms don't improve (where improvement is possible), so too did ancient philosophers think philosophy had failed to do its job if our lives were not made better as a result of our practicing philosophy. To put it bluntly, if practicing philosophy showed no positive change in your life, provided no improvements, then you weren't doing it right!

*I think there is no one who has rendered worse service to the human race than those who have learned philosophy as a mercenary trade.*[126]

Here, the Stoic Seneca is distinguishing genuine philosophers—those who pursue philosophy for the sake of wisdom and living an excellent life—from intellectual mercenaries such as the Sophists. The Sophists were notorious for demanding payment for their instruction, and for their general willingness to argue any position if the price was right. But, for Seneca and other philosophers,

---

[124] Plutarch, *Whether a Man Should Engage in Politics When He Is Old.*
[125] Epicurus, *Extant Remains*, Fragment #221.
[126] Seneca, *Letters to Lucilius.*

philosophy was no game or sport, nor even an intellectual diversion.

*Philosophy is no trick to catch the public; it is not devised for show. It is a matter, not of words, but of facts. It is not pursued in order that the day may yield some amusement before it is spent, or that our leisure may be relieved of a tedium that irks us. It moulds and constructs the soul; it orders our life, guides our conduct, shows us what we should do and what we should leave undone; it sits at the helm and directs our course as we waver amid uncertainties. Without it, no one can live fearlessly or in peace of mind. Countless things that happen every hour call for advice; and such advice is to be sought in philosophy.*[127]

Philosophy was not, for Seneca, merely a mentally stimulating exercise—it was the means by which we navigate life's challenges, find direction, and, ultimately, seek to live a better life.

With a few quotations behind us, setting the tone, I now want to take a "vocabulary break" and introduce you to several terms that will help us to refine our understanding of philosophy, as it was conceived in Greece and Rome.

*Areté* (ἀρετή): human excellence/goodness/virtue
*Askesis* (ἄσκησις): spiritual exercise/training/practice
*Bios* (bioß): way of life/manner of living
*Ergon* (ἔργον): product/deed/action
*Eudaimonia* (εὐδαιμονία): well-being/flourishing/happiness
*Logos* (λόγος): rational explanation/theory/argument/principle
*Philosophia* (φιλοσοφία): love of wisdom
*Telos* (τέλος): end/purpose/goal
*Technē* (τέχνη): art/craft/skill/expertise

For many ancient philosophers, philosophy (φιλοσοφία) was conceived as a skill/art (τέχνη), whose goal (τέλος) was instilling excellence/virtue (ἀρετή) in its practitioner, and thereby achieving flourishing/happiness (εὐδαιμονία). Like other skills, philosophy requires both theoretical understanding (λόγος) as well as training (ἄσκησις) in order that the philosophy be manifested in action (ἔργον) and transform one's life (*bioß*). The Stoic Epictetus does a wonderful job of illustrating this view of philosophy by means of two different analogies.

*Those who have learned the principles and nothing else are eager to throw them up immediately, just as persons with a weak stomach throw up their food. First digest your principles, and then you will surely not throw them up this way. Otherwise they are mere vomit, foul stuff and unfit to eat. But after you have digested these principles, show us some change in your governing principles that is due to them; as the athletes show their*

---

[127] Ibid.

*shoulders as the results of their exercising and eating.*[128]

*A carpenter does not come up to you and say, "listen to me discourse about the art of carpentry," but he makes a contract for a house and builds it...Do the same thing yourself. Eat like a man, drink like a man...get married, have children, take part in civic life, learn how to put up with insults, and tolerate other people.*[129]

Epictetus has provided us analogies with athletics and carpentry—both being skills (τέχνη). In the first quotation, Epictetus is describing the behavior of every person I have ever known (myself included) when first studying philosophy. At first, students of philosophy become fascinated with whichever philosopher they happen to be reading at the time, and are eager to quote from him (or her), and to demonstrate their understanding of the text or philosopher in question. Usually, there is very little actual understanding involved, just regurgitation. Or, to use Epictetus' colorful imagery: "vomiting."

The mark of philosophical understanding, for Epictetus, is not the ability to recite passages from a philosopher, or even to summarize arguments, but rather the effect that the philosophy has had on the student's life and behavior.

We evaluate the skill of an athlete not by how well she can *talk about* basketball, but by how well she *plays*. If someone merely *tells* us that he is a great dancer, that is far less persuasive than demonstrating some dancing. Talk is cheap for aspiring MMA fighters. Get in the cage and win a fight!

The next quotation offers the same theme. An excellent carpenter isn't one who can speak well about carpentry, but rather someone who can actually work well with wood. If I want to hire a carpenter to build a gazebo for me, I'm far less interested in his lectures on carpentry than with some examples of his previous work.

When it comes to philosophy, the best demonstration of your philosophical progress is not you *telling* me about it, but the way you live an excellent life.

*If philosophical theories seduce you, sit down and go over them again and again in your mind. But never call yourself a philosopher, and never allow yourself to be called a philosopher.*[130]

Those for whom philosophy is merely a mental exercise have missed the point of philosophy, according to Epictetus, and he doesn't want them to use the term "philosopher" for themselves. Perhaps they are philologists (lovers of words), but they are not philosophers (lovers of wisdom). Epictetus claimed that the better demonstration of philosophical progress was in our actions, rather than in our ability to *talk about* philosophy. This is not, however, an indicator that we could somehow get by without theoretical understanding. In a quotation in

---

[128] Epictetus, *Discourses*, III.21.
[129] Ibid.
[130] Ibid.

which Epictetus rehearses a conversation with a student who wants to skip over the education/understanding, and get straight to the practical stuff, Epictetus makes this point clear. I have added some words in brackets to provide further clarity.

> *Tell me then about what I should talk to you: about what matter are you able to listen?—About good and evil [ETHICS]. —Good and evil in what? In a horse? No. Well, in an ox? No. What then? In a man? Yes. Do we know then what a man is [METAPHYSICS], what the notion is which we have of him, or have we our ears in any degree practised about this matter? But do you understand what nature is? [METAPHYSICS] or can you even in any degree understand me when I say, I shall use demonstration to you? How? Do you understand this very thing, what demonstration is, or how any thing I, demonstrated, or by what means; or what things are like demonstration, but are not demonstration? [LOGIC] Do you know what is true or what is false? [EPISTEMOLOGY] What is consequent on a thing, what is repugnant to a thing, or not consistent, or in-consistent? But must I excite you to philosophy, and how? Shall I show to you the repugnance in the opinions of most men, through which they differ about things good and evil, and about things which are profitable and unprofitable, when you know not this very thing, what repugnance (contradiction) is?*[131]

Let us suppose that we agree with Epictetus (and his peers) that philosophy is a skill aimed at producing an excellent life and, ultimately, happiness. How can any of us expect to figure out the recipe for a good life if we haven't figured out what we are, as humans, and therefore what would count as a good life in the first place? For example, your basic metaphysical understanding of "human" will make a big difference with regard to what you think is good *for* humans. If you have a purely naturalistic worldview, and believe that humans are rational animals wrought by the same evolutionary forces that produced every other animal on Earth, you will develop a certain kind of understanding of what would count as a good life as a rational animal. On the other hand, if your worldview includes the existence of God, and a belief in an afterlife for the non-physical soul, you will presumably have a different view. To put it bluntly, the sorts of things that might be valuable if this earthly life is the only existence we'll ever have might amount to "nothing" against the backdrop of an eternal life, and what counts as a good life for a theist might be profoundly different than what counts as a good life for an atheist. In other words, metaphysics matters. You need to acquire a sense of "reality," and how it operates, in order to come up with your value system.

Of course, in order to know what reality is like, we need to know what knowledge is, and how it can be acquired (if at all). This means we need to do some epistemology. And, the various arguments concerning both epistemology and metaphysics are *arguments*. We are in no position to assess those arguments

---

[131] Epictetus, *Discourses* II.24.

unless we understand logic and reasoning, in general. This is just to say that there are no "short cuts" in philosophy. Countless contemporary self-help gurus peddle their books promising to guide you to the good life, but how many of them have actually done the *work* necessary to back up that pledge? One hopes that their vision of the good life is actually built upon a foundation that includes metaphysics, epistemology, and logical reasoning.

While the pay-off in philosophy is the transformation of our deeds and our lives into something excellent, we need to develop the *understanding* necessary for that transformation to occur. To return to our analogy, a carpenter needs to understand the mechanics and principles that explain *why* wood needs to be joined using certain techniques and tools, and certain angles, *why* certain structures support weight while others don't—but ultimately the carpenter has to take that understanding and go build something.

Take your philosophical understanding, and then go build an excellent life.

Books like this one, and courses (like mine) that tend to use books like this one, can only promote the "understanding" component (λόγος) of philosophy. The deeds are up to you.

> *The philosophers first exercise us in theory, where there is less difficulty, and then after lead us to the more difficult matters; for in theory there is nothing which holds us back from following what we are taught, but in the affairs of life there are many things which draw us away.*[132]

> *It is not the person who eagerly listens to and makes notes of what is spoken by the philosophers who is ready for philosophizing, but the person who is ready to transfer the prescriptions of philosophy to his deeds and to live in accord with them.*[133]

This therapeutic, intentional application of philosophy reached new heights in the Hellenistic schools that will be our final subjects of inquiry. In these schools, more so than any other, the practical value of philosophy is evident. Philosophy had truly become a "way of life."

In a book of that name (*Philosophy as a Way of Life*), Pierre Hadot discusses this understanding of philosophy. Philosophy was not treated primarily, let alone exclusively, as an intellectual, academic, or analytical exercise. It was a spiritual (or, perhaps, existential) practice—a way of life. Becoming a member of a philosophical school was tantamount to a religious conversion involving one's entire self. As tends to be the case with actual religious conversions, simply reading, analyzing, and discussing texts (e.g., the Bible) would not normally be sufficient for "conversion." To continue the analogy, it's one thing to merely name oneself a Christian, and quite another thing to live as one. So, too, with ancient philosophical schools.

Aristotle, for example, divided students of philosophy into two categories.

[132] Epictetus, *Discourses*, I.26.3
[133] Arius Didymus, *Epitome of Stoic Ethics*, 2.7.1 1k.

One type is already predisposed to virtue, or at least has benefited from a good education. For these people, reading and listening to philosophical lectures can be helpful in transforming their natural virtues into conscious virtues. The other type, though, is one who is not already virtuous and is, at the time, a slave to her passions. "He who is inclined to obey his passions will listen in vain and without profit, since the goal is not knowledge but practice."[134] For such persons, reading books and listening to lectures will not be enough. "The auditor's soul must be worked on for a long time, in order that it make good use of attractions and repulsions, just as we turn over the earth which will nourish the seeds."[135] This indicates that, for some of us—if not many, something more potent than mere "study" is needed to actually affect a change in behavior. Philosophy couldn't be merely "theoretical" if it was to inspire a personal transformation.

What is that more potent "something" that allows the student of philosophy to actually live out his or her system of values? "Spiritual exercises."

## Spiritual Exercises (*askesis*)

The previously mentioned Pierre Hadot was arguably the foremost expert on these spiritual exercises as they were employed throughout the history of Western philosophy. Then, as now, it is usually not an easy thing to sincerely and authentically live according to one's system of beliefs and values. "Such a transformation of vision is not easy, and it is precisely here that spiritual exercises come in. Little by little, they make possible the indispensable metamorphosis of our inner self."[136]

In whatever system we find them, *spiritual exercises serve to transform the practitioner's life such that he can consistently live as his doctrines prescribe.* But just what are spiritual exercises? Hadot describes spiritual exercises as "practices which could be physical, as in dietary regimes [e.g., Epicurean moderation], or discursive, as in dialogue and meditation [e.g., Stoic death meditations], but which were all intended to effect a modification and transformation in the subject who practiced them."[137] Elsewhere, *he defines spiritual exercises as "voluntary, personal practices intended to cause a transformation of the self."*[138] This brief definition requires explanation, which I shall attempt to provide in the spirit of Hadot, if not in his own words.

Spiritual exercises are personal because they apply to oneself. One cannot perform spiritual exercises on behalf of someone else. They are voluntary because they must be deliberate and intended. While brainwashing might be an

---

[134] Aristotle, *Nicomachean Ethics*, 1095a4-6.

[135] Ibid., 1179b24.

[136] Pierre Hadot. *Philosophy as a Way of Life. Spiritual Exercises from Socrates to Foucault.* Edited by Arnold I. Davidson. Translated by Michael Chase (Oxford: Blackwell Publishers, 1995), 83.

[137] Pierre Hadot, *What is Ancient Philosophy?* Translated by Michael Chase (Cambridge: Harvard University Press, 2002), 6.

[138] Ibid., 179-180.

effective way to change behavior and perspective, brainwashing is not a spiritual exercise. Finally, they are transformative of the self because they involve a modification of one's behavior and perspective with respect to one's values (especially one's moral values). It is useful to quote Hadot at length.

> *"Spiritual exercises." The expression is a bit disconcerting for the contemporary reader. In the first place, it is no longer quite fashionable these days to use the word "spiritual." It is nevertheless necessary to use this term, I believe, because none of the other adjectives we could use— "psychic," "moral," "ethical," "intellectual," "of though t," "of the soul"— covers all the aspects of the reality we want to describe. Since, in these exercises, it is thought which, as it were, takes itself as its own subject- matter, and seeks to modify itself, it would be possible for us to speak in terms of "thought exercises." Yet the word "thought" does not indicate clearly enough that imagination and sensibility play a very important role in these exercises. For the same reason, we cannot be satisfied with "intellectual exercises," although such intellectual factors as definition, division, ratiocination, reading, investigation, and rhetorical amplification play a large role in them. "Ethical exercises" is a rather tempting expression, since, as we shall see, the exercises in question contribute in a powerful way to the therapeutics of the passions, and have to do with the conduct of life. Yet, here again, this would be too limited a view of things. . . . these exercises in fact correspond to a transformation of our vision of the world, and to a metamorphosis of our personality.[139]*

Spiritual exercises may involve thought experiments, meditations, and discourse (especially with oneself), but are identical to none of these things. Spiritual exercises are concerned with "the conduct of life," but not merely with behavior *per se*. Spiritual exercises aim at nothing less than self-transformation, at transforming one's perspective, behavior, and character.

Spiritual exercises, then, are not identical with behavior modification in general—though behavior is modified in both cases. For example, a convicted sex offender who volunteers to undergo chemical castration in order to suppress his deviant sexual impulses will (allegedly) display a change in behavior as a result of the medication, but we would not claim that the chemical castration was therefore a spiritual exercise.

Spiritual exercises require deliberate, self-reflective effort on the part of the practitioner. The practitioner must know what she is doing, and why. Spiritual exercises must be "mental" exercises. This, of course, is not to say that they must be *exclusively* mental (e.g., imaginative exercises), but that they necessarily involve the mind's conscious efforts. Hadot says of Socrates that he was a master of dialogue with himself, and "therefore, a master of the practice of spiritual exercises."[140] He says that the same thing happens in *every* spiritual exercise: "we

---

[139] Hadot, *Philosophy as a Way of Life*, 81-82.
[140] Ibid., 90.

must *let* ourselves be changed, in our point of view, attitudes, and convictions. This means that we must dialogue with ourselves, and hence we must do battle with ourselves."[141] A key *feature* of spiritual exercises, then (though not the only feature), is speaking with oneself—where "speaking" is understood to include "inner" dialogues.

Having provided a general account of what spiritual exercises are, we will consider some examples of the use of spiritual exercises from Epicurus (Epicureanism); and Epictetus, Marcus Aurelius, and Seneca (Stoicism, in all three cases). The procedure, in each case, will be the same: first, to offer a brief overview of the basic doctrines of the system in question; then, consider how each figure or tradition incorporated and employed spiritual exercises, and, when applicable, what we might take from them ourselves.

---

[141]Ibid., 91.

# Chapter 6: Epicureanism

---

*Comprehension questions you should be able to answer after reading this chapter:*

1. What is the *"tetrapharmakos?"* What was its purpose?

2. Why did Epicurus believe that "the gods should not be feared?"

3. What did Epicurus believe happens to us when we die? How does his atomism contribute to that view?

4. What is "hedonism?" What does *"aponia"* refer to? What is the difference between "moving" desires and "static" desires? How does Epicurus' hedonism contribute to his belief that death can't be a bad thing?

5. What are the different kinds of desires, according to Epicurus? How can we tell which kind a particular desire is? How does Epicurus recommend we regulate our desires?

6. Why does Epicurus believe that pain is "easy to bear?"

7. What are some Epicurean spiritual exercises, and what are they supposed to accomplish?

---

Epicurus lived from 341 BCE to 270 BCE and was the founder of the school called (not surprisingly) Epicureanism. Like other ancient philosophers, Epicurus regarded the goal of philosophy to be the pursuit (and attainment) of happiness. Where he differed from other philosophers is his interpretation of that in which happiness consists, and how best to achieve it.

As stated, Epicurus' goal was the attainment of happiness. He was convinced that much of our suffering is both unnecessary and avoidable. We bring much of our pain upon ourselves by virtue of false beliefs, and harmful desires. He was also convinced of philosophy's power to cure what ails us. Any "philosophy" that fails to do so is no true philosophy at all.

> *Vain is the word of a philosopher which does not heal any suffering of man. For just as there is no profit in medicine if it does not expel the diseases of the body, so there is no profit in philosophy either, if it does not expel the suffering of the mind.*[142]

Epicurus provided his students with a simple and easily memorized mnemonic device to remind them of the causes of (most of) our suffering. This brief collection of ideas was referred to as the *"tetrapharmakos"* (four-fold drug)

---

[142] Epicurus, *Extant Remains*, Fragment #221.

and may be paraphrased as follows:

> Don't fear god,
> Don't worry about death;
> What is good is easy to get, and
> What is terrible is easy to endure.[143]

> Ἄφοβον ὁ θεός,
> ἀνύποπτον ὁ θάνατος
> καὶ τἀγαθὸν μὲν εὔκτητον,
> τὸ δὲ δεινὸν εὐεκκαρτέρητον

In essence, Epicurus believed that we suffer from a variety of unnecessary fears and pains: fear of the afterlife, fear of death, fear of not getting what we "need" in life, fear of losing what we already have, the pain of "failure," the pain of envy, etc. The tetrapharmakos serves to remind us of these major categories of fears or pains, and also how to dispel them. We'll consider each component of the tetrapharmakos, starting at the top.

## Don't fear god

Then, as now, people feared the afterlife, and divine punishment. Then, as now, people tried to avert calamity and punishment through prayer, offerings and tithes, ritual observances, etc. Epicurus thought that any anxiety a person felt about the wrath of the gods was an unfortunate and unnecessary waste. Epicurus clearly believed that gods existed, but he thought that the common view of them was mistaken. In his *Letter to Menoeceus* he writes, "For there are gods, and the knowledge of them is manifest; but they are not such as the multitude believe." The gods are not jealous fickle beings easily angered and disposed to punish us. That is the mistaken view of the "multitude." Instead, he presents the following claim about the gods in the first point of his *Principle Doctrines*: "A blessed and indestructible being has no trouble himself and brings no trouble upon any other being; so he is free from anger and partiality, for all such things imply weakness."

The gods are "blessed and indestructible" beings that exist in a state of perfect serenity. To put it bluntly, they couldn't care less about us human beings. They do not answer prayers, they do not punish or reward anyone; indeed, they have nothing whatsoever to do with humanity. Although Epicurus gave lip service to the gods, and thought them good examples of philosophical contemplation at work, he might as well have been an atheist. Epicurus' gods did not create humanity, nor did they have any interaction with us. They were more similar to powerful and superior alien creatures than "gods" as traditionally conceived. Indeed, his atomistic understanding of nature (discussed below) allowed for a mechanistic explanation of events, rather than an appeal to superstition and myth. We needn't be concerned that the gods cause disease and

---

[143] Philodemus, *Herculaneum Papyrus*, 1005, 4.9–14.

disasters as a way to punish us, since those events will be explained by collisions of atoms instead.

Admittedly, Epicurus' argument concerning the gods is likely more applicable to modern day atheists (or perhaps deists) then, say, a Christian or a Muslim. Rather obviously, on the Christian view, for example, God *is* concerned with human behavior, *does* (allegedly) intervene in human history, and *does* supply reward or punishment in the afterlife. For anyone, however, who either believes that there is no God, or at least none that has any concern about human behavior or well-being, we can see how Epicurus' argument was meant to be helpful: if you are pained by your fear of the gods, get over it! There's nothing to fear.

## Don't worry about death

*So death, the most frightening of bad things, is nothing to us; since when we exist, death is not yet present, and when death is present, then we do not exist. Therefore, it is relevant neither to the living nor to the dead, since it does not affect the former, and the latter do not exist. (Letter to Menoeceus)*

*Death is nothing to us: for that which is dissolved is without sensation; and that which lacks sensation is nothing to us. (Principle Doctrine II)*

In these two quotations, Epicurus summarizes his infamous death argument. In order to understand it, we need to understand two key premises held by Epicurus: atomism, and hedonism.

## Atomism

For a more detailed review of atomism, please refer to that section in the earlier chapter on the pre-Socratics. What follows is a shorter summary of the key and relevant ideas.

*Atoms are eternal, indivisible, ungenerated, indestructible, unchanging, solid particles that are infinite in number and that vary in size and shape,* while lacking in color, taste, temperature, odor, etc. Although atoms were thought to vary in size and shape, according to Aristotle's testimony, they are all so small as to be invisible to the naked eye. Atoms are literally indivisible (indeed, "atom" is derived from the Greek ἄτομον (*atomon*), meaning "uncuttable."), being solid and containing no void within them.

These infinite atoms are dispersed throughout an infinite "void," and are in continuous motion. The void is empty space—something necessary for motion to be possible. Atoms generally fall "downward," but sometimes are subject to a random "swerve" (an event that, somehow, makes free will possible. . . ). The swerve also causes atoms to sometimes collide with each other, producing one of two possible effects: rebound or cohere. When they rebound, the atoms bounce off of each other and continue their movement through the void—though presumably with a new trajectory. Some atoms, however, have a "barbed" or "hooked" shape and will cling together rather than rebound. When atoms cohere in this fashion, they form compound bodies. Because atoms are physical (solid), all the bodies in the universe are also physical, and ultimately composed of these atoms. Even so-called "soul" atoms are still physical, and thought to be spherical in shape.

*Change is the result of the collision and interaction of these atoms.* This produces the world of "appearances" that we experience. When things *appear* to go in and out of existence (change), what is *really* happening is that the imperishable atoms are simply dissolving or forming new collections (compound bodies).

The significance of atomism with regard to Epicurus' death argument is that it entailed (for Epicurus) that there was no afterlife. Human beings are particular collections of atoms. When we die, those atoms separate and are recycled and recombined to create new objects. If one agrees with this premise—if one agrees that we are purely physical beings composed of a vast number of tiny particles— then it's hard to imagine how one could continue to exist in any meaningful, identity-preserving fashion, after the death of the body. For this reason, Epicurus believes that we simply cease to exist when we die. No identity is preserved, no self remains to experience being dead. When he said "death is nothing to us," he meant that literally. Death is nothing. Not-a-thing. This is what is known as the "annihilationist" account of death, because the self is "annihilated" at death.

Think of it this way: at any particular moment of time, you are either alive, or dead. If you alive, you are not experiencing being dead—because you're not dead! Pretty obvious, right? What about when you're dead? Well, according to Epicurus, "you" cease to exist as soon as you're dead. So, there is no "you" to experience "you" being dead. Therefore, you don't experience being dead when you're alive, or when you're dead. In other words, neither you, nor anyone else, ever experiences being dead. Why would this mean death isn't bad? To understand that, we need Epicurus' second key premise: hedonism.

## Hedonism

Hedonism conjures up all sorts of associations. Drunkenness. Over-eating. Narcotics. Wanton sexual activity. For many people, to say that someone is a hedonist is not a compliment. Indeed, it's an allegation that someone pursues sensual pleasures too much. This understanding has almost nothing in common with the notion of hedonism that forms a key premise in Epicurus' death argument. *Hedonism, in the Epicurean sense, was simply a recognition that pleasure and pain inform our most fundamental value judgments.*

> *When we say, then, that pleasure is the end and aim, we do not mean the pleasures of the prodigal or the pleasures of sensuality, as we are understood to do by some through ignorance, prejudice, or willful misrepresentation. By pleasure we mean the absence of pain in the body and of trouble in the soul. It is not an unbroken succession of drinking-*

*bouts and of revelry, not sexual lust, not the enjoyment of the fish and other delicacies of a luxurious table, which produce a pleasant life; it is sober reasoning, searching out the grounds of every choice and avoidance, and banishing those beliefs through which the greatest tumults take possession of the soul.*[144]

That is, everything that we claim is "good" is good because, in some way or another, it can be traced back to pleasure. Everything that we claim is "bad" is so because we can, in some way or another, trace it back to pain. Why is friendship a good thing? Ultimately, because it's pleasurable. Why is betraying a friend a bad thing? Ultimately, because it's painful. Pleasure and pain are taken to ground our most fundamental value judgments because our ability to ask "why" seems to stop once we reach pleasure or pain. Moreover, the "pleasure" Epicurus has in mind is really an *absence of pain ("Aponia")*.

> Would it be a good thing or a bad thing if I were to set you on fire?
> "Bad."
> Why is it bad?
> "Because you shouldn't set people on fire. It's wrong."
> Why would it be bad for me to do something wrong to you?
> "Because I don't want to be set on fire!"
> Why don't you want to be set on fire?
> "Because it would hurt!"
> Why is it bad to hurt?
> [Awkward silence.]

How exactly would one answer that? How does one explain why pain is bad, or pleasure is good? For hedonists, in the classical sense, pleasure *just is* good, as a brute fact of our nature, and pain *just is* bad, as a brute fact of our nature. I sometimes refer to this as "cave man ethics." Pain bad. Pleasure good.

Cave man ethics needn't be crude or simple, of course. Hedonists (in the classical sense) recognize the complexity of situations.

> *And since pleasure is our first and native good, for that reason we do not choose every pleasure whatsoever, but will often pass over many pleasures when a greater annoyance ensues from them. And often we consider pains superior to pleasures when submission to the pains for a long time brings us as a consequence a greater pleasure. While therefore all pleasure because it is naturally akin to us is good, not all pleasure is should be chosen, just as all pain is an evil and yet not all pain is to be shunned.*[145]

For example, you might choose to forego a pleasure—but when you do it is presumed that is for the sake of a greater pleasure, or the avoidance of a worse

---

[144] *Letter to Menoeceus*
[145] Ibid.

pain. For example, I might resist the pleasure of a second piece of cake for dessert, but presumably I'm doing so to avoid the pains of indigestion, or obesity. We also might voluntarily submit to pain, but for similar reasons. I go to the dentist a couple times each year. Invariably, it is painful—even if I'm only getting my teeth cleaned. Yet, I go to the dentist anyway because in doing so I'm avoiding the greater pains of tooth decay.

This example, in which we pursue a painful action to avoid even greater pain, helps to illustrate an important aspect of Epicurus' "hedonism." Epicurus understood "happiness" (*eudaimonia*) in terms of the absence of pain (*aponia*) and the resulting tranquility (*ataraxia*) that produces. This idea of tranquility (*ataraxia*) is the same term that was employed by the skeptics—and the goal is the same as well: peace of mind and a tranquil life. The difference, of course, lies in how Epicurus and the skeptics each thought this could be achieved.

Tranquility is to be sought, for Epicureans, *not* in some relentless pursuit of pleasure, but in the avoidance of pain. Epicurus categorized pleasures in several different ways, as we shall see, but one system of sorting pleasures is to distinguish between "moving" pleasures and "static" pleasures.

Moving pleasures occur in the act of satisfying a desire, and are experienced as an active sensation. If you are hungry, then the act of eating a slice of pizza could be an example of a moving pleasure for you. Static pleasures, on the other hand, occur after the desire has been satisfied, and we are no longer in a state of want or need. Using that same example, the feeling of no longer being hungry after having eaten some pizza would be a static pleasure. Of the two, static pleasures are both stable and fulfilling, according to Epicurean doctrine. Later in this chapter, we will see how Epicurus urges moderation of our moving pleasures.

A further layer of complexity can be added when we recognize the distinction between "intrinsic" and "extrinsic" goods (or evils). Something is intrinsically good if it is, itself, pleasurable, at that moment. Conversely, something is intrinsically bad if it is, itself, painful, at that moment. Stepping on a nail is intrinsically bad because it hurts, right then and there. Something is extrinsically good if it *leads* to pleasure, extrinsically bad if it leads to pain. Poverty, for example, is not itself painful—but it might well lead to pain (e.g., the pain of hunger, exposure to the elements due to homelessness, or even just the pain of worrying over how to pay your bills). For classical hedonists, the only way something can be bad is if it is either intrinsically or extrinsically bad, in other words, if it is either painful or leads to pain. If neither, then it is not "bad."

This recognition of the obvious (that pain is bad and pleasure is good), and the judgment that this recognition should inform our decision making (i.e., that we ought to pursue pleasure (good) and avoid pain (bad)) is a very early precursor to the ethical theory known as utilitarianism. For our purposes, however, we need only see how it applies to Epicurus' death argument.

If we combine atomism and hedonism, we get the following:

1. Each person stops existing at the moment of death.
2. If each person stops existing at the moment of death, then no one feels any pain while dead, nor does that person feel any pain later, as a result of being dead.
3. If no one feels any pain while dead, then death is not intrinsically bad for the one who is dead.
4. If death does not lead to any later state of pain, then death is not extrinsically bad for the one who is dead.
5. Therefore, death is neither intrinsically nor extrinsically bad for the one who is dead.
6. Therefore, death is not bad for the one who is dead.

Much like his argument that the gods are not to be dreaded, the effectiveness of this argument will vary greatly based on your worldview. If, for example, you believe that there *is* an afterlife, that there is something essential about us, as persons, that survives the death of the body, then you are unlikely to be soothed by Epicurus' argument. However, if you are a materialist, and believe that human beings are complicated animals who (like all other animals) cease to exist (in any meaningful "you being the same you in the same sense" sort of way) at death, then Epicurus is speaking to you. The claim of the sadly misinformed, according to Epicurus, is that death is a bad thing. Because of that belief, we fear death. We mourn when others die. We suffer at various times and in varying degrees throughout our lives when we contemplate death, or narrowly avoid it, or anticipate its approach. But all of this fear and pain is unnecessary and self-inflicted, according to Epicurus. Giving his understanding of "badness," death *can't* be a bad thing. If it's not bad, then our belief that it is bad is false. All the anxieties and suffering resulting from that false belief are, therefore, misguided. If we could only correct that belief and realize that death isn't bad, much of our fear and suffering would be relieved.

## What is Good is Easy to Get...

Perhaps more so than from our fear of death or of "the gods," we suffer from what Epicurus considers needless and unnatural desires. Then, as now, people craved what they did not have, and craved something new once they had what they previously craved. We desire things we don't need or that are, worse yet, actually harmful to us. We're frustrated when we can't satisfy those desires, but even when we manage to catch what we've been chasing some new desire emerges to initiate the chase and frustration once more. The character Tyler Durden from the 1999 film *Fight Club* expresses this problem well, if not crudely:

*Advertising has us chasing cars and clothes, working jobs we hate so we can buy shit we don't need.... We've all been raised on television to believe that one day we'd all be millionaires, and movie gods, and rock stars.*

Epicurus believed that desires could be broken up into several categories, as described in his Letter to Menoeceus.

> *"We must also reflect that of desires some are natural, others are groundless; and that of the natural some are necessary as well as natural, and some natural only. And of the necessary desires some are necessary if we are to be happy, some if the body is to be rid of uneasiness, some if we are even to live."*

For any desire we may consult the following diagram:

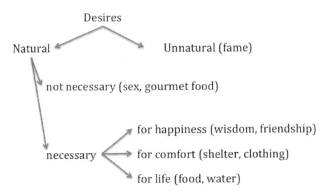

The first division of desires is that of natural as opposed to unnatural desires. How can we distinguish between the two? Natural desires are those which we will all have, simply by virtue of being human. Such desires need not be taught, or acquired, but we find ourselves with them from birth, as it were. These desires will be similar (if not identical) to those of other living creatures. Epicurus recommends that we observe "uncorrupted" samples of creatures and observe their own desires. Consider, for example, the desires of wild (undomesticated) animals. Wild animals desire basic safety and comfort, they desire to eat and drink, they are driven to reproduce—and not much else. Or, consider a newborn human infant. What does it desire? Basic safety and comfort, food and drink—and not much else.

Of those desires that are natural, some are necessary, and others are not. To test our natural desires, Epicurus offers the following tests:

> *One should bring this question to all desires: what will happen to me if what is desired and sought is achieved, and what will happen if it is not?*[146]

> *The desires which do not bring a feeling of pain when not fulfilled are not necessary.*[147]

---

[146] *Vatican Collection,* fragment #71.
[147] *Principle Doctrines,* #26.

The basic test is this: what will be the consequence if you fail to satisfy a particular desire? Suppose, for example, that I desire to eat a fancy seven course dinner with expensive wine paired with each course. What will happen to me if I don't get to eat that particular meal? Will I die? Of course not. Will I get sick, or experience pain? No. Will I suffer? Only if I *make* myself suffer from needless disappointment. Any suffering resulting from failing to experience that meal is self-imposed. Now consider a different example. Suppose my desire is merely to have a modest, inexpensive (but nourishing) meal. What will be the consequence if I fail to satisfy that desire? Will I die? Not if I miss out on such meals only infrequently, but if I am unable to satisfy that desire often enough, I *will* die of starvation. Will I get sick, or experience pain? Quite possibly. Even if I manage to eat just often enough to avoid dying, I will be malnourished and suffer the pain of hunger. What these examples illustrate is that it is natural for us to desire food. All living things naturally require sustenance, and therefore naturally pursue it. But, while it is both natural and necessary (for life itself) that I desire food, it is not necessary that the food be anything "special." I don't *need* steak or lobster, fine wine or artisan cheese. To avoid starvation, plain water and simple food such as fruits and vegetables will suffice. Indeed, despite the modern connotation of an "epicure" being someone with refined taste in food and beverage, Epicurus himself actually advocated the opposite: a simple diet of water and barley bread.

To repeat, those desires that are both natural and necessary are those which, if left unfulfilled, will bring actual harm to the organism. It is both natural and necessary that we desire food and water sufficient for survival. Such things are necessary to remain alive. It is also both natural and necessary that we desire basic comfort, such as shelter from the weather, and sufficient clothing to avoid cold or sunburn. Notice, though, that no special designer label is needed for clothes to keep you warm. You can keep your feet protected from rough ground without needing $14,000 Manolo Blahnik alligator boots. You are protected from wind and rain whether you take shelter in a modest shack, or in a multi-million dollar mansion. (Trivia: you can purchase the "Villa Leopolda" on the French Riviera for a mere $506 million dollars—and then fill the 29,000 square feet with lots of expensive furniture.)

Basic nutrition and shelter are necessary for life itself, and basic comfort— and if these desires are not satisfied, actual pain will come to us (e.g., the pain of hunger or thirst, or the pain of being cold and wet). Epicurus also recognizes that some natural pleasures are necessary for happiness. Friendship, for example, is necessary for a happy life. We are social animals, after all. It is natural for us to seek the company of others. Epicurus' valuing of friendship is unambiguous:

> *Of all the means which wisdom acquires to ensure happiness throughout the whole of life, by far the most important is friendship.*[148]

It is both natural and necessary for us to seek and acquire friendship. Someone who is truly alone in the world will undoubtedly suffer, and be

---

[148] *Principle Doctrines*, #27.

vulnerable. Epicurus claims that "nothing enhances our security so much as friendship."[149] That being said, all that is necessary is that we acquire friends—not any particular friend. I don't need to be friends with Johnny Depp to be happy. My friend Scott will do just fine.

According to Epicurus, we should be grateful that happiness is so easily within our grasp. "Thanks be to blessed Nature because she has made what is necessary easy to supply, and what is not easy unnecessary (*Extant Remains,* fragment #67)." In other words, those things that are truly necessary (e.g., food, water, shelter, friendship) are (generally) easily satisfied. To be sure, some people starve to death, or die of thirst or exposure—and those are all bad things. But, most of us do not face that risk, and even those that do (more often than not) wouldn't need to if the rest of us shared our excess. The things that are harder to acquire, on the other hand (e.g. gourmet food, wealth, a large house, expensive cars, fame) aren't necessary for survival, or even happiness. In some cases, they're not even natural!

It is by virtue of the corrupting influence of society that humans (and other creatures, for that matter) come to desire unnecessary (or unnatural) things, and experience unhappiness when we fail to satisfy them. Only as we grow up do we think that we "need" to be rich, or famous, or to have a particular job, or drive a particular car, or wear particular clothes, or live in a particularly sized house. Infants have no such cravings.

Even non-human animals, once domesticated, can be corrupted in this way. A wild dog will be content with whatever food it can hunt or scavenge on its own.

But, turn a dog into your "pet," and feed him once or twice from your table, and observe how that dog now "needs" *your* food and is unhappy if resigned to only that food in its bowl.

*Our "false" desires come not from Nature but from teaching and socialization.* Natural desires have natural limits and can be satisfied (e.g., my hunger ceases once I'm full), and they aim at the continued and healthy operation of the body. Unnatural desires, on the other hand, are directed at things that are either completely out of reach (e.g., immortality), or difficult to acquire or maintain (e.g., luxury items, fame), or are truly unlimited (e.g., wealth, power).

According to Epicurus' system, there is no afterlife. If, despite that, you desire to never die and, instead, to live forever, you desire the impossible. You are *guaranteed* to be disappointed. Why bring such unnecessary happiness upon yourself? If you desire to be rich, and convince yourself that you can't be happy unless you are, you are setting yourself up for disappointment. It is difficult to become wealthy! Even if one becomes wealthy, wealth is easily lost. What's more, "wealth" is a vague term. How much money is "enough?" Isn't it the case that even

---

[149] Ibid., #28.

"wealthy" people always seem to want more money? How many people who pursue riches reach a point where they can say, honestly, that they have plenty and that they don't desire to make any more money? If you convince yourself that you can only be happy if you become famous, you have set yourself up for unhappiness in the likely event that you fail—or even if you become famous, when you discover that fame is fleeting. If you convince yourself that you can only be happy eating $100 dinners, what will happen should you be unable to afford (or any longer afford) such meals? The theme in each case is that people bring about their own unhappiness by adopting and pursuing unnecessary desires.

A final point of clarification before finishing Epicurus' treatment of desires: Epicurus is *not* claiming that one should never pursue or enjoy "unnecessary" desires. What he is saying is that we shouldn't become dependent upon them. If, for example, you have access to "fancy" food, there is nothing inherently bad about enjoying that fancy food rather than eating only coarse bread and plain water. But, the prudent thing to do, if your goal is to maintain your own peace of mind, is to never come to the false conclusion that you *need* that fancy food in order to be happy, let alone to survive. Detached enjoyment of food, beverage, and luxury items in general is acceptable. The problem, however, is that it is very easy for most of us to lose that "detachment," become accustomed to that level of luxury, and then find that we "need" it. Should that happen, we will be vulnerable to unhappiness in the event that we can no longer afford that lifestyle. As a practical measure, then, it's wiser to avoid those sorts of luxuries altogether. At the least, if you intend to enjoy them, at least train yourself so that you could easily and happily live without them.

## ...and what is Terrible is Easy to Endure.

Epicurus' strategy with regard to regulating our desires is one that focuses on ensuring, as much as is possible, that we will avoid pain. That is, we are to be wary of unnatural or unnecessary desires because the pursuit of them, and attachment to them, results in pain in the event that we fail to satisfy our desires, and the pain of anxiety when we fear losing our ability to satisfy those desires (should we ever be able to satisfy them in the first place). His strategy is defensive, then—a method of minimizing pain in life.

Minimizing is the right way to think of the strategy, as it is impossible to render oneself truly immune to pain (except via suicide, of course—but then there is no "you" who is immune). Some pains are unavoidable. One can regulate one's desires with utmost vigilance, but still get cancer, or be assaulted, or get buried by an earthquake, or acquire arthritis, etc.

Fortunately, Epicurus has a strategy to lessen the impact of even those pains that are unavoidable. Much as he sorted desires, he sorts pains into categories.

*Continuous bodily pain does not last long; instead, pain, if extreme, is present a very short time, and even that degree of pain which slightly exceeds bodily pleasure does not last for many days at once. Diseases of*

An Ancient Way of Life

*long duration allow an excess of bodily pleasure over pain.*[150]

*Pain is usually either continuous, or extreme—but rarely both.* That is, most pains are either long-lasting, but not very intense, or else intensely painful, but tend not to last very long. If you have an ache in a muscle, or a headache, or a toothache, or pain in your joint from arthritis, the pain is very real, and might well last days, or weeks, or even months or years, but such pains are usually not intense. Those sorts of pains (usually) aren't *so* painful that we collapse on the floor, unable to go about our daily business. Painful though they are, they can be endured, and people *do* endure them and still manage to live a decent life. Other sorts of pains take your breath away. They are intensely painful. If you break your arm, or step on a nail, or get shot, it is likely that the pain will be so intense that your ability to function in your everyday life will be diminished, or even fully disrupted. These sorts of pains, however, tend not to last very long. In many cases, the intensity of the pain simply diminishes as the body heals itself, or the initial trauma subsides, or the body acclimates to the experience. Most of us have banged our "funny bone" at some point in our lives. It hurts a lot! When it happens, it's difficult to do anything other than wince, shake out your arm, and catch your breath. But then the pain goes away. Though it might offer only cold comfort, the most intense and traumatic of pains are unlikely to last long if for no other reason than the fact that such pains are likely to result in death. I assume that it is agonizing to be disemboweled, but such a gruesome injury is likely to result in death—at which point the pain ceases.

Epicurus appears to have practiced what he preached. The account of his own death, as offered by Diogenes Laertius, demonstrates his tranquility even in the face of intense pain.

> *I have written this letter to you on a happy day to me, which is also the last day of my life. For I have been attacked by a painful inability to urinate, and also dysentery, so violent that nothing can be added to the violence of my sufferings. But the cheerfulness of my mind, which comes from the recollection of all my philosophical contemplation, counterbalances all these afflictions.*[151]

These words reveal one more strategy to diminish pain: pleasant memories. Though his body was wracked with pain, Epicurus was able to comfort himself with the memories of philosophical conversations with his friends. This is not unlike how those suffering in hospitals may experience some relief when visited by friends or family. The pleasant conversation and good company provides a distraction from the pain.

The only "bad" thing in life is pain. Unavoidable pains are either endurable, or not. If they are not endurable, death will soon release us from that pain—and death is not a bad thing, according to Epicurus. Endurable pains, by definition,

---

[150] Ibid., #4.
[151] Diogenes Laertius, *Lives of Eminent Philosophers*, 10.22.

can be *endured*, and we can diminish their significance with the help of friends and fond memories. All other pains are avoidable, and are experienced usually because we have brought them upon ourselves via needless fears and empty desires. If we can recognize that death is not bad, that "the gods" are not to be feared, and that those things that are truly necessary in life are actually quite easy to obtain, then we can live a life of tranquility.

## Epicurean Spiritual Exercises

This life of tranquility is more easily described than acquired. Epicurus, like many teachers in the ancient philosophical schools, taught that it would not be enough simply to become acquainted with the theories and claims of Epicureanism, if our goal is to benefit from the outlook it offers. We must actively transform ourselves, and the means of doing so is a variety of spiritual exercises.

*Philosophy is to be used to cure us of false beliefs concerning our nature and our happiness.* As the problem is to be found in our beliefs, our treatment must engage our reason. An important difference between Epicurean exercises and those of other schools is that Epicurean exercises are often performed with a mentor, someone more experienced and accomplished in incorporating Epicurus' teachings into daily life. While Epicurean exercises may be performed (in most cases) alone, many of the exercises (for what will be obvious reasons) are better performed with a partner. The Epicurean mentor will tailor her treatment based on the particular condition and needs of her "patient."

One treatment, however, likely to be recommended to *any* aspiring Epicurean involves *memorizing, repeating, and meditating upon summaries of key doctrines.*

> *Meditate therefore on these things and things akin to them night and day by yourself, and with a companion like to yourself, and never shall you be disturbed waking or asleep, but you shall live like a god among men.*[152]

This particular exercise was stressed by Epicurus as essential for understanding his philosophy and making it active in one's life. For example, in Epicurus' letter to Herodotus, he says that "it is necessary to go back on the main principles, and constantly to fix in one's memory enough to give one the most essential comprehension of the truth (section 36)."

To facilitate the memorization and repetition, Epicurus produced short summaries of the key ideas of his own system. For those who are unable "to peruse the larger books which [Epicurus has] composed," he has "already prepared at sufficient length an epitome of the whole system, that they may keep adequately in mind at least the most general principles...in order that as occasion arises they may be able to assist themselves on the most important points (Letter to Herodotus, section 1)." The claim is that by contemplating, memorizing, repeating, and rehearsing the dogmas of Epicureanism, we are able to assimilate

---

[152] *Letter to Meneoceus.*

its teachings within ourselves so as to be able to put them into practice.

The stubbornness of bad habits can only be overcome through repetition. By repeating key doctrines unto memorization, the pupil greatly reduces the risk of getting caught unprepared. More importantly, Epicurus recognizes that some of our false beliefs and values lie beneath the surface of our understanding. Epicurus recommends that we "meditate upon these things" (i.e., the short summaries) and that, as a result, we shall never be disturbed "waking or asleep."

Because of this possibility that some of the adherent's problematic beliefs and values might lie "below the surface," as it were, a second sort of exercise is recommended: confession. This involves not only examining our own conscience and behavior so as to identity our faults and weaknesses in anticipation of correction, but also the sharing of these observations with another Epicurean so that she shares in and assists with the corrective process. Performed with a mentor, the subject is to provide a narrative of her thoughts, desires, actions, and even dreams. The mentor will then be able to analyze the narrative and discern what the subject truly believes and values, and then go about helping her to transform, based on those newly gained insights, so as to achieve a more tranquil "Epicurean" character.

Though often misunderstood and misrepresented, Epicurus presented a philosophical system and life strategy that, in many respects, probably sounds like "common sense" to many today: Pleasure is generally good, and pain is generally bad. We tend to desire things that we don't really need, usually as the result of socialization. We can promote our own happiness by analyzing our desires and regulating them such that we focus only on those things that are truly *necessary* for happiness. Pain can be better endured if we adopt the right perspective. And (for naturalists/materialists, at least), many of our fears concerning death and the afterlife are groundless. Moreover, because living in accordance with these views is easier said than done, we need to train ourselves before the results are manifest. Academically, Epicurus is the philosophical ancestor of Utilitarianism—one of the most well-known and influential ethical systems. Practically, he was an exemplar of someone who pursued and promoted philosophy for therapeutic purposes, as a way of life.

*Epicurus lived from 341 BCE - 270 BCE. The founder of the Epicurean school, only fragments and a few letters remain from his approximately 300 written works. The first selection is his Principle Doctrines, and are a collection of quotations meant to provide a concise summary of the main elements of his ethical theory. The brief quotations indicate several of his important metaphysical assumptions, as well as indicating the key components of his value system. In the Letter to Menoeceus, we find a more narrative summary of those same doctrines.*

# Principal Doctrines
# Epicurus

1. A blessed and indestructible being has no trouble himself and brings no trouble upon any other being; so he is free from anger and partiality, for all such things imply weakness.
2. Death is nothing to us; for that which has been dissolved into its elements experiences no sensations, and that which has no sensation is nothing to us.
3. The magnitude of pleasure reaches its limit in the removal of all pain. When such pleasure is present, so long as it is uninterrupted, there is no pain either of body or of mind or of both together.
4. Continuous bodily pain does not last long; instead, pain, if extreme, is present a very short time, and even that degree of pain which slightly exceeds bodily pleasure does not last for many days at once. Diseases of long duration allow an excess of bodily pleasure over pain.
5. It is impossible to live a pleasant life without living wisely and honorably and justly, and it is impossible to live wisely and honorably and justly without living pleasantly. Whenever any one of these is lacking, when, for instance, the man is not able to live wisely, though he lives honorably and justly, it is impossible for him to live a pleasant life.
6. In order to obtain protection from other men, any means for attaining this end is a natural good.
7. Some men want fame and status, thinking that they would thus make themselves secure against other men. If the life of such men really were secure, they have attained a natural good; if, however, it is insecure, they have not attained the end which by nature's own prompting they originally sought.
8. No pleasure is a bad thing in itself, but the things which produce certain pleasures entail disturbances many times greater than the pleasures themselves.
9. If every pleasure had been capable of accumulation, not only over time but also over the entire body or at least over the principal parts of our nature, then pleasures would never differ from one another.
10. If the things that produce the pleasures of profligate men really freed them from fears of the mind concerning celestial and atmospheric

phenomena, the fear of death, and the fear of pain; if, further, they taught them to limit their desires, we should never have any fault to find with such persons, for they would then be filled with pleasures from every source and would never have pain of body or mind, which is what is bad.

11. If we had never been troubled by celestial and atmospheric phenomena, nor by fears about death, nor by our ignorance of the limits of pains and desires, we should have had no need of natural science.

12. It is impossible for someone to dispel his fears about the most important matters if he doesn't know the nature of the universe but still gives some credence to myths. So without the study of nature there is no enjoyment of pure pleasure.

13. There is no advantage to obtaining protection from other men so long as we are alarmed by events above or below the earth or in general by whatever happens in the boundless universe.

14. Protection from other men, secured to some extent by the power to expel and by material prosperity, in its purest form comes from a quiet life withdrawn from the multitude.

15. The wealth required by nature is limited and is easy to procure; but the wealth required by vain ideals extends to infinity.

16. Chance seldom interferes with the wise man; his greatest and highest interests have been, are, and will be, directed by reason throughout his whole life.

17. The just man is most free from disturbance, while the unjust is full of the utmost disturbance.

18. Bodily pleasure does not increase when the pain of want has been removed; after that it only admits of variation. The limit of mental pleasure, however, is reached when we reflect on these bodily pleasures and their related emotions, which used to cause the mind the greatest alarms.

19. Unlimited time and limited time afford an equal amount of pleasure, if we measure the limits of that pleasure by reason.

20. The flesh receives as unlimited the limits of pleasure; and to provide it requires unlimited time. But the mind, intellectually grasping what the end and limit of the flesh is, and banishing the terrors of the future, procures a complete and perfect life, and we have no longer any need of unlimited time. Nevertheless the mind does not shun pleasure, and even when circumstances make death imminent, the mind does not lack enjoyment of the best life.

21. He who understands the limits of life knows that it is easy to obtain that which removes the pain of want and makes the whole of life complete and perfect. Thus he has no longer any need of things which involve struggle.

22. We must consider both the ultimate end and all clear sensory evidence, to which we refer our opinions; for otherwise everything will be full of uncertainty and confusion.

23. If you fight against all your sensations, you will have no standard to which to refer, and thus no means of judging even those sensations which you claim are false.

24. If you reject absolutely any single sensation without stopping to distinguish between opinion about things awaiting confirmation and that which is already confirmed to be present, whether in sensation or in feelings or in any application of intellect to the presentations, you will confuse the rest of your sensations by your groundless opinion and so you will reject every standard of truth. If in your ideas based upon opinion you hastily affirm as true all that awaits confirmation as well as that which does not, you will not avoid error, as you will be maintaining the entire basis for doubt in every judgment between correct and incorrect opinion.

25. If you do not on every occasion refer each of your actions to the ultimate end prescribed by nature, but instead of this in the act of choice or avoidance turn to some other end, your actions will not be consistent with your theories.

26. All desires that do not lead to pain when they remain unsatisfied are unnecessary, but the desire is easily got rid of, when the thing desired is difficult to obtain or the desires seem likely to produce harm.

27. Of all the means which wisdom acquires to ensure happiness throughout the whole of life, by far the most important is friendship.

28. The same conviction which inspires confidence that nothing we have to fear is eternal or even of long duration, also enables us to see that in the limited evils of this life nothing enhances our security so much as friendship.

29. Of our desires some are natural and necessary, others are natural but not necessary; and others are neither natural nor necessary, but are due to groundless opinion.

30. Those natural desires which entail no pain when unsatisfied, though pursued with an intense effort, are also due to groundless opinion; and it is not because of their own nature they are not got rid of but because of man's groundless opinions.

31. Natural justice is a pledge of reciprocal benefit, to prevent one man from harming or being harmed by another.

32. Those animals which are incapable of making binding agreements with one another not to inflict nor suffer harm are without either justice or injustice; and likewise for those peoples who either could not or would not form binding agreements not to inflict nor suffer harm.

33. There never was such a thing as absolute justice, but only agreements made in mutual dealings among men in whatever places at various times providing against the infliction or suffering of harm.

34. Injustice is not an evil in itself, but only in consequence of the fear which is associated with the apprehension of being discovered by those appointed to punish such actions.

35. It is impossible for a man who secretly violates the terms of the agreement not to harm or be harmed to feel confident that he will remain undiscovered, even if he has already escaped ten thousand times; for until his death he is never sure that he will not be detected.

36. In general justice is the same for all, for it is something found mutually beneficial in men's dealings, but in its application to particular places or other circumstances the same thing is not necessarily just for everyone.

37. Among the things held to be just by law, whatever is proved to be of advantage in men's dealings has the stamp of justice, whether or not it be the same for all; but if a man makes a law and it does not prove to be mutually advantageous, then this is no longer just. And if what is mutually advantageous varies and only for a time corresponds to our concept of justice, nevertheless for that time it is just for those who do not trouble themselves about empty words, but look simply at the facts.

38. Where without any change in circumstances the things held to be just by law are seen not to correspond with the concept of justice in actual practice, such laws are not really just; but wherever the laws have ceased to be advantageous because of a change in circumstances, in that case the laws were for that time just when they were advantageous for the mutual dealings of the citizens, and subsequently ceased to be just when they were no longer advantageous.

39. The man who best knows how to meet external threats makes into one family all the creatures he can; and those he can not, he at any rate does not treat as aliens; and where he finds even this impossible, he avoids all dealings, and, so far as is advantageous, excludes them from his life.

40. Those who possess the power to defend themselves against threats by their neighbors, being thus in possession of the surest guarantee of security, live the most pleasant life with one another; and their enjoyment of the fullest intimacy is such that if one of them dies prematurely, the others do not lament his death as though it called for pity.

# Letter to Menoeceus
# Epicurus

### [Translated by Robert Drew Hicks.]

Epicurus to Menoeceus, greetings:

Let no one be slow to seek wisdom when he is young nor weary in the search of it when he has grown old. For no age is too early or too late for the health of the soul. And to say that the season for studying philosophy has not yet come, or that it is past and gone, is like saying that the season for happiness is not yet or that it is now no more. Therefore, both old and young alike ought to seek wisdom, the former in order that, as age comes over him, he may be young in good things because of the grace of what has been, and the latter in order that, while he is young, he may at the same time be old, because he has no fear of the things which are to come. So we must exercise ourselves in the things which bring happiness, since, if that be present, we have everything, and, if that be absent, all our actions are directed towards attaining it.

Those things which without ceasing I have declared unto you, do them, and exercise yourself in them, holding them to be the elements of right life. First believe that God is a living being immortal and blessed, according to the notion of a god indicated by the common sense of mankind; and so believing, you shall not affirm of him anything that is foreign to his immortality or that is repugnant to his blessedness. Believe about him whatever may uphold both his blessedness and his immortality. For there are gods, and the knowledge of them is manifest; but they are not such as the multitude believe, seeing that men do not steadfastly maintain the notions they form respecting them. Not the man who denies the gods worshipped by the multitude, but he who affirms of the gods what the multitude believes about them is truly impious. For the utterances of the multitude about the gods are not true preconceptions but false assumptions; hence it is that the greatest evils happen to the wicked and the greatest blessings happen to the good from the hand of the gods, seeing that they are always favorable to their own good qualities and take pleasure in men like themselves, but reject as alien whatever is not of their kind.

Accustom yourself to believing that death is nothing to us, for good and evil imply the capacity for sensation, and death is the privation of all sentience; therefore a correct understanding that death is nothing to us makes the mortality of life enjoyable, not by adding to life a limitless time, but by taking away the yearning after immortality. For life has no terrors for him who has thoroughly understood that there are no terrors for him in ceasing to live. Foolish, therefore, is the man who says that he fears death, not because it will pain when it comes, but because it pains in the prospect. Whatever causes no annoyance when it is present, causes only a groundless pain in the expectation. Death, therefore, the most awful of evils, is nothing to us, seeing that, when we are, death is not come, and, when death is come, we are not. It is nothing, then, either to the living or to the dead, for with the living it is not and the dead exist no longer.

But in the world, at one time men shun death as the greatest of all evils, and at another time choose it as a respite from the evils in life. The wise man does not deprecate life nor does he fear the cessation of life. The thought of life is no offense to him, nor is the cessation of life regarded as an evil. And even as men choose of food not merely and simply the larger portion, but the more pleasant, so the wise seek to enjoy the time which is most pleasant and not merely that which is longest. And he who admonishes the young to live well and the old to make a good end speaks foolishly, not merely because of the desirability of life, but because the same exercise at once teaches to live well and to die well. Much worse is he who says that it were good not to be born, but when once one is born to pass quickly through the gates of Hades. For if he truly believes this, why does he not depart from life? It would be easy for him to do so once he were firmly convinced. If he speaks only in jest, his words are foolishness as those who hear him do not believe.

We must remember that the future is neither wholly ours nor wholly not ours, so that neither must we count upon it as quite certain to come nor despair of it as quite certain not to come.

We must also reflect that of desires some are natural, others are groundless; and that of the natural some are necessary as well as natural, and some natural only. And of the necessary desires some are necessary if we are to be happy, some if the body is to be rid of uneasiness, some if we are even to live. He who has a clear and certain understanding of these things will direct every preference and aversion toward securing health of body and tranquillity of mind, seeing that this is the sum and end of a blessed life. For the end of all our actions is to be free from pain and fear, and, when once we have attained all this, the tempest of the soul is laid; seeing that the living creature has no need to go in search of something that is lacking, nor to look for anything else by which the good of the soul and of the body will be fulfilled. When we are pained because of the absence of pleasure, then, and then only, do we feel the need of pleasure. Wherefore we call pleasure the alpha and omega of a blessed life. Pleasure is our first and kindred good. It is the starting-point of every choice and of every aversion, and to it we come back, inasmuch as we make feeling the rule by which to judge of every good thing.

And since pleasure is our first and native good, for that reason we do not choose every pleasure whatsoever, but will often pass over many pleasures when a greater annoyance ensues from them. And often we consider pains superior to pleasures when submission to the pains for a long time brings us as a consequence a greater pleasure. While therefore all pleasure because it is naturally akin to us is good, not all pleasure is should be chosen, just as all pain is an evil and yet not all pain is to be shunned. It is, however, by measuring one against another, and by looking at the conveniences and inconveniences, that all these matters must be judged. Sometimes we treat the good as an evil, and the evil, on the contrary, as a good.

Again, we regard independence of outward things as a great good, not so as in all cases to use little, but so as to be contented with little if we have not much, being honestly persuaded that they have the sweetest enjoyment of luxury who stand least in need of it, and that whatever is natural is easily procured and only the vain and worthless hard to win. Plain fare gives as much pleasure as a costly diet, when once the pain of want has been removed, while bread and water confer the highest possible pleasure when they are brought to hungry lips. To habituate one's self, therefore, to simple and inexpensive diet supplies all that is needful for health, and enables a man to meet the necessary requirements of life without shrinking, and it places us in a better condition when we approach at intervals a costly fare and renders us fearless of fortune.

When we say, then, that pleasure is the end and aim, we do not mean the pleasures of the prodigal or the pleasures of sensuality, as we are understood to do by some through ignorance, prejudice, or willful misrepresentation. By pleasure we mean the absence of pain in the body and of trouble in the soul. It is not an unbroken succession of drinking-bouts and of revelry, not sexual lust, not the enjoyment of the fish and other delicacies of a luxurious table, which produce a pleasant life; it is sober reasoning, searching out the grounds of every choice and avoidance, and banishing those beliefs through which the greatest tumults take possession of the soul. Of all this the beginning and the greatest good is wisdom. Therefore wisdom is a more precious thing even than philosophy; from it spring all the other virtues, for it teaches that we cannot live pleasantly without living wisely, honorably, and justly; nor live wisely, honorably, and justly without living pleasantly. For the virtues have grown into one with a pleasant life, and a pleasant life is inseparable from them.

Who, then, is superior in your judgment to such a man? He holds a holy belief concerning the gods, and is altogether free from the fear of death. He has diligently considered the end fixed by nature, and understands how easily the limit of good things can be reached and attained, and how either the duration or the intensity of evils is but slight. Fate, which some introduce as sovereign over all things, he scorns, affirming rather that some things happen of necessity, others by chance, others through our own agency. For he sees that necessity destroys responsibility and that chance is inconstant; whereas our own actions are autonomous, and it is to them that praise and blame naturally attach. It were better, indeed, to accept the legends of the gods than to bow beneath that yoke of destiny which the natural philosophers have imposed. The one holds out some faint hope that we may escape if we honor the gods, while the necessity of the naturalists is deaf to all entreaties. Nor does he hold chance to be a god, as the world in general does, for in the acts of a god there is no disorder; nor to be a cause, though an uncertain one, for he believes that no good or evil is dispensed by chance to men so as to make life blessed, though it supplies the starting-point of great good and great evil. He believes that the misfortune of the wise is better than the prosperity of the fool. It is better, in short, that what is well judged in action should not owe its successful issue to the aid of chance.

Exercise yourself in these and related precepts day and night, both by yourself and with one who is like-minded; then never, either in waking or in dream, will you be disturbed, but will live as a god among men. For man loses all semblance of mortality by living in the midst of immortal blessings.

# Chapter 7: Stoicism

---

*Comprehension questions you should be able to answer after reading this chapter:*

1.  How did the Cynics contribute to Stoicism, and what did they mean by each of the following terms: *askesis, autarkeia, karteria, adiaphoria*?

2.  What are some Stoic contributions to logic?

3.  What do the Stoics mean by Fate?

4.  How do the Stoics understand human freedom? What is the difference between a "principle cause" and an "initiating cause?" How does this fit with their understanding of Fate?

5.  According to Epictetus, what sorts of things are "up to us?" What things are not? Why should we focus on the things that are up to us?

6.  What do the Stoics mean by each of the following:
    a. Representation
    b. Judgment
    c. Presentation
    d. Assent

7.  Why do they believe we should not "add to appearances?"

8.  What are "externals?" Why is their value "indifferent?" In what way are some "indifferents" nevertheless to be "preferred?"

9.  What does it mean to "act under reserve?"

10. What are some Stoic spiritual exercises, and what is their purpose? Be sure to be able to explain each of the following:
    a. Not "adding to appearances"
    b. Purely physical definitions
    c. Identifying what is up to us, and not up to us
    d. Understanding the "nature" of a thing
    e. Anticipating "evils"
    f. The "view from above"

---

Epicureanism was named for its founder, Epicurus. Stoicism was named for a porch. That's right. The words "stoic" and "stoicism" are derived from "stoa," meaning a covered walkway (similar to the *peripatoi* from which Aristotle's followers acquired their name). Specifically, the "stoa" at the Agora in Athens is where the philosophers later to be named "stoics" would loiter and lecture.

Stoicism can be divided into two rough periods: First, there was the (Greek) "theoretical" period of its founder Zeno of Citium in Cyprus (344 – 262 BCE), as well as his successors, Cleanthes (330 – 230 BCE) and Chrysippus (279 – 206 BCE)(all dates are approximate). Then, there was the (Roman) "therapeutic" period represented by Seneca (4 BCE – 65 CE), Musonius Rufus (20 – 101 CE[153]), Epictetus (55 – 135 CE) and the Emperor Marcus Aurelius (121 – 180 CE). We will consider these two periods under the headings of "theory" and "therapy." However, before addressing either theory or therapy, we will take a brief detour into a lesser-known group of philosophers to whom the Stoics owe much: the Cynics.

## The Cynics

The Stoics liked to trace their lineage from their founder (Zeno) all the back to Socrates himself, but this lineage traces to him only via several Cynic philosophers. One of Socrates' known close associates was Antisthenes (445 - 365 BCE). While Antisthenes did not himself adopt the Cynic lifestyle, his teachings did exercise considerable influence on Cynic values.

In the first few years after Socrates' death (for which Antisthenes was present), Antisthenes was regarded as the foremost presenter of Socrates' moral teachings and legacy. From Socrates, he emphasized "endurance" (*karteria*), and self-sufficiency (*autarkeia*). He also inherited from Socrates the belief that virtue is sufficient for happiness. Antisthenes passed along these beliefs and values to Diogenes "The Dog" of Sinope (410 – 323 BCE).

Diogenes was the most notorious of the Cynics in terms of appearance and shocking behavior. Diogenes neglected his personal hygiene, bathing rarely and allowing his hair and beard to become tangled and matted. He had no home, living outdoors and scavenging (or begging) for food. He possessed only a heavy cloak (suitable for both clothing and bedding), a sack to carry whatever food he gathered, and a walking staff to support him once he grew old enough to need it. According to our accounts of him, he at one time also possessed a wooden bowl

for water and food—until he saw a child drinking water out of his hands and realized he didn't actually need the bowl either. He would do scandalous things in public, including both defecation and masturbation, in order to shock the sensibilities of onlookers. Of course, Diogenes was not just an eccentric homeless man, he was a philosopher. Accordingly, he followed the model  of Socrates and would "teach" passers-by in public places—whether they invited his teaching or not, and whether or not they appreciated his blunt "lessons!"

Notorious or not, Diogenes was so well-known in Athens that when the wooden tub in which he slept broke, the city voted to replace it at public expense, that he might have a new place to sleep. Although his nickname ("the dog") was meant to be an insult, Diogenes embraced his title, pointing out that dogs are

---

153 These dates are largely speculative.

easily satisfied, and live a simple and pleasant existence. Many events of Diogenes' life are legendary, such as his alleged encounter with Alexander the Great, but many of these same events are also regarded as apocryphal—meaning they probably didn't actually happen, but they make for a good story.

What seems to be well-established is that Diogenes was the teacher of Crates of Thebes (365 - 285 BCE). Crates' conversion to the Cynic lifestyle is especially interesting given that he started out as a wealthy landowner. He truly gave up "everything" in order to possess "nothing," and pursue virtue. Despite being a penniless Cynic, and despite having a hunchback, Crates nevertheless inspired the love of a beautiful woman from a respected family. Her family (perhaps not surprisingly) resisted such a union, so Hipparchia (350 - 280 BCE) threatened suicide. Even after Crates joined her parents in urging her to abandon her love for him, she refused to relent. Crates cautioned her that to marry him would require that she live as he did: as a Cynic—and she did exactly that. They embraced the lifestyle together, including living and sleeping together in public. Hipparchia was especially "shocking" as a Cynic due to the social expectations of her gender.

It is through Crates that we finally reach the Stoics, as Crates was the teacher of Zeno of Citium (344 - 262 BCE). But, before we turn to the Stoics and perceive how they inherited some of the teachings of the Cynics, we must first address just what those teachings were. Up to this point, the only thing we know about the Cynics is that they were socially awkward homeless people!

The Cynics urged people to *"live according to Nature"*—a principle obviously inherited by the Stoics, as you will soon learn. To live in agreement with our Nature is our *telos* (our "end" or goal). Therefore, living in according with Nature is the key to our happiness (*eudaimonia*). However, living according to Nature is much more easily said than done. To do so requires training (*askesis*). This training focused on several key Cynic values.

1.  Self-sufficiency (*autarkeia*)
2.  Endurance (*karteria*)
3.  Detachment (*adiaphoria*)

To develop self-sufficiency, Cynics trained themselves to live as simply as possible. This is why they emulated the simplicity of animals, and why they had so few possessions. To build endurance (essential for maintaining tranquility in the face of life's challenges), Cynics would condition themselves to hardship by walking barefoot year round, intentionally sleeping on hard ground, and exposing themselves to heat and cold (e.g., by embracing cold statues in winter, or rolling in hot sand in the summer). Part of developing endurance was also enduring ridicule. To this end, Cynics would intentionally provoke insults in public so they could train themselves to endure abuses of all kinds. Finally, and relatedly, they practiced detachment to socially-valued goods, claiming that virtue was the only true good. They scorned wealth, status, honor, possessions of all kinds, and flouted social conventions with their crass and outrageous behaviors. They even scorned traditional philosophical values such as having a proper "school," and enquiry into logic, metaphysics, and epistemology.

In summary, the Cynics believed that if we train (*askesis*) to be "self-sufficient" (*autarkeia*), to endure (*karteria*), and to be detached (*adiaphoria*) from the false "goods" of society, we will be able to fulfill our *telos*—and that is what they understood virtue to be. Virtue is the ability to fulfill our nature (our *telos*,) and therein is found true "happiness" (*eudaimonia*).

While the Stoics did not adopt the Cynic lifestyle, many major Stoic philosophers (especially Epictetus) respected the Cynics for their commitment and toughness, and the Stoic system certainly incorporated several Cynic ideas, such as their belief that only virtue is intrinsically good, and that *eudaimonia* consists in living in agreement with Nature. Let us turn then, to the Stoics.

## Stoic Theory

Early Stoicism was heavily theoretical, abstract, detailed, and painstakingly developed. Stoicism benefitted not only from its Cynic heritage, but, ironically, from sustained and systematic attacks by the Skeptic school. Briefly, classical Skeptics claimed that knowledge is impossible, that nothing can be known with certainty. Instead, they believed we must frame all our claims as "appearances," and live according to them. Any claim that presumed to go beyond how things appeared (to the observer, at that moment) were deemed "dogma." The Skeptics developed a sophisticated method of attacking dogma, wherever they found it—and they found a lot of it in Stoicism. Their persistent challenges forced the Stoics to develop their own, comparatively sophisticated counter-arguments.

The Stoic system may be divided into three disciplines: logic, "physics," and "ethics." Although Aristotle is often credited for his development of what we now call "logic," a strong case can be made that the Stoics were more important and influential in this field. They developed what we now call "propositional logic," tests for validity, and several rules of inference including *modus ponens* and *modus tollens*. They also developed careful analyses of concepts, and language in general—all of which was intended to be put to use in their pursuit of *eudaimonia*.

The second category ("physics") involves the Stoic understanding of the cosmos and how it operates. This can get very complicated, but we will consider just enough detail (I hope) to motivate our understanding of the therapeutic application of Stoicism. The two most central ideas (for our purposes) from this category are the Stoic concepts of Fate and Freedom.

### Fate and Freedom

The Stoics believed that "God," or "Zeus" (or Nature, or Fate, depending on which Stoic is writing) is immanent throughout the cosmos. To avoid confusing their concept of the divine with the Judeo-Christian concept, I will hereafter use the term "Fate." The physical universe is Fate's "body." Fate is identical with the cosmos. This view is often referred to as "pantheism." The universe itself is Fate's body, and matter was thought to be inert. *Fate is recognized not only as the "body" (to which the cosmos is identical), but also as the "logos" (eternal Reason) that moves and governs all the operations of the universe and the unfolding of history.* All events, therefore, are manifestations of Fate's "will." Moreover, Fate was thought to be perfectly rational. As such, all events transpire in accordance with perfect Reason. This assumption allows the Stoics to go from mere determinism, to "Providence." *All that happens is fated to happen, but all that happens is for the best, and couldn't have turned out any other, or better, way*

Although the transition from this Stoic concept of Fate to the western theistic (e.g., Christian, Muslim, or Jewish) concept of Providence is an easy transition to make (and an appealing one, for some contemporary Stoics), we must be careful not to impose contemporary views of the divine onto the ancient Stoics. Fate, unlike the Judeo-Christian God, is identical to creation, not its transcendent Creator. And, while Fate is perfectly rational (and therefore a mind), Fate is not "personal" in the way the Judeo-Christian God is thought to be, nor is Fate responsive to human needs or prayers. All events occur (and will occur) as they *must* occur, according to the perfectly rational will of Fate. Praying that events might turn out a certain way is a futile effort—if your hope is to bring about an event that is contrary to the will of Fate. Instead, the Stoics thought we should attempt to align our own will with Fate (more on that later).

Because *all* events are the manifestation of Fate's will, human events are no exception. All the events in your life, and all the actions you take, are fated to occur exactly as they do, and could not have turned out any other way. Nevertheless, Stoics believed that there is something different and special about human beings, and a sense in which we are "free" and accountable for our actions, even though all events are the product of Fate. It is generally recognized that the Stoics (specifically, Chrysippus) were the first "compatibilists" with regard to determinism and free will. *That is to say that the Stoics believed that all events are determined (fated) to occur exactly as they do, but there is, nevertheless, a sense in which we are "free"—and that freedom (and responsibility) is "compatible" with determinism (Fate).*

Contemporary compatibilists identify free actions (i.e., those for which we may rightfully be held responsible) as being the effects of internal causes. An easier way to think about this is to ask, of any action you take, "did I do it because I wanted to?" If the answer is yes, you acted on an internal cause (i.e., something about *you*). If the answer is no, you likely acted on an external cause (i.e., something "outside" of you). For an obvious example, consider the difference between murder and suicide. Imagine that a person is standing on a balcony, twenty stories up in a tall building. Imagine that this person falls from that balcony to his death below. Now consider two different versions of that story. In one, the person is seriously depressed and wants to end his life. As a result, he leaps over the balcony. In the other version, he is simply admiring the view when another person (for some reason) rushes up behind him and tosses him over the edge. In the first case, the cause was "internal" (the man's own desire to die). In the second, the cause was "external" (the shove from the murderer). Note that we interpret these events very differently, even though the physical descriptions are quite similar (i.e., a body falling to its death). The first example is an example of suicide, and we say (with however much sympathy and compassion we might be able to generate) that it is his own fault that he's dead. He's responsible for his actions. The second example is an example of murder, and we do not claim that it's his own fault that he's dead. Instead, the responsibility is found with the person who pushed him. Why there? Because the murderer is the one who was acting from an internal cause (in this case, apparently, a desire to kill).

Although the Stoics didn't describe their compatibilism in exactly the same way, their system involves the same basic idea: we are responsible for our actions when those actions stem from something about us, as opposed to something wholly external to ourselves. To use the Stoic vocabulary, "externals" can be "initiating causes" (antecedent causes), but are not "principle causes."

Their most famous example used to illustrate this was that of a cylinder rolling down a hill. To make it a bit more visually appealing, instead of a cylinder, think of a tire. If you are standing atop the hill with that tire, and you give it a

shove, you have provided the "initiating cause." However, that tire isn't going to roll down the hill unless it has a shape that is conducive to rolling. The "principle cause," therefore, of the tire rolling down the hill is its own shape. After all, you could provide the same initiating cause to an anvil and that anvil won't roll down the hill. Because not all objects will respond to the initiating cause in the same way, the "responsibility" for the event lies in the primary cause, rather than the initiating cause—though, to be sure, the event wouldn't have taken place if not for that initiating cause.

Now, apply this same kind of reasoning to people, and our own behavior. Events that occur around us serve as initiating causes for events. However, to the extent that our own actions are the result of ourselves (as a principle cause), we are responsible for those actions. Consider your reaction to the image of the shirtless man.

The sight of that model was an initiating cause of whatever reaction you had. Your reaction would not have occurred if not for that initiating cause. However, I'm confident that not every reader responded in exactly the same way. Let's break it down to just one (and perhaps the most obvious) response: attraction (or not). Some of you might have deemed the model to be physically attractive, but others did not. The model is the same initiating cause for both groups of responses, so the difference must be found not in the model but in *you*. Although the sight of the model was the initiating cause of your response, the principle cause was something about *you* that facilitated attraction, or not. Rather obviously, if you are heterosexual female (or a gay male) you're presumably much more likely to find that model sexually attractive than if you are heterosexual male (or gay female). Even if the sexuality "lines up," there are still matters of personal taste.

Perhaps that model just isn't "your type?" The point, of course, is that your response to that model is "up to you" in the sense that your actions stem from something about you, as opposed to something wholly external to you.

As another example, consider two politicians both being offered an identical bribe by the same lobbyist. One politician accepts the bribe, while the offer refuses. Both experienced the same initiating cause (the bribe), but their reactions were different. Wherein is to be found the difference? In *them*, of course! There is something about the one that makes him susceptible to bribes, and something about the other that makes him resistant. Their actions, therefore, are attributable to themselves, as principle causes, rather than the bribes, as initiating causes. Just to be clear, compatibilists (include Stoics) acknowledge that the sort of person we are (i.e., our nature as a principle cause) is also the product of Fate—in other words, the sort of person we are, just like everything else in the cosmos, is the will of Fate, and couldn't have been any other way. Nevertheless, when it comes to personal responsibility, what we seek (according to compatibilists) is *not* some ability to somehow defy Fate (or causal determinism, in less "spiritualized" versions of compatibilism), but simply the ability to be able to trace our actions back to our own character, as opposed to something wholly external to us. We blame someone for having an extra million dollars in her bank account when it's the result of accepting a bribe. We don't blame that person if it was the result of an error in a bank computer. The first example can be traced back to her character, the second cannot.

The Roman Stoic, Epictetus, famously delineates those things that are "up to us" from those that are not in the very first paragraph of the *Encheiridion*.

> There are things which are within our power, and there are things which are beyond our power. Within our power are opinion, aim, desire, aversion, and, in one word, whatever affairs are our own. Beyond our power are body, property, reputation, office, and, in one word, whatever are not properly our own affairs.

Notice that those few things "within our power" are all "internal," all mental activities stemming from the sort of person we are: "opinion, aim, desire, aversion." Notice also that those things described as being "beyond our power" are all "external" to us: body, property, reputation, office. You might immediately wonder how your own body is listed as being beyond your power. After all, it seems obvious that one can control one's body to make it do as we wish. Tell that to someone with cerebral palsy, or a broken leg, or arthritis, or who is suffering from a stroke, or who is in the midst of a heart attack, or who is pinned underneath the rubble of a collapsed building. You can "will" any number of things, but whether or not those things come to be depends upon the cooperation of things not under your control—including the operations of your own body.

You might wonder how "property" is not under your control. After all, your property is *your* property, to dispose of as you see fit—unless someone steals it. Or it's destroyed in an earthquake, or eaten by termites. "But isn't my reputation under my own control?" No. Your reputation is always the product of your actions and the judgments of others. Those judgments are not under your control. Your behavior might be interpreted as "confidence" by one person and "arrogance" by another. What if the person judging you is racially biased, or sexist?

While traditional ("orthodox") Stoics believed that all events are fated to occur exactly as they do, some contemporary readers might be uncomfortable with the idea of Fate, or Providence, or even the plainly secular notion of causal determinism. Indeed, some contemporary Stoics offer a revised version of what is "up to us" that doesn't place so much emphasis on Fate.

William Irvine, for example, suggests that we should interpret Epictetus' "dichotomy of control" as a "trichotomy of control," instead.[154] A traditional reading of Epictetus' passage above would delineate those things over which we have complete control (e.g., opinion, desire, goal-setting, etc.), from those over which we do not have complete control (e.g., the outcome of events). Irvine, however, thinks these divisions are not sufficiently subtle (or accurate). Instead, he proposes three categories:

1. Things over which we have complete control (e.g. goal-setting).
2. Things over which we have no control at all (e.g., whether or not the sun will rise tomorrow, or events in the past).
3. Things over which we have some control, but not complete control (e.g., whether we win a competition).

Some things are obviously completely beyond our control, and it seems futile to worry about them. It is in no way "up to me" whether the sun rises tomorrow. Similarly, events that have already occurred are obviously beyond my control. Obsessing over something that happened yesterday, or a few years ago, is a waste (except, perhaps, if all we're talking about is learning a lesson so as to be less likely to repeat a similar mistake in the future). Wringing our hands over what happened in the past is not a good use of time or resources, as nothing can be done to change the past.

Other things are things of which we are in complete control. Although Epictetus includes desires and aversions in this category, Irvine thinks him mistaken, if we assume the common understanding of those terms. In a great many cases, desires and aversions simply occur, rise up within us whether we would want them to, or not. If I am hungry, and see some food, it doesn't seem fully under my control whether or not I desire to eat. Similarly, if I am uncomfortable around spiders (as I am), it doesn't seem fully under my control whether or not I will be startled and uncomfortable (to say the least) should a big spider drop onto my face while I'm sleeping. Irvine thinks that desires and aversions actually belong in the third category (see above). If so, what remains for the category of things fully under our control? Irvine's answer is goal-setting and personal values. Goal-setting is completely under our control in the sense

---

[154] See William Irvine's book, *A Guide to the Good Life*—and specifically his chapter entitled "The Dichotomy of Control."

that although we are not in full control over whether we achieve our goals, we are in control of what goals we set for ourselves in the first place. If my goal is to win a sparring match in a martial arts tournament, I have set for myself a goal that is not fully under my control. After all, my opponent is going to have some say as to the outcome of our match! He might be much more skilled than I. My body might not cooperate. I might twist an ankle, or have a heart attack in the middle of the fight. I can't guarantee that I will win the fight, as "winning the fight" is a goal that exceeds my control. But, if my goal is, instead, to fight as well as I'm able, given the circumstances, it seems I have a set a goal that is within my control. After all, my own effort seems "up to me," even in the compatibilist sense favored by traditional Stoics.

Values are also under my control, according to Irvine. Whether or not I become wealthy is not fully up to me, but whether or not I value wealth is—at least in the compatibilist sense that it stems from my character as a principle cause. To the extent that our values stem from, and define, our character, our own character is fully up to us as well.

What remains are all those things that are "somewhat" up to us—neither wholly beyond our control, nor wholly under our control. Let's return to the sparring match, as it illustrates precisely the sorts of actions Irvine thinks belong to this category. As mentioned, the outcome of the match is not fully under my control, but it's also not wholly *outside* of my control, according to Irvine. After all, my own preparation and effort surely play some causal role in determining the outcome of the match. Needless to say, if I have trained hard, and if I fight to the best of my ability, I am more likely to win the match than if I hadn't trained at all, or if I half-heartedly compete.[155]

To summarize, (orthodox) Stoics believed that all events are fated to occur exactly as they do by virtue of the perfectly rational will of Fate. Nevertheless, there is a sense in which we are responsible for our actions, and our proper focus should be on those things that are "up to us" rather than those that are not. Even a more contemporary (less "fatalistic") interpretation acknowledges that there are degrees of control we can exercise over various things. Recognizing this, and regulating our mental life on that basis, leads us to Stoic "ethics."

Stoic "ethics" has a misleading name. Most of us, today, when we think of "ethics," think either of a list of moral commandments ("thou shalts" and "thou shalt nots") or else a formalized study of moral concepts. Stoic ethics didn't so much address moral rules governing our behavior with others (though such things were certainly derived from their system) as it addressed an understanding of how best to achieve *eudaimonia* ("happiness"—understood by the Stoics as tranquility). Stoicism was more "self-help" than "ethics" (as most

---

[155] I feel it important to point out that this trichotomy is *not* orthodox Stoic thought, but Irvine's own, modified, version. A traditional Stoic would likely counter that the outcome of that match (for example) is not even partially under my control, as I could get in a car accident on the way to the tournament, or have a heart attack moments before it begins, etc.

understand the term today).

"Ethics" involved the proper use of what is "up to us"—namely, the judgments we make concerning events as they transpire. According to orthodox Stoicism, given Fate, whatever happens was fated to occur, and could not have turned out any other way. Similarly, whatever *will* happen is also the unavoidable will of Fate. What is up to us is the extent to which we align our will with Fate. What is at stake is our own tranquility. The Stoics offered what would become a famous analogy to illustrate our relationship to Fate. Imagine a dog leashed to a cart (or, today, a slow-moving car). The dog is being pulled, and will be pulled, in whatever direction the cart (or car) goes. Resistance is futile. The cart (or car) *will* "win." In other words, the dog is going to end up wherever he is taken. Now consider the difference between the dog that is being dragged, and the one that is happily following the cart. Both end up at the same destination, but one has a miserable trip. So too with us, and Fate. Our lives will transpire however Fate wills them to unfold. There is nothing we can do about *that*. What is up to us, however, is whether we align our will with Fate and walk, or get dragged. It makes no difference to Fate, but it makes a lot of difference to us. Needless to say, our lives will be much more pleasant if we avoid getting dragged. Now that we have shifted our emphasis to living a pleasant life, we can (gradually) shift from theory, to therapy.

## Stoic Therapy

Why is it that so many of us get "dragged" along by Fate? Largely because of an improper use of our faculties of "assent" and "desire." Similar to Epicureanism, Stoicism claims that we suffer from false beliefs (judgments) and improper desires. To understand the process by which we form false judgments, we need to understand how the Stoics thought we formed judgments in the first place. Our minds process information in three steps.

1) <u>Representation</u>: The mind receives the images (impressions) that come through our bodily sensations.
2) <u>Judgment</u>: An almost involuntary/unconscious judgment concerning the representation, shaped by the person's dispositions, preconceptions, and mental habits.
3) <u>Presentation</u>: Presentation of the impression and judgment to the conscious mind. In effect, the soul tells itself what a given impression *is*.
4) <u>Assent</u>: Formation of desires and impulses to action based upon our judgments about a thing. We give "assent" to the representation by acting upon it in a certain way.

Imagine that someone returns to a parking lot to discover her car has been keyed. As might be typical, she gets very upset. What has happened here? First, she received an "impression"—namely, the sight of her car with a scratch across its paint. Then, she has a (presumably quick) "conversation" with herself in which she interprets that impression. Judging from her reaction, it's obvious that she formed some sort of negative judgment in response to that impression. "Someone keyed my car? Son of a bitch! This sucks!" She then "assents" to that judgment by virtue of her actions (e.g., swearing, physiological responses such as an increased pulse rate or a headache, throwing her purse down, etc.).

One of Epictetus' most famous sayings is that people "are disturbed not by things, but by the views which they take of things." In other words, things and events are not good or bad, in themselves. They take on the quality of good or bad by virtue of the judgments that we *add* to them.

## Great Minds Think Alike!

One of Epictetus' key ideas is that it is not things themselves that are good or bad, but our judgment of them that makes them good or bad. Thousands of miles to the East, Wonhyo said something extraordinarily similar, roughly 500 years after Epictetus did.

Wonhyo lived from 617 – 686 CE. He was born in Amnyang (present-day South Korea), but went to China when young to study Buddhism. He was a prolific writer, writing almost 90 philosophical works. His most famous for his story of his experience in a cave.

According to his account, he'd been traveling for a long time and grew tired and thirsty. He found a cave and crawled into it for the night. Reaching around in the darkness, he felt a bowl filled with rainwater and he drank it before going to sleep. The next morning he woke up and discovered that he was sleeping in a tomb rather than a cave, and that the bowl he had drank water from was actually a rotting skull filled with water, rotting leaves, and maggots. He initially vomited from disgust, but then achieved an epiphany: the disgusting skull was the "bowl" he had been so grateful to find the night before, and the repulsive tomb had been the cave that had granted him shelter.

The only difference between those things was his own judgment.

One interpretation of them made them "good," and another made them "bad," even though nothing had changed about the things themselves. He concluded (strongly analogously to Epictetus) that "thinking makes good and bad." In other words, it is our own perception and judgment of things that makes them "good" or "bad" rather than the objects themselves.

Allegedly, his experience in the cave/tomb convinced him that the world he experienced with his senses is an illusion, determined by his perceptions and the influences of others. Ultimately, if we could abandon those acquired "lenses," we would recognize the Unity of everything and the illusion of differences/distinctions.

In thinking that the reality most of us experience is an illusion, and that only an enlightened person can see existence for what it truly is, his philosophy also bears a resemblance to Plato's, specifically as described in the "allegory of the *cave*" in the *Republic*.

The controversial rejection of emotion attributed to Stoicism stems from this. *Emotions are thought to be our "assent" to judgments.* When we cry in response to an event, we have assented to the judgment that there is something bad about what happened. When we fume in anger, that anger *is* our assent to the judgment that some event is worthy of our anger. Traditional Stoics believe that that is simply not true. If I get angry at the sight of my keyed car, my anger is my assent to the judgment that it's a bad thing that my car has been keyed. *Stoics believe that we should not "add" to appearances, but accept them as they are presented to us.* As Epictetus says, "Right from the start, get into the habit of saying to every harsh appearance," 'You are an appearance, and not the only way of seeing the thing that appears.' Then examine it and test it by the yardsticks you have." Being angry that my car was keyed implies that I have added a judgment ("this is bad") to an appearance (the literal sight of my car, now with an irregular line through the paint). There is nothing inherently bad about a car with a line scratched through its paint. What makes it bad is my own belief that it is bad. If I don't add that judgment to the appearance, I won't be angered by the sight of it, and my tranquility will be preserved.

"But it *is* a bad thing that your car got keyed!" you might respond. "Now it's worth less, and it doesn't look as good, and you'll have to pay to get the paint fixed, or at least fix it yourself, and that will be a hassle. Some jerk vandalized your property, and he didn't have that right."

So, I should give him control over my soul, in addition to control over my paint job? According to Stoicism, externals are not up to me. My car is an external. I can't control whether or not it remains in pristine condition. Even accepting Irvine's trichotomy of control, at best the appearance of my car is something over which I have some, but not total, control. For example, I might make it a point to park it only in "good" areas, with ample lighting, and in so doing try to reduce the risk of vandalism. Even then, the best I can achieve is risk reduction, not risk elimination. In an obvious, common-sense, sort of way I am not in control of the other 7 billion (or so) people in the world. If someone wants to key my car, there is no way I can guarantee it won't happen unless I don't have a car—in which case the person could just vandalize other of my property instead. Stoicism holds that externals (my car) are not under my control, but my response to events is (at least in the sense that it's based on my character). A vandal has sufficient power to damage my car, but that vandal doesn't have sufficient power to make me upset. I must give him that power. Again we can appeal to Epictetus: "For another cannot hurt you, unless you please. You will then be hurt when you consent to be hurt." When a vandal damages my car, he damages an external—something that was never under my control to begin with. When I become upset at the vandalism, I have let the vandal damage my virtue. "If a person had delivered up your body to some passer-by, you would certainly be angry. And do you feel no shame in delivering up your own mind to any reviler, to be disconcerted and confounded?"

*Remember that the primary function of philosophy, of all these efforts, according to Stoicism, is eudaimonia—happiness, understood as a state of tranquility that we can achieve when we live "according to Nature." We live according to Nature when we are governed by Reason, when we employ what is up to us (our judgments) properly, by recognizing what is up to us and what is not, and by aligning our will with that of "Fate" with regard to those things not up to us.* If your goal is something different, their advice and strategies are unlikely to make much sense. If, for example, your goal in life is to maintain a car with an unblemished surface, you will probably not agree with their advice. Good luck with that. Vandals are numerous—as are branches, rocks tossed by other cars, birds, wind and other erosive elements, etc. If your happiness is based on whether or not you can keep your car sufficiently pretty, you are setting yourself up for a lifetime of challenge and frustration. If, on the other hand, you prefer tranquility to an impeccably painted car, then the Stoic strategy might be right for you.

While specific exercises will be addressed in the next section, we can presently outline how Stoics believed we should exercise that which is up to us: our judgments. In the first place, there is the process of disciplining our assent. Recall that for Stoics, "assent" occurs when we accept an appearance as true. However, most of us, much of the time, do not merely accept the appearance as it is presented to us, but "add" to the appearance (e.g., the mere sight of my now-scratched car transforms into the angrily entertained thought that my car has been scratched—with the anger indicating the addition of the judgment that it's a bad thing for my car to have been scratched). Generally speaking, then, we should resist adding to appearances.

In addition to regulating our assent to appearances, we ought to regulate our desires. Given the Stoic belief in Fate, the proper use of desire is to desire whatever is fated to occur. As Epictetus says, "Demand not that events should happen as you wish; but wish them to happen as they do happen, and you will go on well." We have already discussed the Stoic notions of freedom and Fate. If you accept the doctrine of Fate, the Stoic advice seems like common sense. If there is a conflict between your desires, and reality, there are only two ways to resolve that conflict: either change reality, or change your desires. But, given the Stoic doctrine of Fate, it is not within our power to change reality. Events will transpire as they have been fated to transpire. So, the only remedy within my power is to change my desires instead. What should I desire? Whatever it is that actually transpires! If I "embrace fate" and desire things to happen as they do, in fact, happen, then my desires will always be satisfied, and I will never be frustrated. Even if one accepts Irvine's modified Stoicism with its trichotomy of control instead, and acknowledge that there are things that are up to us (e.g., judgments), other things not at all up to us (i.e., externals, in general), and other things that are not fully up to us (e.g., externals to which we contribute, such as the outcome of a competition), we can still recognize that there is a way to regulate our desires so as to promote our own tranquility.

Imagine that I am going to participate in a sparring match with another fighter. Suppose my desire is to win the fight. If one believes in Fate, I am either fated to win the fight, or not. If I am not fated to win the fight, and I desire to win, then I desire something not under my control, and am setting myself up for frustration. So, a safer (and more appropriate) desire would be to desire whichever outcome is fated to happen. In that way, I will be satisfied either way.

Even if we are reluctant to accept the doctrine of Fate, there is still a plausible sense in which desiring victory is unwise. Even if the outcome is not fated, it nevertheless remains not fully under my control. Using Irvine's categories, I contribute to the outcome of the fight by virtue of my preparation and performance, but it's not fully under my control by any stretch of the imagination. My opponent will presumably want to win, too. Desiring to "win" is to desire something beyond my control, but desiring something like "doing my best, under the circumstances" is more realistic. Even if I "lose," I can still satisfy my desire if only I do the best I can. This is similar to the folk wisdom behind encouraging someone to "do your best." If my desire is to remain loved by my wife and married to her for another fifty years, I'm setting myself up for disappointment. Setting aside the notion of Fate, it should be obvious that satisfying that desire is beyond my control. Either one of us might die before fifty years pass. Even if we set aside the duration requirement, even desiring to be loved by my wife is not fully under my control. People change. Feelings change. Her heart might grow cold, despite my best efforts. So, a more appropriate desire would focus on my best efforts. I should desire to be the best husband I am capable of being, the most worthy of love that I can manage. If that is my desire, then it remains possible for me to satisfy that desire, even should I "fail" to, in fact, retain her love.

At this point, some of you might rightly be wondering if this strategy doesn't just amount to paralysis in the face of life. "Desire what happens?" How does anyone *do* anything, then? It's not as if I can sit back and watch my own sparring match to see its outcome, and then quickly desire that particular outcome. It's not as if, when I get sick, I can just wait to see what happens so I know which outcome (recovery, or death) to desire.

According to Stoicism, "externals" have no true value. Only that which is up to us (our own virtue) has any value. All other things (all externals) are, strictly speaking, "indifferent." Cars are indifferent, having no value (positive or negative). This is why a proper Stoic will not be disturbed if his car gets scratched. It had no value to begin with! All "things" in our lives (e.g., clothes, furniture, phones, etc.) are indifferent, in this sense. More controversially, even such things as friends, health, and reputation, in that they are externals, are likewise "indifferent."

That being said, some externals, while being "indifferent," are nevertheless "preferred." Things that are "preferred" are those things that are consistent with our nature as rational animals and that are generally conducive to flourishing (though not necessary for it). Eating, for example, is "preferred" over starving. Being healthy is preferred to being sick. Being financially secure is preferable to desperate poverty. Having good friends is preferable to being lonely. Having a good reputation is preferable to being slandered. With regard to things that are preferred, in this sense, it is appropriate for us to pursue them—though we should recognize that they remain "indifferent," remember that our happiness does not depend on them, and "embrace Fate" with regard to them.

How does a Stoic do this? By acting "under reserve." Stoics, like everyone else, have to make plans, have to make decisions, have to actually live their lives. Yet, Stoics are supposed to desire that things happen as they are fated to happen.

A Stoic reconciles these demands by forming conditional desires in the following general form: "I want X, if Fate permits" (where "X" is something to be preferred).

Before delving into this notion in greater detail, please note the obvious similarity between "*acting under reserve*" and the Muslim and Christian notion of "God willing." Muslims will often say, of some future event they intend, "insha'Allah" (God willing). "And never say of anything, 'I shall do such and such thing tomorrow. Except (with the saying): 'If God wills!'"[156] In the Christian New Testament, we find the same idea: "Now listen, you who say, 'Today or tomorrow we will go to this or that city, spend a year there, carry on business and make money.' Why, you do not even know what will happen tomorrow. What is your life? You are a mist that appears for a little while and then vanishes. Instead, you ought to say, 'If it is the Lord's will, we will live and do this or that.'"[157]

What the Muslim, Christian, and Stoic systems have in common in this respect is that each recognizes a power far greater that controls what transpires, and each recognizes the value of aligning your own will with that power. *A Stoic, then, will pursue preferable things, but recognize that those things are not under her control (at least not fully), and will also recognize that not even those things have true value.* Health is preferable to sickness, and I will pursue it as such. I will even desire health—if Fate permits (or, God willing). If I find myself sick instead of healthy, I will pursue recovery and desire it—if Fate permits. Whatever happens, sickness or health, recovery or decline, is beyond my control, and none of those outcomes is a prerequisite for the only thing of true value: virtue. I can be virtuous (by regulating my assent, and aligning my will with Nature) whether I am sick or healthy—though it's preferable to be healthy.

So, there is no need to think that Stoics must curl up into a fetal position, awaiting Fate and unsure of what they should desire. They will live and choose in ways outwardly similar to everyone else. They will pursue friendship and health, prosperity and love. When they do so, however, they recognize what is up to them, and what it not, and they regulate their desire so as to desire only what Fate permits. They guard themselves from attachment to "indifferents," and they discipline themselves in ways that preserve and promote their own tranquility in the face of whatever Fate has in store.

Now that we have shifted our emphasis to living a pleasant life, and now that we have acquired a proper theoretical understanding of the world (*logos*), we can (gradually) shift from theory, to therapy, and begin to employ some exercises to address death. Before doing so, however, we need just a bit more "theory"— namely, the part of the stoic system that explains *how* stoic spiritual exercises actually work.

To understand the mechanism by which stoic *askesis* is thought to work, we have to develop just a bit more stoic ontology. According to the stoic worldview, there are only two kinds of things: "corporeals" and "incorporeals."

---

[156]Surat Al Kahf (18):23-24.
[157]James 4:13-15.

"Corporeals" are "bodies," as we normally understand that term. They are physical objects. According to stoicism, only bodies/corporeals truly "exist." "Incorporeals" technically don't "exist," but only "subsist" (an abstract sort of existence, analogous to how relations such as "taller" "exist"). According to the stoics, an example of an incorporeal were the "lekta." Literally "sayables," the lekta are the claims being conveyed in acts of speech. Speech, as a sound, is physical, but the idea being represented by the sound is, technically, incorporeal.

The point of this is that for something to truly *exist*, it must be physical. In order to *exist*, then, wisdom and virtue must be physical—existing inside the material soul (*psyche*) of a person. That means that to become wise/virtuous involves a *physical* alteration of the soul.

You might think that "souls" are incorporeal, but that is to impose a decidedly "modern" (Christian?) interpretation onto a stoic worldview where it does not belong. The "soul," for the stoics, was just as physical as the body. Indeed, according to stoicism, all physical objects (corporeals) involve two basic principles: matter, and "breath" (*pneuma*).

*Pneuma* is equally material, as matter, and pervades *all* physical objects—not just humans. Indeed, the qualities of physical objects are the result of the "tension" of the *pneuma* within it. Higher degrees of tension generate more complex properties of corporeals, as follows:

1. Cohesion (inanimate objects)
2. Growth (plants)
3. Soul (psyche) (animals)
4. Rational soul (rational adult humans)

Note that there is no substantive difference in kind among these four types, but merely increasing degrees of "tension." When it comes to human beings, philosophy, and virtue, it can rightly be said that it's good to be "tense!" The more wise someone is, the more tension in their soul. Stoic *askesis literally* strengthens the soul, by increasing the tension of the *pneuma* that is the material soul. Physically-altered souls will serve as different/new internal causes of behavior, thereby changing ones dispositions to behave. Admittedly, however, this is easier said, than done. Accordingly, Stoicism had numerous exercises with which to make such a life possible.

## Stoic Spiritual Exercises

*Every habit and faculty is maintained and increased by the corresponding actions: the habit of walking by walking, the habit of running by running. If you would be a good reader, read; if a writer, write. But when you shall not have read thirty days in succession, but have done something else, you will know the consequence. In the same way, if you shall have lain down ten days, get up and attempt to make a long walk, and you will see how your legs are weakened. Generally, then, if you would make anything a habit, do it; if you would not make it a habit, do not do it, but accustom yourself to do something else in place of it.*

*So it is with respect to the affections of the soul: when you have been angry, you must know that not only has this evil befallen you, but that you have also increased the habit, and in a manner thrown fuel upon fire. When you have been overcome in sexual intercourse with a person, do not reckon this single defeat only, but reckon that you have also nurtured, increased your incontinence. For it is impossible for habits and faculties, some of them not to be produced, when they did not exist before, and others not be increased and strengthened by corresponding acts.[158]*

Perhaps no other school has a more documented usage of spiritual exercises than Stoicism. We find multiple and lengthy examples of exercises in Epictetus, Marcus Aurelius, and Seneca. In each, the fundamental assumption is the same: spiritual exercises are to be used so that the Stoic may successfully and sincerely digest and express his values through his acts.

One of the reasons why humans suffer is because we "add to appearances." We've already discussed this earlier in this chapter, but it's important enough to warrant some review. As Epictetus famously claimed, "Men are disturbed not by things, but by the views which they take of things. Thus death is nothing terrible, else it would have appeared so to Socrates. But the terror consists in our notion of death, that it is terrible."[159] An important exercise, then, will be one which serves to correct our judgments.

*One way of correcting our judgments is to continually remind ourselves of the "nature" of a thing.*

*With regard to whatever objects either delight the mind, or contribute to use, or are tenderly beloved, remind yourself of what nature they are, beginning with the merest trifles: if you have a favorite cup, that it is but a cup of which you are fond, – for thus, if it is broken, you can bear it; if you embrace your child, or your wife, that you embrace a mortal, – and thus, if either of them dies, you can bear it.[160]*

In this example, Epictetus first considers a cup. Part of the nature of a cup is that it is fragile. Cups are the sorts of things that can be (and often are, eventually) broken. If you expect your cup to never break, you have forgotten the kind of thing that it is. If you get upset that there is heavy traffic on the freeway, you have forgotten the "nature" of freeways (namely, that they tend to suffer from heavy traffic, at least here in Southern California!). Perhaps shockingly, Epictetus uses the examples of one's own wife and child, and reminds us that it is part of the nature of mortals that we die. In a certain sense, then, if you are shocked and

---

[158] Epictetus, *Discourses*, Book 2, chapter 18.
[159] Epictetus, *Encheiridion*, section V.
[160] Ibid., section III.

grief-stricken that a loved one dies, you have forgotten the kind of thing that that person was (i.e., mortal). He continues this same line of thought by observing that "If you wish your children and your wife and your friends to live forever, you are foolish; for you wish things to be in your power which are not so; and what belongs to others to be your own."[161]

To help us understand the nature of a thing, and to not "add" to it, *Marcus Aurelius advises us to construct purely "physical" definitions of objects that present themselves to us.* "Look at the object itself as it is in its essence, in its nudity, and tell yourself the name which is peculiar to it."[162] Sometimes shocking in its blunt results, this exercise serves to strip things of any imposed values. For example, "sexual union is the rubbing together of abdomens, with the spasmodic ejaculation of a sticky fluid."[163]

> ### Exercise Break
>
> Identify a physical object in your life that holds great value to you. It could be anything: a house, a car, a piece of jewelry, a photo album, or even a human being. Now, construct a "purely physical" definition of that thing in the style Marcus provides above. Try to eliminate any judgments or emotional investments in your description, and describe it the way a scientist might, or perhaps the way an utterly alien being from another world might.

We also suffer because we attribute a greater value to things or events than they deserve. This understanding doesn't even require that accept the Stoic doctrine that only virtue is (truly) "good," and all other things are (technically) "indifferent." Even if you reject this Stoic value system, we can still recognize that we sometimes take things "too seriously," or blow things "out of proportion."

To correct this tendency, *another exercise employed by the Stoics involves adopting a "cosmopolitan" view, or a "view from above," in order to achieve proper perspective.* We do this through an exercise of the imagination in which we picture ourselves rising up and seeing the things and events of the world from an ever-higher perspective. The idea behind this exercise is that the significance of many of our problems can be diminished if we keep the long view in mind. If we consider the event or problem against the backdrop of our whole life, let alone against the backdrop of history, we will likely realize that the problem just isn't as serious as we initially judged it to be.

---

[161] Ibid., section XIV.

[162] Marcus Aurelius Antonius, *The Meditations*. Translated, with an introduction, by G.M.A. Grube (Indianapolis: Hackett, 1983), III.11.

[163] Ibid., VI.13.

---

### Exercise Break

Cognitive Behavioral Therapy is a contemporary approach to therapy that draws heavily and unmistakably from Stoic insights and exercises. Donald Robertson provides an excellent example of this exercise in his 2010 book, The Philosophy of Cognitive-Behavioural Therapy: Stoic Philosophy as Rational and Cognitive Psychotherapy. You can find the transcript of his guided mediation here: http://donaldrobertson.name/2011/08/13/the-view-from-above-stoic-meditation-script/
   If you prefer to listen to it, you can do so here:
https://soundcloud.com/drobertson-uk/view-from-above/sets

---

If, as an exercise, we try to adopt that "view from above," and we observe the world and our lives from afar, we can also imagine how we would observe change occurring.

To use a cinematic analogy, as we rise "above" our lives it's as though the camera is pulling away from the scene. We can also imagine the film speeding up, in which case we would see persons born, maturing, dying, and decaying in a matter of moments; buildings being constructed, weathering, and crumbling to ruin in mere moments; entire civilizations rising and falling before our eyes. "Acquire a method for contemplating how all things transform themselves into one another. Concentrate your attention on this without ceasing, and exercise yourself on this point. Observe every object, and imagine that it is dissolving and in full transformation; it is rotting and wasting away."[164]

The idea is the same: by situating a problem or event in the "grand scheme of things," against the backdrop of the entire cosmos and all of time, whatever problem we're facing is likely to appear as an infinitesimal speck against such a backdrop. If we just adopt the long view, nothing is truly very bad.

Yet another Stoic exercise *involved preparing ourselves in advance for "unpleasantries" by imagining them happening to us.* By *not* making use of such exercises, we make ourselves vulnerable to emotional upset. "Because we never anticipate any evil before it actually arrives, but, imagining that we ourselves are exempt and are travelling a less exposed path, we refuse to be taught by the mishaps of others that such are the lot of all. So many funerals pass our doors, yet we never think of death!"[165] So, too, with respect to wealth. We never imagine losing ours, even though others lose theirs all the time. "Of necessity, therefore, we are more prone to collapse; we are struck, as it were, off our guard; blows that are long foreseen fall less violently."[166] Epictetus offers examples ranging from

---

[164]Ibid., X.11,18.
[165]Seneca, "To Marcia on Consolation." Section VIII.
[166]Ibid.

anticipating being splashed at a public bath, [167] to the much more shocking example of whispering to yourself, while kissing your child goodnight, "tomorrow you will die."[168] Morbid though it might sound, Epictetus is not advocating that we dwell on death as though we want the person to die! Rather, it's an extension of remembering the nature of a thing (e.g., human nature is to be mortal), and also building up resilience to unpleasant events by having already contemplated them beforehand. "Let death and exile, and all other things which appear terrible, be daily before your eyes, but death chiefly; and you will never entertain any abject thought, nor too eagerly covet anything."[169]

We are to remind ourselves constantly that all "fortuitous things" such as children, honors, fame, wealth, and noble and beautiful spouses are "not our own but borrowed trappings; not one of them is given to us outright."[170] Employing the same metaphors used by Epictetus, Seneca describes such things as lent "properties that adorn life's stage" and which must "go back to their owners."[171] A one-time mention of this will prove insufficient. "Often must the heart be reminded—it must remember that loved objects will surely leave, nay, are already leaving."[172] *Repetition, then, is key to self-transformation.*

For most of us, the mere anticipation (let alone the experience) of sickness, injury, poverty, ridicule, loss, and death causes us to suffer and be afraid.

*Will you, then, realize that this epitome of all the ills that befall man, of his ignoble spirit, and his cowardice, is not death, but it is rather the fear of death? Against this fear, then, I would have you discipline yourself, toward this let all your reasoning tend, your exercises, your reading; and then you will know that this is the only way in which men achieve freedom.[173]*

Another powerful and well-known use of Spiritual Exercises by the Stoics was designed to provide one with tranquility specifically in the face of death. Epictetus advises us to closely consider that nature of death, to uncover what it is, without adding to appearances. We are encouraged to "turn it about" as if we held it in our hand and see that death "does not bite."[174]

---

[167]Epictetus, *Encheiridion*, section IV.
[168]Epictetus. *The Discourses Books III-IV.Fragments.Encheiridion.*Vol. 2. Translated by W.A. Oldfather (Cambridge: Harvard University Press, 2000), III.24.
[169] Epictetus, *Encheiridion*, section XXI.
[170]Seneca, "To Marcia on Consolation." Section X.
[171]Ibid.
[172]Ibid.
[173]Epictetus. *The Discourses Books III-IV.Fragments.Encheiridion.*Vol. 2. Translated by W.A. Oldfather (Cambridge: Harvard University Press, 2000), III.26.
[174]Epictetus, *The Discourses as Reported by Arrian.* Vol. 1.Translated by W.A. Oldfather. Reset and reprinted edition (Cambridge: Harvard University Press, 1998), II.1.

The description of what occurs at death is meant to diminish the gravity of dying. The inevitability of death is stressed. "The paltry body must be separated from the bit of spirit, either now or later, just as it existed apart from it before."[175] The Stoic can argue that, given death's inevitability, it seems to make little sense to be concerned with whether one dies sooner rather than later. "Why are you grieved, then, if it be separated now? For if it be not separated now, it will be later."[176] Epictetus also provides a concrete example of a death-scenario to picture in one's mind. Imagine being on a ship that is sinking into the ocean.

*What, then, have I to do? What I can; that is the only thing I do; I drown without fear, neither shrieking nor crying out against God, but recognizing that what is born must also perish.... What difference, then, is it to me how I pass away, whether by drowning or by a fever? For by something of the sort I must needs pass away.*[177]

Put another way, "what concern is it to you by which road you descend to the House of Hades? They are all equal."[178]

In the face of a perceived loss, such as the death of a son, we can combat our initial grief by pointing out to ourselves, based on the Stoic belief in Fate, that grieving his death means placing blame "back to the time when he was born, for his death was proclaimed at birth; into this condition was he begotten, this fate attended him straightway from the womb."[179] The assumption is that to lament one aspect of someone's life (e.g., the time and manner of their death) is to lament their entire life. Given Fate, the son could not have died at any time other than he did. To wish otherwise would be to wish he had not been born when he was, or have been the person that he was. By reminding ourselves of these claims time and again, we can actually come to express sincerely (through our behavior) the belief that death is not a bad thing.

By reframing each of these so-called hardships through continual spiritual exercises, the Stoic learns how to change his reaction to them. Given perseverance, it is claimed that the Stoic will achieve inner calm even in the face of what the rest of us would fear.

What all such exercises have in common is their presumed practicality. These are not esoteric practices with abstract aims. Rather, they serve to prepare one's character for transformation and, little by little, to transform it. They reinforce core principles in the adherent's mind. They make the relevant beliefs more "actionable," more "efficacious." The point of all such exercises is to *train* oneself to adopt certain attitudes and make certain judgments. The nature of the training is designed such that through constant repetition, the desired response becomes second-nature to the adherent.

---

[175]Ibid., II.1.
[176]Ibid.
[177]Ibid., II.5.
[178]Ibid., II.6.
[179]Seneca, "To Marcia on Consolation," section X.

An analogy may be taken from the martial arts (or from any athletic activity for that matter). A martial artist does not become a proficient fighter by looking at pictures of techniques, or by listening to his *Sensei* describe how to punch and kick. Essential to martial training is exhausting repetition. After having punched with the correct form thousands of times, the artist has trained his body to automatically punch correctly. A theoretical discussion of how to block a punch to the face is useless to the fighter when a punch is actually thrown. However, by practicing with a partner thousands of times, the fighter's body will automatically react when a punch is thrown and execute the block. In this case, practice really does make perfect.

The same line of thought extends to spiritual exercises, and from their earliest inception, such exercises had an apt comparison in physical exercises. The Stoic philosopher Musonius Rufus says that we will exercise both the body and soul "if we accustom ourselves to the cold, to heat, to hunger, to frugal nourishment, to hard beds, to abstinence from pleasant things, and to tolerance of unpleasant things."[180] The body will become hardened to pain, while the soul becomes more temperate and steadfast. Pierre Hadot says that "just as the athlete gave strength and form to his body by means of repeated bodily exercises, so the philosopher developed his strength of soul by means of philosophical exercises, and transformed himself. This analogy was all the more clear because it was precisely in the gymnasium—the place where physical exercises were practiced—that philosophy lessons were often given as well."[181]

After being told one time that death should not be feared, it is doubtful that the Stoic will have experienced the inner transformation such that, when confronted with death, he will truly be unafraid. For example, according to Tacitus' account, when Seneca was committing suicide by the order of Nero, his friends became upset (reminiscent of the death of Socrates). "Where had their philosophy gone, [Seneca] asked, and that resolution against impending misfortunes which they had devised over so many years?" Even in the presence of a great Stoic philosopher, it was difficult (apparently) for his like-minded friends to *act* as if they truly believed death was not a terrible thing.

---

### Exercise Break

Read the following account of Seneca's death. Do you think you could face your own death with the same calm and dignity? What sorts of exercises from above do you think might have prepared Seneca for his own death?

---

*Then followed the destruction of Annaeus Seneca,...*

*Seneca, quite unmoved, asked for tablets on which to inscribe his will, and,*

---

[180]Quoted in Hadot, *What is Ancient Philosophy?*, 189.
[181]Hadot, *What is Ancient Philosophy?*, 189.

*on the centurion's refusal, turned to his friends, protesting that as he was forbidden to requite them, he bequeathed to them the only, but still the noblest possession yet remaining to him, the pattern of his life, which, if they remembered, they would win a name for moral worth and steadfast friendship. At the same time he called them back from their tears to manly resolution, now with friendly talk, and now with the sterner language of rebuke. "Where," he asked again and again, "are your maxims of philosophy, or the preparation of so many years' study against evils to come? Who knew not Nero's cruelty? After a mother's and a brother's murder, nothing remains but to add the destruction of a guardian and a tutor."*

*Having spoken these and like words, meant, so to say, for all, he embraced his wife; then softening awhile from the stern resolution of the hour, he begged and implored her to spare herself the burden of perpetual sorrow, and, in the contemplation of a life virtuously spent, to endure a husband's loss with honourable consolations.*  *She declared, in answer, that she too had decided to die, and claimed for herself the blow of the executioner. There upon Seneca, not to thwart her noble ambition, from an affection too which would not leave behind him for insult one whom he dearly loved, replied: "I have shown you ways of smoothing life; you prefer the glory of dying. I will not grudge you such a noble example. Let the fortitude of so courageous an end be alike in both of us, but let there be more in your decease to win fame."*

*Then by one and the same stroke they sundered with a dagger the arteries of their arms. Seneca, as his aged frame, attenuated by frugal diet, allowed the blood to escape but slowly, severed also the veins of his legs and knees. Worn out by cruel anguish, afraid too that his sufferings might break his wife's spirit, and that, as he looked on her tortures, he might himself sink into irresolution, he persuaded her to retire into another chamber. Even at the last moment his eloquence failed him not; he summoned his secretaries, and dictated much to them which, as it has been published for all readers in his own words, I forbear to paraphrase.*

*Nero meanwhile, having no personal hatred against Paulina and not wishing to heighten the odium of his cruelty, forbade her death. At the soldiers' prompting, her slaves and freedmen bound up her arms, and stanched the bleeding, whether with her knowledge is doubtful. For as the vulgar are ever ready to think the worst, there were persons who believed that, as long as she dreaded Nero's relentlessness, she sought the glory of sharing her husband's death, but that after a time, when a more soothing prospect presented itself, she yielded to the charms of life. To this she added a few subsequent years, with a most praise worthy remembrance of her husband, and with a countenance and frame white to a degree of pallor which denoted a loss of much vital energy.*

*Seneca meantime, as the tedious process of death still lingered on, begged Statius Annaeus, whom he had long esteemed for his faithful friendship and medical skill, to produce a poison with which he had some time before provided himself, same drug which extinguished the life of those who were condemned by a public sentence of the people of Athens. It was brought to him and he drank it in vain, chilled as he was throughout his limbs, and his frame closed against the efficacy of the poison. At last he entered a pool of heated·water, from which he sprinkled the nearest of his slaves, adding the exclamation, "I offer this liquid as a libation to Jupiter the Deliverer." He was then carried into a bath, with the steam of which he was suffocated, and he was burnt without any of the usual funeral rites. So he had directed in a codicil of his will, when even in the height of his wealth and power he was thinking of his life's close.[182]*

Seneca's own death provides a perfect example of philosophy in practice. Due to his philosophical views and *training*, Seneca faced death with dignity. Let us use the example of death for one final application of Stoic *askesis*.

Seneca's "Letter to Marcia, on Consolation," is a letter offering philosophical therapy, but also an opportunity to promote Stoic principles. The letter begins with Seneca reminding Marcia that she has been grief-stricken for three years already. Although she has faced, and recovered from grief in the past (e.g., the death of her father), she is currently seemingly inconsolable in the face of the death of her son. All other attempts at consolation, including the ministrations of friends, diversions such as literature, and even the passage of time, had failed to help her overcome her grief.

*All means have been tried in vain : the consolations of your friends, who are weary of offering them, and the influence of great men who are related to you: literature, a taste which your father enjoyed and which you have inherited from him, now finds your ears closed, and affords you but a futile consolation, which scarcely engages your thoughts for a moment. Even time itself, nature's greatest remedy, which quiets the most bitter grief, loses its power with you alone.[183]*

---

[182] Tacitus: *Annals*, Book 15, Translated by Alfred John Church and William Jackson Brodribb. Slightly adapted. Full text online at http://classics.mit.edu/Tacitus/annals.html

[183] All of the remaining quotations from Seneca are from his "Letter to Marcia, On Consolation," unless otherwise indicated.

Seneca will now apply philosophy to the task of unburdening Marcia from her grief. To begin with, he provides examples of two different grieving mothers: Octavia (the sister of Augustus Caesar), and Livia (the wife of Augustus Caesar). Octavia became a grief-stricken recluse, while Livia faced grief with a dignified (Stoic) resolve.

*Choose, therefore, which of these two examples you think the more commendable: if you prefer to follow the former, you will remove yourself from the number of the living; you will shun the sight both of other people's children and of your own, and even of him whose loss you deplore; you will be looked upon by mothers as an omen of evil; you will refuse to take part in honourable, permissible pleasures, thinking them unbecoming for one so afflicted; you will be loath to linger above ground, and will be especially angry with your age, because it will not straightway bring your life abruptly to an end. I here put the best construction on what is really most contemptible and foreign to your character. I mean that you will show yourself unwilling to live, and unable to die. If, on the other hand, showing a milder and better regulated spirit, you try to follow the example of the latter most exalted lady, you will not be in misery, nor will you wear your life out with suffering. Plague on it! what madness this is, to punish one's self because one is unfortunate, and not to lessen, but to increase one's ills!*

Seneca's treatment goes far beyond merely encouraging Marcia to emulate the more "noble" example of grieving, however. He proceeds to evaluate her grief with a series of exercises drawing upon basic Stoic principles. Many of his exercises and encouragements involve challenging "appearances," and offering new and different perspectives.

He points out, for example, that her friends don't know to behave around her, implying that she should consider the perspectives of those friends.

*In the next place, I pray and beseech you not to be self-willed and beyond the management of your friends. You must be aware that none of them know how to behave, whether to mention Drusus in your presence or not, as they neither wish to wrong a noble youth by forgetting him nor to hurt you by speaking of him. When we leave you and assemble together by ourselves, we talk freely about his sayings and doings, treating them with the respect which they deserve: in your presence deep silence is observed about him, and thus you lose that greatest of pleasures, the hearing the praises of your son, which I doubt not you would be willing to hand down to all future ages, had you the means of so doing, even at the cost of your own life.*

Seneca suggests that grief can become, in some people (such as Marcia herself?) a perverse form of pride, that people can take an odd sort of pride or pleasure in demonstrating their misery. "Do not, I implore you, take a perverse pride in appearing the most unhappy of women." Nor should Marcia force herself to continue to grieve, as opposed to letting time (if nothing else) ease her sorrows.

*Yet there is a great difference between allowing and forcing yourself to grieve. How much more in accordance with your cultivated taste it would be to put an end to your mourning instead of looking for the end to come, and not to wait for the day when your sorrow shall cease against your will: dismiss it of your own accord.*

If Marcia is ready to "dismiss" her grief, then, instead of taking pride in misery, Marcia should keep in mind that adversity is an opportunity to display her virtue and strength.

*... there is no great credit in behaving bravely in times of prosperity, when life glides easily with a favouring current- neither does; a calm sea and fair wind display the art of the pilot . some foul weather is wanted to prove his courage.*

Not only is adversity an opportunity to display virtue, but there is nothing to be gained from grieving—it's not as if her tears and misery will bring her son back from the dead!

*...if fate can be overcome by tears, let us bring tears to bear upon it: let every day be passed in mourning, every night be spent in sorrow instead of sleep: let your breast be torn by your own hands, your very face attacked by them, and every kind of cruelty be practised by your grief, if it will profit you. But if the dead cannot be brought back to life, however much we may beat our breasts, if destiny remains fixed and immoveable forever, not to be changed by any sorrow, however great, and death does not loose his hold of anything that he once has taken away, then let our futile grief be brought to an end.*

As another example of questioning judgments, and considering different perspectives, Seneca asks Marcia about the nature of her complaint. Is she upset because she received no pleasure from her son's life, or just that she would have received more if he had lived longer? If she received no pleasure at all from him, then why is she complaining? She lost something that was of no value to her anyway! If she did receive pleasure from knowing him, then she should be grateful rather than resentful. If her complaint is that she would have preferred to receive more pleasure (by virtue of him living longer), then what would have been "long enough?"

*"But," say you, "it might have lasted longer." True, but you have been better dealt with than if you had never had a son, for, supposing you were given your choice, which is the better lot, to be happy for a short time or not at all? It is better to enjoy pleasures which soon leave us than to enjoy none*

*at all."*

It is better to have had a son than to have had none at all, and better to have lost a son (at a young age) who was good and virtuous, than see a son live longer, and perhaps suffer a lesser quality of life or character. Besides, her son (like all humans) was mortal. This entailed that he would die *someday*. If he had not died the day he did, he would have died some other day instead. Which day would have been acceptable to her? Indeed, if Marcia accepts the Stoic doctrine of Fate, then *no other day* was possible.

> *To each man a varying length of days has been assigned: no one dies before his time, because he was not destined to live any longer than he did. Everyone's end is fixed, and will always remain where it has been placed: neither industry nor favour will move it on any further. . . . so you need not burden yourself with the thought, "He might have lived longer." His life has not been cut short, nor does chance ever cut short our years: every man receives as much as was promised to him: the Fates go their own way, and neither add anything nor take away anything from what they have once promised. Prayers and endeavours are all in vain : each man will have as much life as his first day placed to his credit: from the time when he first saw the light he has entered on the path that leads to death, and is drawing nearer to his doom: those same years which were added to his youth were subtracted from his life.*

Even if Marcia didn't want to accept the Stoic doctrine of Fate, other exercises might be useful. Even if we reject "Fate," it is nevertheless useful to keep in mind the "nature" of a thing—in this case, a human being.

Humans are, by their very nature, *mortal*. We are each making "progress" towards death from the day we are born.

> *If you grieve for the death of your son, the fault lies with the time when he was born, for at his birth he was told that death was his doom: it is the law under which he was born, the fate which has pursued him ever since he left his mother's womb.*

In a sense, to lament the death of her son is to lament his birth, since he was dying from the moment he was born, and because he was born a mortal man, it was his "destiny" to die. For Marcia to wish he would not die is, in effect, to wish he not be born—since it is in the nature of anything born that it must die. Seneca repeats this theme numerous times throughout his letter.

> *Your son has died: in other words he has reached that goal towards which those whom you regard as more fortunate than your offspring are still hastening. this is the point towards which move at different rates all the crowds which are squabbling in the law courts, sitting in the theatres, praying in the temples. Those whom you love and those whom you despise*

*will both be made equal in the same ashes. This is the meaning of that*
*command, KNOW THYSELF, which is written on the shrine of the Pythian*
*oracle. What is man? a potter's vessel, to be broken by the slightest shake*
*or toss: it requires no great storm to rend you asunder: you fall to pieces*
*wherever you strike.*

The language here is perhaps disturbingly poetic. Humans are "a potter's
vessel to be broken by the slightest shake or toss." In other words, it is in our
nature to be fragile, mortal, subject to disease, injury, and death. If Marcia
expected her son to live forever, she had forgotten what kind of thing her son
was: a mortal man.

*"Still, it is a sad thing to lose a young man whom you have brought up, just*
*as he was becoming a defence and a pride both to his mother and to his*
*country." No one denies that it is sad: but it is the common lot of mortals.*

Here Seneca softens for a moment, and acknowledges that it might well be a
sad experience to lose a loved on. But, sad or not, it is inevitable, and to be
expected of each and every one of us.

*...all our relatives, both those who by the order of their birth we hope will*
*outlive ourselves, and those who themselves most properly wish to die*
*before us, ought to be loved by us as persons whom we cannot be sure of*
*having with us forever, nor even for long. We ought frequently to remind*
*ourselves that we must love the things of this life as we would what is*
*shortly to leave us, or indeed in the very act of leaving us.*

Having focused on the nature of human beings (i.e., our mortality), Seneca
now sneaks in some advice: given that every human is mortal, and that it is in our
nature to die, we should remind ourselves that every person important to us will
"shortly leave us"—if not "today," then "someday." This reminder might inspire
us to cherish and appreciate them more while they remain in our lives, but also
connects to another important Stoic exercise: anticipating "evils."

*It is because we never expect that any evil will befall ourselves before it*
*comes, we will not be taught by seeing the misfortunes of others that they*
*are the common inheritance of all men, but imagine that the path which*
*we have begun to tread is free from them and less beset by dangers than*
*that of other people. How many funerals pass our houses? yet we do not*
*think of death. How many untimely deaths?...When, therefore, misfortune*
*befalls us, we cannot help collapsing all the more completely, because we*
*are struck as it were unawares: a blow which has long been foreseen falls*
*much less heavily upon us...."I never thought it would happen!" How can*
*you think that anything will not happen, when you know that it may*
*happen to many men, and has happened to many? That is a noble verse,*
*and worthy of a nobler source than the stage:— "What one hath suffered*

*may befall us all." That man has lost his children: you may lose yours.*

Drawing an analogy from physical combat, Seneca observes that unexpected blows strike us more severely. Suppose that someone sucker-punches you in the stomach. Because you didn't see the blow coming, you had no chance to prepare yourself, and will likely get the wind knocked out of you. But now imagine that you know, in advance, that someone is about to punch you. You have time to tighten your abdominal muscles, control your breathing, and receive the blow. Even better, suppose you have been exercising your abdominal muscles for years, in preparation, and they are now rock-hard as a result? In such a case, perhaps the punch doesn't even hurt you at all? Similarly, with regard to life events, Seneca observes that we are more vulnerable when taken by surprise. This is commonsense, I suspect, in certain cases. If a loved one dies suddenly, without warning, it is a shocking event—but if that loved one dies from cancer, several months after being diagnosed, and having informed his family members, there is nothing "shocking" about the death. Everyone saw it coming. They might still be sad, but the "blow" is presumably "lessened."

Seneca explains Marcia's grief, in part, by claiming that had not adequately prepared, in advance, for her don's death. Did she have any specific reason to believe he was going to die? None of which we (the readers) are aware—but she had a *general reason* to believe he was going to die: he was mortal! In the future, then, Marcia can strengthen herself against grief by reminding herself (in advance) that all other loved ones in her life are equally mortal, and that they too will one day die.

*My Marcia, all these adventitious circumstances which glitter around us, such as children, office in the state, wealth, large halls, vestibules crowded with clients seeking vainly for admittance, a noble name, a well-born or beautiful wife, and every other thing which depends entirely upon uncertain and changeful fortune, are but furniture which is not our own, but entrusted to us on loan: none of these things are given to us outright: the stage of our lives is adorned with properties gathered from various sources, and soon to be returned to their several owners: some of them will be taken away on the first day, some on the second, and but few will remain till the end. We have, therefore, no grounds for regarding ourselves with complacency, as though the things which surround us were our own: they are only borrowed: we have the use and enjoyment of them for a time regulated by the lender, who controls his own gift...*

Finally, Seneca offers an exercise of perspective that will be made even more famous by the emperor Marcus Aurelius: the "view from above."

*Born for a very brief space of time, we regard this life as an inn which we are soon to quit that it may be made ready for the coming guest. Do I speak of our lives, which we know roll away incredibly fast? Reckon up the centuries of cities: you will find that even those which boast of their antiquity have not existed for long. All human works are brief and fleeting; they take up no part whatever of infinite time. Tried by the standard of the universe, we regard this earth of ours, with all its cities, nations, rivers, and sea-board as a mere point: our life occupies less than a point when compared with all time, the measure of which exceeds that of the world, for indeed the world is contained many times in it. Of what importance, then, can it be to lengthen that which, however much you add to it, will never be much more than nothing? We can only make our lives long by one expedient, that is, by being satisfied with their length: you may tell me of long-lived men, whose length of days has been celebrated by tradition, you may assign a hundred and ten years apiece to them: yet when you allow your mind to conceive the idea of eternity, there will be no difference between the shortest and the longest life, if you compare the time during which any one has been alive with that during which he has not been alive.*

Marcia laments that her son died "young." But, Seneca asks, against the backdrop of eternity, whose life is *long*? When compared to the age of the universe, and the span of all time, *every* human life is but the briefest, infinitesimal "specks." In the grand scheme of things, what difference does it make if someone lives 20 years, or 40 years, or a hundred years, when we're dealing in the scale of billions of years? Or eternity? A facet of our nature as human beings is not only that we're mortal, but that our life spans are very brief, if we expand our perspective. It should come as no surprise, then, when someone dies "young." We all do.

Seneca had at least two ambitions in his Letter to Marcia: demonstrate Stoic philosophy, and help Marcia deal with her grief. To that end, he reframes her judgments concerning her son's death, and offers several exercises to help her conquer her grief with "stoic" resolve. Seneca did not merely seek to take away some of the sting of death, however. He also sought to use our knowledge of the inevitability of death to live a better life. For those of you interested in those lessons, I encourage you to read the second letter included at the end of this chapter: "On the Shortness of Life."

## Conclusion

Philosophy, as it is perceived and practiced by most today, conjures associations of abstract and esoteric conversations that are, at best, intellectually stimulating, and, at worst, a waste of time better spent on more practical pursuits. What I hope to have demonstrated by the end of this final chapter of this work is that such need not be the only interpretation of philosophy available, and that such an interpretation bears no resemblance to philosophy as it was practiced amongst its ancient Greek and Roman developers.

Although I personally find great solace in Stoicism and Stoic spiritual exercises, and can attest to the positive transformations they have brought to my life, it is not my goal to have converted all (or even any) of you readers to a Stoic mindset. Instead, I hope merely to have brought to your attention the practical value of philosophy, and demonstrated how philosophy can be put to work in our lives.

Philosophy was once regarded as the means by which we may strive to live an excellent life, to flourish as a human being. It allows us to fulfill our potential, to be more fully awake and engaged with our lives, and to achieve a measure of the happiness that so often eludes us. Regardless of whether you continue to study philosophy in the formal sense, my sincere hope is that your exposure to philosophy, and your continued use of it (even as an "amateur"), will help you to achieve *eudaimonia*.

### Exercises for Wisdom and Growth

1. Identify a "problem" in your life. Using the Stoic exercises covered in this chapter, analyze and treat that "problem." Use the following questions or instructions to help you with this process:

   a. What is the problem?

   b. Describe the problem in "purely physical" terms, as an "appearance," without adding any judgments.

   c. What judgments, if any, had you added to the appearance *before* this exercise?

   d. Try to look at your problem from the perspective of all of space and time, using the "view from above" exercise. In the "grand scheme of things," how serious is this problem? Imagine how you (or others) will view this problem a day from now, a week from now, a month from now, a year from now, a decade from now, fifty years from now, one hundred years from now, and a thousand years from now. How "big" is your problem, ultimately?

   e. With regard to your problem: what is under your control, and what is not under your control? List them.

      i. Under my control:

      ii. Not under my control:

   f. How much "good" is it doing you, or will it do you, to worry about or to focus on the parts of your problem that are not under your control?

   g. Is your problem unique, or have others faced it (or something like it) as well? Do you live in a world where things like this happen? Should it surprise you that you could experience such

*Diogenes Laertius (3ʳᵈ century CE) was a biographer of Greek philosophers. Little is known about his own life, but much of what we think we know about ancient Greek philosophers comes from his partially-provided work below.*

# Lives of Eminent Philosophers
# Diogenes Laertius

## [R.D. Hicks, Ed.[184]]

## Chapter 2. DIOGENES (404 - 323 BCE)

[20] Diogenes was a native of Sinope, son of Hicesius, a banker. Diocles relates that he went into exile because his father was entrusted with the money of the state and adulterated the coinage. But Eubulides in his book on Diogenes says that Diogenes himself did this and was forced to leave home along with his father. Moreover Diogenes himself actually confesses in his *Pordalus* that he adulterated the coinage. Some say that having been appointed to superintend the workmen he was persuaded by them, and that he went to Delphi or to the Delian oracle in his own city and inquired of Apollo whether he should do what he was urged to do. When the god gave him permission to alter the political currency, not understanding what this meant, he adulterated the state coinage, and when he was detected, according to some he was banished, while according to others he voluntarily quitted the city for fear of consequences. [21] One version is that his father entrusted him with the money and that he debased it, in consequence of which the father was imprisoned and died, while the son fled, came to Delphi, and inquired, not whether he should falsify the coinage, but what he should do to gain the greatest reputation; and that then it was that he received the oracle.

On reaching Athens he fell in with Antisthenes. Being repulsed by him, because he never welcomed pupils, by sheer persistence Diogenes wore him out. Once when he stretched out his staff against him, the pupil offered his head with the words, "Strike, for you will find no wood hard enough to keep me away from you, so long as I think you've something to say." From that time forward he was his pupil, and, exile as he was, set out upon a simple life.

[22] Through watching a mouse running about, says Theophrastus in the Megarian dialogue, not looking for a place to lie down in, not afraid of the dark, not seeking any of the things which are considered to be dainties, he discovered the means of adapting himself to circumstances. He was the first, say some, to fold his cloak because he was obliged to sleep in it as well, and he carried a wallet to

---

[184] Text courtesy of the following URL:

http://data.perseus.org/citations/urn:cts:greekLit:tlg0004.tlg001.perseus-eng1:6.2

hold his victuals, and he used any place for any purpose, for breakfasting, sleeping, or conversing. And then he would say, pointing to the portico of Zeus and the Hall of Processions, that the Athenians had provided him with places to live in. [23] He did not lean upon a staff until he grew infirm; but afterwards he would carry it everywhere, not indeed in the city, but when walking along the road with it and with his wallet; so say Olympiodorus,[185] once a magistrate at Athens, Polyeuctus the orator, and Lysanias the son of Aeschrio. He had written to someone to try and procure a cottage for him. When this man was a long time about it, he took for his abode the tub in the Metroön, as he himself explains in his letters. And in summer he used to roll in it over hot sand, while in winter he used to embrace statues covered with snow, using every means of inuring himself to hardship.

[24] He was great at pouring scorn on his contemporaries. The school of Euclides he called bilious, and Plato's lectures waste of time, the performances at the Dionysia great peep-shows for fools, and the demagogues the mob's lacqueys. He used also to say that when he saw physicians, philosophers and pilots at their work, he deemed man the most intelligent of all animals; but when again he saw interpreters of dreams and diviners and those who attended to them, or those who were puffed up with conceit of wealth, he thought no animal more silly. He would continually say[186] that for the conduct of life we need right reason or a halter.

[25] Observing Plato one day at a costly banquet taking olives, "How is it," he said,[187] "that you the philosopher who sailed to Sicily for the sake of these dishes, now when they are before you do not enjoy them?" "Nay, by the gods, Diogenes," replied Plato, "there also for the most part I lived upon olives and such like." "Why then," said Diogenes, "did you need to go to Syracuse? Was it that Attica at that time did not grow olives?" But Favorinus in his *Miscellaneous History* attributes this to Aristippus. Again, another time he was eating dried figs when he encountered Plato and offered him a share of them. When Plato took them and ate them, he said, "I said you might share them, not that you might eat them all up."

[26] And one day when Plato had invited to his house friends coming from Dionysius, Diogenes trampled upon his carpets and said, "I trample upon Plato's vainglory." Plato's reply was, "How much pride you expose to view, Diogenes, by seeming not to be proud." Others tell us that what Diogenes said was, "I trample

---

[185] An eminent politician. Pausanias, i. cc. 25, 26, describes a statue of Olympiodorus in the Acropolis, and takes occasion to recount his exploits, how (c. 288 b.c.) he delivered Athens from the Macedonians (cf. Plut. Demetr. c. 46). As to the variant Ἀθηνόδ ωρος, nothing is known of any Athenian politician of that name.

[186] Some of the stories which follow are so much alike that it is charitable to suppose that Laertius drew from more than one collection of the sayings of Diogenes.

[187] Obviously Favorinus was not the author (vide infra) whom Laertius followed here.

upon the pride of Plato," who retorted, "Yes, Diogenes, with pride of another sort." Sotion,[188] however, in his fourth book makes the Cynic address this remark to Plato himself. Diogenes once asked him for wine, and after that also for some dried figs; and Plato sent him a whole jar full. Then the other said, "If someone asks you how many two and two are, will you answer, Twenty? So, it seems, you neither give as you are asked nor answer as you are questioned." Thus he scoffed at him as one who talked without end....

[31] The boys used to get by heart many passages from poets, historians, and the writings of Diogenes himself; and he would practise them in every short cut to a good memory. In the house too he taught them to wait upon themselves, and to be content with plain fare and water to drink. He used to make them crop their hair close and to wear it unadorned, and to go lightly clad, barefoot, silent, and not looking about them in the streets. He would also take them out hunting. They on their part had a great regard for Diogenes and made requests of their parents for him. The same Eubulus relates that he grew old in the house of Xeniades, and when he died was buried by his sons. There Xeniades once asked him how he wished to be buried. To which he replied, "On my face." [32] "Why?" inquired the other. "Because," said he, "after a little time down will be converted into up." This because the Macedonians had now got the supremacy, that is, had risen high from a humble position. Someone took him into a magnificent house and warned him not to expectorate, whereupon having cleared his throat he discharged the phlegm into the man's face, being unable, he said, to find a meaner receptacle. Others father this upon Aristippus. One day he shouted out for men, and when people collected, hit out at them with his stick, saying, "It was men I called for, not scoundrels." This is told by Hecato in the first book of his *Anecdotes.* Alexander is reported to have said, "Had I not been Alexander, I should have liked to be Diogenes."

[33] The word "disabled" (ἀναπήρο υς), Diogenes held, ought to be applied not to the deaf or blind, but to those who have no wallet (πήρα). One day he made his way with head half shaven into a party of young revellers, as Metrocles relates in his *Anecdotes,* and was roughly handled by them. Afterwards he entered on a tablet the names of those who had struck him and went about with the tablet hung round his neck, till he had covered them with ridicule and brought universal blame and discredit upon them. He described himself as a hound of the sort which all men praise, but no one, he added, of his admirers dared go out hunting along with him. When someone boasted that at the Pythian games he had vanquished men, Diogenes replied, "Nay, I defeat men, you defeat slaves."

[34] To those who said to him, "You are an old man; take a rest," "What?" he replied, "if I were running in the stadium, ought I to slacken my pace when approaching the goal? ought I not rather to put on speed?" Having been invited to a dinner, he declared that he wouldn't go; for, the last time he went, his host had not expressed a proper gratitude. He would walk upon snow barefoot and do the other things mentioned above. Not only so; he even attempted to eat meat

---

[188] The point of Sotion's version is best seen if for the indirect τὸν Πλάτων α τὸν κύνα (sc. πατεῖν we substitute the direct speech τὸν Πλάτων α ὁ κύων (sc. πατῶ).

raw, but could not manage to digest it. He once found Demosthenes the orator lunching at an inn, and, when he retired within, Diogenes said, "All the more you will be inside the tavern." When some strangers expressed a wish to see Demosthenes, he stretched out his middle finger and said, "There goes the demagogue of Athens." [35] Someone dropped a loaf of bread and was ashamed to pick it up; whereupon Diogenes, wishing to read him a lesson, tied a rope to the neck of a wine-jar and proceeded to drag it across the Ceramicus.

He used to say that he followed the example of the trainers of choruses; for they too set the note a little high, to ensure that the rest should hit the right note. Most people, he would say, are so nearly mad that a finger makes all the difference. For, if you go along with your middle finger stretched out, someone will think you mad, but, if it's the little finger, he will not think so. Very valuable things, said he, were bartered for things of no value, and *vice versa*. At all events a statue fetches three thousand drachmas, while a quart of barley-flour is sold for two copper coins....

[37] One day, observing a child drinking out of his hands, he cast away the cup from his wallet with the words, "A child has beaten me in plainness of living." He also threw away his bowl when in like manner he saw a child who had broken his plate taking up his lentils with the hollow part of a morsel of bread. He used also to reason thus: "All things belong to the gods. The wise are friends of the gods, and friends hold things in common. Therefore all things belong to the wise." One day he saw a woman kneeling before the gods in an ungraceful attitude, and wishing to free her of superstition, according to Zoïlus of Perga, he came forward and said, "Are you not afraid, my good woman, that a god may be standing behind you?--for all things are full of his presence--and you may be put to shame?" [38] He dedicated to Asclepius a bruiser who, whenever people fell on their faces, used to run up to them and bruise them.

All the curses of tragedy, he used to say, had lighted upon him. At all events he was

A homeless exile, to his country dead.

A wanderer who begs his daily bread.[189]

But he claimed that to fortune he could oppose courage, to convention nature, to passion reason. When he was sunning himself in the Craneum, Alexander came and stood over him and said, "Ask of me any boon you like." To which he replied, "Stand out of my light."[190] Someone had been reading aloud for a very long time, and when he was near the end of the roll pointed to a space with no writing on it. "Cheer up, my men," cried Diogenes; "there's land in sight." To one who by argument had proved conclusively that he had horns, he said, touching his forehead, "Well, I for my part don't see any." [39] In like manner, when somebody declared that there is no such thing as motion, he got up and walked about. When someone was discoursing on celestial phenomena, "How many days," asked Diogenes, "were you in coming from the sky?" A eunuch of bad character had inscribed on his door the words, "Let nothing evil enter." "How

---

[189] Nauck, T.G.F.2, Adesp.284
[190] Cf Plut. Alex. c. 14.

then," he asked, "is the master of the house to get in?" When he had anointed his feet with unguent, he declared that from his head the unguent passed into the air, but from his feet into his nostrils. The Athenians urged him to become initiated, and told him that in the other world those who have been initiated enjoy a special privilege. "It would be ludicrous," quoth he, "if Agesilaus and Epaminondas are to dwell in the mire, while certain folk of no account will live in the Isles of the Blest because they have been initiated."

[40] When mice crept on to the table he addressed them thus, "See now even Diogenes keeps parasites." When Plato styled him a dog, "Quite true," he said, "for I come back again and again to those who have sold me." As he was leaving the public baths, somebody inquired if many men were bathing. He said, No. But to another who asked if there was a great crowd of bathers, he said, Yes. Plato had defined Man as an animal, biped and featherless, and was applauded. Diogenes plucked a fowl and brought it into the lecture-room with the words, "Here is Plato's man." In consequence of which there was added to the definition, "having broad nails." To one who asked what was the proper time for lunch, he said, "If a rich man, when you will; if a poor man, when you can."

[41] At Megara he saw the sheep protected by leather jackets, while the children went bare. "It's better," said he, "to be a Megarian's ram than his son."[191] To one who had brandished a beam at him and then cried, "Look out," he replied, "What, are you intending to strike me again?" He used to call the demagogues the lackeys of the people and the crowns awarded to them the efflorescence of fame. He lit a lamp in broad daylight and said, as he went about, "I am looking for a man." One day he got a thorough drenching where he stood, and, when the bystanders pitied him, Plato said, if they really pitied him, they should move away, alluding to his vanity. When someone hit him a blow with his fist, "Heracles," said he, "how came I to forget to put on a helmet when I walked out?" [42] Further, when Meidias assaulted him and went on to say, "There are 3000 drachmas to your credit," the next day he took a pair of boxing-gauntlets, gave him a thrashing and said, "There are 3000 blows to *your* credit."

When Lysias the druggist asked him if he believed in the gods, "How can I help believing in them," said he, "when I see a god-forsaken wretch like you?" Others give this retort to Theodorus. Seeing someone perform religious purification, he said, "Unhappy man, don't you know that you can no more get rid of errors of conduct by sprinklings than you can of mistakes in grammar?" He would rebuke men in general with regard to their prayers, declaring that they asked for those things which seemed to them to be good, not for such as are truly good. [43] As for those who were excited over their dreams he would say that they cared nothing for what they did in their waking hours, but kept their curiosity for the visions called up in their sleep. At Olympia, when the herald

---

[191] Where the wool was of fine quality, as near Tarentum (Hor. Carm. ii. 6. 10 "pellitis ovibus"), the fleeces were protected by coverings of skin, partly against damage from brambles and partly to preserve the colour (Varro, R.R. ii. 2). We are reminded of what Augustus said when he heard of the execution of Antipater, "It is better to be Herod's pig than his son."

proclaimed Dioxippus to be victor over the men, Diogenes protested, "Nay, he is victorious over slaves, I over men."

Still he was loved by the Athenians. At all events, when a youngster broke up his tub, they gave the boy a flogging and presented Diogenes with another. Dionysius the Stoic says that after Chaeronea he was seized and dragged off to Philip, and being asked who he was, replied, "A spy upon your insatiable greed." For this he was admired and set free.

[44] Alexander having on one occasion sent a letter to Antipater at Athens by a certain Athlios, Diogenes, who was present, said:

Graceless son of graceless sire to graceless wight by graceless squire.

Perdiccas having threatened to put him to death unless he came to him, "That's nothing wonderful," quoth he, "for a beetle or a tarantula would do the same." Instead of that he would have expected the threat to be that Perdiccas would be quite happy to do without his company. He would often insist loudly that the gods had given to men the means of living easily, but this had been put out of sight, because we require honeyed cakes, unguents and the like. Hence to a man whose shoes were being put on by his servant, he said, "You have not attained to full felicity, unless he wipes your nose as well; and that will come, when you have lost the use of your hands."

[45] Once he saw the officials of a temple leading away someone who had stolen a bowl belonging to the treasurers, and said, "The great thieves are leading away the little thief." Noticing a lad one day throwing stones at a cross (gibbet), "Well done," he said, "you will hit your mark."[192] When some boys clustered round him and said, "Take care he doesn't bite us," he answered, "Never fear, boys, a dog does not eat beetroot." To one who was proud of wearing a lion's skin his words were, "Leave off dishonouring the habiliments of courage." When someone was extolling the good fortune of Callisthenes and saying what splendour he shared in the suite of Alexander, "Not so," said Diogenes, "but rather ill fortune; for he breakfasts and dines when Alexander thinks fit."

[46] Being short of money, he told his friends that he applied to them not for alms, but for repayment of his due. When behaving indecently in the marketplace, he wished it were as easy to relieve hunger by rubbing an empty stomach. Seeing a youth starting off to dine with satraps, he dragged him off, took him to his friends and bade them keep strict watch over him. When a youth effeminately attired put a question to him, he declined to answer unless he pulled up his robe and showed whether he was man or woman. A youth was playing cottabos in the baths. Diogenes said to him, "The better you play, the worse it is for you." At a feast certain people kept throwing all the bones to him as they would have done to a dog.[193] Thereupon he played a dog's trick and drenched them....

[49] When someone reproached him with his exile, his reply was, "Nay, it was through that, you miserable fellow, that I came to be a philosopher." Again, when someone reminded him that the people of Sinope had sentenced him to

---

[192] i.e. "some day you'll come to the gallows."

[193] "You would not see so many bones if I were the dog," was Dante's retort when annoyed by similar attentions at the table of Can Grande.

exile, "And I them," said he, "to home-staying." Once he saw an Olympic victor tending sheep and thus accosted him: "Too quickly, my good friend, have you left Olympia for Nemea.[194]" Being asked why athletes are so stupid, his answer was, "Because they are built up of pork and beef." He once begged alms of a statue, and, when asked why he did so, replied, "To get practice in being refused." In asking alms --as he did at first by reason of his poverty-- he used this form: "If you have already given to anyone else, give to me also; if not, begin with me."...

[53] Noticing a good-looking youth lying in an exposed position, he nudged him and cried, "Up, man, up, lest some foe thrust a dart into thy back!" To one who was feasting lavishly he said:

Short-liv'd thou'lt be, my son, by what thou--buy'st.[195]

As Plato was conversing about Ideas and using the nouns "tablehood" and "cuphood," he said, "Table and cup I see; but your tablehood and cuphood, Plato, I can nowise see." "That's readily accounted for," said Plato, "for you have the eyes to see the visible table and cup; but not the understanding by which ideal tablehood and cuphood are discerned."

[54] On being asked by somebody, "What sort of a man do you consider Diogenes to be?" "A Socrates gone mad," said he.[196] Being asked what was the right time to marry, Diogenes replied, "For a young man not yet: for an old man never at all." Being asked what he would take to be soundly cuffed, he replied, "A helmet." Seeing a youth dressing with elaborate care, he said, "If it's for men, you're a fool; if for women, a knave." One day he detected a youth blushing. "Courage," quoth he, "that is the hue of virtue." One day after listening to a couple of lawyers disputing, he condemned them both, saying that the one had no doubt stolen, but the other had not lost anything. To the question what wine he found pleasant to drink, he replied, "That for which other people pay." When he was told that many people laughed at him, he made answer, "But I am not laughed down."...

[56] Being asked if the wise eat cakes, "Yes," he said, "cakes of all kinds, just like other men." Being asked why people give to beggars but not to philosophers, he said, "Because they think they may one day be lame or blind, but never expect that they will turn to philosophy." He was begging of a miserly man who was slow to respond; so he said, "My friend, it's for food that I'm asking, not for funeral expenses." Being reproached one day for having falsified the currency, he said, "That was the time when I was such as you are now; but such as I am now, you will never be." To another who reproached him for the same offence he made a more scurrilous repartee.

[57] On coming to Myndus and finding the gates large, though the city itself was very small, he cried, "Men of Myndus, bar your gates, lest the city should run away." Seeing a man who had been caught stealing purple, he said:

Fast gripped by purple death and forceful fate. (Il. v. 83.)

---

[194] Shepherd's Bush.
[195] Cf. Hom. Il. v. 40, xviii. 95.
[196] i.e. Plato. This anecdote is found in Aelian, Var. Hist. xiv. 33 εἰώθει δέ, φασίν, ὁ Πλάτων περὶ Διογέν ους λέγειν ὅτι μαινόμ ενος οὗτος Σωκράτ ης ἐστίν.

When Craterus wanted him to come and visit him, "No," he replied, "I would rather live on a few grains of salt at Athens than enjoy sumptuous fare at Craterus's table." He went up to Anaximenes the rhetorician, who was fat, and said, "Let us beggars have something of your paunch; it will be a relief to you, and we shall get advantage." And when the same man was discoursing, Diogenes distracted his audience by producing some salt fish. This annoyed the lecturer, and Diogenes said, "An obol's worth of salt fish has broken up Anaximenes' lecture-class."

[58] Being reproached for eating in the market-place, "Well, it was in the market-place," he said, "that I felt hungry." Some authors affirm that the following also belongs to him : that Plato saw him washing lettuces, came up to him and quietly said to him, "Had you paid court to Dionysius, you wouldn't now be washing lettuces," and that he with equal calmness made answer, "If you had washed lettuces, you wouldn't have paid court to Dionysius." When someone said, "Most people laugh at you," his reply was, "And so very likely do the asses at them; but as they don't care for the asses, so neither do I care for them." One day observing a youth studying philosophy, he said, "Well done, Philosophy, that thou divertest admirers of bodily charms to the real beauty of the soul."...

[64] When he was dining in a temple, and in the course of the meal loaves not free from dirt were put on the table, he took them up and threw them away, declaring that nothing unclean ought to enter a temple. To the man who said to him, "You don't know anything, although you are a philosopher," he replied, "Even if I am but a pretender to wisdom, that in itself is philosophy." When someone brought a child to him and declared him to be highly gifted and of excellent character, "What need then," said he, "has he of me?" Those who say admirable things, but fail to do them, he compared to a harp; for the harp, like them, he said, has neither hearing nor perception. He was going into a theatre, meeting face to face those who were coming out, and being asked why, "This," he said, "is what I practise doing all my life."...

[68] Seeing a bad archer, he sat down beside the target with the words "in order not to get hit." Lovers, he declared, derive their pleasures from their misfortune.

Being asked whether death was an evil thing, he replied, "How can it be evil, when in its presence we are not aware of it?" When Alexander stood opposite him and asked, "Are you not afraid of me?" "Why, what are you?" said he, "a good thing or a bad?" Upon Alexander replying "A good thing," "Who then," said Diogenes, "is afraid of the good?" Education, according to him, is a controlling grace to the young, consolation to the old, wealth to the poor, and ornament to the rich. When Didymon, who was a rake, was once treating a girl's eye, "Beware," says Diogenes, "lest the oculist instead of curing the eye should ruin the pupil." On somebody declaring that his own friends were plotting against him, Diogenes exclaimed, "What is to be done then, if you have to treat friends and enemies alike?"

[69] Being asked what was the most beautiful thing in the world, he replied, "Freedom of speech." On entering a boys' school, he found there many statues of the Muses, but few pupils. "By the help of the gods," said he, "schoolmaster, you have plenty of pupils." It was his habit to do everything in public, the works of

Demeter and of Aphrodite alike. He used to draw out the following arguments. "If to breakfast be not absurd, neither is it absurd in the market-place; but to breakfast is not absurd, therefore it is not absurd to breakfast in the marketplace." Behaving indecently in public, he wished "it were as easy to banish hunger by rubbing the belly." Many other sayings are attributed to him, which it would take long to enumerate.[197]

[70] He used to affirm that training was of two kinds, mental and bodily : the latter being that whereby, with constant exercise, perceptions are formed such as secure freedom of movement for virtuous deeds; and the one half of this training is incomplete without the other, good health and strength being just as much included among the essential things, whether for body or soul. And he would adduce indisputable evidence to show how easily from gymnastic training we arrive at virtue. For in the manual crafts and other arts it can be seen that the craftsmen develop extraordinary manual skill through practice. Again, take the case of flute-players and of athletes: what surpassing skill they acquire by their own incessant toil; and, if they had transferred their efforts to the training of the mind, how certainly their labours would not have been unprofitable or ineffective.

[71] Nothing in life, however, he maintained, has any chance of succeeding without strenuous practice; and this is capable of overcoming anything. Accordingly, instead of useless toils men should choose such as nature recommends, whereby they might have lived happily. Yet such is their madness that they choose to be miserable. For even the despising of pleasure is itself most pleasurable, when we are habituated to it; and just as those accustomed to a life of pleasure feel disgust when they pass over to the opposite experience, so those whose training has been of the opposite kind derive more pleasure from despising pleasure than from the pleasures themselves. This was the gist of his conversation; and it was plain that he acted accordingly, adulterating currency in very truth, allowing convention no such authority as he allowed to natural right, and asserting that the manner of life he lived was the same as that of Heracles when he preferred liberty to everything.

[72] He maintained that all things are the property of the wise, and employed such arguments as those cited above. All things belong to the gods. The gods are friends to the wise, and friends share all property in common; therefore all things are the property of the wise. Again as to law: that it is impossible for society to exist without law; for without a city no benefit can be derived from that which is civilized. But the city is civilized, and there is no advantage in law without a city; therefore law is something civilized. He would ridicule good birth and fame and all such distinctions, calling them showy ornaments of vice. The only true commonwealth was, he said, that which is as wide as the universe. He advocated community of wives, recognizing no other marriage than a union of the man who persuades with the woman who consents. And for this reason he thought sons

---

[197] §§ 70-73. As § 74 joins on well to § 69, the intermediate specimens of Cynic maxims(cf.note on § 10) are clearly an insertion, probably from a different source.

too should be held in common....

[74] He became very ready also at repartee in verbal debates, as is evident from what has been said above.

Further, when he was sold as a slave, he endured it most nobly. For on a voyage to Aegina he was captured by pirates under the command of Scirpalus,[198] conveyed to Crete and exposed for sale. When the auctioneer asked in what he was proficient, he replied, "In ruling men." Thereupon he pointed to a certain Corinthian with a fine purple border to his robe, the man named Xeniades above-mentioned, and said, "Sell me to this man; he needs a master." Thus Xeniades came to buy him, and took him to Corinth and set him over his own children and entrusted his whole household to him. And he administered it in all respects in such a manner that Xeniades used to go about saying, "A good genius has entered my house."

[75] Cleomenes in his work entitled *Concerning Pedagogues* says that the friends of Diogenes wanted to ransom him, whereupon he called them simpletons; for, said he, lions are not the slaves of those who feed them, but rather those who feed them are at the mercy of the lions : for fear is the mark of the slave, whereas wild beasts make men afraid of them. The man had in fact a wonderful gift of persuasion, so that he could easily vanquish anyone he liked in argument. At all events a certain Onesicritus of Aegina is said to have sent to Athens the one of his two sons named Androsthenes, and he having become a pupil of Diogenes stayed there; the father then sent the other also, the aforesaid Philiscus, who was the elder, in search of him; but Philiscus also was detained in the same way. [76] When, thirdly, the father himself arrived, he was just as much attracted to the pursuit of philosophy as his sons and joined the circle--so magical was the spell which the discourses of Diogenes exerted. Amongst his hearers was Phocion surnamed the Honest, and Stilpo the Megarian, and many other men prominent in political life.

Diogenes is said to have been nearly ninety years old when he died. Regarding his death there are several different accounts. One is that he was seized with colic after eating an octopus raw and so met his end. Another is that he died voluntarily by holding his breath. This account was followed by Cercidas of Megalopolis (or of Crete), who in his meliambics writes thus:

Not so he who aforetime was a citizen of Sinope,
That famous one who carried a staff, doubled his cloak, and lived in the open air.

[77] But he soared aloft with his lip tightly pressed against his teeth
And holding his breath withal. For in truth he was rightly named
Diogenes, a true-born son of Zeus, a hound of heaven.

Another version is that, while trying to divide an octopus amongst the dogs, he was so severely bitten on the sinew of the foot that it caused his death. His friends, however, according to Antisthenes in his *Successions of Philosophers*, conjectured that it was due to the retention of his breath. For he happened to be living in the Craneum, the gymnasium in front of Corinth. When his friends came

---

[198] "Harpalus" according to Cic. N.D. iii. 34. 83.

according to custom and found him wrapped up in his cloak, they thought that he must be asleep, although he was by no means of a drowsy or somnolent habit. They therefore drew aside his cloak and found that he was dead. This they supposed to have been his deliberate act in order to escape thenceforward from life.

[78] Hence, it is said, arose a quarrel among his disciples as to who should bury him : nay, they even came to blows; but, when their fathers and men of influence arrived, under their direction he was buried beside the gate leading to the Isthmus. Over his grave they set up a pillar and a dog in Parian marble upon it. Subsequently his fellow-citizens honoured him with bronze statues, on which these verses were inscribed:

Time makes even bronze grow old : but thy glory, Diogenes, all eternity will never destroy. Since thou alone didst point out to mortals the lesson of self-sufficingness and the easiest path of life.[199]

[79] We too have written on him in the proceleusmatic metre :
a. Diogenes, come tell me what fate took you to the world below?
d. A dog's savage tooth.[200]

But some say that when dying he left instructions that they should throw him out unburied, that every wild beast might feed on him, or thrust him into a ditch and sprinkle a little dust over him. But according to others his instructions were that they should throw him into the Ilissus, in order that he might be useful to his brethren.

Demetrius in his work *On Men of the Same Name* asserts that on the same day on which Alexander died in Babylon Diogenes died in Corinth. He was an old man in the 113th Olympiad.[201] [80]...

---

[199] Anth. Pal. xvi. 334.
[200] Anth. Pal. vii. 116.
[201] 324-321 b.c.

*The following work from Epictetus, "The Enchiridion," is provided in its entirety. It provides a brief and helpful survey of key stoic themes, especially those that were emphasized in the Roman period of stoicism. Epictetus (55 CE – 135 CE) was a former "house slave" of Epaphroditos—a secretary to the Emperor Nero. Indeed, we don't know "Epictetus'" real name, as Epictetus (epíktetos/(ἐπίκτητος) literally means "acquired" in Latin—undoubtedly a reference to his slave status. His owner allowed him to study philosophy under the Stoic Musonius Rufus. He was freed after Nero's death in 68 CE, and began to teach philosophy in Rome, but migrated to Nicopolis in Greece after the Emperor Domitian banished philosophers from Rome in 93 CE. That both a slave (Epictetus) and a Roman Emperor (Marcus Aurelius) would both be devoted to stoicism is a testimony to its broad appeal.*

# *The Enchiridion*
## ("The Manual" or "The Handbook" of Epictetus)

### [Translated by Thomas Wentworth Higginson.]

I.

There are things which are within our power, and there are things which are beyond our power. Within our power are opinion, aim, desire, aversion, and, in one word, whatever affairs are our own. Beyond our power are body, property, reputation, office, and, in one word, whatever are not properly our own affairs.

Now, the things within our power are by nature free, unrestricted, unhindered; but those beyond our power are weak, dependent, restricted, alien. Remember, then, that if you attribute freedom to things by nature dependent, and take what belongs to others for you own, you will be hindered, you will lament, you will be disturbed, you will find fault both with gods and men. But if you take for your own only that which is your own, and view what belongs to others just as it really is, then no one will ever compel you, no one will restrict you, you will find fault with no one, you will accuse no one, you will do nothing against your will; no one will hurt you, you will not have an enemy, nor will you suffer any harm.

Aiming therefore at such great things, remember that you must not allow yourself any inclination, however slight, towards the attainment of the others; but that you must entirely quit some of them, and for the present postpone the rest. But if you would have these, and possess power and wealth likewise, you may miss the latter in seeking the former; and you will certainly fail of that by which alone happiness and freedom are procured.

Seek at once, therefore, to be able to say to every unpleasing semblance, "You are but a semblance and by no means the real thing." And then examine it by those rules which you have; and first and chiefly, by this: whether it concerns the things which are within our own power, or those which are not; and if it concerns anything beyond our power, be prepared to say that it is nothing to you.

II.

Remember that desire demands the attainment of that of which you are desirous; and aversion demands the avoidance of that to which you are averse; that he who fails of the object of his desires is disappointed; and he who incurs the object of his aversion is wretched. If, then, you shun only those undesirable things which you can control, you will never incur anything you shun; but if you shun sickness, or death, or poverty, you will run the risk of wretchedness. Remove [the habit of] aversion, then, from all things that are not within our power, and apply it to things undesirable, which are within our power. But for the present altogether restrain desire; for if you desire any of the things not within our own power, you must necessarily be disappointed; and you are not yet secure of those which are within our power, and so are legitimate objects of desire. Where it is practically necessary for you to pursue or avoid anything, do even this with discretion, and gentleness, and moderation.

III.

With regard to whatever objects either delight the mind, or contribute to use, or are tenderly beloved, remind yourself of what nature they are, beginning with the merest trifles: if you have a favorite cup, that it is but a cup of which you are fond, – for thus, if it is broken, you can bear it; if you embrace your child, or your wife, that you embrace a mortal, – and thus, if either of them dies, you can bear it.

IV.

When you set about any action, remind yourself of what nature the action is. If you are going to bathe, represent to yourself the incidents usual in the bath, – some persons pouring out, others pushing in, others scolding, others pilfering. And thus you will more safely go about this action, if you say to yourself, "I will now go to bathe, and keep my own will in harmony with nature." And so with regard to every other action. For thus, if any impediment arises in bathing, you will be able to say, "It was not only to bathe that I desired, but to keep my will in harmony with nature; and I shall not keep it thus, if I am out of humor at things that happen."

V.

Men are disturbed not by things, but by the views which they take of things. Thus death is nothing terrible, else it would have appeared so to Socrates. But the terror consists in our notion of death, that it is terrible. When, therefore, we are hindered, or disturbed, or grieved, let us never impute it to others, but to ourselves; that is, to our own views. It is the action of an uninstructed person to reproach others for his own misfortunes; of one entering upon instruction, to reproach himself; and of one perfectly instructed, to reproach neither others or himself.

VI.

Be not elated at any excellence not your own. If a horse should be elated, and say, "I am handsome," it might be endurable. But when you are elated, and say, "I have a handsome horse," know that you are elated only on the merit of the horse. What then is your own? The use of phenomena of existence. So that when you are in harmony with nature in this respect, you will be elated with some reason; for you will be elated at some good of your own.

VII.

As in a voyage, when the ship is at anchor, if you go on shore to get water, you may amuse yourself with picking up a shell-fish or a truffle in your way, but your thoughts ought to be bent towards the ship, and perpetually attentive, lest the captain should call, and then you must leave all these things, that you may not have to be carried on board the vessel, bound like a sheep; thus likewise in life, if, instead of a truffle or shell-fish, such a thing as a wife or a child be granted you, there is not objection; but if the captain calls, run to the ship, leave all these things, and never look behind. But if you are old, never go far from the ship, lest you should be missing when called for.

VIII.

Demand not that events should happen as you wish; but wish them to happen as they do happen, and you will go on well.

IX.

Sickness is an impediment to the body, but not to the will, unless itself pleases. Lameness is an impediment to the leg, but not to the will; and say this to yourself with regard to everything that happens. For you will find it to be an impediment to something else, but not truly to yourself.

X.

Upon every accident, remember to turn towards yourself and inquire what faculty you have for its use. If you encounter a handsome person, you will find continence the faculty needed; if pain, then fortitude; if reviling, then patience. And when thus habituated, the phenomena of existence will not overwhelm you.

XI.

Never say of anything, "I have lost it;" but, "I have restored it." Has your child died? It is restored. Has your wife died? She is restored. Has your estate been taken away? That likewise is restored. "But it was a bad man who took it." What is it to you by whose hands he who gave it has demanded it again? While he permits you to possess it, hold it as something not your own; as do travellers at an inn.

XII.

If you would improve, lay aside such reasonings as these: "If I neglect my affairs, I shall not have a maintenance; if I do not punish my servant, he will be good for nothing." For it were better to die of hunger, exempt from grief and fear, than to live in affluence with perturbation; and it is better that your servant should be bad than you unhappy.

Begin therefore with little things. Is a little oil spilt or a little wine stolen? Say to yourself, "This is the price paid for peace and tranquillity; and nothing is to be had for nothing." And when you call your servant, consider that it is possible he may not come at your call; or, if he does, that he may not do what you wish. But it is not at all desirable for him, and very undesirable for you, that it should be in his power to cause you any disturbance.

### XIII.

If you would improve, be content to be thought foolish and dull with regard to externals. Do not desire to be thought to know anything; and though you should appear to others to be somebody, distrust yourself. For be assured, it is not easy at once to keep your will in harmony with nature, and to secure externals; but while you are absorbed in the one, you must of necessity neglect the other.

### XIV.

If you wish your children and your wife and your friends to live forever, you are foolish; for you wish things to be in your power which are not so; and what belongs to others to be your own. So likewise, if you wish your servant to be without fault, you are foolish; for you wish vice not to be vice, but something else. But if you wish not to be disappointed in your desires, that is in your own power. Exercise, therefore, what is in your power. A man's master is he who is able to confer or remove whatever that man seeks or shuns. Whoever then would be free, let him wish for nothing, let him decline nothing, which depends on others; else he must necessarily be a slave.

### XV.

Remember that you must behave as at a banquet. Is anything brought round to you? Put out your hand, and take a moderate share. Does it pass by you? Do not stop it. Is it not come yet? Do not yearn in desire towards it, but wait till it reaches you. So with regard to children, wife, office, riches; and you will some time or other be worthy to feast with the gods. And if you do not so much as take the things which are set before you, but are able even to forego them, then you will not only be worthy to feast with the gods, but to rule with them also. For, by thus doing, Diogenes and Heraclitus, and others like them, deservedly became divine, and were so recognized.

### XVI.

When you see any one weeping for grief, either that his son has gone abroad, or that he has suffered in his affairs, take care not to be overcome by the apparent evil; but discriminate, and be ready to say, "What hurts this man is not this occurrence itself, – for another man might not be hurt by it, – but the view he chooses to take of it." As far as conversation goes, however, do not disdain to accommodate yourself to him, and if need be, to groan with him. Take heed, however, not to groan inwardly too.

### XVII.

Remember that you are an actor in a drama of such sort as the author chooses, – if short, then in a short one; if long, then in a long one. If it be his pleasure that you should enact a poor man, see that you act it well; or a cripple, or a ruler, or a private citizen. For this is your business, to act well the given part; but to choose it, belongs to another.

### XVIII.

When a raven happens to croak unluckily, be not overcome by appearances, but discriminate, and say, – "Nothing is portended to *me*; but either to my paltry body, or property, or reputation, or children, or wife. But to *me* all portents are lucky, if I will. For whatsoever happens, it belongs to me to derive advantage therefrom."

### XIX.

You can be unconquerable, if you enter into no combat in which it is not in your own power to conquer. When, therefore, you see any one eminent in honors or power, or high esteem on any other account, take heed not to be bewildered by appearances and to pronounce him happy; for if the essence of good consists in things within our own power, there will be no room for envy or emulation. But, for your part, do not desire to be a general, or a senator, or a consul, but to be free; and the only way to this is a disregard of things which lie not within our own power.

### XX.

Remember that it is not he who gives abuse or blows who affronts; but the view we take of these things as insulting. When, therefore, any one provokes you, be assured that it is your own opinion which provokes you. Try, therefore, in the first place, not to be bewildered by appearances. For if you once gain time and respite, you will more easily command yourself.

### XXI.

Let death and exile, and all other things which appear terrible, be daily before your eyes, but death chiefly; and you will never entertain any abject thought, not too eagerly covet anything.

### XXII.

If you have an earnest desire towards philosophy, prepare yourself from the very first to have the multitude laugh and sneer, and say, "He is returned to us a philosopher all at once;" and "Whence this supercilious look?" Now, for your part, do not have a supercilious look indeed; but keep steadily to those things which appear best to you, as one appointed by God to this particular station. For remember that, if you are persistent, those very persons who at first ridiculed will afterwards admire you. But if you are conquered by them, you will incur a double ridicule.

### XXIII.

If you ever happen to turn your attention to externals, for the pleasure of any one, be assured that you have ruined your scheme of life. Be contented, then, in everything, with being a philosopher; and if you with to seem so likewise to any one, appear so to yourself, and it will suffice you.

### XXIV.

Let not such considerations as these distress you: "I shall live in discredit, and be nobody anywhere." For if discredit be an evil, you can no more be involved in any evil through another, than in baseness. Is it any business of yours, then, to get power, or to be admitted to an entertainment? By no means. How, then, after all, is this discredit? And how is it true that you will be nobody anywhere; when you ought to be somebody in those things only which are within your own power, in which you may be of the greatest consequence? "But my friends will be unassisted." What do you mean by unassisted? They will not have money from you; nor will you make them Roman citizens. Who told you, then, that these are among the things within our own power, and not rather the affair of others? And who can give to another the things which he has not? "Well, but get them, then, that we too may have a share." If I can get them with the preservation of my own honor and fidelity and self-respect, show me the way, and I will get them; but if you require me to lose my own proper good, that you may gain what is no good, consider how unreasonable and foolish you are. Besides, which would you rather have, a sum of money, or a faithful and honorable friend? Rather assist me, then, to gain this character, than require me to do those things by which I may lose it. Well, but my country, say you, as far as depends upon me, will be unassisted. Here, again, what assistance is this you mean? It will not have porticoes nor baths of your providing? And what signifies that? Why, neither does a smith provide it with shoes, or a shoemaker with arms. It is enough if every one fully performs his own proper business. And were you to supply it with another faithful and honorable citizen, would not he be of use to it? Yes. Therefore neither are you yourself useless to it. "What place, then," say you, "shall I hold in the state?" Whatever you can hold with the preservation of your fidelity and honor. But if, by desiring to be useful to that, you lose these, how can you serve your country, when you have become faithless and shameless?

### XXV.

Is any one preferred before you at an entertainment, or in courtesies, or in confidential conversation? If these things are good, you ought to rejoice that he has them; and if they are evil, do not be grieved that you have them not. And remember that you cannot be permitted to rival others in externals, without using the same means to obtain them. For how can he who will not haunt the door of any man, will not attend him, will not praise him, have an equal share with him who does these things? You are unjust, then, and unreasonable, if you are unwilling to pay the price for which these things are sold, and would have them for nothing. For how much are lettuces sold? An obolus, for instance. If another, then, paying an obolus, takes the lettuces, and you, not paying it, go without them, do not imagine that he has gained any advantage over you. For as he has the lettuces, so you have the obolus which you did not give. So, in the present case, you have not been invited to such a person's entertainment, because you have not paid him the price for which a supper is sold. It is sold for praise; it is sold for attendance. Give him, then, the value, if it be for your advantage. But if you would at the same time not pay the one, and yet receive the other, you are unreasonable, and foolish. Have you nothing, then, in place of the supper? Yes, indeed, you have: not to praise him whom you do not like to praise; not to bear the insolence of his lackeys.

XXVI.

The will of Nature may be learned from things upon which we are all agreed. As, when our neighbor's boy has broken a cup, or the like, we are ready at once to say, "These are casualties that will happen;" be assured, then, that when your own cup is likewise broken, you ought to be affected just as when another's cup was broken. Now apply this to greater things. Is the child or wife of another dead? There is no one who would not say, "This is an accident of mortality." But if any one's own child happens to die, it is immediately, "Alas! how wretched am I!" It should be always remembered how we are affected on hearing the same thing concerning others.

XXVII.

As a mark is not set up for the sake of missing the aim, so neither does the nature of evil exist in the world.

XXVIII.

If a person had delivered up your body to some passer-by, you would certainly be angry. And do you feel no shame in delivering up your own mind to any reviler, to be disconcerted and confounded?

XXIX.

In every affair consider what precedes and follows, and then undertake it. Otherwise you will begin with spirit indeed, careless of the consequences, and when these are developed, you will shamefully desist. "I would conquer at the Olympic games." But consider what precedes and follows, and then, if it be for your advantage, engage in the affair. You must conform to rules, submit to a diet, refrain from dainties; exercise your body, whether you choose it or not, at a stated hour, in heat and cold; you must drink no cold water, and sometimes no wine, – in a word, you must give yourself up to your trainer as to a physician. Then, in the combat, you may be thrown into a ditch, dislocate your arm, turn your ankle, swallow abundance of dust, receive stripes [for negligence], and, after all, lose the victory. When you have reckoned up all this, if your inclination still holds, set about the combat. Otherwise, take notice, you will behave like children who sometimes play wrestlers, sometimes gladiators, sometimes blow a trumpet, and sometimes act a tragedy, when they have seen and admired these shows. Thus you too will be at one time a wrestler, at another a gladiator; now a philosopher, now an orator; but nothing in earnest. Like an ape you mimic all you see, and one thing after another is sure to please you, but is out of favor as soon as it becomes familiar. For you have never entered upon anything considerately, nor after having surveyed and tested the whole matter; but carelessly, and with a half-way zeal. Thus some, when they have seen a philosopher, and heard a man speaking like Euphrates, – though indeed who can speak like him? – have a mind to be philosophers too. Consider first, man, what the matter is, and what your own nature is able to bear. If you would be a wrestler, consider your shoulders, your back, your thighs; for different persons are made for different things. Do you think that you can act as you do, and be a philosopher; that you can eat, drink, be angry, be discontented, as you are now? You must watch, you must labor, you must get the better of certain appetites; must quit your acquaintance, be despised by your servant, be laughed at by those you meet; come off worse than others in everything, – in offices, in honors, before tribunals. When you have fully considered all these things, approach, if you please; if, by parting with them, you have a mind to purchase serenity, freedom, and tranquillity. If not, do not come hither; do not, like children, be now a philosopher, then a publican, then an orator, and then one of Caesar's officers. These things are not consistent. You must be one man either good or bad. You must cultivate either your own Reason or else externals, apply yourself either to things within or without you; that is, be either a philosopher, or one of the mob.

### XXX.

Duties are universally measured by relations. Is a certain man your father? In this are implied, taking care of him; submitting to him in all things; patiently receiving his reproaches, his correction. But he is a bad father. Is your natural tie, then, to a *good* father? No, but to a father. Is a brother unjust? Well, preserve your own just relation towards him. Consider not what *he* does, but what *you* are to do, to keep your own will in state conformable to nature. For another cannot hurt you, unless you please. You will then be hurt when you consent to be hurt. In this manner, therefore, if you accustom yourself to contemplate the relations of neighbor, citizen, commander, you can deduce from each the corresponding duties.

### XXXI.

Be assured that the essential property of piety towards the gods lies in this, to form right opinions concerning them, as existing, and as governing the universe justly and well. And fix yourself in this resolution, to obey them, and yield to them, and willingly follow them amidst all events, as being ruled by the most perfect wisdom. For thus you will never find fault with the gods, nor accuse them of neglecting you. And it is not possible for this to be effected any other way than by withdrawing yourself from things which are not within our own power, and by making good or evil to consist only in those which are. For if you suppose any of the things to be either good or evil, it is inevitable that, when you are disappointed of what you wish, or incur what you would avoid, you should reproach and blame their authors. For every creature is naturally formed to flee and abhor things that appear hurtful, and that which causes them; and to pursue and admire those which appear beneficial, and that which causes them. It is impractical, then, that one who supposes himself to be hurt should rejoice in the person who, as he thinks, hurts him; just as it is impossible to rejoice in the hurt itself. Hence, also, a father is reviled by his son, when he does not impart the things which seem to be good; and this made Polynices and Eteocles mutually enemies, that empire seemed good to both. On this account the husbandman reviles the gods; the sailor, the merchant, or those who have lost wife or child. For where our interest is, there too is piety directed. So that whoever is careful to regulate his desires and aversions as he ought is thus made careful of piety likewise. But it also becomes incumbent on every one to offer libations and sacrifices and first-fruits, according to the customs of his country, purely, and not heedlessly nor negligently; nor avariciously, nor yet extravagantly.

XXXII.

When you have recourse to divination, remember that you know not what the event will be, and you come to learn it of the diviner; but of what nature it is you knew before coming; at least, if you are of philosophic mind. For if it is among the things not within our power, it can by no means be either good or evil. Do not, therefore, bring with you to the diviner either desire or aversion, – else you will approach him trembling, – but first clearly understand that every event is indifferent, and nothing to *you*, of whatever sort it may be; for it will be in your power to make a right use of it, and this no one can hinder. Then come with confidence to the gods as your counsellors; and afterwards, when any counsel is given you, remember what counsellors you have assumed, and whose advice you will neglect, if you disobey. Come to divination, as Socrates prescribed, in cases of which the whole consideration relates to the event, and in which no opportunities are afforded by reason, or any other art, to discover the matter in view. When, therefore, it is our duty to share the danger of a friend or of our country, we ought not to consult the oracle as to whether we shall share it with them or not. For though the diviner should forewarn you that the auspices are unfavorable, this means no more than that either death or mutilation or exile is portended. But we have reason within us; and it directs, even with these hazards, to stand by our friend and country. Attend, therefore, to the greater diviner, the Pythian god, who once cast out of the temple him who neglected to save his friend.

XXXIII.

Begin by prescribing to yourself some character and demeanor, such as you may preserve both alone and in company.

Be mostly silent; or speak merely what is needful, and in few words. We may, however, enter sparingly into discourse sometimes, when occasion calls for it; but let it not run on any of the common subjects, as gladiators, or horse-races, or athletic champions, or food, or drink, – the vulgar topics of conversation; and especially not on men, so as either to blame, or praise, or make comparisons. If you are able, then, by your own conversation, bring over that of your company to proper subjects; but if you happen to find yourself among strangers, be silent.

Let not your laughter be loud, frequent, or abundant.

Avoid taking oaths, if possible, altogether; at any rate, so far as you are able.

Avoid public and vulgar entertainments; but if ever an occasion calls you to them, keep your attention upon the stretch, that you may not imperceptibly slide into vulgarity. For be assured that if a person be ever so pure himself, yet, if his companion be corrupted, he who converses with him will be corrupted likewise.

Provide things relating to the body no farther than absolute need requires; as meat, drink, clothing, house, retinue. But cut off everything that looks towards show and luxury.

Before marriage, guard yourself with all your ability from unlawful intercourse with women; yet be not uncharitable or severe to those who are led into this, not frequently boast that you yourself do otherwise.

If any one tells you that such a person speaks ill of you, do not make excuses about what is said of you, but answer: "He was ignorant of my other faults, else he would not have mentioned these alone."

It is not necessary for you to appear often at public spectacles; but if ever there is a proper occasion for you to be there, do not appear more solicitous for any other than for yourself; that is, wish things to be only just as they are, and only the best man to win: for thus nothing will go against you. But abstain entirely from acclamations and derision and violent emotions. And when you come away, do not discourse a great deal on what has passed, and what contributes nothing to your own amendment. For it would appear by such discourse that you were dazzled by the show.

Be not prompt or ready to attend private recitations; but if you do attend, preserve your gravity and dignity, and yet avoid making yourself disagreeable.

When you are going to confer with any one, and especially with one who seems your superior, represent to yourself how Socrates or Zeno would behave in such a case, and you will not be at a loss to meet properly whatever may occur.

When you are going before any one in power, fancy to yourself that you may not find him at home, that you may be shut out, that the doors may not be opened to you, that he may not notice you. If, with all this, it be your duty to go, bear what happens, and never say to yourself, "It was not worth so much." For this is vulgar, and like a man bewildered by externals.

In society, avoid a frequent and excessive mention of your own actions and dangers. For however agreeable it may be to yourself to allude to risks you have run, it is not equally agreeable to others to hear your adventures. Avoid likewise an endeavor to excite laughter. For this may readily slide you into vulgarity, and, besides, may be apt to lower you in the esteem of your acquaintance. Approaches to indecent discourse are likewise dangerous. Therefore when anything of this sort happens, use the first fit opportunity to rebuke him who makes advances that way; or, at least, by silence and blushing and a serious look, show yourself to be displeased by such talk.

### XXXIV.
If you are dazzled by the semblance of any promised pleasure; guard yourself against being bewildered by it; but let the affair wait your leisure, and procure yourself some delay. Then bring to your mind both points of time, – that in which you shall enjoy the pleasure, and that in which you will repent and reproach yourself, after you have enjoyed it, – and set before you, in opposition to these, how you will rejoice and applaud yourself, if you abstain. And even though it should appear to you a seasonable gratification, take heed that its enticements and allurements and seductions may not subdue you; but set in opposition to this, how much better it is to be conscious of having gained so great a victory.

### XXXV.
When you do anything from a clear judgment that it ought to be done, never shrink from being seen to do it, even though the world should misunderstand it; for if you are not acting rightly, shun the action itself; if you are, why fear those who wrongly censure you?

### XXXVI.
As the proposition, *either it is day, or it is night*, has much force in a disjunctive argument, but none at all in a conjunctive one; so, at a feast, to choose the largest share is very suitable to the bodily appetite, but utterly inconsistent with the social spirit of the entertainment. Remember, then, when you eat with another, not only the value to the body of those things which are set before you, but also the value of proper courtesy toward your host.

### XXXVII.
If you have assumed any character beyond your strength, you have both demeaned yourself ill that, and quitted one which you might have supported.

### XXXVIII.
As in walking you take care not to tread upon a nail, or turn your foot, so likewise take care not to hurt the ruling faculty of your mind. And if we were to

guard against this in every action, we should enter upon action more safely.

### XXXIX.

The body is to every one the proper measure of its possessions, as the foot is of the shoe. If, therefore, you stop at this, you will keep the measure; but if you move beyond it, you must necessarily be carried forward, as down a precipice; as in the case of a shoe, if you go beyond its fitness to the foot, it comes first to be gilded, then purple, and then studded with jewels. For to that which once exceeds the fit measure there is no bound.

### XL.

Women from fourteen years old are flattered by men with the title of mistresses. Therefore, perceiving that they are regarded only as qualified to give men pleasure, they begin to adorn themselves, and in that to place all their hopes. It is worth while, therefore, to try that they may perceive themselves honored only so far as they appear beautiful in their demeanor, and modestly virtuous.

### XLI.

It is a mark of want of intellect, to spend much time in things relating to the body; as to be immoderate in exercises, in eating and drinking, and in the discharge of other animal functions. These things should be done incidentally and our main strength be applied to our reason.

### XLII.

When any person does ill by you, or speaks ill of you, remember that he acts or speaks from an impression that it is right for him to do so. Now, it is not possible that he should follow what appears right to you, but only what appears so to himself. Therefore, if he judges from false appearances, he is the person hurt; since he too is the person deceived. For if any one takes a true proposition to be false, the proposition is not hurt, but only the man is deceived. Setting out, then, from these principles, you will meekly bear with a person who reviles you; for you will say upon every occasion, "It seemed so to him."

### XLIII.

Everything has two handles: one by which it may be borne, another by which it cannot. If your brother acts unjustly, do not lay hold on the affair by the handle of his injustice, for by that it cannot be borne; but rather by the opposite, that he is your brother, that he was brought up with you; and thus you will lay hold on it as it is to be borne.

### XLIV.

These reasonings have no logical connection: "I am richer than you; therefore I am superior." "I am more eloquent than you; therefore I am your superior." The true logical connection is rather this: "I am richer than you; therefore my possessions must exceed yours." "I am more eloquent than you; therefore my style must surpass yours." But you, after all, consist neither in property nor in style.

### XLV.

Does any one bathe hastily? Do not say that he does it ill, but hastily. Does any one drink much wine? Do not say that he does ill, but that he drinks a great deal. For unless you perfectly understand his motives, how should you know if he acts ill? Thus you will not risk yielding to any appearances but such as you fully comprehend.

### XLVI.

Never proclaim yourself a philosopher; nor make much talk among the ignorant about your principles, but show them by actions. Thus, at an entertainment, do not discourse how people ought to eat; but eat as you ought. For remember that thus Socrates also universally avoided all ostentation. And when persons came to him, and desired to be introduced by him to philosophers, he took them and introduced them; so well did he bear being overlooked. So if ever there should be among the ignorant any discussion of principles, be for the most part silent. For there is great danger in hastily throwing out what is undigested. And if any one tells you that you know nothing, and you are not nettled at it, then you may be sure that you have really entered on your work. For sheep do not hastily throw up the grass, to show the shepherds how much they have eaten; but, inwardly digesting their food, they produce it outwardly in wool and milk. Thus, therefore, do you not make an exhibition before the ignorant of your principles; but of the actions to which their digestion gives rise.

### XLVII.

When you have learned to nourish your body frugally, do not pique yourself upon it; nor, if you drink water, be saying upon every occasion, "I drink water." But first consider how much more frugal are the poor than we, and how much more patient of hardship. If at any time you would inure yourself by exercise to labor and privation, for your own sake and not for the public, do not attempt great feats; but when you are violently thirsty, just rinse your mouth with water, and tell nobody.

### XLVIII.

The condition and characteristic of a vulgar person is that he never looks for either help or harm from himself, but only from externals. The condition and characteristic of a philosopher is that he looks to himself for all help or harm. The marks of a proficient are that he censures no one, praises no one, blames no one, accuses no one; says nothing concerning himself as being anybody, or knowing anything. When he is in any instance hindered or restrained, he accuses himself; and if he is praised, he smiles to himself at the person who praises him; and if he is censured, he makes no defence. But he goes about with the caution of a convalescent, careful of interference with anything that is doing well, but not yet quite secure. He restrains desire; he transfers his aversion to those things only which thwart the proper use of our own will; he employs his energies moderately in all directions; if he appears stupid or ignorant, he does not care; and, in a word, he keeps watch over himself as over an enemy and one in ambush.

### XLIX.

When any one shows himself vain, on being able to understand and interpret the works of Chrysippus, say to yourself: "Unless Chrysippus had written obscurely, this person would have had nothing to be vain of. But what do I desire? To understand Nature, and follow her. I ask, then, who interprets her; and hearing that Chrysippus does, I have recourse to him. I do not understand his writings. I seek, therefore, one to interpret *them*." So far there is nothing to value myself upon. And when I find an interpreter, what remains is to make use of his instructions. This alone is the valuable thing. But if I admire merely the interpretation, what do I become more than a grammarian, instead of a philosopher, except, indeed, that instead of Homer I interpret Chrysippus? When any one, therefore, desires me to read Chrysippus to him, I rather blush, when I cannot exhibit actions that are harmonious and consonant with his discourse.

### L.

Whatever rules you have adopted, abide by them as laws, and as if you would be impious to transgress them; and do not regard what any one says of you, for this, after all, is no concern of yours.

### LI.

How long, then, will you delay to demand of yourself the noblest improvements, and in no instance to transgress the judgments of reason? You have received the philosophic principles with which you ought to be conversant; and you have been conversant with them. For what other master, then, do you wait as an excuse for this delay in self-reformation? You are no longer a boy, but a grown man. If, therefore, you will be negligent and slothful, and always add procrastination to procrastination, purpose to purpose, and fix day after day in which you will attend to yourself, you will insensibly continue to accomplish nothing, and, living and dying, remain of vulgar mind. This instant, then, think yourself worthy of living as a noun grown up and a proficient. Let whatever appears to be the best, be to you an inviolable law. And if any instance of pain or pleasure, glory or disgrace, be set before you, remember that now is the combat, now the Olympiad comes on, nor can it be put off; and that by one failure and defeat honor may be lost – or won. Thus Socrates became perfect, improving himself by everything, following reason alone. And though you are not yet a Socrates, you ought, however, to live as one seeking to be a Socrates.

### LII.

The first and the most necessary topic in philosophy is the practical application of principles, as, *We ought not to lie*; the second is that of demonstrations, as, *Why it is that we ought not to lie*; the third, that which gives strength and logical connection to the other two, as, *Why this is a demonstration.* For what is demonstration? What is a consequence; what a contradiction; what truth; what falsehood? The third point is then necessary on account of the second; and the second on account of the first. But the most necessary, and that whereon we ought to rest, is the first. But we do just the contrary. For we spend all our time on the third point, and employ all our diligence about that, and entirely neglect the first. Therefore, at the same time that we lie, we are very ready to show how it is demonstrated that lying is wrong.

LIII.
Upon all occasions we ought to have these maxims ready at hand: –
"Conduct me, Zeus, and thou, O Destiny,
Wherever your decrees have fixed my lot.
I follow cheerfully; and, did I not,
Wicked and wretched, I must follow still."[1]
"Whoe'er yields properly to Fate is deemed
Wise among men, and knows the laws of Heaven."[2]
And this third: –
"O Crito, if it thus pleases the gods, thus let it be.
Anytus and Melitus may kill me indeed; but hurt me they cannot."[3]

---

[1] Cleanthes, *Hymn to Zeus*, quoted by Seneca, Epistle 107.
[2] Euripides, Fragment 965 Nauck.
[3] Plato, *Crito* 43d; *Apology* 30c–d.

*Lucius Annaeus Seneca (4 BCE – 65 CE) was a Roman Stoic who was not only a philosopher, but a politician, writer, and tutor/advisor to the Emperor Nero. A prolific and talented writer, some of his "personal letters" serve as "essays in disguise." Though they are thought to be genuine letters, it is also believed they were intended for publication, and served as a new medium with which Seneca could deliver his ideas. In what follows, you will find selections from two of Seneca's letters. One is entitled "On the Shortness of Life," and addresses both the sting of death as well as providing inspiration to live fully while we still can. The other, entitled "To Marcia, On Consolation," is an application of Stoic philosophy to the problem of grief.*

# The Sixth Book of Dialogues of L. Annaeus Seneca, Addressed to Marcia. On Consolation.

**[From: *L. Annaeus Seneca, Minor Dialogs Together with the Dialog "On Clemency"*; Translated by Aubrey Stewart, M.A., Late Fellow of Trinity College Cambridge, pp. 162-203]**

I.

DID I not know, Marcia, that you have as little of a woman's weakness of mind as of her other vices, and that your life was regarded as a pattern of antique virtue, I should not have dared to combat your grief, which is one that many men fondly nurse and embrace, nor should I have conceived the hope of persuading you to hold fortune blameless, having to plead for her at such an unfavorable time, before so partial a judge, and against such an odious charge. I derive confidence, however, from the proved strength of your mind, and your virtue, which has been proved by a severe test. All men know how well you behaved towards your father, whom you loved as dearly as your children in all respects, save that you did not wish him to survive you: indeed, for all that I know you may have wished that also: for great affection ventures to break some of the golden rules of life. You did all that lay in your power to avert the death of your father, Aulus Cremutius Cordus ;[1] but when it became clear that, surrounded as he was by the myrmidons of Sejanus, there was no other way of escape from slavery, you did not indeed approve of his resolution, but gave up all attempts to oppose it; you shed tears openly, and choked down your sobs, yet did not screen them behind a smiling face; and you did all this in the present century, when not to be unnatural towards one's parents is considered the height of filial affection. When the changes of our times gave you an opportunity, you restored to the use of man that genius of your father for which he had suffered, and made him in real truth immortal by publishing as an eternal memorial of him those books which that bravest of men had written with his own blood. You have done a great service to Roman literature: a large part of Cordus's books had been burned; a great service to posterity, who will receive a true account of events, which cost its author so dear; and a great service to himself, whose memory flourishes and ever will flourish, as long as men set any value upon the facts of Roman history, as long as any one lives who wishes to review the deeds of our fathers, to know what a true Roman was like—one who still remained unconquered when all other necks were broken in to receive the yoke of Sejanus, one who was free in every thought, feeling, and act. By Hercules, the state would have sustained a great loss if you had not brought him forth from the oblivion to which his two splendid qualities, eloquence and independence, had consigned him: he is now read, is popular, is received into men's hands and bosoms, and fears no old age: but as for those who butchered him, before long men will cease to speak even of their crimes, the only things by which they are remembered. This greatness of mind in you has forbidden me to take into consideration your sex or your face, still clouded by the sorrow by which so many years ago it was suddenly overcast. See; I shall do nothing underhand, nor try to steal away your sorrows: I have reminded you of old hurts, and to prove that your present wound may be healed, I have shown you the scar of one which was equally severe. Let others use soft measures and caresses; I have determined to do battle with your grief, and I will dry those weary and exhausted eyes, which already, to tell you the truth, are weeping more from habit than from sorrow. I will effect this cure, if possible, with your goodwill: if you disapprove of my efforts, or dislike them, then you must continue to hug and fondle the grief which you have adopted as the survivor of your son. What, I pray you, is to be the end of it? All means have been tried in vain : the consolations of your friends, who are weary of offering them, and the influence of great men who are related to you: literature, a taste which your father enjoyed and which you have inherited from him, now finds your ears closed, and affords you but a futile consolation, which scarcely engages your thoughts for a moment. Even time itself, nature's greatest remedy, which quiets the most bitter grief, loses its power with you alone. Three years have already passed, and still your grief has lost none of its first poignancy, but renews and strengthens itself day by day, and has now dwelt so long with you that it has acquired a domicile in your mind, and actually thinks that it would be base to leave it. All vices sink into our whole being, if we do not crush them before they gain a footing; and in like manner these sad, pitiable, and discordant feelings end by feeding upon their own bitterness, until the unhappy mind takes a sort of morbid delight in grief. I should have liked, therefore, to have attempted to effect this cure in the earliest stages of the disorder, before its force was fully developed; it might have been checked by milder remedies, but now that it has been confirmed by time it cannot be beaten without a hard struggle. In like manner, wounds heal easily when the blood is fresh upon them: they can then be cleared out and brought to the surface, and admit of being probed by the finger: when disease has turned them into malignant ulcers, their cure is more difficult. I cannot now influence so strong a grief by polite and mild measures: it must be broken down by force.

II.

I am aware that all who wish to give any one advice begin with precepts, and end with examples: but it is sometimes useful to alter this fashion, for we must deal differently with different people. Some are guided by reason, others must be confronted with authority and the names of celebrated persons, whose brilliancy dazzles their mind and destroys their power of free judgment. I will place before your eyes two of the greatest examples belonging to your sex and your century: one, that of a woman who allowed herself to be entirely carried away by grief; the other, one who, though afflicted by a like misfortune, and an even greater loss, yet did not allow her sorrows to reign over her for a very long time, but quickly restored her mind to its accustomed frame. Octavia and Livia, the former Augustus's sister, the latter his wife, both lost their sons when they were young men, and when they were certain of succeeding to the throne. Octavia lost Marcellus, whom both his father-in-law and his uncle had begun to depend upon, and to place upon his shoulders the weight of the empire—a young man of keen intelligence and firm character, frugal and moderate in his desires to an extent which deserved especial admiration in one so young and so wealthy, strong to endure labour, averse to indulgence, and able to bear whatever burden his uncle might choose to lay, or I may say to pile upon his shoulders. Augustus had well chosen him as a foundation, for he would not have given way under any weight, however excessive. His mother never ceased to weep and sob during her whole life, never endured to listen to wholesome advice, never even allowed her thoughts to be diverted from her sorrow. She remained during her whole life just as she was during the funeral, with all the strength of her mind intently fixed upon one subject. I do not say that she lacked the courage to shake off her grief, but she refused to be comforted, thought that it would be a second bereavement to lose her tears, and would not have any portrait of her darling son, nor allow any allusion to be made to him. She hated all mothers, and raged against Livia with especial fury, because it seemed as though the brilliant prospect once in store for her own child was now transferred to Livia's son. Passing all her days in darkened rooms and alone, not conversing even with her brother, she refused to accept the poems which were composed in memory of Marcellus, and all the other honours paid him by literature, and closed her ears against all consolation. She lived buried and hidden from view, neglecting her accustomed duties, and actually angry with the excessive splendour of her brother's prosperity, in which she shared. Though surrounded by her children and grandchildren, she would not lay aside her mourning garb, though by retaining it she seemed to put a slight upon all her relations, in thinking herself bereaved in spite of their being alive.

III.

Livia lost her son Drusus, who would have been a great emperor, and was already a great general: he had marched far into Germany, and had planted the Roman standards in places where the very existence of the Romans was hardly known. He died on the march, his very foes treating him with respect, observing a reciprocal truce, and not having the heart to wish for what would do them most service. In addition to his dying thus in his country's service, great sorrow for him was expressed by the citizens, the provinces, and the whole of Italy, through which his corpse was attended by the people of the free towns and colonies, who poured out to perform the last sad offices to him, till it reached Rome in a procession which resembled a triumph. His mother was not permitted to receive his last kiss and gather the last fond words from his dying lips: she followed the relics of her Drusus on their long journey, though every one of the funeral pyres with which all Italy was glowing seemed to renew her grief, as though she had lost him so many times. When, however, she at last laid him in the tomb, she left her sorrow there with him, and grieved no more than was becoming to a Caesar or due to a son. She did not cease to make frequent mention of the name of her Drusus, to set up his portrait in all places, both public and private, and to speak of him and listen while others spoke of him with the greatest pleasure: she lived with his memory; which none can embrace and consort with who has made it painful to himself.[2] Choose, therefore, which of these two examples you think the more commendable: if you prefer to follow the former, you will remove yourself from the number of the living; you will shun the sight both of other people's children and of your own, and even of him whose loss you deplore; you will be looked upon by mothers as an omen of evil; you will refuse to take part in honourable, permissible pleasures, thinking them unbecoming for one so afflicted; you will be loath to linger above ground, and will be especially angry with your age, because it will not straightway bring your life abruptly to an end. I here put the best construction on what is really most contemptible and foreign to your character. I mean that you will show yourself unwilling to live, and unable to die. If, on the other hand, showing a milder and better regulated spirit, you try to follow the example of the latter most exalted lady, you will not be in misery, nor will you wear your life out with suffering. Plague on it! what madness this is, to punish one's self because one is unfortunate, and not to lessen, but to increase one's ills! You ought to display, in this matter also, that decent behaviour and modesty which has characterised all your life: for there is such a thing as self-restraint in grief also. You will show more respect for the youth himself, who well deserves that it should make you glad to speak and think of him, if you make him able to meet his mother with a cheerful countenance, even as he was wont to do when alive.

IV.
I will not invite you to practise the sterner kind of maxims, nor bid you bear the lot of humanity with more than human philosophy; neither will I attempt to dry a mother's eyes on the very day of her son's burial. I will appear with you before an arbitrator: the matter upon which we shall join issue is, whether grief ought to be deep or unceasing. I doubt not that you will prefer the example of Julia Augusta, who was your intimate friend: she invites you to follow her method: she, in her first paroxysm, when grief is especially keen and hard to bear, betook herself for consolation to Areus, her husband's teacher in philosophy, and declared that this did her much good; more good than the thought of the Roman people, whom she was unwilling to sadden by her mourning; more than Augustus, who, staggering under the loss of one of his two chief supporters, ought

not to be yet more bowed down by the sorrow of his relatives; more even than her son Tiberius, whose affection during that untimely burial of one for whom whole nations wept made her feel that she had only lost one member of her family. This was, I imagine, his introduction to and grounding in philosophy of a woman peculiarly tenacious of her own opinion :—"Even to the present day, Julia, as far as I can tell—and I was your husband's constant companion, and knew not only what all men were allowed to know, but all the most secret thoughts of your hearts — you have been careful that no one should find anything to blame in your conduct; not only in matters of importance, but even in trifles you have taken pains to do nothing which you could wish common fame, that most frank judge of the acts of princes, to overlook. Nothing, I think, is more admirable than that those who are in high places should pardon many shortcomings in others, and have to ask it for none of their own. So also in this matter of mourning you ought to act up to your maxim of doing nothing which you could wish undone, or done otherwise.

V.

"In the next place, I pray and beseech you not to be self-willed and beyond the management of your friends. You must be aware that none of them know how to behave, whether to mention Drusus in your presence or not, as they neither wish to wrong a noble youth by forgetting him nor to hurt you by speaking of him. When we leave you and assemble together by ourselves, we talk freely about his sayings and doings, treating them with the respect which they deserve: in your presence deep silence is observed about him, and thus you lose that greatest of pleasures, the hearing the praises of your son, which I doubt not you would be willing to hand down to all future ages, had you the means of so doing, even at the cost of your own life. Wherefore endure to listen to, nay, encourage conversation of which he is the subject, and let your ears be open to the name and memory of your son. You ought not to consider this painful, like those who in such a case think that part of their misfortune consists in listening to consolation. As it is, you have altogether run into the other extreme, and, forgetting the better aspects of your lot, look only upon its worse side: you pay no attention to the pleasure you have had in your son's society and your joyful meetings with him, the sweet caresses of his babyhood, the progress of his education: you fix all your attention upon that last scene of all: and to this, as though it were not shocking enough, you add every horror you can. Do not, I implore you, take a perverse pride in appearing the most unhappy of women: and reflect also that there is no great credit in behaving bravely in times of prosperity, when life glides easily with a favouring current- neither does; a calm sea and fair wind display the art of the pilot . some foul weather is wanted to prove his courage. Like him, then, do not give way, but rather plant yourself firmly, and endure whatever burden may fall upon you from above; scared though you may have been at the first roar of the tempest. There is nothing that fastens such a reproach [3] on Fortune as resignation." After this he points out to her the son who is yet alive: he points out grandchildren from the lost one.

VI.

It is your trouble, Marcia, which has been dealt with here: it is beside your couch of mourning that Areus has been sitting: change the characters, and it is you whom he has been consoling. But, on the other hand, Marcia, suppose that you have sustained a greater loss than ever mother did before you: see, I am not soothing you or making light of your misfortune: if fate can be overcome by tears, let us bring tears to bear upon it: let every day be passed in mourning, every night be spent in sorrow instead of sleep: let your breast be torn by your own hands, your very face attacked by them, and every kind of cruelty be practised by your grief, if it will profit you. But if the dead cannot be brought back to life, however much we may beat our breasts, if destiny remains fixed and immoveable forever, not to be changed by any sorrow, however great, and death does not loose his hold of anything that he once has taken away, then let our futile grief be brought to an end. Let us, then, steer our own course, and no longer allow ourselves to be driven to leeward by the force of our misfortune. He is a sorry pilot who lets the waves wring his rudder from his grasp, who leaves the sails to fly loose, and abandons the ship to the storm: but he who boldly grasps the helm and clings to it until the sea closes over him, deserves praise even though he be shipwrecked.

VII.

"But," say you, "sorrow for the loss of one's own children is natural." Who denies it? provided it be reasonable? for we cannot help feeling a pang, and the stoutest-hearted of us are cast down not only at the death of those dearest to us, but even when they leave us on a journey. Nevertheless, the mourning which public opinion enjoins is more than nature insists upon. Observe how intense and yet how brief are the sorrows of dumb animals: we hear a cow lowing for one or two days, nor do mares pursue their wild and senseless gallops for longer: wild beasts after they have tracked their lost cubs throughout the forest, and often visited their plundered dens, quench their rage within a short space of time. Birds circle round their empty nests with loud and piteous cries, yet almost immediately resume their ordinary flight in silence; nor does any creature spend long periods in sorrowing for the loss of its offspring, except man, who encourages his own grief, the measure of which depends not upon his sufferings, but upon his will. You may know that to be utterly broken down by grief is not natural, by observing that the same bereavement inflicts a deeper wound upon women than upon men, upon savages than upon civilized and cultivated persons, upon the unlearned than upon the learned: yet those passions which derive their force from nature are equally powerful in all men: therefore it is dear that a passion of varying strength cannot be a natural one. Fire will burn all people equally, male and female, of every rank and every age: steel will exhibit its cutting power on all bodies alike: and why? Because these things derive their strength from nature, which makes no distinction of persons. Poverty, grief, and ambition,[4] are felt differently by different people, according as they are influenced by habit: a rooted prejudice about the terrors of these things, though they are not really to be feared, makes a man weak and unable to endure them.

VIII.

Moreover, that which depends upon nature is not weakened by delay, but grief is gradually effaced by time. However obstinate it may be, though it be daily renewed and be exasperated by all attempts to soothe it, yet even this becomes weakened by time, which is the most efficient means of taming its fierceness. You, Marcia, have still a mighty sorrow abiding with you, nevertheless it already appears to have become blunted: it is obstinate and enduring, but not so acute as it was at first: and this also will be taken from you piecemeal by succeeding years. Whenever you are engaged in other pursuits your mind will be relieved from its burden: at present you keep watch over yourself to prevent this. Yet there is a great difference between allowing and forcing yourself to grieve. How much more in accordance with your cultivated taste it would be to put an end to your mourning instead of looking for the end to come, and not to wait for the day when your sorrow shall cease against your will: dismiss it of your own accord.

IX.

"Why then," you ask, "do we show such persistence in mourning for our friends, if it be not nature that bids us do so?" It is because we never expect that any evil will befall ourselves before it comes, we will not be taught by seeing the misfortunes of others that they are the common inheritance of all men, but imagine that the path which we have begun to tread is free from them and less beset by dangers than that of other people. How many funerals pass our houses? yet we do not think of death. How many untimely deaths? we think only of our son's coming of age, of his service in the army, or of his succession to his father's estate. How many rich men suddenly sink into poverty before our very eyes, without its ever occurring to our minds that our own wealth is exposed to exactly the same risks? When, therefore, misfortune befalls us, we cannot help collapsing all the more completely, because we are struck as it were unawares: a blow which has long been foreseen falls much less heavily upon us. Do you wish to know how completely exposed you are to every stroke of fate, and that the same shafts which have transfixed others are whirling around yourself? Then imagine that you are mounting without sufficient armour to assault some city wall or some strong and lofty position manned by a great host, expect a wound, and suppose that all those stones, arrows, and darts which fill the upper air are aimed at your body: whenever anyone falls at your side or behind your back, exclaim, "Fortune, you will not outwit me, or catch me confident and heedless: I know what you are preparing to do: you have struck down another, but you aimed at me." Whoever looks upon his own affairs as though he were at the point of death? which of us ever dares to think about banishment, want, or mourning? who, if advised to meditate upon these subjects, would not reject the idea like an evil omen, and bid it depart from him and alight on the heads of his enemies, or even on that of his untimely adviser? "I never thought it would happen!" How can you think that anything will not happen, when you know that it may happen to many men, and has happened to many? That is a noble verse, and worthy of a nobler source than the stage:—

"What one hath suffered may befall us all."

That man has lost his children: you may lose yours. That man has been convicted: your innocence is in peril. We are deceived and weakened by this delusion, when we suffer what we never foresaw that we possibly could suffer: but by looking forward to the coming of our sorrows we take the sting out of them when they come.

X.

My Marcia, all these adventitious circumstances which glitter around us, such as children, office in the state, wealth, large halls, vestibules crowded with clients seeking vainly for admittance, a noble name, a well-born or beautiful wife, and every other thing which depends entirely upon uncertain and changeful fortune, are but furniture which is not our own, but entrusted to us on loan: none of these things are given to us outright: the stage of our lives is adorned with properties gathered from various sources, and soon to be returned to their several owners: some of them will be taken away on the first day, some on the second, and but few will remain till the end. We have, therefore, no grounds for regarding ourselves with complacency, as though the things which surround us were our own: they are only borrowed: we have the use and enjoyment of them for a time regulated by the lender, who controls his own gift: it is our duty always to be able to lay our hands upon what has been lent us with no fixed date for its return, and to restore it when called upon without a murmur: the most detestable kind of debtor is he who rails at his creditor. Hence all our relatives, both those who by the order of their birth we hope will outlive ourselves, and those who themselves most properly wish to die before us, ought to be loved by us as persons whom we cannot be sure of having with us forever, nor even for long. We ought frequently to remind ourselves that we must love the things of this life as we would what is shortly to leave us, or indeed in the very act of leaving us. Whatever gift Fortune bestows upon a man, let him think while he enjoys it, that it will prove as fickle as the goddess from whom it came. Snatch what pleasure you can from your children, allow your children in their turn to take pleasure in your society, and drain every pleasure to the dregs without any delay. We cannot reckon on tonight, nay, I have allowed too long a delay, we cannot reckon on this hour: we most make haste: the enemy presses on behind us: soon that society of yours will be broken up, that pleasant company will be taken by assault and dispersed. Pillage is the universal law: unhappy creatures, know you not that life is but a flight? If you grieve for the death of your son, the fault lies with the time when he was born, for at his birth he was told that death was his doom: it is the law under which he was born, the fate which has pursued him ever since he left his mother's womb. We have come under the dominion of Fortune, and a harsh and unconquerable dominion it is: at her caprice we must suffer all things whether we deserve them or not. She maltreats our bodies with anger, insult, and cruelty: some she burns, the fire being sometimes applied as a punishment and sometimes as a remedy: some she imprisons, allowing it to be done at one time by our enemies, at another by our countrymen: she tosses others naked on the changeful seas, and after their struggle with the waves will not even cast them out upon the sand or the shore, but will entomb them in the belly of some huge sea-monster: she wears away others to a skeleton by diverse kinds of disease, and keeps them long in suspense between life and death: she is as capricious in her rewards and punishments as a fickle, whimsical, and careless mistress is with those of her slaves.

XI.

Why need we weep over parts of our life? the whole of it calls for tears: new miseries assail us before we have freed ourselves from the old ones. You, therefore, who allow them to trouble you to an unreasonable extent ought especially to restrain yourselves, and to muster all the powers of the human breast to combat your fears and your pains. Moreover, what forgetfulness of your own position and that of mankind is this? You were born a mortal, and you have given birth to mortals: yourself a weak and fragile body, liable to all diseases, can you have hoped to produce anything strong and lasting from such unstable materials? Your son has died: in other words he has reached that goal towards which those whom you regard as more fortunate than your offspring are still hastening. this is the point towards which move at different rates all the crowds which are squabbling in the law courts, sitting in the theatres, praying in the temples. Those whom you love and those whom you despise will both be made equal in the same ashes. This is the meaning of that command, KNOW THYSELF, which is written on the shrine of the Pythian oracle. What is man? a potter's vessel, to be broken by the slightest shake or toss: it requires no great storm to rend you asunder: you fall to pieces wherever you strike. What is man? a weakly and frail body, naked, without any natural protection, dependent on the help of others, exposed to all the scorn of Fortune; even when his muscles are well trained he is the prey and the food of the first wild beast he meets, formed of weak and unstable substances, fair in outward feature, but unable to endure cold, heat, or labour, and yet falling to ruin if kept in sloth and idleness, fearing his very victuals, for he is starved if he has them not, and bursts if he has too much. He cannot be kept safe without anxious care, his breath only stays in the body on sufferance, and has no real hold upon it; he starts at every sudden danger, every loud and unexpected noise that reaches his ears. Ever a cause of anxiety to ourselves, diseased and useless as we are, can we be surprised at the death of a creature which can be killed by a single hiccup? Is it a great undertaking to put an end to us? why, smells, tastes, fatigue and want of sleep, food and drink, and the very necessaries of life, are mortal. Whithersoever he moves he straightway becomes conscious of his weakness, not being able to bear all climates, falling sick after drinking strange water, breathing an air to which he is not accustomed, or from other causes and reasons of the most trifling kind, frail, sickly, entering upon his life with weeping: yet nevertheless what a disturbance this despicable creature makes! what ideas it conceives, forgetting its lowly condition! It exercises its mind upon matters which are immortal and eternal, and arranges the affairs of its grandchildren and great-grandchildren, while death surprises it in the midst of its far-reaching schemes, and what we call old age is but the round of a very few years.

## XII.

Supposing that your sorrow has any method at all, iIs it your own sufferings or those of him who is gone that it has in view? Why do you grieve over your lost son? is it because you have received no pleasure from him, or because you would have received more had he lived longer? If you answer that you have received no pleasure from him you make your loss more endurable: for men miss less when lost what has given them no enjoyment or gladness. If, again, you admit that you have received much pleasure, it is your duty not to complain of that part which you have lost, but to return thanks for that which you have enjoyed. His rearing alone ought to have brought you a sufficient return for your labours, for it can hardly be that those who take the greatest pains to rear puppies, birds, and such like paltry objects of amusement derive a certain pleasure from the sight and touch and fawning caresses of these dumb creatures, and yet that those who rear children should not find their reward in doing so. Thus, even though his industry may have gained nothing for you, his carefulness may have saved nothing for you, his foresight may have given you no advice, yet you found sufficient reward in having owned him and loved him. "But," say you, "it might have lasted longer." True, but you have been better dealt with than if you had never had a son, for, supposing you were given your choice, which is the better lot, to be happy for a short time or not at all? It is better to enjoy pleasures which soon leave us than to enjoy none at all. Which, again, would you choose? to have had one who was a disgrace to you, and who merely filled the position and owned the name of your son, or one of such noble character as your son's was? a youth who soon grew discreet and dutiful, soon became a husband and a father, soon became eager for public honours, and soon obtained the priesthood, winning his way to all these admirable things with equally admirable speed. It falls to scarcely any one's lot to enjoy great prosperity, and also to enjoy it for a long time: only a dull kind of happiness can last for long and accompany us to the end of our lives. The immortal gods, who did not intend to give you a son for long, gave you one who was straightway what another would have required long training to become. You cannot even say that you have been specially marked by the gods for misfortune because you have had no pleasure in your son. Look at any company of people, whether they be known to you or not: everywhere you will see some who have endured greater misfortunes than your own. Great generals and princes have undergone like bereavements: mythology tells us that the gods themselves are not exempt from them, its aim, I suppose, being to lighten our sorrow at death by the thought that even deities are subject to it. Look around, I repeat, at every one: you cannot mention any house so miserable as not to find comfort in the fact of another being yet more miserable. I do not, by Hercules, think so ill of your principles as to suppose that you would bear your sorrow more lightly were I to show you an enormous company of mourners: that is a spiteful sort of consolation which we derive from the number of our fellow-sufferers: nevertheless I will quote some instances, not indeed in order to teach you that this often befalls men, for it is absurd to multiply examples of man's mortality, but to let you know that there have been many who have lightened their misfortunes by patient endurance of them. I will begin with the luckiest man of all. Lucius Sulla lost his son, yet this did not impair either the spitefulness or the brilliant valour which he displayed at the expense of his enemies and his countrymen alike, nor did it make him appear to have assumed his well-known title untruly that he did so after his son's death, fearing neither the hatred of men, by whose sufferings that excessive prosperity of his was purchased, nor the ill-will of the gods, to whom it was a reproach that Sulla should be so truly The Fortunate. What, however, Sulla's real character was may pass among questions still undecided: even his enemies will admit that he took up arms with honour, and laid them aside with honour: his example proves the point at issue, that an evil which befalls even the most prosperous cannot be one of the first magnitude.

XIII.

That Greece cannot boast unduly of that father who, being in the act of offering sacrifice when he heard the news of his son's death, merely ordered the flute-player to be silent, and removed the garland from his head, but accomplished all the rest of the ceremony in due form, is due to a Roman, Pulvillus the high priest. When he was in the act of holding the doorpost [5] and dedicating the Capitol the news of his son's death was brought to him. He pretended not to hear it, and pronounced the form of words proper for the high priest on such an occasion, without his prayer being interrupted by a single groan, begging that Jupiter would show himself gracious, at the very instant that he heard his son's name mentioned as dead. Do you imagine that this man's mourning knew no end, if the first day and the first shock could not drive him, though a father, away from the public altar of the state, or cause him to mar the ceremony of dedication by words of ill omen? Worthy, indeed, of the most exalted priesthood was he who ceased not to revere the gods even when they were angry. Yet he, after he had gone home, filled his eyes with tears, said a few words of lamentation, and performed the rites with which it was then customary to honour the dead, resumed the expression of countenance which he had worn in the Capitol.

Paulus,[6] about the time of his magnificent triumph, in which he drove Perses in chains before his car, gave two of his sons to be adopted into other families, and buried those whom he had kept for himself. What, think you, must those whom he kept have been, when Scipio was one of those whom he gave away? It was not without emotion that the Roman people looked upon Paulus's empty chariot:[8] nevertheless he made a speech to them, and returned thanks to the gods for having granted his prayer: for he had prayed that, if any offering to Nemesis were due in consequence of the stupendous victory which he had won, it might be paid at his own expense rather than at that of his country. Do you see how magnanimously he bore his loss ?he even congratulated himself on being left childless, though who had more to suffer by such a change? he lost at once his comforters and his helpers. Yet Perses did not have the pleasure of seeing Paulus look sorrowful.

## XIV.

Why should I lead you on through the endless series of great men and pick out tbe unhappy ones, as though it were not more difficult to find happy ones? For how few households have remained possessed of all their members until the end? what one is there that has not suffered some loss? Take any one year you please and name the consuls for it: if you like, that of [8] Lucius Bibulus and Gaius Caesar; you will see that, though these colleagues were each other's bitterest enemies, yet their fortunes agreed. Lucius Bibulus, a man more remarkable for goodness than for strength of character, had both his sons murdered at the same time, and even insulted by the Egyptian soldiery, so that the agent of his bereavement was as much a subject for tears as the bereavement itself. Nevertheless Bibulus, who during the whole of his year of office had remained hidden in his house, to cast reproach upon his colleague Caesar on the day following that upon which he heard of both his sons' deaths, came forth and went through the routine business of his magistracy. Who could devote less than one day to mourning for two sons? Thus soon did he end his mourning for his children, although he had mourned a whole year for his consulship. Gaius Caesar, after having traversed Britain, and not allowed even the ocean to set bounds to his successes, heard of the death of his daughter, which hurried on the crisis of affairs. Already Gnaeus Pompeius stood before his eyes, a man who would ill endure that any one besides himself should become a great power in the state, and one who was likely to place a check upon his advancement, which he had regarded as onerous even when each gained by the other's rise: yet within three days' time he resumed his duties as general, and conquered his grief as quickly as he was wont to conquer everything else.

## XV.

"Why need I remind you of the deaths of the other Caesars, whom fortune appears to me sometimes to have outraged in order that even by their deaths they might be useful to mankind, by proving that not even they, although they were styled "sons of gods," and "fathers of gods to come," could exercise the same power over their own fortunes which they did over those of others? The Emperor Augustus lost his children and his grandchildren, and after all the family of Caesar had perished was obliged to prop his empty house by adopting a son: yet he bore his losses as bravely as though he were already personally concerned in the honour of the gods, and as though it were especially to his interest that no one should complain of the injustice of Heaven. Tiberius Caesar lost both the son whom he begot and the son whom he adopted, yet he himself pronounced a panegyric upon his son from the Rostra, and stood in full view of the corpse, which merely had a curtain on one side to prevent the eyes of the high priest resting upon the dead body, and did not change his countenance, though all the Romans wept: he gave Sejanus, who stood by his side, a proof of how patiently he could endure the loss of his relatives. See you not what numbers of most eminent men there have been, none of whom have been spared by this blight which prostrates us all: men, too, adorned with every grace of character, and every distinction that public or private life can confer. It appears as though this plague moved in a regular orbit, and spread ruin and desolation among us all without distinction of persons, all being alike its prey. Bid any number of individuals tell you the story of their lives: you will find that all have paid some penalty for being born.

## XVI.

I know what you will say, "You quote men as examples: you forget that it is a woman that you are trying to console." Yet who would say that nature has dealt grudgingly with the minds of women, and stunted their virtues? Believe me, they have the same intellectual power as men, and the same capacity for honourable and generous action. If trained to do so, they are just as able to endure sorrow or labour. Ye good gods, do I say this in that very city in which Lucretia and Brutus removed the yoke of kings from the necks of the Romans? We owe liberty to Brutus, but we owe Brutus to Lucretia—in which Cloelia, for the sublime courage with which she scorned both the enemy and the river, has been almost reckoned as a man. The statue of Cloelia, mounted on horseback, in that busiest of thoroughfares, the Sacred Way, continually reproaches the youth of the present day, who never mount anything but a cushioned seat in a carriage, with journeying in such a fashion through that very city in which we have enrolled even women among our knights. If you wish me to point out to you examples of women who have bravely endured the loss of their children, I shall not go far afield to search for them: in one family I can quote two Cornelias, one the daughter of Scipio, and the mother of the Gracchi, who made acknowledgment of the birth of her twelve children by burying them all: nor was it so hard to do this in the case of the others, whose birth and death were alike unknown to the public, but she beheld the murdered and unburied corpses of both Tiberius Gracchus and Gaius Gracchus, whom even those who will not call them good must admit were great men. Yet to those who tried to console her and called her unfortunate, she answered, "I shall never cease to call myself happy, because I am the mother of the Gracchi." Cornelia, the wife of Livius Drusus, lost by the hands of an unknown assassin a young son of great distinction, who was treading in the footsteps of the Gracchi, and was murdered in his own house just when he had so many bills half way through the process of becoming law: nevertheless she bore the untimely and unavenged death of her son with as lofty a spirit as he had shown in carrying his laws. Will you not, Marcia, forgive fortune because she has not refrained from striking you with the darts with which she launched at the Scipios, and the mothers and daughters of the Scipios, and with which she has attacked the Caesars themselves? Life is full of misfortunes; our path is beset with them: no one can make a long peace, nay, scarcely an armistice with fortune. You, Marcia, have borne four children: now they say that no dart which is hurled into a close column of soldiers can fail to hit one,—ought you then to wonder at not having been able to lead along such a company without exciting the ill-will of Fortune, or suffering loss at her hands? "But," say you, "Fortune has treated me unfairly, for she not only has bereaved me of my son, but chose my best beloved to deprive me of." Yet you never can say that you have been wronged, if you divide the stakes equally with an antagonist who is stronger than yourself: Fortune has left you two daughters, and their children: she has not even taken away altogether him who you now mourn for, forgetful of his elder brother: you have two daughters by him, who if you support them ill will prove great burdens, but if well, great comforts to you. You ought to prevail upon yourself, when you see them, to let them remind you of your son, and not of your grief. When a husbandman's trees have either been torn up, roots and all, by the wind, or broken off short by the force of a hurricane, he takes care of what is left of their stock, straightway plants seeds or cuttings in the place of those which he has lost, and in a moment—for time is as swift in repairing losses as in causing them— more nourishing trees are growing than were there before. Take, then, in the place of your Metilius these his two daughters, and by their two-fold consolation lighten your single sorrow. True, human nature is so constituted as to love nothing so much as what it has lost, and our yearning after those who have been taken from us makes us judge unfairly of those who are left to us: nevertheless, if you choose to reckon up how merciful Fortune has been to you even in her anger, you will feel that you have more than enough to console you. Look at all your grandchildren, and your two daughters: and say also, Marcia:—"I should indeed be cast down, if everyone's fortune followed his deserts, and if no evil ever befell good men: but as it is I perceive that no distinction is made, and that the bad and the good are both harassed alike."

XVII.

"Still, it is a sad thing to lose a young man whom you have brought up, just as he was becoming a defence and a pride both to his mother and to his country." No one denies that it is sad: but it is the common lot of mortals. You were born to lose others, to be lost, to hope, to fear, to destroy your own peace and that of others, to fear and yet to long for death, and, worst of all, never to know what your real position is. If you were about to journey to Syracuse, and someone were to say :—"Learn beforehand all the discomforts, and all the pleasures of your coming voyage, and then set sail. The sights which you will enjoy will be as follows: first, you will see the island itself, now separated from Italy by a narrow strait, but which, we know, once formed part of the mainland. The sea suddenly broke through, and

'Sever'd Sicilia from the western shore.' [9]

Next, as you will be able to sail close to Charybdis, of which the poets have sung, you will see that greediest of whirlpools, quite smooth if no south wind be blowing, but whenever there is a gale from that quarter, sucking down ships into a huge and deep abyss. You will see the fountain of Arethusa, so famed in song, with its waters bright and pellucid to the very bottom, and pouring forth an icy stream which it either finds on the spot or else plunges it under ground, conveys it thither as a separate river beneath so many seas, free from any mixture of less pure water, and there brings it again to the surface. You will see a harbor which is more sheltered than all the others in the world, whether they be natural or improved by human art for the protection of shipping; so safe, that even the most violent storms are powerless to disturb it. You will see the place where the power of Athens was broken, where that natural prison, hewn deep among precipices of rock, received so many thousands of captives: you will see the great city itself, occupying a wider site than many capitals, an extremely warm resort in winter, where not a single day passes without sunshine: but when you have observed all this, you must remember that the advantages of its winter climate are counterbalanced by a hot and pestilential summer: that here will be the tyrant Dionysius, the destroyer of freedom, of justice, and of law, who is greedy of power even after conversing with Plato, and of life even after he has been exiled; that he will burn some, flog others, and behead others for slight offences; that he will exercise his lust upon both sexes You have now heard all that can attract you thither, all that can deter you from going: now, then, either set sail or remain at home!" If, after this declaration, anybody were to say that he wished to go to Syracuse, he could blame no one but himself for what befell him there, because he would not stumble upon it unknowingly, but would have gone thither fully aware of what was before him. To everyone Nature says: "I do not deceive any person. If you choose to have children, they may be handsome, or they may be deformed; perhaps they will be born dumb. One of them may perhaps prove the saviour of his country, or perhaps its betrayer. You need not despair of their being raised to such honour that for their sake no one will dare to speak evil of you: yet remember that they may reach such a pitch of infamy as themselves to become curses to you. There is nothing to prevent their performing the last offices for you, and your panegyric being spoken by your children: but bold yourself prepared nevertheless to place a son as boy, man, or greybeard, upon the funeral pyre: for years have nothing to do with the matter, since every sort of funeral in which a parent buries his child must alike be untimely.[10] If you still choose to rear children, after I have explained these conditions to you, you render yourself incapable of blaming the gods, for they never guaranteed anything to you."

XVIII.

You may make this simile apply to your whole entrance into life. I have explained to you what attractions and what drawbacks there would be if you were thinking of going to Syracuse: now suppose that I were to come and give you advice when you were going to be born. "You are about," I should say, "to enter a city of which both gods and men are citizens, a city which contains the whole universe, which is bound by irrevocable and eternal laws, and wherein the heavenly bodies run their unwearied courses: you will see therein innumerable twinkling stars, and the sun, whose single light pervades every place, who by his daily course marks the times of day and night, and by his yearly course makes a more equal division between summer and winter. You will see his place taken by night by the moon, who borrows at her meetings with her brother a gentle and softer light, and who at one time is invisible, at another hangs full faced above the earth, ever waxing and waning, each phase unlike the last. You will see five stars, moving in the opposite direction to the others, stemming the whirl of the skies towards the West: on the slightest motions of these depend the fortunes of nations, and according as the aspect of the planets is auspicious or malignant, the greatest empires rise and fall: you will see with wonder the gathering clouds, the falling showers, the zigzag lightning, the crashing together of the heavens. When, sated with the wonders above, you turn your eyes towards the earth, they will be met by objects of a different yet equally admirable aspect: on one side a boundless expanse of open plains, on another the towering peaks of lofty and snow-clad mountains: the downward course of rivers, some streams running eastward, some westward from the same source: the woods which wave even on the mountain tops, the vast forests with all the creatures that dwell therein, and the confused harmony of the birds: the variously-placed cities, the nations which natural obstacles keep secluded from the world, some of whom withdraw themselves to lofty mountains, while others dwell in fear and trembling on the sloping banks of rivers: the crops which are assisted by cultivation, and the trees which bear fruit even without it: the rivers that flow gently through the meadows, the lovely bays and shores that curve inwards to form harbours: the countless islands scattered over the main, which break and spangle the seas. What of the brilliancy of stones and gems, the gold that rolls amid the sands of rushing streams, the heaven-born fires that burst forth from the midst of the earth and even from the midst of the sea; the ocean itself, that binds land to land, dividing the nations by its three-fold indentations, and boiling up with mighty rage? Swimming upon its waves, making them disturbed and swelling without wind, you will see animals exceeding the size of any that belong to the land, some clumsy and requiring others to guide their movements, some swift and .moving faster than the utmost efforts of rowers, some of them that drink in the waters and blow them out again to the great perils of those who sail near them: you will see here ships seeking for unknown lands: you will see that man's audacity leaves nothing unattempted, and you will yourself be both a witness and a sharer in great attempts. You will both learn and teach the arts by which men's lives are supplied with necessaries, are adorned, and are ruled: but in this same place there will be a thousand pestilences fatal to both body and mind, there will be wars and highway robberies, poisonings and shipwrecks, extremes of climate and excesses of body, untimely griefs for our dearest ones, and death for ourselves, of which we cannot tell whether it will be easy or by torture at the hands of the executioner. Now consider and weigh carefully in your own mind which you would choose. If you wish to enjoy these blessings you must pass through these pains. Do you answer that you choose to live? 'Of course.' Nay, I thought you would not enter upon that of which the least diminution causes pain. Live, then, as has been agreed on. You say, "No one has asked my opinion." Our parents' opinion was taken about us, when, knowing what the conditions of life are, they brought us into it.

XIX.
But, to come to topics of consolation, in the first place consider if you please to what our remedies must be applied, and next, in what way. It is regret for the absence of his loved one which causes a mourner to grieve: yet it is clear that this in itself is bearable enough; for we do not weep at their being absent or intending to be absent during their lifetime, although when they leave our sight we have no

more pleasure in them. What tortures us, therefore, is an idea. Now every evil is just as great as we consider it to be: we have, therefore, the remedy in our own hands. Let us suppose that they are on a journey, and let us deceive ourselves: we have sent them away, or, rather, we have sent them on in advance to a place whither we shall soon follow them.[11] Besides this, mourners are wont to suffer from the thought, "I shall have no one to protect me, no one to avenge me when I am scorned." To use a very disreputable but very true mode of consolation, I may say that in our country the loss of children bestows more influence than it takes away, and loneliness, which used to bring the aged to ruin, now makes them so powerful that some old men have pretended to pick quarrels with their sons, have disowned their own children, and have made themselves childless by their own act. I know what you will say: "My own losses do not grieve me:" and indeed a man does not deserve to be consoled if he is sorry for his son's death as he would be for that of a slave, who is capable of seeing anything in his son beyond his son's self. What then, Marcia, is it that grieves you? is it that your son has died, or that he did not live long? If it be his having died, then you ought always to have grieved, for you always knew that he would die. Reflect that the dead huffier no evils, that all those stories which make us dread the nether world are mere fables, that he who dies need fear no darkness, no prison, no blazing streams of fire, no river of Lethe, no judgment seat before which he must appear, and that Death is such utter freedom that he need fear no more despots. All that is a phantasy of the poets, who have terrified us without a cause. Death is a release from and an end of all pains: beyond it our sufferings cannot extend: it restores us to the peaceful rest in which we lay before we were born. If anyone pities the dead, he ought also to pity those who have not been born. Death is neither a good nor a bad thing, for that alone which is something can be a good or a bad thing: but that which is nothing, and reduces all things to nothing, does not hand us over to either fortune, because good and bad require some material to work upon. Fortune cannot take hold of that which Nature has let go, nor can a man be unhappy if he is nothing. Your son has passed beyond the border of the country where men are forced to labour; he has reached deep and everlasting peace. He feels no fear of want, no anxiety about his riches, no stings of lust that tears the heart in guise of pleasure: he knows no envy of another's prosperity, he is not crashed by the weight of his own; even his chaste ears are not wounded by any ribaldry: he is menaced by no disaster, either to his country or to himself. He does not hang, full of anxiety, upon the issue of events, to reap even greater uncertainty as his reward: he has at last taken up a position from which nothing can dislodge him, where nothing can make him afraid.

## XX.

O how little do men understand their own misery, that they do not praise and look forward to death as the best discovery of Nature, whether because it hedges in happiness, or because it drives away misery: because it puts an end to the sated weariness of old age, cuts down youth in its bloom while still full of hope of better things, or calls home childhood before the harsher stages of life are reached: it is the end of all men, a relief to many, a desire to some, and it treats none so well as those to whom it comes before they call for it. Death frees the slave though his master wills it not, it lightens the captive's chains: it leads out of prison those whom headstrong power has forbidden to quit it: it points out to exiles, whose minds and eyes are ever turned towards their own country, that it makes no difference under what people's soil one lies. When Fortune has unjustly divided the common stock, and has given over one man to another, though they were born with equal rights, Death makes them all equal. After Death no one acts any more at another's bidding: in death no man suffers any more from the sense of his low position. It is open to all: it was what your father, Marcia, longed for: it is this, I say, that renders it no misery to be born, which enables me to face the threatenings of misfortune without quailing, and to keep my mind unharmed and able to command itself. I have a last appeal. I see before me crosses not all alike, but differently made by different peoples: some hang a man head downwards, some force a stick upwards through his groin, some stretch out his arms on a forked gibbet. I see cords, scourges, and instruments of torture for each limb and each joint: but I see Death also. There are bloodthirsty enemies, there are overbearing fellow-countrymen, but where they are there I see Death also. Slavery is not grievous if a man can gain his freedom by one step as soon as he becomes tired of thralldom. Life, it is thanks to Death that I hold thee so dear. Think how great a blessing is a timely death, how many have been injured by living longer than they ought. If sickness had carried off that glory and support of the empire Gnaeus Pompeius, at Naples, he would have died the undoubted head of the Roman people, but as it was, a short extension of time cast him down from his pinnacle of fame: he beheld his legions slaughtered before his eyes: and what a sad relic of that battle, in which the Senate formed the first line, was the survival of the general. He saw his Egyptian butcher, and offered his body, hallowed by so many victories, to a guardsman's sword, although even had he been unhurt, he would have regretted his safety: for what could have been more infamous than that a Pompeius should owe his life to the clemency of a king? If Marcus Cicero had fallen at the time when he avoided those daggers which Catiline aimed equally at him and at his country, he might have died as the saviour of the commonwealth which he had set free: if his death had even followed upon that of his daughter, he might have died happy. He would not then have seen swords drawn for the slaughter of Roman citizens, the goods of the murdered divided among the murderers, that men might pay from their own purse the price of their own blood, the public auction of the consul's spoil in the civil war, the public letting out of murder to be done, brigandage, war, pillage, hosts of Catilines. Would it not have been a good thing for Marcus Cato if the sea had swallowed him up when he was returning from Cyprus after sequestrating the king's hereditary possessions, even if that very money which he was bringing to pay the soldiers in the civil war had been lost with him? He certainly would have been able to boast that no one would dare to do wrong in the presence of Cato: as it was, the extension of his life for a very few more years forced one who was born for personal and political freedom to flee from Caesar and to become Pompeius's follower. Premature death therefore did him no evil: indeed, it put an end to the power of any evil to hurt him.

## XXI.

"Yet," say you, "he perished too soon and untimely." In the first place, suppose that he had lived to extreme old age: let him continue alive to the extreme limits of human existence: how much is it after all? Born for a very brief space of time, we regard this life as an inn which we are soon to quit that it may be made ready for the coming guest. Do I speak of our lives, which we know roll away incredibly fast? Reckon up the centuries of cities: you will find that even those which boast of their antiquity have not existed for long. All human works are brief and fleeting; they take up no part whatever of infinite time. Tried by the standard of the universe, we regard this earth of ours, with all its cities, nations, rivers, and sea-board as a mere point: our life occupies less than a point when compared with all time, the measure of which exceeds that of the world, for indeed the world is contained many times in it. Of what importance, then, can it be to lengthen that which, however much you add to it, will never be much more than nothing? We can only make our lives long by one expedient, that is, by being satisfied with their length: you may tell me of long-lived men, whose length of days has been celebrated by tradition, you may assign a hundred and ten years apiece to them: yet when you allow your mind to conceive the idea of eternity, there will be no difference between the shortest and the longest life, if you compare the time during which any one has been alive with that during which he has not been alive. In the next place, when he died his life was complete: he had lived as long as he needed to live: there was nothing left for him to accomplish. All men do not grow old at the same age, nor indeed do all animals: some are wearied out by life at fourteen years of age, and what is only the first stage of life with man is their extreme limit of longevity. To each man a varying length of days has been assigned: no one dies before his time, because he was not destined to live any longer than he did. Everyone's end is fixed, and will always remain where it has been placed: neither industry nor favour will move it on any further. Believe, then, that you lost him by advice: he took all that was his own,

"And reached the goal allotted to his life,"

so you need not burden yourself with the thought, "He might have lived longer." His life has not been cut short, nor does chance ever cut short our years: every man receives as much as was promised to him: the Fates go their own way, and neither add anything nor take away anything from what they have once promised. Prayers and endeavours are all in vain : each man will have as much life as his first day placed to his credit: from the time when he first saw the light he has entered on the path that leads to death, and is drawing nearer to his doom: those same years which were added to his youth were subtracted from his life. We all fall into this mistake of supposing that it is only old men, already in the decline of life, who are drawing near to death, whereas our first infancy, our youth, indeed every time of life leads thither. The Fates ply their own work: they take from us the consciousness of our death, and, the better to conceal its approaches, death lurks under the very names we give to life: infancy changes into boyhood, maturity swallows up the boy, old age the man: these stages themselves, if you reckon them properly, are so many losses.

XXII.

Do you complain, Marcia, that your son did not live as long as he might have done? How do you know that it was to his advantage to live longer? whether his interest was not served by this death? Whom can you find at the present time whose fortunes are grounded on such sure foundations that they have nothing to fear in the future? All human affairs are evanescent and perishable, nor is any part of our life so frail and liable to accident as that which we especially enjoy. We ought, therefore, to pray for death when our fortune is at its best, because so great is the uncertainty and turmoil in which we live, that we can be sure of nothing but what is past. Think of your son's handsome person, which you had guarded in perfect purity among all the temptations of a voluptuous capital. Who could have undertaken to keep that clear of all diseases, so that it might preserve its beauty of form unimpaired even to old age? Think of the many taints of the mind: for fine dispositions do not always continue to their life's end to make good the promise of their youth, but have often broken down: either extravagance, all the more shameful for being indulged in late in life, takes possession of men and makes their well-begun lives end in disgrace, or they devote their entire thoughts to the eating-house and the belly, and they become interested in nothing save what they shall eat and what they shall drink. Add to this conflagrations, falling houses, shipwrecks, the agonizing operations of surgeons, who cut pieces of bone out of men's living bodies, plunge their whole hands into their entrails, and inflict more than one kind of pain to effect the cure of shameful diseases. After these comes exile; your son was not more innocent than Rutilius: imprisonment; he was not wiser than Socrates: the piercing of one's breast by a self-inflicted wound; he was not of holier life than Cato. When you look at these examples, you will perceive that nature deals very kindly with those whom she puts speedily in a place of safety because there awaited them the payment of some such price as this for their lives. Nothing is so deceptive, nothing is so treacherous as human life; by Hercules, were it not given to men before they could form an opinion, no one would take it. Not to be born, therefore, is the happiest lot of all, and the nearest thing to this, I imagine, is that we should soon finish our strife here and be restored again to our former rest. Recall to your mind that time, so painful to you, during which Sejanus handed over your father as a present to his client Satrius Secundus: he was angry with him about something or other which he had said with too great freedom, because he was not able to keep silence and see Sejanus climbing up to take his seat upon our necks, which would have been bad enough had he been placed there by his master. He was decreed the honour of a statue, to be set up in the theatre of Pompeius, which had been burned down and was being restored by Caesar. Cordus exclaimed that "Now the theatre was really destroyed." What then? should he not burst with spite at a Sejanus being set up over the ashes of Gnaeus Pompeius, at a faithless soldier being commemorated within the memorial of a consummate commander?

The inscription was put up:[12] and those keen-scented hounds whom

Sejanus used to feed on human blood, to make them tame towards himself and fierce to all the world beside, began to bay around their victim and even to make premature snaps at him. What was he to do? If he chose to live, he must gain the consent of Sejanus; if to die, he must gain that of his daughter; and neither of them could have been persuaded to grant it: he therefore determined to deceive his daughter, and having taken a bath in order to weaken himself still further, he retired to his bed-chamber on the pretence of taking a meal there. After dismissing his slaves he threw some of the food out of the window, that he might appear to have eaten it: then he took no supper, making the excuse that he had already had enough food in his chamber. This he continued to do on the second and the third day: the fourth betrayed his condition by his bodily weakness; so, embracing you, "My dearest daughter," said he, "from whom I have never throughout your whole life concealed aught but this, I have begun my journey towards death, and have already travelled half-way thither. You cannot and you ought not to call me back." So saying he ordered all light to be excluded from the room and shut himself up in the darkness. When his determination became known there was a general feeling of pleasure at the prey being snatched out of the jaws of those ravening wolves. His prosecutors, at the instance of Sejanus, went to the judgment-seat of the consuls, complained that Cordus was dying, and begged the consuls to interpose to prevent his doing what they themselves had driven him to do; so true was it that Cordus appeared to them to be escaping: an important matter was at stake, namely, whether the accused should lose the right to die. While this point was being debated, and the prosecutors were going to attend the court a second time, he had set himself free from them. Do you see, Marcia, how suddenly evil days come upon a man? and do you weep because one of your family could not avoid dying? one of your family was within a very little of not being allowed to die.

XXIII.

Besides the fact that everything that is future is uncertain, and the only certainty is that it is more likely to turn out ill than well, our spirits find the path to the Gods above easiest when it is soon allowed to leave the society of mankind, because it has then contracted fewest impurities to weigh it down : if set free before they become hardened worldlings, before earthly things have sunk too deep into them, they fly all the more lightly back to the place from whence they came, and all the more easily wash away the stains and defilements which they may have contracted. Great minds never love to linger long in the body: they are eager to burst its bonds and escape from it, they chafe at the narrowness of their prison, having been wont to wander through space, and from aloft in the upper air to look down with contempt upon human affairs. Hence it is that Plato declares that the wise man's mind is entirely given up to death, longs for it, contemplates it, and through his eagerness for it is always striving after things which lie beyond this life. Why, Marcia, when you saw him while yet young displaying the wisdom of age, with a mind that could rise superior to all sensual enjoyments, faultless and without a blemish, able to win riches without greediness, public office without ambition, pleasure without extravagance, did you suppose it would long be your lot to keep him safe by your side? Whatever has arrived at perfection, is ripe for dissolution. Consummate virtue flees away and betakes itself out of our sight, and those things which come to maturity in the first stage of their being do not wait for the last. The brighter a fire glows, the sooner it goes out: it lasts longer when it is made up with bad and slowly burning fuel, and shows a dull light through a cloud of smoke: its being poorly fed makes it linger all the longer. So also the more brilliant men's minds, the shorter lived they are: for when there is no room for further growth, the end is near. Fabianus tells us, what our parents themselves have seen, that there was at Rome a boy of gigantic stature, exceeding that of a man: but he soon died, and every sensible person always said that he would soon die, for he could not live to reach the age which he had assumed before it was due. So it is: too complete maturity is a proof that destruction is near and the end approaches when growth is over.

XXIV.
Begin to reckon his age, not by years, but by virtues: he lived long enough. He was left as a ward in the care of guardians up to his fourteenth year, and never passed out of that of his mother: when he had a household of his own he was loath to leave yours, and continued to dwell under his mother's roof, though few sons can endure to live under their father's. Though a youth whose height, beauty, and vigour of body destined him for the army, yet he refused to serve, that he might not be separated from you. Consider, Marcia, how seldom mothers who live in separate houses see their children: consider how they lose and pass in anxiety all those years during which they have sons in the army, and you will see that this time, none of which you lost, was of considerable extent: he never went out of your sight: it was under your eyes that he applied himself to the cultivation of an admirable intellect and one which would have rivaled that of his grandfather, had it not been hindered by shyness, which has concealed many men's accomplishments: though a youth of unusual beauty, and living among such throngs of women who made it their business to seduce men, he gratified the wishes of none of them, and when the effrontery of some led them so far as actually to tempt him, he blushed as deeply at having found favour in their eyes as though he had been guilty. By this holiness of life he caused himself, while yet quite a boy, to be thought worthy of the priesthood, which no doubt he owed to his mother's influence; but even his mother's influence would have had no weight if the candidate for whom it was exerted had been unfit for the post. Dwell upon these virtues, and nurse your son as it were in your lap: now he is more at leisure to respond to your caresses, he has nothing to call him away from you, he will never be an anxiety or a sorrow to you. You have grieved at the only grief so good a son could cause you: all else is beyond the power of fortune to harm, and is full of pleasure, if only you know how to make use of your son, if you do but know what his most precious quality was. It is merely the outward semblance of your son that has perished, his likeness, and that not a very good one; he himself is immortal, and is now in a far better state, set free from the burden of all that was not his own, and left simply by himself: all this apparatus which you see about us

of bones and sinews, this covering of skin, this face, these our servants the hands, and all the rest of our environment, are but chains and darkness to the soul: they overwhelm it, choke it, corrupt it, fill it with false ideas, and keep it at a distance from its own true sphere: it has to struggle continually against this burden of the flesh, lest it be dragged down and sunk by it. It ever strives to rise up again to the place from whence it was sent down on earth: there eternal rest awaits it, there it will behold what is pure and clear, in place of what is foul and turbid.

XXV.

You need not, therefore, hasten to the burial-place of your son : that which lies there is but the worst part of him and that which gave him most trouble, only bones and ashes, which are no more parts of him than clothes or other coverings of his body. He is complete, and without leaving any part of himself behind on earth has taken wing and gone away altogether: he has tarried a brief space above us while his soul was being cleansed and purified from the vices and rust which all mortal lives must contract, and from thence he will rise to the high heavens and join the souls of the blessed: a saintly company will welcome him thither, — Scipios and Catos; and among the rest of those who have held life cheap and set themselves free, thanks to death, albeit all there are alike akin, your father, Marcia, will embrace his grandson as he rejoices in the unwonted light, will teach him the motion of the stars which are so near to them, and introduce him with joy into all the secrets of nature, not by guesswork but by real knowledge. Even as a stranger is grateful to one who shows him the way about an unknown city, so is a searcher after the causes of what he sees in the heavens to one of his own family who can explain them to him. He will delight in gazing deep down upon the earth, for it is a delight to look from aloft at what one has left below. Bear yourself, therefore, Marcia, as though you were placed before the eyes of your father and your son, yet not such as you knew them, but far loftier beings, placed in a higher sphere. Blush, then, to do any mean or common action, or to weep for those your relatives who have been changed for the better. Free to roam through the open, boundless realms of the ever-living universe, they are not hindered in their course by intervening seas, lofty mountains, impassable valleys, or the treacherous flats of the Syrtes: they find a level path everywhere, are swift and ready of motion, and are permeated in their turn by the stars and dwell together with them.

XXVI.

Imagine then, Marcia, that your father, whose influence over you was as great as yours over your son, no longer in that frame of mind in which he deplored the civil wars, or in which he forever proscribed those who would have proscribed him, but in a mood as much more joyful as his abode now is higher than of old, is saying, as he looks down from the height of heaven, "My daughter, why does this sorrow possess you for so long? why do you live in such ignorance of the truth, as to think that your son has been unfairly dealt with because he has returned to his ancestors in his prime, without decay of body or mind, leaving his family flourishing? Do you not know with what storms Fortune unsettles everything? how she proves kind and compliant to none save to those who have the fewest possible dealings with her? Need I remind you of kings who would have been the happiest of mortals had death sooner withdrawn them from the ruin which was approaching them ?or of Roman generals, whose greatness, had but a few years been taken from their lives, would have wanted nothing to render it complete? or of men of the highest distinction and noblest birth who have calmly offered their necks to the stroke of a soldier's sword? Look at your father and your grandfather: the former fell into the hands of a foreign murderer: I allowed no man to take any liberties with me, and by abstinence from food showed that my spirit was as great as my writings had represented it. Why, then, should that member of our household who died most happily of all be mourned in it the longest? We have all assembled together, and, not being plunged in utter darkness, we see that with you on earth there is nothing to be wished for, nothing grand or magnificent, but all is mean, sad, anxious, and hardly receives a fractional part of the clear light in which we dwell. I need not say that here are no frantic charges of rival armies, no fleets shattering one another, no parricides, actual or meditated, no courts where men babble over lawsuits for days together, here is nothing underhand, all hearts and minds are open and unveiled, our life is public and known to all, and that we command a view of all time and of things to come. I used to take pleasure in compiling the history of what took place in one century among a few people in the most out-of-the-way corner of the world: here I enjoy the spectacle of all the centuries, the whole chain of events from age to age as long as years have been. I may view kingdoms when they rise and when they fall, and behold the ruin of cities and the new channels made by the sea. If it will be any consolation to you in your bereavement to know that it is the common lot of all, be assured that nothing will continue to stand in the place in which it now stands, but that time will lay everything low and bear it away with itself: it will sport, not only with men—for how small a part are they of the dominion of Fortune? — but with districts, provinces, quarters of the world: it will efface entire mountains, and in other places will pile new rocks on high: it will dry up seas, change the course of rivers, destroy the intercourse of nation with nation, and break up the communion and fellowship of the human race: in other regions it will swallow up cities by opening vast chasms in the earth, will shake them with earthquakes, will breathe forth pestilence from the nether world, cover all habitable ground with inundations and destroy every creature in the flooded world, or burn up all mortals by a huge conflagration. When the time shall arrive for the world to be brought to an end, that it may begin its life anew, all the forces of nature will perish in conflict with one another, the stars will be dashed together, and all the lights which now gleam in regular order in various parts of the sky will then blaze in one fire with all their fuel burning at once. Then we also, the souls of the blest and the heirs of eternal life, whenever God thinks fit to reconstruct the universe, when all things are settling down again, we also, being a small accessory to the universal wreck,[13] shall be changed into our old elements. Happy is your son, Marcia, in that he already knows this."

## Endnotes

[1] See Merivale's "History of the Romans under the Empire," ch. Xiv

[2] If it is a pain to dwell upon the thought of lost friends, of course you do not continually refresh the memory of them by speaking of them

[3] See my note on *invidiam facere alicui* in Juv. 15.—J. E. B. Mayor

[4] Koch declares that this cannot be the true reading, and suggests *deminutio*, 'degradation.'

[5] This seems to have been part of the ceremony of dedication. Pulvillus was dedicating the Temple of Jupiter in the Capitol. See Livy ii. 8; Cic.Pro Domo, paragraph cxxi.

[6] Lucius -Æmilius Paullus conquered Perses, the last King of Macedonia, B.C. 168

[7] "For he had four sons, two, as has been already related, adopted into other families, Scipio and Fabius; and two others, who were still children, by his second wife, who lived in his own house. Of these, one died five days before Æmilius's triumph, at the age of fourteen, and the other, twelve years old, died three days after it: so that there was no Roman that did not grieve for him," &e.—Plutarch, "Life of Æmilius, *ch. xxxv.*

[8] A. U. C. 695, B.C. 59

[9] Virg. XL. III. 418

[10] See Mayor's note on Juv. i., and above, c. 16, § 4

[11] Lipsius points out that this idea is borrowed from the comic poet Antipbanes. See Meineke's "Comic Fragments," p. 3

[12] This I believe to be the meaning of the text, but Koch reasonably conjectures that the true reading is *editur subscriptio* "an indictment was made out against him." See "On Benefits," iii. 26.

[13] *Ruinae*; Koch's *urinae* is a misprint

# *On the Shortness of Life*
# L. Annaeus Seneca,

**[Translated by John W. Basore, *Loeb Classical Library*.[202]]**

I. The majority of mortals, Paulinus,[1] complain bitterly of the spitefulness of Nature, because we are born for a brief span of life, because even this space that has been granted to us rushes by so speedily and so swiftly that all save a very few find life at an end just when they are getting ready to live. Nor is it merely the common herd and the unthinking crowd that bemoan what is, as men deem it, an universal ill; the same feeling has called forth complaint also from men who were famous. It was this that made the greatest of physicians exclaim that "life is short, art is long;"[2] it was this that led Aristotle,[3] while expostulating with Nature, to enter an indictment most unbecoming to a wise man—that, in point of age, she has shown such favour to animals that they drag out five or ten lifetimes,[4] but that a much shorter limit is fixed for man, though he is born for so many and such great achievements. It is not that we have a short space of time, but that we waste much of it. Life is long enough, and it has been given in sufficiently generous measure to allow the accomplishment of the very greatest things if the whole of it is well invested. But when it is squandered in luxury and carelessness, when it is devoted to no good end, forced at last by the ultimate necessity we perceive that it has passed away before we were aware that it was passing. So it is—the life we receive is not short, but we make it so, nor do we have any lack of it, but are wasteful of it. Just as great and princely wealth is scattered in a moment when it comes into the hands of a bad owner, while wealth however limited, if it is entrusted to a good guardian, increases by use, so our life is amply long for him who orders it properly.

II. Why do we complain of Nature? She has shown herself kindly; life, if you know how to use it, is long. But one man is possessed by an avarice that is insatiable, another by a toilsome devotion to tasks that are useless; one man is besotted with wine, another is paralyzed by sloth; one man is exhausted by an ambition that always hangs upon the decision of others, another, driven on by the greed of the trader, is led over all lands and all seas by the hope of gain; some are tormented by a passion for war and are always either bent upon inflicting danger upon others or concerned about their own; some there are who are worn out by voluntary servitude in a thankless attendance upon the great; many are kept busy either in the pursuit of other men's fortune or in complaining of their own; many, following no fixed aim, shifting and inconstant and dissatisfied, are plunged by their fickleness into plans that are ever new; some have no fixed principle by which to direct their course, but Fate takes them unawares while they loll and

---

[202] Text courtesy of the following URL:
http://www.forumromanum.org/literature/seneca_younger/brev_e.html

yawn—so surely does it happen that I cannot doubt the truth of that utterance which the greatest of poets delivered with all the seeming of an oracle: "The part of life we really live is small."[5] For all the rest of existence is not life, but merely time. Vices beset us and surround us on every side, and they do not permit us to rise anew and lift up our eyes for the discernment of truth, but they keep us down when once they have overwhelmed us and we are chained to lust. Their victims are never allowed to return to their true selves; if ever they chance to find some release, like the waters of the deep sea which continue to heave even after the storm is past, they are tossed about, and no rest from their lusts abides. Think you that I am speaking of the wretches whose evils are admitted? Look at those whose prosperity men flock to behold; they are smothered by their blessings. To how many are riches a burden! From how many do eloquence and the daily straining to display their powers draw forth blood! How many are pale from constant pleasures! To how many does the throng of clients that crowd about them leave no freedom! In short, run through the list of all these men from the lowest to the highest—this man desires an advocate,[6] this one answers the call, that one is on trial, that one defends him, that one gives sentence; no one asserts his claim to himself, everyone is wasted for the sake of another. Ask about the men whose names are known by heart, and you will see that these are the marks that distinguish them: A cultivates B and B cultivates C; no one is his own master. And then certain men show the most senseless indignation—they complain of the insolence of their superiors, because they were too busy to see them when they wished an audience! But can anyone have the hardihood to complain of the pride of another when he himself has no time to attend to himself? After all, no matter who you are, the great man does sometimes look toward you even if his face is insolent, he does sometimes condescend to listen to your words, he permits you to appear at his side; but you never deign to look upon yourself, to give ear to yourself. There is no reason, therefore, to count anyone in debt for such services, seeing that, when you performed them, you had no wish for another's company, but could not endure your own.

III. Though all the brilliant intellects of the ages were to concentrate upon this one theme, never could they adequately express their wonder at this dense darkness of the human mind. Men do not suffer anyone to seize their estates, and they rush to stones and arms if there is even the slightest dispute about the limit of their lands, yet they allow others to trespass upon their life—nay, they themselves even lead in those who will eventually possess it. No one is to be found who is willing to distribute his money, yet among how many does each one of us distribute his life! In guarding their fortune men are often closefisted, yet, when it comes to the matter of wasting time, in the case of the one thing in which it is right to be miserly, they show themselves most prodigal. And so I should like to lay hold upon someone from the company of older men and say: "I see that you have reached the farthest limit of human life, you are pressing hard upon your hundredth year, or are even beyond it; come now, recall your life and make a reckoning. Consider how much of your time was taken up with a moneylender, how much with a mistress, how much with a patron, how much with a client, how much in wrangling with your wife, how much in punishing your slaves, how much in rushing about the city on social duties. Add the diseases which we have caused by our own acts, add, too, the time that has lain idle and unused; you will see that you have fewer years to your credit than you count. Look back in memory and consider when you ever had a fixed plan, how few days have passed as you had intended, when you were ever at your own disposal, when your face ever wore its natural expression, when your mind was ever unperturbed, what work you have achieved in so long a life, how many have robbed you of life when you were not aware of what you were losing, how much was taken up in useless sorrow, in foolish joy, in greedy desire, in the allurements of society, how little of yourself was left to you; you will perceive that you are dying before your season!"[7] What, then, is the reason of this? You live as if you were destined to live forever, no thought of your frailty ever enters your head, of how much time has already gone by you take no heed. You squander time as if you drew from a full and abundant supply, though all the while that day which you bestow on some person or thing is perhaps your last. You have all the fears of mortals and all the desires of immortals. You will hear many men saying: "After my fiftieth year I shall retire into leisure, my sixtieth year shall release me from public duties." And what guarantee, pray, have you that your life will last longer? Who will suffer your course to be just as you plan it? Are you not ashamed to reserve for yourself only the remnant of life, and to set apart for wisdom only that time which cannot be devoted to any business? How late it is to begin to live just when we must cease to live! What foolish forgetfulness of mortality to postpone wholesome plans to the fiftieth and sixtieth year, and to intend to begin life at a point to which few have                                                                    attained!

IV. You will see that the most powerful and highly placed men let drop remarks in which they long for leisure, acclaim it, and prefer it to all their blessings. They desire at times, if it could be with safety, to descend from their high pinnacle; for, though nothing from without should assail or shatter, Fortune of its very self comes crashing down.[8]

The deified Augustus, to whom the gods vouchsafed more than to any other man, did not cease to pray for rest and to seek release from public affairs; all his conversation ever reverted to this subject—his hope of leisure. This was the sweet, even if vain, consolation with which he would gladden his labours—that he would one day live for himself. In a letter addressed to the senate, in which he had promised that his rest would not be devoid of dignity nor inconsistent with his former glory, I find these words: "But these matters can be shown better by deeds than by promises. Nevertheless, since the joyful reality is still far distant, my desire for that time most earnestly prayed for has led me to forestall some of its delight by the pleasure of words." So desirable a thing did leisure seem that he anticipated it in thought because he could not attain it in reality. He who saw everything depending upon himself alone, who determined the fortune of individuals and of nations, thought most happily of that future day on which he should lay aside his greatness. He had discovered how much sweat those blessings that shone throughout all lands drew forth, how many secret worries they concealed. Forced to pit arms first against his countrymen, then against his colleagues, and lastly against his relatives, he shed blood on land and sea.

Through Macedonia, Sicily, Egypt, Syria, and Asia, and almost all countries he followed the path of battle, and when his troops were weary of shedding Roman blood, he turned them to foreign wars. While he was pacifying the Alpine regions, and subduing the enemies planted in the midst of a peaceful empire, while he was extending its bounds even beyond the Rhine and the Euphrates and the Danube, in Rome itself the swords of Murena, Caepio, Lepidus, Egnatius, and others were being whetted to slay him. Not yet had he escaped their plots, when his daughter[9] and all the noble youths who were bound to her by adultery as by a sacred oath, oft alarmed his failing years—and there was Paulus, and a second time the need to fear a woman in league with an Antony.[10] When be had cut away these ulcers[11] together with the limbs themselves, others would grow in their place; just as in a body that was overburdened with blood, there was always a rupture somewhere. And so he longed for leisure, in the hope and thought of which he found relief for his labours. This was the prayer of one who was able to answer the prayers of mankind.

V. Marcus Cicero, long flung among men like Catiline and Clodius and Pompey and Crassus, some open enemies, others doubtful friends, as he is tossed to and fro along with the state and seeks to keep it from destruction, to be at last swept away, unable as he was to be restful in prosperity or patient in adversity—how many times does he curse that very consulship of his, which he had lauded without end, though not without reason! How tearful the words he uses in a letter[12] written to Atticus, when Pompey the elder had been conquered, and the son was still trying to restore his shattered arms in Spain! "Do you ask," he said, "what I am doing here? I am lingering in my Tusculan villa half a prisoner." He then proceeds to other statements, in which he bewails his former life and complains of the present and despairs of the future. Cicero said that he was "half a prisoner." But, in very truth, never will the wise man resort to so lowly a term, never will he be half a prisoner—he who always possesses an undiminished and stable liberty, being free and his own master and towering over all others. For what can possibly be above him who is above Fortune?

...

VII.

...

Finally, everybody agrees that no one pursuit can be successfully followed by a man who is busied with many things—eloquence cannot, nor the liberal studies—since the mind, when its interests are divided, takes in nothing very deeply, but rejects everything that is, as it were, crammed into it. There is nothing the busy man is less busied with than living: there is nothing that is harder to learn. Of the other arts there are many teachers everywhere; some of them we have seen that mere boys have mastered so thoroughly that they could even play the master. It takes the whole of life to learn how to live, and—what will perhaps make you wonder more—it takes the whole of life to learn how to die. Many very great men, having laid aside all their encumbrances, having renounced riches, business, and pleasures, have made it their one aim up to the very end of life to know how to live; yet the greater number of them have departed from life confessing that they did not yet know—still less do those others know. Believe me, it takes a great man and one who has risen far above human weaknesses not to allow any of his time to be filched from him, and it follows that the life of such a man is very long because he has devoted wholly to himself whatever time he has had. None of it lay neglected and idle; none of it was under the control of another, for, guarding it most grudgingly, he found nothing that was worthy to be taken in exchange for his time. And so that man had time enough, but those who have been robbed of much of their life by the public, have necessarily had too little of it.

And there is no reason for you to suppose that these people are not sometimes aware of their loss. Indeed, you will hear many of those who are burdened by great prosperity cry out at times in the midst of their throngs of clients, or their pleadings in court, or their other glorious miseries: "I have no chance to live." Of course you have no chance! All those who summon you to themselves, turn you away from your own self. Of how many days has that defendant robbed you? Of how many that candidate? Of how many that old woman wearied with burying her heirs?[16] Of how many that man who is shamming sickness for the purpose of exciting the greed of the legacy-hunters? Of how many that very powerful friend who has you and your like on the list, not of his friends, but of his retinue? Check off, I say, and review the days of your life; you will see that very few, and those the refuse. have been left for you. That man who had prayed for the fasces,[17] when he attains them, desires to lay them aside and says over and over: "When will this year be over!" That man gives games,[18] and, after setting great value on gaining the chance to give them, now says: "When shall I be rid of them?" That advocate is lionized throughout the whole forum, and fills all the place with a great crowd that stretches farther than he can be heard, yet he says: "When will vacation time come?" Everyone hurries his life on and suffers from a yearning for the future and a weariness of the present. But he who bestows all of his time on his own needs, who plans out every day as if it were his last, neither longs for nor fears the morrow. For what new pleasure is there that any hour can now bring? They are all known, all have been enjoyed to the full. Mistress Fortune may deal out the rest as she likes; his life has already found safety. Something may be added to it, but nothing taken from it, and he will take any addition as the man who is satisfied and filled takes the food which he does not desire and yet can hold. And so there is no reason for you to think that any man has lived long because he has grey hairs or wrinkles; he has not lived long—he has existed long. For what if you should think that that man had had a long voyage who had been caught by a fierce storm as soon as he left harbour, and, swept hither and thither by a succession of winds that raged from different quarters, had been driven in a circle around the same course? Not much voyaging did he have, but much tossing about.

VIII. I am often filled with wonder when I see some men demanding the time of others and those from whom they ask it most indulgent. Both of them fix their eyes on the object of the request for time, neither of them on the time itself; just as if what is asked were nothing, what is given, nothing. Men trifle with the most precious thing in the world; but they are blind to it because it is an incorporeal thing, because it does not come beneath the sight of the eyes, and for this reason it is counted a very cheap thing—nay, of almost no value at all. Men set very great store by pensions and doles, and for these they hire out their labour or service or effort. But no one sets a value on time; all use it lavishly as if it cost nothing. But see how these same people clasp the knees of physicians if they fall ill and the danger of death draws nearer, see how ready they are, if threatened with capital punishment, to spend all their possessions in order to live! So great is the inconsistency of their feelings. But if each one could have the number of his future years set before him as is possible in the case of the years that have passed, how alarmed those would be who saw only a few remaining, how sparing of them would they be! And yet it is easy to dispense an amount that is assured, no matter how small it may be; but that must be guarded more carefully which will fail you know not when.

Yet there is no reason for you to suppose that these people do not know how precious a thing time is; for to those whom they love most devotedly they have a habit of saying that they are ready to give them a part of their own years. And they do give it, without realizing it; but the result of their giving is that they themselves suffer loss without adding to the years of their dear ones. But the very thing they do not know is whether they are suffering loss; therefore, the removal of something that is lost without being noticed they find is bearable. Yet no one will bring back the years, no one will bestow you once more on yourself. Life will follow the path it started upon, and will neither reverse nor check its course; it will make no noise, it will not remind you of its swiftness. Silent it will glide on; it will not prolong itself at the command of a king, or at the applause of the populace. Just as it was started on its first day, so it will run; nowhere will it turn aside, nowhere will it delay. And what will be the result? You have been engrossed, life hastens by; meanwhile death will be at hand, for which, willy nilly, you must find leisure.

IX. Can anything be sillier than the point of view of certain people—I mean those who boast of their foresight? They keep themselves very busily engaged in order that they may be able to live better; they spend life in making ready to live! They form their purposes with a view to the distant future; yet postponement is the greatest waste of life; it deprives them of each day as it comes, it snatches from them the present by promising something hereafter. The greatest hindrance to living is expectancy, which depends upon the morrow and wastes to-day. You dispose of that which lies in the hands of Fortune, you let go that which lies in your own. Whither do you look? At what goal do you aim? All things that are still to come lie in uncertainty; live straightway! See how the greatest of bards cries out, and, as if inspired with divine utterance, sings the saving strain:

The fairest day in hapless mortals' life.Is ever first to flee.[19]

"Why do you delay," says he, "Why are you idle? Unless you seize the day, it flees." Even though you seize it, it still will flee; therefore you must vie with time's swiftness in the speed of using it, and, as from a torrent that rushes by and will not always flow, you must drink quickly. And, too, the utterance of the bard is most admirably worded to cast censure upon infinite delay, in that he says, not "the fairest age," but "the fairest day." Why, to whatever length your greed inclines, do you stretch before yourself months and years in long array, unconcerned and slow though time flies so fast? The poet speaks to you about the day, and about this very day that is flying. Is there, then, any doubt that for hapless mortals, that is, for men who are engrossed, the fairest day is ever the first to flee? Old age surprises them while their minds are still childish, and they come to it unprepared and unarmed, for they have made no provision for it; they have stumbled upon it suddenly and unexpectedly, they did not notice that it was drawing nearer day by day. Even as conversation or reading or deep meditation on some subject beguiles the traveller, and he finds that he has reached the end of his journey before he was aware that he was approaching it, just so with this unceasing and most swift journey of life, which we make at the same pace whether waking or sleeping; those who are engrossed become aware of it only at the end.

X. Should I choose to divide my subject into heads with their separate proofs, many arguments will occur to me by which I could prove that busy men find life very short. But Fabianus,[20] who was none of your lecture-room philosophers of to-day, but one of the genuine and old-fashioned kind, used to say that we must fight against the passions with main force, not with artifice, and that the battle-line must be turned by a bold attack, not by inflicting pinpricks; that sophistry is not serviceable, for the passions must be, not nipped, but crushed. Yet, in order that the victims of them nay be censured, each for his own particular fault, I say that they must be instructed, not merely wept over.

Life is divided into three periods—that which has been, that which is, that which will be. Of these the present time is short, the future is doubtful, the past is certain. For the last is the one over which Fortune has lost control, is the one which cannot be brought back under any man's power. But men who are engrossed lose this; for they have no time to look back upon the past, and even if they should have, it is not pleasant to recall something they must view with regret. They are, therefore, unwilling to direct their thoughts backward to ill-spent hours, and those whose vices become obvious if they review the past, even the vices which were disguised under some allurement of momentary pleasure, do not have the courage to revert to those hours. No one willingly turns his thought back to the past, unless all his acts have been submitted to the censorship of his conscience, which is never deceived; he who has ambitiously coveted, proudly scorned, recklessly conquered, treacherously betrayed, greedily seized, or lavishly squandered, must needs fear his own memory. And yet this is the part of our time that is sacred and set apart, put beyond the reach of all human mishaps, and removed from the dominion of Fortune, the part which is disquieted by no want, by no fear, by no attacks of disease; this can neither be troubled nor be snatched away—it is an everlasting and unanxious possession. The present offers only one day at a time, and each by minutes; but all the days of past time will appear when you bid them, they will suffer you to behold them and keep them at your will—a thing which those who are engrossed have no time to do. The mind that is untroubled and tranquil has the power to roam into all the parts of its life; but the minds of the engrossed, just as if weighted by a yoke, cannot turn and look behind. And so their life vanishes into an abyss; and as it does no good, no matter how much water you pour into a vessel, if there is no bottom[21] to receive and hold it, so with time—it makes no difference how much is given; if there is nothing for it to settle upon, it passes out through the chinks and holes of the mind. Present time is very brief, so brief, indeed, that to some there seems to be none; for it is always in motion, it ever flows and hurries on; it ceases to be before it has come, and can no more brook delay than the firmament or the stars, whose ever unresting movement never lets them abide in the same track. The engrossed, therefore, are concerned with present time alone, and it is so brief that it cannot be grasped, and even this is filched away from them, distracted as they are among many things.

XI. In a word, do you want to know how they do not "live long"? See how eager they are to live long! Decrepit old men beg in their prayers for the addition of a few more years; they pretend that they are younger than they are; they comfort themselves with a falsehood, and are as pleased to deceive themselves as if they deceived Fate at the same time. But when at last some infirmity has reminded them of their mortality, in what terror do they die, feeling that they are being dragged out of life, and not merely leaving it. They cry out that they have been fools, because they have not really lived, and that they will live henceforth in leisure if only they escape from this illness; then at last they reflect how uselessly they have striven for things which they did not enjoy, and how all their toil has gone for nothing. But for those whose life is passed remote from all business, why should it not be ample? None of it is assigned to another, none of it is scattered in this direction and that, none of it is committed to Fortune, none of it perishes from neglect, none is subtracted by wasteful giving, none of it is unused; the whole of it, so to speak, yields income. And so, however small the amount of it, it is abundantly sufficient, and therefore, whenever his last day shall come, the wise man will not hesitate to go to meet death with steady step.

XII. Perhaps you ask whom I would call "the engrossed"? There is no reason for you to suppose that I mean only those whom the dogs[22] that have at length been let in drive out from the law-court, those whom you see either gloriously crushed in their own crowd of followers, or scornfully in someone else's, those whom social duties call forth from their own homes to bump them against someone else's doors, or whom the praetor's hammer[23] keeps busy in seeking gain that is disreputable and that will one day fester. Even the leisure of some men is engrossed; in their villa or on their couch, in the midst of solitude, although they have withdrawn from all others, they are themselves the source of their own worry; we should say that these are living, not in leisure, but in busy idleness.[24] Would you say that that man is at leisure[25] who arranges with finical care his Corinthian bronzes, that the mania of a few makes costly, and spends the greater part of each day upon rusty bits of copper? Who sits in a public wrestling-place (for, to our shame I we labour with vices that are not even Roman) watching the wrangling of lads? Who sorts out the herds of his pack-mules into pairs of the same age and colour? Who feeds all the newest athletes? Tell me, would you say that those men are at leisure who pass many hours at the barber's while they are being stripped of whatever grew out the night before? while a solemn debate is held over each separate hair? while either disarranged locks are restored to their place or thinning ones drawn from this side and that toward the forehead? How angry they get if the barber has been a bit too careless, just as if he were shearing a real man! How they flare up if any of their mane is lopped off, if any of it lies out of order, if it does not all fall into its proper ringlets! Who of these would not rather have the state disordered than his hair? Who is not more concerned to have his head trim rather than safe? Who would not rather be well barbered than upright? Would you say that these are at leisure who are occupied with the comb and the mirror? And what of those who are engaged in composing, hearing, and learning songs, while they twist the voice, whose best and simplest movement Nature designed to be straightforward, into the meanderings of some indolent tune, who are always snapping their fingers as they beat time to some song they have in their head, who are overheard humming a tune when they have been summoned to serious, often even melancholy, matters? These have not leisure, but idle occupation. And their banquets, Heaven knows! I cannot reckon among their unoccupied hours, since I see how anxiously they set out their silver plate, how diligently they tie up the tunics of their pretty slave-boys, how breathlessly they watch to see in what style the wild boar issues from the hands of the cook, with what speed at a given signal smooth-faced boys hurry to perform their duties, with what skill the birds are carved into portions all according to rule, how carefully unhappy little lads wipe up the spittle of drunkards. By such means they seek the reputation of being fastidious and elegant, and to such an extent do their evils follow them into all the privacies of life that they can neither eat nor drink without ostentation. And I would not count these among the leisured class either—the men who have themselves borne hither and thither in a sedan-chair and a litter, and are punctual at the hours for their rides as if it were unlawful to omit them, who are reminded by someone else when they must bathe, when they must swim, when they must dine; so enfeebled are they by the excessive lassitude of a pampered mind that they cannot find out by themselves whether they are hungry! I hear that one of these pampered people—provided that you can call it pampering to unlearn the habits of human life—when he had been lifted by hands from the bath and placed in his sedan-chair, said questioningly: "Am I now seated?" Do you think that this man, who does not know whether he is sitting, knows whether he is alive, whether he sees, whether he is at leisure? I find it hard to say whether I pity him more if he really did not know, or if he pretended not to know this. They really are subject to forgetfulness of many things, but they also pretend forgetfulness of many. Some vices delight them as being proofs of their prosperity; it seems the part of a man who is very lowly and despicable to know what he is doing. After this imagine that the mimes[26] fabricate many things to make a mock of luxury! In very truth, they pass over more than they invent, and such a multitude of unbelievable vices has come forth in this age, so clever in this one direction, that by now we can charge the mimes with neglect. To think that there is anyone who is so lost in luxury that he takes another's word as to whether he is sitting down! This man, then, is not at leisure, you must apply to him a different term—he is sick, nay, he is dead; that man is at leisure, who has also a perception of his leisure. But this other who is half alive, who, in order that he may know the postures of his own body, needs someone to tell him—how can he be the master of any of his time?...

XIV. Of all men they alone are at leisure who take time for philosophy, they alone really live; for they are not content to be good guardians of their own lifetime only. They annex ever age to their own; all the years that have gone ore them are an addition to their store. Unless we are most ungrateful, all those men, glorious fashioners of holy thoughts, were born for us; for us they have prepared a way of life. By other men's labours we are led to the sight of things most beautiful that have been wrested from darkness and brought into light; from no age are we shut out, we have access to all ages, and if it is our wish, by greatness of mind, to pass beyond the narrow limits of human weakness, there is a great stretch of time through which we may roam. We may argue with Socrates, we may doubt[32] with Carneades, find peace with Epicurus, overcome human nature with the Stoics, exceed it with the Cynics. Since Nature allows us to enter into fellowship with every age, why should we not turn from this paltry and fleeting span of time and surrender ourselves with all our soul to the past, which is boundless, which is eternal, which we share with our betters?

Those who rush about in the performance of social duties, who give themselves and others no rest, when they have fully indulged their madness, when they have every day crossed everybody's threshold, and have left no open door unvisited, when they have carried around their venal greeting to houses that are very far apart—out of a city so huge and torn by such varied desires, how few will they be able to see? How many will there be who either from sleep or self-indulgence or rudeness will keep them out! How many who, when they have tortured them with long waiting, will rush by, pretending to be in a hurry! How many will avoid passing out through a hall that is crowded with clients, and will make their escape through some concealed door as if it were not more discourteous to deceive than to exclude. How many, still half asleep and sluggish from last night's debauch, scarcely lifting their lips in the midst of a most insolent yawn, manage to bestow on yonder poor wretches, who break their own slumber[33] in order to wait on that of another, the right name only after it has been whispered to them a thousand times!

But we may fairly say that they alone are engaged in the true duties of life who shall wish to have Zeno, Pythagoras, Democritus, and all the other high priests of liberal studies, and Aristotle and Theophrastus, as their most intimate friends every day. No one of these will be "not at home," no one of these will fail to have his visitor leave more happy and more devoted to himself than when he came, no one of these will allow anyone to leave him with empty hands; all mortals can meet with them by night or by day.

XV. No one of these will force you to die, but all will teach you how to die; no one of these will wear out your years, but each will add his own years to yours; conversations with no one of these will bring you peril, the friendship of none will endanger your life, the courting of none will tax your purse. From them you will take whatever you wish; it will be no fault of theirs if you do not draw the utmost that you can desire. What happiness, what a fair old age awaits him who has offered himself as a client to these! He will have friends from whom he may seek counsel on matters great and small, whom he may consult every day about himself, from whom he may hear truth without insult, praise without flattery, and after whose likeness he may fashion himself.

We are wont to say that it was not in our power to choose the parents who fell to our lot, that they have been given to men by chance; yet we may be the sons of whomsoever we will. Households there are of noblest intellects; choose the one into which you wish to be adopted; you will inherit not merely their name, but even their property, which there will be no need to guard in a mean or niggardly spirit; the more persons you share it with, the greater it will become. These will open to you the path to immortality, and will raise you to a height from which no one is cast down. This is the only way of prolonging mortality—nay, of turning it into immortality. Honours, monuments, all that ambition has commanded by decrees or reared in works of stone, quickly sink to ruin; there is nothing that the lapse of time does not tear down and remove. But the works which philosophy has consecrated cannot be harmed; no age will destroy them, no age reduce them; the following and each succeeding age will but increase the reverence for them, since envy works upon what is close at hand, and things that are far off we are more free to admire. The life of the philosopher, therefore, has wide range, and he is not confined by the same bounds that shut others in. He alone is freed from the limitations of the human race; all ages serve him as if a god. Has some time passed by? This he embraces by recollection. Is time present? This he uses. Is it still to come? This he anticipates. He makes his life long by combining all times into one.

XVI. But those who forget the past, neglect the present, and fear for the future have a life that is very brief and troubled; when they have reached the end of it, the poor wretches perceive too late that for such a long while they have been busied in doing nothing. Nor because they sometimes invoke death, have you any reason to think it any proof that they find life long. In their folly they are harassed by shifting emotions which rush them into the very things they dread; they often pray for death because they fear it. And, too, you have no reason to think that this is any proof that they are living a long time—the fact that the day often seems to them long, the fact that they complain that the hours pass slowly until the time set for dinner arrives; for, whenever their engrossments fail them, they are restless because they are left with nothing to do, and they do not know how to dispose of their leisure or to drag out the time. And so they strive for something else to occupy them, and all the intervening time is irksome; exactly as they do when a gladiatorial exhibition is been announced, or when they are waiting for the appointed time of some other show or amusement, they want to skip over the days that lie between. All postponement of something they hope for seems long to them. Yet the time which they enjoy is short and swift, and it is made much shorter by their own fault; for they flee from one pleasure to another and cannot remain fixed in one desire. Their days are not long to them, but hateful; yet, on the other hand, how scanty seem the nights which they spend in the arms of a harlot or in wine! It is this also that accounts for the madness of poets in fostering human frailties by the tales in which they represent that Jupiter under the enticement of the pleasures of a lover doubled the length of the night. For what is it but to inflame our vices to inscribe the name of the gods as their sponsors, and to present the excused indulgence of divinity as an example to our own weakness? Can the nights which they pay for so dearly fail to seem all too short to these men? They lose the day in expectation of the night, and the night in fear of the dawn.

XVII. The very pleasures of such men are uneasy and disquieted by alarms of various sorts, and at the very moment of rejoicing the anxious thought comes over them: How long will these things last?" This feeling has led kings to weep over the power they possessed, and they have not so much delighted in the greatness of their fortune, as they have viewed with terror the end to which it must some time come. When the King of Persia,[34] in all the insolence of his pride, spread his army over the vast plains and could not grasp its number but simply its measure,[35] he shed copious tears because inside of a hundred years not a man of such a mighty army would be alive.[36] But he who wept was to bring upon them their fate, was to give some to their doom on the sea, some on the land, some in battle, some in flight, and within a short time was to destroy all those for whose hundredth year he had such fear. And why is it that even their joys are uneasy from fear? Because they do not rest on stable causes, but are perturbed as groundlessly as they are born. But of what sort do you think those times are which even by their own confession are wretched, since even the joys by which they are exalted and lifted above mankind are by no means pure? All the greatest blessings are a source of anxiety, and at no time is fortune less wisely trusted than when it is best; to maintain prosperity there is need of other prosperity, and in behalf of the prayers that have turned out well we must make still other prayers. For everything that comes to us from chance is unstable, and the higher it rises, the more liable it is to fall. Moreover, what is doomed to perish brings pleasure to no one; very wretched, therefore, and not merely short, must the life of those be who work hard to gain what they must work harder to keep. By great toil they attain what they wish, and with anxiety hold what they have attained; meanwhile they take no account of time that will never more return. New engrossments take the place of the old, hope leads to new hope, ambition to new ambition. They do not seek an end of their wretchedness, but change the cause. Have we been tormented by our own public honours? Those of others take more of our time. Have we ceased to labour as candidates? We begin to canvass for others. Have we got rid of the troubles of a prosecutor? We find those of a judge. Has a man ceased to be a judge? He becomes president of a court. Has he become infirm in managing the property of others at a salary? He is perplexed by caring for his own wealth. Have the barracks[37] set Marius free? The consulship keeps him busy. Does Quintius[38] hasten to get to the end of his dictatorship? He will be called back to it from the plough. Scipio will go against the Carthaginians before he is ripe for so great an undertaking; victorious over Hannibal, victorious over Antiochus, the glory of his own consulship, the surety for his brother's, did he not stand in his own way, he would be set beside Jove[39]; but the discord of civilians will vex their preserver, and, when as a young man he had scorned honours that rivalled those of the gods, at length, when he is old, his ambition will lake delight in stubborn exile.[40] Reasons for anxiety will never be lacking, whether born of prosperity or of wretchedness; life pushes on in a succession of engrossments. We shall always pray for leisure, but never enjoy it....

XIX. Do you retire to these quieter, safer, greater things! Think you that it is just the same whether you are concerned in having corn from oversea poured into the granaries, unhurt either by the dishonesty or the neglect of those who transport it, in seeing that it does not become heated and spoiled by collecting moisture and tallies in weight and measure, or whether you enter upon these sacred and lofty studies with the purpose of discovering what substance, what pleasure, what mode of life, what shape God has; what fate awaits your soul; where Nature lays us to rest When we are freed from the body; what the principle is that upholds all the heaviest matter in the centre of this world, suspends the light on high, carries fire to the topmost part, summons the stars to their proper changes—and ether matters, in turn, full of mighty wonders? You really must leave the ground and turn your mind's eye upon these things! Now while the blood is hot, we must enter with brisk step upon the better course. In this kind of life there awaits much that is good to know—the love and practice of the virtues, forgetfulness of the passions, knowledge of living and dying, and a life of deep repose.

The condition of all who are engrossed is wretched, but most wretched is the condition of those who labour at engrossments that are not even their own, who regulate their sleep by that of another, their walk by the pace of another, who are under orders in case of the freest things in the world—loving and hating. If these wish to know how short their life is, let them reflect how small a part of it is their own.

XX. And so when you see a man often wearing the robe of office, when you see one whose name is famous in the Forum, do not envy him; those things are bought at the price of life. They will waste all their years, in order that they may have one year reckoned by their name.[44] Life has left some in the midst of their first struggles, before they could climb up to the height of their ambition; some, when they have crawled up through a thousand indignities to the crowning dignity, have been possessed by the unhappy thought that they have but toiled for an inscription on a tomb; some who have come to extreme old age, while they adjusted it to new hopes as if it were youth, have had it fail from sheer weakness in the midst of their great and shameless endeavours. Shameful is he whose breath leaves him in the midst of a trial when, advanced in years and still courting the applause of an ignorant circle, he is pleading for some litigant who is the veriest stranger; disgraceful is he who, exhausted more quickly by his mode of living than by his labour, collapses in the very midst of his duties; disgraceful is he who dies in the act of receiving payments on account, and draws a smile from his long delayed[45] heir. I cannot pass over an instance which occurs to me. Sextus[46] Turannius was an old man of long tested diligence, who, after his ninetieth year, having received release from the duties of his office by Gaius Caesar's own act, ordered himself to be laid out on his bed and to be mourned by the assembled household as if he were dead. The whole house bemoaned the leisure of its old master, and did not end its sorrow until his accustomed work was restored to him. Is it really such pleasure for a man to die in harness? Yet very many have the same feeling; their desire for their labour lasts longer than their ability; they fight against the weakness of the body, they judge old age to be a hardship on no other score than because it puts them aside. The law does not draft a soldier after his fiftieth year, it does not call a senator after his sixtieth; it is more difficult for men to obtain leisure from themselves than from the law. Meantime, while they rob and are being robbed, while they break up each other's repose, while they make each other wretched, their life is without profit, without pleasure, without any improvement of the mind. No one keeps death in view, no one refrains from far-reaching hopes; some men, indeed, even arrange for things that lie beyond life—huge masses of tombs and dedications of public works and gifts for their funeral-pyres and ostentatious funerals. But, in very truth, the funerals of such men ought to be conducted by the light of torches and wax tapers,[47] as though they had lived but the tiniest span.

1 It is clear from chapters 18 and 19 that, when this essay was written (in or about A.D. 49), Paulinus was *praefectus annonae*, the official who superintended the grain supply of Rome, and was, therefore, a man of importance. He was, believably, a near relative of Seneca's wife, Pompeia Paulina, and is usually identified with the father of a certain Pompeius Paulinus, who held high public posts under Nero (Pliny, *Nat. Hist.* xxxiii. 143; Tacitus, *Annals*, xiii. 53. 2; xv.

2 The famous aphorism of Hippocrates of Cos: ὁ βίος βραχύς, ἡ δὲ τέχνη μακρή.

3 An error for Theophrastus, as shown by Cicero, Tusc. Disp. iii. 69: "Theophrastus autem moriens accusasse naturam dicitur, quod cervis et cornicibus vitam diuturnam, quorum id nihil interesset, hominibus, quorum maxime interfuisset, tam exiguam vitam dedisset; quorum si aetas potuisset esse longinquior, futurum fuisse ut omnibus perfectis artibus omni doctrina hominum vita erudiretur."

4 *i.e.*, of man. *Cf.* Hesiod, *Frag.* 183 (Rzach): Ἐννέα τοι ζώει γενεὰς λακέρυζα κορώνη ἀνδρῶν γηράντω· ἔλαφος δέ τε τετρακόρωνος.

5 A prose rendering of an unknown poet. *Cf.* the epitaph quoted by Cassius Dio, lxix. 19: Σίμιλις ἐνταῦθα κεῖται βιοὺς μὲν ἔτη τόσα, ζήσας δὲ ἔτη ἑπτά.

6 Not one who undertook the actual defense, but one who by his presence and advice lent support in court.

7 Literally, "unripe." At 100 he should "come to his grave in a full age, like as a shock of corn cometh in in his season" (Job v. 26); but he is still unripe.

8 The idea is that greatness sinks beneath its own weight. *Cf.* Seneca, *Agamemnon*, 88 *sq.*: Sidunt ipso pondere magna ceditque oneri Fortuna suo.

9 The notorious Julia, who was banished by Augustus to the island of Pandataria.

10 In 31 B.C. Augustus had been pitted against Mark Antony and Cleopatra; in 2 B.C. Iullus Antonius, younger son of the triumvir, was sentenced to death by reason of his intrigue with the elder Julia.

11 The language is reminiscent of Augustus's own characterization of Julia and his two grandchildren in Suetonius (*Aug.* 65. 5): "nec (solebat) aliter eos appellare quam tris vomicas ac tria carcinomata sua" ("his trio of boils and trio of ulcers").

12 Not extant.

13 As tribune in 91 B.C. he proposed a corn law and the granting of citizenship to the Italians.

14 Throughout the essay *occupati*, "the engrossed," is a technical term designating those who are so absorbed in the interests of life that they take no time for philosophy.

15 *i.e.*, the various types of *occupati* that have been sketchily presented. The looseness of the structure has led some editors to doubt the integrity of the passage.

[16] *i.e.*, she has become the prey of legacy-hunters.

[17] The rods that were the symbol of high office.

[18] At this time the management of the public games was committed to the praetors.

[19] Virgil, *Georgics*, iii. 66 *sq.*

[20] A much admired teacher of Seneca.

[21] An allusion to the fate of the Danaids, who in Hades forever poured water into a vessel with a perforated bottom.

[22] Apparently watch-dogs that were let in at nightfall, and caught the engrossed lawyer still at his task.

[23] Literally, "spear," which was stuck in the ground as the sign of a public auction where captured or confiscated goods were put up for sale.

[24] *Cf.* Pliny, *Epistles*, i. 9. 8: "satius est enim, ut Atilius noster eruditissime simul et facetissime dixit, otiosum esse quam nihil agere."

[25] For the technical meaning of *otiosi*, "the leisured," see Seneca's definition at the beginning of chap. 14.

[26] Actors in the popular mimes, or low farces, that were often censured for their indecencies.

[27] The ancient codex was made of tablets of wood fastened together.

[28] Such, doubtless, as Marius, Sulla, Caesar, Crassus.

[29] Pliny (*Nat. Hist.* viii. 21) reports that the people were so moved by pity that they rose in a body and called down curses upon Pompey. Cicero's impressions of the occasion are recorded in *Ad Fam.* vii. 1. 3: "extremus elephantorum dies fuit, in quo admiratio magna vulgi atque turbae, delectatio nulla exstitit; quin etiam misericordia quaedam consecuta est atque opinio eiusmodi, esse quandam illi beluae cum genere humana societatem."

[30] *i.e.*, *Magnus.*

[31] A name applied to a consecrated space kept vacant within and (according to Livy, i. 44) without the city wall. The right of extending it belonged originally to the king who had added territory to Rome.

[32] The New Academy taught that certainty of knowledge was unattainable.

[33] The *salutatio* was held in the early morning.

[34] Xerxes, who invaded Greece in 480 B.C.

[35] On the plain of Doriscus in Thrace the huge land force was estimated by counting the number of times a space capable of holding 10,000 men was filled (Herodotus, vii. 60).

[36] Herodotus, vii. 45, 46 tells the story.

[37] *Caliga*, the boot of the common soldier, is here synonymous with service in the army.

[38] His first appointment was announced to him while he was ploughing his own fields.

[39] He did not allow his statue to be placed in the Capitol.

[40] Disgusted with politics, he died in exile at Liternum.

[41] Probably an allusion to the mad wish of Caligula: "utinam populus Romanus unam cervicem haberet!" (Suetonius, *Calig.* 30), cited in *De Ira*, iii. 19. 2. The logic of the whole passage suffers from the uncertainty of the text.

[42] Three and a half miles long, reaching from Baiae to the mole of Puteoli (Suetonius, *Calig.* 19).

[43] Xerxes, who laid a bridge over the Hellespont.

[44] The Roman year was dated by the names of the two annual consuls.

[45] *i.e.*, long kept out of his inheritance.

[46] Tacitus (*Annals*, i. 7) gives the *praenomen* as Gaius.

[47] *i.e.*, as if they were children, whose funerals took place by night (Servius, *Aeneid*, xi. 143).

# Notes

# Notes

# Notes

# Notes

# Notes

# Notes

Made in the USA
Columbia, SC
06 January 2023

73632702R00241